PERSONALITY DYNAMICS AND

EFFECTIVE BEHAVIOR

JAMES C. COLEMAN

Associate Professor of Psychology
The University of California at Los Angeles

Selected readings prepared by
Alvin Marks, Assistant Professor of Psychology
Los Angeles State College

SCOTT, FORESMAN AND COMPANY

Chicago, Atlanta, Dallas, Palo Alto, Fair Lawn, N.J.

PREFACE

In presenting a theoretical and practical approach to problems of human "adjustment," *Personality Dynamics and Effective Behavior* starts from the premise that man has an inborn capacity for responsible self-direction. The behaviorist view of man as a reactive organism which responds more or less mechanically to the various stimuli impinging upon it has been greatly modified to take into account man's capacity to select and evaluate stimuli in terms of his needs, to assign value and meaning to experience, to think creatively, and to initiate action.

The approach of this text reflects a new concept of the human organism that has been gradually emerging from experimentation and theory in psychology and such related fields as biology, physiology, biophysics, anthropology, and sociology. Man is viewed as an *energy system* whose behavior is determined partly by its own structural and functional characteristics and partly by forces in its environmental field, with which it continually interacts. The human organism cannot be understood as an isolated entity; it is, in the terminology of systems theorists, an "open system" whose behavior originates in the interplay between (a) its own physical and psychological needs and (b) the demands, limitations, and opportunities of its environment. The success of adjustive behavior is measured by how well the individual satisfies his various needs within the context of his particular physical and sociocultural field.

Like all living energy systems, the human organism seems to have an important "need" or tendency not only to maintain itself against harm but also to fulfill its innate potentialities. For the human being these include potentialities for intellectual, social, and emotional development as well as for physical growth. Thus effective adjustment cannot be equated with absence of illness or lack of tension and conflict; it implies continuing and integrated progress toward self-fulfillment.

Personality Dynamics and Effective Behavior builds on this scientifically based picture of man to provide a meaningful approach to problems of human adjustment. Part 1 (three chapters) considers the basic nature of man and the development of human potentialities through maturation and learning in a physical and sociocultural environment. Part 2 (five chapters) focuses on the dynamics of individual and group behavior—motivation, stress, adjustive and maladjustive behavior, group-individual interaction. Part 3 (five chapters) applies the principles of personality dynamics to a discussion of ways to increase personal effectiveness. Part 4, a selection of readings, offers a first-hand introduction to some promising—and sometimes contradictory—approaches to the study of personality and behavior.

The author is indebted to many scientists whose work he has drawn upon in preparing this book. His theoretical position has been strongly influenced by such men as Gordon Allport, Hadley Cantril, Arthur Combs, Sigmund Freud, Erich Fromm, J. P. Guilford, A. H. Maslow, Margaret Mead, James Miller, O. H. Mowrer, Gardner Murphy, Carl Rogers, and Donald Snygg. On a more personal level he is indebted to many colleagues who have helped him to clarify various systematic and technical points. His special thanks go to Dr. Ralph Timmer for his assistance on the chapter dealing with professional resources and to Dr. Alvin Marks for his work in preparing the reading selections.

James C. Coleman
Los Angeles, California

Contents

PROLOGUE

Science and personal adjustment

Never before in history has man enjoyed such physical luxuries and such opportunities for fulfilling himself as a human being as does the average individual in the United States today. He lives in a home that provides unparalleled living comfort. He is served by a myriad of slaves—powered by electricity instead of human labor—which remove much of the drudgery from his everyday living and give him more time for creative pursuits. He can eat like a gourmet, experience the stimulating rewards of travel, and enjoy the finest literature, music, and art. He has opportunities for sports and other leisure-time activities which were formerly available only to a chosen few. Through motion pictures and television, he is entertained by spectacles that would have taxed the imagination of ancient kings. His achievements in medicine have made him the healthiest man of all time and have greatly increased his life span. His educational opportunities and his freedom for self-determination are almost unlimited. He lives in an exciting age of scientific wonders which have placed him on the threshold of conquering space. In fact, man has never possessed such opportunity for enjoying life to its fullest and for fulfilling himself as a human being. To all external appearances, it would seem that he is entering upon a Golden Age.

PROGRESS AND PANIC

Despite his enviable position, modern man has found that all is not going exactly as he might hope and expect. Paradoxically, the same progress that has made this a kind of Golden Age has also posed many new problems and threats and created the need for new adjustive skills. Hunting and the craft skills required for survival in earlier times have given way over the centuries to skills in getting along with diverse peoples, in achieving technological proficiency, in coping with propaganda, and in keeping track of the innumerable details of everyday living. Modern methods of communication and transportation have reduced the "size" of the world so that the individual is affected by events occurring in areas remote from where he lives. And wherever he looks, he sees his world changing with incredible rapidity—and established customs, traditions, and values changing with it. Indeed, one of our major problems today is having to adjust to continual change itself, for the world has altered probably more in the last fifty years than in all the preceding years of human history.

Superimposed upon the problems created by rapid change are the tensions created by the fear of international conflict and even global destruction. Thus, instead of being able to relax and enjoy the material utopia he has created, man finds himself tense, anxious, and under continual strain. The impact of our scientific age upon the hopes and fears of modern man has been well described by the psychologist Hadley Cantril (1958, pp. vii-viii):

"As more and more people throughout the world become more and more enmeshed in a scientific age, its psychological consequences on their thought and behavior become increasingly complicated. The impact comes in a variety of ways: people begin to feel the potentialities for a more abundant life that modern technology can provide; they become aware of the inadequacies of many present political, social, and religious institutions or practices; they discern the threat which existing power and status relationships may hold to their own development; they vaguely sense the inadequacy of many of the beliefs and codes accepted by their forefathers and perhaps by themselves at an earlier age.

"The upshot is that more and more people are acquiring both a hope for a 'better life' and a feeling of frustration and anxiety that they themselves may not experience the potentially better life they feel should somehow be available to them. They search for new anchorages, for new guide lines, for plans of action which hold a promise of making some of their dreams come true, some of their aspirations become experientially real. They are, in short, seeking something to believe in. They are seeking a faith."

Thus the problems of global unrest, conflict, and change form the background against which we in the United States function. And although the problems of the more primitive peoples are somewhat different—since they are concerned primarily with achieving industrialization and technological proficiency as a means of solving their pressing problem of physical survival—the basic theme is still one of changing values, new adjustive patterns, and the search for a satisfying faith.

The strain of modern life in our own society is revealed in the billions of dollars' worth of alcoholic beverages and the incredible amounts of tranquilizing drugs which Americans consume each year. It is revealed in the way many people eagerly seize upon each new popular book which purports to show how they can solve all their problems by some type of "right thinking." It is revealed in the vast new literature on the "lost selves," the "lonely crowd," the "beat generation." In an even more dramatic way, perhaps, it is revealed in the statistics on personality maladjustment: over one half of all our hospital beds are occupied by mental patients, and some two thirds of all the people who go to see medical doctors are suffering from ailments precipitated largely by emotional factors. It is a period when peptic ulcers and other psychosomatic ailments have become almost as prevalent as the common cold, when juvenile delinquency and adult crime have reached alarming proportions. In fact, the prevention and cure of psychopathology has become the number one health problem in the United States. Obviously this is an Age of Anxiety as well as a Golden Age.

Although it would be foolish to maintain that man was always happy and had satisfactory values in "the good old days," he did in the main have a more stable position in the community and a more secure religious faith to give his life meaning. In the smaller community in which he lived, the individual felt himself an important part of the group; he had a definite position in it and was concerned with contributing his share to the group welfare. And in a predominantly agricultural society, man lived close to the land and was familiar with its plant and animal life and with the events of birth, growth, and death—an existence which helped him to feel his kinship with the world of nature.

The shift in population during the last hundred years from small agricultural communities to great urban centers has provided a majority of Americans with growing opportunities for economic well-being, leisure time, cultural pursuits, health, occupational advancement, and personal growth. However, it has also posed problems for the individual: problems of trying to feel himself a person in his own right and not just a unit in a swarming ant heap; of trying to find a secure position in the group and a feeling that he really belongs; of trying to compensate through marriage or in some other way for the loss of emotional support that in a small community typically comes from the extended family of parents and relatives; and, most important of all, of trying to find values that will make his new way of life seem worth while and meaningful.

It might even be said that in solving the problems of physical survival and launching an economy of abundance, modern science and technology have left man more directly and inescapably confronted with questions of value, purpose, and ultimate meaning than ever before. The difficulty of finding answers has been pointed up by the development of existentialism, a philosophy based on the assumption that life *has* no ultimate meaning, or at least none which man is capable of discerning. According to Rudolph Ehrenburg, the theologian and physiologist, "Life is that process which produces corpses." The existentialist maintains that man, faced with his own death and ultimate aloneness, is only what he makes of himself and therefore must commit himself to a policy of action for the here and now.[1] Other modern thinkers, however, feel that science has revealed increasingly the order and meaning of the universe, and they look forward optimistically to a future that is not even contemplated by the existentialist. Whether he finds them or not, modern man is searching vigorously—sometimes almost desperately— for values and meanings that will hold firm in the light of his new knowledge and pattern of living. He does not accept easily the doctrine of despair, so dramatically portrayed in the lines of Shakespeare, that life "is a tale/Told by an idiot, full of sound and fury,/Signifying nothing."

In pointing out the problems of modern man, we are not advocating a return to "the old ways." In many areas we have come far toward realizing a utopian way of life, and few would care to exchange the benefits of modern civilization even for the greater stability of an earlier age. In any case, we have set out upon a path of change and can find no road back. Our hope lies not in reversing change or in holding the line but rather in developing new modes of adjustment that are appropriate to a rapidly changing world. As we face this challenge, we should remember that modern science has not only complicated the problems of existence but at the same time provided new information and tools for our use in reaching toward effective solutions.

MAN'S UNIQUE PROBLEM
OF SELF-DIRECTION

Throughout his long history, man has pitted his abilities against the world in his struggle to survive. In this he is not unique, for all living things strive to maintain themselves, to resist destruction, and to grow and function in accordance with their inner natures. The process by which an organism attempts to meet the demands placed upon it by its own nature and by its environment is called *adjustment*. Living things never cease to adjust. Adjustive behavior may be more or less *successful*, in terms of how well it meets external demands and satisfies the needs of the organism, but it goes on continuously. It is as basic to life as breathing—itself a form of adjustment.

In the universal struggle for survival and growth, many different adjustive patterns have emerged in the animal world. Some species man-

---

[1]For a discussion of existentialism, see William Barrett's article on page 514.

age to survive by sheer number of offspring; others rely heavily upon defensive armaments such as poisons, camouflage, or speed. Though widely different, these various patterns have one thing in common: they rely upon "built-in" adjustive know-how. While most animals are capable of some learning, their behavior is determined primarily by adjustive patterns that are instinctive. We might say that they come factory-equipped with adjustive know-how.

With man, however, nature has tried out a dramatically different solution to the problems of adjustment. Endowed with superior mental capacities, man has few, if any, instinctive behavior patterns beyond the level of the simplest reflex. He must rely instead on his ability to learn and reason in working out the most satisfactory mode of adjustment, continually modifying his behavior to meet the demands of new situations. The superior mental gifts—and, consequently, the superior adaptability—of man have enabled him to become the unchallenged master of the animal kingdom and to go far toward conquering his physical environment. But man's unique gifts have also created unique problems, for man alone is faced with the responsibility of determining his own behavior—of evaluating and choosing the "best" course of action and of developing the competencies or skills essential for carrying it out. In short, man is faced with the necessity of *self-direction,* and this places a heavy demand upon him to determine the type of creature he is and the basic "role" he should play as a human being. As the Overstreets (1956, pp. 240-241) put it:

"Although he has a role to play—a form to grow into, a function to carry out—he is unlike every other creature in the fact that he does not grow into this role naturally, by just staying alive long enough. He has to decide for himself what his own basic role is. . . .

"Here is where our chief troubles have arisen. We have been as confused about ourselves, often—as uncertain about what our human nature is and what it requires of us—as an acorn would be if it were not sure whether its proper destiny was to be an oak or a cabbage. . . .

"But we are most deeply of all at odds with ourselves and our situation when, being human, we do not know what it basically means to be human—what this demands of us and also grants us."

In directing the "human enterprise" then, man must not only acquire information about himself and his world and develop the competencies for dealing with his problems, but he must also come to grips with the problem of value—of what is good for him and what is not—and ultimately with the problem of the meaning of his existence—of just what his role in the universe is. For our purposes, we may think of these problems in terms of two simple categories: "know-how" and "know-why."

The Problem of "Know-How"

To direct his behavior effectively, man must first of all acquire *information* about himself and his world. He must learn about his needs, his potentialities, his rational and irrational tendencies, and the many other facets of his nature which enable him to fill in a realistic self-picture. Man must also learn about the world in which he lives—not only the inanimate world, but the world of plants and animals and human groups. He must learn about its dangers, its potentialities for meeting his needs, and the principles inherent in its operation—information that will enable him to understand his world and to some extent control it.

Man's views of himself and his world, whether accurate or inaccurate, are primary determiners of his behavior. For the goals he strives after and the means he selects for trying to achieve them are largely determined by what he conceives himself to be, by what he conceives himself able to become, and by the way he pictures the opportunities and limitations of the world around him. People who view human nature as basically kind and good are likely to behave in different ways from those who view human nature as basically cruel and selfish. Similarly, people who view their environment as hostile and dangerous are likely to behave differently from those who view it as friendly and full of opportunity.

In addition to acquiring information about himself and his world, man must also acquire the competencies requisite for getting along in human society and for carrying out his individual purposes. Without such competencies he is all theory and no practice, and however desirable his goals, he is not likely to accomplish very much. Of course, the specific competencies a person needs vary considerably from one society to another and even among individuals within the same society. But as we shall see, there appear to be certain general competencies that are necessary for all men if they are to adjust successfully.

Each of us must spend a major portion of his life acquiring the information and competencies required for adjustive behavior—in acquiring the know-how for living. And as man's scientific and technological progress continues, the amount of information and the complexity of skills he needs continue to increase. Thus, the problem of acquiring know-how for living becomes increasingly difficult and more and more time-consuming.

The Problem of "Know-Why"

Achieving effective adjustment is not simply a matter of acquiring information and developing necessary competencies. Man must also solve the problem of "know-why"—he must find a comprehensive value system to give him a sense of purpose and to guide his adjustive behavior in specific situations. From among the many goals, means, and ways of living that are available to him, he must choose those he thinks will best meet his needs. His choices are inevitably based upon his assumptions or judgments concerning value—upon what he thinks is right and will lead to his greatest satisfaction and well-being. As Clyde Kluckhohn (1954, p. 403) notes: "Surely one of the broadest generalizations to be made by a natural historian observing the human species is that man is an evaluating animal. Always and everywhere men are saying, 'This is good'; 'that is bad'; 'this is better than that'; 'these are higher and those lower aspirations.'" Thus while information helps man to see what *is* or *could* be, values are concerned with the *desirable*—with what *ought* to be.

Over the years man has worked out many reliable values to guide his behavior in simple choice situations. We are all familiar with such maxims as "Honesty is the best policy," and "It is better to be safe than sorry." However, the question of what type of life is best suited for man—will contribute most to his personal satisfaction as well as to the progress of the group—is a far more complex problem. To answer it, man must try to fathom the whole meaning of human existence. He must discover his role in the universe. He must answer the baffling question of "Why?"

In his pursuit of values, man is thus inescapably confronted with the problem of *meaning*—with the question of what life is all about. This concern with meaning, so basic to human thought and action, is unique to man. The behavior of other species is determined primarily by their natural tendencies toward survival. Lacking self-awareness, they have no problem of choosing real from false values and no concern about what they are doing in this world or the destiny of their species. Nor are they concerned with—or probably even aware of—their finite existence here on earth. As the noted psychiatrist Erich Fromm (1955, pp. 23-24) puts it, "Man is the only animal who finds his own existence a problem which he has to solve and from which he cannot escape."

"Animal existence is one of harmony between the animal and nature; not, of course, in the sense that the natural conditions do not often threaten the animal and force it to a bitter fight for survival, but in the sense that the animal is equipped by nature to cope with the very conditions it is to meet. . . .

"Self-awareness, reason and imagination disrupt the 'harmony' which characterizes animal existence. Their emergence has made man into an anomaly, into the freak of the universe. . . . Being aware of himself, he realizes his powerlessness and the limitations of his existence. He visualizes his own end: death."

Thus for the first time in the entire history of the animal kingdom, psychological problems centering around values and meaning enter into and complicate the adjustive process.

THREE KEY QUESTIONS

We have already spoken of man's problem of self-direction—of his need to determine and develop the adjustive patterns which are best suited to his nature and his environment. Now we must translate our concept of self-direction from Homo sapiens to the individual man, in terms of the specific know-how and know-why he needs for effective self-direction.

In this context we may think in terms of three key questions which each individual must attempt to answer if he is to become personally effective and fulfill his potentialities:

Who am I?
Where am I going?
Why?

These questions deal with our identity, our assets and liabilities, our goals, our means, our values, and our way of life or "life style." The meaningfulness of these questions will, of course, vary somewhat depending upon the individual's opportunities for self-direction. In many parts of the world the individual's opportunities may be severely curtailed by the ever present struggle to meet his physical needs or by authoritarian forms of social organization which answer many of these questions for him. But in the United States, the individual's opportunities for self-development and self-direction are almost unlimited.

Who Am I?

By delineating the characteristics common to all men, we can understand much about ourselves, for we are all members of the human species. We can fill in a few more details by studying the patterns and values of the specific culture in which we have been reared. But each individual is unique and therefore has the problem of getting to know and understand *himself*. Berrill (1955, p. 251) states the problem of finding one's identity as a double question: "What am I as a human being and what kind of individual am I?"

It is an interesting facet of our educational system that we study almost everything else before getting around to studying ourselves. Yet we must live with ourselves and work with our own resources in making our lives satisfying and productive. As Selye (1956, p. 253) has pointed out, "Since man is essentially a rational being, the better he knows what makes him tick, the more likely he will be to make a success of life."

We can readily see the benefits of understanding our bodily functions. The achievements of modern medicine have provided us with information about disease and physical hygiene that make for healthier and longer life. By practicing good hygiene we can now avoid needlessly damaging our bodies, and we no longer need to worry about minor symptoms which ignorance used to exaggerate into major illnesses. On a psychological level, there are equally good reasons for insuring adequate self-understanding. This focusing on self is not expected to result in the individual's becoming a psychological hypochondriac who examines his every thought, act, and dream for its possible implications. In fact, genuine self-understanding tends to *lessen* self-involvement, preoccupation, and concern. As Lehner (1957, p. iii) has pointed out, ". . . the better you know yourself, the better you will be able to forget yourself, for it is the things you do NOT know about yourself that cause you to bog down."

The person who does not have a realistic view of himself is like a general who lacks an accurate picture of his men, his equipment, and the fighting strength of his forces. Such an individual is handicapped in meeting life's problems, just as the general would be handicapped in battle. The following cases illustrate some of the difficulties to which inadequate self-knowledge can lead.

Is This What I Wanted?

Sally Dolan's childhood was literally "hate-full" and spent in rebellion. One thought carried her through the years—that things would be different when she grew up. She would escape poverty, she would throw off her religious ties, she would never have children, and if she married at all it would be with the clear understanding that she would continue to be her own boss. Life would be a bowl of cherries.

The dream has seemed to come true. Sally's job supports Jim, her would-be-actor husband, and gives Sally both independence and authority. Jim agrees that children are mainly a nuisance and that religion is only a crutch. Like Sally, he has prized his freedom to do and think as he pleases. Life is a bowl of cherries. . . .

Sally can't say when it began to occur to her that the cherries were not all sweet. All she knows is that nothing she has or does makes much sense to her now, even though her life is just the way she thought she wanted it. She is depressed and frightened by the way she feels when each day begins, as though it were a meaningless chore fraught with unknown dangers. By the end of the day she feels worn-out from having accomplished nothing but too restless to fall easily asleep. Often she is made more anxious by her dreams—of finding herself in church without clothes on, of standing on a precipice with a strong wind at her back, of looking in a mirror and seeing nothing. Jim laughs at her and says she needs more vitamins, but her feelings of depression and "lostness" increase.

What's the Matter with Me?

Henry Robinson feels that he's an attractive male, but he can't get dates for dances and other social activities at his school. The fault obviously isn't his, for he has tried hard to make himself popular by playing the "clown" in class and at parties and by talking up his various accomplishments. He often discusses with his acquaintances the shortcomings of other boys who nevertheless have no trouble getting all the dates they want. Henry has concluded that most of the girls at his college are snobs because he rarely finds one who will go out with him more than once. Recently he has been concentrating on entering freshmen, whom he tries to impress with his senior standing. But the results have been discouraging.

Why Do These Things Happen to Me?

Mr. Butler flunked out of college seven years ago. He doesn't regard this as a personal failure but attributes it to the unfairness of his teachers and his refusal to cheat on tests the way most of the other students did. Since leaving college he has had several sales jobs, but in each case he had to resign because of difficulties with customers or other sales people. He explains this as due to "cranks" and to the envy of competing salesmen. Recently he received a traffic ticket for speeding—thanks to his wife, who had made them late in leaving for a dinner engagement.

It can be seen that without adequate self-knowledge we may be confused as to who we are and feel a sense of being lost, of futility and despair. We may fail to realize that being "grown-up" is not a matter of reaching voting age but involves knowing what one really wants and acting accordingly. Without adequate self-knowledge we may never recognize ourselves the way we really are. We may remain unaware of annoying habits—such as talking incessantly about ourselves or continually belittling others —which drive people away and leave us hurt and bewildered by their rejection. Or we may blame our failures on other people while regarding ourselves as faultless, at the heavy price of being unable to analyze and profit from our mistakes. Such cases are illustrated above. Again, if we do not understand ourselves, we may be plagued by unnecessary worry about our innermost desires and thoughts. We may have fantasies of killing people or dreams of a homosexual nature which make us wonder if we are "normal." Or we may simply be bewildered by some of the apparently irrational things we do. The latter point is made humorously by Rebecca McCann in a little poem called "Inconsistency":

"I'm sure I have a noble mind
And honesty and tact
And no one's more surprised than I
To see the way I act!"

The need for a realistic and clear-cut sense of "who we are" has become particularly crucial in modern society, where the individual often feels himself a puppet in the hands of impersonal economic, political, and social forces. Erich Fromm (1955, p. 120) speaks of the "alienation" of man in our society:

"By alienation is meant a mode of experience in which the person experiences himself as an alien. He has become, one might say, estranged from himself. He does not experience himself as the center of his world, as the creator of his own acts. . . ."

Whether or not we entirely agree with Fromm's conclusion that most of us are ruled by the "anonymous authority" of social pressure toward conformity, the symptoms he cites are certainly familiar. Thus we can see that an answer to the question "Who am I?" is of critical importance in determining not only whether we successfully adjust to specific life situations but also whether we become self-directing and creative individuals, capable of actualizing our potentialities.

Where Am I Going?

The question "Where am I going?" centers around our *goals*, the *means* we select for achieving them, and the *hazards* we are likely to encounter on the way.

Goals focus our energy and effort, guide the competencies we need to develop, and provide us with criteria for deciding between alternate courses of action. Often it is convenient to think in terms of long-range and short-range goals. Long-range goals usually require the attainment of many short-range goals or subgoals. Thus becoming a doctor would be a long-range goal requiring the completion of a premedical course in college, a certain grade-point average, admission to a medical school, and so on. Long-term goals may be thought of as the primary direction-finders for our behavior, but short-term goals are the ones that ordinarily occupy most of our attention and effort.

The delineation of long-range goals is particularly important for modern man, who has many more choices to make than his ancestors did and more leisure in which to contemplate his future. He must have a clear idea of where he is going if he is to choose appropriate subgoals and effective means for achieving them. Yet many people drift through life with little or no sense of direction other than that of meeting their immediate needs. Such individuals usually feel a vague sense of dissatisfaction, of aimlessness or being "lost."

It is readily apparent that some goals are superior to others in the satisfactions they afford and that some are more appropriate than others in relation to the individual's personal resources and environmental opportunities. The pursuit of unrealistically high goals leads to failure and frustration; the pursuit of goals that are too low in aspiration level leads to wasted opportunities and lost satisfaction; the pursuit of "false" goals that fail to yield satisfaction when they are attained leads to disillusionment and discouragement.

The Budding Actress

Alice Kendall views herself as a very gifted young actress who will someday make a name in the movies or possibly even on Broadway. She is failing in her drama class but feels that her native ability makes formal study unimportant. She obtained a small part in the last school play but had to be replaced because of her poor diction. The drama coach says her chances of ever becoming a successful actress are very small because of her appearance, immaturity, and lack of sensitivity. Alice, however, feels that he is unqualified to judge her natural talent.

The Man Who Lived Down to His Reputation

Rather than admit that a Richardson was not college material, Dwayne's parents financed their "black sheep" for four years at a small eastern university. But they were not surprised that he barely managed to get his degree. Nor were they surprised at his taking a blue-collar job with a contracting firm or at his marrying a girl with little educational or social background. That was Dwayne for you.

But neither Dwayne's marriage nor his job lasted long. His boss reacted to Dwayne's suggestions for improving the firm with, "If you know so much, get out and start your own outfit," and all his wife wanted out of life was fun. After his job folded, Dwayne almost went into business with an ambitious, energetic school friend but at the last minute decided it was too great a risk and took a job as a salesman instead. He also almost married a friend of his sister, a teacher, but decided that he could never measure up to what she wanted and drifted into marriage with a twenty-five-year-old girl who was still at home with her mother.

At thirty, after two failures at marriage and continued shifting from job to job, Dwayne senses that maybe he has been shooting too low. But he is so accustomed to failure that he's afraid to try anything that seems more ambitious. "I can eat," he jokes, but inwardly he is disturbed that there is nothing worth while in either his past or his future.

The Unhappy Politician

Bruce Elevan, a handsome young man in his late twenties, makes an immediate good impression on everyone he meets but finds that most people soon lose interest in him, even though he is careful never to offend anyone. He has finished law school and is trying to make his way up in politics, a career in which his father enthusiastically supports him (as he refused to do in the career Bruce had half hoped to pursue, that of combining music with teaching). His father maintains that success is inevitable if Bruce will make a friend of every man and use a little common sense in making necessary compromises. Bruce has always respected his father's dynamic forcefulness and relied heavily on his judgment, but he is not happy. He is unable to express himself freely with people, partly because he is afraid of offending them, and he can feel them withdrawing in the face of his emptiness. He has never been able to find any real common ground with other politicians and has begun to dread going forward in his chosen career. But how can he turn back now, after all that education . . . and the way his father feels?

Cases such as these point up the importance of selecting goals that are both realistic and satisfying. But an answer to the question "Where am I going?" involves *means* as well as goals. Thus in delineating both long-range and short-range goals we must determine what general and specific competencies we will need to develop. Although the specific skills necessary for effective adjustment and the achievement of life goals will vary greatly with the individual's culture and his specific life situation, certain general competencies seem basic:

1. Physical competencies—the practice of good physical hygiene and the use of medical resources to keep the body functioning as efficiently as possible.

2. Intellectual competencies—the achievement not only of broad knowledge and understanding, but even more important, a high degree of competency in learning, problem solving, and decision making.

3. Emotional competencies—the ability to cope with the fears and anxieties of modern life and to meet life with the enthusiasm and sense of wonder that our emotional apparatus makes possible.

4. Social competencies—the ability to deal effectively with other people and build satisfying interpersonal relationships.

These basic competencies enter in various ways into almost everything we do and open up countless avenues for increased personal growth and self-fulfillment. Failure to develop them, however, can prevent us from "getting where we want to go." Of course many goals are out of our reach because we have personal limitations that cannot be changed—a physical handicap, inferior ability in some area of activity, or a situational limitation such as low social status or unusual family responsibilities. These are all liabilities that we must realistically assess in setting up our goals. But just as often we fail to achieve goals that are *within* our reach, for no other reason than that we fail to develop our assets. Despite our power to reason—the priceless possession of man alone—many of us are crippled by inaccurate information, emotional prejudices, and lack of training in evaluating and solving problems. Often we are burdened with unnecessary fears and anxieties which take most of the fun out of living. And often we fail to achieve the maturity in our social relationships that would make for fully satisfying relations with those close to us. Many marriages, for example, drag along for want of the knowledge that might make them rich and satisfying experiences.

A final consideration in answering the question "Where am I going?" is trying to anticipate some of the hazards we may meet along the way. Although we cannot foresee all the problems we will have to face during our lifetime, there are certain types of adjustment—such as getting married, bringing up children, earning a living, finding a satisfying philosophy of life, and growing old gracefully—that most of us will want to make. We can increase the probability of success if we know what hazards may be involved, what factors will be within our control, what pitfalls can be avoided, and what skills and attitudes we will need. Much as the soldier learns in military training about the problems he will be likely to encounter in combat, we can learn about the problems we are likely to meet in an ordinary life span and prepare ourselves to meet them.

Why?

The problem of goals is intimately related to that of values. What kind of life is good or bad for human beings in general and for me as an individual? Why is this way of life more desirable than that way? Why is this goal to be valued more highly than that one? Why is honesty the best policy? Ultimately, of course, the individual can answer these questions only in relation to a much larger "Why"—the meaning of his existence. For until he begins to answer this question to his own satisfaction, he lacks a general framework or perspective for making specific value judgments and choices. As Cantril (1950, p. 37) puts it, values "are the compass which gives man his direction both as to how he should act and what his action is for."

Lacking a satisfactory system of values, a person may waste the best of his resources and find himself drifting pointlessly. The following case may be all too typical:

Bill Archer is referred to by his friends as the "man of distinction" because of his striking good looks. In other ways, too, he is the very picture of success. His wife is feminine and beautiful, a thoughtful wife and mother, a gracious hostess. As a junior executive in a city bank, he has a secure and promising future. The commuting service from his suburb is so good that he can sleep until nearly eight and be in his office by nine. Bill has "fallen into" most of his good fortune by always doing what was expected of him—first by his parents, later by his wife and his employers. He feels that he has every reason to be proud of his accomplishments, but recently has begun to experience a growing anxiety that life is rushing aimlessly past him. Outwardly he presents a picture of self-confidence, but he has the uneasy feeling that, far from being in command of his own destiny, he is "on the outside looking in." He can't think what he might want that he doesn't already have, but he wishes that something would really matter to him. Bill's wife and friends consider him one of the "best-adjusted" people they know.

Obviously a surface commitment to "the good life" is not enough. To find happiness and satisfaction, a person must have some purpose for being and a system of values in which he can really believe. The degree to which he trusts the soundness of his values will determine how much he actually relies on them in making his choices, how much satisfaction he gains from following them, how free he will be from inner conflict, how successfully he can cope with setbacks and frustrations, and how much effort he will put forth in working toward his goals.

Although value patterns vary from individual to individual and, even more, from culture to culture, it is a mistake to assume that the selection of values must always be arbitrary. In the light of science, religion, and the experience of the human race, we can point to certain basic values that are clearly more realistic and satisfying than certain others. Modern science, for example, is continually helping man in his search for reliable values by obtaining more and more information about man's basic nature, his strivings, the universe in which he lives, and the environmental conditions that are conducive to his maintenance and growth. In accumulating such knowledge, the physical and biological and social sciences have substantially increased the likelihood of our selecting more reliable values. For as we learn more about what is "good" for man, in the sense of maintaining and improving his physical and psychological health, we become less dependent upon arbitrary—and sometimes false—assumptions of value.

A SCIENTIFIC APPROACH
TO ADJUSTMENT

Most people would consider it sheer folly to attempt to climb a high mountain peak without procuring the necessary equipment, studying the possible routes that might be taken, and obtaining a clear understanding of the hazards to be faced. Yet these same people expect that inadequate knowledge, competencies, and values will carry them successfully through the journey of life—a far more difficult undertaking than the conquest of a mountain peak.

Most People Muddle Through

Living, for most people, is a matter of muddling through. Instead of using the knowledge and resources which science and human history have put at our disposal, we go through life making many costly and needless mistakes and wasting much of our potential for self-fulfillment. And even today, literally millions of people guide their lives by super-stitions or "common-sense" notions of human nature which science has proved to be false. They prepare for the wrong occupations, choose incompatible mates, and bring up their children with a naïve hope that good intentions will be sufficient. But behind the brave front of confidence that they present to the world are apt to lie deep-seated feelings of bewilderment, inadequacy, and unhappiness. The price of muddling through is a high one. At the very least, it can lead to an incredible and unnecessary waste of human resources. And more commonly it takes a high toll in unnecessary failures, lost satisfactions, and emotional wear and tear on the human body. It is a curious fact that one of the most frustrating of all man's experiences is that of lost satisfactions—of "what *might* have been."

Although we often seem to manage quite well by simply muddling through, the mistakes we make because of ignorance and immaturity have a way of catching up with us in the long run. Violations of the laws of man's nature are inevitably punished. As Herrick (1956, p. 148) notes:

"Transgression of these laws brings its own penalty. No prosecutor is required. If you drink whisky to excess, your health is impaired. If you drink wood alcohol, you die. . . . The wages of sin is death, if not of the person, certainly of his richest values and satisfactions. And ignorance of the law excuses no man."

Modern Psychology Can Help

Today the findings of psychology are reducing man's "ignorance of the law." In much the same way that the findings of modern medicine have contributed to man's physical health, so the findings of modern psy-chology are contributing to his mental health—and to his ability to make more effective and satisfying adjustments. As we have noted, it is becoming increasingly possible for us to develop values and to pattern our behavior on the basis of scientifically sound knowledge rather than superstition, custom, or common sense. This is not to say, of course, that psychology—or science as a whole—can fully answer the questions of *Who*, *Where*, and *Why* or provide an infallible guide for "right living." But psychology *can* give us some partial answers, and it can reduce the probability of our getting unrealistic and invalid answers.

Already the findings of psychology—still a very young and incomplete science—have made themselves felt in almost every area of human behavior. They have provided new and generally effective guides in child rearing, education, marriage, and vocational planning and adjustment. They have brought promising results in the diagnosis, treatment, and prevention of personality disorders. They have contributed to the better understanding of how groups function and to methods for improving group efficiency. They have been useful in selecting and training personnel in business, industry, and the military services. In studying the dynamics of human behavior—how both individuals and groups develop and function—psychology has discovered many basic principles that have direct application to man's adjustment, in terms of both the know-how and the know-why for modern living.

In understanding the workings and contributions of modern psychology, it is instructive to note the tasks that psychology faces as a field of science.

1. Gathering facts. The first big task of psychology is to gather information about man and his behavior. Psychology relies heavily upon two basic approaches in making its observations and gathering needed data— the *clinical* and *experimental.*

The clinical method involves the intensive study of the personality make-up of a given individual. Various techniques may be employed here, including psychological tests, dream analysis, developmental records, and personal interviews. In addition to yielding information about the personality traits and adjustment problems of particular individuals, the clinical method—by collecting and analyzing data on a great many individuals—has contributed substantially to our understanding of human behavior in general.

The experimental method involves the formulation and carefully controlled testing of hypotheses about specific aspects of behavior. The experimental psychologist may design an experiment, for example, to investigate the effects of anxiety on man's ability to solve problems. As with the clinical method, a wide range of techniques and tools may be utilized, ranging from mechanical measuring devices to psychological tests to opinion surveys. The crucial feature of the experimental method, however, is that the investigator tries to design his experiment in such a way as to hold constant all conditions or variables except one *independent variable* (e.g., anxiety), which is allowed to change systematically so that its effects upon a *dependent variable* (e.g., performance in solving problems) can be studied. If more than one variable were allowed to change (e.g., level of fatigue as well as level of anxiety), it would be impossible for the experimenter to determine which of these variables—or what combination of them—was responsible for whatever variations occurred in the subject's performance.

The experimental method makes possible more precise measurement of human behavior than does the clinical method, because it can test its hypotheses under carefully controlled conditions. Furthermore, these conditions can later be duplicated if an investigator wishes to verify his results by repeating the experiment. The clinical method, on the other hand, is better suited than the experimental for assessing the total personality make-up of a given individual and studying how he behaves in actual life situations. Thus the experimental and clinical methods provide complementary approaches to scientific inquiry in psychology.

2. Formulating principles. Facts, to be useful, must be not only gathered but interpreted. Thus the scientist tries to integrate his data into meaningful principles which, in turn, can be systematically related to one another in a theoretical framework that will explain all the known facts.

Since facts owe no prior allegiance to any scientist, they can sometimes be interpreted in several different ways. This is especially true in a relatively new science such as psychology, where data are far from complete. Thus we find considerable differences in the theoretical positions of such "schools" of psychologists as the behaviorists and psychoanalysts. But even though current theories of human behavior must be regarded as highly tentative, they are of inestimable value in helping psychologists to organize their thinking about the facts now available and to design additional research that may support or correct their present conclusions. Every theory is potentially useful so long as it is held open to question and is used as a stepping stone to additional knowledge. Indeed, the progress of psychology as a science may well be accelerated by having different groups of psychologists work on the same central problem—a comprehensive understanding of man's structure and functioning—from complementary or even contradictory points of view.[1]

3. Applying the findings. It is apparent that scientific facts and principles are of little value unless they can eventually be given some practical application. For a long time most psychologists were reluctant to go beyond the theoretical level in discussing their findings for fear of making premature applications and falling into the same booby traps as many of the popular books on "right thinking" and "personality adjustment." As modern psychology has amassed a growing body of experimental support for its findings, however, it has begun to take a much more active role in disseminating its conclusions and applying them to human problems. While caution is still very necessary, it has become increasingly apparent that man cannot afford to wait until psychology has turned in its final report.

The purpose of the present book, then, is to present the core findings of modern psychology (and of allied biological and social sciences) as

---

[1]For a discussion of some basic considerations in theory construction, see Melvin H. Marx's article on p. 426.

they relate to a better understanding of ourselves and others and to the development of resources for effective living in today's complicated world. This will lead us to an inquiry about man's basic nature; his physical, intellectual, and emotional development; how he perceives his environment and is motivated to act; the kinds of problems he faces and how he goes about resolving them. Although the emphasis will be on scientific information and principles, we will try to point up the significance of these findings in relation to the problem of values—in relation to know-why as well as know-how.

It is not proposed, of course, that personal effectiveness can be achieved by reading a book. People continually seek easy and oversimplified answers to their problems, but unfortunately there are no known short cuts to effective adjustment. Modern psychology can help by providing a considerable body of knowledge about some of the key elements in successful adjustment. The mastery and effective use of this knowledge is up to the individual.

In his book, *Man's Emerging Mind*, John Berrill (1955) discusses man in the perspective of evolutionary time. Although this is a different emphasis from that in the present book, Berrill's beautifully expressed statement of purpose encompasses our present intent as well.

"I am a human being, whatever that may be. I speak for all of us who move and think and feel and whom time consumes. I speak as an individual unique in a universe beyond my understanding, and I speak for man. I am hemmed in by limitations of sense and mind and body, of place and time and circumstance, some of which I know but most of which I do not. I am like a man journeying through a forest, aware of occasional glints of light overhead, with recollections of the long trail I have already traveled, and conscious of wider spaces ahead. I want to see more clearly where I have been and where I am going, and above all I want to know why I am where I am and why I am traveling at all" (p. 1).

REFERENCES

The following list includes both the references cited in this chapter and a selected number of additional books and articles for outside reading.

Berrill, N. J. 1955. *Man's Emerging Mind.* New York: Dodd, Mead & Company. Copyright © 1955 by N. J. Berrill. Published by Dodd, Mead & Company, Inc., New York, and reprinted with their permission.

Cantril, Hadley. 1950. *The "Why" of Man's Experience.* New York: The Macmillan Company.

Cantril, Hadley. 1958. *The Politics of Despair.* New York: Basic Books, Inc. Reprinted by permission of the publishers.

Fromm, Erich. 1955. *The Sane Society.* New York: Rinehart & Company, Inc.

Herrick, C. Judson. 1956. *The Evolution of Human Nature.* Austin: University of Texas Press.

Kluckhohn, Clyde. 1954. "Values of Value-Orientations in the Theory of Action: An Explanation in Definition and Classification." *Toward a General Theory of Action.* Talcott Parsons and Edward A. Shils, eds. Cambridge, Mass.: Harvard University Press.

Lehner, George F. J. 1957. *Explorations in Personal Adjustment.* 2nd ed. Englewood Cliffs, N. J.: Prentice-Hall, Inc.

McCann, Rebecca. 1932. "Inconsistency." *Complete Cheerful Cherub.* New York: Covici, Friede, Inc. Copyright 1932 by Covici, Friede, Inc. Reprinted by permission of Crown Publishers, Inc., New York.

Maslow, Abraham H., ed. 1959. *New Knowledge in Human Values.* New York: Harper & Brothers.

May, Rollo, Ernest Angel, and Henri F. Ellenberger, eds. 1958. *Existence: A New Dimension in Psychiatry and Psychology.* New York: Basic Books, Inc.

Overstreet, Harry and Bonaro. 1956. *The Mind Goes Forth.* New York: W. W. Norton & Company, Inc.

Riesman, David, and others. 1950. *The Lonely Crowd: A Study of the Changing American Character.* New Haven, Conn.: Yale University Press.

Selye, Hans. 1956. *The Stress of Life.* New York: McGraw-Hill Book Company, Inc. Copyright © 1956 by Hans Selye. By permission of McGraw-Hill Book Company, Inc., New York, and Longmans Green & Co., Ltd., London.

Whyte, Willam H., Jr. 1956. *The Organization Man.* New York: Simon and Schuster.

THE
HUMAN
SYSTEM

The Problem of Man's Basic Nature

Determinants of Human Development

Growth Toward Maturity

INTRODUCTION

In order to understand the dynamics of human behavior and the factors that lead to effective or ineffective adjustment, we must know something about the human system itself. Thus Part 1 begins with a consideration of man's basic nature and the way it develops under the influence of inner and outer pressures toward growth and change.

As a first step toward defining the fundamental characteristics of man, Chapter 1 examines some of the conflicting evidence about "human nature." Is man basically cooperative and loving or selfish and aggressive? Is his behavior primarily rational or irrational? Is he capable of self-direction or is he the helpless pawn of influences beyond his control? These age-old questions are seen from a new perspective when we look at man as an "energy system" which continually interacts with—and therefore is constantly being changed by—an environmental field. The development and fulfillment of man's basic nature may be either encouraged or thwarted, depending upon the individual's experiences in his particular environment.

Chapter 2 goes further toward explaining the seeming diversity in human nature by showing how development and behavior (structure and functioning) are shaped by the combined influence of genetic factors, environmental influences, and the unique self-structure which each individual gradually develops. These determinants operate to make each individual both similar to and different from all other human beings. Every change thus produced in the individual influences his subsequent development and behavior.

Chapter 3 continues the story of human development by outlining characteristic patterns of growth toward physical, psychological, and social maturity. Recognizing that any adequate definition of "normality" or "maturity" must leave room for individual and cultural variations, the text traces seven general trends of growth that seem universally characteristic of healthy personality development. The chapter concludes with a discussion of some of the key conditions that may promote or block healthy growth. With this background, we shall be ready to take a closer look at the dynamics of adjustive behavior.

THE PROBLEM OF
MAN'S BASIC NATURE

Conflicting Views of Man's Basic Nature

Man As an Energy System

Despite man's steadily increasing knowledge about his biological antecedents and his place in the universe, there is still no satisfactory answer to the question, "What is human nature?" For the underlying nature of man has been all but obscured by the tremendous diversity of human behavior. Consider, for example, the people we read about in the daily newspaper—the embezzler, the public-spirited businessman, the father who beats his child to death, the social climber, the sex deviate, the kindly priest. It is difficult to see what "human nature" these fellow citizens have in common, and when we expand our horizons to include the people of other cultures, we find even greater differences—in values, goals, and ways of life.

Is there a hidden order beneath this diversity, comparable to the order that scientists have found in the rest of nature? Just what sort of creature is man "down underneath"? This question is not an idle one, for on its answer hinges the type of life man should lead, the form of government that is best suited to him, and the kind of world he should try to construct for himself.

CONFLICTING VIEWS
OF MAN'S BASIC NATURE

Man's attempts to find order in the diversity of human behavior have extended over many centuries. Long before modern science entered the arena, philosophers, theologians, and politicians had been arguing among themselves and with each other over the problem of man's basic nature. From a welter of conflicting views, three questions seem to have consistently recurred—whether man is basically *good or evil; rational or irrational;* and *active or reactive* (i.e., whether he is an active and relatively free agent in determining his own behavior or a passive creature whose behavior is determined by outside influences).

Good or Evil

Some people have asserted that man is basically self-seeking. Others have denied this. Some have seen him as competitive by nature, others as cooperative. Some have maintained that his "real" nature is hostile and cruel, others that it is friendly and kind. All these issues become involved in the larger one of whether man's nature is basically good or evil.

Negative views of human nature. The view that man is a basically "sinful" creature has received substantial support over the centuries from both religion and science—as well as from the experience of the human race. The Christian doctrine of original sin has taught that man, once capable of living a good and perfect life, was corrupted by the Fall. Without divine help, he is unable to resist the temptations of evil. Genesis (8:21) tells us, "the imagination of man's heart is evil from his youth." And St. Paul (Rom. 7:19) confesses, "I do not do the good that I want, but the evil that I do not want, that I do."

This view of human nature as basically sinful has dominated much of Western thought. As Montagu (1955, pp. 402-403) sums it up:

". . . in the western world it is generally believed man is a 'cussed' and 'ornery' creature. There is good and evil in him, but the good is so shot through with the evil, that one must constantly be policing the evil in order to give the good an opportunity to express itself. . . .

"The secular experience of humanity during the last 2,000 years, the internecine wars, the bloodshed, plunder and treachery, the general inhumanity of man to man has in almost every way served to confirm the Church Fathers' view of the natural depravity of man."

While contradicting the traditional Christian explanation of the origin and nature of mankind, Charles Darwin's theory of evolution seemed to lend scientific support to a view of man as basically cruel and evil. Darwin's *On the Origin of Species by Means of Natural Selection,* published in 1859, pictured the natural world as the battleground for a ruthless struggle for survival in which man as well as the lower animals participated. In this universal struggle, the fittest would always win out at the expense of their weaker rivals.

Darwinian theory had a tremendous impact on nineteenth-century thought and was quickly extended to the field of human affairs, where it was used to justify war, racism, and political and economic exploitation. Actually, most so-called social Darwinism was based upon a misinterpretation of Darwin, who maintained that the progress of natural selection worked "solely by and for the good of each being" and that all human endowments would therefore "tend to progress towards perfection." But the general impact of the theory of evolution was to strengthen belief in the essential cruelty and aggressiveness of man.

The theories and writings of Sigmund Freud seemed to validate further this unflattering conception of human nature. In his *Civilization and Its Discontents* Freud (1955, pp. 85-86) depicts man as follows:

". . . men are not gentle, friendly creatures wishing for love, who simply defend themselves if they are attacked, but . . . a powerful measure of desire for aggression has to be reckoned as part of their instinctual endowment. The result is that their neighbor is to them not only a possible helper or sexual object, but also a temptation to them to gratify their aggressiveness, . . . to seize his possessions, to humiliate him, to cause him pain, to torture and to kill him; . . . who has the courage to dispute it in the face of all the evidence in his own life and in history? . . . Anyone who calls to mind the atrocities of the early migrations, of the invasion by the Huns or by the so-called Mongols under Jenghiz Khan and Tamurlane, of the sack of Jerusalem by the pious crusaders, even indeed the horrors of the last world-war, will have to bow his head humbly before the truth of this view of man."

Human nature as "neutral." But despite man's deplorable record of pillage, rape, betrayal, torture, and destruction of his fellow human beings, often on a grandiose scale, there is another side to the picture. Anthropology gives us evidence that there are many peoples in the world who are friendly and kind. The Arapesh of New Guinea, for example, are a peaceful people who think that "all human beings . . . are naturally unaggressive, self-denying, . . . concerned with growing food to feed growing children" (Mead, 1939, p. xix).

Maslow (1954, p. 175) describes a similar lack of aggressiveness among the Northern Blackfoot Indians. He found a record of only five fist fights in fifteen years among this group (which has a constant population of about eight hundred) and no other signs of overt hostility.

"The humor was friendly rather than malicious, the gossip substituted for newspapers rather than for backbiting, the magic, the sorcery, the religion were almost all for the good of the whole group or for healing pur-

"HUMAN NATURE" UNDER STRESS

"In the history of American arms, the most revealing chapter as to the nature of the human animal does not come from any story of the battlefield but from the record of 23 white men and two Eskimos who, on August 26, 1881, set up in isolation a camp on the edge of Lady Franklin Bay to attempt a Farthest North record for the United States."

"The Expedition under command of First Lt. A. W. Greeley, USA, expected to be picked up by a relief ship after 1 year, or 2 years at most. Its supply could be stretched to cover the maximum period. . . .

". . . June of the second year came and passed, and no relief ship arrived. In August, Greeley decided on a retreat, intending to fall back on bases which were supposed to hold food stores. Thereafter disaster was piled upon disaster. . . . When the Greeley Expedition was at last rescued at Cape Sabine on June 22, 1884 . . . seven men remained alive. Even in these, the spark of life was so feeble that their tent was down over them and they had resigned themselves to death. . . .

". . . That any survived was due to the personal force and example of Sgt. (later Brig. Gen.) David L. Brainard, who believed in discipline as did Greeley, and supported his chief steadfastly, but also supplied the human warmth and helping hand which rallied other men, where Greeley's strictures only made them want to fight back. Brainard was not physically the strongest man in the Expedition, nor necessarily the most self-sacrificing and courageous. But he had what counted most—mental and moral balance.

"Among the most fractious and self-centered of the individuals was the camp surgeon, highly trained and educated, and chosen because he seemed to have a way among men. Greeley was several times at the point of having him shot; the surgeon's death by starvation saved Greeley that necessity.

"Among the most decent, trustworthy, and helpful was Jens, the simple Eskimo, who died trying to carry out a rescue mission. He had never been to school a day in his life.

"There were soldiers in the party whom no threat of punishment, or sense of pity, could deter from taking advantage of their comrades, rifling stores, cheating on duty and even stealing arms in the hope of doing away with other survivors. . . .

"But in the greater number, the sense of pride and of honor was stronger even than the instinct for self-preservation. . . .

"Private Schneider, a youngster who loved dogs and played the violin, succumbed to starvation after penning one of the most revealing deathbed statements ever written: 'Although I stand accused of doing dishonest things here lately, I herewith, as a dying man, can say that the only dishonest thing I ever did was to eat my own sealskin boots and the part of my pants.'

"Private Fredericks, accused in the early and less-trying period of meanness and injustice to his comrades, became a rock of strength in the weeks when all of the others were in physical collapse or coma. . . .

"There is still an official report on file in the Department of the Army which describes Sergeant Rice as the 'bravest and noblest' of the Expedition. He is identified with most of its greatest heroisms. The man was apparently absolutely indomitable and incorruptible. He died from freezing on a last forlorn mission into the Arctic storm to retrieve a cache of seal meat for his friends. . . .

"Such briefly were the extremes and the middle ground in this body of human material. . . ."

Department of Defense, 1950, pp. 99-102.

poses rather than for destructiveness, aggression, or revenge. . . . Even today children are rarely punished physically, and the whites are despised for the cruelty with which they treat their children and their fellows. . . . These were not weak people by any means. The Northern Blackfoot Indians are a prideful, strong, upstanding, self-valuing group. They are simply apt to regard aggression as wrong or pitiful or crazy."

This and similar anthropological evidence has led many social scientists to the conclusion that man is a highly educable animal who is neither good nor bad by nature but has potentialities to develop in either direction. Whether he becomes cruel, selfish, and warlike or kindly, self-sacrificing, and peaceful will depend largely upon the culture in which he is reared. Although anthropological evidence alone cannot prove this theory, since hereditary differences might account for some of the observed variations among ethnic groups, it certainly lends strong support to the belief that man's basic nature is highly malleable. This is essentially the point of view taken by the behaviorists, who view human behavior as primarily the result of conditioning.

Evidence for goodness as "natural."
Swinging still further from the negative view of man as essentially evil is the positive conception of the basic goodness of man. The Judaic-Christian tradition, while recognizing man's tendencies to sinfulness, has also taught that man was created in the likeness of God and that there is a divine spark in each of us. Jesus said, "The Kingdom of heaven is within you."

Belief in man's essential goodness was particularly strong in the late eighteenth and early nineteenth centuries and was forcefully expressed in the writings of many Romantic poets and philosophers, who believed that if men were allowed to live "naturally," much

of the evil in the world would disappear. For example, in *Émile*, a treatise on education published in 1762, Jean Jacques Rousseau struck a surprisingly modern note by maintaining that the aim of education should be self-expression rather than the suppression of natural tendencies—that the chief function of the school was to provide the individual child with opportunities to develop his natural gifts, unhampered by the corrupting influences of society.

While taking a more realistic approach to the problems of human development, a growing number of psychologists are coming to accept a similarly positive view of man's essential nature: Man is basically good if permitted to develop his natural propensities. Only when his nature is distorted by pathological conditions, rejecting parents, constant failure and rebuff, or a repressive culture does he become aggressive and cruel. This general position has been forcefully delineated by Maslow (1954, p. 340):

"First of all and most important of all is the strong belief that man has an essential nature of his own, some skeleton of psychological structure that may be treated and discussed analogously with his physical structure, that he has needs, capacities, and tendencies that are genetically based, some of which are characteristic of the whole human species, cutting across all cultural lines, and some of which are unique to the individual. These needs are on their face good or neutral rather than evil. Second, there is involved the conception that full health and normal and desirable development consist in actualizing this nature, in fulfilling these potentialities, and in developing into maturity along the lines that this hidden, covert, dimly seen essential nature dictates, growing from within rather than being shaped from without. Third, it is now seen clearly that psychopathology in general results from the denial or the frustration or the twisting of man's essential nature."

A theory of man's basic tendency toward goodness would seem to receive support from our common experience of being happiest and most content when we are being loving or "good"; hostility and aggressiveness, on the other hand, rarely yield us real or lasting satisfaction. Allport (1954, p. xiv) makes a similar point:

"Normal men everywhere reject, in principle and by preference, the path of war and destruction. They like to live in peace and friendship with their neighbors; they prefer to love and be loved rather than to hate and be hated. . . . While wars rage, yet our desire is for peace, and while animosity prevails, the weight of mankind's approval is on the side of affiliation."

On the physiological level, too, it has been shown that the body functions most efficiently in joy, whereas the visceral activity accompanying unpleasant emotions such as hostility and anger—although useful in coping with many emergencies—disrupts the normal functioning of the body and, over a continued period of time, can actually damage bodily tissues.

Cultural implications. If we adopt the view that man is basically good, then we must modify the old notion that human beings must be "socialized" by severe pressures and controls. Techniques of restriction and control largely give way to techniques designed to encourage fulfillment of potentialities. The implications of this new approach are summed up by Maslow (1954, p. 352):

"The key concepts in the newer dynamic psychology are spontaneity, release, naturalness, self-acceptance, impulse-awareness, gratification. They *used* to be control, inhibition, discipline, training, shaping, on the principle that the depths of human nature were dangerous, evil, predatory, and ravenous. Education, family training, bringing up children, acculturation in general were all seen as a process of bringing the darker forces within us under control.

"See how different are the conceptions of society, law, education, and family that are generated by these two different conceptions of human nature. In the one case, they are restraining and controlling forces, in the other they are gratifying and fulfilling."

The work of Slavson (1943) with a group of delinquent children serves as a dramatic illustration of what is meant by Maslow's viewpoint. These children had come to view the world as a hostile and hurtful place and had become hostile and retaliatory in return. They had fought, stolen, burned property, smashed windows, broken rules, and otherwise shown unwillingness to abide by established social rules. Slavson and his associates concluded that the most important need was to help the children realize that the world was not hostile. Previous attempts to accomplish this by means of personal kindness, talks on right and wrong, praise, rewards, and so on had met with little success.

Slavson and his associates proceeded to contrive an environment for these children in which all social controls were to be abandoned—in which they were not told what to do but could do as they pleased. It was a daring plan, since the apparent "crime" of these children was that they already did as they pleased rather than as parents and other authority figures told them to do. Nevertheless, the children were organized into play groups in which the adult present was not to lead or direct the group but simply to pick up the broken pieces. The children were permitted to do as they pleased with the food, materials, and tools in the room. No adult rules or restraints were imposed other than seeing to it that the children did not severely injure each other. Everything else was considered expendable.

The results were slow, but the group improved steadily and remarkably. An antisocial boy took an interest in what another boy was making and voluntarily helped him instead of trying to destroy it as he would probably have done before. These children gradually found their own hostility decreasing and friendly cooperative impulses emerging instead. In a reasonably favorable environment, an inner tendency toward "healthy" development apparently had reasserted itself.

The success of this experiment does not imply that children growing up in normal circumstances should be given complete freedom to do as they please, for healthy growth requires a certain amount of guidance from without. Being social creatures, we must learn to live within the structure of our society. The children in Slavson's study had been severely twisted by an unfavorable environment and thus required rather drastic treatment before they could be free to develop more normally and to learn more effective techniques of adjustment. In helping these children overcome their feelings of hostility, the experimenters accomplished only an important first step.

The diverse views of human nature as evil or neutral or good have important cultural implications. Whichever view one accepts, it is apparent that man is a highly educable creature and that his development for good or evil can be greatly influenced by cultural conditions. But here the agreement ends. If man is by nature hostile and aggressive, society must shape him into a social creature by exerting stringent controls; if, on the other hand, man's natural tendencies are for good, society can best achieve its purposes by structuring the environment in such a way as to allow the individual considerable freedom for spontaneity and self-direction.

Rational or Irrational

The indictment of man over the ages has not been confined to evidences of his selfishness, cruelty, and aggression. Man has also been characterized as stupid, irrational, and lazy. Political dictators from the time of the Romans to our own day have belittled the ability of the masses and have given them great public spectacles to divert their attention from complex political and social problems which allegedly were beyond their comprehension. In every age there have been those who scoffed at man's much-touted gift of reason. The seventeenth-century satirist, John Wilmot, Earl of Rochester, in "A Satire Against Mankind" spoke of,

> "Reason, which fifty times to one does err,
> Reason, an *ignis fatuus* of the mind."

Even our own Alexander Hamilton spoke with contempt of "the imprudence of democracy, where the people seldom judge or determine right." The ordinary person, he insisted, is governed by emotion and is changeable and unpredictable.

Democratic faith in reason. But reason has also had its champions, and our entire democratic social organization is based on the belief that man, given sufficient information and opportunity, can direct his own affairs and those of society with wisdom and responsibility. In the eighteenth century reason was elevated almost to the level of a cult, as poets, philosophers, and statesmen expressed their faith in man's capacity to achieve perfection by exercising his own superior reason. The American and French revolutions reflected and enhanced a widespread spirit of optimism about the ability of the common man to guide his own destiny. Thomas Jefferson, an aristocrat by birth, maintained that the average person could reason and judge rightly if he were given access to the facts: "Enlighten the people generally, and tyranny and oppressions of body and mind will vanish like spirits at the dawn of day." In his first inaugural address Lincoln expressed a similar faith when he asked: "Why should there not be a patient confidence in the ultimate justice of the people? Is there any better or equal hope in the world?"

Depreciation of reason in modern times. Our own age has seen this faith in man's innate good sense and rationality questioned and depreciated. Current research in psychology and the social sciences has delineated many cultural, emotional, and motivational factors which can distort man's thinking and lead to irrational approaches to his problems. Modern advertisers and political propagandists give daily proof of their ability to influence people's thinking and behavior. Irrational and irresponsible behavior is not uncommon even among individuals who have the necessary knowledge to think soundly on current issues.

Interestingly enough, two of the early schools of psychological thought—behaviorism and psychoanalysis—contributed to the modern loss of faith in man's rationality. In his *Psychopathology of Everyday Life*, for example, Freud emphasized the unconscious and irrational influences that permeate our thinking and behavior. Reading of repressed sex drives, of "unconscious" hostility, of rationalizations, of "irrational" emotions, many people came to the seemingly obvious conclusion that man's behavior is inherently self-deceptive and irrational. Apparently man's motives are something other than they appear on the surface; and his thinking is easily distorted by inner desires and passions of which he may not even be aware. In fact, according to this view, man's "finer" sentiments and strivings are only sublimations of

animal instincts which lurk just beneath the surface of his civilized veneer. Man is thus the victim of instinctual drives and unconscious processes which distort his reason.

Although differing with Freud on many aspects of psychoanalytic theory, the noted Swiss psychiatrist Carl Jung has also contributed materially to the view of man's basic irrationality. Jung not only agrees with Freud concerning the magnitude of the unconscious and irrational forces in man's make-up, but he views man's unconscious as even more archaic and dangerous than did Freud. According to Jung, mental illness results from the overwhelming of the conscious by forces rising up from the unconscious, and wars and revolutions are nothing less than "psychic epidemics" over which man as yet has little rational control (Jung, 1953; Munroe, 1955). Jung also points out that the mass of mankind live within the safe confines of group convention—with little sense of individuality or ability to evaluate problems on their own. In order for the individual to become a rational, thinking person in his own right, he must exert a heroic effort. Not only must the "hero" have the courage to break through the confines of group conformity and go his own way, but he must also come to grips with his archaic unconscious and integrate it with his conscious self. In Jung's thinking, the individual can arrive at the fulfillment of his human potential and become a rational being only as he accomplishes these difficult and painful tasks.

Both Freud and Jung have thus emphasized the unconscious and irrational in man's thinking, and both have pointed to man's need to understand and master the unconscious side of his make-up if he is to cope with his personal and group problems in rational ways. Progoff (1953, p. xiv) summarizes the implications of this general view: "As long as we have not mastered the unconscious side of mental life, we must be at its mercy. This uncomfortable fact hangs over us like a sword on a slim thread, a constant threat to the vaunted achievements of our scientifically rational world."

Although less negative in its implications than psychoanalytic theory, the school of psychology known as behaviorism has also tended to undermine faith in man's rationality. While denying the overwhelming force of unconscious and hence irrational forces in man's thinking, the behaviorists have viewed man as a malleable creature whose thinking and behavior are shaped by his culture through the mechanical process of conditioning. The behaviorists allow room for the possibility of rational thinking, providing man's conditioning is in that direction, but they question the existence of any inherent rational force in man's make-up. According to this view, man is essentially a puppet, manipulated by the strings of his social and cultural conditioning.

Continuing evidence of man's rationality. Although faith in man's rationality has been substantially weakened in the last fifty or hundred years, it is by no means lost. Many modern psychologists believe that man's natural tendencies are toward reason and common sense, just as they are toward "goodness" and love—though in both cases these tendencies can be distorted by environmental influences. Man can be misled by false information, all but stupefied by repetitious and blatant stimuli from the mass communication media, restricted by his cultural background, overwhelmed by the complexity of the issues he is expected to act upon, and handicapped by a lack of training in problem solving. Even his vaunted science, with its worship of scientific objectivity, can mislead him if it causes him to regard as nonexistent or meaningless all aspects of human experience that cannot be studied objectively.

The achievements of modern science, nevertheless, indicate man's capacity and inclina-

tion for dealing with his problems in rational ways. His unremitting efforts to probe the secrets of the universe and make sense of his world mark him as a rational creature. Man is a builder, using simple objects to make more complex ones, striving to establish order in both his physical surroundings and his social relationships, developing ever higher levels of abstraction, and striving for continuity, improvement, and growth. These propensities seem to come naturally, without teaching. We see them already in operation in every healthy toddler.

Active or Reactive

In his everyday life man has always operated on the assumption that he is free to make decisions and choose his own course of action, at least within certain limits. Yet many philosophers, theologians, and scientists have raised the question of whether this freedom of action is *real* or merely *illusory*—whether man is in fact an active and responsible agent with "free will" or a puppet whose behavior is determined by forces beyond his control.

Determinism in philosophy, religion, and science. Various kinds and degrees of determinism have been argued since ancient times. The great dramatic tragedies of Aeschylus and Sophocles, for example, are pervaded by the ancient Greek belief that man, for all his nobility, is in the last analysis a pawn of fate. There is an inevitability in his action, an end from which he cannot escape. This fatalism is clearly illustrated in the well-known legend of Oedipus, who in trying to avoid fulfilling the oracle's prophecy that he would kill his father and marry his mother turned headlong into fate's trap and unwittingly did as was prophesied. The Calvinist doctrine of predestination, which holds that at the time of his birth every individual has already been elected to salvation or condemned to damnation, is a more modern example of religious or philosophic determinism.

Modern science is also concerned with the problem of determinism. In the field of atomic physics, some investigators have concluded that the inner workings of atoms obey simple and exact laws, and they reason that if we could make measurements with infinite accuracy, we could predict the future in every conceivable detail. Others feel that there is a certain amount of indeterminism, or "freedom," in the inner workings of atoms which makes it possible to predict only within certain degrees of probability and hence makes strict determinism untenable.

In the field of psychology, modern determinists have taken their lead from the seventeenth-century English philosopher John Locke, who concluded that the human mind at birth is a *tabula rasa,* or blank tablet, on which learning and experience write their script, giving the mind its content and structure. This view of man as an essentially passive, reactive organism is exemplified by the behaviorist school of psychology. In its most extreme form behaviorism has regarded the individual as a sort of mental robot, the helpless pawn of whatever influences happen to shape him. Thus, the very concepts of self-determination and freedom of choice are illusory; consciousness itself is regarded as only a by-product of "real" events—neurological processes—and thus is assumed to have no power to influence behavior.

Although behaviorists today do not necessarily hold to a strict determinism, American psychologists have by and large favored the view of man as a reactive organism. For evidence they have pointed to the diverse customs and habits of peoples throughout the world, all shaped by cultural conditioning. They have emphasized the experimental findings that the beliefs and values of people can be manipulated by society through punish-

ment and reward and that suggestion and imitation are important forces shaping man's values and opinions. Particular emphasis has been given to the importance of early conditioning as the basis on which subsequent conditioned reactions are built. Recent findings on the effects of subliminal stimulation—or "hidden advertising"—in eliciting desires and action have seemed to lend some further support to a deterministic view of human behavior.

Man viewed as active and purposive. There is, however, another important school of psychological thought that looks upon man as a purposive and striving creature, continuously engaged in the meaningful activities of choosing, judging, and organizing. While acknowledging that human behavior is influenced by the individual's culture, this school of thought emphasizes that a personal factor also operates—that there is a subjective side of culture. Thus the effect of external stimuli on individual behavior is always partially determined by the way the individual views his group, by his ability to accept some ideas and reject others, by his tendency to behave in ways which are consistent with his concept of himself, and by his ability to objectify his experience and to be critical of his own values—to be self-aware and to strive for self-enhancement and self-growth.

This viewpoint, of course, is more consistent with our subjective experience of having freedom to evaluate and choose than is the behaviorist view of man as a purely reactive organism. The American clergyman Harry Emerson Fosdick (1943, p. 7) sees the issue as a question of response as opposed to reaction:

"Things act under the influence of stimuli; they may even be said to *react* to stimuli, but persons can *respond.* Reaction is mechanical, while response is personal, and the endeavors of materialists to reduce the latter to the former are unconvincing because in actual experience the two are so radically different. Billiard balls react; persons can do more. A sneeze is a reaction, but the triumphant answers which some personalities make to life's difficult situations cannot be convincingly subsumed under such a category. Socrates' reply to his judges was not a sneeze, but a response."

The view of man as having a large potential for freedom also ties in with our approach to government—the democratic conviction that the average man, given access to the "facts," can evaluate public issues with some degree of objectivity and rationality rather than as a robot conditioned to think and behave in certain ways. We assume that the freedom granted by democracy to the individual to make decisions is not just an illusion. The view of man as free and active is likewise basic to our philosophy of education, with its emphasis upon developing young adults capable of rational problem solving, creativity, and critical evaluation and with its premise that the more information the individual has at his disposal, the more likely he is to choose and behave wisely.

An eminent American psychologist, Gordon Allport (1955, pp. 82-83), points up the need for psychology and the other behavioral sciences to come to grips with the problem of man's apparent freedom for self-direction:

"One may look through a hundred successive American books in psychology and find no mention of 'will' or 'freedom.' It is customary for the psychologist, as for other scientists, to proceed within the framework of strict determinism, and to build barriers between himself and common sense lest common sense infect psychology with its belief in freedom. For the same reason barriers are erected against theology. But to our discomfort recent events have raised the issue all over again. Existentialism insists on freedom;

much of the psychotherapy now in vogue presupposes it; psychology's new concern with values is at bottom a concern with choices, and therefore revives the problem of freedom."[1]

Allport (p. 100) later goes on to discuss the question of free will versus determinism as it relates to the problems of democracy:

"Up to now the 'behavioral sciences,' including psychology, have not provided us with a picture of man capable of creating or living in a democracy. These sciences in large part have imitated the billiard ball model of physics, now of course outmoded. They have delivered into our hands a psychology of an 'empty organism,' pushed by drives and molded by environmental circumstances. What is small and partial, what is external and mechanical, what is early, what is peripheral and opportunistic—have received the chief attention of psychological system builders. But the theory of democracy requires also that man possess a measure of rationality, a portion of freedom, a generic conscience, [personal] ideals, and unique value. We cannot defend the ballot box or liberal education, nor advocate free discussion and democratic institutions, unless man has the potential capacity to profit therefrom. . . .

"Curiously enough, many of the ardent adherents to the 'empty organism' theory of human nature are among the most zealous fighters for democracy. No paradox is more striking than that of the scientist who as citizen makes one set of psychological assumptions and in his laboratory and writings makes opposite assumptions respecting the nature of man."

Allport is not advocating, of course, that our democratic ideals should dictate our sci-

[1] See Allport's article, "Freedom," on page 520.

entific findings. Rather, he is pointing out that psychologists, in their efforts to be rigorously scientific, have often tended to concern themselves with relatively peripheral and fragmentary phenomena that happen to be amenable to objective and controlled scientific investigation. The result has been to focus scientific attention on those aspects of behavior which can be explained in terms of conditioned responses. This, in turn, has produced a deterministic view of man and tended to obscure the fact that, in real life, people do not seem to function entirely as reactive organisms. Much of human behavior, certainly, *is* determined by conditioning: our opinions, values, and ways of behaving all reflect the experiences we have had and thus the culture in which we live. But this does not seem to tell the whole story. Man is also creative and purposeful.

In maintaining that man is active as well as reactive, we are once again talking about the way man's inner nature tends to work under "normal" conditions—conditions that allow the individual adequate freedom to develop and use his inner potentialities. According to this viewpoint, an autocratic culture which seeks to indoctrinate its members with a uniform value orientation and political viewpoint may be regarded as a "pathological" condition under which man's inner tendencies toward self-direction are considerably thwarted. That such efforts have never been wholly or lastingly successful may be evidence that they are counter to an inborn characteristic of the human energy system—to evaluate rather than just to react mechanically.

Fortunately, modern psychology is gradually developing the scientific tools for tackling the complex problems of values, "free will," and purpose. The results of this broadened research are gradually leading to the emergence of a more realistic picture of man as "endowed with a sufficient margin of reason, autonomy, and choice to profit from living in a free society" (Allport, 1955, p. 101).

MAN AS AN ENERGY SYSTEM

Despite conflicting views of man's basic nature, psychologists assume that there is an order underlying the diversity of human behavior and that continued research will tell us more about the common denominators of human nature, about its potentialities, and about how these potentialities can best be realized. Their methods of approaching these problems, however, have been as varied as their theoretical positions. Some psychologists maintain that the clinical method offers the greatest promise of "explaining" man, while others place their confidence in the experimental method; some insist we must study each facet of man's make-up in great detail, while others feel that only study of the "whole man" can be really fruitful; some place their emphasis upon the external stimuli that have shaped man, while others claim that we must focus our attention on man's motives and thought processes; some feel the study of animals has many implications for understanding human behavior, while others prefer to study only human subjects. We shall examine the contributions of these and other approaches in the course of the present book. For the moment, however, we need a starting point—a broad definition of "human nature" upon which most modern psychologists would agree. Such a definition can be framed if we look at man objectively as an *energy system*.

In essence, an energy system is simply an assemblage of parts which are held together by some force of interaction or interdependence. Thus, we may talk about nonliving systems, such as our solar system, or about living systems, such as plants and animals. Living systems range in complexity from a simple virus to a human society involving hundreds of millions of people.

Physical and biological scientists have long been accustomed to thinking in terms of energy systems, and recently many behavioral scientists have come to approach their study of man in much the same way—viewing him as an energy system which should be studied both in relation to the subsystems that compose it (nervous and glandular systems, for example) and in relation to the larger field or environment of which it is inevitably a part. This approach is a promising one, for it is apparent that human behavior makes sense only as we understand both its component parts and the context in which it takes place.[1]

General Properties of Energy Systems

All energy systems, whether living or nonliving, complex or simple, have *structural, functional,* and *field* properties. A consideration of these basic characteristics will provide us with a general perspective for the study of human personality and behavior.

Structural properties. Every energy system has a definite structure, composed of parts or subsystems. Subsystems in the human body, for example, include glands, bones, musculature, and the nervous system. These subsystems are organized so that the body functions as an integrated unit.

Each energy system also has a boundary of some kind. The boundary of the human body is more clear-cut than that of many energy systems. A political, military, or social group, for example, though operating as a unified

system, may have a boundary that is both intricate and fluid. The systems theorist James G. Miller (1955, p. 515) provides the following illustration: "A naval task force maneuvering blind at sea can be a system, even though its boundary is complicated and in continual flux. It is a system organized by communications. . . ." If a typhoon were to come up, however, and wipe out radio and radar contact, then the task force would no longer be a system since its usual functional interrelationships would be impossible.

The structure of any system provides certain potentialities for action. These potentialities vary greatly, of course, from one type of system to another—the behavior potentialities of a virus or a fish are obviously quite different from those of a man. This is why it is important to understand the structure of a system if we are to understand its behavior.

Functional properties. Energy systems have a built-in tendency to maintain themselves and to resist disintegration. Gravitational forces, for example, keep our solar system from flying apart into space. If a system's equilibrium is disturbed, it tends automatically toward restoring itself. The Navy task force dispersed by a storm will strive to reorganize itself into a functioning system as soon as weather conditions permit the restoration of communications. Even a lowly sponge shows this tendency: if it is reduced to a pulp, rolled flat, and then centrifuged until no trace of its original form remains, it will reconstitute itself into an organized sponge. The amazing ability of a mutilated sponge to restore itself was demonstrated many years ago by the biologist H. V. Wilson, whose remarkable experiment with "scrambled" sponges is described on page 37. Every plant and animal seems to be constituted with self-regulating mechanisms that operate more or less effectively to maintain its characteristic structure and functioning.

---

[1] For a fuller discussion of systems theory in the behavioral sciences, see James G. Miller's article on page 433.

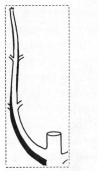

Side shoot becoming vertical

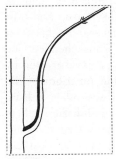

Branch tied up

Branch tied down

Living systems tend to develop according to a pattern that is characteristic for their species and to resist disintegration or distortion. This tendency has been shown dramatically in studies with pine trees and sponges. When the vertical leader (terminal shoot) at the top of a pine tree is cut off, one of the lateral branches turns up to form a new leader (figure a). Sometimes two or more branches compete briefly, but when one takes over as the vertical leader, the others drop back and grow again at the normal angle for side shoots. If a branch is tied up or down, the free end tends to resume the normal direction (figures b and c). In such studies it has been found that a reddish substance called reaction wood *forms on the side of the branch away from the direction in which it needs to bend in order to restore the characteristic growth pattern of the tree. The branch curves away from the reaction wood, because its cells have greater lengthwise extension than other wood cells. The formation of reaction wood is controlled by a hormone,* auxin, *but the regulatory mechanism which, in turn, controls the secretion of auxin is still unknown (Sinnott, 1952).*

Wilson's classic study of sponges (below) provides an even more remarkable demonstration of self-regulatory mechanisms. A sponge was cut up finely and forced through fine bolting cloth into a container of sea water. The minute particles sank to the bottom and promptly began to form small conglomerations and then larger ones. After eight days the new mass had formed the characteristic internal structure of the original sponge (Wilson, 1910).

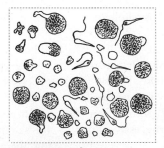

Cells just pressed out

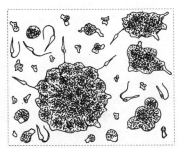

Ten minutes

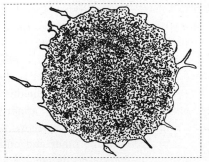

1 hour after being pressed out

Eight days later

Although the ability to resist disintegration is most striking in the lower forms of life, the human system shows a similar tendency to maintain itself. When a man suffers limited brain damage, intact parts can often take over the functions which the damaged parts are no longer capable of performing. When the body is invaded by disease germs, antibodies are formed to fight the invaders. If there is an oversupply of sugar in the blood stream, an increased flow of insulin helps the body to metabolize the sugar and restore its chemical equilibrium. Comparable maintenance tendencies also operate on the psychological level. A person thrown badly off balance by the sudden loss of a loved one or by some other traumatic experience usually regains his equilibrium over a period of time and is much the same person as before. If a man's feelings of adequacy and worth are threatened by repeated failures, he may rationalize his failures or blame them on other people. By the use of such ego defense mechanisms, he maintains the intactness of his "self" system and the integration of his psychological functioning.

Another functional characteristic of living systems is their tendency to grow in accordance with their inherited potentialities—to *actualize* their potentialities. This inner growth tendency is in the direction of greater complexity, as illustrated by the progressive differentiation, specialization, and increasingly complex integration of parts of plants and animals as they develop toward maturity. In human beings this tendency toward growth becomes incredibly complex, for it involves not only physical growth but intellectual, emotional, and social development as well. In later chapters we shall have frequent occasion to note the important role of these inner growth tendencies in human motivation and adjustment.

Field properties. Just as each system, down to the atom, is composed of subsystems, so each is also a part of a larger system or *field*. Thus, a cell is a subsystem of an organ; an organ a subsystem of an individual; an individual a subsystem of a group; and the group a subsystem of society. From this point of view we see persons not as completely separate and distinct from their environment but rather as integral parts of it, both influencing and influenced by the surrounding field.

So far as scientists have been able to discover, there is no such thing as a completely closed system. Each system is in continual transaction with its environmental field as well as with its own subsystems, and this constant interchange influences the behavior of both system and field. Thus chemical imbalances in the body, such as those created by lack of food, may affect the functioning and even the structure of various other subsystems; singly and in combination these changes will affect the behavior of the individual; and the individual may in turn use the resources of his environment to restore the balance of his system—for example, by procuring food.

Even in this simple illustration the individual has both altered his environment and in turn been altered by it. Normally, of course, the transactions between man and his environment—both physical and social—are much more complex than this. His life goals, for example, and the opportunities for achieving them may be largely determined by his environment. Or he may take an active role in modifying the basic structure of his environment by working for political, economic, and social changes. As we shall note shortly, one of the unique characteristics of man as an energy system is the richness of his transactions with his field.

It is readily apparent that to understand the human system, we will have to study both the inner and outer factors that together determine its condition and behavior. Its behavior will always be partly the result of its own particular inner make-up and tendencies and partly the result of outside forces which are acting upon it, interacting with it, or simply providing opportunities or limitations for its actions.

Special Characteristics of the Human System

Although all energy systems share the basic structural, functional, and field properties outlined above, different types or levels of systems—physical, biological, psychological, or social—also reveal many unique characteristics. Living systems are different in many ways from nonliving systems, and as we go up the scale from simple to complex living systems we find that new structural and functional properties begin to appear. It often happens that properties present in rudimentary form at lower levels of life become further refined and more influential at higher levels. The evolvement of the nervous system, for example, can be traced from a very simple segmental apparatus in a worm to the highly complex brain of man.

While sharing many general characteristics with lower-level systems, man reveals many characteristics that are relatively unique. Among the most significant are his self-awareness and self-direction; his ability to modify his behavior to meet varied situations; his use of symbols; the richness of his transactions with his environment; and his concern with information, values, and meaning.

Self-awareness and self-direction. Responsiveness to stimulation—sometimes called *irritability*—is a property of all living things. Though it is impossible to know at what point in the scale of life irritability becomes associated with consciousness, there can be no doubt that man's consciousness reaches a stage of depth and precision far beyond the types of awareness that exist in

lower animals. Man is aware both of his world and of himself—and being thus aware, goes on to evaluate what he sees and to act with forethought and purpose. To a far greater extent than any other species, he has the ability to shape his own future and control his own destiny.

Modifiability of action. Acute awareness of problems to be solved and needs to be met would be of little use to man if he were limited to reflex or instinctive behavior. Of all creatures, man is the least bound by such patterns and the most capable of flexibility and modifiability. By storing information, by developing new skills, concepts, and tools, by reasoning and imagining, and by learning from experience, man can adjust his efforts to meet the particular requirements of each new situation. His resources for doing this are far superior to those of the lower animals.

Use of symbols. Other creatures show some flexibility and even resourcefulness in dealing with perceived situations, but there is little evidence that they can deal in any complex way with absent situations by thinking about them. Man's thought processes, on the other hand, may be concerned largely or entirely with ideas—symbols of absent or even imaginary objects. This makes possible creativeness, inventiveness, the prediction of consequences, and hence the intelligent planning of future activity.

Our highly developed ways of communicating with each other are possible only because of our ability to use symbols. Many animals can signal approaching danger, but it is doubtful if they can describe the danger to each other in detail or discuss alternate ways of handling it. Our ability to speak and write precise ideas gives us an incalculable advantage over them.

Man's ability to use symbols has also made it possible for him to store information, accumulate ideas from one generation to the next, and transfer the results of experience from one person to another. Greek writers, dead for over two thousand years, can still spark our thinking through their writings. Each new generation has a little more to build on than any previous generation and thus need not repeat actions that have already been shown to lead to blind alleys.

Richness of transactions with field. Whereas the lower animals must usually eat what they can find or starve and must shiver on cold days and swelter on hot ones, man is not so limited. In fact, there seems to be almost no end to the ways in which he can change and control his surroundings. As a consequence, his relationships and transactions with his environment have become far more rich and complex than those of other creatures.

MAN AS AN ENERGY SYSTEM

Common Characteristics of Energy Systems		*Examples in Man*
Structural	Internal structure, subsystems	Bodily equipment, constitution, personality structure
	Changes in structure with time	Maturation, learning, aging
Functional	Energy sources	Motives, drives, emotions
	Stabilizing resources	Homeostatic mechanisms, healing and restoration after damage
	Adjustive resources	
	a) Information handling	Perception, evaluation, decision
	b) Information storing	Memory
	c) Modification of behavior	Learning, reasoning
	d) Emergency resources	Emotions, compensation
	e) Communication devices	Neural and chemical (within system); language, other symbols (with field)
	Reproduction	Reproductive system
Field	Relations with lower-order systems	Relations with animals and inanimate objects
	Relations with same-order systems	Relations with other individuals
	Relations with higher-order systems	Individual-group and group-group relations

Adapted by permission from Grinker, 1956, p. 303.

This is especially true of man's social environment. Though some animals have societies, they can hardly be said to have cultures. The standards and values, the loyalties, and the many material and nonmaterial creations and forms of expression of a human society have no counterpart in animal groups. They are possible at the human level because of the greater richness of transactions possible to man in both the physical and social spheres.

Such transactions have several characteristic qualities. First, as indicated above, they are purposive: they represent attempts by the human system to maintain itself and to achieve its goals. Second, they involve information gathering by the system, a prerequisite to any effective action. And third, they involve feelings, sentiments, and emotions. These are basic aspects of human experience and are often referred to as man's striving, thinking, and feeling—or, more technically, as the *conative, cognitive,* and *affective* dimensions of human behavior. They are present in the definition of psychology as the science of why we act, think, and feel as we do. They used to be represented in the psychology books by separate chapters on "the will," "reason," and "emotions," but now we conceive of them as dimensions of all activity rather than as separate entities.

Concern with information, value, and meaning. Since man's behavior is not limited to instinctual, built-in patterns of adjustment, he may decide for himself what goals to pursue and then attempt to get the information and know-how he needs to achieve them. To choose his goals and decide what means will achieve them, he must not only process vast quantities of information but also decide what is valuable and what is not. And inevitably, he sooner or later finds himself trying to understand the significance of his own existence. These concerns are uniquely human. They can arise only when a high degree of flexibility and choice is possible for the system.

Changes in the System with Time

Changes inside the system or in its field bring corresponding changes in the overall system and its behavior. Such changes may be minor or drastic, slow or fast, reversible or permanent.

In man, as in other living systems, some changes come as part of a predictable life cycle, genetically determined and more or less automatic. In the early phases of this life cycle the changes are toward increased size and complexity and toward the development of new abilities; in the later phases the changes include deterioration and disintegration.

But not all the changes in the human system are genetically determined. Some may be caused by accident or disease. Others, especially on the psychological level, come as the result of experience and involve both choice and learning. This makes it impossible to predict the exact psychological structure that an individual will develop, nor is there any guarantee that the path he takes will be the "natural" one in terms of fulfilling his best potentials. It can only be predicted that he will probably emerge with a fairly consistent structure of assumptions, attitudes, and values which will guide his behavior and lead to a life style that is characteristic for him.

It can also be predicted that a person's emerging psychological structure will itself become an increasingly important influence on his further learning. He will tend to learn what is consistent with his past learning and to ignore or deny new experiences which do not fit. Environmental demands, expectations, rewards, and opportunities therefore tend to exercise their greatest influence during childhood, before the personality becomes well defined. By adulthood the psychological structure is usually so well developed and stable that, although it may continue to change in minor ways, only a radical upheaval in a person's environment or in his outlook will bring about a major change in his life style.

Although understanding man's basic nature is a very complex problem, science has cleared away many misconceptions and has provided much useful information. In the present chapter we have tried to see through the diversity of human behavior in order to pick out a few of the most fundamental characteristics of human nature. We have concluded that man, while sharing certain basic properties with all other energy systems, has unique characteristics which both broaden and complicate his potentials for development.

Man is a highly educable creature, shaped in different ways as the result of his complex transactions with his environmental field. Lacking built-in mechanisms to guide most aspects of his psychological and social development, he may become many things. But like other systems, he seems to have *tenden-*

cies to grow in certain directions when environmental conditions permit. His general tendency toward health and toward fulfilling and actualizing his potentialities as a human being seems to be revealed in tendencies to be loving, cooperative, rational, active, and purposeful in guiding his own behavior. Our view of man as an energy system, operating within an environmental field that provides opportunities, limitations, and demands, helps us to understand how these tendencies may be either encouraged or thwarted.

To understand why people behave as they do—and the likenesses and differences among them—we must examine the structural, functional, and field properties of the human system in more detail. In the next two chapters dealing with personality development we shall be primarily concerned with structural properties and how they come into being; in Part Two, on the dynamics of individual and group behavior, we shall be concerned primarily with functional properties; and throughout, we shall emphasize the interaction between system and field, particularly the social field.

REFERENCES

The following list includes both the references cited in this chapter and a selected number of additional books and articles for outside reading.

Allport, Gordon W. 1954. *The Nature of Prejudice.* Boston: Beacon Press, Inc.

Allport, Gordon W. 1955. *Becoming: Basic Considerations for a Psychology of Personality.* New Haven, Conn.: Yale University Press.

Department of Defense. 1950. *The Armed Forces Officer.* Washington D. C.: United States Government Printing Office.

Fosdick, Harry Emerson. 1943. *On Being a Real Person.* New York: Harper & Brothers.

Freud, Sigmund. 1954. *Psychopathology of Everyday Life.* 2nd ed. London: Ernest Benn, Ltd.

Freud, Sigmund. 1955. *Civilization and Its Discontents.* Westport, Conn.: Associated Booksellers.

Grinker, Roy R., ed. 1956. *Toward a Unified Theory of Human Behavior.* New York: Basic Books, Inc.

Jung, Carl G. 1953. *The Development of Personality. Collected Works*, Vol. 17. Herbert Read and others, eds. New York: Pantheon Books, Inc.

Maslow, A. H. 1954. *Motivation and Personality.* New York: Harper & Brothers.

Mead, Margaret. 1939. *From the South Seas: Studies of Adolescence and Sex in Primitive Societies.* New York: William Morrow & Company, Inc.

Miller, James G. 1955. "Toward a General Theory for the Behavioral Sciences." *The American Psychologist, 10*, No. 9, 513-531.

Montagu, M. F. Ashley. 1955. "Man—and Human Nature." *The American Journal of Psychiatry, 112*, No. 6, 401-410.

Munroe, Ruth L. 1955. *Schools of Psychoanalytic Thought.* New York: The Dryden Press, Inc.

Progoff, Ira. 1953. *Jung's Psychology and Its Social Meaning.* New York: The Julian Press, Inc.

Sinnott, Edmund W. 1952. "Reaction Wood and the Regulation of Tree Form." *American Journal of Botany, 39*, No. 1, 69-78.

Sinnott, Edmund W. 1955. *The Biology of the Spirit.* New York: The Viking Press, Inc.

Slavson, Samuel R. 1943. *Introduction to Group Therapy.* New York: The Commonwealth Fund.

Wilson, H. V. 1910. "Development of Sponges from Dissociated Tissue Cells." *Bulletin of the Bureau of Fisheries, 30*, 1-30.

DETERMINANTS OF HUMAN DEVELOPMENT

Man's Genetic Endowment

Physical and Sociocultural Environment

Self As a Third Determinant

In discussing man as an energy system, we noted that the structural, functional, and field properties of the human system are constantly changing. Although we can see a remarkable continuity in the behavior and life style of most people over a period of years, no person has exactly the same structural and functional characteristics that he had yesterday or will have tomorrow. These are continuously being modified by maturation and learning, under the combined influence of internal and external pressures toward growth and change.

Thus, to understand why people behave as they do—and the likenesses and differences among them—we must study not only the basic structural properties of the human system but the ways in which the system changes with time. In this chapter we shall first examine man's genetic endowment, which provides the potentialities for growth and behavior. Next we shall note the role of environmental opportunities, limitations, and pressures in determining what the individual *makes* of his potentialities. And finally we shall see how the individual's sense of personal identity and purpose—his *self-structure* —comes to act as a third important influence on development. Working together, the forces of heredity, environment, and self shape us all into the recognizable mold of human beings and, paradoxically, make each of us a little different from everybody else.

MAN'S GENETIC ENDOWMENT

At conception each new human being receives a genetic inheritance which provides all the potentialities for his behavior and development throughout his lifetime. This endowment includes potentialities for the individual's bodily equipment; for the development of specific skills, abilities, and kinds of behavior; and for patterns of growth and change throughout a predictable life cycle.

The Mechanics of Heredity

At fertilization, the male and female germ cells unite to form a fertilized ovum containing about forty-six chromosomes, half from each parent.[1] The chromosomes are minute, threadlike structures containing many hundreds of ultramicroscopic particles called *genes*, which are the real carriers of a person's heredity. Together, the chromosomes probably contain from ten to fifteen thousand genes, each of them a complex molecule consisting of thousands of atoms in special arrangements. The genes carry the blueprint for the individual's development and direct his growth from a one-celled fertilized ovum to a multibillion-celled adult. Within this inherited structure, too, are the potentialities for behavior.

Ethnic (group) differences. Although the entire human race receives a characteristic genetic inheritance that is different in important respects from that of any other species, there are noticeable differences from one group to another. The peoples of the world have customarily been classified, for example, into three racial strains: the Mongoloid or yellow, the Negroid or black, and the Caucasian or white. This classification has been based primarily upon consistent differences in physical traits (such as body size and shape,

[1]On the basis of current research, we cannot say for sure whether the number of chromosomes in a human cell is forty-six or forty-eight, or whether it varies. The number has long been thought to be forty-eight, but some recent investigators—using a new technique of "spreading" the chromosomes, plus highly refined photomicrography—have found forty-six predominant (Tjio and Levan, 1956). The issue is by no means settled, but for our purposes here the important point is that a fertilized egg contains an equal number of chromosomes from each of the two parents.

skin color, hair color and texture, eye shape, and the distribution of blood types) which seem to be genetically determined. Consistent differences are also found among smaller ethnic groups—often even among national groups.

The extent to which psychological differences among ethnic groups are genetically determined is obscured by the difficulty of distinguishing culturally determined traits from hereditary ones. If observed differences in such traits as competitiveness, introversion, and submissiveness are influenced by genetic factors, the underlying genetic differences may be the result of the selective survival of individuals best adapted to a given environment. The long-term results of inbreeding may also be a factor.

In general, it would appear that all racial and ethnic groups are basically the same in biological make-up and that the differences *between* groups in respect to any trait are less than the range of differences *within* given groups. Because identification as a member of a particular ethnic group may lead to differences in role, status, and opportunity, however, there are often wider differences in development than genetic inheritance alone would seem to explain

Family and individual differences. Important genetic differences are found not only within ethnic groups but even within a single family. To understand the basis for such differences, it is necessary to understand the process of *reduction division*.

Germ cells—both sperms and ova—contain only half the number of chromosomes that other body cells do. Thus, when a sperm and ovum unite, the resulting fertilized cell (and each of the cells subsequently formed by subdivision) has the characteristic full number of chromosomes. Reduction division is the process of random selection by which each germ cell receives one or the other of each pair of chromosomes. It is impossible to pre-dict, of course, which chromosomes a particular sperm or ovum will carry, and different germ cells from the same individual may have very different selections of chromosomes—much like the different hands that can be dealt from a deck of cards. In the mating of any two parents, there are 8,388,608 possible combinations between the twenty-three chromosomes of the mother and the twenty-three of the father—and the likelihood that any one of these combinations would occur more than once is so small as to be virtually nonexistent.

Thus, a tremendous range of individual differences is possible among children of the same parents, even though in every case they receive half their chromosomes from the mother and the other half from the father. In *very* rare instances brothers and sisters may not be related to each other genetically at all—each may receive an entirely different selection of chromosomes. At the other extreme are identical twins, who grow from a single fertilized ovum and thus have identical genetic endowments. On the average, however, we might expect about half the chromosomes of brothers and sisters to be alike.

Differences in genetic endowment among members of the same family provide somewhat different potentials for development, both physical and psychological. And as we go from the immediate family to grandparents, cousins, and other more distant relatives, we find that differences in genetic make-up increase—for, by the laws of chance, the average number of shared chromosomes becomes smaller. Random selection also makes it theoretically possible, of course, for cousins or other fairly distant relatives to be more alike in genetic make-up than brothers and sisters are, but this happens only rarely. Finally, as we come to people who are unrelated, we find no common chromosomes at all.

The operation of dominant and recessive genes accounts for further differences within families. When the ovum is fertilized, the genes from each parent arrange themselves in corresponding pairs—for example, the genes which determine eye color from the paternal side become paired with the genes for eye color from the maternal side. But suppose genes for brown eye color are paired with genes for blue eye color. In this case, because the brown-eye genes are *dominant* genes, the offspring's eyes will be brown. The *recessive* blue-eye genes still remain a part of the new individual's chromosome structure, however, and may show up in later generations if the person marries someone who also carries genes for blue eye color. By this mechanism, recessive traits that are not visibly evident in either parent may show up in their children.

It thus becomes apparent that our genetic inheritance makes ample provision for widespread individual differences while at the same time insuring a common hereditary core which is characteristic of the entire human species.

The Role of Heredity in Development

In Chapter 1 we summarized some of the unique characteristics of the human energy system—self-awareness and self-direction, modifiability of action, the use of symbols, richness of transactions with field, and concern with information, values, and meaning. We also noted that the human organism, like all living systems, tends to maintain itself and to fulfill its inherent potentialities. These characteristics are the product of our hereditary endowment, as it unfolds through experience.

It is clearly impossible to list all the specific potentialities our genetic endowment provides. In this section we shall content ourselves with a brief discussion of heredity's role in establishing the overall pattern of growth and change that is typical of the human life cycle; in determining our general

potentials for behavior; and in establishing certain constitutional tendencies characteristic of each individual.

Potentials for growth. Although normal growth is always dependent upon a minimally favorable environment, it is initiated from *within*, by man's genetic endowment, and it operates toward fulfilling the potentialities of the human system. The course of development from conception to maturity is incredibly complex. In many ways the life cycle of the human being, especially in its early phases, repeats the evolution of the species. As Gesell (1953, pp. 51-52) puts it:

". . . the human life cycle as of today remains biologically a most complicated and even an awe-inspiring spectacle. Into the early sectors of this cycle are compressed millions upon millions of years of prehuman evolution. The germinal cells which initiate a cycle of growth are, in a sense, very new, but each has a phyletic history which recedes into remote geologic epochs. By the same token, the embryo, fetus, and newborn infant are biologically very ancient. The toddler walks and leans with a posture which suggests primitive mankind. Yet he is at the same time so untutored in our modern culture that we rightfully regard him as something unique and recent under the sun."

We are all aware that physical growth follows a definite pattern from infancy to adulthood. We often fail to realize, however, that intellectual, emotional, and social growth also follow a developmental sequence whose general outline is determined by man's genetic endowment—even though the specific details are shaped by environmental factors. Every growing individual acquires increasing information about himself and his world, for example, and gradually achieves competence in reasoning and problem solving. Similarly, emotional and social behavior progress from immature and relatively undifferentiated patterns of response to the more complicated and subtle ones required for adult living. In short, although development in these areas is heavily dependent on learning, its broad outlines seem to be established by hereditary factors.

Heredity provides for significant differences as well as likenesses in growth. Individuals vary widely in both the rate and the quality of their development, especially during childhood. Some children grow more slowly than average and may be somewhat at a disadvantage with respect to others of their own age group; others mature more rapidly, so that at each chronological stage they have a better than average potential for achievement. As a rule, different areas of growth tend to parallel each other, regardless of whether the overall rate of growth is rapid or slow, but sometimes development is uneven. For example, one child may be precocious in speaking and slow in walking, whereas another may walk early but be slow in talking. Spurts of growth, especially noticeable in adolescence, may also upset the balance temporarily. Such variations in growth patterns are determined primarily by inherited make-up.

Developmental variations make individual differences more and more apparent with time. Minor differences existing early in the developmental sequence tend to become more pronounced as development proceeds, largely as a result of social influences. For example, a stronger than average child may be encouraged to develop athletically, while a frail child is excused from strenuous physical activities. Original differences between the two children are thus increased.

Behavior potentials. We may think of the inherited properties of the human system as providing such general behavior potentials as those for:

Learning and thinking—receiving, integrating, and storing information and using it creatively in symbolizing, reasoning, and problem solving.

Feeling—experiencing fear, anger, love, joy, and other emotional patterns that help motivate action and give meaning to conscious experience.

Striving—setting goals and initiating purposeful behavior.

Acting—channeling energy toward the achievement of goals and executing adjustive responses.

Making automatic responses—adjusting automatically to repetitive situations through the mechanisms of reflex and habit, thus leaving conscious thought processes free to cope with more difficult problems.

Making emergency responses—mobilizing physical and psychological resources to deal with emergency situations.

To a large extent, these are behavior potentials of all higher animals, but they are considerably broader for the human being than for any other species because man's mental equipment is far more complex and refined. A normal human being has an almost limitless capacity for learning. He can symbolize, reason, and imagine; he can evaluate, integrate, and communicate vast quantities of information; he can anticipate his future needs and act purposefully to meet them. His emotional potentials, too, are infinitely greater than those of other species and make possible a vast richness of conscious experience. Only man among all living creatures talks, tells jokes, laughs, prays, worries about dying, writes of his experiences, and strives for future improvement.

As we have already suggested, the characteristic that most clearly sets man apart from lower species is his great potential for responding appropriately to new situations—he is not restricted to built-in adjustive patterns. In this connection it is interesting to compare man with another remarkable species, the ant. Ants can lift more than twenty times their own weight and perform numerous other remarkable feats. The famed leaf-cutting parasol ants of Latin America have mastered a simple type of gardening: they gather leaves, chew them to a pulp, and make an underground compost heap in which to grow mushroom spores.

Even the social structure of ants may be well organized and complex. The carnivorous driver ants of Africa, for example, march in orderly formations flanked by larger "officer ants" who organize, discipline, and direct the troops. Scouts bring back reports on the territory to be invaded and then act as an advance guard for the expedition. The ants move rapidly through the jungle devouring every edible thing in their path. If their route is exposed to the burning sun, they escape death by quickly throwing up a covered archway of earth and march on (Crompton, 1954).

All driver ants behave in this way, for their behavior is determined by built-in, genetically determined mechanisms. Given a favorable environment, they function effectively, at their level, and can meet their needs automatically; but they have virtually no capacity for changing their behavior in the light of experience.

Man, on the other hand, has worked out countless forms of social organization—some more successful than others, but all made possible by his capacity for modifying his behavior. The variety of responses possible to man is both an advantage and a disadvantage, for while it gives him freedom to work out appropriate behavior at a much higher level than other species can, it also presents him with the worry and responsi-

The members of a given species and sometimes of larger taxonomic groups inherit not only potentials for structure but also potentials for characteristic behavior. For example, most of the Amniota (reptiles, birds, and mammals, whose embryos develop in an amniotic sac) scratch their heads in the same way—with a hindlimb crossed over a forelimb. This is true even of the few birds that have learned to eat by raising their claws directly to their mouths: they still scratch their heads in the clumsy, over-the-wing way and cannot be taught to do it differently (Lorenz, 1958). Inherited potentials for behavior are also shown in the nest-building of birds, different for each species, and in the propensity of newborn ducklings to learn to follow their mothers (or substitutes). Man's propensities for upright posture and verbal communication are equally insistent, though most human behavior potentials require complex learning to reach fruition.

bility of finding the most effective patterns. Man has no assurance that even his most basic needs will be met; he *must* learn in order just to stay alive.

Constitutional tendencies. Even before birth, genetic factors seem to contribute a uniqueness to each developing human being. As Gesell and Amatruda (1945, p. 248) summarize it: "Every embryo is unique. The uniqueness is so fundamental that it pervades the whole life cycle. It expresses itself in psychic constitution, temperament, motor demeanors, and distinctive modes of growth." This uniqueness continues and is elaborated after birth, as the result not only of experience but of the continuing action of genetic factors. Traits such as intelligence, sensitivity, vigor, resiliency, and even temperament seem to have a constitutional basis. To be sure, there is no positive way to prove that such traits are genetically based, but we may tentatively assume that a characteristic is constitutional when (1) it appears immediately after birth and subsequently remains fairly stable or (2) its appearance at a later stage of development seems independent of the environment and particular experiences of the child (Witmer and Kotinsky, 1952).

Some constitutional traits, such as intelligence, influence development primarily in terms of the level of potential they provide; others, such as physical appearance, exert their influence primarily in terms of the reactions of other people; and still others, such as sensitivity, appear to be responsible for basic patterns of reactivity which appear very early and are relatively consistent throughout a given individual's life span. The following constitutional traits seem particularly important in contributing to developmental differences.

1. Intelligence. Inherited differences in intelligence are important in determining learning rate, interests, and the complexity of problems the individual can handle. Low intelligence obviously places many limitations on what a person can do, particularly in terms of education and occupation. And by influencing success or failure in competition, differences in intelligence also help shape a person's feelings of self-confidence and worth.

Contrary to popular notions, intellectual superiority tends to be accompanied by better than average physical and emotional health. Referring to the findings of Terman, who tested a group of gifted children and followed their development over a period of some thirty years, Gough (1955, p. 1) says:

"Intellectually gifted persons tend to excel in nearly all that they do. Since the publication of the classic studies on intellectually superior children by Lewis M. Terman and his associates, we have known that such children are healthier, happier, more mature emotionally, more stable, and more likely to achieve in both educational and social activities than their less advantaged counterparts. Furthermore, these differences continue on into adult life, and in some respects are even increased. The gifted child grown up is indeed a fortunate individual. He is physically healthier, freer from psychiatric illness, delinquency, and alcoholism, more likely to attain marital happiness, better-educated, better paid, and better fitted to his job and his station in life than the average man."

Although we place a great deal of emphasis upon intelligence in our society, it is by no means the only important characteristic of the individual, nor does a high level of intelligence by itself insure either successful adjustment or happiness. Motivation, maturity, acquired competencies, and many other factors enter into total adjustment.

2. Sensitivity. Even during the first few weeks of life, babies differ greatly in their general sensitivity to stimulation. Some are startled by even slight sounds or cry or whimper if sunlight hits their faces. Others are seemingly insensitive to such stimulation. Thus the same environment may have different effects on different babies; conditions that one can tolerate may be quite upsetting or even overwhelming to another. Apparently many babies and young children who seem "nervous" and "high-strung" react as they do because of a constitutionally higher than average sensitivity and would show these traits regardless of the child-rearing practices to which they were subjected. Such sensitivity can be aggravated or minimized by parental handling, but it always carries over to some degree and continues to influence development and behavior throughout life.

3. Vigor. Brief observation of any group of infants clearly reveals that they vary considerably in their vigor and activity level. This may be reflected in marked differences in exploratory activity and in the tendency of infants with a high level of vigor to deal with their problems in a more active, aggressive manner than less energetic babies. Such basic differences are often noticeable even between two children of the same family. They seem to continue throughout development and will affect the needs and satisfactions of the individual at every turn.

Differences in vigor may also markedly affect the way parents relate to a child. A highly vigorous and active child born into a rather phlegmatic family may prove difficult for the parents to understand and cope with; similarly, a relatively passive child born into an active and vigorous family may prove disappointing to his parents and difficult for them to understand. In such ways the child's constitutional characteristics may elicit reactions from others which in turn affect his subsequent development.

4. Temperament. The term *temperament* refers to the individual's emotional disposition and prevailing moods. Some individuals tend from early childhood to be relatively stable in emotional make-up and are not easily aroused to intense fear, anger, joy, or anxiety. Others tend to overreact emotionally to even minor setbacks or successes. Most individuals are also characterized by what may be termed a prevailing mood pattern—as, for example, of cheerfulness and well-being or dejection and gloom—though some people characteristically show rather marked fluctuations in mood.

5. Resistance. Babies show marked differences in their vulnerability to both physical and psychological upsets and in their ability to recuperate from such disturbances. Besides these overall differences in level of resistance, consistent variations have also been observed in more specific reactions. For example, in response to a minor infection, some babies characteristically develop a fever; others, a digestive disturbance; still others, a skin infection. Apparently a particular subsystem of the body is frequently more vulnerable than others and is most likely to show a reaction to any disturbance in the overall functioning of the organism.

This tendency continues into adulthood: although few illnesses are congenital, constitutional factors seem to predispose certain individuals to particular manifestations of physical or psychological disturbance. Thus, under conditions of stress some persons develop peptic ulcers whereas others are afflicted with allergies or migraine headaches or other disorders.

6. Other constitutional tendencies. Characteristics such as physical appearance (including physique), the fact of being male or female, and physical deformities are also important in total personality development. Several psychologists have even attempted to show the existence of a systematic relationship between physical build and such seemingly unrelated aspects of development as temperament. Probably the best known of these body-type theories at present is that of W. H. Sheldon (1954). Sheldon postulates three body types based on a predominance of development of one of the three embryonic layers: (1) the visceral layer, associated with a soft, rounded physique and social, comfort-loving temperament; (2) the bone and muscle layer, associated with an athletic physique and energetic temperament; and (3) the neural layer, associated with tall, thin, delicate physique and sensitive, intellectual temperament. Although it is difficult to say which is cause and which is effect in relationships between physique and temperament, Seltzer (1946) found in his study of 256 "normal" college men that uneven body proportions—hips broad for width of shoulders, stature tall for body weight, and so on—were more frequently associated with traits indicating instability than were more "harmonious" bodily proportions.

Whatever the exact cause-effect relation between physical constitution and other traits, it is apparent that our general physical appearance may have a great deal to do with how other people react to us (witness the response of men to a pretty girl and a homely one) and thus affect our self-confidence, feelings of worth, and other aspects of development. Similarly, the fact of being male or female—while making little difference, apparently, in our inherent capacity for most types of achievement—contributes significantly to individuality because of differing cultural expectations for men and women. Thus we find fairly consistent differences between the sexes in such characteristics as interests, athletic and intellectual abilities, aggressiveness, and emotional responses. Finally, being born with a physical handicap such as blindness, deafness, or deformity affects widely varied aspects of personality development, for the handicapped individual faces many adjustment problems that the average person never encounters.

Although much remains to be discovered about the role of constitutional tendencies in human development, their special significance lies in their influence on the way the individual tends to react to his environment and hence to be influenced by it.

PHYSICAL AND SOCIOCULTURAL ENVIRONMENT

No trait is so dependent on heredity as not to require certain minimal environmental conditions for its development. This is true even of physical traits and certainly much more so of intellectual, social, and emotional ones. At any given moment an individual is the product of countless interactions between his genetic endowment and his physical and sociocultural environment. By physical environment we refer to the natural world surrounding the individual: climate, terrain, food supplies, disease germs, and so on. By sociocultural environment we mean the world of people, customs, values, and man-made objects.

Physical Environment

Peoples of the earth live under diverse conditions of climate, terrain, and natural resources. Some live in dense jungles and others on barren deserts; some live on high mountains and others on flat prairie lands. Some live where it is extremely cold and others where it is oppressively hot; some live where it rains most of the time and others where there is chronic drought. In some places food and other resources are plentiful; in others they are so scarce that most of the individual's life must be spent in eking out a bare subsistence. Some areas are infested with disease and other hazards to physical safety; others are relatively free of disease and danger.

Climate and terrain. Peoples inhabiting areas where conditions of climate or terrain are unfavorable tend to undergo adaptive physiological changes. For example, the circulatory system of the Eskimo tends to lie deep within a protective fatty layer which conserves his body heat. The native Indians who work the tin mines of Bolivia in the thin atmosphere of mountains as high as eighteen thousand feet have a greater number of red corpuscles than we do and a lung capacity about twice as efficient as ours.

The effects of climate and terrain on psychological development are less well understood. The extent to which the reputed emotionality of the Latins and the stolidness of the Scandinavians are a function of climate is a matter of speculation. It has been suggested that the long winter darkness may have a depressing effect on people who live near the Arctic Circle and that people who live in mountain valleys may feel more secure and hence be less aggressive than those who live on open plains. As yet, however, the possible relationships have not been studied systematically.

Scarcity, disease, and other unfavorable conditions. Even today many millions of people live in areas where disease is rife and food supplies are inadequate. Such conditions take a tremendous toll in reduced physical vigor, bodily damage, and loss of life. Because adverse physical conditions influence the way a group lives, we may assume that they also exert some effect, at least

indirectly, on the personality development of individual members. However, the precise effect is difficult to assess, for again we typically find cultural factors complicating the total situation.

An extreme example is provided by the Sirono Indians of eastern Bolivia, who live in thick, tropical rain forests where food is very scarce. This nomadic group lives in an almost perpetual state of semistarvation. Food and the quest for food—game, fish, nuts, berries, fruit—have assumed prime significance. The effects of this centering of their existence around food are reflected in their customs, values, and general personality make-up. Women do not marry for love but are wooed by promises of fat meat or wild-bee honey. Wives usually do not resent their husbands making love to another woman unless he gives her food. To avoid sharing food with others, they lie about how much they have and eat mainly at night so that they can consume more without others knowing about it. Their goal in eating seems to be to swallow the most food in the least time. The thoughts, chants, and dreams of these primitive Indians are mainly of hunting and food. Although the Sironos reveal stable personality development, they are selfish and completely unconcerned with others —usually refusing even to help anyone in trouble. When a Sirono grows too old or sick to hunt or obtain food, he is abandoned to die (*Science News Letter*, 1950).

Although the unfavorable physical environment undoubtedly influenced the development of these cultural and personality patterns, it is difficult to assess its influence accurately or to explain Sirono practices which seem inconsistent with their dominating concern for food. For example, these Indians have failed to develop methods of storing food, and they hunt only when their immediate food supply is exhausted. In addition, they refuse to eat snakes—which are edible and plentiful in Bolivia—regardless of how hungry they are. Nor can we overlook the fact that certain other peoples who live in areas where food is scarce have become highly cooperative and friendly.

It thus becomes very difficult to evaluate the effects of physical environment on individual and group differences in development. Except in cases where unfavorable conditions lead to actual bodily damage, as in malnutrition and disease, the role of the physical environment seems far less important than that of the sociocultural environment.

Sociocultural Environment

In much the same sense that man receives a genetic heritage which is the end product of countless millions of years of evolutionary history, so he receives a sociocultural heritage which is the end product of many thousands of years of social evolution. This heritage varies dramatically from one social group to another, but the various cultures of the world have enough in common to enable us to speak meaningfully of "human culture." Every group, for example, has its language, family and social structure, customs, values, music, and art. These "institutions" are characteristically human and tend to be transmitted by similar means in every society. Sometimes instruction is deliberate, but just as often it is not. In the following pages we shall consider group membership and instruction, status and role, and interpersonal relationships as the chief means by which the sociocultural environment exerts its influence on individual development.

Group membership and instruction. Both deliberately and unconsciously, each society teaches its concepts, values, and accepted behaviors to its children. This instruction is largely accomplished by social institutions such as the home, school, and church —or their equivalent in primitive societies.

Such systematic instruction, together with the examples set by adults or other "models," tends to make for some degree of uniformity and to establish what may be called the *basic personality type* of the particular society.

Societies can shape the development of their members in very different ways. Margaret Mead (1949) has contrasted the personality types of two New Guinea tribes who live in the same general area. The Arapesh she describes as a kindly, peaceful, cooperative people who accept human nature as essentially good and emphasize permissiveness, nonaggressiveness, and helpfulness in their relations with each other. The Mundungumor, on the other hand, are a warlike, aggressive, competitive, vengeful people who are suspicious and jealous of each other and inclined toward violence.

The individual's basic personality structure is affected not only by the larger social group but also by the various *subgroups* to which he belongs—groups based upon his family membership, religion, occupation, social class, age, and sex. Each subgroup tends to foster certain values, beliefs, and approved behavior patterns which may in turn be subject to the restrictions imposed by society as a whole. The fact that each individual belongs to a somewhat different pattern of subgroups tends to produce individual differences, just as common membership in the larger cultural group makes everyone somewhat alike.

The groups with which an individual identifies, or with which he would *like* to be identified, are called his *reference groups*— for it is in reference to their norms and values that he sets his goals, models his behavior, and evaluates his worth. Sometimes reference groups from which the individual is excluded have greater influence than membership groups. Thus a boy from "the wrong side of the tracks" may adopt the values, attitudes, and mannerisms of a more privileged group, divorcing himself insofar as possible from his own family and social class.

Status and role. In every social structure there are a variety of distinguishable positions—doctor, teacher, carpenter, parent, student, child, and so forth—each of which contributes in some way to the total group functioning and is accorded a certain social rank or *status*. Status brings with it both privileges and responsibilities. The medical doctor, for example, has the privilege of practicing medicine and also is held in high regard by other members of society. In return, he is expected to follow the ethical code of his profession; if he fails to do so, he may have his medical license revoked and be relegated to an inferior social standing. Thus, in much the same way that parents shape the personality development of a growing child by administering various rewards and punishments, society enforces its basic rules of behavior by conferring and withdrawing the privileges of status.

To clarify what is expected of a person with a given position and status, society establishes various *roles* for its members to play, each associated with a certain pattern of expected behavior.[1] Thus the role of the army general calls for loyalty, decisiveness, courage, and resourcefulness; the medical doctor is expected not only to conduct an ethical practice but also to be sympathetic, wise, authoritative, and dedicated to the welfare of his patients. Each person, young or old, tends to develop the skills, behavior, and values that his role seems to demand. If he deviates too far from what is expected of him, he is likely to run into difficulties in his social relationships. Society may even, in effect, revoke his status if it feels that his behavior violates the obligations of his role and is detrimental to the welfare of the group as a whole.

Everyone must play a great variety of roles, depending on the different subgroups to which he belongs. A young person may play simultaneously the roles of son, student, boy scout, and team captain; an older person, the roles of lawyer, father, husband, scoutmaster, and civic leader. Usually the individual thinks of his various roles within the context of some broad role that he considers more important than others—the one with which he most closely identifies his "real self," the one that carries the highest status, or perhaps the one that seems to represent the personality type preferred by his society, such as that of being "a good American." But the specific—and sometimes conflicting—demands made by *each* of the roles he plays are influential in shaping his development and behavior.

The extent to which role expectations can influence personality development is well illustrated by Margaret Mead's study (1949) of the Tchambuli, a New Guinea tribe in which the sex roles are practically the reverse of ours. Women are supposed to earn the living, handle business transactions, take the initiative in courtship, and in general head the family. Men, on the other hand, are expected to be coquettish, graceful, prone to gossip, good homemakers, and interested in dancing and theatricals. The established roles for men and women among the Tchambuli obviously tend to channel personality development along lines very different from those in our own culture.

We shall presently examine various other aspects of social roles, including the significance of role conflicts, of roles which the individual finds uncomfortable, and of differences between the way the individual sees his role and the way others see it. First, however, we must examine still another

[1]Some psychologists and sociologists make a distinction between *role* and *role behavior*. They define role as a "pattern of expectancies" regarding behavior; role behavior, on the other hand, is the actual behavior of an individual as he plays his role.

A child's drawings offer clues not only to his individual personality but also to the characteristic values and habits of his culture. For example, the two sketches at left, drawn by a Balinese boy, portray mythological characters familiar to all Balinese and show the stereotyped poses and facial expressions, lacking individuality or indication of emotion, that Balinese children are taught to adopt. The painting at right, showing a funeral procession on a busy street, was done by a French girl; it reveals the seriousness, meticulous care, and attention to precise, literal detail that are fostered in French children (Mead and Wolfenstein, 1955).

means by which man's sociocultural environment shapes his development.

Interpersonal relationships. Man is a social creature, and much of his personality development reflects his experiences with other people. In many societies a certain pattern of interpersonal relationships may predominate over others—for example, the norm may be for competition or cooperation, hostility or friendliness. In general, however, interpersonal relationships contribute to *individuality* rather than similarity of development, for no two of us have exactly the same acquaintances nor do we have an identical relationship with the people we

do know in common. Even parents relate to their various children in somewhat different ways. The experiences of love and hate, of friendship and distrust, of shared experience and misunderstanding which mark our associations with other people are in each case unique.

Although we have many kinds of interpersonal relationships in the course of our lives, those that have the greatest influence in shaping our development are those with our parents and with members of our peer groups.

1. Parent-child relationships. Parents may be warm and accepting or cold and rejecting, rigid disciplinarians or given to over-indulgence. Each particular patterning of parent-child relationship tends to shape personality development in a somewhat different way. A child whose parents make him feel loved and wanted and who allow him freedom to be himself will develop a picture of himself and the world—and patterns of behavior—very different from those of a child who feels rejected, misunderstood, and unreasonably constrained. Too, the child who has been treated with love and affection will ordinarily be able to establish warm friendships and a loving relationship in his own marriage, whereas the child who has been "frosted" may find difficulty in giving and receiving affection in his later relationships with people outside his family.

Psychoanalysts have long pointed to the crucial role in personality formation of the child's early emotional relationships with his parents. We shall examine the specific effects of various types of parent-child relationships in more detail in Chapter 3.

2. Peer-group relationships. As the child grows older and participates increasingly in activities outside the family, his relationships with people outside his family become increasingly important in his development. The child who is intimidated and bullied by other children, for example, may lose his self-confidence and come to feel that his only "safe" role is a submissive one. This, in turn, may lead to problems in handling hostility.

As the child reaches adolescence, his peer group becomes increasingly important to him. The adolescent's success or failure in winning social acceptance from both boys and girls is a major influence on his further development. Later, the type of relationship the individual establishes in his marriage becomes a crucial one for both his immediate happiness and his continued growth.

Although we have singled out parent-child and peer-group relations as perhaps the most important, it is apparent that many other types of interpersonal relationships—with brothers and sisters, grandparents, teachers, neighbors—may play a significant part in shaping personality. Even a chance meeting with someone may change the direction of our lives.

The Role of Environment in Development

The crucial importance of environmental factors in shaping personality development has been well summarized by anthropologist Margaret Mead (1953, pp. 377-378):

". . . the functioning of every part of the human body is moulded by the culture within which the individual has been reared—not only in terms of diet, sunlight, exposure to contagious and infectious diseases, overstrain, occupational . . . hazards, catastrophes, and traumatic experiences, but also by the way he, born into society with a definite culture, has been fed and disciplined, fondled and put to sleep, punished and rewarded. . . .

"Culture is seen . . . as a principal element in the development of the individual, which will result in his having a structure, a type of functioning, and a pattern of irritability different in kind from that of individuals who have been socialized within another culture. . . ."

In the preceding pages we examined the physical, cultural, and social dimensions of environment. We observed that under ordinary conditions the sociocultural environment plays a far more crucial role than physical surroundings in shaping personality development. We also examined some of the mechanisms by which the sociocultural environment exerts its influence on the individual. Now we shall look more closely at the impact of sociocultural factors in determining the individual's frame of reference, the competencies he develops, and the likenesses and differences between him and other members of his sociocultural group.

Frame of reference. On the basis of his experiences in his particular environment, the growing individual gradually develops a coherent *frame of reference* which he uses in evaluating new experiences and selecting appropriate modes of behavior. The key elements in a person's frame of reference are his basic *assumptions* about himself and his world—about his personal worth, his abilities, his deficiencies, the kind of world he lives in, what is good and bad, what can be changed, and so on. We make such assumptions on the basis of whatever information we have gathered in the course of living, but ordinarily our knowledge is far from complete. We therefore must interpret the information we do have and make inferences that go beyond it. For example, when we decide to marry a certain person, we never have sufficient evidence to guarantee that we will be happy, but we assume on the basis of what we know (and a little wishful thinking perhaps) that we will make a happy marriage. The more nearly complete our information, the more sure we can be of making reliable assumptions.

On the basis of his assumptions about himself in relation to his world, the individual adopts certain *attitudes*—positions or postures—toward various objects, events, and situations. If we were to ask a man about his attitude toward women voting, he might reply that he was opposed (attitude) because women are not so well informed on political matters as men (assumption). Similarly, the individual may make the assumption that premarital sexual relations are immoral and hence take an attitude opposing such behavior; or he may make the assumption that a person should "sow his wild oats" before marriage and hence favor premarital

sexual relations. Typically, the individual takes an attitude favoring or opposing, but attitudes may take many other forms such as suspicion, caution, and so on.

The assumptions that make up a person's frame of reference can be classified into three basic categories: assumptions concerning fact, value, and possibility.

1. Assumptions concerning fact—the individual's concept of reality, of how things *really are*. Included in this category are the individual's assumptions about his own assets and liabilities, the sort of people who inhabit his world, and the opportunities and limitations of his environment. Such assumptions may be based on sources as varied as scientific information, custom, superstition, and wishful thinking. Usually people try to use various sources of information to check their assumptions of fact, subjecting them to continual elaboration, refinement, and correction.

2. Assumptions concerning value—the individual's concept of how things *should* be, incorporating his judgments of what is good and bad, desirable and undesirable, right and wrong. Value assumptions may be based upon religious or ethical beliefs (it is good for man to live by the golden rule), scientific information (it is good for man to eat a balanced diet), or human experience (it is good for man to share in the responsibility of government). Value assumptions are usually more resistant to change than are assumptions of fact.

3. Assumptions concerning possibility—the individual's concept of how things *could* be, of possibilities for change and improvement. Thus the student may look forward to the completion of his college work so that he can get a job, marry, and raise a family. The peoples of underdeveloped lands may assume that they can achieve a better way of life by becoming industrialized and technologically proficient.

All these assumptions are integrated into a coherent whole which provides the individual with an "inner picture" of himself and the world around him. Any assumption may be relatively valid or invalid, depending upon how well it accords with objective "reality." It may be relatively conscious or unconscious, have various types and degrees of emotional involvement, and be held with more or less conviction. All assumptions are subject to modification with experience, but some are much more resistant to change than others.

Because the individual perceives, thinks, and acts in reference to his basic assumptions, a realistic frame of reference becomes crucial to successful adjustment. The goals men strive for, their desires and aspirations, the things they value, their views of work and play, the type of relations they establish with others—in short, their life styles—are largely determined by the pattern of assumptions they acquire. In a general sense, a person's frame of reference—together with the various competencies he develops—represents his learned know-how and know-why for coping with the world.

The sociocultural environment plays the primary role in filling in the individual's pattern of assumptions and hence in shaping his thinking and behavior; it largely determines the type and amount of information available to the individual, the assumptions he is encouraged to make from this information, and the attitudes he is encouraged to adopt from these assumptions. A vivid contrast in the assumptions fostered by different cultures is provided by the Arapesh and the Mundungumor (p. 54) and the Sironos (p. 53). Like us, they think they evaluate situations objectively and are following the dictates of common sense. But their views of "reality" are shaped largely by their experiences in their own particular sociocultural environment.

Curiously enough, the individual is usually so deeply immersed in his culture that he is scarcely aware of it as a shaping force in his life. As someone has remarked, "The fish will be the last to discover water." People who know no other cultural patterns but their own tend to regard them as God-given and intrinsically right. Only as we become aware that different groups have solved the same basic life problems in different ways do we see culture in perspective as simply a combination of man-made arrangements for living. We are then in a position to examine

SAMPLE INFORMATION—ASSUMPTION—ATTITUDE CHAIN

Information	*Possible Assumptions*	*Possible Attitudes*
Little girl discovers father had wanted a boy	Boys are more valuable There's something wrong with me	Feelings of inadequacy, timidity Resentment toward boys and men Contempt for girls and women as beings of lesser worth

our basic assumptions and to modify them if we find more accurate and realistic ones.

Competencies. As we noted in the Prologue, every society requires that its members develop basic physical, intellectual, social, and emotional competencies. Although there are many common denominators, the specific competencies that are required or encouraged vary greatly from culture to culture. Whereas skills in hunting or fishing, for example, may be essential to survival in the economy of a primitive tribe, the only physical competencies necessary in contemporary American society are those that can be roughly equated with good health. Our economy requires, rather, the development of technological proficiency and skills in dealing effectively with people. Even the social and emotional competencies necessary for "getting along" may be quite different in different cultures. Mundungumor children, to meet the expectations of their society, must develop social skills different from those of the Arapesh; and the requirements of both of these groups are very different from those of our own society. Significant differences are found even among contemporary Western cultures. Many is the traveler who finds himself socially inept when he visits a foreign country.

In the area of intellectual competencies, sociocultural influences make themselves felt primarily in the amount of opportunity and encouragement they provide for intellectual growth. In some societies people live under such primitive conditions that their opportunities for acquiring any kind of broad knowledge or for developing their intellectual capacities are meager indeed. At a different extreme, people living under some dictatorships are subjected to rigid indoctrination and otherwise discouraged from thinking for themselves except in limited areas. In still other societies men have considerable opportunity for intellectual development,

while women are merely trained for performing household duties. A few societies are so saturated with superstitions and taboos that the individual's opportunities for learning to think objectively are very limited. Even in our own society the protection and fostering of freedom of thought and inquiry have become matters of concern.

Likenesses and differences. In general, the more uniform and consistent the cultural environment, the more alike the members of the group will be—the more nearly they will approximate the personality type fostered by that culture. Dictatorships take advantage of this principle by systematically indoctrinating their young people with rigid political and economic beliefs which tend to produce a "mass man." Isolated and self-contained cultures, such as those of many so-called primitive groups, also tend to produce considerable uniformity. In such cultures, the values of society as a whole and of various subgroups tend to be consistent. Children usually experience little difficulty in growing into their adult roles, for roles are clearly delineated and fixed. In short, the basic personality type emerges as clear-cut and standardized.

In our own rapidly changing and heterogeneous society, on the other hand, we often find church, school, family, and other groups pulling us in different directions and trying to teach contradictory values. The reckless behavior that wins an adolescent boy the admiration of his friends may shock and upset his parents. The cutthroat competition of his business life may disturb an individual who has strong religious and ethical values. The serious student from a poorly educated family may find himself at odds with his parents. Indeed, each individual must reconcile conflicting pressures and work out his own role.

The degree of heterogeneity in a person's culture is a significant factor in his development, providing important opportunities or limitations for his growth as an individual. The benefits we reap from having no fixed molds and standards are freedom from regimentation, almost unlimited diversity, and a degree of personal responsibility and self-direction not otherwise possible. But the penalties we often pay for these advantages are worry, bewilderment, and conflict, for while in theory heterogeneity is not inconsistent with harmony, in actual fact it usually leads to the development of conflicting values and goals. On the other hand, unless he is exposed to more than one set of values, the individual becomes increasingly time- and culture-bound and thus less capable of objectivity.

In some respects American culture is considerably more homogeneous today than at any previous time in its history. Modern methods of transportation and communication have greatly reduced regional differences and increased our number of common interests, while class distinctions have been lessened by the broadening of educational and economic opportunities. Yet religious, regional, occupational, and class differences continue to foster important differences in development.

Class differences alone are responsible for differing views of marriage, sex, politics, education, and many other aspects of living. For example, members of the upper class tend to attach high importance to family tradition and prestige, send their children to private schools, and expect them to prepare for positions of leadership. Middle-class values stress education, hard work, economic stability, professional training, and a good marriage. Lower-class patterns put more value on "earthiness" and spontaneity, less on restraint and ambition. The well-known Kinsey studies (1948, 1953) on the sexual behavior of American men and women offer evidence that sexual patterns also differ significantly from one social class to another. Other researchers have gathered evidence of differences in attitudes toward fighting and physical violence, levels of aspiration, concepts of child rearing, regard for the law, and so on (see chart on p. 62).

Thus, while we may speak meaningfully of an "American culture" which fosters many similarities in development, we must realize too that individuals participate in that culture from very different vantage points; they occupy different positions, have different social rank and status, and play different roles. Contrast, for example, the status and role differences between a minister and a jazz band leader, a diplomat and a janitor. Strikingly different attitudes, values, and behavior are expected of them. This factor of *differential participation* is highly important in understanding individual differences within a culture.

SELF AS A THIRD DETERMINANT

In our discussion of man's genetic endowment we discussed the role of constitutional differences in fostering individual differences. Then in the section on environmental influences we noted the effects of uniformity or heterogeneity of sociocultural conditions on individuality. Now as we proceed to a discussion of "self" as the third determinant of personality development, we shall discover still another factor that contributes to the uniqueness of every human being. For as the individual achieves a sense of his own identity, he tends to view each situation in the light of *his* motives, assumptions, and feel-

DIFFERING ATTITUDES
AT VARIOUS SOCIOECONOMIC LEVELS

Attitudes Toward:	Upper	Middle	Lower
Family	Family tightly knit; emphasis on maintaining family name and prestige.	Considerable emphasis on independence; family ties often less close and less permanent than at upper levels.	Family less closely knit than average family in higher socioeconomic groups and homes more apt to be broken.
Education	Emphasis on quality of education and prestige of schools; training for high-level administration rather than financial gain.	Great emphasis on grades and concern about failure; education seen as the road to advancement and security.	Family's needs often given priority over child's education; school usually regarded as unpleasant; low premium put on good grades.
Aggression and Destruction	Value of property stressed; destruction and fighting discouraged.	Value of property stressed; guilt and anxiety over open expression of anger, but "fighting back" sometimes encouraged at school age.	Children often permitted or encouraged to settle differences by fighting; physical prowess valued; less emphasis on value of property.
Sex	Inhibition of sexual behavior during early years but considerable freedom by later adolescence.	Severe inhibition in early years, with accompanying anxiety over sexual impulses; adolescent sexual activity usually limited to petting and masturbation.	Sex accepted as matter of course; tendency to early sexual experience, often regarded by boys as proof of masculinity; petting and masturbation often regarded as perversion.
Recreation	Relatively exclusive sports common, like golf, sailing, horseback riding; strong tendency to participate in community activities; reading and TV viewing common.	Considerable emphasis on social skills like dancing, ping-pong, tennis; tendency to join organized community activities; reading and TV viewing common.	Basketball, softball, boxing popular; little reading; TV viewing common.

These are generalizations that have emerged from many studies including Davis and Havighurst, 1946; Davis, 1948; Kinsey and others, 1948; Sears, Maccoby, and Levin, 1957; Bronfenbrenner, 1958. There are wide individual variations, of course.

ings. Thus, the effects of a particular environment become increasingly dependent upon the way it is *experienced* by the individual.

In introducing the concept of self as the third major determinant of man's development, we must be careful to avoid the idea of some "little man" sitting up in the brain deciding how we should behave. When psychologists refer to "self" they are thinking in terms of a *conceptual* structure rather than a physical one. Like gravity, the self cannot be observed directly but is inferred from various phenomena which *can* be observed and which seem to operate according to some unifying principle. The self, in other words, is not a mystical entity but a useful and seemingly necessary construct for explaining many aspects of individual behavior. Hall and Lindzey (1957, p. 468) state it thus:

"The self, whether it be conceived as object or as process or both, is not an homunculus or 'man within the breast' or soul; rather it refers to the object of psychological processes or to those processes themselves, and these processes are assumed to be governed by the principle of causality. In other words, the self is not a metaphysical or religious concept; it is a concept that falls within the domain of a scientific psychology. Self theory represents a serious attempt to account for certain phenomena and to conceptualize one's observations of certain aspects of behavior."

In examining the self-structure more closely, we shall focus on two aspects of the individual's experience of self: (1) *self as object*, referring to the individual's perception and evaluation of himself as something distinct from other persons and things; and (2) *self as process*, referring to the individual's perception of himself as a knower, striver, and doer with facilities for perceiving, evaluating, choosing, and planning in reference to himself. We shall see that both of these views of self provide us with important conceptual tools for understanding human development and behavior.[1]

Self As Object

When we refer to self as object, we are talking about the individual's self-image. This image incorporates the individual's perception of what he is really like (self-identity), his value as a person (self-evaluation), and his aspirations for growth and accomplishment (self-ideal). From this point of view, we can regard the self as the core of the individual's frame of reference—his assumptions concerning facts, values, and possibilities.

Self-identity. Man is not born with a sense of self. In fact, the newborn infant apparently does not even know where his own body leaves off and his environment begins. Only gradually does he learn to recognize his body parts, name, feelings, and behavior as integral parts of a single *me* and to build up a cluster of assumptions about himself. It is this self-structure that provides the individual with a stable sense of his own identity and a central reference point for his adjustive behavior. It is in terms of his awareness of himself as something unique that he sets goals, hopes, prays, fears, and makes decisions. *He* exists as the center of a changing world of experience, and most events in his world are perceived and dealt with in relation to the *I* and *me*.

As the individual's experience broadens, his self-image gradually extends to include certain things outside of himself with which he feels personal involvement. When we think of the *me* or *my*, we may include possessions such as our home, the people we

[1]See pages 437 and 449 for theories of personality structure as developed by Freud and Rogers.

love, the groups we are loyal to, and the values we believe in. Many parents identify so completely with their offspring that they experience any reward or humiliation to the child as if it were their own. Although such complete identification with another person can interfere with individual growth, normally the process of *ego-extension* works beneficially. Allport (1955, p. 45) describes the process more fully:

"A child . . . who identifies with his parent is definitely extending his sense of self, as he does likewise through his love for pets, dolls, or other possessions, animate or inanimate.

"As we grow older we identify with groups, neighborhood, and nation as well as with possessions, clothes, home. They become matters of importance to us in a sense that other people's families, nations, or possessions are not. Later in life the process of extension may go to great lengths, through the development of loyalties and of interests focused on abstractions and on moral and religious values."

The individual's sense of identity is shaped partly by the social roles he plays. If the group regards him as a leader, a solid citizen, or a menial, he tends to regard himself in the same way. He also tends to adopt the values and attitudes that are expected of one in his position, as well as those fostered by the groups to which he belongs or would like to belong. These attitudes, often adopted quite unconsciously, make him different from others with the same original potential who happen to be cast in other roles.

The effect of role on one's sense of identity is vividly portrayed in Barrie's *The Admirable Crichton*. At the beginning of this play, Crichton, the butler, plays the stereotype of the humble servant whose only thought is to do the bidding of the noble family to whom he owes all the good things of his life. When he and the family are shipwrecked

on an island and his ingenuity keeps them alive, their roles and social status are reversed: now he is the somewhat arrogant leader and they the subservient, self-effacing subordinates. When rescue comes, the characters' roles and self-pictures suddenly revert to what they were originally.

As we noted earlier in this chapter, most of us have several roles at once—and sometimes feel as though we have several "selves." The same man may be a shrewd, tight-fisted businessman, a devout and generous member of his church, and a henpecked husband. Often when we become accustomed to seeing a person in a particular role, we are quite surprised to discover that he is "a different person" in a different setting. When his conflicting roles cannot be integrated into a coherent "master role" of some sort, the individual may have difficulty in establishing a stable sense of identity. An example is the young woman who tries to assume an adult role in her marriage but reverts to the role of a child with her parents. In such cases of confused identity, adjustment to any one master role becomes exceedingly difficult.

Although everyone's self-image is influenced by the roles he plays, people identify themselves with their roles to very different degrees. Occasionally a person's sense of identity is so closely associated with a particular role that he goes to pieces when he loses it. This partially explains the behavior of the business tycoon who, losing his fortune and prestige, commits suicide.

In later chapters we shall have more to say about some of the interacting forces that help shape a person's sense of identity. For now, we shall simply emphasize that the self, once it is delineated clearly, becomes the very core of individual existence. Without a sense of identity, we would be like machines capable of performing complicated tasks but without the capacity to enjoy the richness of human experience. It is our awareness of self that makes existence meaningful, providing continuity between past, present, and future.

Self-evaluation. The individual's sense of personal identity can be equated roughly with his reality assumptions about himself—his assumptions about what he is really like. Because these assumptions naturally include an assessment of his assets and liabilities, they tie in closely with his feelings of self-worth.

As a child comes to achieve a clear sense of self-identity, he begins to evaluate himself as superior or inferior, worthy or unworthy, adequate or inadequate. Whether these feelings about self are positive or negative depends upon the child's experiences—most particularly, upon his relationships with other people, for during the early years of his development he has no other standards for measuring his adequacy than those supplied by his parents and other important people in his life. If their words and behavior label him as inadequate and unworthy of love, he has little choice but to accept that evaluation as true. If, on the other hand, he is warmly accepted and receives verbal assurances that he is essentially "a good boy," his self-evaluation will probably be positive. As Combs and Snygg (1959, p. 136) point out, these early evaluations of self-worth have a continuing effect on personality development:

"In his interaction with father, mother, and siblings, the young child begins his differentiations of self as liked or unliked, wanted or unwanted, acceptable or unacceptable, able or unable, worthy or unworthy, adequate or inadequate. These are the kind of perceptions through which the individual is able to symbolize his own degree of self actualization. The more positive self definitions he acquires, the greater is the feeling of adequacy and need satisfaction; and, conversely, the more negative self definitions he acquires, the more frustrated and unhappy he becomes. Experience later in life may change the concepts developed as a product of family living but never easily or quickly. The most basic of such self concepts may be so deeply rooted in the individual's organization that they cannot easily be changed even by the most drastic of later experiences."

Thus the child who grows up thinking of himself as inferior to other children or as unworthy of his family because he cannot live up to their high expectations will need many experiences of success and acceptance before he begins to evaluate himself in generally positive terms. He will interpret even the small failures that are inevitable in anyone's life as adding to the already overwhelming proof of his inadequacy. The child who grows up feeling adequate and secure, on the other hand, can take considerable failure in stride and realistically accept many personal shortcomings without altering his basic self-picture.

Obviously there is no one-to-one relationship between a person's ability and the way he evaluates himself. The highly talented individual may be the one with deep feelings of inferiority; the mediocre one may feel proud and self-satisfied. Our feelings of personal worth and adequacy—or their opposites—are more closely related to our self-image than to our actual achievement.

Self-ideal. The self as object includes not only the individual's view of himself in terms of his identity and worth but also his aspirations for growth and accomplishment. Implicit in the individual's self-ideal are his assumptions of possibility—his notion of what he should be able to achieve or become—and his assumptions about what is desirable. And of course this ideal image is built in relation to the way the individual sees himself now, or his assumptions of fact.

Depending upon whether a person's aspirations are difficult or easy to achieve in relation to his abilities, we say that he has a high or low *level of aspiration*. As we shall see, it is important that the individual's level of aspiration be realistic, for if it is too high it will lead to failure and self-devaluation, and if it is too low, to a waste of personal resources and opportunities. Ideally, the individual selects goals that are appropriate to his interests, aptitudes, and opportunities, but outside pressures often tend to push him in other directions. Family expectations, for example, may influence the "C" student to set his heart on graduate school and a professional career—or the "A" student to quit school and get out and make a living. The economic competitiveness of American society can pressure the would-be farmer or artist or missionary to divert his energies into a business career and compete for such symbols of status as automobiles, homes, clothes, and club memberships. Family and social expectations can work constructively as incentives for the individual to achieve the best of his potentialities; but when they allow too little room for individuality, they can force him to accept as "ideal" goals that are incompatible with his abilities, temperament, and values.

Often our self-ideals are related to *identifications* we make with various models—parents, teachers, television personalities, athletes, national heroes, or other persons whom we admire and would like to emulate. The identifications we make in childhood, especially those with the parent of our own sex, are the source of many of our most basic goals for self-growth and are important in providing direction for development. Although the mechanism of identification can continue to work constructively in later years, the mature person is more likely to set his aspirations in terms of thought-out values and a realistic assessment of himself as an

individual. When a person accepts too easily the manners, attitudes, and goals of others, it may indicate that he lacks a clear sense of identity and an integrated frame of reference.

Self As Process

Theoretically, the human organism could function on a mechanical level without a self-structure, as other living energy systems do. But once the sense of self develops in the human being, the individual always behaves in reference to it and comes to perceive himself as an active agent in determining his own behavior—as indicated, for example, by such typical statements as "I know," "I understand," "I think," "I intend," "I will do it." Our experience of inner direction involves the self as a knower, striver, and doer.

Self as knower. Basic to all functions associated with self as process is the ability of the human organism to perceive itself somewhat as it would another object. Indeed, all the knowing activity of the human being is carried on in relation to self. The vast quantity of information we receive from our internal and external environment is evaluated, integrated, and stored with reference to its perceived significance for us as individuals.

The things that we "know" about ourselves and about other persons, events, objects, and ideas as they relate to ourselves comprise the frame of reference that we use in choosing and carrying out any course of action. Thus, for the human organism to behave effectively, the self must function effectively as a knower, building a frame of reference which is essentially accurate and realistic. To the degree that our "knowledge" is distorted, we will be unable to cope successfully with situations as they really are.

Self as striver. Each of us is motivated to seek or avoid things in terms of their meaning for us—whether they promise to benefit us in some way or seem to threaten our physical or psychological well-being. And regardless of the many external influences that press in on us, we perceive the *self* as the active force in initiating our strivings. It is *I* who want or need this and who try to avoid that.

Because the self-structure is experienced as the very core of existence, its maintenance and enhancement become matters of very special concern. If our assumptions concerning self and the world in relation to self were to crumble all at once, we would be lost indeed, for we would have no reference points to guide our behavior. For this reason, we tend to defend our existing assumptions from attack and to relinquish them only if different ones have equal or greater appeal—for example, if they raise our feelings of personal worth and adequacy. In many large and small ways we strive to maintain and enhance the good picture we have of ourselves. We set goals for self-improvement; we try to do a good job; we toot our own horns so that others will notice our achievements; we try to dress attractively, to be witty and charming, and to make a good impression on others so that we can have a good impression of ourselves. These are perfectly normal techniques for making us feel more secure and confident in coping with everyday situations.

Although we continually strive for self-enhancement, we often encounter situations which threaten to undermine our self-image. When failure comes or the self is otherwise threatened with devaluation, we usually have to rely on various unconscious defense mechanisms to protect ourselves from hurt. Thus we may alter facts to fit our prejudices or rationalize our defects as moral victories. Our own faults may be projected so that they become the faults of others. In Chapters 6 and 7 we shall examine these and other mechanisms of self-defense and their significance for human adjustment.

Self as doer. The typical pattern of adjustive behavior in the human organism involves perceiving the situation; processing all the information received from inner and outer sources—evaluating its significance, integrating it with previous knowledge, deciding what course of behavior it dictates; and pursuing a course of action that seems best suited to meeting the requirements of the situation. All these processes take place with reference to the individual's perception of himself as an active and responsible agent with conscious intent—as a doer with the capacity for self-direction. A child's "discovery" of himself as an active agent is a key step in the emergence of his self-concept. The negativism which is typical of children at about two is nothing more than a testing of independent power and, as such, is basic to self-development.

In viewing the self as a knower, striver, and doer, we are focusing on the key processes involved in self-direction. We shall elaborate on these processes in our next section on the role of self in development. However, two additional points may be made here. First, we have emphasized the conscious experience of self and the role of the self in integrating behavior. We shall shortly see that many processes focusing around this system, such as our ego defense mechanisms, operate without awareness. Secondly, we may note that as the self-structure emerges and other psychological subsystems are organized around it, it becomes a highly selective factor in shaping the course of subsequent behavior and development.

The Role of Self in Development

The emergence of self adds a new dimension to human development. In our discussion of self as object and process, we suggested various ways in which the self-structure functions to shape individual development. A few major points, however, deserve some further elaboration.

Interpreting new experiences. The self is at the center of a world of changing experiences, and each new experience is interpreted in relation to the existing self-structure —in terms of its meaning and significance to the individual. Rogers (1951, p. 503) describes it this way:

"As experiences occur in the life of the individual, they are either (a) symbolized, perceived and organized into some relationship to the self, (b) ignored because there is no perceived relationship to the self-structure, (c) denied symbolization or given a distorted symbolization because the experience is inconsistent with the structure of the self."

As a consequence of this "screening" process, by which information is selected, organized, and perhaps distorted, each individual experiences environmental conditions in a somewhat personal way. His perception of "reality" and his responses to it reflect his frame of reference, especially his attitudes about himself. The failure to be invited to an "important" party may constitute a major crisis for one girl but may be brushed off as inconsequential by another with more self-confidence or different values; a raise of a thousand dollars a year may be seen as a major pay increase to a man in a middle-income bracket but as an insult to the business executive in the six-figure bracket.

Obviously, then, we must examine the way the individual perceives situations if we are to understand his reactions to them. Often a situation which seems objectively favorable to us is highly stressful to another person; and although his response may seem irrational to us, it will be relevant to the situation as he understands it. As Combs and Snygg (1959, p. 17) point out:

"People do not behave according to the facts as *others* see them. They behave according to the facts as *they* see them. . . .

"From the point of view of the behaver himself behavior is caused. It is purposeful. It always has a reason. Sometimes the reasons are vague and confused, in which case his behavior is equally vague and uncertain; sometimes the meanings are extremely clear and definite. But everything we do seems reasonable and necessary at the time we are doing it. When we look at other people from an external, objective point of view, their behavior may seem irrational because we do not experience things as they do. Even our own behavior may, in retrospect, seem to have been silly or ineffective. But at the instant of behaving, each person's actions seem to him to be the best and most effective acts he can perform under the circumstances. If, at that instant, he knew how to behave more effectively, he would do so."

Thus, the individual responds *not* to an objective reality but to situations as he *perceives* them. This unique world of personal experience has been called the *perceptual field—"the entire universe, including himself, as it is experienced by the individual at the instant of action"* (Combs and Snygg, 1959, p. 20).[1] The individual's perceptual field is in a continual state of change, and he is immediately aware of only a small portion of it at any given moment—depending largely upon the immediate needs of the organism. But it also has a stability that comes from the organism's compelling tendency to impose order and meaning on its universe. This private world of experience is the only "reality" in terms of which individual behavior can be understood.

In trying to understand why people respond differently to highly similar situations,

[1]For a further discussion by Combs and Snygg on the relationship between perception and behavior, see their article on page 466.

we should also note that the particular parts of the environment with which one individual feels self-involvement may be quite different from those which seem important to another person. .In general, activities, objects, and events that potentially enhance or threaten the self are the ones that command our attention and exert the most significant influence on our development. Conversely, experiences that are not perceived as touching upon our purposes, feelings of worth, and self-ideals have relatively little influence on the shaping of personality.

Self-consistency and continuity. Because the ongoing activities of the human system are organized and integrated in relation to self, each individual tends to establish a relatively consistent life style. He has a characteristic way of doing, thinking, reacting, and growing that tends to distinguish him from everyone else. He puts his personal stamp on every role he plays and every situation he encounters. He is fairly consistent in regarding people as honest or as untrustworthy, in regarding life as exciting or as threatening or perhaps as a constant struggle, in seeking certain experiences and avoiding others. These typical patterns of behavior are always consistent with his self-concept.

As we have noted, a child learns to regard himself as important, lovable, clever, pretty, naughty, fragile, undependable, or clumsy —depending largely upon the reactions of other people but also upon his own evaluation of his accomplishments. Whether or not his self-evaluation is realistic, he assumes it is and acts accordingly. A child who is taught to feel he is better than the other children in the neighborhood is likely to become arrogant toward them and to expect special recognition from his teachers and other adults. A girl who is continually criticized for being clumsy and stupid will develop an unflattering picture of herself that will influence how she acts and how she develops. A boy who is told he is a "good-for-nothing" may not try to make anything of himself.

Obviously, children with such different self-images will have different relationships with other people, different experiences, and different learnings. And since each day's learning necessarily builds upon what has gone before, there emerges an increasingly unique individual whose growth is slanted in the direction of his existing self-structure. Thus the self-structure provides not only for consistency of life style but also for continuity of growth.

Consistency and continuity do not, however, imply rigidity. Indeed, it is a sign of healthy self-development when new experiences and new information—about one's self and one's world—can be assimilated into the self-structure without disturbing its basic integrity. In general, the more realistic an individual's frame of reference is, the more readily he will be able to modify his assumptions and reintegrate his self-structure in the light of new experience. Rogers (1958, p. 16) describes this "openness to experience" as one of the outcomes of successful psychotherapy:

"The individual becomes more openly aware of his own feelings and attitudes as they exist in him at an organic level. He also becomes more aware of reality as it exists outside of himself, instead of perceiving it in preconceived categories. He sees that not all trees are green, not all men are stern fathers, not all women are rejecting, not all failure experiences prove that he is no good, and the like. He is able to take in the evidence in a new situation, *as it is*, rather than distorting it to fit a pattern which he already holds. As you might expect, this increasing ability to be open to experience makes him far more realistic in dealing with new people, new situations, new problems. It means that his beliefs are not rigid, that he can tolerate ambiguity."

The person with an essentially false picture of himself and his world will find himself continually confronted with experiences which seem inconsistent with his self-structure and therefore threatening. In such cases the self-structure tends to become more rigidly organized in order to maintain itself. A threatening experience may be denied consciousness or perceived in such a distorted fashion that it no longer seems threatening. As a result, of course, the self-structure becomes increasingly out of tune with reality and must depend upon a spiraling system of defenses for its maintenance. We shall have more to say in later chapters about how such vicious circles come into being—and how they can often be broken in the threat-free atmosphere of psychotherapy.

Degree of self-differentiation. In some societies the individual is so immersed in the group that he seems to develop very little sense of self. Fromm (1955, p. 61) theorizes that "the degree to which man is aware of himself as a separate self depends on the extent to which he has emerged from the clan and the extent to which the process of individuation has developed. The member of a primitive clan might express his sense of identity in the formula 'I am we'; he cannot yet conceive of himself as an 'individual,' existing apart from the group."

The natives of Kenya in Africa offer one example of a contemporary society in which there is little self-differentiation. In a study of these Kenya tribesmen, Carothers (1947) found that social roles were rigidly prescribed and that most behavior was group determined, with individual achievement being discouraged. Where there is little need or opportunity for self-direction, there is little reason for self-criticism or a sense of personal responsibility. It is hardly surprising, therefore, that Carothers found the Kenyans virtually free from the use of ego defense mechanisms and from feelings of anxiety, depression, and guilt, all of which are dependent on a strong sense of self.

In our own society, on the other hand, every effort is made to encourage individuality. Each person is held responsible for his own acts from an early age and is encouraged to develop and use his own unique capacities. Though there are many pressures toward conformity, we tend to deplore them and, in principle at least, to value differences. This deep-rooted emphasis on individuality and encouragement of personal responsibility inevitably sharpen our sense of self and thus increase the differences among us. The result is a greater opportunity for achievement and satisfaction but also a greater possibility for experiencing anxiety and personal failure.

In this chapter we have seen how our genetic endowment sets the limits for development by providing our potentials for growth, our potentials for behavior, and certain basic constitutional tendencies which influence the ways we interact with our environment. Environment, the second major determinant of human development, is largely responsible for directing the unfolding of these hereditary potentials. While physical conditions provide the necessary background for growth, our sociocultural environment plays the significant role in shaping the development of distinctly human characteristics. Through experience, the self emerges to become a third major influence on development. As the individual begins to experience himself as a unique entity capable of self-direction, his self-structure becomes his "operational center"—the center which screens and interprets incoming information, gives goals their meaning, and coordinates, integrates, and evaluates the individual's activity.

DETERMINANTS OF DEVELOPMENT

	Heredity	*Environment*	*Self-Structure*
Universal Level	Potentials for physical characteristics of human species Potentials for growth, aging (life cycle) Potentials for behavior (self-awareness, self-direction, modifiability by learning, concern with values and meaning, use of symbols, rich transactions with field) Resources for both routine and emergency response	Physical setting, requiring adaptation Cultural setting, with prescribed roles, mores, values, language, family and social structure, ideology Social setting (relationships with family members and others)	Awareness and evaluation of self Development of basic assumptions and attitudes about (1) what is real or true, (2) what is valuable, important, good, and (3) what is possible Tendency to screen, evaluate, and distort perceptions in ways consistent with own attitudes and needs
Communal (Community) Level	Racial characteristics (e.g., skin color, endemic diseases) Family characteristics; genes for particular recessive and dominant traits	Resources or limitations of the particular setting (e.g., climate, food supply) Need for particular competencies Sociocultural structure and social climate of particular group (e.g., values stressed, opportunities and limitations)	Assumptions and values held in common with other members of group—"basic personality type" Motives and goals typical of group Characteristic degree of self-differentiation and sense of responsibility
Individual Level	Unique physical characteristics Unique pattern of psychological capacities Constitutional reaction tendencies (e.g., temperament, sensitivity, energy level, resistance, resilience) Male or female	Membership in unique pattern of subgroups Unique role demands Unique relationships with other individuals Unique satisfactions and frustrations from interaction with physical and sociocultural environment	Unique frame of reference (assumptions and attitudes about self and the world in relation to self) Unique pattern of abilities, habits, interests Unique "life style" (generally consistent way of behaving)

Psychologists who view man primarily as a *reactive* organism have tended to emphasize heredity and environment as the chief determinants of human development; *active* theorists, on the other hand, have emphasized the role of self. Actually, of course, we must view heredity, environment, and self as *interactive* forces that continually work together in shaping individual development. Heredity does not complete its role at birth but operates throughout the lifetime of the individual, his genetic potentials unfolding as he interacts with his environment. His environment, in turn, is meaningful in terms of shaping the basic personality pattern of the individual and providing opportunities for self-growth.

In examining heredity, environment, and self as the forces which shape human development, we have seen that they operate to produce both likenesses and differences in development. Conditions that obtain for all human beings are said to operate on the *universal* level. An example is the common genetic inheritance that distinguishes mankind from all other species and the general features of human society. Conditions that influence all members of one sociocultural group but are not characteristic of other groups are said to operate at the *communal* (community) level. Examples are special climatic conditions, particular tribal customs, gene combinations producing a particular skin color, and so on. Conditions that influence one member of the group but not another are said to operate at the *individual* level. Examples are hereditary variations among members of a family, different roles in the culture, and the somewhat unique set of experiences that each person has, through which he develops his own set of attitudes, assumptions, and skills. The end result is that "every man is like all other men, is like some other men, is like no other man."

REFERENCES

The following list includes both the references cited in this chapter and a selected number of additional books and articles for outside reading.

Allport, Gordon W. 1955. *Becoming.* New Haven: Yale University Press.

Bronfenbrenner, U. 1958. "Socialization and Social Class Through Time and Space." *Readings in Social Psychology.* Eleanor E. Maccoby, Theodore M. Newcomb, and Eugene L. Hartley, eds. New York: Henry Holt and Co.

Carothers, J. C. 1947. "A Study of Mental Derangement in Africans, and an Attempt to Explain Its Peculiarities, More Especially in Relation to the African Attitude of Life." *Journal of Mental Science,* 93, 548-597.

Combs, Arthur W., and Donald Snygg. 1959. *Individual Behavior.* Rev. ed. New York: Harper & Brothers. Copyright © 1959 by Arthur W. Combs and Donald Snygg. Published by Harper & Brothers, New York, and reprinted with their permission.

Crompton, John. 1954. *Ways of the Ant.* Boston: Houghton Mifflin Company.

Davis, Allison. 1948. *Social-Class Influences upon Learning.* Cambridge, Mass.: Harvard University Press.

Davis, Allison, and Robert J. Havighurst. 1946. "Social Class and Color Differences in Child-Rearing." *American Sociological Review, 11,* 698-710.

Fromm, Erich. 1955. *The Sane Society.* New York: Rinehart & Company, Inc.

Gesell, Arnold. 1953. "Human Infancy and the Embryology of Behavior."

Contributions Toward Medical Psychology, Vol. 1. Arthur Weider, ed. New York: Ronald Press. Copyright 1953 by The Ronald Press Company.

Gesell, Arnold, and Catherine Amatruda. 1945. *The Embryology of Behavior.* New York: Harper & Brothers.

Gough, Harrison G. 1955. "Factors Relating to Differential Achievement Among Gifted Persons." Paper presented at the annual meeting of the American Psychological Association in San Francisco, California, September 1, 1955.

Hall, Calvin S., and Gardner Lindzey. 1957. *Theories of Personality.* New York: John Wiley & Sons, Inc. Copyright © 1957 by John Wiley & Sons., Inc., New York, and reprinted with their permission.

Harsh, Charles M., and H. G. Schrickel. 1950. *Personality: Development and Assessment.* New York: The Ronald Press Company.

Honigmann, John Joseph. 1954. *Culture and Personality.* New York: Harper & Brothers.

Kinsey, Alfred C., and others. 1948. *Sexual Behavior in the Human Male.* Philadelphia: W. B. Saunders Company.

Kinsey, Alfred C., and others. 1953. *Sexual Behavior in the Human Female.* Philadelphia: W. B. Saunders Company.

Linton, Ralph. 1945. *The Cultural Background of Personality.* New York: Appleton-Century-Crofts, Inc.

Lorenz, Konrad Z. 1958. "The Evolution of Behavior." *Scientific American, 199,* No. 6, 67-78.

Mead, Margaret. 1949. *Male and Female.* New York: William Morrow & Company, Inc.

Mead, Margaret. 1953. "The Concept of Culture and the Psychosomatic Approach." *Contributions Toward Medical Psychology*, Vol. I. Arthur Weider, ed. New York: Ronald Press. Copyright 1953 by The Ronald Press Company.

Mead, Margaret, and Martha Wolfenstein, eds. 1955. *Childhood in Contemporary Cultures.* Chicago: The University of Chicago Press.

Moustakas, Clark, ed. 1956. *The Self.* New York: Harper & Brothers.

Rogers, Carl R. 1951. *Client-Centered Therapy.* Boston: Houghton Mifflin Company. Copyright 1951 by Carl R. Rogers.

Rogers, Carl R. 1958. *Becoming a Person.* Austin: The Hogg Foundation for Mental Hygiene, The University of Texas.

Scheinfeld, Amram. 1956. *Human Heredity Handbook.* New York: Longmans, Green and Company.

Science News Letter. 1950. "Hunger Regulates Lives." *58,* No. 2, 21-22.

Sears, Robert R., Eleanor E. Maccoby, and Harry Levin. 1957. *Patterns of Child Rearing.* Evanston, Ill.: Row, Peterson and Company.

Seltzer, Carl C. 1946. "Body Disproportions and Dominant Personality Traits." *Psychosomatic Medicine, 8,* 75-97.

Sheldon, William H., and others. 1954. *Atlas of Men: A Guide for Somatotyping the Adult Male at All Ages.* New York: Harper & Brothers.

Sherif, Muzafer, and Hadley Cantril. 1947. *The Psychology of Ego-Involvements.* New York: John Wiley & Sons, Inc.

Tjio, J. H., and A. Levan. 1956. "The Chromosome Number of Man." *Hereditas, 43,* 1-6.

Witmer, Helen L., and Ruth Kotinsky, eds. 1952. *Personality in the Making.* New York: Harper & Brothers.

GROWTH
TOWARD MATURITY

Variations in Development

Goals of Human Development

The Patterning of Development

Some Key Conditions of Growth

In the preceding chapter we have examined the forces that shape our development—our genetic endowment, our physical and sociocultural environment, and our self-structure. And we have seen that one characteristic of the human species is a predictable life cycle with an unusually long period of immaturity and special susceptibility to change through learning and experience. In the present chapter we shall focus on this formative period of the life cycle to see how growth is patterned and scheduled under the combined influences of inner and outer determinants. We shall see that, within limits, human development seems to follow an inner timetable and to proceed in a certain general direction, but that maintenance of this developmental schedule is heavily dependent on the learning of essential knowledge and competencies along the way.

VARIATIONS IN DEVELOPMENT

In order to make valid generalizations about patterns of human development, we must study vast numbers of individuals, each of them somewhat different from all the others in physical appearance, rate of growth, intelligence, temperament, interests, attitudes, and almost any characteristic that could be named. Some of the differences among people, such as sex differences, are qualitative, or differences in kind. But in most ways people differ quantitatively, or in degree. Everybody has *some* intelligence, *some* height, and *some* musical ability, for example, but certain individuals have more than others.

To understand either individual development or the broader patterns of human growth, we must compare people in terms of such differences. Although ideally we should like to compare one person as a whole with another person as a whole, the complexity of human personality makes it impossible to do this accurately. We can, however, make useful and accurate comparisons in terms of particular traits such as height, intelligence, honesty, or self-confidence.

As psychologists use the term, a *trait* is any distinguishable and relatively enduring characteristic of the individual. A given trait may be very general (such as intelligence) or very specific (such as liking to play ten-

nis); it may refer to biological or psychological structure or functioning; and it may be determined by heredity or learning or both. Going a step further, we may define *personality* as the individual's unique pattern of traits—the pattern that distinguishes him as an individual and accounts for his unique and relatively consistent ways of interacting with his environment.[1] Personality patterns are sometimes shown graphically on a trait profile, or *psychograph*, as illustrated on page 76.

Studying Trait Variability

In using the concepts of trait and trait pattern, psychologists are faced with the problem of selecting and defining the traits to be used in describing personality. In general, they try to select primary traits which refer to some demonstrable and significant personality characteristic, such as intelligence or honesty, and then to define each of these primary traits in terms of the factors or more specific traits which it includes. Intelligence, for example, is made up of such factors as

[1] These definitions, and much of the material on trait variability, are based on Guilford (1959). For a further discussion of trait theory and its contribution to the study of personality, see the selection from Guilford on page 461.

perceptual speed and verbal comprehension. An effort is made to keep the number of traits selected to a minimum consistent with a full and adequate description of personality structure.

In studying trait patterns, it is often helpful to classify particular traits in terms of the following broad areas of individual difference:

1. Physical appearance—physique, hair color, eye color, facial features, and other characteristics of bodily equipment.

2. Temperament—prevailing mood pattern.

3. Capacity—potential for development in a given area.

4. Ability—actual competency or skill of performance in a given area.

5. Interest—degree of attraction toward any activity.

6. Aptitude—a propensify for doing well in a particular area of activity (e.g., in medicine or in law).

7. Attitude—a propensity to react in a given way (e.g., favorably, unfavorably, cautiously) to a given object or situation.

8. Character—the moral and ethical dimensions of personality.

9. Stress tolerance—level of resistance to physical and psychological stress.

10. Action patterns—broadly characteristic ways of interacting with one's environment (e.g., as an extrovert or introvert, aggressively or submissively).

A trait can be measured either in terms of an individual's performance on a specially designed test or in terms of his behavior in ordinary life situations. Obviously, not all traits can be measured by the same method, and some measurements are necessarily less accurate than others. It is impossible, for example, to measure such traits as honesty and sociability as exactly as we can measure verbal comprehension or manual dexterity.

The *amount* of a particular trait which an individual possesses, as indicated on some measurement scale, is called his *trait position*. Often trait position is shown by a centile score, which states a person's exact position on a given trait in comparison to others who have been measured—a centile score of 90, for example, means that 90 per cent of the cases measure below this point and only 10 per cent above it. The average or norm on this type of trait scale is 50.

PSYCHOGRAPHS

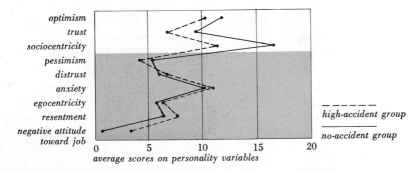

These trait patterns were found for two groups of industrial workers matched for ability and working conditions; one had a high accident rate and the other no accidents (Davids and Mahoney, 1957).

Patterns of Variation

In measuring various kinds of individual differences, psychologists find that traits typically are distributed among the population along a continuum, with most measures clustering around a midpoint and the number of cases rapidly falling off toward either extreme of the range. This pattern can be seen pictorially in the graph at the bottom of this page; psychologists refer to it as a *normal distribution.* In any large group selected at random, most traits—general intelligence, artistic ability, height, sociability—would be distributed according to this pattern. Thus we can think of personality traits as dimensions which vary from person to person rather than as all-or-nothing categories into which some people fall and others do not.

In considering trait variability, we must also take into account such factors as the *consistency* and *durability* of a particular trait—how much it fluctuates from day to day (or from situation to situation) and how much it changes over a period of years. In general, traits determined largely by heredity (such as intelligence and temperament) are likely to be most consistent, whereas those shaped primarily by learning (such as honesty and self-confidence) are likely to fluctuate considerably from situation to situation and with time. Even with respect to learned traits, however, the same individual may be highly consistent in some traits but highly inconsistent in others. For example, he may typically be honest and industrious but be sociable in some situations and unsociable in others. Trait consistency tends to be greatest in situations where the individual is ego-involved—when he perceives the situation as directly related to his purposes and values.

In the matter of durability, a majority of traits remain relatively fixed from the start of adulthood until the onset of senescence, but even here there are individual variations, and some traits may change considerably as the result of new learning experiences. In individual cases, major changes may be effected by a religious conversion or psychotherapy or some major alteration in a person's life situation. Thus it is important to know both the short- and long-range stability of a trait as well as the individual's trait position at any given time or in any situation.

A NORMAL CURVE OF DISTRIBUTION

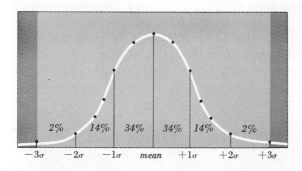

In any normal distribution, regardless of how much the "scores" spread, about 68 percent of cases fall within the middle third of the range—statistically, within one standard deviation (σ) above or below the mean.

The Significance of Trait Differences

The significance of trait differences for behavior depends upon such considerations as the type of trait in question, its strength and stability, and its relation to the overall personality, or total trait pattern.

Type of trait. It is apparent that some traits have far more significance for human behavior than others. For example, honesty is vastly more important than interest in art when it comes to determining a person's behavior and relationships with other people. In general, the more *inclusive* the trait—that is, the more subtraits the trait includes—the greater its significance. Individual differences in intelligence, an inclusive trait, are thus likely to be more important than differences in perceptual speed or verbal comprehension, which are two of the many subtraits involved in intelligence.

The *generality* of a trait, or the extent to which it is evident in a person's behavior, must also be considered in assessing its significance. Some traits—such as fear of heights, swimming ability, dislike of large groups—can operate only in a relatively small range of situations. At the other extreme, highly general traits such as self-control, nervousness, and ability to face reality are significant in almost every situation a person encounters.

Trait position and stability. If the individual's trait position is very much above or below the average, the trait in question is likely to play a more important role in his total adjustment than if his trait position falls near the norm. The trait of intelligence, for example, has far more significance both for the genius and for the mental defective than it has for someone who falls within the average range. Extreme deviations in mental capacity, whether above or below the average, have implications that extend into almost every aspect of the individual's life situation. The same thing is true with the upper and lower extremes of honesty, self-confidence, sociability, or any other inclusive trait.

As we have noted, the trait positions of a given individual are not perfectly stable but may vary from situation to situation and from year to year. In general we may say that consistent and durable traits have the greatest implications in determining a person's characteristic patterns of adjustment, although inconsistency itself may become an important consideration.

Relation to total trait pattern. The extent to which a given trait influences behavior also depends upon the way it is related to the individual's overall trait pattern. For example, a high degree of aggressiveness means something quite different in the context of a personality with strongly developed ethical values from what it does when it occurs with poorly developed ethical values and a high level of hostility toward society.

When we consider the practically limitless variety in the properties of specific traits and in overall trait patterns, we gain some perspective on the vast range of individual differences in personality make-up. An understanding of the complexity of the individual personality—and its uniqueness—is basic to any discussion of development and adjustment.

GOALS OF HUMAN DEVELOPMENT

In talking about variations in development, we tacitly assume that some ways of developing are better—or healthier—than others. Otherwise there would be no cause for concern over the "proper" education and training of children. But what are our criteria for "healthiness"? When are individual differences to be regarded as good or bad?

On a *biological* level we have a fairly clear picture of what constitutes healthy or unhealthy development, for physical growth is guided by maturational processes and follows a genetically determined pattern. Under favorable environmental conditions, the body tends automatically toward health and normality. Although *psychological* development also tends toward health and normality, the direction of desirable growth here is not nearly so clear, because development in this area depends heavily on learning and can proceed in any of a number of different directions.

What Is Healthy Development?

Because science cannot provide us with a complete understanding of our human nature and its requirements, we are forced to make certain value judgments in deciding which directions of development are healthy and desirable. A brief examination of the various criteria that have been used for making such judgments may help us formulate a meaningful definition of healthy development.

Development within the normal range. Since most traits follow a normal distribution, we might assume that *healthy development* could be defined simply as "development falling within the normal range" and *unhealthy development* as "development deviating from the normal range." This criterion is fairly satisfactory on a biological level, where it is possible to make rather clear-cut demarcations. The upper and lower limits for healthy blood pressure, endocrine functioning, bodily weight in proportion to height, and so on have been determined by scientific investigations and are generally agreed upon.

On a psychological level, however, deviation from the norm is a far less helpful criterion. A special talent of any kind is a deviation from the norm, yet we would hardly call it unhealthy. Furthermore, norms in psychological characteristics depend on what happens to be typical or conventional in a given society. Social groups differ considerably in their emphasis on traits like industriousness, competitiveness, and aggressiveness in personality development. Among the natives of Dobu Island in northwestern Melanesia, anthropologist Ruth Benedict (1934) found that ill-will, suspiciousness, and treachery were the recognized virtues. Whereas most societies have minimized extreme forms of animosity and hostility by their institutions, Dobuan institutions exalted them to the highest degree. The good man, the successful man, was one who had cheated another out of his place.

"The Dobuan lives out without repression man's worst nightmares of the ill-will of the universe, and according to his view of life virtue consists in selecting a victim upon whom he can vent the malignancy he attributes alike to human society and to the powers of nature. All existence appears to him as a cutthroat struggle in which deadly antagonists are pitted against one another in a contest for each one of the goods of life. Suspicion and cruelty are his trusted weapons in the strife and he gives no mercy, as he asks none" (p. 172).

The culture of Dobu offers a striking illustration of the fact that traits considered essential for normal development by one social group may be the very ones that are deplored and discouraged by other groups.

Even if the norms of a particular society seem to be essentially good ones, we cannot say for sure how much deviation is healthy. It is rather startling to note that in Dobuan society the naturally friendly individual was considered abnormal. Benedict cites the case of a Dobuan "simpleton" who did not seek to overthrow or punish other people but was openly friendly and readily agreed to do what anyone asked of him. Thinking in terms of our own society, we might ask ourselves such questions as whether a mathematical genius of twelve who seems perfectly happy without friends and dislikes athletic activities should be made to play baseball, join a scout troop, and take dancing lessons. We tend to feel that being "well-rounded" is desirable, but when a person has a towering gift in one line, how far are we justified in insisting that his energies be divided? Only long-range scientific investigations can provide the kind of data that will enable us to distinguish the range of psychological development that can be called healthy.

Until such experimental evidence is forthcoming, it would appear desirable to leave room for a reasonable amount of variation. As LaBarre (1954) has pointed out, animals whose behavior patterns become too standardized or specialized become inflexible and unable to adapt successfully to change. This, apparently, is what happened to many extinct species of animals such as the dinosaurs. In terms of human society, LaBarre's thesis would suggest that until man can find ultimate answers to the *who, where,* and *why* of his existence, he should allow room for reasonable variations in both individual and cultural patterns of behavior, with the idea that the best patterns will prove themselves and the less desirable will drop out.

Personality integration and adjustment. Another possible criterion of healthy development is that of personality integration—the smooth coordination of all parts. Unhappy, ineffective people seem to be those who are torn by inner conflicts and anxieties; in our mental hospitals are many individuals who have almost literally "gone to pieces." Effective, confident people, on the other hand, seem to have achieved an inner harmony and integration—a wholeness. Their assumptions, motives, values, and actions form a well-coordinated pattern.

Certainly a healthy personality will be a well-integrated one, but is an integrated personality necessarily healthy? What if the end result is a clever, unscrupulous, fearless criminal? He might have no qualms or misgivings, no conflict of desires or values; yet we would regard his development as unhealthy. Evidently our criterion must include something more than inner stability and integration.

Closely related to the concept of integration is that of adjustment. Implied in this term is not only the *inner harmony* of personality integration but also an *outer harmony,* or freedom from serious conflict with the environment. By this criterion, an individual who was in continual conflict with those around him would not be considered a well-adjusted personality however well integrated he might be.

But if we took social adjustment as a necessary criterion, we would have to say that Galileo showed unhealthy development because he was out of harmony with his times. Any innovator, coming into conflict with established ideas or customs, would have to be called unhealthy. We would find ourselves back at a statistical norm as the standard for healthy development. In a repressive, stultifying society the "healthy" personalities would be those that conformed to the stultifying group norms.

Fulfillment of individual and group potentialities. One clue to a meaningful definition of *healthy* comes from our earlier discussion of human potentialities. As we have noted, living systems seem to have innate tendencies toward health and growth. The developmental goals of the individual organism, then, would seem to be successfully achieving and maintaining health (well-being, wholeness, integrity) and fulfilling the potentialities given by its genetic endowment—becoming what it is capable of becoming. We may summarize these as the general goal of personal *maturity*—the full development of one's capacities and potentialities.

Important as they are, however, the inner goals of the human system tell us only half the story. We are social beings, and the goals of our development are determined partly by the needs and demands of the social group in which we grow up. A hunting society tries to turn out able hunters; a farming community, able farmers. Societies also differ in the value they place upon such things as industry and self-reliance, family affection, religious piety, esthetic sensitivity, and respect for authority. From the standpoint of society, there is no universal agreement on what constitutes a "grown-up" person.

Although we lack sufficient knowledge to assess all group differences objectively, the systematic study of history and the findings of our modern social sciences have shown us that not all customs and attitudes are equally valid. This is not to say that certain customs and standards are best for all people everywhere but only that those which promote individual and group welfare are better than those which do not. As Benedict (1934, p. 248) has pointed out, "It is possible to scrutinize different institutions and cast up their cost in terms of social capital, in terms of the less desirable behavior traits they stimulate, and in terms of human suffering and frustration." A particular cultural pattern may be right in one setting and wrong in another; but under no circumstances can such practices as human sacrifice, self-mutilation, hate-mongering, and physical or intellectual oppression be considered healthy, however prevalent or "normal" they may be in a given society. They are harmful not only to given individuals but to the long-range interests of the group. On the other hand, we can say that love and understanding *are* healthy, because they lead to smoother physiological functioning, more workable patterns of group living, greater flexibility, and greater creativity than hate and fear.

To define what we mean by healthy development, then, we must consider not only the potentialities of the human system, with its innate tendencies toward health and personal fulfillment, but the potentialities of man as a social creature. Healthy development is that which produces a mature, well-integrated person capable of actualizing his own potentialities and contributing to the long-range welfare of his group. Simply stated, the major goals of human development are personal and social maturity.

Trends Toward Maturity

Although each social group has its own ideal of maturity and does its best to guide the development of its youth toward certain fairly specific goals, there are, nevertheless, certain broad trends that seem to characterize healthy development in any culture. In this section we shall briefly examine seven such trends which have received considerable emphasis in scientific studies: the trends from (1) dependence to self-direction, (2) pleasure to reality, (3) ignorance to knowledge, (4) incompetence to competence, (5) diffuse sexuality to heterosexuality, (6) amorality to morality, and (7) self-centeredness to other-centeredness. Although these trends may be expressed in terms of quite different traits or goals in various societies, they seem characteristic of healthy human development in any culture.

Dependence to self-direction. One of the most obvious pathways to maturity is that by which we progress from the nearly total dependency of infancy to the point where we become independent, self-directing adults. To become self-directing we must not only mature physically and acquire adult competencies but also develop a system of values to guide our behavior. Self-direction, in other words, implies a good deal more than freedom from outside authority. The adult who remains the victim of his own impulses and immaturities is really no more free to direct his own life than the child whose behavior is restricted by the authority and prohibitions of his parents.

Self-direction also involves a willingness to make decisions and to abide by the consequences of one's actions. The immature person is inclined to lean on others for his decisions because he is unsure of himself and because he does not want to assume the blame if the decision turns out to be a wrong one. Decision making always involves some degree of risk, but the mature individual reduces that risk—and increases his sense of personal responsibility—by developing the competencies that will help him decide wisely. He accepts whatever comes without resentment or self-recrimination, utilizing his failures as learning experiences which can help him make subsequent decisions.

In a sense, then, self-direction means taking responsibility for oneself and one's actions. But as a member of a family and other social groups, we also find ourselves expected to take on responsibilities that involve the welfare of other people and to work toward group goals as well as individual ones. Indeed, because man is a social creature, complete individualism is self-defeating. As Herrick (1956, p. 8) points out:

"Human patterns of socialized behavior are unworkable without some sacrifice on the part of every one of us of highly prized personal prerogatives. The ends we work for must be judiciously chosen so as to ensure a proper balance between personal profit and the welfare of the community of which we are members and whose prosperity is essential for our own survival and comfort."

To say that we must assume responsibility toward the groups to which we belong is not to say that we are social puppets. While feeling concern for the welfare of others, we must first of all respect ourselves. This means developing our own behavior standards—inner guides we can trust—and following them even when outside pressures try to push us in another direction.

Today, pressures toward conformity seem to be greater than they have ever been in our society. In an age of changing values and increasing uncertainty, we seem to seek security by establishing a close identity with the group. Sociologist David Riesman (1950) speaks of the "outer-directed" man, who seems to him typical of American society—a sort of "radar man" who lives as though he wore a receiving set on his head in order to get signals from everyone else as to what he should believe and how he should behave. He is sensitive to social situations in the sense of wanting to do what is expected, to conform, to avoid ideas or behaviors that might be disapproved. He is dependent on society in much the same way that a child is dependent on his parents. Mature self-direction, though, implies "inner direction" —the ability to formulate and live by an integrated system of personal values. Although the inner-directed man is and should be influenced by the attitudes and behavior of his social group, he does not accept them blindly.

The transition from the complete dependence of childhood to mature self-direction is difficult to make. Even under the best of conditions we are somewhat reluctant to accept adult responsibilities. The inconsistency of adolescent behavior reflects a very real ambivalence: the adolescent wants to be self-directing but is not ready to give up the security and other benefits that go with dependency. "The double threat of fearing to behave like a child and of yearning to behave like a child runs through all adult lives, just as the fear and hope of some day becoming an adult inform the play and fantasies of children" (Mead, 1955, p. 7).

Probably few of us ever lose all childhood desires, attitudes, and dependency needs. We continue to lean upon our parents, friends, and relatives for advice and support. Occasionally we dream of a carefree life on some South Sea island or, in the face of special stress, regress to childish patterns of behavior. But despite conflict and occasional backsliding, most of us move toward increased self-direction, with all it implies in readiness to accept responsibility and make our own decisions.

Pleasure to reality. Believing that human beings tend universally to seek pleasure and to avoid pain and discomfort, Freud postulated a *pleasure principle* as a fundamental force governing human behavior. But this tendency to seek immediate pleasure is gradually superseded, he maintained, by a *reality principle,* as the individual comes to realize that his long-term needs can be met only if he learns to face the realities of life and make the immediate sacrifices required for his long-term goals.

Whether or not we accept Freudian theory *in toto*, we can readily see that the pathway to maturity does indeed involve a growing ability to cope with the demands and expectations of the "real world." This means, first of all, that the individual must develop an ability to delay immediate pleasures and gratifications—even to forego certain ones altogether—in order to achieve long-range goals. For example, the medical student must put in long hours of study which preclude many of the social activities he would enjoy, and often it is a long hard struggle to develop and maintain the self-discipline that is required. Again, every individual learns that the responsibilities of adulthood may require that he sacrifice many of his selfish

desires—that he learn to share, to cooperate, and sometimes to put the needs of others before his own.

Facing the realities of life also implies the development of tolerance and resiliency. The adult must learn to take in stride the many inevitable delays, frustrations, failures, hurts, and disappointments of living. Whereas the young child is completely upset by such experiences, the mature adult has learned to roll with the punches. Otherwise he would find the stresses of adult life overwhelming. This does not mean, of course, that mature people are so emotionally insulated that they do not suffer hurt; on the contrary, they make heavy emotional investments in the things they consider worth while, but they have learned to take inevitable hurts in stride, refusing to fret over what cannot be changed. They have a resiliency that enables them to recover quickly from failure or disappointment and to turn their attention to new tasks.

In large measure, this ability to tolerate frustration stems from a willingness to face and accept reality. Like the scientist, the mature person attempts to learn the truth about himself and his world and to adjust his behavior accordingly. This means, among other things, that he must temper his idealism concerning himself and other people with an acceptance of the fact that the obstacles to perfection are many—and often insurmountable. It means that he must recognize his own feelings and motives for what they are, even when he cannot be altogether proud of them, and attempt to understand why other individuals sometimes fall far short of his ideals. This does not imply disillusionment, cynicism, or apathy. A realistic acceptance of limitations and weaknesses can be a first important step toward improving whatever can be changed.

Ignorance to knowledge. The human infant is born with certain simple reflexes related to survival, such as the sucking motions that enable him to take food, but his ignorance of himself and the world is total. In the classic statement of William James (1890, p. 488), "The baby, assailed by eyes, ears, nose, skin, and entrails at once, feels it all as one great blooming, buzzing confusion."

As he starts to achieve his enormous knowledge potential, the infant rapidly acquires a great deal of isolated and discrete information, but the process of organizing this information into a meaningful whole—into a meaningful picture of himself and his world—is a much slower one. Gradually, however, the child develops an integrated picture of his immediate world—first his crib, then his home, then his neighborhood, and so on. What is at first a very limited world, or several separate worlds, gradually takes on greater meaning as smaller wholes are integrated into increasingly larger ones.

No individual, of course, ever learns all that he could theoretically learn. Although we might postulate certain minimal levels of knowledge as one criterion of maturity, this seems less important than the individual's attitude toward acquiring knowledge and his ability to integrate new information into an ever expanding frame of reference. For as a person extends his frame of reference, he not only extends the range of situations in which he can act effectively but also gains a better perspective for evaluating the meaning of specific events and situations.

Many people, unfortunately, have no interest in learning except to advance their own present interests. Or they may fail to integrate new information with previous knowledge, checking the one against the other and fitting the pieces together in an effort to validate and expand their range of knowledge. Failure to continue searching for broader insights limits a person's effectiveness both as an individual and as a member of society. As Overstreet (1949, p. 69) puts it: "Situations

beyond number are distorted by the indifference of full-grown men and women who still 'see in part and prophesy in part.'"

It is important not only that we extend and integrate our knowledge but also that we have faith in it as a guide to our adjustive actions. As Cantril (1950, p. 96) has pointed out:

"We become suggestible when we are unsure of our assumptions or when we have no assumptions that appear to be relevant in carrying out some action. In these situations we actively seek direction or confirmation. The psychology of mass movements, of rumor, of propaganda, and the like can find much of its explanation in terms of the genesis and function of our assumptive worlds. . . . People labeled 'joiners' are those who need confirmation of their assumptions because of their own lack of surety."

This does not suggest, of course, that we must always rely upon direct, personal experience for our knowledge. On the contrary, a person with a mature attitude toward learning will turn to various reliable sources—people of wide experience in a particular field, books, newspapers, and countless others—to extend his own frame of reference and thus to increase the number of areas in which he can act self-confidently. While having faith in his own assumptions as behavioral guides, he seeks constantly to elaborate and refine his knowledge and understanding.

Incompetence to competence. To a great extent, the process of achieving maturity is one of developing the various competencies necessary for effective adult living in one's particular culture. Teaching these competencies is the task of the home, the school, and other educational institutions; learning them requires a major proportion of a young person's time and, especially in such a rapidly changing culture as ours, continues throughout life.

The competencies essential to maturity can be classified into four areas: *physical* competencies (developing motor skills, keeping physically fit, protecting the body against accident and disease), *emotional* competencies (learning to deal with unpleasant emotions and developing appropriate and satisfying means of emotional expression), *social* competencies (developing effective interpersonal relationships), and *intellectual* competencies (developing proficiency in learning, problem solving, and decision making). In Part Three we shall examine emotional, social, and intellectual competence in detail.

The achievement of most basic competencies follows a general developmental sequence and is dependent upon both maturation and learning. The sequence of emotional development, for example, progresses from the relatively diffuse, transient, and easily aroused emotions of childhood to the differentiated and relatively controlled emotional behavior of adulthood. Although this general pattern of development is directed by maturation, the precise course of emotional growth is determined chiefly by learning, and many people never achieve true emotional maturity. The mature adult understands and accepts his emotions and has learned how to express them in ways that are at once socially acceptable and personally satisfying. His broader and more realistic perspective makes him less subject to the unpleasant emotions of fear, anger, and hostility than a child is; but when emotional tensions do arise, he knows how to recognize them and deal with them constructively, channeling their expression rather than suppressing them. And at the same time, the emotionally mature person continually broadens his capacity to experience positive emotions like love and humor. He regards his emotions, in other words, as potentially

healthy and normal forces that can enrich his life, not as something dangerous and disruptive.

We could similarly trace the sequence of events in the development of intellectual and social competencies, for our skills in problem solving, decision making, and interpersonal relationships are also the products of maturational and learning processes that extend over many years. It should be noted, too, that these various competencies tend to be interdependent—genuine emotional competence, for example, obviously depends somewhat on physical, intellectual, and social maturity. To be well-integrated and effective persons we must achieve reasonable maturity in all areas of competency.

Diffuse sexuality to heterosexuality. The psychoanalysts have put great emphasis on sexual development as an important aspect of a person's growth toward maturity. We now know that sexuality is not some mysterious force that suddenly appears at puberty but is present from early infancy. Its initial expressions are relatively diffuse and generalized, but even infants have been observed to experience pleasure from genital stimulation, and by early childhood, "crushes" that have a high degree of sexual involvement are common. Still later, the growing child may go through a period of normal homosexuality in which his interests and emotional feelings are directed toward another member of the same sex. It is not until the advent of puberty that heterosexuality becomes clearly differentiated.

Sexual behavior thus passes through progressive stages of development (varying with the social roles and training administered by the particular social group) and normally ends in heterosexuality in adulthood. An individual's development may, of course, be arrested at any point, or it may deviate in various directions—as we can readily see in the case of the philanderer, whose sexual development has been arrested at the adolescent level, or the pervert, whose sexual development has deviated from the normal course.

Maturity in sexual behavior eventually involves far more than a satisfying physical relationship with some member of the opposite sex. In marriage, sexual behavior requires the establishment of an intimate and satisfying personal relationship involving mutual respect and feelings of closeness. The individual's sexual maturity is thus limited by his maturity in other life areas.

Amorality to morality. The newborn infant is amoral—he has no concept of "right" or "wrong." Very early, however, he begins to discover that he is loved and rewarded for certain kinds of behavior and punished for others. This early awareness of "good" and "bad" eventually develops into a cluster of ethical assumptions and attitudes which we refer to as the *conscience*, or *superego*. Typically, these attitudes reflect the values of the individual's sociocultural environment, and they are first learned because of social pressures. Eventually, however, they are "interiorized" and become part of the self-structure, providing inner guides for the direction of behavior and thus eliminating much of the need for external controls. When an individual has interiorized the main values of his group, he is said to be *socialized*.

Allport (1955, p. 73) describes this process of conscience development in terms of three stages:

"1. External sanctions give way to internal —a change adequately accounted for by the processes of identification and introjection familiar in Freudian and behavioral theory. 2. Experiences of prohibition, fear, and 'must' give way to experiences of preference, self-respect, and 'ought.' This shift becomes possible in proportion as the self-

image and value-systems of the individual develop. 3. Specific habits of obedience give way to generic self-guidance, that is to say, to broad schemata of values that confer direction upon conduct."

For the mature person, strength of conscience and its effectiveness in guiding behavior depend more on his dedication to his own values than on fear of punishment. The mature individual experiences "guilt" chiefly as self-devaluation, resulting from a realization that he has failed to live up to his self-ideal and possibly has jeopardized his chances of achieving certain long-range goals and satisfactions.

Many adults fail to develop a mature conscience. In some instances, inner controls are not sufficiently strong to guide behavior; thus an individual may say he believes in honesty but nonetheless behave dishonestly whenever it profits him to do so. Because individual controls are often weak, society has had to introduce a system of prohibitions and punishments for enforcing adherence to its values. Unfortunately, many of us behave in approved ways from our fear of social punishment rather than any real understanding and acceptance of the values involved. When driving our automobiles, we are apt to make a boulevard stop or respect the speed limit because we are afraid of getting a ticket rather than because we realize that these things are necessary to safeguard life and property. Sometimes, too, people accept established social values without really thinking them through. This may lead to the interiorization of rigid and unrealistic values which can seriously interfere with successful adjustment. A person who blindly accepts the notion that his sexual desires are sinful, for example, will wage a continual battle to keep them suppressed. Rigid and unrealistic behavioral controls—like weak ones— are a sign of immaturity.

Self- to other-centeredness. One of the most important developmental goals—important to both individual happiness and group welfare—is that of learning to care beyond self. In a child's view of the world, the central and most important character is *I;* but the mature person has gradually extended this view to the point where other people's concerns are as important to him as his own. The experience of the race has been that the ability to care deeply about something outside oneself leads to the highest levels of personal fulfillment and gives human life its richest meaning. It is this other-centeredness that sustains a Dorothea Dix in her long struggle to win more humane care for the mentally ill, that keeps a Florence Nightingale ministering to the needs of wounded and dying soldiers, that keeps an Albert Schweitzer serving in his jungle hospital in Africa.

Other-centeredness does not necessarily require that everyone become a Florence Nightingale or an Albert Schweitzer, but it does seem that each of us needs to build rich and meaningful links with the world. One great strength of religious faith is that it helps the individual to relate meaningfully not only to his family and fellow men but to the whole of being. We find our greatest satisfactions in identifying and sharing with others. As Archibald MacLeish (1936) says in one of his poems:

"The solitary and unshared experience
Dies of itself like the violations of love
Or lives on as the dead live eerily."

The investment of self in other people or in worth-while causes often involves considerable sacrifice of what normally seems best in terms of the *I* and *me*. Yet it is only through caring deeply about something outside of self that the individual reaches his deepest fulfillment and achieves the sense of belonging to the "human enterprise."

THE PATTERNING OF DEVELOPMENT

It should be apparent from our discussion thus far that human development is the product of a constant interplay between maturational processes and learning. This interplay leads to a spiraling sequence of growth which proceeds in general from (a) an undifferentiated level to (b) the differentiation of parts to (c) the reorganization of these parts into larger wholes. Motor activity in the newborn infant, for example, is relatively undifferentiated; but specific purposeful movements gradually develop as the baby learns to reach and grasp, to sit up, and to walk. Eventually these various part reactions are organized into an integrated pattern of bodily action. Similarly, mental development proceeds from an undifferen-tiated level, to the learning of relatively discrete items of information about oneself and one's world, to the articulation of this information into a coherent "global" view.

The Scheduling of Development

Looking through the family album and seeing our pictures as babies and later as children and adolescents, most of us have been intrigued by the way we have changed in size and appearance. We have probably noted, too, that our bodily development followed a rather definite pattern and that our motor skills, such as walking and talking, fitted into this developmental sequence. We are less likely to realize that our psychological development was also following a definite schedule.

One simple way to gain a clearer picture of this growth sequence is to look at it in terms of the various major stages of development. These are not completely separate from each other, for life is an ongoing process—there is no one day or moment when a person ceases to be a child and becomes an adolescent or finishes middle age and begins old age. Yet it is fair to say that there are notable differences between a "child" and an "adolescent" or between an adolescent and a young adult.

Intensive studies of thousands of infants and children have shown that human de-

SOME SEQUENCES IN DEVELOPMENT

Typical at Age:	Telling the Truth	Belief in Santa Claus	Concept of Death
Three		Fears physical Santa.	
Four	Distinguishes little between fact and fiction.	Believes literally in every detail of myth.	Denies death as inevitable or final, sees it as a temporary departure. (4-5)
Five	Still exaggerates and tells fanciful tales; knows when fooling.	Embraces realism of Santa's clothes, laugh, reindeer.	
Six	Distinguishes truth from fiction; may lie or cheat despite telltale evidence.	Believes with emotional intensity; visualizes Santa's wife and workshop.	Personifies death; recognizes its existence but defends self against accepting it; has fantasies of people being carried off by "death man," etc. (5-9)
Seven	Lies less; is concerned about wrongdoing, especially by others.	Has moments of skepticism; may repudiate details of Santa myth.	
Eight	Is essentially truthful, boasts and tells tall tales at times; sizes up audience. (8-9)	Etherealizes idea of Santa but does not give it up.	
Nine			Realistically views death as inevitable process.
Ten		Has usually given up myth without trauma.	

Material in this chart taken from Nagy, 1948; Gesell, 1953; Ilg and Ames, 1955.

velopment follows a definite schedule not only in physical and motor development but in intellectual, emotional, and social development too (Gesell and others, 1940; Gesell and others, 1946; Bayley, 1949; Ilg and Ames, 1955). Not only does the individual crawl and sit up before he begins to walk, but his intellectual development proceeds from fantasies and simple concepts to subtle distinctions and complex ideas of cause and effect; his emotional behavior changes from relatively undifferentiated pleasure or displeasure to the complexities of shame, guilt, and sympathy; and his social behavior evolves from almost exclusive preoccupation with gratifying his own wishes and exploring or exploiting his immediate environment to co-operation, teamwork, and dedication to the welfare of others. Several examples of such sequences are shown on page 88.

The infant who is ahead of the developmental norms for his age group—that is, who walks and talks at a very early age—tends to be superior in intelligence; and conversely, the infant who is behind in relation to the developmental timetable tends to be inferior in intelligence. This principle has proven useful in forecasting the intellectual development of infants when such information is needed—such as when a child is being placed for adoption.

Developmental Tasks

At each stage of development there are certain fairly specific tasks—skills, attitudes, understandings—which are appropriate to that level of maturity and which society expects the individual to master at that time. Major tasks of infancy and early childhood, for example, are learning to walk and talk. During middle childhood the tasks of mastering schoolwork, of learning to get along with others, and of taking responsibility come to the fore. During adolescence the

tasks of establishing a mature sense of identity and of preparing for work and marriage are of crucial importance.

If these tasks are not mastered at the appropriate stage of development, the individual may be at a serious disadvantage in making subsequent adjustments. A child who has not mastered the vocabulary of a normal six-year-old by the time he begins school will be handicapped not only in his schoolwork but in social and emotional adjustment. An adolescent who does not date will miss his best opportunity for learning the social skills and acquiring the information about himself and others that will later help him select a good marriage partner. Some of the major developmental tasks for different life periods are listed on page 90.

Underlying the apparent diversity of these specific tasks we can see certain *general* tasks common to all stages of development. These general tasks focus around:

1. Achieving a realistic frame of reference, with healthy attitudes and accurate assumptions about self and environment.

2. Developing essential competencies, including physical, intellectual, emotional, and social skills.

3. Learning about problems likely to be encountered and about the preparation necessary for dealing with them successfully.

These general tasks are met in different ways at different ages. A four-year-old and a college student should be achieving quite different understandings and skills. But each at his own level should be broadening his horizons and developing physical, intellectual, emotional, and social competencies that he did not have last year in order to be ready for the tasks next year will bring.

Maturation and Readiness

Maturation, the continuing action of heredity after birth, guides the development of

DEVELOPMENTAL TASKS

Early Childhood
0-6 years

Acquiring a sense of trust in self and others. Developing healthy concept of self. Learning to give and receive affection. Identifying with own sex. Achieving skills in motor coordination. Learning to be member of family group. Beginning to learn physical and social realities. Beginning to distinguish right and wrong and to respect rules and authority. Learning to understand and use language. Learning personal care.

Middle Childhood
6-12 years

Gaining wider knowledge and understanding of physical and social world. Building wholesome attitudes toward self. Learning appropriate masculine or feminine social role. Developing conscience, morality, a scale of values. Learning to read, write, calculate, other intellectual skills. Learning physical skills. Learning to win and maintain place among age-mates. Learning to give and take, and to share responsibility.

Adolescence
12-18 years

Developing clear sense of identity and self-confidence. Adjusting to body changes. Developing new, more mature relations with age-mates. Achieving emotional independence from parents. Selecting and preparing for an occupation. Achieving mature values and social responsibility. Preparing for marriage and family life. Developing concern beyond self.

Early Adulthood
18-35 years

Seeing meaning in one's life. Getting started in an occupation. Selecting and learning to live with a mate. Starting a family and supplying children's material and psychological needs. Managing a home. Finding a congenial social group. Taking on civic responsibility.

Middle Age
35-60 years

Achieving full civic and social responsibility. Relating oneself to one's spouse as a person. Establishing adequate financial security for remaining years. Developing adult leisure-time activities, extending interests. Helping teen-age children become responsible and happy adults. Adjusting to aging parents. Adjusting to physiological changes of middle age.

Later Life

Adjusting to decreasing physical strength. Adjusting to retirement and reduced income. Adjusting to death of spouse and friends. Meeting social and civic obligations within one's ability. Establishing an explicit affiliation with age group. Maintaining interests, concern beyond self.

**Tasks at
All Periods**

Developing and using one's capacities. Accepting oneself and developing basic self-confidence. Accepting reality and building valid attitudes and values. Participating creatively and responsibly in family and other groups. Building rich linkages with one's world.

Adapted in part from Erikson (1950) and Havighurst (1952).

our biological structure (changes in the skeleton, muscles, glands, nervous and reproductive systems, and so forth) and contributes directly to the appearance of certain behavior. In a study of emotional development, Goodenough (1932) found that children who had been born blind and deaf, and hence had little opportunity to learn emotional behavior from interaction with others, nevertheless showed recognizable emotional reactions such as fear, anger, and joy. Evidently these reactions appeared through maturation.

In a comparable study, Dennis (1940) has shown the effect of maturation on walking. Using Hopi Indians as subjects, he was able to find sixty-three Hopi mothers who had kept their children on a cradle board from the day they were born until the infants were about nine months of age. The cradle board is a plank about a foot wide and two and one-half feet long to which the baby is firmly bound. Except for short periods when the infant's clothes were being changed, this board greatly restricted his movement. Dennis then compared this group with another group of forty-two Hopi children whose mothers had given up the cradle board and had allowed the children freedom of movement. Curiously enough, the mean age of walking was about fifteen months for each group—indicating that the restricting experience of the cradle board during the first nine months of development had had no retarding effect upon learning to walk.

But although the development of walking and of certain differentiated emotional responses seems to be guided chiefly by maturation, the same is clearly not true of talking: a child who never heard spoken language would not acquire speech simply by reaching the right age. Most human behavior is more like talking than walking in this respect. It depends heavily on experience and

learning, with maturation setting the time when learning can begin. In this sense we can think of maturation as establishing the necessary preconditions for learning to take place. Thus a child cannot learn to read until his nervous system and sense organs have developed to a certain point—with the average child, at about the age of six. To attempt to force him to read before he has reached this level of maturation is useless—and often leads to negativistic behavior and other undesirable results. The individual's readiness for learning any new task depends, of course, on his past learning as well as his level of maturation, for it is these two jointly which make up his structure at the moment when he encounters the new task. Whenever we learn something new, we always build upon what we already know.

Thus although maturation establishes the basic pattern for human development, learning fills in important details and is continually modifying the structure and functioning of the human system. Our previous experience as well as our heredity determines not only what we *are* at any given moment but also what we can *do* and *learn* and *become*.

Development and Learning

Because learning plays some part in almost every facet of our development and behavior, it is useful to know something about the different ways learning takes place. Basically, there seem to be two types of learning—*associative* and *cognitive*. Both are important in shaping the course of human growth, with associative learning playing a particularly significant role during the early years of life.

Associative learning. Much of our early learning is based upon the association of certain stimulus situations with certain response tendencies. When our response to some situation is accompanied by feelings of pleasure or satisfaction (reward), we develop a tendency to repeat this response in similar stimulus situations. If the response continues to bring a reward, the stimulus-response association is reinforced; if not, the pattern tends to break down. Similarly, we may learn to avoid making certain kinds of response that lead to pain or frustration (punishment). Such stimulus-response patterns are usually not verbalized by the learner and are not readily accessible to conscious control.

There is little creativity in associative learning. In essence, the individual is molded by the forces impinging upon him, often without even being aware that he is learning. The emphasis given to associative learning by behaviorists has earned them the popular name of "S-R" (stimulus-response) psychologists. Although there are many theoretical differences among modern associationists, especially concerning the precise nature of associative "bonds" between a stimulus and response and the importance of reward in reinforcing responses, they are in general agreement in their view of man as primarily a *reactive* organism.

Some of the principal types of associative learning are trial and error, conditioning, imitation, and identification.

Trial and error. As the child explores his world and develops basic motor skills and concepts, he frequently learns by random trial and error, blindly trying out various alternative possibilities until something happens to work. He relies less on this type of learning for solving problems, however, as his fund of knowledge and experience grows. Even in novel situations, he may possess enough information to make intelligent guesses or to try out various possible solutions in his imagination and then attempt the one that seems most likely to succeed.

Conditioning. One of the earliest examples of conditioning in human behavior occurs in the nursing situation. When the nipple of

his bottle is put in the infant's mouth, it evokes an automatic sucking response. With time, the infant begins to make anticipatory sucking movements at the mere sight of the bottle, which he has learned to associate with being fed.

Conditioning experiences are common during infancy and childhood, and much of this early learning—particularly where strong emotion is involved—carries over into adult behavior. Conditioned responses that involve the autonomic nervous system, as emotional responses do, seem to be especially persistent. Thus a person may be afraid of the dark during his entire lifetime as a result of some early frightening experience with darkness, even though the memory of the experience itself soon fades out. Many of our fears, values, sentiments, loyalties, likes, and dislikes are grounded in early conditioning.

We can even be conditioned to respond to subliminal stimuli. Our brains somehow register many impressions which are below the threshold of awareness. Baker (1938), for example, presented his subjects with a buzzing sound too weak to be consciously perceived. Simultaneously with this sound, a bright light was flashed into the subject's eye, causing his pupil to contract. Interestingly enough, a conditioned response was soon established in which the pupil contracted at the sound of the buzzer. In another experiment, Smith, Spence, and Klein (1957) utilized pictures with unchanging facial expressions. Each picture was presented once with the word "angry" and once with the word "happy," but the words were flashed on the screen so briefly—for only a few thousandths of a second—that the subjects were conscious only of the pictures. Yet the words apparently registered subliminally, for the subjects thought they saw the face becoming either happy or angry depending upon which word was flashed on the screen with the picture.

Such findings obviously have many implications for the development of human behavior as well as for its manipulation through advertising and propaganda. For example, a child may learn—without being aware of it—to discriminate fine shadings of his father's voice that indicate anger. Later, as a young man, he may experience anxiety when a new acquaintance uses the same vocal inflections. Yet he may have no understanding of his seemingly irrational feeling. Such subliminal impressions may also account for many of our hunches and intuitions, in the sense that cues of which we are unaware register in our brains and lead us to certain conclusions.

In general, our susceptibility to most kinds of conditioning increases up to about four years of age and decreases thereafter. Apparently what happens is that by the age of four a child's intellectual and perceptual capacities have matured to the point where he has a fairly clear picture of himself and his world. The ability to differentiate and interpret experience makes him less susceptible to simple associative learning, and he begins to be more influenced by rational processes and by what he already knows from past experience (Mateer, 1918; Razran, 1935).

Imitation and identification. Consciously and unconsciously, we often adopt other people's values, ideas, mannerisms, and ways of behaving. Learning by imitation and identification is of great importance in personality development, for children, especially, tend to shape themselves in the likeness not only of their parents but of other grown-ups and older children whom they admire. Society, of course, makes the most of this tendency by setting up heroes and legends for us to emulate, thus providing further models for development.

Much of the everyday learning we do is imitative learning. Learning to play baseball, to skate, to cook, to dance, or to shoot a basketball may be largely a matter of copying what we see someone else do. We learn what to do and say and wear in social situations largely from watching and copying what other, more experienced people do and say and wear.

Imitation during adolescence often takes the form of conformity to whatever the gang is doing. Teen-agers follow the latest fad in dress, hair style, and dance, and even their parents tend to follow current fashions in clothes, books, entertaining, and interior decorating. Advertisers, of course, try to take advantage of this tendency by emphasizing the fact that "everyone is doing it" or that "more people buy this or that product than any other."

Although adults may learn from watching the way other people solve problems or may simply conform to the group patterns which happen to be currently in fashion, such imitative learning or behavior tends to be tempered in maturity with more understanding and reason than is characteristic of the blind identifications of earlier years.

Cognitive learning. While acknowledging the undoubted importance of external stimuli in shaping human learning and behavior, psychologists who look upon man as an active, striving organism have tended to deemphasize the role of conditioned stimulus-response associations. They claim that much human learning, especially in adults, involves the acquisition of new insights. By *insight* is meant the perception of new relationships, usually after a period of study in which the individual organizes and reorganizes his experience in terms of the situation at hand. As Parsons and Shils (1954, p. 12) point out: Learning is not merely the acquisition of "information" about one's world, "it is also the acquisition of new 'patterns of orientation.' That is, it involves acquiring new ways of seeing, wanting, and evaluating; these are predispositions to approach or avoid, to seek actively in certain types of situation or to 'lie low' and wait, to keep away from noxious objects or to control them."

In general, we use insightful learning in dealing with the typical problems of everyday living—problems in which we are active participants. Thus the businessman may wrestle with a knotty problem in production; a physicist, with a problem in space travel; a medical doctor, with a problem in diagnosis. In all these examples the person applies his knowledge, memories of past experience, intelligence, and powers of reasoning to the problem. He tries to discover the essential relationships or elements involved and to imagine and evaluate various possible solutions.

Reasoning is made possible by man's superior ability to manipulate symbols and deal with abstractions. This ability gives him a flexibility and creativeness not found in the lower animals, who must rely primarily on associative learning such as imitation or random trial and error for solving problems. Some lower animals, it is true, are capable of insight when problems are simple enough that they can grasp the essential relationships. This was demonstrated in early studies by Köhler (1926) in which chimpanzees were put in several problem situations. In one experiment, food was suspended from the roof of the cage just beyond the animal's reach. To solve the problem—get the food—the animal had to realize that he might move a box which had been placed in the corner of the cage and climb up on it to reach the bananas. Although this would be a simple problem for the average human, it took time for the chimpanzees to work it out, and some were unable to solve the problem at all.

In cognitive learning, what the individual learns will depend to a large extent on what he already knows, what his present motives and purposes are, and how he views the situation at hand. The result of such learning will be a new understanding of himself or his environment—changes in his frame of reference. These changes may modify or reinforce his existing tendencies to respond to his environment and solve problems in a given way, but they do not produce a simple conditioned response. Psychologists who have studied cognitive learning stress the importance of the learner as an active participant.

Actually, of course, associative and cognitive learning are not mutually exclusive but rather represent two extremes on a continuum in which we find passive conditioning at one extreme and reasoning and creative imagination at the other. Both kinds of learning seem to occur throughout life, depending on whether the autonomic or the central nervous system is primarily involved. In general, however, we are most susceptible to conditioning in infancy and early childhood. As we grow older, we become increasingly capable of learning through insight, reasoning, and creative imagination. By school age, we are able to organize and reorganize ideas to achieve new understandings and to solve many problems of everyday living.

The importance of early learning. Our basic personality framework—leading to our habitual ways of feeling, thinking, and acting—is formulated largely during the early years of infancy and childhood. The plasticity of these early years was stated dramatically by the pioneer behaviorist J. B. Watson (1930, p. 104): "Give me a dozen healthy infants, well-formed, and my own specified world to bring them up in and I'll guarantee to take any one at random and train him to become any type of specialist I might select—doctor, lawyer, artist, merchant-chief, and yes, even beggarman and thief. . . ."

Such control does not exist, of course, in real life. Nor do most modern psychologists accept such strict behaviorism, for hereditary and constitutional factors have been shown to have a far greater influence on development than Watson realized. Nevertheless, it is generally agreed by psychologists of both the "active" and "reactive" viewpoints that the early years of life are of crucial importance in shaping the individual's basic attitudes toward himself and his world.

To understand the crucial role of early learning in shaping personality development, it is useful to examine some general aspects of learning: reinforcement, generalization and discrimination, and habits.

Reinforcement of early learning. We have seen that where associative learning involves strong emotion, it may persist indefinitely and be very resistant to change. Conditioned fear reactions, for example, may persist from early infancy and childhood into adult life. In general, however, associative learning requires continual reinforcement if its effects are to endure. The child who learns the capitals of all the states because the teacher demands it or because he wants to get a good grade to please his parents is not likely to remember them very long unless his learning is reinforced by continual review. Thus anyone trying to promote associative learning must plan for adequate reinforcement through repetition and the judicious use of rewards and punishments. Since such reinforcement is important in determining what is learned and how well it is remembered, the concept of reinforcement has become a crucial one in learning theory.

The attitudes and values a child learns from his parents are continually reinforced by his experiences at home. Thus they tend to become habitual at the very period in the individual's life when he is sorting out "reality," developing his basic concepts and making the fundamental assumptions about life on which his subsequent reactions will be based. It is at this time that he develops his basic attitude of trust or distrust toward other people and his feelings of personal worth or inadequacy. He also learns attitudes toward curiosity as good or bad, toward right and wrong, toward sex and love, toward authority and cultural demands. This early, tenacious, often largely unconscious learning affects all later learning.

Generalization and discrimination. The concept of generalization, which grew out of associative learning theory but applies to cognitive learning as well, helps account for the spiraling influence of early learning. By *generalization* is meant the transfer of newly learned patterns of feeling, thinking, or acting to new situations in which they *seem* appropriate. Thus conditioned fears may generalize or spread through association, so that a child bitten by a dog may come to fear not only every dog he sees but cats and other furry animals as well. In the same way, any learned response pattern which has proved rewarding may be applied to a variety of new but seemingly similar situations.

Generalization becomes less a blanket affair as the individual matures and his powers of discrimination grow. If physical and psychological development proceed normally, he becomes increasingly able to recognize the differences between similar situations and to react appropriately. Nevertheless, generalized patterns of response learned during infancy and early childhood form the basis of his characteristic life style. Thus by five or six a child may have learned to take an aggressive attitude toward life or to withdraw and become passive, obtaining service from others by his own helplessness. He may learn that different techniques work in different situations, but his underlying orientation and purposes will be generally consistent. Once attitudes are formed—especially the earliest ones, learned irrationally and often with a high degree of emotional involvement—they serve as reference points for evaluating new experience and guiding response patterns. And with time and repeated reinforcement, they become increasingly resistant to change.

A child's pattern of ego defense also begins to take shape during his early years. One child may be able to examine his failures and profit from them; another may be unable to acknowledge that he has failed and may need to rationalize his failure or project the blame onto others in order to avoid a threat to his feelings of worth and adequacy. The ego defense pattern that emerges during childhood and the extent to which the child relies on it are keys to much of his later behavior.

Habits. Learned ways of thinking, feeling, and acting which are used repeatedly tend to become habitual—they involve less and less conscious attention until they are virtually automatic. Many of the skills we use in everyday living have reached the level of habit —we go through the mechanics of eating, dressing, walking, writing, typing, and driving our cars without conscious effort. As standardized methods for dealing with the routine problems of life, habits greatly facilitate effective adjustment, freeing our attention for problems that require a fresh and more thoughtful approach.

When we become too dependent upon them, however, even good habits can work to our disadvantage—for example, when we drive our automobiles without conscious attention to the hazards of traffic, road conditions, and the like. And, of course, not all habits are good ones, nor can all problems be met effectively by a habitual response. We may have a habit of sulking to get what we want from other people or a habit of withdrawing in the face of any potential threat. Such habitual reaction patterns are often established early in life, when the child is especially susceptible to conditioning. Without conscious thought, he learns that certain ways of behaving accomplish or

defeat his immediate aims and thus establishes persistent habits of response that will affect much of his subsequent learning. This is one reason why childhood experiences can be of such importance to later adjustment.

Faulty Patterns of Development

The tendency of the human organism toward health and normality does not in itself assure healthy development. There are many ways in which both biological and psychological development can get off the track. This is particularly true of psychological development, which is so heavily dependent on learning. Curiously enough, it is much easier to agree on what unhealthy development is than on just what we mean by healthy development.

Three common types of unhealthy personality development are (1) *fixation*, in which development is arrested at some immature level; (2) *regression*, in which the individual goes backward to an earlier and "safer" level of development; and (3) *distortion*, in which development is toward faulty goals.

Fixation. For various reasons, development in one or more areas of growth is sometimes arrested. We all know grown men and women, for example, who have never achieved emotional maturity but react as children or adolescents would to the pleasures and frustrations of life. The middle-aged Don Juan and the "outer-directed" man are other illustrations of fixated development. Sometimes development is totally arrested at a particular level; a more common pattern, however, is for the individual to carry over a residue of immature attitudes and behavior patterns into later developmental stages.

Sometimes growth becomes blocked in a certain area because of a psychological weak spot. Traumatic events in childhood often cause a "psychic wound" which never completely heals, leaving the individual unnaturally fearful of certain experiences and especially vulnerable to stresses associated with them. A child who is rejected or deserted by his parents, for example, may become fearful of rejection in any important relationship thereafter; a child who is painfully embarrassed in public by some real or imagined failure may become self-conscious and shy in groups and find it difficult to establish satisfying social relationships; a child who is severely injured in an accident may become fearful and timid about meeting the ordinary hazards of living. In each case, growth in some important area is blocked. There is no way to predict the lasting effect of childhood traumas, but probably all of us have a more or less vulnerable Achilles heel as a result of our early experiences.

Regression. Sometimes the normal course of development is temporarily or permanently reversed. In emergencies or difficult situations, many of us fall back on earlier, easier ways—petulance, dependence on others, irresponsibility—that we have known to work in the past. It is quite usual for a three- or four-year-old to regress to infantile behavior such as baby talk, bed-wetting, or thumb-sucking when a new brother or sister is born. In much the same way, the bride may run home to Mother when the biscuits burn, and the man who resents his approaching middle age may revert to behavior more appropriate to adolescence. Previous habits often tend to be reinstated under stressful conditions or when more recently acquired habits are not yielding satisfaction. Usually

the regressive behavior clears up when normal growth conditions are reinstated or when the individual finds a more effective way of adjusting to existing conditions. Under unfavorable conditions, however, regression may be permanent.

Distortion. Distortions in development are readily apparent on biological as well as psychological levels. Children born without lower limbs, with extra toes, or with other physical anomalies are examples of distortion on a biological level—although, thanks to the guiding influence of our genetic controls, such anomalies are relatively rare.

On a psychological level, however, some degree of distortion is almost inevitable, partly because we have no very clear understanding of what our "real" nature and destiny are supposed to be. An acorn, presumably, is not plagued by wondering about whether it should grow into a weed or an oak tree. It has no choice in the matter and automatically and predictably grows into the latter. But, metaphorically, a man can grow into either a "weed" or an "oak tree" or any number of other things, depending upon the attitudes and behavior patterns he learns. Distortion may take many forms—juvenile delinquents, adult criminals, homosexuals, ruthless demagogues, all show distorted development—and may reveal varying degrees of severity and resistance to correction.

To prevent distortion and fulfill our best potentials, we need a clearer picture of what we can and should be growing *toward*—and of the conditions that can best foster such growth.

SOME KEY CONDITIONS OF GROWTH

The level of maturity a person achieves depends largely upon the conditions of his growth. A pine tree will be stunted if it is

growing near the timber line, more fully developed farther down the mountain side, and lush and green in the valley. Human beings, too, achieve optimal development only under optimal conditions of growth. But the factors operating here are much more complex.

Science has not yet been able to delineate fully the conditions under which we are likely to achieve the most complete fulfillment of our human potentialities, but laboratory and clinical studies of both healthy and unhealthy development have provided many important clues. Because the preponderance of clinical work has been with individuals showing faulty development, our understanding of causal factors here is somewhat more complete than our understanding of factors important in normal growth, but many of the latter can be inferred from an understanding of "what went wrong." We can also infer some of the favorable conditions of growth by examining the major characteristics of personal maturity, as discussed earlier in this chapter. Growth conditions should be those that encourage the development of a clear sense of identity, well-delineated life goals, a realistic and integrated system of assumptions and values, and the essential competencies for dealing with one's world. In essence, we are trying to foster the development of individuals who will have reasonably adequate answers to the questions of *who, where,* and *why.*

It should be emphasized from the start that none of the factors influencing growth operates independently. There is always a *pattern* of favorable and unfavorable conditions. Sometimes two or more conditions reinforce each other; in other cases they tend to balance each other out. Thus, a child's tendency to be sickly may be minimized by wise parents as an obstacle that can probably be overcome with time, or it may be reinforced by oversolicitousness to the extent that the child becomes a hypochondriac. Similarly, a child with a physical handicap who has low intelligence and an unloving mother will probably develop quite differently from a child with the same physical handicap who has high intelligence and a warm, mature mother. Each child faces a somewhat different set of problems with somewhat different resources. The pattern is more important than any one item in it.

Hereditary and Constitutional Factors

As we noted in the last chapter, our genetic endowment establishes both potentialities and limitations for development. For example, inherited differences in intelligence and in specific aptitudes produce differences in learning ability, interests, skills, and general competencies. Although low intelligence need not prevent satisfactory adjustment at a certain level, it seriously limits the individual's developmental and behavioral potentialities. Such a person will have much more than average difficulty in learning and will find it impossible to understand and work with many abstract concepts. The mentally gifted individual, on the other hand, has the potentiality for superior achievement as an individual and for making a greater than average contribution to the group.

Since all behavior is dependent upon our constitutional equipment, the quality of this equipment is always an important factor in personality development. Congenital or acquired defects such as blindness, deafness, paralysis, amputations, or brain damage place serious obstacles in the way of normal development. Yet the individual's reaction to his handicap rather than the handicap itself is the crucial consideration in his psychological development. Many individuals have developed normal and productive personalities despite serious physical limitations.

Our general reaction tendencies apparently are also related to constitutional factors. As we have seen, such dispositional characteristics as sensitivity to stimulation, energy level, temperament, and resistance to physical and psychological disturbances seem to have a genetic basis, manifesting themselves shortly after birth and remaining fairly stable throughout the individual's lifetime. Dispositional differences help account for many differences in development, for in a general way they determine how the individual will react to his environment. Traits such as an extreme sensitivity to stimulation or a low energy level may make healthy development more difficult, especially if environmental conditions are unfavorable. Predispositions to certain illnesses may also contribute to faulty development. Fortunately, we do not inherit physical or mental disease, but we may inherit predispositions that make us vulnerable to specific diseases under certain environmental conditions. For example, there is evidence that some people are prone to develop schizophrenia under severe stress, although under favorable conditions this inherent weakness probably will never show up. The same thing holds true for many other physical and psychological disturbances.

Parent-Child Relationships

The key influence in guiding personality development is the child's relationship with his parents, although teachers and age-mates become increasingly important as time goes by. In assessing the role of parent-child and other interpersonal relationships in healthy and unhealthy development, it should be stressed again that there is no invariable one-to-one relationship between the way a child is reared and the way his personality develops. The effects of any type of parent-child relationship—good or bad—vary considerably with the constitutional make-up of the child, his self-structure, and other factors in his total life situation. One child may become aggressive and destructive because he has been rejected; another may become anxious and withdrawn. Rejection accompanied by strict, punitive discipline will probably have effects different from rejection accompanied by overindulgence. And either of these patterns of rejection will affect a highly sensitive child quite differently from a more phlegmatic one.

"Mothering" in infancy. Research has shown that the early months of life are tremendously important in starting the infant on the pathway of healthy or unhealthy development. Particularly significant during this period is "mothering"—the subtle factor of maternal love and stimulation (Ribble, 1944; Bowlby, 1951; Fischer, 1952; Roudinesco, 1952). How far this factor is biological and how far psychological is not yet certain, but we do know that if the mother (or mother-substitute) is responsive to the infant when he is hungry or cries, protects him from excessive cold and light, and provides him with ample love and stimulation, the infant normally gets off to a good start. The infant who is rejected, treated harshly, or simply ignored, on the other hand, tends to show symptoms of developmental difficulty almost at once.

The effects of inadequate mothering are often seen among infants brought up in orphanages. Bakwin (1949, p. 512) summarizes the typical pattern of symptoms as follows: "Infants under 6 months of age who have been in an institution for some time present a well-defined picture. The outstanding features are listlessness, emaciation and pallor, relative immobility, quietness, unresponsiveness to stimuli like a smile or a coo, indifferent appetite, failure to gain weight properly despite ingestion of diets which, in the home, are entirely adequate, frequent stools, poor sleep, an appearance of unhappiness, proneness to febrile episodes, absence of sucking habits."

The long-range effects of early deprivation of maternal love and stimulation are suggested by the findings of Beres and Obers

(1950) in a study of thirty-eight adolescents who had been institutionalized from approximately three weeks of age until they were three years old. At the time of the study, sixteen to eighteen years after discharge from the orphanage, four were diagnosed as psychotic, twenty-one as having a character disorder, four as mentally retarded, and two as psychoneurotic. Only seven had achieved satisfactory personality development.

McClelland (1955, p. 33) has suggested that the stimulation an infant receives from its mother may be even more important than her "love" during the first months of life, and that the great need of institutionalized babies is for exercise and a change of scene:

"Maybe this is what mothers provide their babies with, and maybe it is what is meant operationally by 'mother love.' If so, the need is more for a kind of biological exercise of function in babies than for a somewhat mystical psychic entity—'mother love'. . . ."

This need for maternal stimulation is by no means confined to the human species. Licking the newborn and other maternal stimulation have been shown to be important in fostering normal physiological development of many mammals. Harlow (1958) has found convincing evidence of a strong need for contact comfort in baby monkeys. Weininger, McClelland, and Arima (1954) even found that rats subjected to gentling (handling and petting) for ten minutes a day for a three-week period following weaning grew bigger and were more active and less fearful than a comparable group of controls. Although the subject has not received adequate study, Montagu (1955) suggests that this need for contact and stimulation may account in part for the fact that physical contact—handshaking, nose-rubbing, kissing, holding hands, and so on—plays such an important role in personal relationships in almost all cultures.

Physical care. The importance of adequate nutrition, exercise, rest, and other conditions essential to maintaining physical health and vigor should hardly need mention. Yet many parents seem to think that adequate physical care consists only of securing medical help in case of illness or some obvious physical defect. As the result of poor physical hygiene, many children suffer unnecessarily from chronic colds, irritability, loss of energy, and other symptoms.

Such symptoms may interfere with development in a variety of ways. A child who is continually tired may dread learning situations that require sustained effort and may tend to give up before completing a task. Frequent colds may lower a child's energy level and make him highly irritable. Such reactions are likely, in turn, to complicate his relationships with his parents, teachers, and peers. The child, on the other hand, who has a healthy body and can operate at a high level of physical efficiency has an automatic advantage in dealing with other people and in coping with his problems.

Love and acceptance or rejection. A child's need for love and acceptance as a condition for healthy development has been demonstrated in studies of children with both healthy and unhealthy personality traits. In an intensive study of 261 well-adjusted children, for example, Langdon and Stout (1951) concluded that the most important single factor in their good adjustment was satisfaction of the children's need for love and acceptance. The children came from various socioeconomic levels, from different-sized families, and from widely differing kinds of discipline. The one factor they shared was that they were accepted and loved and made to feel that they were wanted.

As in the case of proper physical care, parental love and acceptance pay many subtle dividends in personality development. A child who is loved by others has little difficulty in accepting himself. Love is the best safeguard against fear and anxiety, giving a child the security he needs to explore his environment confidently and to develop new competencies. Many conditions that might seriously impair healthy development—a physical handicap, poverty, unusual strictness on the part of parents—are neutralized for the child who feels loved and accepted.

If, on the other hand, a child feels that nobody really cares about him, he is deprived of his major source of security and will find it hard to regard himself as adequate or lovable. This may result in a variety of behavior problems. One recent study found that coldness on the part of the mother was positively correlated with feeding problems and bed-wetting; that punishment given by a cold parent tended to make the child angry and retaliatory rather than to improve his behavior; and that a cold parent trying to discourage a child's dependency tended instead to increase it (Sears, Maccoby, and Levin, 1957).

It is particularly important that the child develop feelings of confidence and adequacy at the start, for once his self-picture begins to take form, it tends to resist change. Thus the child who feels unloved is apt to carry his feelings of insecurity into adulthood. He may never learn to give and receive affection or be able to establish satisfying relationships with other people.

Protection or overprotection. Although a child needs a great deal of guidance from his parents and their unconditional support, he should not be protected from the ordinary hazards of "learning by doing." In growing toward maturity, he needs practice in self-direction, with opportunities to direct his own activities in areas where he is capable. To protect a child from every danger he might encounter in exploring his world and testing his abilities is to deny him opportunity for developing the initiative and the

competencies he will need—and for learning how to cope with failure. A child who accepts his parents' conviction that he is unable to fend for himself may be passive and dependent for the rest of his life. Or he may become rebellious and aggressive. If the pattern of "smother love" includes overindulgence, as it often does, the child may also become selfish and egocentric, inconsiderate of the needs and feelings of others.

Overprotection may even involve "thinking" for the child. Parents who indoctrinate their children at an early age with rigid political, social, and religious beliefs discourage the development of their capacity for critical thought, which is essential to a mature value structure. Every child needs guidance in developing his values and beliefs, and often he must accept rules and regulations which he is too young to understand. But with every passing year he needs to be given increasing opportunities to form his own opinions and make independent decisions. The concept of freedom commensurate with maturity implies freedom not only to *do* but to *think* for oneself.

Opportunity and stimulation. The infant does not have to learn to be curious. He is constantly exploring—feeling, touching, tasting, looking. As nerves and muscles mature and mental capacities develop, the scope of his exploration broadens; and as soon as he can talk, he begins to ask questions. Yet even though these tendencies toward curiosity, exploration, and learning are seemingly natural and universal, they can be blocked by lack of opportunity and stimulation or by early experiences which teach the child to regard curiosity as dangerous and unrewarding.

Many children come from homes where material resources for learning are meager and parents do nothing to encourage their children's natural curiosity. Some are openly contemptuous of "book learning," caring little whether a child fails or passes his school subjects. A person growing up in such surroundings tends to learn only what he must. Indeed, there has been a tendency in our culture as a whole to disparage intellectual curiosity. Few people want to risk being called a "brain," and we tend to trust "horse sense" more than the "theoretical" knowledge of the scholar.

Since the entire course of personality development is so heavily dependent on learning, it is apparent that early and continuing encouragement of learning will be of crucial importance in fostering healthy development. If a child is to develop his potentials, achieve the understandings and competencies he needs for personal effectiveness, and function effectively as a mature citizen in a democracy, he needs an environment that both stimulates and rewards learning.

Structuring and discipline. We have seen that one of man's deepest needs is to understand and find order in the world around him. As might be expected, children grow and function better in a clearly structured environment in which they know exactly what is expected of them and what is not —what is considered permissible and desirable and what will be disapproved or punished. With such structuring, a child can experience the success and approval that come from living up to his parents' expectations. He does not suffer the frustration of constantly having to test reality in order to find just what he can get away with—trying to find a pattern where none exists.

In recent decades psychologists, educators, and parents have argued the case for permissiveness in child-rearing as opposed to "old-fashioned discipline." There is general agreement today, however, that a child can be just as handicapped—though in a different way—by a lack of discipline as by severe restraints. Too much permissiveness tends to produce a spoiled, inconsiderate

child—and often an insecure one, for children need to know what is expected of them. Unnecessarily rigid structuring and excessively severe discipline, on the other hand, may cause a child to fear and hate authority and to feel overly guilty and anxious about his own mistakes or misdeeds. Finally, inconsistent discipline makes it difficult for a child to establish stable values and behavioral controls. When he is punished one time and ignored or even rewarded the next for doing the same thing, he has no consistent guide to behavior.

Three elements of structuring seem particularly important for healthy development: (1) clear limits, so that the child understands approved goals, procedures, and standards of conduct; (2) adequately defined roles for both older and younger members of the family, so that the child will know what is expected of himself and others; and (3) established methods of handling the child that will encourage desired behavior, discourage misbehavior, and deal with infractions when they occur. The limits and roles established for a child must, of course, be realistic and appropriate to his age, needs, and abilities. And criticism and punishment should always fit the child as well as the misdeed. The same punishment that may help one child develop and maintain desirable behavior patterns may make another child rebellious and still another one insecure and withdrawn.

Guidance and assistance. We take it for granted that a child needs help in learning to read and work arithmetic problems, but we are less likely to realize that he also needs guidance in learning nonacademic skills—in becoming emotionally and socially mature, in developing a sound value structure, in learning to meet obligations. Actually, without guidance a child may not even be able to identify the developmental tasks he faces at a particular period of growth, much less know how to go about mastering them. He is exposed to many ideas, situations, and points of view which he is not yet mature enough to evaluate critically without help. Thus he needs guidance in deciding what is true and real, what is morally right, and what is worth striving for—in developing a reliable frame of reference.

Guidance and assistance do not always take the form of direct instruction, although there are many times when it is necessary to point out details that a child might not notice, to give him information, and to help him see new relationships. Parents and other adults may also guide a child by structuring his environment in such a way as to provide certain kinds of experience. Democratic values, for example, are fostered by a democratic home. The behavioral models provided by parents are another very important form of guidance—for good or bad.

The need for competent and understanding adult guidance is often increased during critical periods of development—for example, when a child starts school or approaches adolescence, when he suffers failures and traumas, when excessive demands are placed upon him. And throughout development, children need help in handling such special problems as hostility and sexual feelings.

Success and recognition. One need only observe a child's eager request of "Watch me, Mommy," as he demonstrates some new achievement, to understand the importance of success and recognition. As Allport (1943, p. 466) points out: "Not only does human learning proceed best when the incentive of praise and recognition is used, but the individual's *capacity* for learning actually seems to expand under this condition."

Although it would be imprudent as well as impossible to protect a child from every failure, healthy development requires that the balance be kept on the side of success. Parents and teachers can help in this respect by furnishing the guidance and instruction necessary to insure a child's readiness for new activities and by not expecting more from him than he is capable of achieving. While calling for real effort, mastering a new task or meeting a behavioral standard should always be within the realm of possibility.

The success of genuine achievement not only bolsters a child's sense of adequacy and worth but also encourages his continued effort. A child who continually fails, on the other hand—in schoolwork, fist fights, competition with other children, and living up to his parents' expectations—is likely to begin regarding himself as personally inadequate and unworthy in the eyes of others. Such self-devaluating attitudes tend, in turn, to breed anxiety and fear and to discourage further effort. Sometimes a child misses the experience of success even when his achievements are above average, because his aspirations—or the standards set by others—are unreasonably high.

Fully as important as experiencing success is learning to use failure constructively. Here again, parents and teachers can help—first, by giving the child enough support to assure him that he is still a worthy person and that his failure is not catastrophic; second, by helping him to profit from his mistake.

Early Frustrations and Traumas

Closely related to failure experiences are severe frustrations and traumas in early childhood. As we noted earlier in this chapter, such experiences often leave psychological wounds or weak spots that never completely heal. In one interesting early experiment, Hunt (1941) found that rats subjected to partial starvation during infancy tended to hoard more food and to eat faster in adulthood—even though ample food had always been available after the infant period —than rats who had received ample food from the start. People who have experienced serious early frustrations often react in much the same way, showing an exaggerated concern for security or achievement in areas where they were frustrated as children. In a sense these are weak spots much like those caused by isolated traumatic events—a serious accident, the death of a parent or sibling, a sexual assault. Problems that seem relatively mild to other people often reopen these wounds.

Perhaps it will help to understand the effects of severe frustration and trauma in childhood if we note that (1) they seriously weaken the individual's feelings of adequacy in the area involved; (2) they involve deep emotional conditioning rather than reasoned or even conscious attitudes, with the result that their reactivation reinstates automatic, conditioned emotional responses rather than calculated or rational ones; and (3) they sometimes lead to anxiety and withdrawal, so that the individual misses opportunities for compensatory experiences.

Investigation has shown that accidents and medical operations are the situations that most frequently precipitate anxiety reactions among children, with frights, separations, sudden privations, births of siblings, and sudden environmental changes also important (Levy, 1949). Whether or not an individual is traumatized by such events is influenced by his age, degree of dependency, state of health, dispositional tendencies, and many other complicating factors. A child who is beaten up by a bully during his first day at school, when he is already under considerable stress, is much more likely to find the experience traumatic than a more self-assured third-grader. In general, children are most predisposed to trauma during transitional periods of development, when a combination of changes temporarily decreases their physical and emotional stability. Early trauma usually has a greater ef-

fect on future behavior than does trauma later in life (Kahn, 1951).

Although traumas often result from unavoidable accidents, many are the product of parental ignorance or unconcern about a child's needs, fears, capabilities, and response tendencies. In the widely publicized case of multiple personality of Eve White (Thigpen and Cleckley, 1957), it was discovered in the course of psychotherapy that Eve had been forced as a young girl to kiss her dead grandmother good-by—a highly traumatic experience that proved significant in the later development of Eve's severe neurosis. This is an extreme example, but it illustrates the point that parents sometimes unknowingly place a child in situations for which he is physically, intellectually, socially, or emotionally unprepared.

Even the wisest parents, of course, cannot always protect a child from trauma. Deaths, accidents, family breakups, self-devaluating failures sometimes are unavoidable. But adults can lessen the long-range effects of a traumatic experience for a child—if they recognize it as such—by giving him the emotional support he needs to feel secure even in disaster and by helping him to cope successfully with subsequent situations. The handicap of a psychological weak spot can often be overcome by early support and guidance in relearning.

Detection and Correction of Defects

Medical science can now do many remarkable things in the early diagnosis and correction of bodily defects—in vision, hearing, glandular balance, and other areas. If such physical defects are not corrected, the child's entire subsequent development may be handicapped.

In a similar way, modern psychology and psychiatry have made notable advances in the early detection and treatment of faulty

KEY INFLUENCES IN DEVELOPMENT

	Common Results If Favorable	*Possible Results If Unfavorable*
Heredity and Constitution	High capacity for achievement; adequate physical and intellectual resources; resiliency.	Restricted capacity for achievement; difficulty in solving life problems; predisposition to illness.
Mothering in Infancy	Physical well-being; feelings of security and self-acceptance; ability to move ahead with developmental tasks.	Poor physical and psychological development; listlessness; feelings of insecurity; high mortality rate in infancy.
Physical Care	Good health; physical and psychological efficiency.	Retarded or stunted growth; poor resistance to illness; lowered efficiency in all areas.
Love and Acceptance	Self-acceptance and self-confidence; trust in others; ability to tolerate failure and disappointment; ability to form warm and open relationships with others.	Feelings of insecurity and inadequacy; withdrawal or retaliation, with accompanying behavior problems; low tolerance for stress; inability to give and receive love.
Protection	Feeling of adequacy; gradual assumption of responsible self-direction, commensurate with level of maturity.	*Overprotection:* passivity and dependency; egocentricity; often rebelliousness. *Underprotection:* failure to develop feelings of adequacy and/or responsibility to others.
Opportunity and Stimulation	Curiosity; eagerness to learn and to expand horizons.	Intellectual apathy and provincialism; minimal intellectual growth.
Structuring and Discipline	Clear values and ethical concepts; strong inner controls; confidence in ability to handle situations.	Confused concepts of right and wrong, of acceptable and unacceptable behavior; weak inner controls.
Guidance and Assistance	Adequate competencies; integrated values; reliable frame of reference; ability to meet developmental tasks.	Continued reliance on trial and error; important gaps in learning; identification with faulty models.
Success and Recognition	Self-confidence; ability to make best use of learning potential; desire for further achievement; ability to tolerate failure and use it constructively.	*Too much failure:* feelings of inadequacy; impaired learning ability. *Too easy success:* unsureness about actual competency; unrealistic aspirations: low tolerance for failure.
Frustration and Trauma	Success in handling moderate stress increases self-confidence and ability to tolerate and handle frustrations.	Feelings of insecurity and inadequacy; withdrawal to avoid further hurt; special vulnerability to later stress.

personality trends. Although the symptoms of unhealthy personality development are less clearly defined than those in physical development, many have been delineated. Excessive shyness, severe inferiority feelings, nail-biting, tics, temper tantrums, lying, the use of unacceptable language, tattling, stealing, bullying other children—all these are usually danger signals.

Unfortunately, developmental defects tend to perpetuate themselves unless they are detected and corrected early. The child who is overly sensitive and tends to withdraw from active participation in social situations, for example, may fail to master needed competencies in dealing with people. This in turn results in further withdrawal—and further loss of opportunity for needed learning. In short, the individual becomes involved in a vicious circle.

Although it may be impossible to undo completely damage such as that caused by early parental rejection or to overcome an early failure to develop adequate moral standards, even the most serious personality damage can often be corrected through a process of relearning. This, of course, is what psychotherapy is. Without relearning, the psychologically damaged individual is likely to be increasingly handicapped at each successive level of development.

Social Climate

The profound effects of social climate on values, on behavior, and even on the basic physiological functioning of the individual are at last beginning to be fully realized. There is evidence, for example, that authoritarian climates tend to elicit far more hostility and less personal dedication to group effort than do democratic climates. The type of social climate is also closely related to the incidence of such psychosomatic afflictions as peptic ulcers, headaches, high blood pressure, and heart trouble. Their frequency among us is a direct reflection of the types of stresses created by the culture in which we are functioning.

Actually, of course, all the conditions discussed in this section are part of the social field. A child's home, his school and community, and his culture as a whole work together to establish values and norms, provide stability or instability, and stimulate or discourage growth toward maturity.

In Part One we have discussed the main forces that shape our development and have outlined the general pattern of growth by which we move toward personal and social maturity. Within this developmental pattern there is a wide range of individual differences caused by differences in the genetic inheritance, learning experiences, and self-structure of each human being. It is difficult to establish criteria for determining which differences in intellectual, social, and emotional development are within the range of healthy development, but we can say that, in general, growth in any area is healthy when it moves the individual toward fulfillment of his potentialities as an individual and as a group member.

In spite of wide cultural differences in the definition of personal and social maturity, there seem to be certain broad trends that characterize healthy development in any society—trends toward self-direction, a reality orientation, expanding knowledge of oneself and one's world, competency in the various areas of living, mature heterosexuality, a positive morality, and other-centeredness. We have examined some of the key conditions of growth which are responsible for guiding development in these directions—or for blocking or distorting normal growth.

In Part One we have been concerned primarily with the structure of the human system—what it is and how it is formed and developed. In Part Two we shall be concerned with the way this system functions —with man's adjustive behavior. Actually, of course, we do not first complete our development and then start behaving. From the beginning, we are functioning while we are developing, and each process is constantly affecting the other. The ways in which we function have cumulative effects on our developing structure, so that the ways in which we have behaved in the past must always be counted among the forces that have made us what we are today. At the same time, our functioning, whatever our age, always depends partly on our development up to that point. Any full explanation of behavior must take into account the capabilities, limitations, and other particular traits that development has built into the personality structure.

REFERENCES

The following list includes both the references cited in this chapter and a selected number of additional books and articles for outside reading.

Allport, Gordon W. 1943. "The Ego in Contemporary Psychology." *Psychological Review, 50,* 451-478.

Allport, Gordon W. 1955. *Becoming: Basic Considerations for a Psychology of Personality.* New Haven, Conn.: Yale University Press.

Baker, L. E. 1938. "The Pupillary Response Conditioned to Subliminal Auditory Stimuli." *Psychological Monographs, 50,* No. 3.

Bakwin, Harry. 1949. "Emotional Deprivation in Infants." *The Journal of Pediatrics, 35,* 512-521.

Bayley, Nancy. 1949. "Consistency and Variability in the Growth of Intelligence from Birth to Eighteen Years." *The Journal of Genetic Psychology, 75,* 165-196.

Benedict, Ruth. 1934. *Patterns of Culture.* Boston: Houghton Mifflin Co.

Beres, David, and Samuel J. Obers. 1950. "The Effects of Extreme Deprivation in Infancy on Psychic Structure in Adolescence: A Study in Ego Development." *The Psychoanalytic Study of the Child,* Vol. 5. Ruth S. Eissler and others, eds. New York: International Universities Press, Inc.

Bowlby, J. 1951. "Maternal Care and Mental Health." *World Health Organization Monograph Series,* No. 3.

Cantril, Hadley. 1950. *The "Why" of Man's Experience.* New York: The Macmillan Company. Reprinted by permission of the publishers.

Cattell, Raymond Bernard. 1957. *Personality and Motivation Structure and Measurement.* Yonkers-on-Hudson, N.Y.: World Book Company.

Davids, Anthony, and James T. Mahoney. 1957. "Personality Dynamics and Accident Proneness in an Industrial Setting." *Journal of Applied Psychology, 41,* 303-306.

Dennis, Wayne, and Marsena G. Dennis. 1940. "The Effect of Cradling Practices upon the Onset of Walking in Hopi Children." *The Journal of Genetic Psychology, 56,* 77-86.

Erikson, E. H. 1950. *Childhood and Society.* New York: W. W. Norton & Company, Inc.

Fischer, Liselotte K. 1952. "Hospitalism in Six-Month-Old Infants." *American Journal of Orthopsychiatry, 22,* 522-533.

Gesell, Arnold. 1953. "Human Infancy and the Embryology of Behavior." *Contributions Toward Medical Psychology,* Vol. I. Arthur Weider, ed. New York: The Ronald Press Company.

Gesell, Arnold, and others. 1940. *The First Five Years of Life: A Guide to the Study of the Preschool Child.* New York: Harper & Brothers.

Gesell, Arnold, and others. 1946. *The Child from Five to Ten.* New York: Harper & Brothers.

Getzels, J. W. 1957. "A Stable Identity in a World of Shifting Values." *Educational Leadership, 14,* 237-240.

Goodenough, Florence L. 1932. "Expression of the Emotions in a Blind-Deaf Child." *The Journal of Abnormal and Social Psychology, 27,* 328-333.

Guilford, J. P. 1959. *Personality.* New York: McGraw-Hill Book Company, Inc.

Harlow, Harry F. 1958. "The Nature of Love." *The American Psychologist, 13,* 673-685.

Havighurst, R. J. 1952. *Developmental Tasks and Education.* New York: Longmans, Green and Company.

Herrick, Judson C. 1956. *The Evolution of Human Nature.* Austin: University of Texas Press.

Hunt, J. McV. 1941. "The Effects of Infant Feeding-Frustration upon Adult Hoarding in the Albino Rat." *The Journal of Abnormal and Social Psychology, 36,* 338-360.

Ilg, F. L., and L. B. Ames. 1955. *Child Behavior.* New York: Harper & Brothers.

James, William. 1890. *The Principles of Psychology.* New York: Henry Holt and Company.

Kahn, Marvin W. 1951. "The Effect of Severe Defeat at Various Age Levels on the Aggressive Behavior of Mice." *The Journal of Genetic Psychology, 79,* 117-130.

Köhler, Wolfgang. 1926. *The Mentality of Apes.* New York: Harcourt, Brace and Company.

LaBarre, Weston. 1954. *The Human Animal.* Chicago: The University of Chicago Press.

Langdon, Grace, and I. W. Stout. 1951. *These Well-Adjusted Children.* New York: The John Day Company.

Levy, David M. 1949. "On Evaluating the 'Specific Event' As a Source of Anxiety." *Anxiety,* Vol. 4. Proceedings of the 39th Annual Meeting of the American Psychopathological Association, June 1949. Paul H. Hoch and Joseph Zubin, eds. New York: Grune & Stratton, Inc.

McClelland, David C. 1955. "Comments on Professor Maslow's Paper." *Nebraska Symposium on Motivation.* Marshall R. Jones, ed. Lincoln: University of Nebraska Press.

MacLeish, Archibald. 1936. "Speech to Those Who Say Comrade." *Public Speech.* New York: Rinehart & Company, Inc.

Martin, William E., and Celia Burns Stendler. 1959. *Child Behavior and Development.* New York: Harcourt, Brace and Company.

Mateer, Florence. 1918. *Child Behavior: A Critical and Experimental Study of Young Children by the Method of Conditioned Reflexes.* Boston: Richard G. Badger.

Mead, Margaret. 1955. "Theoretical Setting—1954." *Childhood in Contemporary Cultures.* Margaret Mead and Martha Wolfenstein, eds. Chicago: The University of Chicago Press.

Montagu, M. F. Ashley. 1955. *The Direction of Human Development.* New York: Harper & Brothers.

Mussen, Paul Henry, and John Janeway Conger. 1956. *Child Development and Personality.* New York: Harper & Brothers.

Nagy, Maria. 1958. "The Child's Theories Concerning Death." *The Journal of Genetic Psychology, 73,* 3-27.

Overstreet, Harry. 1949. *The Mature Mind.* New York: W. W. Norton & Company, Inc.

Parsons, Talcott, and Edward A. Shils, eds. 1954. *Toward a General Theory of Action.* Cambridge, Mass.: Harvard University Press.

Rasey, Marie I. 1956. "Strength Which Can Be Developed from Within." *Merrill-Palmer Quarterly, 2,* 84-88.

Rasey, Marie I., and J. W. Menge. 1956. *What We Learn from Children.* New York: Harper & Brothers.

Razran, Gregory H. S. 1935. "Conditioned Responses: An Experimental Study and a Theoretical Analysis." *Archives of Psychology,* No. 191.

Ribble, Margaret A. 1944. "Infantile Experiences in Relation to Personality Development." *Personality and the Behavior Disorders,* Vol. 2. J. McV. Hunt, ed. New York: The Ronald Press Company.

Riesman, David, and others. 1950. *The Lonely Crowd: A Study of the Changing American Character.* New Haven, Conn.: Yale University Press.

Roudinesco, Jenny. 1952. "Severe Maternal Deprivation and Personality Development in Early Childhood." *Understanding the Child, 21,* 104-108.

Sears, Robert R., Eleanor E. Maccoby, and Harry Levin. 1957. *Patterns of Child Rearing.* Evanston, Ill.: Row, Peterson and Company.

Seidman, Jerome M., ed. 1958. *The Child: A Book of Readings.* New York: Rinehart & Company, Inc.

Skard, Aase Gruda. 1955. "Recent Trends in Child Psychology in U.S.A." *Courier, 5,* 341-349.

Smith, Gudmund J. W., D. P. Spence, and George S. Klein. 1957. "Effects of Subliminally Exposed Words upon Conscious Impressions of a Face." *The American Psychologist, 12,* 394.

Sontag, L. W. 1951. "Dynamics of Personality Formation." *Personality: Symposium on Topical Issues, 1,* 119-130.

Terman, L. M., and M. A. Merrill. 1937. *Measuring Intelligence.* Boston: Houghton Mifflin Company.

Thigpen, C. H., and H. M. Cleckley. 1957. *The Three Faces of Eve.* New York: McGraw-Hill Book Company, Inc.

Watson, J. B. 1930. *Behaviorism.* Rev. ed. New York: W. W. Norton & Company, Inc.

Weininger, Otto, W. J. McClelland, and R. K. Arima. 1954. "Gentling and Weight Gain in the Albino Rat." *Canadian Journal of Psychology, 8,* 147-151.

THE DYNAMICS OF HUMAN BEHAVIOR

Human Motivation

Problems of Adjustment

The Dynamics of Adjustive Behavior

Faulty Patterns of Adjustment

The Social Setting of Behavior

INTRODUCTION

In Part 1 we examined the structure of the human system and showed how human potentialities develop through maturation and learning. The traits that development thus builds into the individual's structure have an important influence on how he behaves, but this is not the whole story. As we shall see in Part 2, human behavior is caused by a complicated interplay of continually changing inner and outer determinants.

Chapter 4 takes up the question of motivation. What moves an individual to act at all, and what determines the particular goals he will seek? Despite their seemingly endless diversity, all human motives can be seen as serving one or both of two basic purposes: (1) the maintenance of physiological and psychological equilibrium and (2) the actualization or fulfillment of inherent potentialities. At any given moment an individual's behavior is geared toward satisfying a complicated pattern of short-term and long-term motives, reflecting both maintenance and growth needs. His selection of particular goals and means for satisfying these basic needs is influenced heavily by the opportunities, limitation, and demands of his physical and sociocultural environment.

Behavior is nearly always complicated by frustrations, conflicts, or pressures that interfere with the attainment of goals and thus create stress. In discussing problems of adjustment, Chapter 5 shows how the severity of stress is determined not only by the characteristics of the adjustive demand but by the way the individual perceives it and the resources he has available for meeting it.

Chapters 6 and 7 examine the dynamics of effective and ineffective adjustment, showing how all behavior—even when it turns out to be seriously maladjustive—represents an attempt of the organism to meet both inner and outer demands. If the individual has adequate resources at his command and feels generally competent to handle a problem of adjustment, his behavior will be geared toward overcoming the problem and moving on to achieve his goals. Faulty patterns of adjustment, ranging from an overreliance on ego defenses to a complete breakdown of personality organization, result when the individual's adjustive resources are inadequate for coping with a stress situation as he perceives it.

Chapter 8 examines the social setting of behavior and the dynamics of both organized and unorganized groups. Primary attention is devoted to the structure and functioning of organized groups, which in many ways parallel the structure and functioning of individuals. The chapter concludes with a summary of the important implications of group-individual interaction.

HUMAN
MOTIVATION

Ernest Hemingway (1955, p. 52) introduces his story "The Snows of Kilimanjaro" with the following:

"Kilimanjaro is a snow covered mountain 19,710 feet high, and is said to be the highest mountain in Africa. . . . Close to the western summit there is the dried and frozen carcass of a leopard. No one has explained what the leopard was seeking at that altitude."

This dramatic introduction implies two interesting points: (1) that the behavior of the leopard was purposive—that there was some reason for his climbing to the top of a snow-covered mountain—and (2) that to understand the leopard's behavior, we would have to understand his purpose—what he was seeking. This concept of the purposiveness of behavior, whether of lower animals or of man, is fundamental to an understanding of behavior.

But even within this general perspective, there remains the problem of discovering some order in the apparently limitless diversity of behavior. Is there a common principle that can explain the behavior of the student cramming for an exam, the show-off trying to impress people, the commuter gulping down his breakfast before dashing off to catch his train, the cub scout working for a silver arrow, the girl from a good family caught stealing jewelry in the ten-cent store, the boy getting up at six to deliver papers, the minister caring for his flock, the hate-monger fanning fears and prejudices? From the range and variety of behavior of which man seems capable, it would appear at first glance as though human motives would defy classification. Yet all of man's motives can be viewed as serving one or both of two basic purposes: (1) *self-maintenance* and (2) growth toward *actualization* of his potentialities. All our strivings—toward wealth,

status, security, adventure—can be seen as variations on these themes.

In the last two chapters we saw these two forces operating in the development of our structure. We noted that human growth is not random or segmental but rather a persistent, consistent, coordinated unfolding of a pattern established at conception and somehow inherent in the developing organism itself. Behavior seems to be an extension of this directive self-regulation toward fulfilling inner potential. The human system tends to resist disintegration of the structural and functional pattern it has already achieved and, if not blocked or seriously threatened, to press on toward a further unfolding of its potentialities.

Man is not alone in this built-in tendency to strive for maintenance and growth. It is characteristic of lower species too. Frogs—or any other animal we might name—try to survive, grow, and function in accordance with their potentialities. Yet there are important differences in the forms these strivings take in man as compared with lower forms. First, man shows more variability, flexibility, and precision in the specific goals he learns to seek and in the means by which he learns to achieve them. Second, in the case of man living under reasonably favorable circumstances, maintenance strivings seem to be generally less important in the motivation of behavior than do fulfillment or growth strivings. In fact, it is in man's attempts at creative expression and at finding values and meaning that he reveals his most characteristically human capabilities.

Although maintenance and actualization strivings will be discussed separately in this chapter, they should not be regarded as separate kinds of energy stored somewhere within the system. Man is an integrated, ongoing energy system, and his strivings at any given moment represent what seems most important to the total organism at that time.

SOME THEORIES OF MOTIVATION

The comparatively recent insight that all behavior is caused has brought a new attitude: if there are causes, we should be able to find out what they are; then, to the extent that they can be changed, we should be able to change and control behavior. This is the perspective of the psychologist.

In the comparatively brief history of psychology, the problem of why people are motivated to behave in particular ways has been a matter of major concern. Various theories of motivation have been put forth, but none seems to explain all the facts. Some of the approaches that have received wide support and have contributed substantially to our understanding of human behavior are discussed below.

Primary and Secondary Drives

One popular theory has maintained that there are a few basic, inborn, physiological drives with which every member of the species begins life. The diversity of the motivation in everyday behavior is regarded as the result of the conditioning of these inborn urges to new goals. Thus a motive for love or power or esthetic enjoyment is considered as really a disguised hunger or sex drive, for example. Any drives or motives except the original, primitive, physiological ones are thus *secondary* since, supposedly, they are built on the *primary* ones. This is the position maintained by such otherwise unlike groups as the psychoanalysts and the stimulus-response psychologists.

This theory makes three assumptions as yet not established experimentally: (1) that our only inborn motive power is biological—drives powered by hunger, sex, and other tissue needs; (2) that there is no qualitative change in our drives with learning—that the

underlying motive power remains the original hunger or sex drive and that the only way our motivation can be changed through learning is by attaching new goals to unchanged drives; and (3) that conditioning can in fact account for all the kinds of motives we see in operation.

All these assumptions are open to question. For example, there is considerable evidence for a psychological substratum of strivings, and needs comparable to the biological ones. Thus although men seek for love and approval and status in very different ways in different cultures, these seekings seem to be common to people everywhere, and studies like those reported by Bowlby (1951) seem to indicate that even in the early months of life, unmet psychological needs can lead to illness and death even when physiological needs are adequately met.

Further evidence of the inadequacy of this position as an explanation of all motivation comes from the work of Harlow (1953). His studies with baby monkeys demonstrate that very early in life exploratory and manipulatory motives appear that are clearly not conditioned from other drives, that do not follow the patterns of arousal and satiation typical of hunger and sex, and that frequently take precedence over the biological drives.

Finally, there is nothing in conditioning theory to explain how a supposedly conditioned drive could become stronger than or antithetical to the original one, whereas we have examples every day of biological satisfactions being denied or deferred for psychological and social reasons. This seemingly would be impossible if all our psychological and social motives were derived from biological ones. Monkeys can be taught to work for tokens which they can then exchange for food, but they never come to prefer the tokens to the food. Yet a man can choose to die rather than recant his beliefs or can give up affluence to devote his life to inadequately paid work that he feels is important. The truth may be sought even when it repeatedly fails to lead to biological satisfactions, and the striving to preserve one's self-esteem can take precedence over any and all biological needs. All in all, the theory that all adult motives are derived from biological ones through conditioning to new goals not only is unproven but is not in agreement with all the known facts.

Motives As Tension-Reducing Devices

Some psychologists have explained motives as devices for reducing tension and restoring equilibrium—as devices for bodily maintenance. Deprivation or disequilibrium is conceived as setting up an unpleasant tension which the organism then strives to reduce. For example, when the organism needs nourishment, hunger sends it out in search of food. Then, when it finds food, tension is reduced, the hunger drive is sated, the motivated state ceases, and the organism is quiescent until something else comes along to upset it.

Much of our biological functioning does obviously follow this pattern, and the discovery of the homeostatic mechanisms for maintaining physiological equilibrium has been extremely useful in helping us to understand behavior like food seeking. Yet human beings do not seem to be concerned solely with maintenance of the status quo or removal of all tension. Few people are content to live like vegetables. Instead, they go out of their way to work long hours at fulfilling their potentialities, to create, to explore, to build, to improve, to increase the complexity of their lives. These activities cannot be satisfactorily explained as attempts

to reduce tension. So again we seem to have a theory that does not explain all the facts.

Push and Pull Theories

A number of approaches to motivation can be labeled "push" theories or "pull" theories. The push theories emphasize man's inner drives or strivings, his own purposes, his essentially active nature. His behavior is seen as the result of his attempts to meet his needs, to express himself, to make sense out of his world, to achieve his purposes. The environment may provide what he needs or put obstacles in his way, but the action is initiated by forces and conditions within him: he is an active, striving, purposeful agent.

The pull theories, on the other hand, emphasize environmental stimuli as the primary forces that induce and channel behavior. Our behavior is conceived as a response to demands and pressures, rewards and punishments, deprivations, dangers, and inducements—in any case a response to some initiating stimulus in the environment.[1].

Thus the push theories emphasize the *active* side of man; the pull theories, the *reactive* side. Whereas the push theories find the essential motive power *within* the individual in impelling urges, the pull theories find it largely in forces *outside* him, manipulating the strings, with man as more or less a puppet.

It seems evident that neither of these positions is sufficient by itself. Man is both active and reactive. His behavior, like that of other energy systems, is the result of both (a) his inner structural and functional properties and (b) the conditions and forces of his field, or environment. Some things we do because of inner demands; some, because of

[1]To allow for action clearly initiated within the organism, some stimuli are assumed to arise in the "inner environment," though where the organism ends and its inner environment begins is not always clear.

social dictates or other field demands. Both the instigation of behavior and the form it takes are joint results of our own personality and the field in which the action takes place. If either the doer or the field were different, the action would be different.

An Eclectic Approach

While we cannot completely accept any of the three approaches outlined, we will incorporate useful concepts from all of them. Although we do not accept the notion of primary and derived drives as a full explanation of our motives, it is clear that learning does play a tremendous part in human motivation, and an understanding of motivation must thus delineate the role of conditioning and other kinds of learning. Although we do not accept a tension-reduction theory of motivation as being the whole story, we will apply it to the kinds of behavior where it does seem to fit reasonably well. And finally, although neither push nor pull theories are complete alone, the insights of both will be needed to show how inner strivings and field forces together direct our behavior.

In the present chapter we will be using the general term *motive* to refer to any striving toward a specific goal, regardless of how it may have been initiated. The goal may be an object, an experience, an activity, or a situation. Other terms, like *drive* and *need*, will be explained as we go along.

STRIVINGS TOWARD MAINTENANCE

It is apparent that preserving the integrity of one's body is the prime requisite for survival and that countless activities within the body work together toward this end. Digestion, circulation, endocrine action, and breathing all play their part, as do built-in mechanisms for combating disease, insuring normal blood chemistry, maintaining proper body temperature, and sending us out in search of food. All these processes are part of the continuous endeavor of the body to maintain internal conditions within the limits necessary for survival and health—an endeavor referred to by Cannon (1939) as *homeostasis.*

Some of these homeostatic mechanisms are automatic and involve no awareness or conscious effort on our part. This is the case, for example, with the mechanisms for fighting bacteria and maintaining normal blood chemistry. Such mechanisms are primarily the concern of the field of medicine rather than of psychology. In many cases, however, as in the drives for hunger, thirst, and sleep, the homeostatic mechanisms do lead to awareness and conscious effort and even come to include complicated learned behavior.

Although the concept of homeostasis was developed in connection with physiological processes, it has a parallel on the psychological level. Here, too, man strives to maintain his integrity or integration—in this case his feelings of worth and adequacy and his ability to think and feel and act in organized, coherent ways. Damage to his self-structure, as in the case of severe guilt or inadequacy feelings, can disable him just as surely as can disruption of his physiological functioning. Patients in mental hospitals have been disabled in this way. So man puts considerable effort into maintaining and strengthening his psychological structure—especially his self-structure, which, as we have seen, serves as his basic anchorage point. And unconsciously he develops defense mechanisms like rationalization and projection to protect himself from threats to his feelings of personal worth and adequacy.

On both biological and psychological levels, maintenance of smooth functioning is possible only if certain basic requirements are met. What we call *maintenance-directed behavior* is behavior aimed at meeting these requirements. It is initiated when a deprivation of some kind occurs, or is anticipated, and it ceases when the missing requirement has been supplied. Thus it may aptly be called *deficiency* motivation since it dominates our behavior only when a deficiency occurs or is anticipated.

Organisms may of course operate at different levels of efficiency. In a concentration camp, where the inmates receive only a few hundred calories a day and no psychological or social satisfactions, life may continue at a bare subsistence level. Many ordinary physical and psychological requirements are not being met, yet the individual may hang on to life for many months or even years. Thus it should be emphasized that the requirements we shall be discussing are requirements for normal functioning, not for bare survival. They are requirements for a certain quality of living as human beings, though not in every case requirements for life itself.

Our first task, then, will be to review some of the generally agreed-on requirements—biological and psychological needs—that must be met for normal functioning and to see the typical chain of events by which these requirements are met. It should be stressed that when we talk of requirements or needs, we are referring to actual, objective needs, not felt needs; often the individual is aware of his needs, but sometimes he is not.

Bodily Needs

The human body needs many substances, conditions, and activities, ranging from vitamins to sexual release. Some needs, such as our need for food and water, may be clearly and frequently felt; others, such as our need for air, are felt only under conditions of serious deprivation; still others, such as our need for vitamin A, we know about only intellectually—if we are seriously deficient in vitamin A, we may realize that something is wrong, but we may not know what it is and in any case do not have a specific, conscious longing for the particular element that our body needs. Yet a certain "body wisdom" will help us if we let it. In various studies, especially with animals and infants, the subjects have chosen from an assortment of foods the ones that contained the elements they most needed (Davis, 1928; Richter, 1942). Thiamine-deficient rats will cut down their carbohydrate intake and increase their fat intake (thiamine is essential in carbohydrate metabolism); and when thiamine is restored to their diet, they will go back to their usual proportions of fats and carbohydrates (Richter and Hawkes, 1941). People with an adrenal deficiency tend to put salt on everything, even pie, thus aiding their metabolism. Infants make good selections if they are given a choice between natural foods, but if sweets are introduced, their judgment is upset.

Bodily needs can be classified in various ways. The following kinds of needs seem particularly pertinent to an understanding of human behavior:

1. Visceral needs—needs for food, water, oxygen, sleep, elimination of wastes, and other substances, conditions, and activities necessary for keeping the organism alive.

2. Safety needs—needs relating to the avoidance of bodily harm.

3. Sex needs—needs basic to the perpetuation of the species and important to individual fulfillment.

4. Sensory and motor needs—needs for using bodily equipment if it is to function properly.

Of these four types of bodily needs, the last—the sensory and motor needs—perhaps require special comment. We have long been aware that failure to use muscles leads to their atrophy. Now experiments have shown that integration of thought processes is dependent upon sensory stimulation, or "feed-in" from the environment (Lilly, 1956; Heron, Doane, and Scott, 1956). In other words, to prevent disorganization of thought processes, a certain level of sensory stimulation is essential. If incoming stimulation is greatly reduced for a period of several hours, an individual's thought processes become disoriented and he begins to have hallucinations. In addition, he becomes prone to accept any information that is "fed in," a tendency which suggests why brainwashing can be effective. After a prolonged period without sensory stimulation, performance on intelligence and other psychological tests is temporarily lowered, and time is necessary to restore normal mental functioning.

The organism's tendency to use its bodily equipment is also shown in the child's urge to explore his environment, to learn to walk, to engage in vigorous bodily activities, and to enjoy sound and sights, including music and colorful pictures. Not much is known about man's esthetic needs, but his enjoyment of music, dancing, and art is thought to be closely related to his sensory-motor make-up —complicated, of course, by cultural conditioning.

Psychological Needs

On the psychological level, any attempt to classify basic requirements is arbitrary at best, for psychogenic processes are so heavily infused with learning that it is almost impossible to pick out an inborn core. Our list therefore will include some requirements that apparently involve little or no learning and some that tend to develop to some extent in all people but may be primarily the result of a similarity of experience. Whether learned or unlearned, conscious or unconscious, these needs play an important part in human motivation, and deprivation of them leads to disturbances in the integration of overall functioning.

Although we will discuss five psychological requirements that fit this description,

---

THE NEED FOR SENSORY STIMULATION

	In Development	In Behavior
Function of Stimulation	Needed for acquiring (1) information and concepts—a "cognitive map" of one's world—and (2) strategies for coping with novel situations.	May initiate action. Provides feedback for evaluating accuracy of information and concepts and effectiveness of action.
Results of Deprivation	Inadequate basis for identifying significant cues out of barrage of stimuli. Inadequate strategies for coping with new problems.	Disorientation and sometimes panic. Tendency to accept any information fed in. Skill on psychological tests sometimes lowered temporarily.

they are not actually so separate or independent of each other as such a discussion implies. In some cases, in fact, they seem to be more like aspects of each other than separate requirements.

An integrated frame of reference. A profoundly felt psychological need is that of developing a meaningful picture of our world and our place in it. As Cantril (1950, p. 65) says:

". . . we cannot learn how to carry on until we learn to select from the environment around us those aspects that are significant in terms of our own purposes. We have to learn what things are edible . . . , what things will aid or harm us, what people are friendly and unfriendly, what activities within our group structure will bring rewards or punishments."

In short, man cannot act effectively until he builds up a fairly stable frame of reference concerning his world and himself which enables him to evaluate new situations and to anticipate the effect of his actions. To be effective, this frame of reference must be accurate. But accurate or inaccurate, man develops a frame of reference because he must. Human beings do not like ambiguity, lack of structuring, chaos, or any events which seem beyond their understanding and control and which place them at the mercy of alien forces.

Our perceptual processes operate in such a way as to help us maintain the consistency and stability of our world. When contradictions occur, we try not to notice them; if we cannot avoid recognizing the contradictions, we are uncomfortable until we can somehow reconcile them. Festinger (1958) points out that a contradiction is a motivating condition in the same way that hunger is a motivating condition. In both cases, activity is initiated toward reducing or eliminating the problem, and success is experienced as satisfying. Trying to go along with contradictory pictures of our world would be like trying to drive on a highway with multiple, incompatible pictures of oncoming traffic. In such a situation we would be thrown into hopeless confusion as to what to do.

This striving toward order and a consistent picture applies also to our assumptions about ourselves and accounts for much of our forgetting, rationalizing, and lack of self-understanding. As Fromm (1955, p. 65) notes, we have a great need to believe we are behaving rationally:

"However unreasonable or immoral an action may be, man has an insuperable urge to rationalize it, that is, to prove to himself and to others that his action is determined by reason, common sense, or at least conventional morality. He has little difficulty in acting irrationally, but it is almost impossible for him not to give his action the appearance of reasonable motivation."

To face the possibility that our own behavior may be irrational or disorganized would disable us seriously—we then could not depend on ourselves.

Feelings of adequacy and security. Everyone needs to feel basically capable of dealing with his problems. When our adjustive resources seem inadequate for coping with a situation, we tend to become confused and disorganized; we are upset by apprehension of disaster which we feel helpless to avert. This pattern is perhaps most dramatically shown in the disorganization of panic reactions, but felt inadequacy in any situation can interfere with integrated, effective behavior.

Many experimental studies with animals have shown the effects on behavior of severe conditions of inadequacy. In such studies the animal is faced with a problem situation in which he is forced to act but for which his adjustive capacities are inadequate. The result is the development of a disturbance in behavior referred to as an "experimental neurosis" or "nervous breakdown" (Liddell, 1944). We do not put human beings into experimental situations that will induce such a breakdown, but life often does, and the factors seem to be much the same.

Feelings of adequacy are heavily dependent on the development of a reliable frame of reference and of essential skills for dealing with specific types of problems. Our tendencies to test reality, to learn, to master, and to improve our situation all seem closely related to our strivings toward feelings of adequacy. The normal infant is continually exploring the possibilities and limitations of his physical and social environment. By such testing of reality he acquires the practical knowledge and skills he needs to be independent and adequate.

Security is, in a sense, assurance of adequacy in the future. Because we know that failure to meet our needs is acutely unpleasant, we try to maintain conditions that insure future as well as present gratification.

Our effort to achieve security is reflected in our preference for jobs with tenure, disability insurance, and retirement benefits. As we noted in our discussion of personality development, achievement of a sense of security during early infancy is important because without a basic trust in people and in his general environment, the child cannot have courage to explore his world and learn to meet its challenges and hazards.

Physical well-being plays a more important part in feelings of security than we sometimes realize. A low energy level, an acute illness, the loss of an arm or an eye, or the feeling that we are physically unattractive may seriously undermine our sense of security and adequacy.

The more adequate we feel, the less awareness we have of our need for security and adequacy. Conversely, the more inadequate or insecure we feel, the stronger our felt need to be more adequate and secure. In one study, for example, it was found that people who identified themselves with the "working class" expressed a desire for security as their

PSYCHOLOGICAL NEEDS

	Low Acceptance of Others	*High Acceptance of Others*
High Self-Acceptance	Group A	Group B
Low Self-Acceptance	Group C	Group D

Our need for adequacy, self-esteem, and love can be inferred from our functioning with and without them. In one study, subjects in the four categories shown took several personality tests. Group A expressed complacency about their social status but were uneasy and defensive. Group C were definitely troubled. Group D tended to be timid and to underestimate their popularity. Group B were the healthiest and happiest. They were optimistic, had faith in mankind, and showed a high level of personal responsibility (Fey, 1957).

major value in life, possibly because they had been at the mercy of economic fluctuations. On the other hand, the subjects who identified themselves with the "middle class" and who in most cases probably had a more secure economic position typically considered a desire for self-expression or actualization as being more important to them (Cantril, 1950).

Learning, too, may affect the relative importance of security to a marked degree. Through learning, people may come to value the exploration of unfamiliar roads—leaving the safe security of the known to look for richer experiences and new, better ways of doing things. But evidently this happens only when the individual has developed underlying feelings of inadequacy so that he can tolerate change and uncertainty without undue panic and fear.

Feelings of belonging and approval. The growing infant is completely dependent for his existence on the approval and assistance of others. He soon learns that socially approved behavior is rewarded, while socially disapproved behavior is punished. As he grows older, he finds that being approved and accepted in the group becomes increasingly important, for only through group participation can he ordinarily meet his needs for security, love, self-esteem, and a meaningful frame of reference. So he strives to become and remain an approved member in his social surroundings. As Sherif and Cantril (1947, p. 5) summarize it:

"Every individual strives to place or to anchor himself as an acceptable member in his social milieu or in some social setting. . . . This is true for any individual in any culture, whether highly competitive or highly co-operative, whether primitive or advanced. There is an unmistakable striving on the part of the individual *to belong* to his group or to some aspired group."

Man's need for social belonging and approval was well brought out many years ago by William James (1890, pp. 293-294):

"No more fiendish punishment could be devised . . . than that one should be turned loose in society and remain absolutely unnoticed by all the members thereof. If no one turned around when we entered, answered when we spoke, or minded what we did, but if every person we met 'cut us dead,' and acted as if we were non-existing things, a kind of rage and impotent despair would ere long well up in us, from which the cruelest bodily tortures would be a relief. . . ."

Rare indeed is the person who can long maintain his morale in complete isolation from other people or in the face of continual disapproval from all others. Most of us strive to achieve an approved position in the group and are alert for ways to better our position or status.

Feelings of self-esteem and worth. Closely related to our needs for feelings of adequacy and social approval is our need to feel—and to have others feel—that we are important and that we possess whatever traits we and they have learned to regard as valuable. As we learn our society's values and standards concerning education, physical appearance, economic status, and right and wrong, we apply these standards in evaluating ourselves. We try to measure up so we can approve of ourselves and feel worth while. If we see ourselves as falling short, we tend to feel worthless, guilty, insecure.

Self-esteem has its early grounding in the mastery of developmental tasks and in successful problem solving, and it receives continual nourishment from a feeling of competency in areas that gain us social approval. Thus being a football star or earning a Phi Beta Kappa key or simply feeling we are doing our job well contributes to our self-esteem. Lacking a sense of personal worth, we tend to become negative in our general approach, to criticize and belittle others, to be discouraged and apathetic, and to see little meaning or challenge in life.

Experiences of love and relatedness. We have already mentioned the importance of maternal love for the normal physiological and psychological development of the infant. Numerous studies have shown that deprivation of love during later life periods also tends to block self-fulfillment and happiness. In fact, many psychologists believe that the thwarting of the need for love is the most common basis for personality maladjustments in our society. The title of a recent book—*Love or Perish*—states succinctly the choice we seem to have psychologically. Evidently human beings both develop better and function more effectively in a warm and loving environment.

Ordinarily our basic love needs are met in the intimate relations of marriage and family. Unfortunately, however, many individuals grow up in homes that deprive them of adequate warmth and love so that they may later have difficulty in giving and receiving love. In some cases such individuals are overly possessive of the persons they love and are almost insatiable in their need to be assured that others love them. More typically, they become "insulated" or "frosted" and tend to remain aloof and self-contained. Often they admit to feelings of loneliness and isolation—of somehow not being able to feel close to others.

It can be readily seen that we are not using the term *love* as synonymous with sex but rather as including all warm, accepting interpersonal relationships. Ordinarily, of course, love enters into the motivation toward mating, but the psychological requirement for love has a much broader range (Fromm, 1956).

Often the need for love is thought of simply as a need *to be loved,* but our need *to love* is fully as great. We need to care about people and things outside ourselves if we are to function properly and grow.

The Sequence
of Maintenance-Directed Behavior

When either physiological or psychological needs are not being met, there is a disturbance in the overall equilibrium of the organism. If the situation continues, symptoms of the deficiency appear and increase. On the biological level, the symptoms of a need for food are hunger pangs and changes in blood chemistry and, much later, emaciation. On the psychological level, symptoms of deprivation of love or security in a child might be exaggerated attention seeking and bullying of younger children. Ordinarily, the imbalance sets up a sequence of action aimed at restoring equilibrium by supplying the missing element. Any or all of the following events may be involved.

Energy mobilization. First of all, with deprivation or anticipation of deprivation there is a general mobilization of energy. This may be experienced as unpleasant tension, the degree and unpleasantness of the tension being generally proportional to the degree of the disturbance. In any case, action is taken toward restoring equilibrium.

In the case of visceral deprivations, specific physiological drives are triggered. For example, when the stomach empties, contractions set in and become increasingly stronger and more frequent as the time for the next meal approaches. These stomach contractions we experience as "hunger pangs"; they are unpleasant and tend to drive us to do something about getting food. Although we have to learn from experience what foods we need and how to get them, the hunger drive, when active, helps to channel and direct our activity, even commandeering other physical and psychological resources in its behalf.

When drive and tension become very intense, we experience pain. Pain is unpleasant and leads to additional arousal and mobilization of bodily resources for emergency action. Pain is a primary agent in protecting the body from hurt, and the individual tends to avoid situations or activities in which he has experienced pain in the past.

When psychological requirements are not being met, there are no automatic drives to give direction to our search. We have to learn from experience both what we are lacking and how to get it. Thus with deprivation on the psychological level, the mobilized energy is not automatically channeled into the appropriate behavior. Instead, it may lead to the arousal of unpleasant emotions—such as anger, fear, or resentment—or to the use of unconscious ego defense mechanisms (Chapter 6) which protect the individual from having to face his own deficiency. A person whose psychological needs are not being met also typically feels chronically anxious—the anxiety serving as an indication that his psychological well-being is under threat, much as pain gives warning of a threat to one's physical well-being. Anxiety, in fact, is often called "psychic pain." But here the parallel ends, for commonly the individual does not understand what it is that is making him anxious.

But although anxiety, negative emotions, and the use of defense mechanisms commonly result when psychological needs are not met, their appearance is not inevitable. With a realistic appraisal of the difficulty, constructive action is possible, and the individual may learn to be as successful in meeting his psychological needs as his physiological ones. A course such as this can help you by increasing your understanding of what your normal human needs are and by showing you how to recognize the symptoms of unmet needs in yourself and others.

Goal-directed action. As we have seen, maintenance-directed behavior begins with the energy mobilization that occurs when basic requirements are not being met. Normally the organism then undertakes some action toward a specific goal which promises to meet the need. This goal may be an object, like food, or an experience, like making a good impression on a blind date. It may also be merely avoidance of something unpleasant. Its choice is heavily influenced both by cultural sanctions and by the alternatives the environment has to offer. Thus a hungry man in Boston has a somewhat different choice from a hungry man in Burma. And even two Bostonians, surrounded by the same objective possibilities, may select quite different foods as a result of religious beliefs, family or ethnic habits, or esthetic considerations. So even the built-in hunger drive becomes highly complicated by learning. Instead of a simple need for food, we develop a set of preferences for certain foods and a certain style of cooking, for eating at certain times, for not eating certain items on certain days or in certain seasons, and for eating with other people in attractive surroundings.

Yet variable as are the goals and means by which we can learn to satisfy our hunger need, they are very restricted as compared with the variability that is possible in meeting our psychological needs. Only food of some kind can eventually satisfy the hunger drive, but an almost infinite number of situations can give rise to the experience of love and relatedness, for example. The many different cultures that man has developed over the centuries in different parts of the world give us some hint of the variety in psychological and social arrangements that can meet basic human needs.

The goal selected usually depends on the individual's own past experience. Rarely are we confronted with a situation so novel that we have no clues to guide us. Usually we try what has worked reasonably well on similar past occasions—something that has met the need and reduced the tension. In a familiar situation where our customary goals are readily available, our action may be almost automatic, largely directed by habit. If there are new elements to be appraised or if our usual goals are not available, problem solving is called for, with careful thought, observation, and testing of likely hypotheses.

Restoration of equilibrium. The action, if successful, reduces the original tension by supplying the missing requirement. The action then comes to an end and the individual experiences pleasure, or at least cessation of the unpleasant state that started the whole sequence. He also learns that the action worked, and next time he will probably try the same thing again. By the same token, unsuccessful tries will teach him what *not* to try again. In the parlance of psychologists, some responses are *reinforced* and retained; those that are not reinforced tend to drop out.

Unfortunately, in the process of tension reduction we can learn actions that are in the long run ineffective and maladjustive. The child who finds he can get his way by crying or temper tantrums learns how to lessen one tension, but does so by creating others. In the same way, the man who steals food may lessen his hunger but increase his feelings of worthlessness, and the hot-rodder who tries to prove that he is clever, brave, and skillful may do so only by considerable build-up of inner tension and great threat to his safety needs.

Since the reduction of drive and tension and the accompanying return to a state of equilibrium are usually experienced as pleasurable, we soon learn to anticipate such pleasure, and this anticipation may come to be a powerful force in motivating our behavior.

Often we go to great lengths to attain pleasurable stimulation. The Romans, in their quest for pleasure, even went so far as to regurgitate their food deliberately in order to be able to start the pleasurable process of eating all over again.

Because the experience of pain accompanies nearly every strong drive state and the experience of pleasure accompanies the reduction of drive and tension, some theorists have been led to the conclusion that all human behavior is motivated by the desire to avoid pain and achieve pleasure. But pain and pleasure are no longer considered the only motivational agents underlying behavior. Although pleasure is one end result of successful activity, it seldom is the conscious goal toward which people strive, and there seems no way of proving whether or not the course of action a person chooses is actually the one with the highest pleasure potential for him. When he reduces one tension by increasing another, the resulting balance of pleasure and pain is hard to assess. Thus pain and pleasure may be regarded chiefly as reinforcers of behavior directed toward other goals.

In general, the pleasure that comes from the successful meeting of maintenance needs is brief and transient. Sometimes it is better described as relief than as actual pleasure. In any case the deep satisfaction and elation that come from mastering a difficult new skill or realizing one's creative potentialities seem to be lacking. The person who strives only for "creature comforts" may be repeatedly frustrated by finding that they never quite satisfy him.

The emphasis on pleasure and pain in motivation theory has been a logical outgrowth of the deficiency concept of motivation—the assumption that any motivated state signalizes an unmet need and hence is automatically and inevitably unpleasant, something to avoid or escape as soon as possible.

Actually, if we have usually been able to meet our needs in the past and have reason to expect this state of affairs to continue, the tension and drive accompanying visceral deprivation is not necessarily painful or even unpleasant. A healthy appetite is welcome and enjoyable when a good meal is imminent. And in the case of actualization-motivated behavior, as we shall see, there seems little to support the concept of a motivated state as an unpleasant tension which must be alleviated.

STRIVINGS TOWARD ACTUALIZATION

Motivation theory in psychology, as already mentioned, has long been dominated by the concept of maintenance strivings in which man's primary motivation has been seen as directed toward meeting whatever deficiency arises and thus returning to a state of equilibrium and relative passivity. But needs related to survival and good health are clearly only a small part of our motivational structure. Such needs cannot explain the mountain climber or the explorer, the scientist or the inventor, the Einstein or the Schweitzer, or any man who throws himself into his work with zest and enthusiasm.

Such actions are expressions of actualization strivings. Actualization, essentially, is growth—physical, intellectual, emotional, spiritual. Whereas maintenance strivings help the organism to *keep the status quo*, actualization strivings tend to *improve the system or its situation* by making it more attractive, more capable, more useful, or otherwise of greater real or apparent worth. Both kinds of strivings are typical of human beings in a reasonably favorable environment.[1]

Only as our maintenance needs are met are we free to move on to more rewarding and meaningful activities. The more adequately our maintenance needs are being met, the more capable we are of direction from within toward growth and fulfillment. When the life situation is so unfavorable

that a person's primary energies must be devoted to meeting his basic bodily needs, he is apt to experience a sense of frustration, dissatisfaction, and meaninglessness in his life. For deep satisfaction he needs to feel he is "getting somewhere," improving himself or his situation.

Growth is not without pain, but it is stimulating and rewarding in a way that meeting deficiency needs is not. Our human nature seems to be such that we actually function more smoothly and more happily when we are active, questing, challenging, stimulated. When we go out of our way to expand our interests and our knowledge, we gain a sense of satisfaction; when we narrow our interests and cease to grow, we feel dissatisfied. We are bored with a vegetative existence that offers no challenge.

From all sides comes evidence of man's desire to develop and use his talents, to broaden his affiliations and interests, to know even though knowledge calls for effort and may bring pain. If his maintenance needs are met, he seeks not desirelessness but stimulation and action. The feeling of effort is itself satisfying. In fact, the achievement of a goal, instead of bringing contentment, often simply opens the way for new desires to make themselves felt. Huxley (1953, pp. 162-163) says:

"Human life *is* a struggle—against frustration, ignorance, suffering, evil, the mad-

---

[1] See Maslow's article about deficiency motivation and growth motivation on page 475.

dening inertia of things in general; but it is also a struggle *for* something. . . . And fulfillment seems to describe better than any other single word the positive side of human development and human evolution—the realization of inherent capacities by the individual and of new possibilities by the race; the satisfaction of needs, spiritual as well as material; the emergence of new qualities of experience to be enjoyed; the building of personalities."

We have described the need for meaning, value, and organization and the need for love and relatedness as maintenance needs because they must be met for normal integration and healthy psychological functioning. They are also actualization needs, however, in that much of our actualization takes place as we broaden the scope of our knowledge and understanding and expand our relatedness to other people.

Forms of Actualization Strivings

Although any categorization is somewhat artificial, we can delineate five closely related forms that actualization strivings typically take. These can be described as a striving for greater value in one's experiences, a striving for self-enhancement, a striving to develop one's capacities, a striving to become a "real person," and a striving to create rich linkages with one's world.

Finding increased satisfactions. As Cantril (1950) has pointed out, an outstanding characteristic of man is his capacity to see value in his experiences—and his tendency to expect a certain level of satisfaction from everything he does. When we go out to dinner, we expect the food to meet certain standards in quality and variety. When we go to a movie, we expect it to meet certain standards of plot, character portrayal, and photography. When we start out on a career,

we have expectations regarding our earnings, responsibilities, and usefulness. The norms that we use in evaluating these and other new experiences as "worth while" or "disappointing" are based on the satisfactions we have received from our experiences in the past. We also use such standards in deciding which new experiences to choose and which ones to avoid. We avoid a party, a television program, a trip, a lecture, or a course if we think it will not make a sufficient return in value received on our investment of time and participation.

But this is not all. We are never satisfied for long but seem to suffer from what the poets call "divine discontent." What was perfectly satisfying yesterday seems a little flat today, and we are constantly trying to improve the quality of our experience. We wait in line to see the movie that the critics have given a top rating and feel cheated if it is not above the usual standard. New cars and new washing machines must have new, better features each year to compete for our attention. We become dissatisfied with our jobs unless we have a chance to grow in them. The increased satisfaction that we find in any new experience becomes a part of our new standard for judging the value of subsequent experiences.

As our standards become higher, increments of satisfaction may become increasingly hard to achieve and may entail struggle and sacrifice. Yet one of our most persistent urges seems to be to build, to improve, to go beyond previous achievements and understandings, to reach just a little higher and farther than we did yesterday.

Enhancing self-worth. The concept of self-enhancement is so broad as to be almost a substitute for the term *actualization*, but we will limit its meaning here to an enhancement of the perceived self. The forms it takes are, of course, heavily influenced by sociocultural standards: the large, stretched lips that enhance a Ubangi woman's feeling of worth would not have that effect for us.

On a relatively simple level, this striving toward self-enhancement can be seen in the use of cosmetics, the wearing of stylish clothes, the joining of exclusive clubs, and the driving of prestige cars. This type of behavior (though of course taking different forms) is common to people all over the world. The striving toward self-enhancement is also seen in our attempt to improve our performance to make a better showing. Our efforts in this cause may range from learning to wiggle our ears at ten to later learning to walk with poise or to dance or ski or play the piano well.

Many of these attempts at self-enhancement result in real self-improvement, but because of the importance we attach to improving our worth in other people's eyes, the means we choose may improve our attractiveness to other people without actually changing us "inside" or improving our capabilities. Some psychologists find the source of much of modern man's anxiety in precisely this problem: in trying to develop the traits and behavior and appearance that will please other people, we often are untrue to ourselves. As Fromm (1955) points out, we tend to develop a "marketing" orientation, in which the worth of a trait is gauged by its market value, instead of a "productive" orientation, in which the individual's genuine capacities for creative functioning are highly prized. We are afraid to be ourselves and to grow in the directions our inner natures dictate. When self-enhancement strivings are limited to externals, they do not carry us far toward actualization.

Developing and using potentials. The most obvious and potent form of striving to fulfill our potentials is seen in our physical growth, in which, without conscious effort, our bodies move toward the fulfillment of the pattern inherent in the original genes.

An acorn grows into an oak tree; a fertilized human ovum into an adult human being. The intermediate changes can be viewed as a continuing progress toward fulfillment of original potentialities.

Most of our psychological potentialities get no such automatic fulfillment. Yet intellectually, emotionally, and spiritually, as well as physically, there is an urge to grow, to improve, to become more capable.

One of the chief ways in which this urge is evident is in the common attempt to make better sense of our world. We listen and read to find out what is going on and what has gone on and what others have thought about it. We try to broaden our viewpoint, sometimes just for the sake of knowing but sometimes to be better able to cope with life problems. We try to expand our basic assumptions and generalizations about what is true, what is important, and what is possible. We also try to improve our understanding by redefining and reorganizing the ideas and assumptions we already have, looking for new relationships, and trying to achieve a better integration of contradictory elements.

Another important way in which we fulfill our potentialities is through building new competencies and improving old ones, developing whatever capacities we have into greater actual abilities, and using these abilities for creative self-expression. If we have special talents for music or writing, we may be quite miserable if prevented from developing them and expressing ourselves through them. Even with more modest capacities we want to develop and use what proficiencies we can, and most of us want to improve our present level of skills. We may persist in working at what we have a special bent for even when it is a skill not especially prized in our group.

Developing our potentials for physical, intellectual, emotional, and social competencies is so important that several chapters will be devoted to it in Part Three. Continuing growth not only increases our ability to master the problems of living but also is satisfying in its own right.

Becoming a person. Closely allied with the striving to develop one's potentials but not quite the same thing is the striving to become a person—to find and be one's "real self." Rogers (1958, pp. 9-10) says:

"As I follow the experience of many clients in the therapeutic relationship which we endeavor to create for them, it seems to me that each one has the same problem. Below the level of the problem situation about which the individual is complaining—behind the trouble with studies, or wife, or employer, or with his own uncontrollable or bizarre behavior, or with his frightening feelings lies one central search. It seems to me that at bottom each person is asking: 'Who am I, *really*? How can I get in touch with this real self, underlying all my surface behavior? How can I become myself?'

". . . it appears that the goal the individual most wishes to achieve, the end which he knowingly or unknowingly pursues, is to become himself."

The Danish philosopher Soren Kierkegaard described this search for self more than a century ago. He pointed out that the most common despair is in being unwilling to be one's self, but that the deepest form of despair is choosing to be other than one's self.

Each of us has an inner nature in part uniquely his and in part common to the species. When this essential core is denied expression, the individual becomes physically or mentally sick—sometimes in obvious ways, sometimes in devious, subtle ways. As Maslow (1956, p. 233) points out:

"This inner nature is not strong and overpowering and unmistakable like the instincts of animals. It is weak and delicate and subtle and easily overcome by habit, cultural pressure, and wrong attitudes." But, ". . . though weak, it never disappears in the normal person—perhaps not even in the sick person. Even though denied, it persists underground forever pressing for actualization."

Becoming a person seems to be bound up with a striving toward wholeness, toward inner consistency and resolution of warring inner tendencies, toward integration and self-direction.

Building rich linkages with the world. One of the ways we seek to grow is through the associations we form with our world, and especially with other people. We have a deep capacity for caring for others, for protecting, encouraging, and teaching others, and for helping *them* grow and find meaning and satisfaction in their lives. Unless we use this capacity we feel incomplete, unsatisfied. This is a particularly human characteristic, and the person who does not develop and use it falls short of his potential stature as a human being. And, paradoxically, caring deeply for something outside oneself is one of the most gratifying and self-fulfilling of human experiences.

Many of the experiences we value most highly are those we have shared with others close to us. We treasure our family jokes and anecdotes and our family traditions. Louise Rich, in her autobiographical novel, *Happy the Land* (1946, p. 19), says:

"Of Plymouth Rock, I may tell my children: 'This is where the Pilgrims landed.' Of the rock by the side of the road, halfway up Wangan Hill, I say 'Right here is where your father found the little deer that time.'"

Throughout our lives we build landmarks of this kind which enrich our lives and add to their meaning and value by increasing our sense of relatedness to the world around us. We cherish the memory of an event shared with a group of friends or of a place where we were once very happy. The bond we feel toward others with whom we have shared a crisis or a joy or even just an hour of silence is an enriching thing that broadens our base of self.

Self-centeredness or narrow concern with self leads to a restriction of energy and an impoverishment of meaning in one's life. Asch (1952, pp. 320-321) says:

"The ego [self] is not dedicated solely to its own enhancement. It needs and wants to be concerned with its surroundings, to bind itself to others, and to work with them. The ego needs to have interests wider than itself, not to be always looking at itself, not to be always watching its feelings and looking out for its interests.

". . . When the possibilities of entering into appropriate relations with others are barred, the ego turns its potentialities for care upon itself. Avarice, greed, ruthless ambition often are the answer the ego gives when it fails to find in the surroundings the opportunity for its outgoing needs."

One of the most important means of establishing rich linkages with the world is to build satisfying love relationships with others. Implied here is not the deficiency-motivated love of the affection-starved child, which is possessive, jealous, and insatiable, but an outgoing love, accepting of others as they are and concerned with their needs. Such a love is not limited to a striving for self-gratification but is directed toward the fulfillment and happiness of the loved one. This implies no loss of one's personal identity but an extension of self, an ability to care beyond one's personal welfare and to take an active role in improving one's world. Fromm (1955, pp. 31-32) states:

"*Love is union* with somebody, or something, outside oneself, *under the condition of retaining the separateness and integrity of one's own self*. It is an experience of sharing, of communion, which permits the full unfolding of one's inner activity. . . .

"Love is one aspect of what I have called the productive orientation: the active and creative relatedness of man to his fellow man, to himself, and to nature."

Christianity and other religions see such an outgoing love as the basic motivating force that should underlie all our behavior. It is brotherly love that is stressed—the need to love others as we do ourselves. In this sense, in fact, love is even more than a matter of warm relationships with particular people —it is a basic orientation of concern for others and for one's world.

Drive Forces Toward Actualization

Actualization strivings, like maintenance strivings, seem to be initiated from within. They "come naturally" without having to be learned and are characteristic of human beings in widely differing cultures. Yet prevalent as is this growth motivation, growth is not universal. The neurotic is too busy defending himself to be free to grow; the person who must struggle hard for mere physical survival has little time or energy left for social or spiritual growth.

Actualization strivings, like maintenance strivings, seem to follow a general sequence of arousal, energy mobilization, goal-directed behavior, and, if successful, feelings of satisfaction. But here satisfaction comes through increased effort, through mobilization of energies and abilities, through a welcoming of stimulation and activity rather than through the removal of tension or the cessation of need, as with activity aimed at maintenance. In fact, the growing person, though mobilized for increased energy output and hence supposedly under constant tension, is usually happier, healthier, and more efficient in both bodily and psychological functioning than the person whose energies are devoted only to maintenance (Maslow, 1954).

Although actualization strivings may not appear unless minimal maintenance needs have been met, these actualization strivings, once aroused, may take precedence over the supposedly more basic maintenance needs. The scientist may go without food and sleep in the excitement of a crucial experiment; the man with unpopular political or social ideas may pursue them even though they bring him social ostracism and cost him his job; Socrates chose the hemlock rather than give up his devotion to truth. This seeming anomaly of actualization strivings taking precedence over even survival needs is probably the exception rather than the rule; it is possible only because so little of our behavior is automatic and so much of it is mediated by evaluation and choice. Instead of reacting mechanically to stimuli, we screen, sort, interpret, weigh, and compare and then select action that is in keeping with our self-picture and with our assumptions, attitudes, and values.

Because man is a creature of choice rather than instinct, he *can* choose even what is not good for him—including stagnation instead of growth. Thus, even when maintenance needs are met some people exhibit little growth-motivated behavior. Whether through habit or fear or failure to recognize the alternatives, they stick to the comfortable rut of familiar routine and seek only goals related to maintenance and creature comforts. Only in childhood does the urge to grow seem to be so potent that growth can be called virtually automatic; thereafter it takes decision and effort. Nevertheless, actualization strivings remain a part of our equipment that must be reckoned with. We ignore them at our peril.

FIELD FORCES IN MOTIVATION

Psychologists have been so concerned with instincts, needs, drives, motives, and other inner sources of motive power that they have sometimes tended to overlook the importance of outside influences in motivating our behavior. We may eat because food is offered, even when we are not hungry. We may be aroused sexually by seeing a lurid movie. We can be talked into wanting—and striving to attain—roast beef, school integration, the latest style dress or car, or a filtered cigarette. In an excited crowd at a football game we may hear ourselves shouting for someone to kill the officials or for the coach to take some bumbling player out of the game. A patriotic symbol may motivate us to salute; a religious one may move us to pray. In all these cases our behavior is induced by something which is in our environment.

This may seem at first like a contradiction of everything we have been saying. Actually it is a qualification and elaboration—a step toward a broader view in which we can see the roles played by both inner and outer factors. Just as we found environment to be an important force in shaping personality development, so we find it shaping and channeling our motives in important ways.

Goals and Means for Meeting Our Needs

Virtually any action to meet an inner need involves some interaction with animate or inanimate objects around us; we utilize what

The channels through which psychological needs are met are as varied as the world's standards of beauty and value. In eastern Burma, where a girl's wealth is measured by the number of copper coils she wears around her neck (left), a girl gains satisfaction and self-esteem from behavior that would bring only discomfort and disapproval to an American girl. And whereas American girls often spend long hours acquiring a deep bronze in summer, girls in Taiwan (right), where a light skin is prized, take elaborate precautions to protect their skins from the sun.

is available, adapt what is not suitable, and ward off what could hurt us. Even when the motive power is completely from within, the goal is usually outside us. We are so dependent on external objects that our motives cannot help but incorporate them.

The most obvious way in which external factors affect our motivation is by providing certain goals and activities through which we can meet our needs and by not providing certain others. These provisions are both physical and cultural and vary greatly from one place to another and from one society to another. Groups that stay in one place can achieve feelings of security from the permanence of buildings and lands of their own, whereas nomadic groups must keep physical belongings to a minimum and depend instead on their resourcefulness and mutual cooperation. Members of one group

learn to achieve feelings of self-esteem through deceiving and tricking rival groups; members of another group achieve self-esteem through accumulating great wealth.

Some cultures offer rich opportunities for psychological satisfactions and fulfillment of potentialities. Others are limiting, repressive, rigid. Some provide fulfillment opportunities for certain groups but not others—the leaders but not the followers, the wealthy but not the poor, the men but not the women. But in any group both the goals that a person learns to seek and the means by which he learns to achieve them—including the special skills required—depend on the opportunities and limitations of his local setting and on his own role in the group. They are chosen from among those physically possible in accordance with the rules and values of the groups to which he feels loyalty, although, because he is an evaluator and not a rubber stamp, there will also be the impress of individuality in his goals and means.

Because our choice of goals is channeled by the standards of our own group, incentives that have a high value in one social group often have no value at all in another. The monetary incentives that are so motivating to the average American would inspire no effort among the members of a monastic order. One teacher who had used the urge to win as an incentive among white children found that, with Indian children, when a prize was offered for the first one through his lesson, all contrived to finish at the same time so no one would have to be so rude as to beat the others. People everywhere learn which goals and which action sequences will enable them to meet their needs for acceptance, approval, and secure status in their own social group.

Sometimes the goals and action sequences we learn take strange twists. We adopt them because they have the sanction of our group, even though on occasion they actually threaten some of our own important needs. The custom of defending one's honor by dueling seems almost as strange and self-destructive to us now as the custom among the Kwakiutl Indians of British Columbia of proving one's worth by destroying or giving away more personal property than one's neighbors could afford to or the custom among a Bolivian tribe of cutting off one's fingers to show anger toward others. In following such customs people are under the same compulsion as the teen-ager who feels he must play "chicken." The goals and means prescribed by our social group are usually the ones we must adopt if we want the approval of that group.

Arousal and Reduction of Strivings

The external field affects not only the goals we can readily choose and the means we can use for achieving them but also the arousal and reduction of the drives themselves and the relative strength of different strivings. In the socialization of an individual and the later control of his behavior, each group tends to inhibit certain strivings and to encourage certain others. For example, most societies put controls on physical aggression and sexual behavior that tend to inhibit these particular drives. Thus in our own society we tend to disapprove of masturbation and premarital sexual relationships, and young people are encouraged to inhibit their sexual urges until after marriage. Our society also frowns on extramarital sexual relationships. Other societies encourage somewhat different patterns, but all tend to set up restrictions against uncontrolled sexuality.

In a comparable way, groups differ in their encouragement or inhibition of other strivings, such as those for love and relatedness, security, and fulfillment of individual potentialities. In some social groups material security is regarded as the greatest good; marriages are so contracted and business so conducted as to serve this dominant goal. In some societies, such as the Dobu (p. 79), suspiciousness and self-centeredness are encouraged; in others, a premium is placed on affection, trust, and mutual helpfulness. The end result of such continuing social inhibition of some strivings and encouragement of others is the production of somewhat uniform motive patterns among the members of a given group. As a group they may be warlike or peaceful, friendly or suspicious, energetic or indolent.

The social setting not only influences our characteristic motive patterns but also tends to increase or reduce individual motives in our everyday behavior. Many external stimuli acquire the power to set off or inhibit strivings originally controlled entirely by internal mechanisms. Thus whereas food-seeking activity may at first start only when we feel hunger, it can later come to be aroused by the sight of attractive food, a mouth-watering menu, an announcement that a food shortage is imminent, or watching others eat.

A number of interesting experiments have shown that chickens, rats, monkeys, and other animals, after eating to the point of satiation, will start to eat again if they see hungry companions doing so (Allee, 1958). Hungry rats eat more when fed in pairs than when fed alone. Likewise it has been found that increasing the amount of food offered leads to a continuation of eating past the point of physiological need. We probably all have had the experience of having a heartier appetite and eating more with good friends in an attractive setting than by ourselves in the kitchen. Our appetite is a function of more than our actual inner need for food.

Sexual appetite, too, is whetted by external stimulation, both in lower animals and in humans (Allee, 1958). One study found that among hens, sexual activity increased when sexual stimulation was increased. With humans, the results of exposure to pornographic art—or even to more subtle sexual stimulation—are well known. Sexual appetite, like the appetite for food, is not solely a function of inner need but is greatly influenced by external factors.

Drives may also be *reduced* by environmental factors, even though the goal has not been gained and the physiological need remains unchanged. We may lose our appetite in a hurry if we find the dishes and tablecloth are dirty or if we see a fly fall into the soup. Our sexual appetite is limited by our standards of attractiveness and our group's rules and values. Under normal circumstances a person's attractiveness to us sexually may be less dependent on our degree of physiological deprivation than on his or her appearance and personality, our probable compatibility, the setting, the opinions and standards of our friends, and other external factors.

Demands on Us

External forces not only channel the individual's own strivings and affect their strength but also present him with certain demands to which he responds. He is not only active but also reactive, and his behavior is instigated jointly by his own strivings and the demands made on him by his field.

Such demands are of two main kinds. First, there are the needs of other people, who, like us, are also continuously trying to meet their own needs. Social living involves a constant give and take with mutual efforts to help one another. When we care about these other people, helping them may seem no sacrifice, for their happiness makes us happy too; but whether we care for them or not, we are often dependent on their efforts and they on ours. One man's car gets stuck in a ditch, and three other men stop to help him push it out. A woman starts to fall getting off a bus, and people nearby reach out to catch and support her. Children are hurt in a school fire, and strangers from miles around send money to help them. Periodically, most of us take time to encourage and help others, listen to their problems, and share our resources with them, even at some inconvenience to ourselves.

Our legal structure is based on a recognition of our shared responsibility for each other's welfare. Often it is couched in negative terms—what we cannot do—restraints against interference with our neighbor's pursuit of happiness. But many laws have gone beyond the negative to state the positive duties of citizens toward each other. One of the oldest on record is the Roman law of Biblical fame that a traveler had the right to ask a local inhabitant to go a mile with him to show him the way. The second mile counseled by Jesus implied even further responsibility for the welfare of others. In our own day, laws state the duties of parties entering into a contract and say what drivers of cars, public officials, and others in special roles must do for the benefit of others whose lives they touch.

But not all responsibilities are legal ones. Labor and management recognize that they have moral responsibilities to each other as do members of different ethnic groups living in the same community, though often there is disagreement as to just what these responsibilities are. Teachers acknowledge responsibilities to their pupils and to the community where they teach, over and above their goals for personal maintenance and growth. No one living in a social group can be concerned only with meeting his own needs and be callous to the needs of people around him.

Second, there are the needs of the groups to which we belong. Our country may require two years of our lives for military service, or our firm may want us to go to a remote spot where the climate is not good for our health. Our government may ask us to accept austerities for the long-term good of the country, or if we live in a dictatorship, we may be forced to give up a cherished career to work in an uncongenial field where we are more needed. In an emergency we may even have to risk our lives for the group's welfare.

Sometimes, of course, there is no conflict, and the action that serves the needs of others and advances the goals of the group also moves us closer to our own goals. But there is no guarantee that this will be so. There may be no relationship at all, or, as in the examples above, what is demanded of us may be at variance with what we had hoped to do.

Much of our motivation for helping other people or for serving the needs of the group undoubtedly comes from identification with those we help, so that their needs become our needs and their values and goals ours too. When we feel closely identified with a group, we feel threatened by whatever we

perceive as threatening to it. As citizens, we are stirred to indignation by corruption in government. In everyday situations we are upset if someone uses poor table manners, laughs out loud in church, or tells a dirty joke to a child. Although such behavior does not threaten us personally, it upsets us because it violates standards we have adopted from our group. Every society strives to induce its members to adopt as their own the needs and values of the group so that they will experience tension when they or others violate its code. When we feel a strong enough identification with and loyalty to our group, we can gain a sense of fulfillment even in surrendering some of our personal well-being if we feel it is for the good of the group.

Demands made on us from outside are not automatically followed, however. Sometimes they are simply ignored or even not recognized; sometimes they are actively rejected. When we choose to accept them, we may transmute or redefine them to make them more palatable or appealing. When we do follow them, we may do so because of fear, because of the self-esteem or social approval that will result, because we have identified ourselves with the person or group making them, or simply because we see something out of order that needs to be put right to work more smoothly. In any case, if we accept them, our behavior takes on directions it would not take if we were powered only by drives toward personal maintenance and growth. Our behavior helps to meet requirements both in us and in our field.

The external situation, then, influences motive patterns by (1) determining what goals and means are available for meeting our needs, (2) encouraging some drives and inhibiting others, and (3) making demands of its own on the individual. The field, however, is always perceived and interpreted from the individual's own frame of reference. He accepts, rejects, adapts, or defends himself against it as it fits in with or threatens his own purposes and values. All these channels of influence create differences in people's motive patterns and behavior, yet the underlying similarity of their strivings remains even more striking than the differences. The differences are only in the means they have learned for meeting their needs as human beings and in the demands made on them by their field.

PATTERNS OF MOTIVATION

Since individual motives are not autonomous entities but all help to subserve the more basic, underlying strivings toward maintenance and fulfillment of potentialities, the operation of any given motive can be understood only as we see its part in the whole motivational pattern at any given time. Several characteristics of motive patterns should be pointed out.

Multiplicity and Interdependence of Motives

You do not need a psychology course to tell you that motives rarely operate singly, one at a time. Usually the motivation behind a bit of behavior is mixed and complex, and a whole pattern of motives is instigating and guiding what you do, though one motive may be dominant. During the days or weeks you struggle to gather data and write a term paper, you are also motivated by needs for food, rest, and companionship (and many others), though as the deadline for the term paper approaches, these other requirements may be temporarily ignored.

One act may serve many motives. Most acts also subserve more than one motive. You may try to write a good term paper not just to complete an assignment but also to demonstrate your skill, to gain commendation, to raise your grade level (and perhaps that of your fraternity), and to have a good record to show prospective employers. In general, behavior that brings social approval also serves to raise your self-esteem and sense of worth. Social contacts may be sought as an expression of affection, as a source of power, as a testing ground for our worth, as a medium for promotion of our ideas, or as a source of relaxation and fun—or perhaps for all these reasons at once. A Don Juan may be as eager to prove his masculinity as to gain sexual satisfaction.

Key motives pervade behavior. Just as one act may express many motives, one motive pattern may find expression through many kinds of behavior. A central motive to excel, for example, will show up in schoolwork, in personal contacts, in group activity, and even in recreation.

Different needs may arouse the same motive. Our various motives are closely related to each other in both arousal and expression. In fact, one drive may even be brought into play by deprivation of needs other than those usually associated with it. For example, the hunger drive, though usually aroused by tissue needs for food, may also be aroused by unmet psychological needs. Children who feel unloved often have a pathological craving for sweets. In the same way, some individuals experience an almost continuous sex drive and engage in promiscuous sexual behavior not primarily out of physical need but rather in an attempt to increase their feelings of being worth while and attractive to others.

Conversely, real tissue need may fail to lead to feelings of hunger or any desire for food in a man whose fiancée has just eloped with his best friend. Or a hungry man may lose his appetite if he is criticized by his boss. Arguments at mealtime are notorious destroyers of appetite. There seems to be no one-to-one relationship between need and either motive or behavior.

Is There a Hierarchy of Motives?

What happens when two or more needs are frustrated at the same time or when one need can be met only at the expense of another? What happens when a man can get food only by stealing it or a promotion only by giving up his evenings and week ends with his wife and children? Among our various strivings, do some regularly have predominance or prepotence over others and, if so, which ones are they?

Maslow (1954) suggests that motives arrange themselves in a hierarchy from the most basic biological needs to the need for self-esteem and self-actualization, which represent the higher development of the personality. With some slight modifications for our present purposes, this hierarchy is envisaged as:

1. Body needs—basic tissue needs such as the need for food
2. Safety needs—protection from harm or injury
3. Needs for love and belonging—for warmth, status, acceptance, approval
4. Needs for adequacy, security, self-esteem, self-enhancement, competencies
5. Needs for self-fulfillment, broader understanding

In terms of our earlier discussion, these may also be grouped as biological maintenance needs, psychological maintenance needs, and actualization needs.

Relative strength under deprivation. Interestingly enough, one order of relative strength seems typical under certain conditions of deprivation, and the reverse order under conditions of reasonable gratification. Thus in extreme deprivation, most (though not all) individuals will sacrifice their higher-level needs for esteem and actualization to meet acceptance, belonging, and other psychological maintenance needs and will sacrifice the latter, in turn, for personal safety and survival. Both in the Nazi concentration camps and in the Japanese prisoner-of-war camps, for example, it was a common pattern for prisoners subjected to prolonged deprivation and torture to lower their moral standards, take food from each other and in other ways surrender the loyalties and values they had held under more normal conditions (Bettelheim, 1943; Nardini, 1952).

Even under experimental conditions, the tremendous force of the hunger drive makes itself readily observable. In a study of the effects of semistarvation carried out during World War II with conscientious objectors, Keys and his associates (1950) found that dramatic personality changes took place. The men became irritable, unsociable, and increasingly unable to concentrate on anything but the thought of food. By the end of the twenty-fifth week, food dominated their thought, their conversation, and their daydreams. They even pinned up pictures of chocolate cake instead of female beauty.

This pattern does not always hold, however. Every catastrophe has had its heroes who sacrificed their own welfare for the good of others and every age its martyrs who remained faithful to their principles and beliefs despite social ostracism, physical deprivation, torture, or certain death. It seems to be possible, through learning, for human relationships, beliefs, and values to become more important to us than our instinctual needs. Also, for many creative people the expression of a special talent has been more important than the mere technicalities involved in having enough to eat regularly.

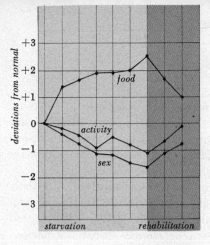

The hierarchy of motives changes with the pattern of available satisfactions. During twenty-four weeks of semistarvation, subjects in the Minnesota experiment (p. 136) were asked to rate the strength of their drives for food, sex, and activity on a scale from −5 (extremely less than normal) to +5 (extremely more than normal). As the graph shows, concern with hunger increased steadily and concern with sex and activity declined during the starvation phase; during the rehabilitation phase, when adequate food was again available, these trends were reversed. The increasing preoccupation with food during the starvation period was accompanied by a decline in table manners. Subjects also developed a new interest in cookbooks, which they collected (right) and read avidly, making files of recipes and planning concoctions like candy bars with chocolate sauce (Keys and others, 1950).

Probably most of us would choose at least *minor* physical deprivations rather than surrender our principles, or minor disapproval rather than give up a cherished ambition. In fact, every day most of us undergo delays, frustrations, and inconveniences rather than violate social conventions to achieve our wishes more directly. We want our creature comforts, but we can forego them when they would cost us approval and self-esteem. Evidently it is a matter of degree and a highly individual matter; only under very extreme conditions, as in the prisoner-of-war camps or under semistarvation, do the lower needs seem to be predominant in directing our behavior.

Relative strength under favorable conditions. Under favorable conditions, the higher-level needs typically become dominant. Needs that are met cease to be active motivators. If we have plenty to eat, a warm house to live in, and assurance of a good income, we are free to be concerned about our relationships with other people and our status in the community; we want others to accept and approve of us and are unhappy if they do not. Then, if there are no severe deprivations to our needs for status, acceptance, and approval to make us focus on self-defense, we may feel restless and start looking for new fields to conquer, new competencies to master, and new meanings and values in what we do.

People who despite adequate resources remain dominated for long by maintenance strivings tend to be unhealthy, physically or psychologically or both, and usually unhappy —a uniquely human predicament. Allport (1953) regards individuals preoccupied with tension reduction as "clearly pathological." Along the same line, Goldstein (1939, p. 197) says:

"In the state of isolation, as in sick people, the discharge of tension is in the foreground: the tendency to *remove* any arising tension prevails. In sound life, however, the result of the normal equalization process is the *formation* of a certain level of tension, that which makes possible further ordered activity.

"The tendency to maintain the existent state is characteristic for sick people and is a sign of anomalous life, of decay of life. The tendency of normal life is toward activity and progress."

Because maintenance-motivated man is more segmentally driven, he is more easily manipulated by anyone who has the power to offer or withhold incentives. Also, since he is concerned primarily with relieving immediate tension, he may hit upon alcohol or drugs as an easy way of achieving relief from his tension. He is, as it were, not a whole man; he is more vulnerable to outside threats because he responds in segments, rather than as a whole person.

In comparing "deficiency-motivated" people with "actualizing" ones, Maslow (1950) discovered that the self-actualizing ones had more efficient perceptions of reality and more comfortable relations with it; could tolerate uncertainty better; were more spontaneous, creative, and accepting of themselves and others; were problem-centered rather than ego-centered; had deeper than average relationships with other people but also valued solitude more; felt kinship with and concern for all humanity; and had a philosophical, unhostile sense of humor.

The Life Style

As we have seen, the developing self-structure of each person gives him a fairly consistent life style; a continuing pattern of assumptions and attitudes makes his behavior somewhat predictable. Rarely is behavior a simple reaction to external stimulation. Usually it incorporates some degree of screening, evaluation, and selection from among alternatives.

Preferred patterns of motives. A further element in this consistent and continuing life style is what Goldstein (1939) calls a *preferred pattern of motives*—what the person is persistently trying to do. Each person develops a unique and continuing pattern of key motives and purposes that helps to make his behavior predictable even in widely differing settings. This pattern is consistent with his concept of himself and his capabilities in relation to the demands he sees being made on him. It may have little relationship to the actual degree of deprivation or gratification of basic needs.

In *The Diary of Anne Frank*, a wartime chronicle of eight people hiding from the Germans for two years under conditions of considerable deprivation and constant fear, each member is portrayed as behaving in ways consistent with his life style before the episode began. The deprivations and fears affected the behavior of all of them but in very different ways and different degrees. Anne herself was far less concerned with (motivated by) the hunger and the danger than with her relationships with other people and her own developing values. Mrs. Van Daan, self-centered and materialistic, behaved consistently in a petty, childish way. Anne's father, for whom immaterial values were all-important, kept himself and the children busy reading, thinking creatively, and broadening their interests and knowledge. The dentist, a pessimist even before going into hiding, never saw anything but irritations and gloomy prospects.

A consistent level of aspiration. Part of any person's life style is his level of aspiration, based partly on the group standards but even more on his interests and needs and his own evaluation of his abilities. Emotionally healthy people tend to have a fairly accurate evaluation of themselves and their world and hence a fairly realistic level of aspiration. Maladjusted people, on the other hand, are typically under pressure to defend themselves from threats to their feelings of worth and to enhance their feelings of self-esteem. Studies show that their level of aspiration tends to be unrealistic—either too high or too low—which in turn leads to inevitable failure or wasted opportunities, with further self-devaluation and an ever growing need for self-defense.

How Motives Form and Change

Obviously the same motive or pattern of motives does not operate day in and day out at the same strength. What makes motives change from day to day and over a longer period of time?

Short-term changes. The motivational pattern is continually changing as given needs are gratified and others make themselves felt. On the biological level this process follows a rhythm based on periodic intensification and reduction in drive strength—a phenomenon resulting from metabolic activity and commonly referred to as *drive cycle* or *periodicity of drive*. This periodic rhythm of biological drives may be observed in the hunger, thirst, and sex drives; with continued frustration (up to a point) the drive becomes intensified, and with gratification its strength is decreased and it drops to a much lower position in the motivational pattern.

A periodic rhythm on the psychological level is less readily apparent either in the maintenance strivings for affection, adequacy, and self-esteem or in the strivings for growth and fulfillment, although moods may swing up and down unaccountably. Yet here, too, when one need is met, its relative felt strength tends to be reduced, and others tend to come to the fore. Thus, however well off we are, we always seem to find some new point of imperfection or dissatisfaction on which to focus our energies. This is often dramatically illustrated when we achieve some long-sought goal in life such as college graduation or marriage, which does in fact gratify certain basic needs, only to find that instead of feeling relaxation and peace we become aware of a whole new set of needs and motives.

Long-term changes. In addition to such short-term changes, we also develop new motives from time to time. Some of these long-term changes seem to result from the appearance of new requirements at different life stages; others come as a result of experience and learning.

We have defined motives as strivings toward particular goals. A persistent problem in motivational theory has been the interpretation of changes in our motivational patterns through experience and learning as we go through life—changes in goals, changes in means for achieving them, changes in our interests. When the camera bug tires of his hobby and becomes a ceramics enthusiast, has he unlearned his old motive and learned a new one?

Some psychologists would say so. Thus Allport (1937) holds that new motives are learned through association with existing ones and then eventually become "autonomous" —able to energize behavior in the absence of the original need. An example of an autonomous motive, according to this view, would be the motive for working. This motive, begun as a source of money to buy food, often continues even if work becomes no longer necessary and perhaps even no longer remunerative. In somewhat the same way, Woodworth (1918) held that habits after a time acquire the power of drives in their own right.

In keeping with our earlier discussion, it seems an equally sound and somewhat simpler interpretation to assume that for the most part our basic requirements remain unchanged and that we merely change the means by which we satisfy them as we find that new goals and new activities will suit the purpose as well or better than old ones. Thus a child abandons his show-off behavior when he is helped to find more constructive ways of getting the attention and acceptance he seeks. According to this view, a man might continue wanting to work after he no longer needed to financially, because work had become for him an important means of meeting his self-esteem and actualization needs.

RELATION OF MOTIVES
TO OTHER PSYCHOLOGICAL PROCESSES

Just as a man's motives are closely related to each other, so his motivational processes and other processes are interrelated. Man, like other organisms, functions as a unit, and the primary business being attended to at the moment determines how other processes operate. During physical combat, digestive processes cease so that more resources can be diverted to the needed physical activity. Perception and the rational processes also subserve both the dominant activity in progress and the individual's long-term motivational patterns.

Motives and Cognitive Processes
Affect Each Other

It is common experience that our motives determine what we pay attention to and what we see. The critical, punitive teacher spots every incipient infraction of the rules; the one who loves children sees their wonderful potentials and their efforts to do the right thing. The girl who is oversensitive and alert for signs of approval or disapproval may see the most innocent chance remark as an evaluation of her worth. People are constantly scanning their surroundings in relation to their current motivational pattern, attending to what is relevant, ignoring what is not.

Reasoning, learning, and remembering. Reasoning, learning, and remembering—crucial processes in problem solving and decision making—are constantly influenced by motivational factors. Our reason is all too easily subverted to a justification of what we want to do or to believe. The slogan "There are no atheists in foxholes" is not so much a proof of God's existence as evidence of the force of the need for safety, which believing helps to satisfy. Similarly, we rationalize to put ourselves in a good light or to justify the foolish thing we would like to do. Dictators may justify their ruthlessness and cruelty by reasoning that what they are doing is really for the people's ultimate good. The possessive mother may find fault with every would-be suitor for her daughter. The man who is afraid of marriage can find many reasons for putting it off.

It is notoriously difficult to think objectively about a situation when our own interests are involved. We may think we are reasoning logically, but we are apt to be blinded by our feelings and desires. This is why we need courts with impartial juries; in all conflicts, the participants tend to start with differing perceptions, and their lines of reasoning are usually further distorted by their motives and feelings. In the same way, marital counseling can often help both husband and wife to see their problems more objectively as a necessary first step to working out appropriate solutions.

Learning and remembering, too, are colored by our motivations. We learn and remember what fills a need for us, what interests us and ties in with our purposes. Material without meaning for us or material counter to our beliefs we find harder to learn than material high in meaning for us and in agreement with our cherished convictions (Levine and Murphy, 1943). Both our long-term attitudes and prejudices and our motivational pattern of the moment help to determine what "gets through" to us and hence what we can learn and remember from any experience.

Assumptions and attitudes. Our motives both influence and are influenced by the assumptions and attitudes we hold. The man who *feels* prejudice against members of another race is quick to assume that they are dirty, stupid, and shiftless and to conclude that allowing them to move into the neighborhood would be an economic threat. The man who feels a strong urge toward unorthodox sexual behavior may develop attitudes and beliefs congenial to his behavior. The woman who has always condemned divorce develops new attitudes about it when she herself feels impelled to leave her husband.

But this is a two-way road, and motives may themselves be encouraged or ignored, expressed or denied expression in keeping with our structure of assumptions and attitudes. Repressing one's sexual feelings, for example, grows out of the assumption that sex is evil. Our strivings are constantly being affected by what we believe is desirable, worth while, and possible.

MOTIVES AFFECT LEARNING AND REMEMBERING

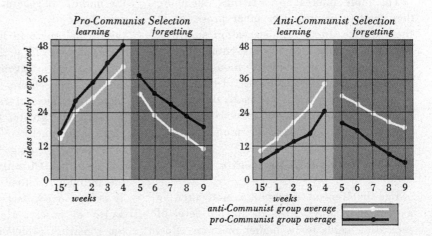

Cognitive processes are not independent of other processes. In one study pro-Communists and anti-Communists of comparable learning ability learned two selections—one favorable to Communism, the other unfavorable. As the graphs show, both groups learned more and remembered better the material that agreed with their own attitudes (Levine and Murphy, 1943).

Dreams. Even our dreams—one important form of thinking—are influenced by our motives. Therapists make good use of clues provided by their patients' dreams in getting at the source of the trouble. Children who live in orphanages commonly dream—both during the day and at night—about being adopted into a happy family. Similarly, the dreams of prisoners tend to be about freedom, and the dreams of hungry, displaced children during World War II were commonly about food. We have all probably had dreams about revenge, sexual activity, and other experiences in which we could readily see the influence of motivational factors.

Emotional arousal. With very strong motives there is usually considerable emotional arousal, which may further distort cognitive processes. Under strong anger or fear, for example, the individual may react with blind rage or panic; in any case, his ability to evaluate the problem objectively and behave calmly and rationally is likely to be impaired.

The more intense our strivings, the more they tend to commandeer other processes in their service. In the semistarvation study, as we have already seen, food eventually came to dominate all the subjects' thoughts. This, of course, is an extreme case. Under more normal circumstances, our motivational pattern is just one of many influences on our perceiving, thinking, and learning.

Ego-Involvement in Motivation

Ego-involvement enters into motivation in a number of ways. First of all, our level of aspiration tends to be higher and our effort greater when we are strongly ego-involved—when we see a goal as related to the enhancement of our self-structure and to the forwarding of our key purposes. We are on our best behavior when we are with people whose opinions matter deeply to us. We work hard for high grades or attention or approval or whatever it is that makes us feel good about ourselves. In a bridge game with strangers we may not try so hard as we would in a game against a disliked rival. The man who got out a huge crowd for an alumni gathering by writing each alumnus and asking him to be on the hospitality committee was taking advantage of the close relationship between feeling ego-involvement and being willing to put forth effort.

Second, several studies have shown that the greater the ego-involvement the more an individual's behavior tends to be consistent with his life style—and thus to be predictable. Where there is little or no ego-involvement, on the other hand, the situation plays a larger role in shaping his behavior, and he tends to react more directly to both inner and outer demands with less mediation by his self-structure. Thus, without ego-involvement, behavior tends to be less consistent and less predictable. This fact probably explains the apparent discrepancy between the finding of general traits like honesty and confidence by some experimenters and the failure of others to find such general traits. As Allport (1943, p. 461) sums it up, "When there is ego-involvement there are general traits; when there is no ego-involvement there are no general traits."

Third, the greater the ego-involvement the greater the likelihood that perception, memory, and reasoning will be commandeered and distorted. Objectivity is more likely when the individual either is not ego-involved or, if ego-involved, feels no threat to his own worth or safety. He can diagnose Cousin Sue's marital problems quite objectively and usually much more accurately than he can diagnose his own. He may function with confidence and objectivity with employees under his supervision but become insecure with his superiors. He may see clearly why the neighbors' children are such "brats" but

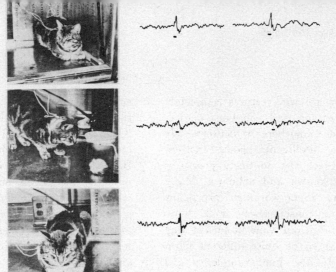

Dots under tracings indicate when clicks occurred.

Incoming stimulation is not received and transmitted mechanically to the brain in proportion to its intensity. Instead, from the barrage of stimuli to which the organism is potentially sensitive at any given moment, some are selected by central mechanisms within the organism for transmission to "headquarters" while others, irrelevant to the purpose of the moment, are screened out or accepted in muted form. In one study (Hernández-Peón, Sherrer, and Jouvet, 1956), the same auditory clicks that gave rise to size-able electrical responses in the cochlear nucleus of a relaxed cat (top) aroused almost no response while the cat was watching two mice in a jar (center), but again produced sizeable responses when the cat's attention was no longer preoccupied (bottom).

be completely mystified at the uncooperative behavior of his own offspring.

And fourth, the degree of ego-involvement in motivation is closely related to the amount of emotional arousal that accompanies our strivings. When we feel a cherished goal is at stake, we are fearful, anxious, or perhaps angry, as the situation warrants. When a long-sought prize is at last within our grasp, we feel elation, triumph, and great joy. With ego-involved strivings, there is not the indifference of the person who is just doing a job or putting in time. We care very much about the outcome, marshal our best effort, and keep anxious tab on our progress.

Finally, ego-involvement breeds interest. We tend to become interested in events, activities, and goals that we see as having some relation to ourselves. The good teacher builds new interests by showing students how a new idea or activity is related to what they already know and care about. People are interested in anything they see as having potential value for them, as meeting their needs, enhancing their satisfactions, or contributing to their worth.

Conscious and Unconscious Motives

Even though we have a highly consistent pattern of behavior that everyone else recognizes as characteristic of us—such as always contriving to lean on someone else or constantly trying to build ourselves up by belittling other people—we ourselves may be quite unaware of the actual purposes of much of our behavior. Sometimes we are puzzled at apparently irrational or inconsistent things we say or do—or wish we could. Although we are not creatures of blind instinct, neither are we creatures completely controlled by reason and conscious choice. We seem to be somewhere in between. We are capable of intelligent, planned action, yet we are subject also to many pressures and influences, known and unknown. Many processes in our "inner workings" are below the level of our consciousness or in some cases screened from our view in such a way that they appear to be quite different from what they really are. For example, a girl may marry a "big shot" because of an unconscious motive to get away from an unsatisfactory home situation or because of a motive to achieve the prestige and status of being his wife while being convinced in her own mind that her motivation is deep and undying love. In the same way, a child who steals from his mother's purse may not realize that it is affection he really wants; a show-off may wonder why he makes such a fool of himself, not realizing that his desire for attention and acceptance is responsible for his behavior.

The ability of unconscious motives to guide behavior has been shown experimentally in hypnotic demonstrations like the following (Erickson, 1939, pp. 340-341):

"During hypnosis the subject was instructed that after he awakened Dr. D. would begin talking to him about some abstruse subject in which he was not at all interested, and that although he would actually be profoundly bored he would try to appear interested. He was told that he would want very much to close the conversation, that he would wish for some way of shutting off this interminable flow of words, that he would look around him in the hope of finding some distraction, and that he would feel that Dr. D. was terribly tiresome. He was then awakened, whereupon Dr. D. began the conversation. Although the subject appeared to be politely attentive, Dr. D. would occasionally

say, 'Perhaps you're not interested?' The subject would reply with excessive emphasis, 'Oh, yes, certainly, I'm very much interested.' Now and then he would interrupt Dr. D., trying to pin him down to some definite point for discussion, but each time this effort was evaded. At length the subject began glancing about the room and was noted casually to observe an open door. Finally he interrupted Dr. D., saying, 'Excuse me, I feel an awful draft,' and got up to close the door. As he did so he was asked what he was doing. He replied, 'The air seems to be awful hot ['hot air!']; I thought I would shut off the draft.' When the hypnotist pretended not to understand and asked him what he was doing the subject replied, 'Why, I just shut the bore.'"

With Freud's revelations of the power and reality of unconscious motivation in our behavior, it was perhaps inevitable that for a time the importance of unconscious factors should be magnified out of all proportion in research and clinical work. Such faith has been placed in projective tests like the Rorschach and other tools for uncovering repressed motives that clinicians have sometimes not even bothered to study the patient's conscious motivational pattern—his interests, purposes, and conscious desires for the future. Yet, as Allport (1953) has pointed out, the subjects in the semistarvation experiment (p. 136), though consciously dominated by longings for and fantasies about food, gave no hint of this in their responses on various projective tests. Allport suggests that, useful as the indirect methods for uncovering repressed, unconscious motives are, such roundabout methods are not needed with healthy personalities, where little has been repressed. In the latter case, assessing the conscious desires and purposes may give an adequate and more accurate picture. In any case, even with unhealthy personalities, a picture of only the unconscious motives is a partial picture at best.

One of the characteristics of an unhealthy personality is that conscious and unconscious elements seem to be at odds with each other. An unhealthy person is unaware of many of the purposes that actually determine his behavior; there seems to be a dissociation and lack of integration. One vivid example is seen in the use of the defense mechanism of reaction formation (p. 202) in which the individual not only is unaware of his real feelings but actually develops conscious ideas diametrically opposed to the repressed ones. Often, for example, a fanatical crusader against vice is actually trying unconsciously to erect a bulwark against his own unacceptable impulses. In psychotherapy the patient is helped to bring such unconscious feelings and motives into consciousness where he can examine them and build a more rational, unified approach to life.

The unconscious elements in our motivation are, of course, what make it so hard for us to change our behavior simply because we want to or know we should. The need to know and accept ourselves is the first step in successful change.

In this chapter we have tried to clarify our perspective on human motivation by classifying all human motives as strivings toward (1) physical and psychological self-maintenance or (2) improvement of oneself and one's situation through growth, fulfillment, and richer satisfactions. In all cultures success in these strivings means meeting certain physiological and psychological needs, or requirements. In addition, people learn to strive for the maintenance and actualization of other individuals and of the groups to which they belong and tend to accept the goals and values of these groups as their own.

Our motivation is influenced by our surroundings in three ways: (1) through the resources or limitations it provides for meeting our needs, (2) through its encouragement of some strivings and discouragement of others, and (3) through its demands on us.

Motives are closely interrelated and rarely operate singly: one motive may be expressed in many acts, and one act may be the expression of several motives. Under conditions of deprivation or threat, the motives involved in self-maintenance and survival tend to take precedence, but under favorable conditions, actualization motives tend to come to the fore.

We all tend to develop a pattern of consistent, long-term key purposes and motives that becomes characteristic of us and part of our life style. Motive patterns change, however, as needs are met. Long-term changes come as we learn new ways of meeting our biological and psychological needs and as our field makes new demands on us.

Motives may commandeer and distort perception, reasoning, and learning—a tendency increased by ego-involvement and perceived threat. With a large degree of ego-involvement, our behavior tends to be heavily determined by personality factors and hence to be highly consistent with the person's life style. With little ego-involvement, situational factors may be most important. Motives affect and are affected by attitudes and assumptions. Only part of our motivation is conscious and rational.

In this chapter we have been discussing energy sources—what makes us move and what goals we tend to seek. But on the way to those goals we often encounter obstacles or other hazards that complicate our lives. In the next chapter we will examine various frustrations, conflicts, and pressures that sometimes keep us from a simple attainment of our goals.

REFERENCES

The following list includes both the references cited in this chapter and a selected number of additional books and articles for outside reading.

Allee, W. C. 1958. *The Social Life of Animals.* Boston: Beacon Press, Inc.

Allport, Gordon W. 1937. "The Functional Autonomy of Motives." *The American Journal of Psychology, 50,* 141-156.

Allport, Gordon W. 1943. "The Ego in Contemporary Psychology." *Psychological Review, 50,* 451-478.

Allport, Gordon W. 1953. "The Trend in Motivational Theory." *American Journal of Orthopsychiatry, 23,* 107-119.

Asch, Solomon E. 1952. *Social Psychology.* New York: Prentice-Hall, Inc.

Bettelheim, Bruno. 1943. "Individual and Mass Behavior in Extreme Situations." *The Journal of Abnormal and Social Psychology, 38,* 417-452.

Bowlby, J. 1951. "Maternal Care and Mental Health." *World Health Organization Monograph Series,* No. 3.

Cannon, Walter Bradford. 1939. *Wisdom of the Body.* New York: W. W. Norton & Company, Inc.

Cantril, Hadley. 1950. *The "Why" of Man's Experience.* New York: The Macmillan Company. Reprinted by permission of the publishers.

Cattell, Raymond Bernard. 1957. *Personality and Motivation Structure and Measurement.* Yonkers-on-Hudson, N.Y.: World Book Company.

Davis, C. M. 1928. "Self Selection of Diet by Newly Weaned Infants." *American Journal of Diseases of Children, 36,* 651-679.

Erickson, Milton H. 1939. "Experimental Demonstrations of the Psychopathology of Everyday Life." *The Psychoanalytic Quarterly, 8,* 338-353.

Festinger, Leon. 1958. "The Motivating Effect of Cognitive Dissonance." *Assessment of Human Motives.* Gardner Lindzey, ed. New York: Rinehart & Company, Inc.

Fey, William F. 1957. "Correlates of Certain Subjective Attitudes Toward Self and Others." *Journal of Clinical Psychology, 13,* 44-49.

Frederick, J. George. 1957. *Introduction to Motivation Research.* New York: Business Bourse.

Fromm, Erich. 1955. *The Sane Society.* New York: Rinehart & Company, Inc.

Fromm, Erich. 1956. *The Art of Loving.* New York: Harper & Brothers.

Goldstein, Kurt. 1939. *The Organism.* New York: American Book Company.

Hall, Calvin S., and Gardner Lindzey. 1957. *Theories of Personality.* New York: John Wiley & Sons, Inc.

Harlow, Harry F. 1953. "Mice, Monkeys, Men, and Motives." *Psychological Review, 60,* 23-32.

Hemingway, Ernest. 1955. *The Short Stories of Ernest Hemingway.* New York: Charles Scribner's Sons.

Hernández-Peón, Raúl, H. Sherrer, and M. Jouvet. 1956. "Modification of Electrical Activity in the Cochlear Nucleus During 'Attention' in Unanesthetized Cats." *Science, 123,* 331.

Heron, Woodburn, B. K. Doane, and T. H. Scott. 1956. "Visual Disturbances After Prolonged Perceptual Isolation." *Canadian Journal of Psychology, 10,* 13-18.

Huxley, Julian. 1953. *Evolution in Action.* New York: Harper & Brothers and London: Chatto & Windus Ltd. By permission of the author and publishers.

James, William. 1890. *Principles of Psychology,* Vol. I. New York: Henry Holt and Company.

Jones, Marshall R., ed. 1959. *Nebraska Symposium on Motivation.* Lincoln: University of Nebraska Press.

Keys, Ancel, and others. 1950. *The Biology of Human Starvation.* Minneapolis: University of Minnesota Press.

Krech, David, and Richard S. Crutchfield. 1958. *Elements of Psychology.* New York: Alfred A. Knopf, Inc.

Levine, Jerome M., and Gardner Murphy. 1943. "The Learning and Forgetting of Controversial Material." *The Journal of Abnormal and Social Psychology, 38,* 507-517.

Liddell, H. S. 1944. "Conditioned Reflex Method and Experimental Neurosis." *Personality and the Behavior Disorders,* Vol. I. J. McV. Hunt, ed. New York: The Ronald Press Company.

Lilly, John C. 1956. "Mental Effects of Reduction of Ordinary Levels of Physical Stimuli on Intact, Healthy Persons." *Psychiatric Research Reports, 5,* 1-9.

Lindzey, Gardner. 1958. *Assessment of Human Motives.* New York: Rinehart & Company, Inc.

Martineau, Pierre. 1957. *Motivation in Advertising: Motives That Make People Buy.* New York: McGraw-Hill Book Company, Inc.

Maslow, A. H. 1950. "Self-Actualizing People: A Study of Psychological Health." *Symposium #1 1950 Values in Personality Research.* Werner Wolff, ed. New York: Grune & Stratton, Inc.

Maslow, A. H. 1954. *Motivation and Personality.* New York: Harper & Brothers.

Maslow, A. H. 1956. "Personality Problems and Personality Growth." *The Self.* Clark E. Moustakas, ed. New York: Harper & Brothers.

Nardini, J. E. 1952. "Survival Factors in American Prisoners of War of the Japanese." *The American Journal of Psychiatry, 109,* 241-248.

Rich, Louise Dickinson. 1946. *Happy the Land.* Philadelphia: J. B. Lippincott Company.

Richter, C. P. 1942. "Total Self-Regulatory Functions in Animals and Human Beings." *Harvey Lectures, 1942-1943, 38,* 63-103.

Richter, C. P., and C. D. Hawkes. 1941. "The Dependence of the Carbohydrate, Fat, and Protein Appetite of Rats on the Various Components of the Vitamin B Complex." *American Journal of Physiology, 131,* 639-649.

Rogers, Carl R. 1958. *Becoming a Person.* Austin: The Hogg Foundation for Mental Hygiene, The University of Texas.

Sherif, Muzafer, and Hadley Cantril. 1947. *The Psychology of Ego-Involvements.* New York: John Wiley & Sons, Inc. Copyright 1947 by John Wiley & Sons, Inc., New York, and reprinted with their permission.

Stacey, Chalmers L., and Manfred F. DeMartino. 1958. *Understanding Human Motivation.* Cleveland: Howard Allen, Inc.

Woodworth, Robert Sessions. 1918. *Dynamic Psychology.* New York: Columbia University Press.

PROBLEMS
OF ADJUSTMENT

Strivings do not always attain their objective, and requirements are not automatically met. Sometimes we can comply successfully with the inner and outer demands made on us, but sometimes we run into difficulty. From time to time we all encounter delays, lacks, failures, losses, disappointments, restrictions, obligations, illnesses, and contradictions in needs. Any such interferences with the attainment of our goals create problems of adjustment. Some are relatively easy to cope with. Others put considerable strain on us. And some are so overwhelming that they overtax our capacities and we break down.

Good adjustment is not a quiescent state in which we feel no pain and no desire; it is a continuing successful meeting of inner and outer requirements, which change from moment to moment and from year to year. Good adjustment does not mean being free from problems of adjustment but learning to cope with them effectively.

Actually any demand made on us is a problem of adjustment and involves some stress and strain, however small. Just as even a single brick put on a bridge puts a stress on the bridge, so any adjustive demand on a human energy system puts a stress on the system. The resulting changes in the system, such as emotional arousal or increased effort, indicate the severity of stress.

If the demand can easily be met by the system's adjustive resources, as in the case of the brick on a bridge, there is no problem. But with heavy demands, the system's adjustive resources may be severely taxed or even overtaxed. In the bridge there may be structural changes like the crystallization and breaking of metal after continual bending; in the human system there may be a breakdown of integrated functioning.

Many of the demands of everyday life are relatively minor ones that we can meet fairly easily: we can size up the situation, see what action is called for, and follow through appropriately. Such adaptive actions involve no *appreciable* degree of strain on the organism, and we shall arbitrarily call them *nonstressful*. But from time to time we all meet problems that render adaptation difficult and put us under considerable strain; here we shall use the term *stressful*. Becoming reconciled to the death of a dearly loved wife or coping with social disgrace, for example, we would call stressful adaptations. It should be remembered, however, that the difference is actually one of degree rather than of kind and that all adjustive demands are *somewhat* stressful.

Stressful situations call for extra effort on the part of the organism if it is to reach its goal. Thus they typically lead to increased tension and to some measure of emotional arousal. We raise our output of energy and, in turn, increase the wear and tear on our system. The more or less chronic stress most of us experience as a result of the hurry and worry of modern living is a serious problem because of its long-term damaging effects on our health and happiness.

TYPES OF ADJUSTMENT PROBLEMS

Problems of adjustment can be classified as *frustrations*—blockings of our strivings toward a goal; *conflicts*—concurrent action tendencies which are contradictory and thus tend to block each other; and *pressures*—demands that call for more than ordinary effort, perhaps for a speeding up or for special persistence or endurance. These categories inevitably overlap somewhat but will be useful for discussion purposes.

Frustration

Frustration is the result of the thwarting of a motive—of the organism's inability, temporarily or permanently, to proceed toward a desired goal. Ongoing activity or desired activity is blocked, and the need is left unsatisfied. Frustrations may be large or small, serious or inconsequential. Minor frustrations may mean only petty irritations whereas severe ones may signal serious threats to our welfare.

In some cases motives are thwarted by obstacles blocking the path to a goal, as when a student who is trying to maintain his grade average to be eligible for medical school runs out of money and has to find a job. Many direct ways of reaching our goals are blocked by social restrictions, and much of our effort goes into trying to find acceptable, alternate ways of satisfying our requirements. In other cases motives are thwarted because no appropriate goal object is available, as when shipwrecked men run out of provisions or famine threatens the land.

Sources of frustration. The barriers to achieving our goals may originate outside us in our environment or within us as a result of our personal characteristics. Environmental conditions that may lead to frustration range from rain when we want to play golf to more serious events like earthquakes, famines, or floods, which put at naught our best planning and effort. Pens that refuse to write, glamorous ads that make us want things we cannot have, red tape that prevents us from taking a course we feel would do us more good than some of those prescribed for our major—these are just a few of the countless environmentally caused frustrations that plague us in ordinary living.

Personal characteristics can also keep us from getting what we want. Physical handicaps, disease, low intelligence, lack of special talents, inadequate competencies (real or imagined), and personal qualities that antagonize other people are all examples of sources of frustration that result from our own limitations. Our desires may also be frustrated by lack of adequate self-control, by rigid overcontrol, or by misdirected control, as when we subject ourselves to continual failure and self-devaluation because we make unrealistic demands on ourselves.

Common frustrations in our culture. In our relatively prosperous and literate culture, few of us suffer from the material frustrations and limitations to fulfillment that still are realities for over half the world's people. Most prevalent among us are frustrations stemming from delays, from discrepancies between what we have and what we would like, from the lack of satisfying values or meaning, from the loss of someone or something precious to us, from failure, guilt, discrimination, and limitations. A complete list, of course, would be endless, but a few of those that cause us special difficulty warrant some discussion.

1. Delays. In our time-conscious culture, where we feel we must make every minute count, delays are especially galling. Yet with our concentrations of population, our specialization, and our high degree of interdependence, many delays are inevitable. We cannot all get through the intersection at the same time but must take our turn. Literally and figuratively, we are continually standing in line waiting for something we would like. We cannot marry when we are physiologically ready but must wait until we have the skills we need to earn a living. Few of us can buy the new car or the house we want the moment we decide we would like it.

Many of our delays—especially those related to material possessions—are made especially difficult by the constant barrage of advertising that keeps stimulating our desires. Necessary as this aspect of modern marketing may be for creating broader markets and greater productivity, it creates a stress for those who cannot keep pace in their purchases with the desires and standards thus created. This stress is often further intensified by our tendency to ignore what we *do* have and preoccupy ourselves with the things that are still lacking.

2. Lacks. Although most of us do not lack the basic necessities of life, probably none of us is completely satisfied with everything he has. We would like a more comfortable home, a newer car, a better class schedule, more becoming or more stylish clothes. We would like to be more poised, more clever, a better conversationalist, a better tennis player. There always seem to be lacks in our material or immaterial resources or in our life situation that we would like to fill.

Lacks that are especially worrisome in our culture are physical shortcomings that limit our chances for fulfillment, absence of satisfying values or meaning in life, not enough money to buy the things we want, and want of approval and status in the community. A lack of dates or other indications that men find her unattractive is frustrating to a girl; lack of freedom to make his own choices is frustrating to any normal young person in our culture. Couples who are eager for children feel deep frustration if they find they are unable to have them. A lack of underlying self-acceptance is one of the most debilitating of frustrations.

3. Losses. Loss of anything that we have possessed and valued is frustrating because it deprives us of a source of gratification or a resource for meeting our needs. Loss of money or time may mean we must forego a cherished dream. Loss of friendship or love may not only deprive us of satisfactions we had come to depend on but also threaten our self-esteem. The death of someone close to us upsets our previous pattern of giving and receiving love and leaves us feeling incomplete. The losses that come with aging—loss of loved ones, loss of financial independence,

loss of valued status in the group, and gradual loss of one's own skills—are all highly frustrating.

Losses are especially frustrating because so often they are beyond our control, and once they have occurred there is nothing we can do about them. They often seem to represent the whim of a cruel and capricious fate.

4. Failure. Even if we did not live in a competitive society, we would sometimes be bound to fail in our endeavors; but by encouraging all of us to aim higher than we all can possibly reach at once, the competitive setting in which we operate increases the frequency of failure and heightens its ability to frustrate us. Even when we do well in the light of our own ability, we may feel we have failed if we have not done so well as someone else. Failure may also come from inadequate effort, lack of necessary skills, chance factors, or behavior on the part of a friend or teacher or supervisor that blocks attainment of our goal. Any failure is frustrating and may threaten our feelings of worth.

5. Guilt. From time to time we all do things that lead to feelings of guilt. Either doing something we feel is wrong or failing to do something we know we should can make us feel guilty. Guilt is a source of frustration because it thwarts our needs for self-esteem and security. We condemn ourselves and may fear that others will condemn and perhaps punish us.

In addition to the common sources of frustration already discussed, several others may be mentioned briefly. Although widely decried in principle, discrimination against various ethnic groups still occurs and is a source of great frustration to its victims, tending to elicit both hostility and feelings of lack of worth. Economic fluctuations and economic uncertainty are highly frustrating to anyone dependent on a regular income for the material necessities of life. Being a misfit in one's career is intensely frustrating not only because one misses the satisfactions of achievement and creativity that a career should bring but also because the individual may be denied the income he would like to support his family adequately. The frustrations that result from an unhappy marriage are especially severe because they permeate one's whole "home base" and threaten one's basic anchorages. And, finally, the knowledge that we are living in a world of nations armed to the teeth with weapons able to destroy all human life gnaws at our feelings of security and is frustrating to our need for safety.

Conflict

Conflict results when contradictory goals or means vie with each other and interfere with the smooth flow of ongoing behavior. You want to go home for the week end, but you also want to stay for the dance. You would like to defer your military service, but you don't want to lose your chance to choose your branch of service. You are interested in taking a certain course, but you don't want any Saturday classes.

Although it is convenient to make a distinction between frustrations and conflicts, it is the underlying threat of frustration that makes a conflict stressful. In a conflict you are threatened with frustration regardless of which course you choose to follow. You have to give up either the dance or the week end at home. If you take a chance on finishing school before you get called for the service, you may be called sooner than you expect. To get the course you want, you may have to give up your free Saturdays.

A conflict may be either between alternative actions for meeting the same need or between contradictory motives, one of which must be frustrated if the other is satisfied. Choosing between steak and roast beef is an example of the first—a choice between two ways of meeting your need for food. But if you can join a high-status group only by indulging in behavior contrary to your ethical standards, then the course of action that will meet your need for social approval will frustrate your need for self-esteem, and you must give up one or the other unless you can find a satisfactory compromise.

Implicit in the concept of conflict is the assumption that the contradictory alternatives are of approximately equal attractiveness or unattractiveness and that some decision is required. Since a gain on either side means a corresponding loss on the other, such a decision is often extremely difficult to make, and it is not surprising that the person in conflict often hesitates, vacillates, and goes through agonies in trying to make up his mind.

Types of conflict. Psychologists usually classify conflicts in terms of the *valence*—the positive or negative value—that the alternatives have for the individual. Thus there are double-approach, approach-avoidance, and double-avoidance conflicts.

1. Double-approach conflicts. As the name suggests, double-approach conflicts involve competition between two or more desirable alternatives. On a simple level, a decision may have to be made between two courses we would like to take, between playing tennis and going swimming, or between two invitations for the same evening. To a large extent, such simple "plus-plus" conflicts result from the inevitable limitations in our time, space, energy, and personal resources. We cannot be in two places at once, we do not have time or energy to do all the things we would like to do, and most of us do not have unlimited funds.

Although even simple decisions—such as whether to buy a blue or a gray sweater—may be hard to make, they do not ordinarily upset us greatly because we are assured of reasonable gratification at the moment and because we can often obtain the other desired alternative at a later time. With more complex conflicts, as when we must choose between loyalty to a mother and to a wife or between two good jobs, a decision may be very difficult and highly stressful.

2. Approach-avoidance conflicts. In an approach-avoidance conflict we have contradictory tendencies toward the same course of action because we see it as desirable for certain reasons but undesirable for others. A woman may feel trapped and denied fulfillment by an unhappy marriage and yet may value the status and security it gives her. A man may feel attracted to a beautiful and intelligent girl while recognizing that her sense of values would limit the success of their marriage. This kind of conflict is sometimes referred to as the "mixed blessing" conflict, because some negative and frustrating features of the goal (or the means involved in obtaining it) must be accepted if we are to enjoy the positive features.

3. Double-avoidance conflicts. In double-avoidance conflicts we are caught between the devil and the deep blue sea and must try to choose the lesser of two evils. We may have to choose between going square dancing and going bowling, neither of which we enjoy, or between letting down the little theater group and not getting a paper written. An employee may have to choose between behaving in ways he feels are unethical and giving up a lucrative job.

When such "minus-minus" conflicts are severe, they can cause serious adjustment problems because even resolution of the conflict will bring frustration rather than relief. Under such conditions, individuals are prone to grasp at unrealistic alternatives that only get them into worse trouble. Often they try to avoid having to make a decision at all by fleeing the conflict situation—either literally, by running away, or imaginatively, by re-

treating to a more pleasant world of fantasy. Minor double-avoidance conflicts are often escaped by a sudden "headache" or "stomach upset" which forces the person to take to his bed until the situation has passed.

It can be readily seen that this classification of conflicts is somewhat arbitrary and that various combinations among these different types are the rule rather than the exception in everyday life. Thus a "plus-plus" conflict between marrying one of two desirable persons may also have its "plus-minus" aspects growing out of the responsibilities and loss of personal freedom entailed in marriage.

Common conflicts in our culture. Each culture, in the social arrangements it prescribes and the resources and limitations it offers, renders certain types of conflicts more common than others. The following are a few of the conflicts especially characteristic in our society today.

1. Inner versus outer direction. The insecurities of our anxious age and the lack of a clear pattern for young people to follow make the development of self-direction and personal responsibility especially hard. It is no easy task to construct a value system and chart a course of action that will meet our needs for both security and growth and for both self-esteem and social approval, for often we encounter contradictory demands and value systems from parents, age-mates, and employers. At the same time, lingering emotional dependence on parents and unsureness of our own powers often pull us back toward the safety of dependence, even while we are feeling strong urges to stand on our own two feet and show what we can do on our own. Or we may simply transfer our dependence from our parents to our age-mates, even though the support of our peers must be paid for with slavish conformity. In either case, the conflict between our desire to have someone to lean on emotionally and our urge to act independently can create a serious conflict.

Several writers of our time—Riesman, Fromm, Whyte—have pointed to the tendency of many people in our anxious age to surrender the risks and pains of independence for the security of authority. Sometimes this authority is tradition; sometimes it is a dictatorship; sometimes it is a corporation; sometimes it is just a vague "they" who become the arbiters of our actions. In the latter case we may choose clothes, cars, furniture, colleges, and even churches because we think other people will approve of them rather than because they satisfy our ideas of value.

In all these examples, other people's values are followed, and the individual judges himself successful or unsuccessful, worthy or unworthy, in proportion to how he sees himself meeting these outer standards. If his own standards of right or beauty or importance coincide with those of the external authority, then of course there is no conflict, but often a person ignores or goes counter to his own experience of value to the extent that he becomes a stranger to his own real feelings. An outer-directed person will feel a deep sense of frustration, for he will be violating a central part of his nature.

2. Love versus hate. The conflict between love and hate—between constructive tendencies and destructive ones—is a key problem in our modern, highly competitive society. For even though we pay lip service to our ideal of "brotherly love," our competition for money and status tends to elicit much envy, frustration, and hostility. As a result, relationships with other people are often fraught with both love and hate—with ambivalent feelings.

An admixture of love and hate usually complicates most of our family relationships. The parents who feed and protect us also frustrate us and hence arouse our anger or hostility. Yet we have usually been indoc-trinated with the belief that hostility is wrong—particularly when directed toward loved ones such as parents, brothers or sisters, or mates, for whom we should presumably feel only pure affection. So when we have feelings of irritation or anger, we feel guilty about them and try to deny them. Actually, of course, bottling up hostile feelings or denying that they exist only compounds the problem. We need to acknowledge them and find constructive or at least harmless ways of expressing them.

3. Sexual conflicts. Although current writers do not consider sexual conflicts the inevitable phenomena that Freud judged them to be, they are common enough to cause considerable grief, especially among young people. The earliest sexual conflict often centers around the practice of masturbation, which has so long been condemned as a vile, enfeebling, immoral habit that even present-day knowledge of its physical harmlessness and of its prevalence at a certain stage in development does not always remove the sense of fear and guilt concerning it.

Another sexual problem in growing up is learning to accept oneself as a man or a woman. In healthy development, the child is usually able to learn and accept an appropriate masculine or feminine role by identifying with the parent of the same sex. When one parent is missing, however, or when for some other reason the desirable identification does not take place and a boy identifies with a feminine role or a girl with a masculine one, great unhappiness may be in store for the individual, and a successful marriage may be impossible.

In later adolescence and young adulthood, sexual conflicts may become full-blown. Especially when marriage must wait, moral codes may conflict seriously with a desire for sexual intimacy. Conflicts are often intensified by such frustrating conditions as a long engagement or the practice of stimulation without gratification. Sexual desires battle against reality restraints as well as ethical ones. There is always the fear of detection, of disease, of pregnancy, and of the social disapproval that any one of these would bring.

These are such strong desires and such effective restraints that it is no wonder sexual conflicts are powerful and distressing ones. To add to the difficulty, there is so much confusion and disagreement in the standards young people encounter that many are genuinely confused as to what is right and wrong, good and bad. "Society" says one thing, but when the noses are counted, it is discovered that "society" has not always followed its own precepts. Exceptions are made, and the mores of one social group do not correspond with those of another.

4. Value conflicts. Values enter into all the conflicts already discussed, for every choice is a choice between values. Many of our most difficult conflicts are those in which we must choose between basic principles or standards or must weigh a standard against advancement of our goals. Conflicts of loyalties, conflicts over whether the end justifies the means, and conflicts engendered by membership in groups with different standards are all value conflicts that we may find very difficult to resolve. In our jobs we may encounter conflicts between turning out a first rate product and making a higher profit by skimping on materials, conflicts between going after "success" and doing work one honestly feels is more important, and conflicts between working overtime to gain promotion and spending time with one's family.

Thinking individuals often find they have conflicting assumptions. For instance, it is assumed that loyalty to a friend is a good thing. Does this mean that you must lend him money? Does it mean that you stand up for him in public if he commits a wrong? If he is fired from his job with good reason, do you recommend him for another?

Some of our conflicts and anxieties reflect rigid or unrealistic assumptions we are making about ourselves. We may feel we *should* be able to get along with everyone, *should* be able to concentrate better, *should never* be impatient or cross with a child, *should* be able to do better than we are doing, *should not* feel the way we clearly do feel. Karen Horney (1950) calls this the "tyranny of the 'should.'"

In many ways, conflicts are the most severe type of stress, for they require all the skills needed for meeting frustration plus those needed for making good decisions under difficult circumstances.

Pressure

Problems of adjustment come not only because our own strivings are frustrated or in conflict but also because of pressures that complicate our journey toward our goals. For example, if our parents have made sacrifices to send us to college and expect us to do well, we may feel under great pressure not to let them down. Such pressures may force us to intensify our effort and to speed up our activity—often to an uncomfortable degree. In short, they may involve severe stress and strain.

Sources of pressure. Pressures, like frustrations, may stem from inner or outer sources. Inner sources typically center around our own aspirations and ego-ideals. Where we have a high level of aspiration in terms of standards to be met and goals to be achieved, the pressure may be fairly continuous and severe. Many of us drive ourselves mercilessly toward such high levels of attainment that we are kept under constant stress and strain. We may be determined to get to the top, to be the best, to achieve perfectionistic standards. Where we strive to be the "best" rather than to better our own previous performance and improve our skill, we subject ourselves not only to sustained pressure but also to probable frustration and failure, with the self-devaluation they bring.

Many pressures arise from environmental demands. Thus our family may put pressure on us to get good grades or to uphold the family reputation for business prowess or community service. Society puts many pressures on us to conform to its written and unwritten rules. Sometimes it seems as though we are constantly under pressure to make decisions, solve problems, increase our knowledge, and meet deadlines.

Outside pressures may be mild or severe. When a friend asks a small favor, the pressure may be quite minor. When a teacher assigns large amounts of outside reading and requires many written reports, students may be put under considerable strain—particularly poorer students or students eager for high achievement.

Common pressures in our culture. In addition to the unique demands and pressures each of us faces, there are certain pressures common to all members of our society. Prevalent among these are pressure to compete, pressure to adjust to constant change, pressures for performance first at school and later on the job, pressure to get along with other people, and, for most of us sooner or later, pressure toward building and maintaining the kind of marriage and family life that are valued in our society. Some of us find these pressures extremely onerous and disconcerting; others of us learn to live with them without undue strain.

1. Competition. We live in a highly competitive society in which we compete for grades, athletic honors, leadership, jobs, financial advantages, social status, marital partners, and almost everything else we want. Although there are certain accepted rules for playing the game, our society places its major emphasis upon success. Even in the more idealistic school atmosphere, the loser is rarely remembered or given status for his

effort or fair play. The losing football team certainly does not attract crowds or gain plaudits for its performance. There simply is no substitute for success. We all are encouraged to "hitch our wagon to a star"—to "think big." Yet not everyone can win all the time, and in striving to do the impossible we only invite frustration and self-devaluation.

Our tendency to have an unrealistically high level of aspiration stems from both external and internal sources. Parents, with great expectations for their children, exert early and continuing pressure on them for high levels of performance. Their teachings are reinforced by those of television programs, newspapers, magazines, and other channels of communication that foster our American stereotype of rags to riches—the idea that you can do it if you try because the United States offers unlimited opportunity for those who are willing to take advantage of it. Very early, most children—especially middle-class ones—learn these values and accept them as standards by which to measure their own achievements.

2. Rapid social change. We live in a period of incredibly rapid change which has created many new problems for us. Jobs, values, social institutions, houses, meals, and amusements are all very different today from what they were even fifty years ago, and change has become almost more common than continuity. Just the constant need to keep making new adjustments puts a strain on us. Furthermore, technological innovations have made the world so much smaller that many complex social problems are superimposed upon the personal problems of the individual. Whether we like it or not, we have to be concerned with what happens in China, Russia, and other parts of the world —for these happenings may directly affect our own security and well-being.

In our changing world we tend to assume that change leads to progress. Change and newness are valued for themselves, and whatever is the latest thing is automatically assumed to be the best. Cars, homes, clothes, and television sets are rapidly outmoded, and we are under considerable pressure to keep up with the Joneses.

3. *Educational, occupational, and marital demands.* Many stressful pressures stem from demands made on us in connection with our education, career, and marriage. The concentration of effort, the long hours of study, the tension of examinations, and the fear of flunking out, and uncertainty perhaps as to the proper direction of one's educational training, create some measure of strain in most students. Coping with the intense competitive demands of our modern educational system can be especially stressful for those who lack good background preparation and efficient study skills or who are lower in intellectual ability than most of the students with whom they have to compete.

Marriage also makes many demands on an individual—demands that may be quite stressful if either partner is immature or if the external situation is not favorable. Marriage calls on the individual to adjust to intimate relationships with another person, to help work out a mutually satisfactory approach to problems, and to resolve value conflicts. With the arrival of children, the problems of parenthood, division of responsibility, type of discipline, and other possible sources of difficulty arise. In short, the achievement of the happy marriage· that

most of us eagerly want requires the solution of many problems, the making of many compromises, and sincere effort. Sometimes these adjustment problems in marriage cause considerable strain. Statistics show that one out of three marriages is unhappy or ends in divorce and that another is likely to reach only a minimal level of satisfaction. Only one marriage in three can be called really happy.

Occupational demands may also be highly stressful. This is true particularly when the individual is very ambitious to get to the top or feels under considerable pressure from parents, wife, or friends to make good. In many business organizations there is a constant jockeying for position to be in line for promotions. Even if the individual is well prepared in terms of both professional and personal competencies, he may find himself under considerable strain in his attempts to move up the ladder. Even if he gets to the top, he may find himself in a job that yields satisfactions in terms of money, status, and worth but makes heavy demands on him in terms of responsibility for problem solving and decision making. And, of course, it is not only the administrative jobs that are high-pressure ones in our society. Many selling jobs put a salesman under continual pressure to meet quotas and to maintain or improve his rating. Any job that requires constant speed and attention to deadlines or other exact standards can put us under continued strain.

WHAT DETERMINES
THE SEVERITY OF STRESS?

The severity of stress is determined partly by the characteristics of the adjustive demand itself and partly by the unique char-

acteristics of the individual involved. Thus on the biological level, the severity of the problem created by invading tuberculosis germs, for example, depends partly on the strength and number of the invaders and partly on the organism's ability to resist. On the psychological level, individual factors play an even more important role in determining the severity of stress, for the seriousness of the adjustive demand itself depends considerably upon how it is perceived by the person involved.

Characteristics of the Adjustive Demand

Several aspects of an adjustive demand affect its severity for almost everyone regardless of his frame of reference or other personal characteristics.

Duration, importance, and multiplicity of demands. Ordinarily the longer a stress situation continues, the more severe will be the strain on the organism. The individual can easily afford to miss a meal or so, but continued hunger puts a severe strain on him. Similarly, he can tolerate uncertainty for a short period, but prolonged uncertainty can be very stressful. With some kinds of stress, however, the individual manages to work out a pattern of adaptation that either lessens the stress or protects him from its effects. Muscles harden if the individual continues to perform heavy physical labor over a long period of time. The skin tans as protection from the sun. On the psychological level, a person may develop new competencies to meet an adjustive demand, or he may lower his level of aspiration so that he no longer feels a need to meet the demand. Such defenses, of course, are possible only when the stress is not overpowering and when the individual has enough time to shield himself from it or increase his adequacy—in either case to reduce the strain it causes. In general, however, the more prolonged the stress situation, the more severe the strain.

The severity of stress also depends on the relative importance of the need or needs be-

ing frustrated or the difficulty of the demand being made. Thus sexual frustration would probably not be as stressful to the individual as a threat to his basic value system. Severity of stress in this sense can be inferred in the laboratory by what an organism is willing to do to rid himself of the stress and by the persistency with which he does it.

The number and intensity of the pressures or the number and importance of the needs being frustrated also have a direct relationship to the severity of stress. An individual who is put into solitary confinement on a bread and water diet after seeing all the members of his family killed is under far more severe strain than he would be if any of these stresses had come separately. In this context it may be pointed out that blocking of one need may also prevent others from being met. For example, sexual satisfaction typically helps to meet status and self-esteem needs as well as physiological ones; hence sexual frustration may have implications for psychological stress that go far beyond the mere frustration of the biological drive.

Sometimes the effects of a series of minor frustrations are cumulative and lead to an overall result similar to that of one larger frustration. A husband may retain his composure through a long series of minor irritations or frustrations brought about by his wife only to explode in the face of a quite inconsequential final straw. The wife may be dumbfounded by the suddenness and violence of this seeming overreaction to such a minor frustration, not realizing that it represents the culmination of a long series of frustrations.

Similarly, a number of minor demands coming at the same time may be more stressful than one major demand to which we can give all our attention. In a high-pressure job, single problems or decisions may be well within our power, but the sheer number of problems and decisions to be dealt with each day greatly increases the strain factor and may overwhelm us.

Strength and equality of conflicting forces. In the case of conflict, the size of the problem depends largely on the strength and equality of the conflicting motives. Conflicts between weak motives or motives with little ego-involvement involve minimal strain, for usually it does not matter greatly to the individual which alternative he chooses. An example here would be having to decide between going to a dance and to a movie. On the other hand, conflicts between important needs or strong motives—such as having to choose between self-esteem and social approval—would subject the individual to much greater strain.

The comparative strength of the opposing forces is also a factor. If an individual finds guilt feelings over sexual misbehavior far more stressful than sexual frustration, the conflict will not be very severe since the decision required to resolve it will be made almost automatically. Where the conflicting forces involve strong motives or needs of about equal strength, however, severe frustration will ensue from either choice.

The attractiveness of a goal is not static and unchanging. Sometimes an obstacle seems to enhance its desirability. Having to meet in secret can make lovers' meetings seem more precious, and the knowledge that a girl is much sought after may enhance her attractiveness and hence increase the severity of the stress if one is turned down by her for a date. Also, the closer we get to a much-wanted goal, the more desirable it seems and the more we want it. But if there are negative aspects, they loom larger too. Thus, if a young man is ambivalent about getting married, both his eagerness and his fear will become more intense as the wedding date approaches, and the stress will mount accordingly.

Interestingly enough, in such a situation the two trends do not increase at the same rate. Typically, the avoidance gradient increases more sharply as the goal draws near, which helps to explain why many people experience a feeling of anxiety or near panic on their wedding day. Suddenly all the underlying doubts seem to well up out of proportion to the positive values, which have increased in attractiveness but not so rapidly. Where a goal has appreciable negative aspects, it may become an essentially negative goal as it comes within reach as shown below (Brown, 1948).

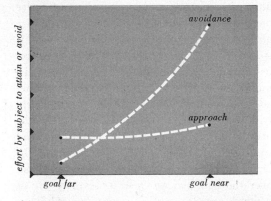

Unfamiliarity and suddenness of the problem. Frustrations, conflicts, and pressures that we have coped with successfully before may cause little stress or strain when we meet them again, for usually we can see a relatively painless way out on the basis of our past experience. But new problems which we have not anticipated, for which we have no ready-made approach, and in which the requirements of the situation may not be clearly understood can put us under severe strain. One reason major catastrophes are so overwhelming is that all one's usual "props" have disappeared and one's knowledge and skills seem totally inadequate and irrelevant to the task at hand. Any problem we do not know how to attack may pose a serious threat.

Individual Factors

Often situations that are acutely stressful for one person are not so stressful for another. The severity of the stress may depend as much on the individual as on the objective situation.

Degree of competence. When we think we can remove a cause of frustration or meet a demand on us with a little additional effort, well within our capacity, the stress is mild and we feel little or no strain. Getting acquainted in college is easier for a friendly, attractive girl than for a shy, unattractive one. The well-trained debater can organize an eloquent rebuttal while his opponent is speaking. A student who is failing a course because he has not studied enough may be under no great strain if he is confident that additional effort before the end of the term will enable him to pass. But when the demands on a person require maximum and sustained effort and he is not sure that he can make the grade, stress is severe. Whatever the problem we face, its severity for us depends partly on the degree to which we have the particular skills it requires. The greater our competence, the less severe the stress.

Interpretation of the problem. An even bigger factor than our actual competence or incompetence is our interpretation of the situation—what the problem is, how serious it is, and how it affects us. For example, we may see failure in a course as proof that we are too stupid for college work, as proof that we should study harder, or as proof that the instructor is unfair and prejudiced. We may see it as a catastrophe or as "just one of those things."

1. Assumptions and attitudes. Anyone's evaluation of a stress situation is dependent largely on his underlying assumptions and attitudes about himself and his world. Often we can see nothing in the life situation of a distraught individual sufficiently stressful to explain his defensiveness and discouragement. Yet to him life may seem intolerable. If he is convinced that he is inadequate and the world is a dangerous, unfriendly place, he is likely to worry constantly, no matter how favorable his actual situation and no matter how adequate his actual competencies. Every minor setback or failure makes him feel more helpless and makes life demands seem more overwhelming. On the other hand, the person who feels generally confident and optimistic (regardless of external realities) can see obstacles as challenges instead of threats and may feel little or no strain even when facing a difficult and complex demand.

2. Ego-involvement and threat. The severity of stress will depend to a large extent upon whether we view the situation as threatening to us or our worth. If we see it as involving a danger to our biological or psychological welfare, it is highly stressful. Otherwise, even though it calls for a skillful adjustment on our part, it is nonstressful or only mildly stressful. Our perception and judgment, or course, may be inaccurate, and the situation may in fact be more threatening than we realize. Thus shipwrecked sailors who think they are about to be rescued are not under such severe stress as they would be if they saw no hope of rescue; this is true whether or not rescue is actually near.

If the individual feels that his worth is at stake in the resolution of a problem, he experiences more stress than if he sees it simply as a requirement to be met, with no overtones of threat to his self-adequacy. For example, the boy who wants a date for a big dance but is turned down by a girl because she is going out of town for the week end with her parents does not experience this frustration as particularly ego-involved or threatening (even though she actually may have been glad of the excuse and might have turned him down anyway). But if she turns him down in order to go out with someone else, his feelings of adequacy and security are directly threatened and he is under considerable stress.

Some immature and anxious people experience an exaggerated self-reference in everything they do and must keep proving their worth to themselves and others. Such people find the world much more stressful than those without such pervasive self-awareness.

Stress tolerance. An additional factor in the individual that determines the severity of stress is his stress tolerance—how much he can take before the strain becomes so great that it seriously disrupts his integrated functioning. Both biologically and psychologically, we vary greatly as to the *amount* of frustration or conflict or pressure we can handle. Prolonged exertion and fatigue that would be only mildly stressful to a young person might prove fatal to someone older or in poor health. Likewise, emergencies, conflicts, and other life problems that one person can take in stride may quite incapacitate another.

Some people are so marginally adjusted that even a minor challenge can precipitate a serious disruption in biological or psychological functioning or both. Patients with serious coronary heart trouble may be endangered by even mild emotional upsets or slight physical fatigue. On a psychological level, if an individual has suffered from very faulty personality development or is in a highly stressful life situation, he may be so precariously adjusted that any increase in the total stress load results in the disorganization of psychological integrative processes and mental disorder. Any stress increase in this case is likely to be the straw that breaks the camel's back.

At the other extreme, there are many mature, capable, confident people who can withstand tremendous stress before they go to pieces. During World War II, approximately ninety per cent of all combat troops survived their battle experiences without showing serious signs of disintegration or becoming operationally ineffective. Yet the study of such combat situations suggests that all of us do have our breaking point—that in the face of severe cumulative stress, we all eventually would reach a point where our adjustive capacities would be inadequate and a process of serious disintegration would begin.

The cumulative effects of severe stresses are well brought out in the following excerpts from the diary of one of our fighting men on Guadalcanal (Stern, 1947, pp. 583-586). The excerpts cover a six-week period:

"Aug. 7, 1942. Convoy arrived at Guadalcanal Bay at approximately 4 A.M. in the morning. Ships gave enemy a heavy shelling. At 9 A.M. we stormed the beach and formed an immediate beachhead, a very successful landing, marched all day in the hot sun, and at night took positions and rested. Enemy planes attacked convoy in bay but lost 39 out of 40 planes.

"Aug. 8, 1942. Continued march in the hot sun and in afternoon arrived at airport. Continued on through the Jap village and made camp for the night. During the night, Jap navy attacked convoy in battle that lasted until early morning. Enemy had terrific losses and we lost two ships. This night while on sentry duty, I mistook a horse for a Jap and killed it.

"Aug. 19, 1942. Enemy cruiser and destroyer came into bay and shelled the beach for about two hours. The cruiser left and the destroyer hung around for the entire morning. We all kept under shelter for the early afternoon a flying fortress flew over, spotting the ship and bombed it, setting it afire we all jumped and shouted with joy. That night trouble again was feared and we again slept in foxholes.

"Aug. 21, 1942. The long waitɛd landing by the enemy was made during the night 1500 troops in all and a few prisoners were taken and the rest were, killed. Bodies were laying all over beach. In afternoon planes again bombed the Island. [Here the writing begins to be shaky, and less careful than previously.]

"Aug. 28, 1942. The company left this morning in higgins Boats to the end of the Island, landed and started through thick Jungle and hills. It was hot and we had to cut our way through. In afternoon we contacted the japs. our squad was in the assault squad so we moved up the beach to take positions the enemy trapped us with machine gun and rifle fire for about two hours. The lead was really flying. Two of our men were killed, two were hit by a hand greade and my corporal received a piece of shrampnel in back, —was wounded in arm, out of the squad of eight we had five causitry. We withdrew and were taken back to the Hospital.

"Sept. 12, 1942. Large jap squadron again bombed Island out of 35 planes sent over our air force knocked down 24. During the raid a large bomb was dropped just sevety yards from my fox hole.

"Sept. 13, 1942. At on o'clock three destroyers and one cruiser shelled us contumally all night. The ships turned surch lights all up and down the beach, and stopped one my foxhole seveal time I'm feeling pritty nervese and scared, afraid I'll be a nervas reack be for long. slept in fox hole all night not much sleep. This morning a 9:00 we had a nother air raid, the raid consisted of mostly fighter planes. I believe we got several, this afternoon. we had a nother raid, and our planes went out to met them, met them someplace over Tulagi, new came in that the aircraft carrier wasp sent planes out to intersept the bombers. This eving all hell

broke lose. Our marines contacted enemy to south of us and keep up constant fire all night through.

"Sept. 14, 1942. This morning firing still going on my company is scaduted to unload ships went half ways up to dock when enemyfire start on docks, were called back to our pososeion allon beach, company called out again to go after japs, hope were lucker than we were last time [part of this illegible.] Went up into hills at 4:00 P.M. found positions, at 7:00 en 8 sea planes fombed and strifed us, 151942 were strifed biy amfibious planes and bombed the concussion of one through me of balance and down a 52 foot hil. I was shaking likd a leaf. Lost my bayanut, and ran out of wathr. I nearves and very jumpy, hop I last out until morning. I hop sevearly machine s guns ore oping up on our left flank there going over our heads

"Sept. 16. this moring we going in to take up new possissons we march all moring and I am very week and nerves, we marched up a hill and ran in to the affaul place y and z company lost so many men I hardly new what I was doing then I'm going nuts.

"Sept. 17. don't remember much of this day.

"Sept. 18. Today I'm on a ship leaving this awful place, called Green Hell. I'm still nearves and shakey."

In general, the best guarantee of a high level of stress tolerance is personal maturity, with all this implies in terms of a realistic frame of reference, an integrated value system, and essential competencies. Such maturity and such capabilities give us the resources we need to solve most normal problems of living, although sometimes natural or man-made crises prove too much for the strongest of us.

We vary not only in the total amount of stress we can tolerate, but also in the particular *type of stress* to which we are most vulnerable. We each have our Achilles heel. We may be able to take criticism and failure but not social rejection, or prejudice and discrimination but not a situation in which we must turn out shoddy merchandise. Any situation is stressful that threatens whatever we have learned to base our feelings of adequacy upon or involves the loss of anything or anyone we closely identify with ourselves. Likewise, situations that reactivate earlier traumas or weak spots in our personality structure are usually particularly difficult for us to handle. For example, if we were starved for recognition and acceptance in childhood, we may be especially vulnerable to threats of disapproval in adulthood.

In summarizing the factors that determine the severity of stress, we may say, in general, that stress becomes more severe:

1. the longer the stress situation continues

2. the more important the need being frustrated or the more difficult the demands of a situation

3. the larger the number of frustrations or pressures

4. the stronger the opposing forces in a conflict and the more equal they are in strength

5. the closer one gets to the goal in an approach-avoidance conflict and the greater the relative strength of the avoidance gradient

6. the more unfamiliar and unexpected the problem

7. the less competent one feels (rightly or wrongly) to cope with the stress situation

8. the more threatening and ego-involving the problem seems to the individual

9. the less tolerance the individual has for problems of a given magnitude or type.

INDIVIDUAL STRESS PATTERNS

Stresses, like motives, usually do not come singly or operate independently of one another. The total stress pattern at any time determines the part any one stress will play and has much to do with how skillful we will be at resolving it. If a student's stress pattern includes fatigue, pressure toward winning a scholarship, a chemistry assignment that he cannot understand, and new competition for the affections of his best girl, he may decide to concentrate on winning back his girl and disregard his fatigue and his schoolwork in a way he would not do if all were well with his love life. At the same time, however, his fatigue may make him more irritable than usual and that plus his uneasiness about his undone schoolwork may make him seem moody and unappealing to his girl, so that his stress load is increased rather than lessened.

Stress Patterns
Are Unique and Changing

To understand any person's behavior, it is important to understand the unique stress pattern with which he is confronted. This pattern will vary in relation to his age, sex, occupation, economic status, special interests and talents, group memberships, and other personal and cultural conditions. The stress pattern of the child is different in many respects from that of an adult; that of the patient with an incurable illness differs from that of the healthy person. The soldier in combat has a different stress pattern from that of the civilian; the woman executive has somewhat different problems from those of a man. Even two similar people faced with the same stressful situation—for example, two middle-aged executives whose firms have gone bankrupt—may be affected quite differently, for each will perceive the situation somewhat uniquely and will have somewhat unique resources for meeting it.

Stress patterns, like motive patterns, change both from day to day and from one period of life to another. Your stress pattern is somewhat different today from what it was a week ago, and it is, as a whole, quite different this year from what it will be when your oldest child is about to be married.

Whatever the nature of the stress and however severe, the vicissitudes of living place all of us under some measure of stress a good deal of the time. Human life is full of frustrations, conflicts, and pressures, and some are never completely resolved. Often there is one key stress or a limited number of them that permeates the life of an individual, particularly his adult life. If we succeed in discovering these key stresses, we have gone a long way toward understanding his behavior. But in any case, mental health and effective functioning come not from lack of stress but from learning to cope with it and the problems it presents.

Stress Patterns May Be Unconscious

Stress patterns, like motive patterns, may not be entirely conscious. Although we are acutely aware of many frustrations, conflicts, and pressures, there are others of which we are only partially or intermittently aware and some that are completely below the level of consciousness. Just as the body may be invaded by microorganisms and may take defensive action against them without our awareness, so psychological needs may be frustrated and defensive behavior undertaken with no awareness or conscious choice on our part. Thus show-off behavior and negativism are usually defensive reactions to the frustration of needs for adequacy, social approval, and acceptance. In some cases, not only the defensive tactics but even the feelings of inferiority that prompt them are below the level of consciousness.

Even when conflict rather than simple need frustration is the problem, we find the same principles operating. The individual may be clearly aware of the nature of his conflict, as when he is trying to decide between two jobs, or the conflict may involve lesser degrees of awareness or actually be unconscious. We shall shortly see how ego defense mechanisms make this possible.

The example given in the last chapter of the hypnotically induced conflict (p. 144) shows dramatically how behavior may be affected by stress of which we are quite unaware. In this case the subject's artificially induced attitudes toward the experimenter functioned on an unconscious level in much the same way as do many of our assumptions and attitudes. Many of us have unconscious attitudes toward sexual behavior, authority demands, marriage, and other life situations that conflict with our conscious wishes and ideas. Unconscious conflicts make intelligible much behavior that on the surface seems irrational or incomprehensible.

SOME EFFECTS OF STRESS

The human system under stress is faced with an adjustive demand that must be met if integrated functioning is not to be impaired. In the next two chapters we shall examine the various possible solutions that may be tried and the effective or ineffective behavior patterns that may emerge. For the moment, however, we will establish a broad background for this discussion by outlining some of the general ways in which stress typically influences behavior.

Characteristic Patterns of Response

As we have seen, stress comes as an interference with ongoing or contemplated action. A motivated individual encounters some obstacle or conflict or other complication to his pursuit of his goal. Sometimes, especially in mild stress or stress that is not ego-involved, the energy that is mobilized is channeled into an increased effort toward the original goal; the problem is solved and the goal is reached. In general, however, some of the individual's attention and energy is diverted from the original goal to defense against the stress itself.

Although many other factors enter in to determine the course of action actually taken, each of the three general types of stress we have discussed tends to induce a characteristic pattern of response.

Some typical responses to frustration. With sustained or seemingly inescapable frustration, the individual tends to reduce the stress by lowering his level of aspiration, accepting whatever goals and satisfactions he can attain. An individual who has been subjected to prolonged semistarvation may eat insects, bark off trees, and practically any other substitute that has nutritional value or tends to assuage his hunger pangs. One of the men in the ill-fated Greeley expedition to the arctic (p. 27) even ate his sealskin boots. In a somewhat similar way, a frustrated individual may tend toward symbolic satisfaction, such as staring at pin-up pictures in lieu of the real thing or gaining some satisfaction from fantasies about the desired goal object.

Of course, the extent to which the individual will accept such substitute and symbolic goals will depend on the character and strength of the barrier and on his motivation, values, and stress tolerance. He is particularly likely to accept substitute goals when the barrier seems insurmountable or requires more effort and sacrifice than the goal appears to warrant.

Some typical responses to conflict. In conflict situations the individual faces all the stress of inevitable frustration plus the stress

COMMON REACTIONS TO STRESS

Reactions to Frustration	*Reactions to Conflict*	*Reactions to Pressure*
Acceptance of substitute goals	Vacillation, indecision	Resistance
Lowered aspiration	Anxiety, discouragement	Defiance, destructiveness
Restricted field of operation	Postponement of decision	Dawdling, helplessness (in children)
Apathy, regression	Inability to accept either alternative whole-heartedly	Increased effort, physical and psychological strain
Fantasy, symbolic satisfactions	Escape through sickness or divertive activities	Apathy, fantasy

of trying to reach a good decision. It is hardly surprising that people in conflict tend to vacillate and be indecisive in a vain effort to avoid the frustration of either choice. The girl who is trying to choose which of two eligible men to marry—one exciting and fun to be with but somewhat irresponsible and the other steady and dependable but a bit dull—may find herself deciding on first one and then the other, perhaps not even seeing the possibility that neither one would make her happy.

The more equally matched the alternatives, the harder the decision. And when the conflict involves serious consequences—where the outcome is very important in terms of our values, needs, and purposes, as when we are considering marriage or an investment of our life's savings—we may hold back on a decision until we are quite sure of the consequences. Where the decision has to be made at once, tension and anxiety mount accordingly, and the integrative functioning of the organism may be seriously impaired.

Sometimes, however, we actually use a conflict as a means of preventing the frustration that would come if we resolved it. We may even carefully keep the alternatives equally strong and contrive *not* to make a decision or to keep postponing it, thereby gaining some of the attractive features of both choices and not having to give up either one entirely.

Sometimes, too, even when a choice is made, it is not a complete, whole-hearted one. Mary may decide to marry George instead of Bill but may not accept George completely: she may reject certain mannerisms and wish he had Bill's sense of humor. When this happens, the conflict is not yet wholly resolved and unhappiness lies ahead.

Some typical responses to pressure. In general, the individual tends to resist pressures on him from external sources. Children often develop highly effective techniques of resistance in coping with perfectionistic parents or teachers. Destructiveness, defiance, and rebelliousness are active forms of resistance, but there are passive forms too. Children who dawdle or remain helpless, refusing to take normal steps toward independence and self-reliance, are often using this behavior to resist parental pressures. Again and again people in authority have found pressure an ineffective means of achieving their goals because it has induced resistance rather than cooperation.

Pressures on a group also tend to elicit resistance, active or passive. Workers may resist a speed-up by petitions to the management or by a slow-down or excessive absenteeism. A class of fourth-graders may resist pressures toward unrealistic quietness and neatness by apathy, by flagrant disregard of the rules, by scapegoating, or by putting tacks on the teacher's chair or hiding a snake in her drawer. Gandhi's India used passive resistance tellingly in its struggle against English rule.

Even where the pressures stem from the individual's own aspirations and motives he may have to keep driving himself mercilessly to achieve his goals. The inner maintenance tendencies of the system appear to resist and oppose excessive pressure on the system whether it originates from within or without.

Commandeering of Cognitive Processes

We have already seen the ways motives can interfere with perception and thought processes. Stress carries this interference and distortion still further.

Narrowing and distortion of perception. In general, stress tends to narrow the perceptual field. The individual tends to withdraw his attention from other areas of the field and to concentrate on the stressful part of it, thus limiting the field to which he can be responsive. Combs (1952) emphasizes both the narrowing and the rigidity of perception under stress. The individual who sees himself in jeopardy tries to hold onto what he has, including his perceptual patterns. It is difficult or impossible for him while under serious stress to reinterpret a situation or see new factors and relationships in it. Disagreements between unions and management and between nations often show this narrowing and rigidity of perception under perceived threat.

Studies with animal subjects have shown that even when the stress situation is changed and new possibilities of solution are made available, the animal that has been under severe stress may not see the new possibilities and instead may continue to follow a rigid, stereotyped, less satisfactory adjustive pattern (Maier, 1949). Other studies have shown that people with a high level of anxiety tend to be rigid and inflexible and to approach new problems in a more stereotyped way than people whose general anxiety level is lower (Cowen, 1952a, 1952b; Jones, 1954). High anxiety is not conducive to creative imagination.

This narrowing of the perceptual field probably explains why people in the throes of a difficult conflict often are unaware of much that is going on around them. They have focused their major attention and energies inward on their conflict and in this sense have withdrawn from the surrounding world. In extreme form this process can be seen in the psychotic patient who is completely preoccupied with his inner world and literally out of contact with the world around him.

Another general effect of stress is a tendency toward distortion of the perceptual field. For example, an individual who feels under pressure from parental demands may become so sensitized to this particular pressure that he sees pressure even in the most permissive parental behavior and also in chance remarks by others where no pressure was intended.

Sometimes the individual manages to protect himself from what would be a stressful situation by perceiving it in a distorted way. With somewhat ambiguous, unstructured stimuli it would not be surprising to find an individual's attitudes distorting his perceptions. But even a quite clear, unambiguous situation can be misinterpreted in this way. Lazarsfeld (1947, pp. 18-19) reports an interesting example of such distortion in the case of a series of cartoons designed to reduce prejudice:

"The purpose of these cartoons was to caricature the intolerance exhibited by Mr. Biggott in a variety of situations. For instance, he was shown refusing to employ an American Indian because he did not like "foreigners and immigrants." In another cartoon, he was pictured standing in a cemetery in which soldiers of the recent war had been buried; in the caption he expressed indignation that Italian and Jewish and good Anglo-Saxon soldiers were buried without proper segregation. Another cartoon showed him on his sickbed, refusing a blood transfusion from anyone but a sixth-generation American.

"A number of people to whom the cartoons had been shown were interviewed to learn how the general reader would respond. Many people had no difficulty understanding the meaning and intent of the cartoons. But a large number of respondents, who, we know from other sources, were intolerant, misinterpreted the cartoon series and so avoided applying its message to themselves. For example, a man with strong isolationist tendencies said that the cemetery scene showed that Mr. Biggott was indignant that so many people had been killed in the war. An anti-Semitic worker interpreted the sickbed scene as demonstrating how rotten the capitalists are: They need special blood for a transfusion. Another respondent considered this cartoon a caricature of up-starts; he himself was a tenth-generation American while the fellow in the cartoon who was making the fuss was only a sixth-generation American.

"Often people turn tolerance propaganda upside down to protect their own prejudices.

When an anti-Semitic respondent was asked who he thought created the Mr. Biggott cartoons, he had a simple answer: some organization that wanted to show that a lot of people dislike Jews so that the rest of the public would feel freer to express their own hostility towards Jews."

If the respondents had perceived the situation more accurately, it would have been

STRESS AND COGNITIVE FUNCTIONS

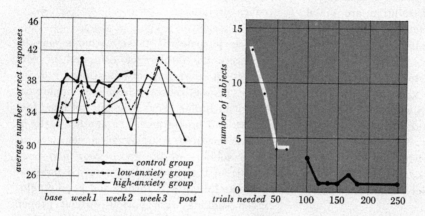

Studies have repeatedly shown that perception, judgment, learning, and remembering are impaired under stress. In one study, for example, air force trainees were given an accuracy-of-perception test daily during three stressful weeks of intense training in parachute jumping (above, left). Not only did they perceive less accurately than a control group, but those found by other criteria to be highest in anxiety made the most errors of all (Korchin and Basowitz, 1954). The same external frustration or pressure, however, may seriously disrupt one person's learning and not another's, depending on their levels of stress tolerance. In another study, college student subjects of comparable ability were frustrated by fifty trials on an unsolvable discrimination problem, then tested on the number of trials needed to learn a solvable one (above, right). The subjects seemed to divide into two groups: three fourths of them (white line) showed unimpaired learning; but the other fourth, as a group (black line), needed almost four times as many trials, and a few were unable to learn at all. Most of this latter group also showed self-deprecation, aggression, inflexibility, discouragement, or other behavioral signs of frustration (Marquart and Arnold, 1952). Evidently their stress tolerance was exceeded.

threatening to their attitudes of prejudice; therefore they unconsciously contrived to defend themselves from such a stress by seeing the situation in a "safer" way.

Hampered reasoning. An individual under stress finds that his reasoning is hampered both by the narrowing and rigidity of perception already discussed and by the disruption of coordination that typically accompanies strong emotion. If the stress is severe, he is likely to resort to fixed, stereotyped, irrational patterns. In fact, we may generalize to the extent of stating that *as stress increases, imaginative, objective thinking and adaptive efficiency decrease.* Ultimately, heavy, long-continued stress leads to fragmented, deviate, and disintegrated thought processes—the integration of the system breaks down.

In some individuals, sustained or very severe stress appears to lead to chemical changes in the blood that further impair the ability to think in an integrated manner. In fact, a disorganization and fragmentation of thought processes characteristic of schizophrenia can even be induced temporarily in normal people by injection of strong drugs such as lysergic acid or mescaline. We shall examine the implications of such chemical changes in more detail in Chapter 7.

Arousal of Emotion

Since stress represents an actual or potential source of danger to the organism, it tends to lead to a general increase in tension and some measure of emotional mobilization for emergency action. The degree of emotionality elicited is roughly equivalent to the severity of the perceived threat.

The problem of emotional mobilization. In an emergency there are a number of physiological changes: the muscles tense, the adrenal glands are activated, the heart quickens its beat, and extra sugar is dumped into the blood to provide added energy for fight or flight. But these changes, helpful under primitive conditions, are not so adaptive for modern man in his complex society, where both physical fight and physical flight may be out of the question. So modern man mobilized for emergency action must solve not only the original problem but the added one produced by all the physiological changes of emotion.

Studies show that with mild stress there is an increased alertness and sensitization to outer conditions that may actually improve the efficiency of behavior, whereas with moderately severe stress the individual tends to become less task-centered and more defensive, less flexible in his perceptions and approaches, and less skillful in his acts. Under very severe stress, his skills may break down altogether. Both physical and psychological functioning are affected, and control and organization of behavior are disrupted.

If emergencies were few and well spaced, we might be able to cope with the extra tension without too much strain and soon get back on an even keel. Sometimes, as we have seen, we even develop a resistance to certain stresses somewhat as we develop immunity to certain bacteria. But for most of us, emergency piles on emergency, and we are almost constantly under pressure and subject to frustration and conflict of some sort. If we feel generally competent to meet these emergencies, the emotional mobilization may be slight and easily handled—just enough to keep us on our toes. But if we keep feeling really threatened, our whole system will keep responding accordingly, and we will be in a state of chronic emotional mobilization. This can have serious consequences, for not only is there constant interference with our ability to solve problems effectively but our bodily equipment itself may suffer from the continued strain. Many psychosomatic ailments have their origin in chronic emotional mobilization.

Different stresses elicit different emotional patterns. Although any stress involves emotional mobilization, the particular pattern is characteristically different for the different forms of stress.

1. Frustration tends to arouse hostility. When someone blocks our efforts, our first reaction is likely to be one of anger whether we show it overtly or not. Thus if we feel we have a good case for getting our grade raised from a C to a B but meet with refusal from our instructor, we are likely to feel anger and resentment toward him.

In a more primitive world, our impulse would be to attack and destroy an obstacle to our goal, but in our civilized world we usually must keep our anger under control. Instead of direct action we may have fantasies about what we would like to do, like getting the instructor fired, or we may work off some of our hostility by telling all our friends what a heel he is. But the important point is that situations, people, or events that get in the way of something we want tend to elicit feelings of hostility in us and impulses toward an aggressive response.

2. Specific dangers tend to arouse fear. Specific dangers that appear to be potentially beyond our defensive powers may elicit fear rather than anger and may induce flight or withdrawal behavior. Thus we may fear the possibility of flunking a test, of being turned down for a date by a very attractive girl, of financial losses stemming from our investments, and so on. And when the possibility becomes a probable or actual danger, the fear reaction is almost certain to occur.

Often we also hate the things we fear, since the feared situation implies the likelihood of frustration. Thus a person in authority who is feared may be cordially hated as well, although we may be careful to conceal both feelings for fear of retaliation.

The degree of fear elicited by the danger will have much to do with the direction and quality of the behavior induced. In the face of intense fear, the individual may panic or freeze and become unable to function in an organized manner at all.

3. Undefined threats tend to arouse anxiety. Whereas a specific danger usually elicits fear, a danger that we cannot pin down and define tends to elicit anxiety. Commonly, too, fear is elicited by an external danger and anxiety by an internal one which is so vague that the individual senses danger but is not sure of its exact nature. For example, if an individual has repressed homosexual desires, he may feel anxiety whenever they threaten to break through into overt behavior or even into consciousness, but being unaware of his repressed desires he will not know what is making him anxious. In the same way, repressed hostility toward a parent or child may give rise to a vague anxiety from time to time. Such anxiety is a subjective warning of danger, but the individual is at a loss to know what the danger is. Approach-avoidence conflicts in which the elements are not clearly delineated are especially potent sources of anxiety.

Breakdown Under Excessive Stress

The effects of sustained stress on the human system vary considerably depending upon whether the system is able to lessen the stress in some way or raise its stress tolerance. If the stress proves excessive and cannot be escaped, it leads to a breakdown of the system.

The general-adaptation-syndrome. A theoretical approach that helps to explain the effects of continued stress on the human system has been formulated by the prominent endocrinologist, Hans Selye (1956).[1] According to Selye's theory, the organism's reaction to severe, unresolved stress occurs in three

[1] For a discussion by Selye of some of the implications of his stress theory, see page 486.

major stages: the *alarm reaction,* the *stage of resistance,* and the *stage of exhaustion.*

1. The alarm reaction. The alarm reaction is a call-to-arms to the body's defense forces in the face of biological or psychological stress. The alarm reaction consists of various biochemical changes mediated primarily by the autonomic nervous system which mobilize the organism's bodily defenses. The emergency mobilization already discussed is part of this process.

The initial physiological changes in response to stress tend to have much the same characteristics regardless of the nature of the stress. This accounts for the similarity of the general symptoms (such as fever, fatigue, and loss of appetite) of people suffering from different specific illnesses. Selye uses the term *general stress reaction* to refer to these changes.

2. The stage of resistance. If the stressful situation continues, the alarm stage is typically followed by the stage of resistance in which the system evidently "learns" how to adapt to the particular stress, and the symptoms that occurred during the alarm stage disappear even though the stress continues. This resistance is achieved largely through increased activity of the anterior pituitary and the adrenal cortex, though more specific adaptations may also be made in blood chemistry, nutrition, or other processes. For example, continued exposure to lowered oxygen content in the air gradually results in an adaptation that permits subjects to perform work at high altitudes which would have been impossible at the beginning.

During the stage of resistance, most of the symptoms which occurred during the alarm reaction disappear, and physiological processes seem to resume normal functioning. If successful adaptation is achieved in this stage, the individual can cope with the stress over a considerable period of time. Sometimes, however, the hormonal defenses overshoot their mark and lead to bodily damage and pathology such as ulcers or other "diseases of adaptation."

EFFECTS OF ANXIETY

Slight Anxiety	*Moderate Anxiety*	*Severe Anxiety*
General alerting	Less spontaneity	Organization of behavior breaks down
Increased sensitivity to outside events	Rigidity, reliance on "safe" habitual responses	Inability to distinguish between safe and harmful stimuli
Physiological mobilization	Reduced ability to improvise	Stereotyped, unadaptive, random-appearing patterns
Effective integration of behavior	More effort needed to maintain adequate behavior	Irritability, distractability
Increase in ability for productive behavior	Narrowing and distortion of perception	Impaired learning, thinking

These generalizations are drawn from many studies including Cannon, 1939; Liddell, 1944; Combs, 1952; Ausubel and others, 1953; Basowitz and others, 1955.

3. The stage of exhaustion. If the stress continues too long or becomes too severe or if the organism is unable to make an effective adaptation during the stage of resistance, the bodily defenses eventually break down, leading to a stage of exhaustion. The anterior pituitary and the adrenal cortex are no longer able to continue secreting their hormones at the increased rate, so that there is a lowering in stress tolerance and a breakdown of whatever adaptation has been achieved. Now many of the symptoms which appeared during the alarm reaction begin to reappear, and the integration of the system is seriously impaired. Further exposure to the stress leads eventually to disintegration and death.

When the stress represents a threat to the self-structure rather than to the body, various psychological defenses are mustered in addition to the physiological ones described by Selye. Thus, the individual may be able to develop resistance to a psychological stress by learning new competencies or increasing his stress tolerance in other constructive ways. Or he may be able to erect defenses stable enough to protect him fairly well from the threat and allow him to maintain coordinated functioning. But any heavy, long-continued stress takes its toll, and eventually it may exceed his adjustive resources. This sequence, with final breakdown, was shown in the Guadalcanal diary reproduced on pages 161-162.

Disintegration on the psychological level is called *decompensation.* The various mental disorders to which it may lead are discussed in Chapter 7.

Adaptation to stress is expensive. Sustained stress, even when it is not excessive, is expensive in (1) reducing our resistance to other stress and (2) using up irreplaceable reserves.

Selye (1950) found that in building up resistance to one stress, the organism typically suffers a lowering of tolerance to other stresses. For example, mice exposed to extremes of cold develop increased resistance to the cold but become unusually sensitive to x-rays. Similarly, soldiers who develop resistance to combat may show a lowering of tolerance for other stresses such as being bossed by superior officers or getting bad news from home. It may be that the defensive resources of the system are limited and that if they are thrown into one area of battle they are not available for coping with other stresses. This would help to explain how sustained psychological stress can lower biological resistance to disease, and how sustained bodily illness can lower psychological resistance so that the individual overreacts to even minor frustrations, conflicts, and pressures.

With sustained or very severe stress there may be a considerable amount of irreversible wear and tear on the system. In Selye's words (1956, pp. 274-275):

"Many people believe that, after they have exposed themselves to very stressful activities, a rest can restore them to where they were before. This is false. Experiments on animals have clearly shown that each exposure leaves an indelible scar, in that it uses up reserves of adaptability which cannot be replaced. It is true that immediately after some harassing experience, rest can restore us almost to the original level of fitness by eliminating acute fatigue. But the emphasis is on the word *almost.* Since we constantly go through periods of stress and rest during life, just a little deficit of adaptation energy every day adds up—it adds up to what we call *aging.*

"Apparently, there are *two kinds of adaptation energy:* the superficial kind, which is ready to use, and the deeper kind, which acts as a sort of frozen reserve. When superficial adaptation energy is exhausted during

Rats repeatedly subjected to stress by being turned in the revolving drum above developed many signs of pathology. Blood vessels in the intestine (a) became greatly thickened (b), contributing to high blood pressure. The adrenal glands, normally small and yellow (c), became enlarged and brown (d). Other changes included a wasted thymus and stomach ulcers (Constantinides and Carey, 1949).

exertion, it can slowly be restored from a deeper store during rest. This gives a certain plasticity to our resistance. It also protects us from wasting adaptation energy too lavishly in certain foolish moments, because acute fatigue automatically stops us. It is the restoration of the superficial adaptation energy from the deep reserves that tricks us into believing that the loss has been made good. Actually, it has only been covered from reserves—and at the cost of depleting reserves. We might compare this feeling of having suf-

fered no loss to the careless optimism of a spendthrift who keeps forgetting that whenever he restores the vanishing supply of dollars in his wallet by withdrawing from the invisible stocks of his bank account, the loss has not really been made good: there was merely a transfer of money from a less accessible to a more accessible form.

". . . Due to the great advances made by classic medicine during the last half century, premature death caused by specific disease-producers (microbes, malnutrition, etc.) has declined at a phenomenal rate. As a result of this, the *average human life-span* increased in the United States from 48 years in 1900 to 69.8 years in 1956. . . . An ever-increasing proportion of the human population dies from the so-called wear-and-tear diseases, or degenerative diseases, which are primarily due to stress."

Thus it behooves us all to learn to deal effectively with stress. Muddling through is more costly than most people realize.

In this chapter we have seen that stress is inescapable; good adjustment consists in coping with it successfully. Although any adjustive demand is actually a stress and results in *some* degree of strain, we are here calling *stressful* only those situations that put the individual under *appreciable* strain —that could seriously disrupt his functioning if not resolved.

Stresses we all meet are frustrations, conflicts, and pressures. In every case the severity of stress is determined not only by the characteristics of the adjustive demand itself but by the way the individual perceives it and by the resources he has for meeting it. The importance of a given stress also depends on the whole stress pattern. No two people face the same pattern of stresses even in the same external situation. Stress and the defenses against it may be partly or wholly unconscious.

If a stress is seen as a threat, the individual may focus on defending himself from the threat rather than on reaching his original goal. Cognitive processes are commandeered and distorted in this effort, and the physiological changes that accompany emotional mobilization may be more disruptive than helpful. With severe, long-continued stress, on either the physiological or the psychological level, the individual may pass through an *alarm stage*, in which defenses are mobilized and various symptoms of disturbance appear; a *stage of resistance*, in which an equilibrium of sorts is regained and symptoms disappear; and a *stage of exhaustion*, with a reappearance of symptoms and a gradual breakdown of integrated functioning. While we are resisting one stress, our ability to resist other stresses is apparently weakened.

With this background we are now ready to examine how the human organism copes with its problems of adjustment. The next two chapters will discuss the dynamics of adjustive behavior and some of the effective and ineffective forms it may take.

REFERENCES

The following list includes both the references cited in this chapter and a selected number of additional books and articles for outside reading.

Ausubel, David P., Herbert M. Schiff, and Morton Goldman. 1953. "Qualitative Characteristics in the Learning Process Associated with Anxiety." *The Journal of Abnormal and Social Psychology, 48,* 537-547.

Basowitz, Harold, and others. 1955. *Anxiety and Stress: An Interdisciplinary Study of a Life Situation.* New York: McGraw-Hill Book Company, Inc.

Brown, Judson S. 1948. "Gradients of Approach and Avoidance Responses and Their Relation to Level of Motivation." *Journal of Comparative and Physiological Psychology, 41,* 450-465.

Cannon, Walter Bradford. 1939. *Wisdom of the Body.* New York: W. W. Norton & Company, Inc.

Combs, Arthur. 1952. "Intelligence from a Perceptual Point of View." *The Journal of Abnormal and Social Psychology, 47,* 662-673.

Constantinides, P. C., and Niall Carey. 1949. "The Alarm Reaction." *Scientific American, 180,* No. 3, 20-23.

Cooper, Eunice, and Marie Jahoda. 1947. "The Evasion of Propaganda: How Prejudiced People Respond to Anti-Prejudice Propaganda." *Journal of Psychology, 23,* 15-25.

Cowen, E. L. 1952a. "The Influence of Varying Degrees of Psychological Stress on Problem-Solving Rigidity." *The Journal of Abnormal and Social Psychology, 47,* 512-519.

Cowen, E. L. 1952b. "Stress Reduction and Problem-Solving Rigidity." *Journal of Consulting Psychology, 16,* 425-428.

Davis, Stanley W. 1956. "Stress in Combat." *Scientific American, 194,* No. 3, 31-35.

Fromm, Erich. 1955. *The Sane Society.* New York: Rinehart & Company, Inc.

Horney, Karen. 1950. Neurosis and Human Growth. New York: W. W. Norton & Company, Inc.

Jones, L. C. T. 1954. "Frustration and Stereotyped Behavior in Human Subjects." *Quarterly Journal of Experimental Psychology, 6,* 12-20.

Korchin, Sheldon J., and Harold Basowitz. 1954. "Perceptual Adequacy in a Life Stress." *Journal of Psychology, 38,* 495-502.

Lazarsfeld, Paul. 1947. "Some Remarks on the Role of the Mass Media in So-Called Tolerance Propaganda." *Journal of Social Issues, 3,* 17-25.

Lazarus, R. S., and R. W. Baker. 1957. "Motivation and Personality in Psychological Stress." *Psychological Newsletter, 8,* 159-193.

Liddell, H. S. 1944. "Conditioned Reflex Method and Experimental Neurosis." *Personality and Behavior Disorders,* Vol. I. J. McV. Hunt, ed. New York: The Ronald Press Company.

Maier, N. R. F. 1949. *Frustration.* New York: McGraw-Hill Book Company, Inc.

Marquart, Dorothy I., and Patricia L. Arnold. 1952. "A Study in the Frustration of Human Adults." *Journal of General Psychology, 47,* 43-63.

Pronko, N. H., and W. R. Leith. 1956. "Behavior Under Stress: A Study of Its Disintegration." *Psychological Reports, 2,* 205-222.

Selye, Hans. 1950. *The Physiology and Pathology of Exposure to Stress.* Montreal: Acta, Inc.

Selye, Hans. 1953. "The General-Adaptation-Syndrome in Its Relationships to Neurology, Psychology, and Psychopathology." *Contributions Toward Medical Psychology,* Vol. I. Arthur Weider, ed. New York: The Ronald Press Company.

Selye, Hans. 1956. *The Stress of Life.* New York: McGraw-Hill Book Company, Inc. Copyright © 1956 by Hans Selye. By permission of McGraw-Hill Book Company, Inc., and Longmans Green & Co. Ltd., London.

Sharma, Sohan Lal. 1955. "Personality Under Stress—Survey of Literature." *Journal of Education and Psychology, 13,* 143-154.

Stern, Robert L. 1947. "Diary of a War Neurosis." *Journal of Nervous and Mental Diseases, 106,* 583-586.

THE DYNAMICS
OF ADJUSTIVE
BEHAVIOR

General Principles of Behavior

"Processing" Stress Situations

Patterns of Adjustive Response

The Use of Feedback Information

All behavior—successful, unsuccessful, wise, foolish, flexible, rigid—is an attempt by the organism to meet the demands facing it, or perceived as facing it. Behavior, in other words, is an attempt to *adjust*. The requirements we try to meet may stem primarily from within (demands for food, rest, affection, understanding, personal accomplishment) or from without (demands for group cooperation, obedience to law, adherence to custom). Depending upon the nature of the demand and our resources for meeting it, we may solve a problem of adjustment easily and effectively—or we may experience considerable stress and, even after sustained effort, meet it with only partial success. In some cases a demand may exceed our adjustive adequacy altogether.

Unfortunately, problems of adjustment do not stand in line and present themselves one at a time. They crowd in upon us, competing for our attention and often getting in each other's way. Thus we are usually trying to meet several demands at the same time. While we are working to earn a living, we may be planning a badly needed vacation, worrying about financial or marital problems, striving to get a promotion, and so on. And even though some of our problems may be solved or may simply disappear with time, others persist, and new problems are constantly arising.

Although this chapter will sometimes discuss a bit of behavior as if it were an isolated act, behavior in actual fact is multiple and continuous. It is usually impossible to pinpoint the beginning or end of an adjustive action, and actions to meet different requirements may be so intertwined that they cannot be separately identified.

GENERAL PRINCIPLES OF BEHAVIOR

Before looking more closely at the actual dynamics of adjustment, we can improve our perspective by re-emphasizing some fundamental principles of behavior—that it is holistic, that it may be relatively conscious or unconscious and automatic, and that it has both inner and outer determinants.

Behavior Is Holistic

An organism develops as a unit and behaves as a unit. Just as arms and legs develop not at random or independently but in keeping with a centrally controlled pattern, so individual psychological processes (perceiving, imagining, remembering, thinking, desiring, feeling) are coordinated with the organism's efforts to meet adjustive demands. The behavior of a healthy organism is not a series of disconnected activities but a unified action, directed toward definite goals. And depending on the activity of the moment, there are variations in such things as the organism's threshold of sensitivity (to sounds, lights, or pain, and so on). A cat watching a mouse hole, for example, is less sensitive than usual to other stimuli. On D-day in World War II one of our paratroopers, frantically cutting himself loose from the tangled lines of his parachute, slashed off the end of his own thumb without feeling it, not realizing until later what he had done. Our threshold of sensitivity is not absolute but shifts, depending on what else is occupying our attention, the degree of stress at the moment, what we have just been doing and are trying to do, and what we are looking for. In the same way, other physiological and psychological processes "go" or "stop," speed up or slow down, depending on the need of the moment and on the overall activity of the organism.

Since all our adjustive behavior must use the same bodily equipment—sense organs, muscles, glands, nervous system, and so on—the overall adjustive demand of the moment determines how it will be used. If there are several competing demands, the one that is most important at the moment commandeers the organism's adjustive resources: certain functions or actions are *inhibited* while others are *facilitated*. This is readily illustrated by the emergency reaction, in which digestion and other bodily processes that are not immediately essential to survival stop or slow down while the organism's resources for increased activity and effort are mobilized—muscle tonus increases, stored sugar goes into the blood stream, adrenalin is secreted. Similarly, on a psychological level a certain desire or impulse may be given immediate and direct expression, or may be inhibited until a more appropriate time, or may be suppressed and pushed out of consciousness each time it appears. If a desire seriously threatens the individual's sense of psychological well-being—as, for example, sexual desires sometimes do—it may be entirely screened out of consciousness by the mechanism of repression. In general, facilitating and inhibiting controls provide the organism with a necessary flexibility in dealing with stress, enabling it to mobilize its resources to meet the most crucial demand of the moment as effectively as possible.

Only under unusual or pathological conditions does the organism function segmentally rather than as an integrated unit. A person threatened with starvation may steal to obtain food, though this may violate his self-concept and his pattern of values. Under the threat of torture and possible death, a prisoner of war may allow himself to betray fellow prisoners. Segmental actions may also occur as a consequence of interference with the integrating

functions of the higher brain centers, which normally inhibit any behavior—such as the uncontrolled expression of sexual impulses or of hostility—that would not be in accord with the individual's value structure. This inhibiting function of the brain may be reduced in mental illness or under the influence of alcohol or drugs. Under usual circumstances, however, the organism is able to inhibit segmental actions in the interests of overall maintenance and actualization, and the acts that forward these overall goals are the ones selected (Goldstein, 1939). The alternative would be disorganized behavior which would disable the individual just as surely as a football team would be disabled if each player did as he pleased instead of functioning as a member of a coordinated team.

Not only do the goals and needs of the whole organism affect the functioning of the parts, but the intactness and efficiency of the parts determine the quality of behavior as a whole. A defective or damaged brain limits the learning and thinking that the individual can carry on. Debilitating illness or fatigue renders him an easy prey to other stresses. On the other hand, a high level of intelligence, emotional stability, relevant skills, and self-confidence give him a better than average ability to meet adjustive demands.

Behavior is also holistic in the sense that a problem of adjustment on either the physiological or psychological level can evoke defenses and impair functioning on the other level. Thus, a soldier terrified at the prospect of combat may become hysterically blind on the day of departure for the front. A harried executive may get ulcers. The recovery of a tuberculosis patient may depend as much on his attitude as on the physical treatment he gets. Allergies may be aggravated by emotional tensions. A brain-damaged patient may develop hallucinations or other symptoms of mental illness. The human organism, despite almost incredible specialization of its parts, functions as a unit: stress, of whatever origin, threatens the whole organism, and both biological and psychological processes are affected.

Behavior May Be
Conscious or Unconscious

The concepts of conscious and unconscious represent the extremes of a continuum of awareness which ranges from sharp focusing of attention at one end to total unawareness (and inaccessibility to awareness) at the other. The behavior by which we attempt to meet adjustive demands may fall anywhere on this continuum: it may be undertaken with full and conscious intent, with only partial awareness, or with no conscious involvement at all. In many ways, our potentials for automatic and conscious functioning represent complementary resources for adjustive behavior.

Kinds of automatic functioning. We have already noted how, in an emergency, our bodily processes are automatically mobilized for action. Other examples of automatic functioning on the biological level are: constancy of blood composition, temperature regulation, repair and replacement of damaged tissue, and other routine maintenance processes. Over a period of time we also adapt automatically to changes in such conditions as altitude, climate, and amount or kind of activity. We even build new antibodies to fight new kinds of invading germs.

Automatic functioning on the psychological level may be habitual behavior like walking, dressing, or eating with a fork, which was once conscious and deliberate but has become so routine that it no longer requires our attention. Another kind of automatic functioning is our use of unconscious defenses against threats to our self-structures. Seeing what we want to see, screening out or distorting threatening ideas, and repressing painful experiences are all examples of automatic, largely unconscious processes.

Needless to say, the automatic processes, though potentially a boon in taking care of routine situations so that our attention is freed for solving more important problems, may not always be suited to the jobs they are allotted. Thus we may judge as "routine" a marital situation that really needs our most concerted and creative efforts. Often, too, we learn ineffective habits but never question their utility, or we carry once useful habits over into new situations where they are no longer appropriate. When a person is not making a satisfactory adjustment to life's problems, it is time for him to examine and analyze his automatic patterns of behavior.

Conscious efforts to adjust. To survive in our complicated, ever changing environment, we must constantly modify our behavior to meet new demands. On the physiological level, as we have noted, the organism adapts automatically to many kinds of change. But on the psychological level we must rely largely upon conscious machinery and must exercise our capacities for learning, reasoning, and imagination. Thus we analyze the unique features in a new situation and either tailor our routine responses to fit the circumstances or develop new ideas and new competencies. By exercising our powers of reason and imagination, we can go far beyond what we have actually experienced to grasp new relationships and invent new devices. With our capacity to see cause-and-effect relationships, we can also analyze the results of our adjustive efforts and, if necessary, modify our behavior to correct our errors.

Man's advantage over lower species rests largely on this ability to attack problems analytically and to modify his behavior, with conscious intent, to meet changing demands. To the extent that unconscious processes take over the direction of anything but the most routine behavior, the individual's flexibility of response—and hence his ability to make effective adjustments—is reduced.

Behavior Has
Inner and Outer Determinants

The ways in which we attempt to adjust are determined both by the structural and functional characteristics of the human system and by the nature of the surrounding field, with which the system continually interacts. Sometimes inner determinants, such as the individual's frame of reference, play the predominant role; at other times outer determinants, such as social expectations or environmental resources, are of primary importance. Any adjustive action, of course, reflects the interplay of a combination of determinants—some more influential than others but all of them operating to make the individual behave as he does.

Since we have encountered most of the determinants of behavior in our discussion of development, motivation, and stress, we need only summarize their role in the present context.

Frame of reference. As we noted in Chapter 2, we begin early in life to build a pattern of information, assumptions, and attitudes about ourselves and our world in regard to (a) what is real or true, (b) what is valuable and right, and (c) what is possible. This frame of reference provides our basic psychological equipment for dealing with life's problems—for our adjustive behavior. It acts as a screen through which incoming information must pass, a yardstick by which it is evaluated, and a control for guiding our behavior into channels that seem appropriate to us.

We deal with stress situations in terms of how we perceive them and in terms of what we think the alternative courses of action are. An example is provided by three girls not invited to join the sorority of their choice at a large university. One transferred to another school: "It was the only possible thing to do!" The second modified her aspirations, joined a different sorority, and made a perfectly happy adjustment. The third felt humiliated and rebuffed and saw the experience as proof that she was totally unattractive. Nobody would want *her* for a friend. By withdrawing into a shell, she made sure that no one could hurt her again. In each case the reaction stemmed from the girl's frame of reference far more than from the objective situation, though each girl saw her behavior as a natural reaction and failed to recognize how much she herself, in her assumptions and attitudes, had added to the situation.

It is probably safe to say that we are rarely aware of all the possibilities of action a situation leaves open to us. The ways that we see to act are the ones consistent with our assumptions about ourselves and our world. Indeed, many of our responses to stressful situations are aimed more at justifying or otherwise protecting our assumptions than at realistically solving the problem. We tend to look for evidence supporting our attitudes and ideas and to ignore, distort, or "forget" information that would undermine them. We create rationalizations for our behavior, prove (to our own satisfaction) that our attitudes are based on simple logic, and become defensive if our basic assumptions are challenged. This selectivity is largely responsible for the characteristic life style that each of us displays—our more or less consistent pattern of behavior. When someone breaks away from his accustomed pattern, we think something is wrong. We say that he is acting "out of character," that he is "not himself."

Without an integrated frame of reference we would respond segmentally to the strongest stimulus or drive of the moment without regard for our overall needs and motives, and our behavior would mirror the strength of these forces rather than being part of a coordinated pattern aimed at overall adjustment. Unfortunately, however, our frame of reference can interfere with effective adjustment to the extent that inaccurate and limited assumptions distort our perception and blind us to possible courses of action.

Motive patterns. All behavior is motivated and involves need-goal relationships that give direction to what we do. Even behavior that is ineffective and, in terms of the total organism, maladjustive may still be motivated by an inner need for self-maintenance or for growth. Frustrations, conflicts, and pressures are stressful only because they interfere with the achievement of our goals.

The strength of a motive helps determine the amount of effort we are willing to expend, the obstacles we are willing to face, and the means we are willing to employ in striving toward a goal. Our motives, as we have seen, may be conscious or unconscious, may push us in harmonious or contrary directions, and may change considerably as time goes by. But whatever their pattern at any given moment, they are a chief determinant of our adjustive action.

Constitutional action tendencies. In Chapter 2 we saw that even newborn infants vary in their basic action tendencies in ways that suggest constitutional differences. Even in the first days in the hospital, one will take milk with long, steady sucks, while another will use short, excited ones; one will adapt placidly to changes in handling, while another will be easily upset by lights, sounds, and any change in routine or handling; one will be vigorous and active almost every waking moment, while another will tire easily or seem listless and phlegmatic.

It is through an interplay of constitutional factors and experience that we develop our characteristic action patterns. Usually, constitutional tendencies are reinforced by experience, so that our ways of responding

to certain kinds of situations become habitual. For example, a child who lacks energy and is easily upset by even minor difficulties may take the path of least resistance until, as an adult, the habit of running away from decisions and putting off difficult tasks becomes firmly entrenched. This habit may be strong enough to determine his behavior even when he is well aware that the demands of the situation and his own needs call for some other course of action. By the same token, an energetic, activity-loving person is likely to develop the habit of regarding most problems as a challenge and tackling them head on.

Constitutional tendencies are always complex, and they may be modified by learning. Indeed, a person's experiences and motivation are occasionally such that he develops action tendencies that actually run counter to his constitutional pattern. In general, however, constitutional tendencies exert a continuing and pervasive influence on behavior, helping to determine not only our susceptibility to various kinds of stress but our ways of responding to them.

General resources for handling stress. The skills, abilities, habits, interests, and other traits that, through the interplay of maturation and learning, become part of our continuing personality structure are the resources with which we meet the problems of life. They are an important group of determinants of our behavior—its direction, its quality, and its probable effectiveness.

Our skills and abilities, for example, are important in determining both what action we can take and how successful it is likely to be. If the situation calls for competencies we do not have, we can hardly meet its demands successfully. The college courses open to us are limited by our high school record. Jobs and promotions later will be limited by the proficiencies we have acquired along the way. Physical, intellectual, emotional, and social competencies all help to determine what doors will be opened to us as we go through life and what ones will be closed.

Both our learned skills and our natural level of capacity are important factors here. The level of capacity in our genetic equipment will set limits on the range within which we *can* function, but even high native capacity will not insure that we *will* function at a high level. Even with great musical talent one does not reach the concert stage without long hours of instruction and practice. And besides the skills to be learned, motives and interests must lead in that direction, and the necessary emotional and temperamental qualities for the rigorous life of a professional musician must be developed.

Since all our behavior is of necessity dependent upon our structural equipment, the quality of this equipment becomes of crucial significance. Low intelligence places severe restrictions on the types of problems that the individual is capable of handling; extreme vulnerability to various types of illness may seriously reduce his overall stress tolerance. Physical handicaps, chronic diseases, or other handicapping conditions can permanently impair the functional efficiency of the body and hence the effectiveness of adjustive behavior.

A person's ability to tolerate stress is another important resource for dealing with problems of adjustment—and hence another important determinant of behavior. As we noted in Chapter 5, each of us is more vulnerable to some types of stress than to others, and each has his own breaking point—the point at which he can no longer function in an integrated way. The individual's level of stress tolerance, whether high or low, seems to be based upon his constitutional make-up, the general degree of success with which he has been able to meet his biological and psychological needs, and the development of traits such as patience, courage, and flexibility. Certain conditions such as illness and fatigue also can affect an individual's stress tolerance temporarily.

Momentary conditions. Our bodily and psychological "structure" at the moment of behavior includes not only the long-term characteristics already mentioned but also various temporary conditions such as our mental set. Thus, what we have just been doing or thinking has much to do with our receptivity to and interpretation of new stimulation. Specific instructions can have the same effect. For example, if you are instructed to respond with words opposite in meaning to words given you, you respond within a narrow, circumscribed, predictable pattern. More often, of course, the current mental set is determined by factors not so evident—a mood of discouragement, a wish to attract favorable attention, an experience of success or frustration, or perhaps an idea or a fear. But whether induced by known or by unknown events, the mental set of the moment has an important influence on both our perceptions and our actions.

The kind and degree of emotional involvement we are experiencing at the moment of action also help to determine the resources available to us. For example, the extra sugar in the blood and the quickened pulse and respiration that come with anger or fear give us extra resources for successful fight or flight.

Just as emotional mobilization gives us extra resources, fatigue or illness may deplete our resources and leave us less able to behave effectively. The weeks of semistarvation in the experiment described on page 136 profoundly affected the subjects' behavior, fantasies, interests, and performance on certain psychological tests. The narrowing of interest which is typical in any severe, long-continued deprivation can in itself affect behavior, both by focusing its direction and by making the individual less flexible and imaginative in solving problems.

ADJUSTIVE DEMANDS AND RESOURCES

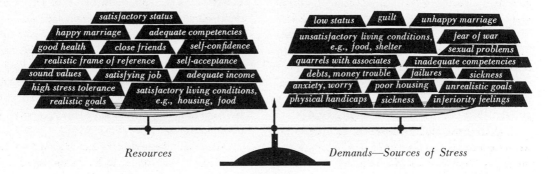

Resources   Demands—Sources of Stress

Adjustive demands and our resources for meeting them can be conceived as weights on a scale. Moderate resources can balance light demands. Heavier demands call for more and better resources. If demands threaten to exceed resources, we focus on defensive measures; if they do exceed our resources, we become disorganized and perhaps mentally ill.

Ability to handle stress always depends on the relation between the severity of the demand and one's resources for handling it, not on either factor alone. Thus in a favorable life situation, Individual A, below, with poor resources but relatively small demands upon him, might show more effective behavior than Individual D, who has better resources but an overwhelmingly severe problem.

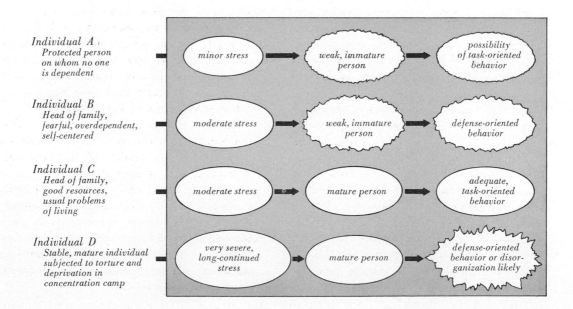

Intoxication, fevers, and certain drugs can also temporarily alter our structural equipment and hence affect our behavior. The role of such factors in impairing normal brain functioning is dramatically illustrated in recent experiments using lysergic acid and other drugs which can temporarily induce symptoms of mental illness in otherwise healthy people (Fabing, 1955; Abramson, 1956).

Environmental resources, limitations, and demands. As we noted in Chapter 1, no energy system is so self-contained but that it has some transactions with its surrounding field and consequently is somewhat affected by it. Field transactions are especially rich in the case of the human system, and many of the ways in which they influence our behavior have been suggested in earlier chapters.

We have seen, for example, how the resources and limitations of both our physical and sociocultural environments are highly important factors in shaping our personality development. Throughout our lives they continue to influence our behavior by providing the structure of relationships, the roles, and the economic and social activities through which we must meet our various needs. Some of these influences are common to all members of our culture and operate to produce common patterns of behavior. But in a society like ours, which permits wide differences among individuals and groups, the individual's own unique group setting is often fully as important as the broader culture in determining how he behaves. If he is in authoritarian subgroups, his freedom of action may be quite limited. His happy or unhappy marriage, congenial or critical associates, high or low financial and social standing, free or restrictive working conditions, and ample or meager educational opportunities are all important in setting up certain channels through which he must act as he tries to meet his needs.

Social roles are as important in affecting behavior as we saw them to be in channeling development. Much of what we do (and don't do) is determined directly by the intricate but usually unwritten social rules as to how a person with our status and various group roles is supposed to behave. The rules of etiquette are only more obvious and clearly formulated examples of these social expectations.

Often our behavior is an attempt to help our group or other individuals meet *their* needs, sometimes even at the expense of meeting some of our own. We may go to a social function we dread or spend the evening with people we dislike in order to please someone we love. We work hard to put our children through college or set aside regular time to spend with a sick friend largely out of concern for other people's satisfaction—though we too may find real satisfaction in the process.

To the extent that we identify with groups or other individuals, we adopt their goals as our own and behave in ways intended to promote their good. But sometimes the field puts demands on us that are heavier than we feel adequate or willing to meet, puts pressure on us to work or think faster than is comfortable, or forces us to make decisions before we are ready. When we see field demands as serious threats to our own well-being, our whole attention may be focused on lessening this threat, and this goal may become the central determinant of our behavior.

All these system and field characteristics, then, jointly determine the direction in which we move and the quality of our behavior. Their patterning, in turn, determines whether we can move ahead easily to reach our goals or whether we face serious problems of adjustment. If the various elements are in good balance, inner motives and outer demands move the individual in the same direction, and inner and outer resources are adequate to permit effective action.

"PROCESSING" STRESS SITUATIONS

In spite of a great deal of research, we know relatively little about what goes on in the human brain as it directs our adjustive behavior, especially about the processing of information that takes place between perception and action. Part of the difficulty lies in the tremendous complexity of man's cognitive, emotional, and volitional processes, which makes research into these activities extremely difficult. It is assumed that all ideas and other psychological events have their correlates on the neurological level, but so far these neurological events have been inaccessible to direct study and can only be inferred from behavior. Psychologists have gained some insights by varying stimulation experimentally and then noting the correlated changes in behavior, but it has been impossible on this basis to establish complete and predictable laws of behavior. Clearly the "black box" of the human brain is more than just a switchboard where stimuli and responses are connected. It seems to be more like an elaborate communications center where incoming information is sorted, arranged, and integrated and where an appropriate response is worked out.

In attempting to understand human behavior, some theoreticians have likened the operation of the brain and nervous system to that of a complex electrical computing machine.[1] The analogy, of course, is far from perfect; but the human brain does seem to work much like an electronic computer in the way it scans the field for relevant information, defines our problems, assesses our resources in relation to meeting these problems, calculates the apparently safest and most rewarding course of action, and checks feed-

back to see if errors must be corrected and compensated for. But our self-aware "human computer" is at once more and less efficient at handling problems than any machine is, being on the one hand more inventive and creative, on the other hand more subject to error. We often come up with wrong answers, not only because of lack of information but also because of urgent time pressures, the need to defend our self-structures, and many other limiting conditions which are peculiarly human. Furthermore, our machinery for processing adjustive demands operates on more than one level of consciousness, so that sometimes we are dealing with our problems thoughtfully and sometimes without the least degree of awareness. And always we are dealing not with an isolated problem but rather with a continuously changing complex of interrelated and sometimes contradictory adjustive demands.

Remembering that at our present stage of knowledge we can do no more than make tentative assumptions about what actually happens on a neurological level during the processing of stress situations, we may find it useful for descriptive purposes at least to think of the human brain as functioning in a series of computer-like operations. These involve (a) perceiving the situation, (b) evaluating the problem, and (c) selecting a response or course of action.

Perceiving the Situation

As we have pointed out in earlier chapters, we are not passive receptors and recorders of the stimulation that keeps coming to us. On the biological level, we are constantly selecting and taking in elements from our surroundings and transforming them to build new tissue, while rejecting noxious or irrelevant elements. On the psychological level,

---

[1]See, for example, Morgan and Stellar's article, "Electrical Analogies for the Brain," on page 499, and Wiener's article, "Cybernetics and Psychopathology," on page 502.

we are constantly scanning both our surroundings and our inner world of memories, ideas, and feelings, screening stimuli impinging on us, selecting and perhaps distorting parts we can use, remembering what fits in and serves our purposes, and rejecting what does not. Often we do not realize how active we are in this process and how much we contribute to what we see. The subjects who misinterpreted the Mr. Biggott cartoons as lending support to their own prejudices (p. 167) only gave a more dramatic than usual example of forces constantly active as we are perceiving.

Perception is the process by which the individual gets information about events going on outside him and within him. What he perceives at any given moment—his unique world of personal experience—is called his *perceptual field* (p. 68). And this, for him, is reality. The perceptual field has three important characteristics: (a) it is selective, (b) it is organized, and (c) it is meaningful.

Selectivity. Our perceptual field includes only a small part of the total range of percepts available as far as the objective situation is concerned. We focus our attention on some parts rather than others, and only a fraction of the stimuli bombarding us gets through to be represented in our consciousness. Although some stimuli are by their nature more likely than others to win in this competition (loud noises, bright lights, or other blatant stimuli), we all tend to make somewhat different selections on the basis of our own interests, needs, assumptions, attitudes, and momentary motive patterns and mental set.

To help explain perceptual selectivity, Bruner and Postman (1947, p. 305) have introduced the concept of *selective vigilance*: "In any given situation, the organism singles out what it considers to be the environment's most relevant aspects—relevant to adaptation in the situation." This formulation emphasizes

the role of perception in adjustment and helps to explain the tendency of stress to command attention, to become the focus of perceptual processes.

The concept of selective vigilance, or differential sensitivity to relevant stimuli, may be extended to explain the phenomenon of *perceptual defense*. Not only do we become increasingly sensitive to stimuli that seem useful in adjustment, but we tend to resist information that is contradictory or threatening. Thus we may be very insensitive to whatever aspects of a situation tend to lower our self-worth or are contrary to our desires and aspirations while, on the other hand, we are unusually sensitive to stimuli or events that tend to support us. Much ineffective behavior is the direct result of our overlooking or screening out important elements of a situation.

Interestingly enough, recent experiments in subliminal conditioning show that although much gets through that we are not aware of at the time, selection and defense are taking place even on this subconscious level. For example, McLeary and Lazarus (1949) exposed subjects to threatening words so rapidly that the subjects were unaware of them; nevertheless, the subjects showed in minor degree some of the usual bodily changes associated with emotional mobilization, such as the galvanic skin response. Undoubtedly much of our selectivity, evaluation, and defense occur at this subconscious level. Such research as this helps to explain the vague anxiety we sometimes experience when we are not aware of any threat.

Organization. Even among the signals that get through to us, some claim our central attention and others remain on the periphery of our consciousness. The perceptual field is not a mass of miscellaneous information or impressions but a coherent pattern with focal points and background. Its organization into *figure* and *ground* occurs spontaneously in

ADJUSTIVE BEHAVIOR:

ANALOGY TO A COMPUTER

INPUT
Stimulation from
within organism
and from field

THROUGHPUT
Processing of adjustive demand by self-aware organism

Perception	*Evaluation*	*Selection*
(selection and organization of input; awareness of meaning)	(definition of adjustive demand and formulation of possible actions)	(choice of action promising best balance of risk, cost, richness of reward.)

Processing influenced by:

1) *Individual's frame of reference*—realistic assumptions make for clear perception, sound evaluation, wise choice of action; unrealistic assumptions lead to cognitive distortion.
2) *Motive pattern and action tendencies*—needs and interests influence which stimuli "get through" and guide choice of action.
3) *Resources for handling problem*—capacities, skills, knowledge, and general competencies gained from experience determine actual ability to cope with the demand and quality of action possible.
4) *Momentary conditions*—mental set affects what stimuli are selected and what possibilities of action are thought of; emotional involvement or fatigue may disrupt effective processing; etc.

OUTPUT
Task-oriented
and/or defense-
oriented action

FEEDBACK
Information which tells organism how processing and action are proceeding.

Human adjustive behavior has certain obvious similarities to the processing of information by a computer, but the analogy is far from perfect. For example, the stimulation which initiates human action—unlike the input of a computer—does not have an unvarying effect: as the diagram suggests, response varies with changes in the individual's frame of reference, motivational state, and other inner factors. A computer, furthermore, cannot set its own goals or discover ways of processing information for which it has not previously been programmed.

perception; the figures we see can be changed through learning, but the tendency to structure any field into figure and ground is one of our innate integrative characteristics. We tend to see "things" rather than discrete spots of color, for example, and to focus our attention on these "things" rather than on the spaces between them, which become part of the ground.

Even when there is no clear pattern in the incoming stimulation, the individual automatically tries to structure it. He sees familiar forms in clouds or inkblots and constantly tries to classify and categorize new experiences and new people. In an ambiguous situation there may be a rapid shifting in the figure-ground relationships as he tries to see some order or meaning. If the situation is incomplete, he may supply enough details out of his imagination for it to make sense. Rumors sometimes start in this way.

The more ambiguous the situation, the more our desires and interests determine its structuring. Thus hungry subjects are more likely than nonhungry ones to give food associations to ambiguous pictures, and thirsty men on the desert may mistake the haze on the horizon for water. When you are waiting for someone in a public place, you often mistake a number of people at a distance for the one you are waiting for. Our tendency to see what we want to see has freest rein in ambiguous situations.

A further feature of our automatic tendency to see and focus on the figures in the perceptual field is the tendency for them to be *magnified* or *accentuated* in our awareness, especially when they have a positive or negative value for us. Whatever we see as potentially satisfying or threatening looms larger to us than it does to observers for whom this positive or negative value is lacking (Bruner and Postman, 1948). This characteristic of our perceiving is evidently at the root of our common habit of exaggerating

dangers and difficulties on the one hand and expected satisfactions on the other.

There is also a *constancy* factor in perception. Once we have structured a situation, we tend to continue to see it that way even when it undergoes considerable change. Thus we often continue to see a business or other institution as it was rather than as it is now; a mother may continue to see her grown daughter as a child; and a happily married couple may not notice each other's gradual aging. Sometimes we find it hard to change our appraisal of a person or situation even when discrepant facts fairly scream at us.

Meaning. The meaning in what we perceive derives partly from the pattern itself and partly from its apparent relationship to us as a potential source of gratification, amusement, enrichment, growth, or, perhaps, danger. This apparent value depends heavily, of course, on both our present pattern of motives and interests and our past experiences with similar perceptions. We are continually trying to identify the essential elements in new situations in terms of the consequences of similar past experiences. As Bruner, Goodnow, and Austin (1956, p. 13) say:

". . . we attempt to find those defining signs that are as sure as possible as early as possible, to give identity to an event. At the barest level of necessity, this is essential to life. We cannot test the edibility of food by eating it and checking the consequences. We must learn ways of anticipating ultimate consequences by the use of prior signs."

Since meaning is so dependent on experience and since members of the same society have many similarities in their background of experience, they often tend to view situations in somewhat similar ways. Yet since no two people have had exactly the same subgroup memberships or other experiences, a situation may be seen as having very different meanings even by people in the same social group. One person suffering a rebuff may see it as a threat to his feelings of worth, while another may see it as an indication of rudeness on the part of the rebuffer. A good report card may be seen as a badge of excellence by a serious student but as something to hide by a student whose friends do not value scholarship. Our own motive patterns and unique frames of reference are always critical factors in determining the meaning a situation has for us. Often, of course, we fail to grasp the significance of social, political, and economic problems because our personal experience has been so narrow that we have no basis for seeing the complete meaning of the broader problems.

All these active, integrative tendencies in our selection and organization of new stimulation influence what we perceive and hence the data on which we must act. It can hardly be overemphasized that the perceptual field is *reality* for the individual and that it is this to which he responds. However accurate or inaccurate his perceptions and evaluations are, they are all he knows of reality. If his perceptual field is accurate in terms of the objective situation, he can make plans that have a good chance of success; if it is inaccurate, he has two strikes against him at the start.

The individuality of perception explains why we can never predict a person's behavior from a knowledge of the stimulus situation alone. We also must understand how he perceives the situation and how accurate his perceptual field is. If he thinks the salt is really sugar, he will put it in his coffee; if he thinks his "enemies" are watching his every move, he will be secretive and suspicious. His behavior can be predicted only on the basis of *his* perceptual field, which may be quite different from our own.[1]

[1]For an elaboration of this point, see Combs and Snygg's article, "The Perceptual View of Behavior," on p. 466.

Evaluating the Problem

When we evaluate incoming information, memories, or ideas so as to solve problems and make decisions, we continue the activities begun in perceiving. On the basis of the original pattern and meaning that come to us automatically in the act of perceiving, we go on—using unconscious processes as well as deliberate effort and thought—to see further relationships and meanings, to clarify and define the adjustive demand, and to formulate alternative possibilities of action.

Categorizing the situation. Our first tendency in defining a problem situation is to assign it to a category if possible. This tendency to classify and categorize is such an important integrative characteristic that it deserves a little elaboration. Bruner, Goodnow, and Austin (1956, p. 1) state it:

"We begin with what seems a paradox. The world of experience of any normal man is composed of a tremendous array of discriminably different objects, events, people, impressions. There are estimated to be more than 7 million discriminable colors alone, and in the course of a week or two we come in contact with a fair proportion of these. . . .

"But were we to utilize fully our capacity for registering the differences in things and to respond to each event encountered as unique, we would soon be overwhelmed by the complexity of our environment. Consider only the linguistic task of acquiring a vocabulary fully adequate to cope with the world of color differences! The resolution of the seeming paradox—the existence of discrimination capacities which, if fully used, would make us slaves to the particular—is achieved by man's capacity to categorize. To categorize is to render discriminably different things equivalent, to group the objects and events and people around us into classes, and to respond to them in terms of their class membership rather than their uniqueness. Our refined discriminative activity is reserved only for those segments of the environment with which we are specially concerned. For the rest, we respond by rather crude forms of categorical placement. In place of a color lexicon of 7 million items, people in our society get along with a dozen or so commonly used color names. . . ."

It thus becomes apparent that our natural tendency to simplify by categorizing is a highly useful one in making our environment less complex; but it is also a possible source of error since much of our behavior is a reaction to the characteristics the current situation shares with other situations rather than to the particular situation in all its uniqueness. Simplification often becomes oversimplification, as seen in our tendency to develop stereotypes of Republicans, Democrats, labor, management, foreigners, old people, children, and many others and also stereotyped reactions to anyone seen as falling into these categories. Anyone classified as a "peddler at the door" gets the treatment we have decided is appropriate for door-to-door peddlers. We may approach all unknown old people with solicitude and a raised voice; unknown children, with condescension and one-syllable words; business executives or television stars, with awe and deference.

Groups we admire can do no wrong; if they behave in strange ways, we give them the benefit of the doubt and go a long way to rationalize or justify their behavior. With groups we disapprove, on the other hand, we expect the worst; whatever they do, good or bad, we tend to interpret in terms of our expectations. With our natural tendency to simplify by categorizing and our further tendency, already discussed, to protect our own attitudes and interests, it becomes doubly easy for us to see things in black and white and often very difficult to see shades of gray.

To the extent that our basic categories or labels are distorted, oversimplified, or otherwise inaccurate, our classification of new situations cannot help leading to ineffective behavior. Error (and therefore ineffective behavior) can come either through faulty perception and interpretation of the common elements on which our categories and stereotypes are built or through reacting only to classes and ignoring the unique elements of each situation.

Structuring an unfamiliar situation. When we face a new kind of solution for which our categories are obviously inadequate, we must analyze it and figure out its key dimensions. As already stated, we feel an imperative need to structure any unfamiliar situation that seems relevant to our needs. Sometimes further information enables us to classify it in one of our established categories, but sometimes we must form new generalizations which, in turn, will be used in later experiences. A situation we cannot categorize may be experienced as a dangerous threat and may induce fear, since we have no ready response pattern for meeting it. Thus the history of warfare has shown that the introduction of new weapons has often led the enemy to panic and disorderly flight. They have experienced terror and disorganization in the face of a threat which they had no way of categorizing and hence no immediately apparent way of defending themselves against.

Whenever time and courage permit and we do not feel we must flee for our lives, we try to identify the important elements and relationships in a new situation as preparation for coping with it appropriately. This tendency to structure and organize our picture of the world, to make it a meaningful whole, is at the root of our ability, in turn, to deal with it as a whole instead of having to react segmentally to individual stimuli.

Formulating possible lines of action. The boundary line between grasping the demands of a situation and seeing possible lines of action is of course nonexistent. Often our definition of the problem to be solved or the decision to be made includes in it some formulation of the possible alternatives. In a familiar situation the whole process of definition, formulation of alternative actions, and choice of action may take place quite automatically with little or no conscious involvement. But a situation with many unfamiliar elements may not be amenable to immediate categorization, and no appropriate response pattern may be evident even when the problem has been defined. Here we may have to use reason, imagination, and other conscious processes to work out possible solutions.

All of us tend to develop a characteristic and fairly consistent way of approaching new problems. Some of us may deny their reality or look the other way as long as we can; some of us become highly emotional; some of us seek advice or help from a more experienced or stronger person; some of us tackle problems head-on as if we were knights of old and they were dragons to be slain. We may also tend to approach different types of problems in different ways. Thus a scientist may be very objective in dealing with scientific problems but very emotional and unobjective in dealing with family problems. Our characteristic approach, or strategy, in dealing with a given type of problem has far-reaching effects on our behavior.

Despite major differences in the general way we approach our problems, there are certain basic considerations that we normally take into account when formulating possible lines of action. Consciously or unconsciously, we ask ourselves such questions as the following —and, on the basis of our answers, weed out the alternatives that are obviously unsatisfactory from those that seem to merit serious consideration.

1. Would this solution be realistic? Some courses of action must be discarded because they are obviously inconsistent with the realities of the situation. If one marriage partner firmly insists on a divorce or legal separation, the other cannot solve his problem by resolving to hold the home together. The homesick G.I. cannot pack up for a two-week vacation with his family. Sometimes, too, lack of time makes an otherwise good solution completely unrealistic.

2. Can I predict the outcome of this action? On the basis of his actual experience in similar situations and his assumptions about himself and his world, the individual tries to anticipate what will happen if he follows a given line of action. Sometimes solutions that would be good are discarded on the sole ground that the individual lacks sufficient information to predict the outcome of his action with any degree of certainty. By the same token, of course, he may feel falsely confident in predicting the consequences of a particular action.

3. Would the risk be too great? In evaluating elements of risk, the individual not only considers the possibility that his prediction of the outcome may turn out to be wrong but weighs this possibility against his chances for gain or loss. If the risk is high and the expected outcome has relatively little to recommend it, a possible course of action may be discarded immediately. However, if the possible rewards are great, the alternative may be considered seriously even though considerable risk is involved. Often, of course, wishful thinking may enter in here and throw off a person's better judgment.

4. Would the action be consistent with my standards? In formulating possibilities of action, the individual considers whether they are in keeping with his standards. He takes into account such standards as those related to his self-concept and aspirations, the level of satisfaction he has come to expect, and the amount of risk he is willing to take. Cultural standards also enter into his evaluation, and many lines of action are discarded as possibilities not so much because they would violate the individual's own standards as because of possible social disapproval.

5. *Would too much effort or anxiety be involved?* Sometimes a person discards possible solutions—even good ones, from the standpoint of meeting a particular problem—on the grounds that too much of his time or effort would be required to work them out, that the risk or uncertainty of outcome would be too worrisome, or that the proposed line of action would create a serious conflict. Especially if the stakes are not high, we tend to take the easy way out.

This formulating and preliminary weighing of possible lines of action may be a conscious process, or it may take place largely without our awareness. A soldier may have an impulse to run away which he consciously rejects, or the impulse itself may be repressed before he becomes aware of it so that he does not even know he has rejected one course of action. Among the solutions possible from an objective point of view, we retain for serious consideration only those that are in keeping with our self-structures and appear to have a fair chance of success without too great a cost.

Selecting a Course of Action

Often after the alternatives are delineated and the unsuitable ones are rejected, there still remain two or more possibilities of action in keeping with our standards and values and apparently suitable in terms of the situation's demands. We must then compare and choose between them, weighing such considerations as our probabilities of success, the degree of satisfaction we will accept, and the cost we are willing to pay.

Playing the probabilities. Other things being equal, the individual tends to select the course of action which seems to offer the greatest probability of success.[1] In figuring the odds, he not only examines the relevant information at his disposal but tends to assess —often unconsciously—the likelihood of chance factors upsetting his calculations or of events beyond his control interfering to prevent him from reaching his goal. As Phillips (1956, p. xvi) puts it:

"The organism selects, as it were, in the way that the gambler selects a number to bet on. We are all betting on life's contingencies all the time, although we do not stop to think about it nor do we conceptualize the odds at every turn."

The better the odds and the bigger the possible winnings, the more ready we usually are to take a chance. But the matter of calculating the odds for success is not always an entirely rational matter. Wishful thinking may lead a person to take untoward risks. He may even bet on responses which have failed consistently in the past, much as the gambler continues despite heavy losses over a period of time. If we knowingly choose to go against the odds, the element of strain involved is very great.

Deciding on an acceptable level of satisfaction. Though we may take bigger risks for bigger potential gains, we do not automatically choose the course which, if successful, would yield the greatest satisfaction. If the most gainful course of action also carries with it the risk of losing everything if we fail, we may settle for an alternative that is less appealing but more sure of bringing us *some* level of satisfaction. We are willing to date a girl less attractive than the much-sought-after campus queen and to accept a good job rather than wait for the better one that may never come through.

[1]This has led some theoreticians to develop an analogy between decision making and the strategy of games. See Oskar Morgenstern's article, "The Theory of Games," on page 493.

A person with a very high level of aspiration may always tend to insist on an optimal level of satisfaction, but most of us are usually content—at least in making our routine decisions—to find a course of action that is "good enough" and will meet whatever level of satisfaction we have come to expect. And when we seek no more than adequate satisfaction, we tend to select the first alternative that meets our criteria. Rarely do we attempt to ascertain every possible course of action and to ferret out the one that promises to yield maximum returns (Simon, 1957).

Even the person who seeks only adequate satisfaction in most areas may insist upon optimal satisfaction in others. The man who is content to go to a mediocre restaurant probably will not be content to choose a mediocre wife. The man who is satisfied with an old car and a modest home may demand excellence in his work.

Balancing risk, satisfaction, and cost. In selecting between alternative courses of action, we do not base our decision on any one factor but must balance the risks—the amount of effort, anxiety, or other cost—against the possible satisfactions. For high stakes and good odds we may be willing to work hard and undergo considerable pain and sacrifice; but if the returns look small and the risk of losing is considerable, we are usually reluctant to exert much effort. And as we have noted, there are also marked differences in the level of satisfaction that different individuals expect, in their willingness to take risks and to exert themselves, and in their tolerance of stress and strain.

The process of evaluating alternatives and making a choice of action is of course influenced by the context in which it takes place. In some situations which are not particularly stressful we can take our time, get more information if we need it, weigh and balance all factors carefully, and emerge with a choice in which we have considerable confidence. But in other situations we may be under time pressure to decide or may be experiencing so much stress that *any* decision seems better than none. In this case we may take the first possible way out even though it promises little in positive satisfaction or even in freedom from later risk and strain. When we must act but have not yet identified a course of action in which we have confidence, we tend to become disorganized and panicky.

In balancing risk, satisfaction, and cost we must also consider the relationship between a single decision and our ultimate goals. Although some choices are likely to arise only once and to have a continuing influence on our lives—for example, whether we go to college and whom we marry—others are relatively unimportant in the long run, even some that seem immensely important at the time, such as whether we buy a new or used car, a provincial or modern home. The mature person realizes, too, that decision making is by necessity a process of taking calculated risks and that he cannot hope to win every time. Small losses must be balanced off against overall gains. As the Overstreets (1956, p. 24) point out:

"After all, we live by batting averages, not by perfect scores. The research scientist does not expect that every hypothesis he sets up will prove out. The teacher does not expect every day's lesson to set aflame the minds of youth. We live by making plans and by making efforts that are, so far as we can see, in line with the results we want; by improving our plans and efforts as experience dictates; and by believing that a fair batting average constitutes enough success to justify our staying on the job."

It should be emphasized that our "human computer" does not invariably make an objective analysis of each problem, objectively formulate and evaluate possible alternatives of action, and objectively select the course of action which best meets the requirements of the overall situation. Faulty assumptions, desires, emotions, lack of adequate information, inability to foresee outcomes, time pressures, and many other factors may lead us to wrong answers. Problems of self-defense may enter into the way the individual perceives and defines a problem, the alternatives he finds acceptable, and the particular course of action he selects. Thus although the human organism tends to the rational processing of problems, there are many possible sources of error. We shall discuss some of these further in the next chapter.

PATTERNS OF ADJUSTIVE RESPONSE

Our behavior when we feel generally competent to handle a problem is quite different from our behavior when we do not. This is true whether the problem is in fact difficult or simple, whether we actually have ample or limited resources, and whether we really are competent or only think we are.

If we feel generally competent to handle the situation, our behavior tends to be *task-oriented*—aimed primarily at meeting the requirements of the situation. If we feel threatened and unsure of our adequacy, our behavior tends to be *defense-oriented*—aimed primarily at protecting ourselves from devaluation and emotional hurt or perhaps at alleviating tension and anxiety. And as we shall see in Chapter 7, in the face of continued or severe stress that exceeds our adjustive resources, our behavior tends to become *decompensatory*—disintegrative and increasingly disorganized rather than integrative and adjustive.

Task-Oriented Behavior

Task-oriented behavior is aimed at meeting adjustive demands realistically. Such behavior tends to be based on an objective appraisal of the situation and to be coordinated, constructive, rational, realistic, and consciously directed. An exception, of course, occurs in the case of the person with a distorted frame of reference. His behavior can still be task-oriented—focused on the task as he sees it—but his faulty perceptions may lead to a quite unrealistic, unobjective solution.

Task-oriented reactions are most typical in situations where there is a simple adjustive demand to be met and no particular stress involved. But they may also be used in stressful situations where the individual, though under strain, still feels generally adequate.

The task may be to meet either an inner demand or an outer one or a combination of both, and task-oriented behavior can mean making changes in either oneself or one's surroundings or, again, in both—whatever the occasion warrants. It can involve attack, withdrawal, or compromise. We are using *behavior* here in its broadest sense: in some cases it may not involve actual motion but may mean working out a reinterpretation or sounder attitudes.

Attack. If the Western hero sees the bad guy about to pull a gun, he may handle the situation by beating him to the draw. This is a simple attack reaction and is the prototype of much of our action. Whether the troublesome element we tackle is in our surroundings or in ourselves, we size up the requirements of the situation and try to meet them quite directly.

Task-oriented attack may involve physical assault, frankness, subtlety, dominance, patience, learning new skills, cooperating, competing, or even, as in Gandhi's case, passive resistance. The possible ways of attacking problems in task-oriented ways are legion, but usually they have the following characteristics:

1. Increased effort—the individual musters his forces to solve the problem or reach his goal.

2. Variation in mode of attack—the individual plans his attack; he assesses the various possible actions, tries the most promising, and if that fails tries another.

3. Learning—the individual seeks to get enough information to assure his full understanding of the problem and tries to develop new competencies that will help him solve it.

When the adjustive demand lies within the range of the individual's adjustive resources, an attack approach usually offers him the best channel for using and coordinating his abilities productively.

Withdrawal. Sometimes it is the better part of valor to withdraw from a situation that is exerting demands we cannot, or prefer not to, meet. An unpleasant job or one without a future may offer so little reward that we can better meet our needs for achievement and growth by looking elsewhere. Sometimes students get half way through medical school or law school only to realize that it is not for them. A realistic, task-oriented solution then usually involves trying to assess their key interests and aptitudes and switching to a more promising field. An ego-defensive reaction, by contrast, might be refusing to admit they had made a mistake or blaming parents or counselors or perhaps the school for their unhappiness and playing a "martyr" role; in either case the situation would hardly be remedied as it would by acknowledging the mistake and trying to correct it by leaving the undesirable setting.

This is not to say, of course, that running away is always a task-oriented solution.

Sometimes it is purely defensive, a refusal to face and solve a problem. But just as when your house is on fire you do not stay inside and argue with the fire, so there are situations in which the cards are stacked against you and the most realistic solution is simply to leave the situation.

Task-oriented withdrawal patterns tend in general to involve four components:

1. Admitting defeat—the individual admits that the situation is too difficult for him.

2. Giving up—the individual decides against trying to continue the unequal struggle.

3. Leaving the field—actual physical or psychological withdrawal from the scene of action takes place.

4. Establishment of new direction—the individual turns his attention and constructive efforts toward a new goal.

Withdrawal is often indicated when the individual finds himself under excessive inner or outer pressures for achievement—and when he can disengage himself without undue frustration. Some stress situations, however, such as conflicts, are usually not amenable to withdrawal but must be dealt with in terms of attack or compromise patterns if they are to be resolved.

Compromise. Most task-oriented behavior is neither pure attack nor pure withdrawal but a compromise. You change what you can in yourself or the situation, separate yourself if you can from impossible elements, and live as best you can with what cannot be changed or escaped. If it becomes apparent that you cannot achieve the exact goal you sought, you settle for the best substitute or approximation you can. If the group will not do things entirely your way, you may trade concessions or try to work out a compromise path that both you and the others can accept in good conscience.

If the compromise succeeds in meeting the essential requirements of the situation, the problem is resolved, and the individual can go on to other activities. If, however, the compromise enforced by today's objective situation turns out tomorrow to be frustrating important needs, then stress will build up, presenting a new problem of adjustment that must be dealt with.

Compromise reactions take many forms. Among the most common in everyday life are:

1. Accepting substitute goals. If a young man is turned down by the girl he would really like to marry, he starts dating someone else. An individual faced with starvation may accept substitute food goals such as worms, bugs, and grass, which he would not ordinarily eat.

2. Lowering level of aspiration. Instead of trying to make all A's in college, the good but not brilliant student learns to strive for "good" grades. Instead of always trying to outperform others, he learns to do his best and accept the results, thus adjusting his aspirations to more realistic levels.

3. Using flexible means. The individual tries to figure all the angles and is willing to surrender his preferred patterns of operation if he sees they will not work and thinks others will. This may even mean resorting to usually disapproved means if he thinks the situation justifies it.

4. Accepting vicarious satisfactions. Satisfaction may be found through vicarious experiences when no direct means of gratification are available. Thus people who cannot travel to the far corners of the world can read about them or watch travel films.

5. Limiting the field. The individual may limit his field of operation to activities in which he feels adequate. For example, if he finds himself ill at ease in large social gatherings, he may avoid them and seek social satisfaction with a few close friends.

Attack, withdrawal, and compromise reaction patterns for dealing with stress may oc-cur in almost endless combinations in our overall behavior. Thus an individual who is going to college to prepare for a career in business (basically an attack approach) may avoid courses which he feels are particularly difficult (withdrawal). The pattern chosen in task-oriented behavior tends to be determined largely by the requirements of the particular situation.

Task-oriented reactions often have emotional components, especially if considerable stress is involved. We may feel zest and exhilaration in a close contest where we know we are making a good showing, hostility toward a person who is blocking our progress, or fear that time may run out or that events beyond our control may negate our efforts. In a very terrifying situation, withdrawal behavior, though still task-oriented, may be complicated by intense fear and hence be less rational and coordinated than usual. In general, however, as long as we feel generally competent to handle the situation, the emotional components do not upset our functioning and may even improve it.

Task-oriented behavior clearly has a better chance than defense-oriented behavior of resolving our problems, but obviously it does not always do so—even when it achieves its immediate goal. For example, stealing, physical assault, sexual misbehavior, and unethical means to our goals may be task-oriented but are not apt to be desirable solutions. Other criteria than task orientation must be taken into account too, and in our next chapter we shall consider the criteria and causes of effective and ineffective adjustive behavior.

Defense-Oriented Behavior

As we have pointed out, an individual under serious stress has two problems: to meet the adjustive demand and to defend himself from the stress itself. When we are put under severe strain by a problem we do not feel competent to solve, our behavior typically becomes geared toward meeting the second objective. Defense-oriented behavior helps protect us from self-devaluation or emotional hurt and alleviates the tension and anxiety associated with frustration, conflict, and pressure.

General characteristics of defensive behavior. Defense-oriented responses tend to be ego-involved, unrealistic (in terms of the objective requirements of the situation), and indirect. They are usually more emotional, more irrational, and more segmental than task-oriented responses, and the choice of action is commonly made below the level of consciousness. Fear and anxiety (or anger) loom larger than the objective requirements of the situation, and we act more to release this tension and lessen the threat than to solve the problem itself. Thus a little child

trying to build a tower that keeps falling down may finally scream and kick the recalcitrant blocks in a furious release of feeling. Although this does not move him toward his goal, it lessens his tensions.

Many other kinds of aggressive behavior usually are defense-oriented—bullying, retaliation, abusive language, sarcasm, tantrums, negativism, and rebelliousness. In fact, aggression—often accompanied by hostility—is one of the most common reactions to frustration. Expressing it may not overcome the barrier but helps the individual to feel better temporarily.

Other patterns of defensive behavior are characterized by a withdrawal from threatening, or potentially threatening, situations. A person who is characteristically shy, seclusive, apathetic, or prone to daydreaming is very likely motivated by a desire—perhaps

DETERMINANTS OF BEHAVIOR

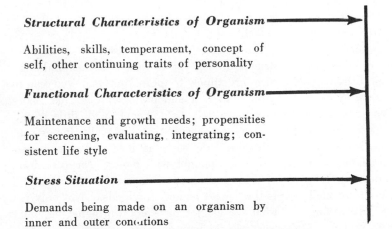

Structural Characteristics of Organism ———————▶

Abilities, skills, temperament, concept of self, other continuing traits of personality

Functional Characteristics of Organism ———————▶

Maintenance and growth needs; propensities for screening, evaluating, integrating; consistent life style

Stress Situation ———————————————————▶

Demands being made on an organism by inner and outer conditions

Behavior

Task-oriented and/or defense-oriented, depending on degree of threat perceived. Specific form and quality depend on resources and limitations of personality and field.

unconscious—to escape difficult situations that might be too much for him to handle, to avoid experiences that might cause failure or emotional hurt. Sickness can be another means of avoiding problems: many is the stomach ache that has magically disappeared as soon as a difficult situation has passed. Sickness may also be used as a means of commanding the sympathy and support of others, as when a possessive mother becomes ill every time her grown son prepares to leave her.

When people show these patterns of behavior, it is important to realize that they are not motivated by meanness or orneriness but by feelings of inadequacy in the face of threat. They are trying, however unwisely and ineffectively, to protect themselves from situations they feel incapable of handling. Any stressful situation they face becomes less threatening if they can either learn to see it differently (mask out or distort the threatening elements) or erect defenses against it that make them feel less vulnerable.

Although defense-oriented actions may be conscious and deliberate, they are usually so illogical that the individual tends to hide them even from himself. When they take place entirely below the level of his consciousness, he not only gains the reward of lowered stress (temporarily at least) but is spared the view of himself as irrational or illogical.

One clue as to whether our behavior has been task-centered or defense-centered is whether or not we become emotional and defensive when it is questioned. We usually are able to examine and discuss a task-centered act calmly, but when a defense-oriented act is challenged, we tend to become anxious and defensive. We feel *ourselves* under attack, because if our defense does not hold, we shall again be exposed to the stress we were trying to escape.

Defense mechanisms. Defense-oriented behavior typically involves one or more automatic, unconscious mechanisms for protecting the self-structure. These mechanisms are brought into operation automatically when the integrity or worth of the self is endangered. Typically they do not alter the stress situation appreciably, but they help allay anxiety by concealing or distorting the threat. Thus we may learn to blame others for our failures or justify our misdoings as "what everybody else does." The following are defense mechanisms commonly used in everyday life.

1. Rationalization. Rationalization is a well-known process in which we justify our behavior by imputing acceptable and logical motivation to it. If we decide to go to a movie when we know we should study for an examination, we can usually think up various reasons to justify our decision: we live only once, we may not have another chance to see the movie, the relaxation will help us feel fresh for the exam. Or we may try to justify cheating by pointing out that others cheat, that there is no virtue in being a sucker, and that, in real life, society doesn't ask too many questions as long as you are successful. By such means we can usually justify about everything we have done, are doing, or propose to do. Many of the other defense mechanisms often involve varying degrees of rationalization.

Rationalization is also used to soften the disappointment of thwarted desires. Balding men are quick to point out that you can't grow both hair and brains or that Don Juan was completely bald. People with little money may emphasize that the really important things in life such as love and friendship cannot be bought with money. An extension of this "sour grapes" form of rationalization is the "sweet lemon" mechanism. Not only is what we cannot have not worth having, but what we do have is remarkably satisfactory. Not only are the most important things in life free, but it is actually better to be poor since money is the root of all evil.

Rationalization is a very complex mechanism and one that is often difficult to detect because rationalizations frequently contain an element of truth. We may suspect that we are rationalizing when we (1) hunt for reasons to justify our behavior or beliefs, (2) are unable to recognize inconsistencies, and (3) become emotional when the reasons for our behavior are questioned. Usually, however, our own rationalizations probably fool us if not other people.

2. Projection. Projection may involve placing the blame for our failures and difficulties on other people or ascribing to others our own unacceptable motivations. The student fails his test because the professor is unfair or incapable of making up a good test. If a person likes to dominate every situation, he may accuse others of always trying to dominate. If he is dishonest, he tends to believe that "you can't trust anybody." A man with strong homosexual tendencies may accuse other men of continually trying to seduce him.

Projections typically center around the alleviation of inferiority feelings resulting from failure and around ethical attitudes relating to hostility, honesty, and sexual desires. The latter use of projection is particularly common among individuals with rigid conscience development and high ego-ideals. Their high personal standards make it impossible for them to accept unethical desires as part of themselves. And since these desires are so threatening and self-devaluating that they usually cannot be handled even by rationalization, they are projected to someone else who now becomes the culprit while the individual himself remains conveniently "pure" in his thoughts, actions, and behavior.

3. Compensation. As the term suggests, the mechanism of compensation involves the substitution of more rewarding traits or activities for ones that make us feel inferior or inadequate. It operates as an unconscious automatic defense against possible feelings of inferiority by giving us grounds for a favorable picture of ourselves. Since a discrepancy between our actual accomplishments and our ego-ideal would tend to lead to inferiority feelings, we unconsciously protect ourselves by downgrading the value of accomplishments in areas where we are weak and focus our attention on areas where we can excel, at the same time putting a high value on success in these new fields. If we know we are neither a beauty nor a brain, for example, we may tend to belittle the value of good looks and scholarship and regard helpfulness and a sense of humor as more important.

Sometimes compensation is undertaken deliberately and consciously as simply a more or less realistic reaction to the situation. For example, a boy who is too frail and sickly for sports may compensate for his lack of athletic prowess by concentrating on winning scholastic prominence. Although in certain instances compensation may thus result in desirable and useful behavior patterns, it is not likely to do so when its primary objective is self-defense. The rejected and insecure child may show off, trying in this way to get some of the attention and approval he so badly needs; the boy who feels inferior and inadequate may become the neighborhood bully; the girl who feels unloved and unwanted may eat too much or resort to fantasy compensations. Insecure adolescent boys sometimes resort to antisocial behavior as a means of demonstrating their bravery and masculinity.

4. Regression. Regression is essentially an unconscious retreat from the present into the past. It alleviates the stress of feelings of failure and inadequacy by providing an escape from the problems and challenges of maturity. Such a retreat may involve either (1) greatly lowered levels of aspiration, or (2) substitution of less mature modes of behavior that brought satisfaction at some earlier stage of development. Sometimes both factors are involved.

We might expect that a person would try out previously successful patterns of response in the face of stresses which do not respond to his current methods of attack. But regression is a more comprehensive mode of response than this, for it is an unconscious retreat to a dependence on immature patterns of behavior that place less demand on the individual and, if successful, permit more ready achievement of satisfaction with little or no effort. Thus the new bride may go home to the protective arms of her mother at the first sign of trouble. A more dramatic example of regressive behavior under stress is provided by Bettelheim's description (1943, pp. 445-446) of the general "regression to infantile behavior" seen in nearly all the prisoners at Dachau and Buchenwald:

"The prisoners lived, like children, only in the immediate present; . . . they became unable to plan for the future or to give up immediate pleasure satisfactions to gain greater ones in the near future. . . . They were boastful, telling tales about what they had accomplished in their former lives, or how they succeeded in cheating foremen or guards, and how they sabotaged the work. Like children they felt not at all set back or ashamed when it became known that they had lied about their prowess."

5. *Denial of reality.* One defense mechanism that many people learn to use for protecting the self from unpleasant or devaluating situations is refusal to face the situation. In much the same way that we turn away from an unpleasant sight, so we may turn away from facing our failures and faults. Or we may refuse to face the faults of others with whom we identify. Mothers are often blissfully unaware of the limitations of their offspring, and a person in love often refuses to see traits in his proposed mate which might conflict with his dreams and hence with his own needs.

One form of this denial of reality is *escapism.* We may escape the need to face reality by procrastinating, by getting sick, by not being in the mood, or by keeping away from any situation in which we think we might fail. We can even "escape into reality" if we manage to keep so busy with work or the social whirl or some form of "busy work" that we have no time to face our real problems. Keeping busy in such seemingly important tasks prevents our having pangs of conscience about not facing more difficult problems.

Denying reality is not the same thing as ignoring it when it is not relevant to our present purposes. Denial consists of falsifying reality either by convincing ourselves it does not exist or by perceiving it in a distorted way. This certainly gives us a prettier picture of our world to look at. But to the extent that we must use our picture for a map to guide our behavior, it should be accurate if we are to get where we want to go.

6. *Fantasy.* Not only do we tend to screen out unpleasant aspects of reality, but we also tend to imagine things as we would like them to be. Many fantasies are ready-made for us in the form of movies, television, soap operas, stories in magazines, and novels; others we create in our daydreams.

Sometimes fantasies involve hostile themes and enable the individual to discharge his hostile tensions by conquering against great odds and, in fantasy, destroying all opposition. Many individuals report daydreams or fantasies in which they punch, machine-gun, or run over their enemies with tanks. Such hostile fantasies are likely to occur after some unsuccessful encounter in which we feel someone has taken advantage of us or embarrassed us. Through imagination, we relive the situation as we would have liked it to be, with us succeeding rather than failing; in so doing, feelings of self-devaluation are lessened, at least temporarily. Such "conquering hero" fantasies are, of course, the fulfillment in fantasy of desires that are frustrated in real life. Thus the fantasy of being a great person enables the individual to enjoy social status and accomplishments which he is denied in real life; fantasies of the destruction of his enemies give safe expression to hostility normally denied expression.

"Suffering hero" fantasies are those in which the individual imagines that he is suffering from some horrible affliction or handicap or is an adopted and abused child; when people find out about the difficulties besetting him, they will be sorry for the way they have treated him and give him the attention he deserves. By such fantasies, the individual avoids the admission of personal inferiority or lack of worth and to some extent also avoids the necessity of striving more strenuously toward his goals. He has actually demonstrated remarkable courage and is highly successful considering the handicaps he has labored under. In short, he merits the sympathy and admiration of all.

Escaping temporarily from the stresses of everyday life into a more pleasant fantasy world relieves us of our burdens for a time and adds the dash of excitement and encouragement that enables us to return to the struggles of everyday living with renewed vigor. But fantasy becomes dangerous if we come to substitute the easier accomplishments of make-believe for real-life endeavors.

7. Displacement. Displacement, as a defense mechanism, is an unconscious shift of emotion and symbolic meaning from one person or object to a substitute. Typically it involves discharging hostility onto a safer person or object than the one which aroused it. Thus a common subject for cartoons is the employee who, instead of expressing his hos-

tility toward his boss—which would be dangerous to his job and economic security—goes home and takes it out on his wife because dinner is a few minutes late. His wife then takes out her feelings of hostility on their child who, in turn, displaces his anger onto the dog or cat.

Displacement often involves other emotions as well as hostility. Fears, for example, may be displaced from the actual source to related situations, as in the case of the irrational fears called *phobias* (p. 226).

Displacement may be of considerable adjustive value when it enables the individual to discharge his hostile tensions without risking loss of love or retaliation from parents or authority figures and without having to recognize the true nature of his feelings toward such individuals. By displacing his hostility onto his wife, the clerk is able to maintain relatively smooth relationships with his boss and even, as far as he is aware, to have admiration and respect for him. But if his marriage relationship suffers, it is an expensive solution. Usually it is more healthful to recognize and acknowledge emotional reactions in their primary form, even when unpleasant, and try to devise constructive channels of expression instead of letting them go underground where we cannot control them.

8. Acting out. Sometimes the individual tries to reduce the tension of unacceptable impulses by giving them quick, direct expression. This is not usually possible unless his ethical controls are relatively weak, since he would otherwise subject himself to devaluating and anxiety-arousing guilt feelings that would be worse than the original anxiety.

As we might expect, many individuals prone to acting out their unacceptable impulses get into difficulties with law-enforcement agencies and other authorities. However, there are times for all of us when particular conflicts build up such high levels of anxiety and tension that almost any action would be a relief, and we may be tempted to take action simply to get the situation over with and reduce our tension.

9. *Repression.* The mechanism of repression blinds the individual to certain unpleasant internal realities by screening out painful memories or desires that are dangerous to his self-esteem or feelings of adequacy. This mechanism is illustrated in a dramatic way by the soldier who has undergone an extremely traumatic battle experience and is brought to the aid station suffering from amnesia. He does not remember the situation or his name or anything about himself. He may, of course, be extremely nervous and depressed and show other signs of his ordeal; but the intolerable battle situation itself is screened from his consciousness, and he is thereby protected from stress that would completely overwhelm him. Sometimes—especially in sudden, very traumatic experiences—such repressive defenses operate only on a temporary basis until time and other factors have somewhat desensitized the individual to the shock of the experience so that he can handle it without extreme ego disruption.

In a less dramatic situation, an individual with strong feelings of hostility toward his parents may have these feelings so well repressed that he is unaware of his hatred. Similarly, sexual desires that the individual considers to be immoral may be blocked from consciousness. Sometimes repressive defenses have to be bolstered by other defense mechanisms. For example, the problem of intense hostility toward an autocratic and feared father may be handled by a combination of repression and displacement.

When repressive defenses are in danger of failing, the individual becomes extremely anxious, for he is again placed under threat. This, in turn, tends to reinforce his defenses or to induce new ones. If his defenses fail and the forbidden material enters his consciousness, the experience is a most traumatic one.

In severe instances, such as those involving repressed homosexuality, the conscious realization of such desires may completely disorganize the person's psychological functioning. In general, repression may be considered one of the more harmful defense mechanisms, for it results in the inadequate handling of relatively severe stresses.

10. *Reaction formation.* In reaction formation a person not only represses his actual, unacceptable attitudes and wishes but develops others on the conscious level that are the exact opposite. Thus people with underlying homosexual desires may strongly condemn such behavior and react with strong disgust and aversion to the very mention of it. People who crusade militantly against loose morals or the evils of alcohol are often helping to safeguard themselves from such errant behavior. Such self-appointed protectors of the public morals may voluntarily devote their lives to ferreting out obscene passages in books, or drawing attention to the inadequate attire of particular burlesque dancers, or otherwise publicly condemning the alleged vice and corruption which they presumably discover. By making such activities their "duty," they undoubtedly gain some vicarious satisfaction of their own unacceptable desires without damage to their self-ideals.

Often, of course, reaction formation is more subtle in its operation. An individual who experiences what he considers immoral sexual attraction to his friend's wife may develop conscious attitudes of antagonism toward her. Or the member of the jury who has had tempting impulses toward embezzling funds from his own company may be unduly severe in condemning the defendant for similar behavior and may demand the most extreme penalty the law permits. By such condemnation and punishment, he helps to hold his own dangerous impulses in check.

Reaction formation, like other defense mechanisms, does help us to maintain socially approved behavior and protects us from the stress of acknowledging that we have anti-social or unethical desires. But the self-deception involved is not conducive to a realistic and effective solution of our problems, and the harshness with which we treat others shows neither understanding nor fairness.

11. Undoing. Undoing is a defense mechanism designed to negate or atone for some disapproved desire, idea, or behavior. It apparently develops out of our early training, in which we are punished or forced to apologize or make restitution for our misdeeds. In adult life we may consciously attempt to atone or make restitution for our misdeeds, or this negating action may take place on an unconscious level. The latter is what is meant by undoing. Thus the unfaithful husband may try to atone by suddenly, and for no apparent reason, bringing his wife flowers and candy. Or the unethical businessman may give large sums of money to his church or to some charitable organization. The rejecting mother commonly showers her child with toys and other material possessions or other external indications of solicitude. Sometimes the only possible atonement for our sins appears to be punishment itself, and we may unconsciously devise ways to "get what's coming to us."

Since it is socially desirable that we make restitution for our misdeeds and since undoing assists us in avoiding devaluating and disturbing guilt conflicts, the use of this defense mechanism may be considered generally beneficial. Again, however, we may unconsciously rely on it too much, at the expense of understanding and improving our behavior.

12. Sublimation. In sublimation we accept socially approved substitute goals for sexual or other drives whose normal goals are blocked. Thus the girl who fails to marry may find some substitute satisfaction in her teaching career, in oil painting, in gardening, or in volunteer work in an orphanage.

There is some doubt, however, as to whether the "energy" that goes into these kinds of activity is the same energy that would go into a sexual relationship, as Freud thought it was. It seems more likely that genuine new interests are developed and that constructive activity reduces sexual tensions rather than rechannels them.

13. Emotional insulation. In emotional insulation the individual withdraws from stress by reducing his degree of emotional involvement in situations that might prove disappointing and hurtful. Thus in looking forward to a date with a very attractive girl, he may not let himself get too excited or enthusiastic about it for fear that something will happen to prevent it or that he will be disappointed in her or she will not like him.

Since we all undergo many disappointments in life, most of us learn to keep our hopes and anticipations within bounds until the hoped-for event is too close to get away. We are careful to avoid premature celebrations or to let our hopes get too high. We are usually careful to hedge our emotional bets somewhat when the hoped-for event is one in which we are deeply ego-involved.

Up to a certain point, emotional insulation is a highly important method of defending ourselves from unnecessary disappointment and hurt. But life involves calculated risks, and most of us are willing to take our chances on participating rather than withdrawing from it. Most of us choose to become actively and emotionally involved in marriage, close friendships, group concerns, and work and play, expecting some disappointments with the satisfactions. Unfortunately, however, individuals who have been badly bruised by life's blows may withdraw from further involvement in which they might be hurt. The sensitive youth who has been badly hurt by a broken love affair may insulate himself to such an extent that he finds it difficult to achieve a close affectional relationship again. This reaction is especially common among people who have been rejected and hurt in early childhood and who by adulthood have learned to insulate themselves with a protective shell of aloofness and detachment that makes it impossible for them to give or receive love or to participate enthusiastically in life.

14. Intellectualization. A mechanism related to both emotional insulation and rationalization is that of intellectualization, in which the emotional charge that would normally accompany certain events is prevented by "rational" explanation. Grief over the senseless death of a child may be softened by the conviction that the good die young. Sometimes we avoid actively dealing with unpleasant aspects of life that would ordinarily make civic and emotional demands on us by becoming cynical or making exhaustive analyses of the situation and letting it go at that. We may argue that there is no point in trying to expose graft or improve political institutions because people are stupid and greedy and you can't change them. Or we may verbally deplore racial discrimination but assume we can do nothing about it.

15. Identification. The mechanism of identification is not only an important guide in development (p. 93) but one of the most successful means of enhancing one's feelings of worth and importance. By identifying himself with his father, a child can lay claim to the traits that make his father so powerful and can get a sense of adequacy from his father's exploits far beyond what comes to him from his own puny achievements. As we grow up, the same mechanism continues. The college we attend, the company for which we work, and the clubs or other elite organizations to which we belong can all enhance our feelings of personal worth, as can living in an exclusive part of town or driving a prestige car. Actually it is often hard *not* to identify ourselves with the organizations or possessions that affect our status. We can conveniently forget that the glory in which we bask as a member of a highly respected group does not all emanate from us personally.

The mechanism of identification is undoubtedly of value as an ego defense mechanism in making us feel more adequate and secure in the face of everyday stresses. Again, however, we can observe dangers. The person who relies on others' accomplishments rather than on his own will in the long run experience a deep sense of frustration.

16. Introjection. Although introjection is really a type of identification, the term refers more specifically to the internalization of attitudes with which the individual may not basically agree but which seem essential to his survival or to the improvement of his status. This is illustrated early in life by the child's learning and accepting ethical values that come to limit his impulsive actions and function as internal controls in directing his behavior. By internalizing society's value attitudes, he acquires inner controls that tend to insure his behaving in approved ways.

Unfortunately the same process occurs whether the social group has healthy or unhealthy values. Much teen-age conformity is a defensive internalizing of values inconsistent with the teen-ager's own real convictions but adopted to bolster his feelings of security. Bettelheim (1943, pp. 447-449) reports that after living for a time as prisoners in the concentration camps of Dachau or Buchenwald, even intelligent, politically well-educated individuals tended in self-defense to adopt the norms of their captors:

"Practically all prisoners who had spent a long time in the camp took over the Gestapo's attitude toward the so-called unfit prisoners. . . . So old prisoners were sometimes instrumental in getting rid of the unfit, in this way making a feature of Gestapo ideology a feature of their own behavior. This was one of the many situations in which old prisoners demonstrated toughness and molded their way of treating other prisoners according to the example set by the Gestapo. That this was really a taking-over of Gestapo attitudes can be seen from the treatment of traitors. Self-protection asked for their elimination, but the way in which they were tortured for days and slowly killed was taken over from the Gestapo.

"Old prisoners who seemed to have a tendency to identify themselves with the Gestapo did so not only in respect to aggressive behavior. They would try to arrogate to themselves old pieces of Gestapo uniforms. If that was not possible, they tried to sew and mend their uniforms so that they would resemble those of the guards. The length to which prisoners would go in these efforts seemed unbelievable, particularly since the Gestapo punished them for their efforts to copy Gestapo uniforms. When asked why they did it they admitted that they loved to look like one of the guards."

Many other examples from ordinary social behavior illustrate this defense mechanism. Sherif and Cantril (1947) for example, point to the introjection of white people's norms by many colored people, who come to look on darker Negroes as inferior and exclude them from social groupings.

Introjection, like other defense mechanisms, takes place without the individual's awareness. It seems to follow the old adage, "If you can't beat 'em, join 'em." Apparently, from the standpoint of self-defense, inner controls—even unethical ones—are less threatening than outer ones. We like to feel we are directing our own enterprise.

There are other defense mechanisms, but these are the most common ones. Once established, they tend to allay anxiety and reduce tension and hence to be reinforced—even though the price for their use is likely to be high.

Overdependence on defense. In defense-oriented action, as we have seen, we are dealing with a self-structure threatened by devaluation, typically in the form of failure, guilt, inadequacy, or lowered worth. Some use of defensive mechanisms is probably universal and is a valuable safety valve for helping us to maintain the self-confidence we must have for task-oriented action. But overdependence on them is dangerous.

Often defense-oriented behavior leads us from one stressful situation right into another. For example, a man may seek to escape the frustration of one unhappy marriage by rushing into a second marriage with a totally incompatible person. A child constantly outshone by a brilliant brother or sister may give up trying for solid achievement and retreat to fantasy or dependence on people stronger than he or may even stop trying to be a cooperative family member and become a skilled obstructionist. In these cases the withdrawal and the substitution of new goals are obviously motivated chiefly by the need to lessen current stress. Sadly enough, the effect is often a compounding of stress.

The individual who relies constantly on defensive patterns is one who rightly or wrongly has deep underlying convictions of his own inadequacy and inferiority. He *has* to be continually on the defensive, for he has so little margin of security and confidence. The more inadequate he feels, the more need he has for these unconscious defenses—but the more he depends on them, the more out of touch he becomes with reality and its requirements and the more inadequate he becomes. It is a dangerous cycle that can lead to the mental hospital. But fortunately it is usually an unnecessary one, for except in cases of catastrophic or very severe, long-continued stress, most of us have or could develop the resources needed for meeting problems in a task-oriented way. The first essential is a realistic picture and acceptance of both our assets and our liabilities so that we have no false picture we must keep protecting. The second is realistic expectations, including the realization that everyone has some experiences in which he feels inadequate—that this is normal and no cause for alarm or flight.

In concluding our discussion of task-oriented and defense-oriented behavior, we should emphasize that though we can usually describe reactions as primarily one or the other, most behavior has some elements of both. Seldom is it *purely* task-oriented or *purely* defense-oriented. Thus even though we react to failure in a generally constructive way, increasing our efforts and improv-

ing our skills for the next time, we may at the same time still protect our self-esteem by rationalizing that *this* time the failure was partly someone else's fault or that we didn't know just what was wanted, and we may feel somewhat anxious and resentful about the whole thing. Often, of course, it is difficult or impossible to separate the strands and tell how far a given act was task-oriented and how far defense-oriented.

It should also be emphasized that the same action may be task-oriented in one set of circumstances and defense-oriented in another. For example, stealing on the part of a slum child or a spy hiding in enemy territory may be a task-oriented act to acquire needed things that there is no other way of

---

TYPICAL PATTERNS OF DEFENSE MECHANISMS

Stress Centering Around:	*Common Ego Defense Mechanisms:*
Failure	Rationalization, projection, compensation
Guilt	Rationalization, projection, undoing
Hostility	Fantasy, displacement, repression, reaction formation
Inferiority	Identification, compensation, fantasy
Disappointment in Love	Insulation, rationalization, fantasy
Personal Limitations	Denial of reality, fantasy, compensation
Sex	Rationalization, repression, reaction formation

getting. Stealing on the part of a boy from a comfortable home, on the other hand, may be a defense-oriented reaction: he may not even want or need what he steals but may be retaliating for lack of love and understanding. In the same way, criticism may be to remedy a bad situation (task-oriented) or to cut someone down to size (defense-oriented). Even destructiveness, disobedience, submissiveness, and conformity, though usually defense-oriented, may sometimes be task-oriented solutions (and even realistic ones in some settings). Usually, however, if we are confident and objective enough to be task-oriented, we can find patterns more likely to be successful than these.

THE USE OF FEEDBACK INFORMATION

The concept of *feedback* has been developed most fully in connection with electronic computers and other servomechanisms such as target-seeking missiles. A *servomechanism* is a self-directing, "purposeful" machine which is error sensitive and, on the basis of information about its actual performance which is fed back to a central regulatory apparatus, compensates automatically for any deviations it makes in pursuing its goal.

Like a self-regulating machine, the human organism continuously modifies its behavior on the basis of return information concerning the progress or outcome of its actions. Our knowledge of results may come from both external and internal stimuli, and it may be wholly or partly unconscious. We are unaware, for example, of most of the kinesthetic feedback which informs us of the position and tension of our muscles and thus enables us automatically to keep our balance and control our body movements. Much of our routine activity involves unconscious feedback of this sort, but in more complex —and uniquely human—activities, conscious feedback plays a predominant role. The grades he receives in school, the happiness of his marriage, the work evaluations he receives on the job, and the attitudes of his friends all represent different kinds of feedback that an individual uses to judge the progress or outcome of his behavior. Unlike servomechanisms, however, the human organism can ignore, screen out, or misinterpret some of the feedback that might help it behave more effectively.

Convergent and Divergent Feedback

Feedback may indicate that we either are on or off the beam. *Convergent* feedback is information telling us that we are making satisfactory progress toward our goal or that the goal has been achieved. When we have little doubt that an action will be successful, we may not even be aware of convergent feedback, simply because we do not expect anything to go wrong. But if the adjustment problem is highly stressful or if we are uncertain about the course of action we have chosen, convergent feedback usually alleviates anxiety, builds self-confidence, and may even lead to accelerated effort. It is a signal that our needs will be met and stress resolved.

Feedback is rarely altogether favorable. When an action is not progressing as satisfactorily as we had anticipated, we get *divergent* feedback, indicating that—because of unforeseen complications or a wrong choice of action—we are not reaching our goal as efficiently as we might be or perhaps even that our behavior is actually making a stress situation worse. Thus a person who shows off to gain attention and approval may be informed, by the negative reactions of other people, that he is not succeeding in his attempt to achieve his ends. Besides signaling the need for a modification of behavior, divergent feedback tends to prolong or intensify stress, anxiety and uncertainty, lowered self-confidence, and the use of ego defenses.

Amount of Feedback

The amount of feedback we receive is determined not only by how much information is actually available concerning the course or outcome of an action but also by our ability to *perceive* such information. A child may not associate a stomach ache with having eaten green apples; an adult may ignore or misinterpret frowns or other signs of social disapproval. For the moment, however, we are concerned chiefly with the objective availability of feedback.

Zero feedback. Zero feedback may mean either that the individual learns nothing at all about the results of his action or, more commonly, that he receives no information until after his action is complete. In terms of this particular action, then, the individual must operate more or less blindly. For example, a person buying stocks must complete his investment before he knows for sure whether he has invested wisely. He gets zero feedback in terms of being able to modify his original investment—though he can use delayed feedback as a guide in making further investments. Similarly, television performers who work without a studio audience have zero feedback until the program is over.

In general, when the individual receives zero feedback he has less confidence in what he is doing and is less efficient in his behavior, because he is committed to whatever course of action he has taken and has no basis for modifying and improving his tactics as he proceeds. The anxiety thus aroused

tends to intensify if zero feedback continues after the action has been completed. Imagine the mental and emotional state of a young man who makes a proposal of marriage by letter—and at the end of two or three weeks has still received no answer!

Limited feedback. The sponsor of a television program usually gets little direct feedback even after a program is over but must infer its degree of success on the basis of increased or decreased sales, the reports of rating services, and so forth. Since the available feedback is limited, sponsors do what they can to increase it by spending considerable sums of money on audience research, in hope of gaining a more reliable guide for evaluating the success of their efforts. Similarly, in our everyday behavior we usually get some return information about the effectiveness of our behavior but not so much as we would like. For example, an acquaintance may respond to something we say or do with a frown, a smile, or a look of puzzlement—without actually telling us whether he understands or approves. Limited feedback is often ambiguous and, especially in ego-involving situations, tends to create anxiety and uncertainty.

Free feedback. In some situations we receive maximal return information and are able to modify the ongoing course of our behavior to make it as effective as possible under the given circumstances. In a football game, the head coach tries to create conditions of maximal feedback by having assistants, spotted in various locations, help him observe the success or shortcomings of given plays, the effectiveness of various team members, the weaknesses of the opposition, and so on as the game progresses. Free feedback tends not only to improved performance but also to increased confidence—unless, of course, it is highly divergent and there is no apparent way to improve the course of action. In individual cases of this latter sort, free feedback may lead to a disorganization of behavior, for it highlights failure without indicating a possible path to success.

Task-Oriented and Defense-Oriented Responses to Feedback

We have noted that the individual may respond to stress situations in a task-oriented or a defense-oriented way. We can make a similar classification of responses to feedback —which involves a repetition of the entire adjustive sequence. As with any other kind of stimulation, we perceive feedback, process it, and take action on the basis of our evaluation. In this context we may note that, by the return of feedback information, each response the individual makes modifies the human system to some extent and hence has implications for his future behavior.

When an individual perceives divergent feedback fairly accurately and takes a task-oriented approach to it, he will analyze the source of trouble and modify his behavior to make it more effective. Thus, poor grades in a course may lead him to evaluate and improve his study habits; marital friction may lead him to seek the help of a marriage counselor or other means to improve his marital relationship; a traffic ticket for speeding may lead him to change his driving habits. When a person feels generally adequate to cope with a situation, he can tolerate a considerable amount of divergent feedback without becoming unduly discouraged, and he tends to use it in a task-oriented way.

A defense-oriented response to feedback is typical of individuals who feel generally inadequate and insecure or who lack confidence in their ability to handle a particular situation in which they are ego-involved. The insecure person may be unreasonably elated by convergent feedback, whereas divergent feedback may seem so threatening to him that he gives up or, more commonly perhaps,

uses unconscious defenses to blind himself to the signs of his failure. In social situations, for example, unfavorable reactions from other people may be screened from consciousness altogether or may be perceived in such a distorted way that they no longer seem threatening: a lack of response to a joke may be taken as a sign that the *other* person has no sense of humor rather than as evidence that *we* somehow haven't told the story well. In general, as the amount of divergent feedback increases in ego-involving situations, there is a tendency for the individual to shift from a task-oriented to a defense-oriented approach.

If there is a continued failure to make use of divergent feedback, a pattern of behavior may become fixed even though it fails to pay off. In a sense, we try to prove we are right by sticking to our guns. Unfortunately, the tendency to rigidity that characterizes defensive behavior is reinforced by our normal tendency toward *inertia*—that is, our tendency to follow established patterns of perceiving, thinking, and acting simply because it requires energy to modify them. When a person's behavior patterns are inadequate to cope with the demands of life, the failure to use feedback—and the resultant rigidity and circularity of response—may lead to an eventual breakdown of integrated, adjustive behavior.

In this chapter we have seen that all behavior—whether effective or not—is an attempt by the organism to meet inner and outer demands. In its efforts to adjust, the healthy organism behaves as an integrated unit, using the biological, psychological, and social resources at its disposal to meet adjustive demands in the best way it knows how. Sometimes adjustive behavior is automatic, but the superior adaptability of man rests on his ability to use reasoning and imagination to work out the most effective patterns of behavior.

In dealing with a problem of adjustment, the individual consciously and unconsciously processes the information available to him in a complex operation that involves perception, evaluation, and decision making. After embarking on a course of action, he normally modifies his behavior as he goes along on the basis of feedback information which informs him of the actual effectiveness of the course he has undertaken. Although we tend to approach problems rationally and to work out a pattern of behavior that promises a maximum of satisfaction with a minimum of risk and effort, we often fail to adopt the most effective course of action because of limiting conditions such as the inadequacy or inaccuracy of available information, time pressures, and our ever present need to defend our self-structure.

When his resources are adequate and he feels generally competent to meet a problem of adjustment, the individual tends to respond to the situation in a task-oriented way. If he lacks confidence in his ability to meet demands and feels threatened by them, his behavior tends to be ego-defensive. This classification of behavior as task-oriented or defense-oriented is in terms of the person's conscious or unconscious intentions at the time of acting—whether he is primarily trying to meet an adjustive demand or to defend his feelings of adequacy and worth from threat. Task-oriented behavior tends to be more conscious, rational, unemotional, and well coordinated than ego-defensive behavior and is generally more effective in terms of overall adjustment. All of us rely to some extent on defense mechanisms, however, as shock absorbers to soften the blows of failure and disappointment. Their use becomes dangerous only when an individual becomes dependent upon them to the extent that he is no longer able to face his adjustive demands and cope with them effectively.

In the next chapter we shall consider the criteria of effective and ineffective behavior, the factors that lead to success or failure in our attempts to adjust, and the main types of seriously maladaptive behavior.

REFERENCES

The following list includes both the references cited in this chapter and a selected number of additional books and magazines for outside reading.

Abramson, Harold A. 1956. "Some Observations on Normal Volunteers and Patients." *Lysergic Acid Diethylamide and Mescaline in Experimental Psychiatry.* Louis Cholden, ed. New York: Grune & Stratton, Inc.

Barrett, Eric, and Geoffrey Post. 1950. "Introduction to Some Principles of Applied Cybernetics." *The Journal of Psychology, 30,* 3-10.

Bettelheim, Bruno. 1943. "Individual and Mass Behavior in Extreme Situations." *The Journal of Abnormal and Social Psychology, 38,* 417-452.

Bruner, Jerome S., and Leo Postman. 1947. "Tension and Tension Release As Organizing Factors in Perception." *Journal of Personality, 15,* 300-308.

Bruner, Jerome S., and Leo Postman. 1948. "Symbolic Value As an Organizing Factor in Perception." *Journal of Social Psychology, 27,* 203-208.

Bruner, Jerome S., Jacqueline J. Goodnow, and George A. Austin. 1956. *A Study of Thinking.* New York: John Wiley & Sons, Inc. Copyright © 1956 by John Wiley & Sons, Inc., New York, and reprinted with their permission.

Buswell, Guy Thomas, and B. Y. Kersh. 1956. "Patterns of Thinking in Solving Problems." *Publications in Education, 12,* No. 2, 63-148.

Combs, Arthur W., and Donald Snygg. 1959. *Individual Behavior: A Perceptual Approach to Behavior.* Rev. ed. New York: Harper & Brothers.

Davidson, Donald, Patrick Suppes, and Sidney Siegel. 1957. *Decision Making: An Experimental Approach.* Stanford: Stanford University Press.

Edwards, Ward. 1953. "Probability-Preferences in Gambling." *The American Journal of Psychology, 66,* 349-364.

Fabing, Howard D. 1955. "New Blocking Agent Against the Development of LSD-25 Psychosis." *Science, 121,* 208-210.

Goldstein, Kurt. 1939. *The Organism.* New York: American Book Company.

Hebb, Donald Olding. 1949. *The Organization of Behavior: A Neuropsychological Theory.* New York: John Wiley & Sons, Inc.

Johnson, Donald McEwen. 1955. *The Psychology of Thought and Judgment.* New York: Harper & Brothers.

Koch, Sigmund, ed. 1959. *Psychology: A Study of a Science.* New York: McGraw-Hill Book Company, Inc.

Levitt, Eugene E. 1950. "Cognitive Distortion and Ego-Involvement." *Journal of Personality, 19,* 212-220.

Luce, Robert Duncan, and Howard Raiffa. 1957. *Games and Decisions: Introduction and Critical Survey.* New York: John Wiley & Sons, Inc.

McCleary, Robert A., and Richard S. Lazarus. 1949. "Autonomic Discrimination Without Awareness: An Interim Report." *Journal of Personality, 18,* 171-179.

Mackworth, J. F., and N. H. Mackworth. 1956. "The Overlapping of Signals for Decisions." *The American Journal of Psychology, 69,* 26-47.

Mayzner, M. S. 1957. "Bibliography on Cognitive Processes: XII Problem-Solving." *Psychological Newsletter, 8,* 77-82.

Overstreet, Harry and Bonaro. 1956. *The Mind Goes Forth.* New York: W. W. Norton & Company, Inc.

Phillips, E. Lakin. 1956. *Psychotherapy.* New York: Prentice-Hall, Inc.

Rogers, Carl R. 1951. *Client-Centered Therapy.* Boston: Houghton Mifflin Company.

Sherif, Muzafer, and Hadley Cantril. 1947. *The Psychology of Ego-Involvements.* New York: John Wiley & Sons, Inc.

Simon, Herbert Alexander. 1957. *Models of Man: Social and Rational.* New York: John Wiley & Sons, Inc.

Vinacke, William Edgar. 1952. *The Psychology of Thinking.* New York: McGraw-Hill Book Company, Inc.

Wassermann, Paul, and Fred S. Silander. 1958. *Decision-Making: An Annotated Bibliography.* Ithaca, N.Y.: Graduate School of Business and Public Administration, Cornell University.

Wiener, Norbert. 1948. *Cybernetics.* Cambridge, Mass.: Technology Press.

Wiener, Norbert. 1954. *The Human Use of Human Beings: Cybernetics and Society.* Boston: Houghton Mifflin Company.

Williams, J. D. 1954. *The Compleat Strategyst; Being a Primer on the Theory of Games of Strategy.* New York: McGraw-Hill Book Company, Inc.

FAULTY PATTERNS
OF ADJUSTMENT

We have seen that behavior is an attempt by the organism to adapt to inner and outer demands. This is as true of maladjustive behavior as it is of smooth, effective, successful behavior. Both represent answers to the same questions—how best to protect one's well-being, to develop one's potentialities, and to meet social demands. To distinguish between effective behavior and ineffective behavior then, we must look not at the purposes—which are the same—but at other criteria.

CRITERIA OF EFFECTIVE ADJUSTMENT

The particular acts that are judged effective vary greatly in different cultural and situational settings. Nevertheless, it is possible to make some generalizations about effective and ineffective behavior that apply to human beings in any setting—from Madison Avenue to the tropical rain forests of the upper Amazon.

Does the Action Meet the Demands of the Situation?

Some seemingly adjustive actions do not help resolve the stress situation but merely provide the individual with some temporary relief. Thus the individual who resorts to tranquilizers as a means of alleviating the anxiety and tension associated with his problems accomplishes nothing with respect to solving the problems themselves. Of course there are some stress situations, such as the death of loved ones or disappointment in love, where time tends to heal the wound and hence temporary defensive measures may be of value—particularly if the individual is in danger of being overwhelmed by the stress. But even in these instances, such defenses may simply delay inevitable hurt and grief.

Most defense-oriented behavior, in fact, only puts off the day of reckoning. Indeed, in the long run it may even increase the stress and the difficulty of successfully meeting the adjustive demand. For example, the individual who escapes from an unhappy home situation by resorting to alcohol not only fails to solve his problem but usually makes his situation worse; similarly, the individual who unconsciously relies on defense mechanisms to cope with stress situations is likely to escape only temporarily and often finds his ability to handle problems deteriorating over a period of time. One criterion of effective adjustment, then, is that it meets the objective requirements of the situation.

Does the Action Meet the Overall Needs of the Individual?

Sometimes an action seems to meet the demands of the situation but fails to meet the maintenance or actualization needs of the individual. Thus the youth who wants to be a teacher but gives in to his father's wish for him to go into the family business may relieve the stress of parental pressures at the expense of frustrating his need for self-fulfillment. Far from being an effective adjustment, such a decision is likely to create inner conflict and to cause more difficult problems of adjustment later on.

Another factor to consider in determining whether behavior is effective or ineffective is how much it costs in terms of wear and tear. A high-pressure executive job may offer a man rich rewards in money, prestige, and fulfillment of his potentialities, but if it makes him constantly anxious about making good or resentful of the time and energy he must expend, the cost is probably too great and his behavior pattern ineffective in terms of his total adjustment. Likewise, defenses like repression—though they may relieve anxiety temporarily—are costly because they require an excessive amount of energy to maintain and because they impair a person's ability to cope with related problems constructively. As we saw in Chapter 5, any long-term, costly adjustment to stress seems to lessen a person's ability to cope with other stresses.

Is the Action Compatible with Group Welfare?

Ideally, effective adjustment means that the individual copes with his problems in such a way as to maintain harmony with his environment as well as to maintain his own integrity and well-being. If he satisfies his needs at the expense of other people, his action cannot be considered truly adjustive.

Not only is it harmful to the group, but in the long run it may frustrate the needs of the individual by causing him to be isolated, rejected, and perhaps severely punished.

The ability to maintain both inner harmony and harmonious relations with one's surroundings presupposes a "normal" environment in which the same acts *can* forward both individual and group goals. But where the group is repressive or otherwise pathological, it may be impossible for an individual to maintain his own integrity and meet his needs without running counter to group demands. Thus while freedom fighters in a dictatorship might be regarded as enemies of the state, from a broader perspective of human welfare they might be behaving in an adjustive way. Any ultimate definition of effective and ineffective adjustment must take into consideration both the optimal development of the individual and the fostering of social conditions which are compatible with group welfare.

THE CONTINUUM OF EFFECTIVE-INEFFECTIVE ADJUSTMENT

A small group of people make highly effective adjustments to life, achieving a large degree of self-fulfillment as well as coping successfully with the problems they encounter. A much larger middle group muddle through with varying degrees of inefficiency and ineffectiveness. At the lower end of the scale are those people whose methods of adjusting are so unsuccessful and even incapacitating that we call them mentally ill. A given individual may fall anywhere on this continuum of effective-ineffective adjustment, and his position on the continuum may change with time. For example, his adjustment may deteriorate under continued and

severe stress, or his adjustment may improve when his general life situation improves or when he learns to cope more effectively with certain kinds of problems. Some people adjust well in certain areas of living and poorly in others.

Balancing Success and Failure

In applying our criteria for effective adjustment, we must recognize that people rarely if ever find perfect answers to life's problems and that occasional failures are inevitable for even the most effective person. All of the variables cannot be controlled, and chance factors may determine the outcome of even the most carefully thought-out decisions. In the well-known lines of Robert Burns, "The best-laid schemes o' mice an' men/Gang aft agley."

Quite aside from chance factors, everyone is subject to errors in perception and judgment and occasionally chooses a course of action that is ineffective or maladjustive. In general, however, such errors are not serious if they are considered in the context of the individual's overall adjustment and if the individual utilizes divergent feedback so that he does not keep making the same mistakes over and over.

In evaluating the success of adjustive behavior, we must remember, too, that sometimes the choice is not between an entirely effective and an ineffective pattern of behavior but rather between two or more courses of action which for one reason or another are not completely desirable. When an individual can satisfy one important need only by frustrating another or must choose between meeting inner and outer demands, completely effective adjustment is not possible. Here the most he can do is try to choose the best of the possibilities, realizing that it is not a perfect answer and that some stress will continue. Often such situations pass, or better opportunities for more adjustive action become available later on. If a severe stress situation continues indefinitely and no real solution is possible, the individual's adjustive resources may finally be exceeded and a breakdown may occur. This will be discussed later in this chapter.

A large part of effective adjustment is knowing where to concentrate one's efforts. Since an individual must typically deal with a number of stress situations at the same time, the deployment of his adjustive resources becomes a matter of crucial strategic importance. He cannot hope to win every battle; he must concentrate on winning the crucial ones while permitting some of the less important ones to go by default. Obviously the individual can take many minor losses if he wins the key battles. And, conversely, minor victories mean little if he fails in such key areas as marriage and work.

Probably little behavior is *entirely* effective or ineffective in terms of overall adjustment. We say that behavior is effective when it meets the individual's basic needs fairly well and in a generally approved way. Usually the most one can expect is to keep the balance well on the side of success.

Minor Difficulties in Adjustment

Examples of ineffective behavior in everyday living are legion. We make wrong decisions, overreact to small things, assume inappropriate roles, worry unnecessarily, rely excessively on defense mechanisms, behave selfishly or dishonestly, and so on. Any of these behavior patterns represents "error" in terms of the criteria we have established for effective adjustment. Some are "spot" errors, occurring only in one area of adjustment or under a certain set of circumstances; others are consistent and habitual. Although the individual can usually manage to muddle through in spite of such errors, all of them interfere to some degree with effective adjustment, and some are quite costly for both the individual and society. Most could be prevented by developing better understandings and more adequate competencies.

Common patterns of ineffective behavior. *Deceit*—ranging from fibs to major dishonesties—is one common pattern of maladjustive behavior. Although it may enable the individual to achieve certain goals that otherwise would be inaccessible or to get out of stressful situations, he usually must justify such antisocial behavior by rationalization or other ego defense mechanisms. Trading one's integrity for short-term gains is always a poor bargain. Also, deceit almost invariably leads to a deterioration of interpersonal relationships.

Impulsiveness, another way to lessen immediate stress or take a short cut to desired goals, may also have unhappy results. Many individuals seem to prefer risking a high percentage of mistakes to putting forth the effort needed for gathering relevant information and making decisions carefully and rationally. But when major life decisions are made impulsively, mistakes may be very costly both to the individual and to others around him.

Selfishness is still another common error in adjustment. As we have pointed out, human beings need to feel involvement with other people and things if they are to achieve personal fulfillment. Often people tend to confuse what *appears* to be self-interest with genuine self-interest. In *Peer Gynt,* Henrik Ibsen portrays a man who devotes his entire life to pursuing what he believes to be his own best interest, only to discover at the end of his life that he has lost everything of real value.

Overconformity, envy, resentment, and belittling are other examples of behavior patterns which are commonly considered normal but which alienate an individual from other people and often stand in the way of really effective adjustment. When such patterns become habitual and unconscious, they are somewhat akin to the stage of resistance in the general-adaptation-syndrome (p. 170). The individual has achieved equilibrium of a sort but is paying a heavy price for it. He may do a fair job of meeting most of his maintenance needs and keeping out of serious trouble, but his behavior is usually less effective than it might be, and if new and severe stresses come along, he may be unable to handle them.

Sources of error. Ignorance or misconceptions about oneself or one's world are at the root of many adjustment difficulties. Failure to recognize important realities makes the individual vulnerable to stresses against which he can hardly defend himself, and reacting to distorted pictures and to perceived but nonexistent threats consumes an inordinate amount of his energy.

The "human computer" can hardly be expected to give correct answers if the assumptions on which it bases its answers are inaccurate. For example, if the individual wrongly assumes that he is a person of great talent and therefore sets his aspirations too high, he will subject himself to continual failure and self-devaluation. Even his very creditable accomplishments will fail to meet his perfectionist standards. Similarly, wrong assumptions about other people, about environmental opportunities and limitations, or about appropriate means for achieving given goals make it impossible for anyone to behave effectively.

If the individual perceives the original situation inaccurately, he is also likely to misinterpret the feedback that keeps coming in from his actions. And as his inaccurate frame of reference is reinforced and elaborated by distorted feedback, he becomes involved in a vicious circle that makes effective adjustment increasingly difficult.

Failure to develop basic physical, intellectual, emotional, and social competencies also can seriously impair the individual's ability to behave effectively and to cope with the problems of living. For example, poor habits of personal hygiene may leave the individual with little energy and drive and with lowered resistance to both physical and psychological stresses. Similarly, the individual who is not competent in learning, reasoning, and creative thinking may make very poor use of the resources normally at his command. Lack of emotional competencies may mean an inability to give and receive love, to handle one's fears and hostilities, or to tolerate failure and disappointment. And, finally, inadequate social competencies may lead to disturbed interpersonal relationships, which almost inevitably cause serious adjustment problems.

Serious Difficulties in Adjustment

Serious adjustive difficulties result when the individual experiences more stress than he can successfully handle with the resources available to him.[1] Some problems make such heavy demands that even the most mature, capable person finds them too difficult; others which could be handled easily by most people cause excessive stress for the individual whose personal resources are deficient. Fixations or distortions in development, a faulty frame of reference, weak inner controls, inadequate competencies, ineffective habits—all these are handicaps which, under certain conditions, may help push an individual across the borderline from muddling through to behavior so unadaptive that coordinated functioning breaks down altogether.

Damaged or otherwise faulty bodily equipment may also be a factor in some types of maladjustment. Thus brain damage, endocrine malfunction, and other chemical conditions can so lower an individual's adjustive resources that he is incapable of normal adjustive behavior. Apparently, too, some individuals inherit a constitutional make-up that predisposes them to mental disorders under conditions of severe stress.

The complex and interrelated factors that determine the severity of stress were summarized on page 163 of Chapter 5. It should be emphasized again that an individual's ability to make effective adjustments depends on both sides of the balance sheet—his assets and his liabilities. The greater his resources,

the larger the "expenses" he can handle without depleting his reserves. And by the same token, even a minor expense can break him if his resources are inadequate.

Decompensation. When stress becomes excessive and the individual is unable to cope with it by his usual means, he may be forced into a self-defeating pattern of exaggerated defenses. The disintegration of personality organization and of adjustive ability under conditions of excessive stress is sometimes referred to as *decompensation*. Although dramatic symptoms of mental disorder sometimes appear seemingly without warning, decompensation is usually gradual, characterized by a progressive inability to cope effectively with one's problems. Only under unusual conditions of acute and overwhelming stress does personality disorganization come about suddenly.

Decompensation may result in any of several patterns of mental or emotional disorder. Those that we shall discuss in the remaining sections of this chapter are (1) transient personality disorders brought about by acute or special stress, (2) neurotic disorders, (3) functional psychotic disorders, (4) disorders associated with brain pathology, (5) character disorders, and (6) psychosomatic disorders, or physical ailments precipitated largely by psychological causes. These classifications have been generally accepted by the psychiatric profession and are very useful for purposes of study and discussion, but they are not absolute. Mental and emotional disorders cannot always be classified clearly either by symptom or cause: many of the same symptoms appear in several of the disorders, while the causes are usually multiple and often obscure.

General characteristics of maladjustive behavior. The various patterns of decompensation which we shall discuss have in common some or all of the following general characteristics.

[1]In his article on page 502, Norbert Wiener speculates on some implications of computer analogies for an understanding of mental disorders.

THE DEVELOPMENT OF THE STRESS REACTION

Although long-continued, severe stress can deplete one's resources and lead to a breakdown, there is evidence that an organism needs some stressful experiences to develop its physiological and psychological potentials for coping with the inevitable stresses of living. In the study illustrated here, one group of infant rats were given mild electric shocks every day for three weeks (left), a second group were put into small compartments for a few minutes each day (center), and a third group were simply left in the nest and not handled at all. It was expected that the early traumatic experience of the first group would result in symptoms of emotional disorder in adulthood, but surprisingly it was the nonstimulated rats that showed deviations in both behavior and development. From this and subsequent investigations it was discovered that: (1) The shocked and manipulated rats matured more rapidly—opened their eyes sooner, achieved motor control sooner, gained weight more rapidly, had more hair sooner, had a higher resistance to an injection of leukemia cells; and developed sensitivity to cold and other stimuli several days earlier. (2) Both groups of stimulated rats showed in adulthood a more normal and adaptive stress response—a quick response of sympathetic nervous system and adrenals followed by a quick return to normal—whereas the nonstimulated rats showed a more sluggish and much longer-lasting stress response. (3) The nonstimulated rats showed a stress response in unfamiliar but otherwise neutral situations. As is seen in the multiple exposure photograph above (right), a nonstimulated rat would cower fearfully in a corner while a stimulated one would explore freely with no physiological stress response (Levine, 1960).

1. Predominance of irrational and unconscious reactions. The individual usually lacks insight into his problems and behavior and reacts in ways that seem obviously inappropriate to the outside observer. His precarious structure of ego defenses can be maintained only by an inflexible and unrealistic approach to his problems. Even where the individual realizes that his behavior is maladjustive, he is usually unable to correct it without psychiatric help.

2. Anxiety and exaggerated ego defenses. When a threatening stress situation gives rise to anxiety, or psychic pain, the individual may focus his energy on building up defenses against this anxiety instead of meeting the basic adjustive demand in a task-oriented way. Sometimes, however, his defenses do not hold, and the anxiety threatens to break through again. Second-line defenses may then be developed to reinforce the first ones. If simple rationalization is not enough, projection or displacement may be added; if repressed ideas threaten to reappear, a phobia may be developed to make the repression more effective.

Rationalization, projection, and other ego defense mechanisms may be used to such an extreme that the individual becomes seriously out of touch with reality. In a sense, the system breaks down from the weight and expense of its "defensive armaments" much as a hard-pressed country might do.

3. Vicious circles. As defense piles on defense, the individual's frame of reference becomes more and more unrealistic, and he becomes increasingly incapable of effective, task-oriented action. He acts on the basis of his faulty assumptions and perceptions; divergent feedback is screened out or distorted so that it fits his original false perception of the situation; and his maladjustive behavior continues. This way of dealing with contradictory facts is not only ineffective from a practical standpoint, but it tends to create

further anxiety—and thus causes a further narrowing and distortion of perception.

4. Lowered integration of behavior. Unless the individual's defenses hold at some point, his behavior becomes increasingly disorganized, fragmented, and segmental. Such disorganization is especially typical of the psychoses and of shock reactions. The lowered integration in many abnormal behavior patterns is associated with lowered cortical control: segmental reactions that are normally coordinated in the cerebral cortex occur without regard to the overall needs of the individual or to the demands of the situation—and apparently without the individual's awareness of their inappropriateness. Thus a person may become preoccupied with sexual fantasies and make overtures to strangers, or he may become violent and abusive. Psychotic disorders characteristically involve such a lowering of cortical controls.

5. Symptoms. The various symptoms of mental disorder are signs that something is wrong in the "human computer," just as fever, headache, and stomach upset indicate some physical ailment. And as in physical illnesses, two people may show similar symptoms but have different underlying disorders, or they may have similar disorders but show quite different symptoms. Some symptoms, like delusions, usually indicate serious pathology; others, like confusion under conditions of acute stress, are less cause for concern. In general, the meaning and importance of a given symptom depends on the whole context in which it appears.

Other characteristics of personality decompensation might also be mentioned here —for example, a tendency toward deficiency rather than growth motivation and a tendency for the individual to be exclusively preoccupied with his own needs. Again it should be emphasized that there are different patterns of decompensation and that in any given case some of these characteristics may not apply.

Our discussion of the various mental and emotional disorders will focus on their general symptom patterns and the conditions that may bring them about. We shall not attempt here to describe their treatment or to make anything more than very general statements about chances for recovery. It may be noted, however, that modern methods of chemotherapy and psychotherapy have made possible the rehabilitation of many cases previously considered hopeless and have drastically reduced the average length of hospitalization for the mentally ill. In fact, despite an increase in the number of patients being treated for mental disorders, many of our mental hospitals are finding for the first time that their rate of discharges is higher than their rate of admissions.

TRANSIENT PERSONALITY DISORDERS

Under conditions of overwhelmingly severe stress—such as terrifying accidents, military combat, internment in a concentration camp, or sudden loss of vision or limbs—temporary personality disorders may develop even in previously normal, stable people. The personality decompensation may be sudden, as in the case of a fire or other catastrophe, or more gradual, as in a prison camp or a very unsatisfactory life situation. If the individual is removed from the stressful situation, he usually shows rapid recovery, though in some cases there may be residual damage to the self-structure.

Transient personality disorders are commonly grouped into three categories: (1) reactions to combat, (2) civilian shock reactions, and (3) situational reactions.

Reactions to Combat

Combat reactions have been common throughout the history of warfare, but only recently have they been studied scientifically. The clinical picture of combat exhaustion during World War II varied somewhat depending on the branch of service, the duration of combat, and the nature of the combat trauma. In some cases the personality decompensation was sudden, but more typically it occurred gradually as a result of many months of combat. Hypersensitivity, irritability, and sleep disturbances commonly signaled the first stage of combat exhaustion. In some cases the personality decompensation went no further until additional stress upset the already unstable equilibrium.

The clinical picture in the full-blown combat reaction typically involved dejection, tearfulness, and overwhelming anxiety:

"In the majority of cases they followed a stereotyped pattern: 'I just can't take it any more'; 'I can't stand those shells'; 'I just couldn't control myself.' They varied little from patient to patient. Whether it was the soldier who had experienced his baptism of fire or the older veteran who had lost his comrades, the superficial result was very similar. Typically he appeared as a dejected, dirty, weary man. His facial expression was one of depression, sometimes of tearfulness. Frequently his hands were trembling or jerking. Occasionally he would display varying degrees of confusion, perhaps to the extent of being mute or staring into space" (Menninger, 1948, p. 143).

In unusually severe cases the symptom picture often included temporary amnesia for the traumatic experience. The defensive mechanism of repression was clearly demonstrated here, for the battle experience could be brought to consciousness under hypnosis or drugs like sodium pentothal.

The diary of the marine on Guadalcanal cited on page 161 gives an unusually clear portrayal of the cumulative effects of combat stresses. In this case, the frightful pressure, with constant danger and inadequate

FACTORS DETERMINING
TYPE OF DISORDER

Mental disorder results when the stress, however great or small, is too much for the resources of the individual. The more immature and unstable the individual, the more precarious his adjustment and the less the stress needed to upset it. Interestingly enough, the kind of disorder that appears depends on the relative importance of the two factors—stress and personality weakness—in precipitating the trouble. With little stress but moderate personality instability, obsessive-compulsive neuroses or phobias are common, whereas with less personality weakness but moderately severe stress, an acute anxiety state or other acute but temporary symptoms of neurosis are more likely. When either stress or personality instability is very severe, psychotic patterns may develop. With a highly unstable personality, character disorders or chronic schizophrenia may develop even with very mild stress. With a highly stable personality, very extreme stress may bring on psychotic reactions such as those we see in combat exhaustion, but these reactions are likely to be acute and transient. As the diagram indicates, a mature and stable individual can withstand a considerable amount of stress while still maintaining good mental health (Marmor and Pumpian-Mindlin, 1950).

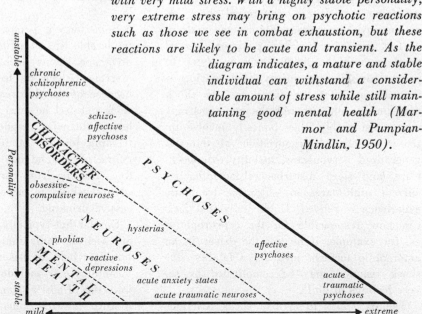

rest, had continued about six weeks when the man finally had to be removed from combat. Most victims of combat exhaustion responded quickly to therapy once they were taken out of the stressful combat situation.

Many predisposing factors tend to lower the overall stress tolerance of a soldier and pave the way for a possible breakdown. Among these are fatigue, feelings of personal vulnerability which come from seeing friends killed or wounded, disturbing letters from home, and lack of faith in either the long-range goals or the immediate objectives for which he is fighting. Factors that tend in the other direction—toward higher resistance and stress tolerance—are a feeling of esprit de corps, pride at being a part of an efficient combat unit, and confidence in commanding officers.

Civilian Shock Reactions

In civilian life, people exposed to airplane crashes, automobile accidents, explosions, fires, earthquakes, sexual assaults, or other terrifying experiences may reveal shock reactions involving personality decompensation. At first the individual may panic or "freeze" or show considerable ingenuity in trying to protect himself from injury. Then, during or immediately after the experience, the shock reaction sets in. Although the symptoms may vary considerably, they typically involve intense anxiety, disorganization of thought, generalized nervousness, inability to concentrate, and sleep disturbances including recurrent nightmares in which the traumatic experience is relived. If the individual feels somehow responsible for the catastrophe—as, for example, if he was the driver in an automobile accident involving a fatality—the shock reaction may be complicated by severe feelings of guilt.

The dynamics in civilian shock reactions are similar to those in combat reactions ex-

cept that the civilian has not been prepared for the situation and also lacks such support as the soldier gets from being part of a fighting unit and from having confidence in his leaders. For the civilian, the experience is not only terrifying but completely unexpected, and the resultant disorganization of personality is apt to be both sudden and severe.

Although some individuals are considerably more vulnerable to shock reactions than others, most people who undergo such reactions—even severe ones—are relatively well adjusted and stable and thus tend to recover rapidly once the crisis is past. They regain confidence in their ability to handle most situations and are able to accept the traumatic experience without allowing it to upset their self-structures. Occasionally, however, an individual seems to be "broken" by a catastrophe and, even after a considerable period of time, suffers residual symptoms of personality disorganization.

Situational Reactions

Sometimes a person finds himself in an intolerable life situation from which he sees no escape. He may feel trapped in an unhappy marriage which he feels he must maintain because of the children, or he may hate his work but feel he must stick to it because of heavy financial responsibilities or lack of training for any other kind of job. In the course of time, he may develop various symptoms ranging from chronic fatigue and lack of enthusiasm to serious inefficiency or excessive drinking.

Similar but typically more severe reactions are seen in individuals serving long prison terms or held as prisoners of war. Here the symptoms may include apathy, depression, a lowering of ethical standards, and a tendency to turn inward. Some of the ways ego defense mechanisms protect the self in these continuing stressful situations were described in Chapter 6.

The symptoms in situational reactions reveal both the individual's inability to function effectively in the situation and his attempts to find action patterns that will relieve his mounting tensions. Here, too, predisposing factors such as rigidity, low stress tolerance, or lack of faith in his frame of reference may enter into the total picture.

NEUROTIC DISORDERS

The stress that precipitates a neurotic reaction may be an inner conflict, such as trying to handle hostility or sexual desires in ways compatible with one's self-concept, or an outer condition, such as social disapproval or oppressive group demands. In either case, the individual is face to face with a situation he evaluates as threatening to his integrity and worth and with which he feels inadequate to cope. His reaction is essentially defense-oriented, and his main effort goes into emergency measures to allay his anxiety and defend himself from devaluation. Although neurotic defenses may help the individual save face, they do nothing to solve his real problems—instead, they serve to complicate his difficulties.

General Characteristics

Neurotic disorders usually have their origin in faulty personality development. Typically the individual is immature in key areas of development, has an unrealistic frame of reference, and lacks some of the necessary competencies for handling life's problems. In his background, one or more of the following are usually found: (1) an overly protective, anxious parent who by his overprotectiveness taught the individual not to trust his own competence; (2) a perfectionist parent who expected and demanded so much that the individual learned to feel incapable of doing anything right; (3) an overly strict parent who made the individual mistrust and be ashamed of his natural impulses; (4) a rejecting parent who taught the individual to feel that he was worthless and unlovable. Handicapped by feelings of inadequacy, the individual may engage in a series of complicated neurotic maneuvers to avoid further damage to his self-integrity.

The neurotic typically lacks a clear-cut sense of identity and shows a considerable discrepancy between his idealized and actual self. He constantly keeps an eye on the kind of person he feels he *should* be rather than the kind of person he actually is. His attitudes and approaches to his problems are apt to be equally unrealistic. He is baffled and frightened by the demands of adult life and unready for the responsibility they entail.

It is hardly surprising that the neurotic's attention and energy are centered on his own conflicts and problems. He is continually and often painfully aware of his own feelings, hopes, ambitions, and disappointments. He is apt to have a variety of complaints—fatigue, discouragement, anxiety, tension, and general feelings of unhappiness. Often he becomes preoccupied with the side-effects of prolonged anxiety or emotional tensions, misinterpreting these bodily symptoms as heart trouble or some other physical illness.

Neurotics usually can get along well enough to keep out of a mental hospital—indeed, they may show adequate or even superior ability to cope with many kinds of problems. In general, however, the neurotic's effectiveness is seriously restricted.

Types of Reaction

It is difficult to generalize about neurotic behavior patterns, for they vary greatly not only in their severity but also in the specific symptoms manifested. All of them, however, seem to develop in something like the following sequence:

1. Perception of common life stresses as terribly threatening; arousal of intense and painful anxiety.

2. Development of exaggerated ego defenses to cope with threat and allay anxiety.

3. A vicious circle of inadequacy, defense, more inadequacy, and a building up of secondary defenses to protect the original ones.

Unless the vicious circle can be broken, the neurotic may develop symptoms of severe personality decompensation. His perception becomes increasingly distorted and he loses his capacity to respond flexibly to changing situations. Irrational fears and obsessive thoughts may become dominant in his consciousness and behavior. Some common patterns of serious neurotic disorder are described briefly below.

Anxiety reaction. In addition to the generalized feelings of anxiety and apprehensiveness characteristic of most neuroses, many neurotics experience acute anxiety attacks in which feelings of foreboding and panic are characteristically accompanied by such physical symptoms as heart palpitations, profuse sweating, and dryness of the mouth. Such attacks may last from a few seconds to a few hours and vary greatly in intensity.

The actual source of the neurotic's anxiety is repressed. An attack may be brought on by (1) unacceptable feelings or desires

INCIDENCE OF MALADJUSTIVE
BEHAVIOR IN THE UNITED STATES

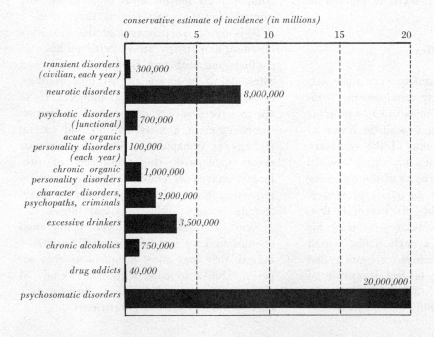

conservative estimate of incidence (in millions)

transient disorders (civilian, each year)	300,000
neurotic disorders	8,000,000
psychotic disorders (functional)	700,000
acute organic personality disorders (each year)	100,000
chronic organic personality disorders	1,000,000
character disorders, psychopaths, criminals	2,000,000
excessive drinkers	3,500,000
chronic alcoholics	750,000
drug addicts	40,000
psychosomatic disorders	20,000,000

threatening to break through into consciousness or into behavior inconsistent with the self-image; (2) reactivation of an early psychic wound, as when a person rejected as a child is criticized by his employer; or (3) a threatened breakdown of ego defenses. Sometimes such a breakdown is threatened by the individual's own mounting rebellion against the defenses that are hemming him in and stifling his normal growth.

The following case history of a neurotic anxiety reaction is fairly typical. An attractive woman in her twenties sought psychological help, complaining of severe anxiety attacks which had occurred about once a week over a period of three months. The attacks usually came on during the evenings when her husband worked late at the office, and they usually lasted throughout the night or until she could reduce the tension somewhat with alcohol and sleeping tablets. She stated that during these attacks she felt incredibly tense and apprehensive, and was terrified that she was going to die or experience some horrible catastrophe. She said that she had often contemplated suicide during the attacks but that "of course, I am not the type of person to really go through with it." When her husband returned home, usually quite late, he was unable to help her; she found some comfort, however, in calling a close girl friend and talking to her on the phone for half an hour or more. During her last attack neither her friend nor her husband was available, and this made her realize that she must get help. In addition, her husband was becoming increasingly concerned over the possibility that, if the attacks continued, she might become an alcoholic.

In the course of therapy it became apparent that the patient, despite her youth, dreaded the prospect of growing old and feared that she was no longer sexually attractive to her husband, who was becoming increasingly preoccupied with his work and often did not come home until quite late at night. Although she apparently feared that he was going out with another woman, she was unable to verbalize this to the therapist, insisting that her husband was not the type of man who would be unfaithful. It came out that her father had left her mother when the patient was nine years old and that this had been a terribly traumatic experience for both her mother and herself—both had felt rejected, devaluated, and hurt. Although it became apparent that the patient's anxiety attacks stemmed from her doubts about her own ability to hold a husband and maintain a marriage, this entire problem—related to the earlier trauma of her parents' breakup —was so painful to face that it had been repressed from consciousness. It made itself known, however, by the recurrent anxiety attacks. In short, the stresses in this young woman's life situation had come to focus on her particular Achilles heel.

Repression is the primary mechanism underlying anxiety reactions, but over a period of time it is usually reinforced by other neurotic defenses which make it increasingly difficult for the individual to cope with his problems effectively.

Dissociative reaction. In a dissociative reaction the individual escapes from conflicts or other threats by blocking certain parts of his life from consciousness. Three subtypes are distinguished.

1. Amnesia. The amnesic patient has total or partial inability to remember past experience. A neurotic individual who finds himself in an intolerable life situation, such as an unhappy marriage or job, may develop total amnesia, which enables him to escape the situation without self-devaluation. In partial amnesia a traumatic episode, such as combat experience or sexual assault, may be screened from consciousness until time reduces the trauma. The amnesia may last for days, weeks, or even years.

2. *Fugue.* In a fugue reaction, amnesia is accompanied by actual physical flight. The patient becomes amnesic and wanders away; then, perhaps, he may suddenly find himself in a strange place with no memory of how he got there or what he has been doing. During the period of the fugue, he retains his basic skills and habit patterns, but he takes on a new identity and does not know who he is or where he has come from.

3. *Multiple personality.* For most of us, the various roles we play are related to and fairly consistent with each other. But sometimes a neurotic is unable to reconcile the role he feels he *must* play, in order to live up to his self-ideal, with a contradictory role that he would *like* to play. In rare cases the repressed traits, which are inconsistent with his usual role, crowd to the surface and take over for a time. Thus a moralistic, timid personality may alternate with an outgoing, promiscuous, fun-loving one. Typically, the two or more roles are kept separate from each other, so that the individual is aware only of the role he is playing at the moment. In some cases, however, one personality is aware of another and may even play tricks on it.

In all dissociative reactions the individual avoids a difficult and threatening conflict by blocking it from consciousness and keeping the contradictory parts separate from each other. These are such spectacular reactions that they have received considerable public attention, but they actually have little defensive value and are relatively rare.

Conversion reaction (hysteria). In a conversion reaction the individual resolves his conflict or difficulty by developing the symptoms of some disease or disability. For example, he may go blind, become deaf or paralyzed, develop coughing or sneezing spells, lose his sensitivity to touch and pain in some body area, or even simulate the symptoms of pregnancy or some disease like malaria. Yet no organic pathology underlies his symp-toms. Sometimes, however, the picture is complicated by the fact that the symptoms are superimposed on actual organic damage, as when an individual with a history of impaired hearing suddenly becomes totally deaf.

As with other neurotic reactions, the particular stress that precipitates hysteric symptoms is a situation in which the individual feels hopelessly inadequate and faced with self-devaluation. The apparent disability of the conversion hysteric brings him sympathy and attention and enables him to avoid the threatening situation. Yet he is not malingering or putting on an act. The symptoms are real, and he is as baffled by them as anyone else, though he typically does not show the concern one would expect to see in someone actually going blind or afflicted with a paralyzed arm.

The physiological mechanisms involved in conversion reactions are not fully understood, though interestingly enough such symptoms can be removed or changed under hypnosis. There may also be some selectivity in the symptoms, as when an allegedly blind patient avoids a baseball thrown at him or when a patient with a paralyzed arm uses it to turn over during sleep.

In an age and a society in which there is no longer belief in being "struck" dumb or blind, conversion reactions are much rarer than they used to be, though they still are common in certain less sophisticated cultures.

Phobic reaction. A phobia is a persistent, unwarranted fear of something which presents either no danger at all to the individual or a minor danger that he magnifies out of all proportion. The fear has been displaced from the object or event that is the real source of his anxiety; thus the new fear acts as a sort of camouflage. For example, the individual who is afraid of failing on his new job may develop a fear of elevators or something else that makes it impossible for him to continue in the job. The phobia enables him to quit without the self-devaluation that would come from admitting failure. He realizes that his phobia is irrational, but he has no control over it and must yield to it to avoid overpowering anxiety.

The original fear may also originate from inner dangers. For example, a neurotic housewife who is unhappily married but would be horrified to think she could want to kill her husband may develop such a fear of knives that she will not have one in the house. It is as though the neurotic in his immaturity equates the thought with the deed.

Obsessive-compulsive reaction. In an obsessive-compulsive reaction the individual is seemingly victimized by persistent irrational thoughts that he cannot drive away or by a compulsion to carry out certain acts. Next to anxiety reactions, this is the most common neurotic type.

Obsessions run the gamut from a fear that one is going to shout some obscene word in a public gathering to a persistent wish that a loved one would drop dead. To the individual such obsessive thoughts seem not only irrational but horrifying. Although immorality and violence are common in obsessions, the individual's rigid conscience usually prevents their being carried out in action.

In some cases obsessions seem to represent the breakthrough into consciousness of actual thoughts or desires simply as ideas, without emotional or motivational reinforcement. Thus if the individual has repressed resentment and hostility toward his mother, such feelings may break through into dreams or fantasies of her being killed in which his desire for this event has been left out. In other cases reaction formation seems to be involved. For example, an individual with an urge to engage in some sexual act that he considers immoral develops obsessive fears of syphilis or becomes obsessed with the need for catching and punishing all sexual offenders.

Compulsions are sometimes means of counteracting obsessive thoughts. An individual who cannot rid himself of thoughts of masturbating and considers such thoughts immoral may have a compulsion to wash his hands every few minutes, thus symbolically cleansing or purifying himself. In other cases, as when an individual develops a compulsion for orderliness and must follow endless rituals in everything he does, his behavior seems to be serving the purpose of structuring his behavior so completely that he is kept safe from any temptation or danger.

In general, obsessive-compulsive reactions seem to help the insecure individual maintain inner control, protect himself from inner or outer threats, and lessen guilt and anxiety somewhat by the mechanism of undoing. An obsessive-compulsive pattern of defense is clearly evident in the following case of a twenty-four-year-old man who sought psychiatric treatment. The patient complained of recurrent fears that he had a venereal disease. He felt compelled to wash his hands repeatedly and was afraid to touch people or go out with girls because he thought he would contaminate them. His symptoms had begun some ten years previously when he began to masturbate a great deal. A partial evaluation of his case follows (Posner, 1951 pp. 71-72, 74):

"He has been taught that 'sex is evil' and so he repressed his 'dreams, hopes, and desires' for they make him feel 'unclean and decrepit.' Sex is mysterious to him and it becomes something to be feared. He is 'afraid to venture into the unknown and get what he wants, for he'd be lost.' He sets up idealistically high standards for the female. She becomes something 'good, pure, and beautiful,' untinged by sexuality. Women are unable to live up to these ideals, and he finds that he cannot establish successful relationships with them. He finds it necessary to depend upon bribery with 'dates and presents' in order to gain the female's attention. He is constantly disappointed in women, but he recognizes to some extent that the situation arises because of some inadequacy within himself. He is not aware of the specific mechanisms involved, but he feels responsible for 'tarnishing' them in some way. He derogates men, in general, for he holds them, as well as himself, to blame for depriving the female of purity and goodness by virtue of their sexual urges. Since he has constructed a situation where he can gain little sexual satisfaction from the female, he turns to the male. But this is even more taboo. The solution to his problems, he feels, would be marriage. This would provide an acceptable outlet for his sexual energy and he could become 'clean, pure, and useful' again. He is afraid that old age will come upon him before he has reaped all the advantages of youth.

"His self-picture is one in which he sees himself as 'a self-pitying sort of baby who wants someone to come along and sympathize with him.' He is aware that he has a problem, but he 'always looks away from things he wants to look at and closes his eyes to make . . . sure he doesn't see.' . . .

"Rather than face what is troubling him, he retreats into a concern with the petty details of life and satisfies himself with a superficial approach to problems."

The symptoms of this patient not only reveal his underlying difficulties but represent his attempt to control his inner urges by obsessive-compulsive patterns of behavior. Thus the obsessive fear of contaminating others helps him to control his "evil" sexual impulses; and his compulsive hand-washing is a ritual which helps "cleanse" him. There were indications, however, that the patient's neurotic defenses were breaking down and that personality decompensation was becoming progressively more serious.

Asthenic reaction. The asthenic reaction, formerly called *neurasthenia*, centers around chronic fatigue, discouragement, and apathy, usually with numerous vague aches, pains, and bodily complaints. It used to be ascribed to "nerve weakness" and was thought to be brought on by overwork, but the psychological basis of the symptoms is revealed in the way they drop away and energy and enthusiasm appear when the individual is doing something in which he is interested and for which he feels adequate. His customary fatigue is his way of coping with what seems to be a hopelessly difficult life situation; a "sick" person obviously cannot be expected to achieve much or be able to solve difficult problems.

Neurotic depressive reaction. In a neurotic depressive reaction the individual is deeply depressed and berates himself for mistakes or setbacks that most people would take in stride. Often he complains of restlessness, inability to concentrate, feelings of extreme unworthiness, and great tension.

Neurotic depressive reactions are often associated with ambivalent feelings toward someone the individual feels he should love. If he has resented a domineering mother and wished she were dead, he may feel somehow responsible for her death when she dies. It is not uncommon for a soldier to be secretly glad that an exploding shell gets someone else instead of him. But to a neurotic, the realization of having such an "immoral" thought may bring feelings of guilt and apprehension that he will be punished, perhaps by death or mutilation.

The individual who develops neurotic depressive reactions is typically a person with an immature but rigid conscience, vivid ideas about sin and guilt, and a tendency to self-blame when anything goes wrong. The self-recrimination and self-depreciation in this reaction may serve as a form of punishment that atones for the individual's sinful thoughts, thus representing an exaggerated use of the normal ego defense mechanism of undoing.

In summary it may be said that neurotic reactions seldom involve such clear-cut patterns of symptoms as we have outlined here. Except for a relatively few classic cases, most neurotics manifest a combination of symptoms and cannot be pigeonholed strictly as one type or another. The severity of neurotic reactions also covers a wide range, from those which interfere only with a limited area of activity to those which are severely handicapping. Finally, it should be emphasized again that the individual who behaves in a seemingly irrational, self-defeating manner is not doing so deliberately. Neurotic defenses come into operation unconsciously and are maintained without conscious reasoning. Despite the fact that they bring great suffering and frustration, the neurotic clings to them because the only other alternatives he sees appear more threatening still.

DIFFERENCES BETWEEN NEUROSES AND PSYCHOSES

	Neuroses	*Psychoses*
General Behavior	Mild degree of personality decompensation; perspective and efficiency impaired but fairly adequate social functioning possible.	Severe degree of personality decompensation; reality contact markedly impaired; individual incapacitated in social functioning.
Nature of Symptoms	Anxiety, bodily complaints, and psychosomatic symptoms common but no delusions, hallucinations, or other markedly deviate behavior.	Wide range of psychosomatic symptoms with delusions, hallucinations, distorted emotional reactions, fragmented thought processes, and other severely deviate behavior.
Social Aspects	Behavior rarely injurious or dangerous to individual or to society.	Behavior frequently injurious or dangerous to individual or to society.
Insight	Individual often has some insight into inappropriateness of his behavior.	Individual rarely has insight concerning his behavior, does not realize he is sick.
Treatment	Individual rarely needs institutional care, psychotherapy usually the only treatment necessary.	Individual usually requires institutional care; physical and psychological therapy commonly needed.

Adapted from Thorpe and Katz (1948).

FUNCTIONAL PSYCHOTIC DISORDERS

In psychotic disorders there are such severe disturbances in thinking, feeling, and behavior that the individual's contact with reality is seriously impaired. Hospitalization is usually necessary. The term *insanity* is sometimes used in referring to psychotic disorders, but this is a legal term rather than a psychiatric one.

It was formerly thought that psychoses were inherited by way of recessive genes, and members of families with a history of psychotic disorders were fearful of becoming psychotic themselves or having psychotic children. It is now believed that psychoses are not inherited directly but that genetic factors can have an influence in two ways: (1) by producing constitutional differences in resistance to stress and (2) by helping to determine which specific pattern appears if the individual *does* become psychotic. For example, some people seem constitutionally more prone to develop schizophrenic reactions than manic-depressive ones, and vice versa.

General Characteristics

The several specific psychotic reactions usually share the following characteristics:

1. Personality disorganization. Psychotics show serious personality disorganization, though the degree varies greatly from one patient to another and even in the same patient from time to time. There is a marked impairment of contact with reality, which may show itself in disorientation as to time and place, in overexcitement or overdepression, or in misinterpretation of events. Often the disorganization and lowering of cortical controls bring a release of primitive desires, resulting in inappropriate behavior—for example, profane language, indiscriminate sexual overtures, or physical or verbal attacks.

2. Delusions and hallucinations. Delusions are false beliefs that the patient defends despite their logical absurdity and all contrary evidence. Hallucinations are perceptions of objects, smells, sounds, or other sensory phenomena without any appropriate sensory stimulation. Both symptoms are typical of psychotic disorders.

There are several kinds of delusions. Most frequent are (1) delusions about having committed some unforgivable sin; (2) hypochondriacal delusions about having some horrible disease; (3) delusions of persecution in which enemies are plotting against the individual, talking about him, or influencing him in some way; and (4) delusions of grandeur, in which the individual thinks he is some important and remarkable person, perhaps a great leader who has been appointed to save the world from destruction. These delusions may be transient and disorganized, or they may be organized into enduring, coherent, logical systems.

The most common hallucinations are auditory ones, but other sensory modes are commonly involved. The patient may taste poison in his food, smell poison gas that his enemies are using to try to kill him, or feel small bugs running around under his skin. Not all psychotics have hallucinations, of course, and the same patient may have them at one time but not at another.

Delusions and hallucinations may result primarily from (1) exaggerated ego defense mechanisms such as projection; (2) lowered personality integration and removal of cortical controls, permitting release of segmental processes; or (3) chemical substances like lysergic acid that are secreted into the blood in some individuals prone to psychotic reactions. The temporary disorganization of thought processes that lysergic acid can cause has been demonstrated by injecting it into the blood of normal people. One graduate student who participated in such an experiment described his reaction as follows (Fabing, 1955, p. 209):

"I had very little by way of visual hallucinations, but what *I* consider the important thing that—well, what's a word to describe it—dissociated, plagued, pounded, weighed—all these are inadequate to describe the horrible state I was in, all of them put together. Perhaps the central thing was suspicion and fear that you would find out about me, or perhaps think things that were not true. On and on and ON this went, and, as was no doubt obvious, I decided to do as little as possible so I wouldn't make any mistakes."

It is hoped that further study of body chemistry in relation to the psychoses will give us a better understanding of psychotic disorders and suggest improved methods of treating them.

Types of Reaction

Psychotic disorders are classified as *functional* or *organic*. In functional disorders there is a breakdown in adaptive functioning in an apparently intact organism; in organic disorders there is some organic pathology. Actually psychotic disorders seem to fall along a continuum, with those of psychogenic origin at one end and those of organic origin at the other. Once a psychotic reaction develops, from whatever origin, both psychological and physiological factors may aggravate it. At the present time, research on glandular imbalances and chemical changes is pointing up the importance of organic factors in many cases formerly ascribed entirely to psychological processes.

Among the functional psychotic disorders there are four quite different patterns, each with several subtypes.

Schizophrenic reactions. Schizophrenia is the most common of the psychotic disorders and accounts for about a fifth of all first admissions to mental hospitals. It occurs most commonly during young adulthood but may occur in childhood or in later life.

Schizophrenic reactions usually develop gradually over a period of several years. The full-blown reaction is characterized by withdrawal from reality, emotional blunting and distortion, disorganization of mental processes, and deterioration of personal habits and ethical controls.

The following case study illustrates the gradual development of a schizophrenic reaction in a young girl who, at the age of nineteen, made headlines by shooting a major league baseball player in a Chicago hotel room. In the course of a psychiatric examination ordered by the court, the following case history was pieced together (Haines and Esser, 1950, pp. 739-742):

The patient was born in 1929. She was cheerful and happy as a child and did well in school, but during adolescence she seemed to change in many ways, becoming extremely nervous and self-conscious. She did not want people to look at her and felt very uncomfortable in crowds. She graduated from a commercial school at seventeen and, after failing to get a job as a private secretary, finally obtained a position as a typist and billing clerk. She was a hard worker and well liked by her employers.

While attending a major league baseball game on April 27, 1947, the patient noticed Eddie, one of the players, when a fan shouted "Hello, funny face" at him. After that he became her only interest. She attended all the games she could and began to celebrate the twenty-seventh of every month as their "anniversary." She clipped pictures of Eddie and stories about him from the newspapers and kept one photo with her always, putting it under her pillow at night. Because his number was 36, she bought records made in 1936; because he came from Boston, she ate baked beans; because he was of Lithuanian descent, she studied the language, read books on Lithuania, and listened to Lithuanian music. Her father, her employer, men on the street reminded her of Eddie.

". . . When asked if she wanted to marry [Eddie] she replied she seemed to want to mother him. She wanted to be with his mind and with his intellect. Sexual matters were never discussed. When [it was] suggested that she meet Eddie socially she replied that she couldn't stand it, that she 'knew she would spill all over herself if she were face to face with him.' "

In discussing with the psychiatrist why she shot Eddie, the patient summarized:

" 'It's a mixture of things. First of all I think I shot him because I liked him a great deal and knew I never could have him and if I couldn't have him neither could anybody else. Secondly, I had the idea that if I shot him I would have to shoot myself. [The patient had often spoken to her parents of suicide, but they had not taken her seriously.] In the third place I wanted publicity and attention for once. . . . About the first year I was crazy about him. The second year . . . I pretended he was with me and I talked to him, not out loud, it was in a mental sense, not physical, and we walked down the street together. Whenever I walked home from my mother's home, she used to say "Take the street car home." I said, I didn't want to because I had Eddie with me. I didn't tell her that. She would have laughed at me. I told my girl friend. I have never joked about it. I remember one day, that was the 27th— that is our anniversary . . . I was reading [the newspaper] and saw his picture. He was holding a gun. He as much as told me to go, right there on the picture. I told him you got me coming there on the 27th, what a nice

anniversary present. . . . I used to go to all the ball games I could . . . and all the time I was watching him I was forming the idea in my mind of killing him.' "

When Eddie's team came to town, the patient checked into the hotel with a rifle she had bought in a pawn shop. The next day she went to the game, stayed until the seventh inning, and then returned to the hotel. She gave a bell boy a note to leave in Eddie's room, telling the ball player that she wanted to see him. Between 6:30 p.m. and 10:30 she had three drinks, listened to the radio, and debated what she would do—kill him or give herself up. At 10:30 she decided that Eddie wasn't coming and that she would go to bed and leave the hotel in the morning without seeing him. No sooner had she fallen asleep than Eddie phoned, inquiring what she wanted. She asked if she could see him in the morning; he said this was impossible but agreed to come to her room for a few minutes that evening.

" '. . . I remember when he knocked on the door, I was scared stiff but I thought to myself I would settle this once and for all and really kill him. That time I had a knife in my skirt pocket and I was going to use that on him. When I opened the door he came rushing in right past me. . . . I was kind of mad that he came right in and sat down and didn't give me a chance to stab him. He looked at me surprised and said, "What do you want to see me about?" I said wait a minute I have a surprise for you. I went to the closet and got out the gun. I took it out, pointed it at him and he had such a silly look on his face. He looked so surprised. I was pretty mad at him. . . . He just stood there stuttering and stammering and he asked me again, "What is this all about, what have I done?" and I said, for two years you have been bothering me and now you are going to die, and then I shot him. For a minute I didn't think I shot him because he just stood there and then he crashed against the wall. . . . He kept saying, "Baby why did you do that?" and then I said, I don't believe I shot you, because he was still smiling. Then I knelt down next to him. He had his hand stretched out, I put my hand over his. He said something to the effect, "You like that don't you?" I took my hand away from his when he said that. . . . I thought, well, now's the time to shoot myself . . . but I couldn't find [the bullets] and then I lost my nerve. I was frantic by that time and I called the operator to call the doctor. When he kept moaning, "Why did you do it, oh baby, why did you do it?", he was groaning and I didn't like to hear it. So I went out in the hall and waited for the doctor. The doctor came and the police. After the doctor came the house detective came too. It was so silly, nobody came out of their rooms. You think they would come rushing out. I got mad. I kept telling them I shot Eddie. . . .' "

After her arrest, she said of Eddie:

" 'He is with me in jail. . . . We talk about the whole thing. I said, what are you going to do about me now? You wanted me to do this. He usually answers my questions. This time he evaded me. Finally he said to me, "Don't you think it would be better to go to some hospital?" I told him I would rather do time . . . than go to a psychopathic ward. . . . I'm not insane. I'll probably go to the Psychopathic Hospital because I said he is with me but it isn't fair. He should get me out of this mess. He got me in, now let him get me out. . . . I didn't want to kill him, not his real self not the self that was with me. His unconscious self. There are two parts of him, his other self does know he is with me. The man himself doesn't know anything about this. It doesn't do anything to me, it just walks and talks and keeps me company. He's like an invisible friend.

"When questioned about the next time: 'If I ever get out of here I'll kill him for sure if he ever got married. He's the only one worth shooting. I wouldn't shoot anybody else.' "

The patient was indicted for the shooting but was declared legally insane and committed to a state mental hospital.

The dynamics in schizophrenic reactions may be exceedingly complex and, of course, vary considerably from one case to another. Often there is a background of disturbed family relationships and early psychic traumas that have resulted in a failure of socialization and in the development of ineffective behavior patterns, such as withdrawal in the face of hurt. Studies have indicated that the mothers of schizophrenic patients are often rejecting, overanxious, overpossessive, moralistic, and perfectionistic. As children, patients had commonly been so well indoctrinated with the evils of sex and hostility that they found such impulses and desires unacceptable and self-devaluating and strove to repress them. Often they had been regarded as "good boys" or "good girls."

This concept of the "good" child is very important for an understanding of how schizophrenic reactions develop. It means that the individual has accepted for himself the role and values his parents and society have chosen for him and has learned to judge himself by those values. Sexual desires and hostility in particular are usually taboo. But his conscience development is immature and rigid, and in order to remain "good," he must maintain a fiction, denying that certain parts of him exist. Meanwhile, the repressed feelings keep injecting themselves directly or indirectly into his thoughts and behavior, threatening his picture of himself as "good." The result is intense and continuing inner turmoil, self-condemnation, and self-devaluation.

Although symptoms are not always clear-cut, there are four main subtypes of schizophrenia, each involving a somewhat different strategy for coping with conflict and anxiety. In *simple schizophrenia* the individual solves his problem by withdrawing and insulating himself from life. He simply gives up caring or trying to achieve anything. In *hebephrenic schizophrenia* withdrawal and decompensation reach their ultimate, and silliness, fragmentation of thought processes, delusions, and hallucinations attest to the complete disintegration of the personality. In *catatonic schizophrenia* the individual seems to be still struggling desperately to save himself. He typically alternates between periods of stupor, during which he may maintain odd postures and follow stereotyped ritualistic patterns, and periods of intense excitement and activity. In *paranoid schizophrenia* the individual tries to maintain his feelings of adequacy by blaming his difficulties on others. He may assert that his impure thoughts have been elicited by others, who control his mind with electronic devices, that his failures are due to enemies who are plotting against him. But his delusions are poorly systematized and do not protect him from further self-devaluation and decompensation.

Paranoid reactions. In a paranoid reaction the patient develops a set of delusions but otherwise shows no evidence of serious personality disorganization. Because paranoid individuals seem so normal in other respects, they are often able to avoid being hospitalized. Less than 2 percent of first admissions to mental hospitals are paranoiacs.

Paranoid delusions are intricate and highly systematized. Usually they center around one theme, such as financial matters, a job, or an unfaithful wife. Paranoid reactions typically center around delusions of persecution —the individual feels that he is being taken advantage of, lied to, mistreated, plotted against, or otherwise persecuted. Some paranoiacs develop delusions of grandeur, fancying themselves to be someone with an important mission to perform for the benefit of mankind.

Although the "evidence" on which the paranoiac bases his delusions is extremely tenuous, he is firm in maintaining his own interpretation of the facts. He may be convinced of his wife's unfaithfulness because she has suddenly taken to buying perfume guaranteed to make her attractive to men. When he tells his friends about her unfaithfulness and they question his assumptions, he is sure they have turned against him and gone over to his wife's side—have become his enemies. Thus with time, more and more of his world comes to be integrated into his delusional system.

A regular *paranoid reaction* develops slowly and occurs most often in late middle age. There also are *paranoid states*—transient and less well-systematized paranoid delusions that occur in response to some particularly traumatic event. In such cases there is neither the degree of systematization that characterizes so-called true paranoia nor the disordered thought and personality disorganization of the paranoid schizophrenic.

Paranoid individuals typically have a childhood background that fostered rigidity, suspiciousness, high aspirations, repressed hostility, and intense feelings of inferiority. Personality characteristics that often foreshadow paranoia are aloofness and an overly critical attitude toward other people, hypersensitivity to criticism, craving for praise and recognition, formal adherence to socially approved behavior, overzealous attention to the most minute details of work, and an almost complete lack of a sense of humor. These personal qualities lead the individual to one failure after another in critical life situations, until eventually he constructs a delusional system based on projection to defend himself against the intense pain of continued failure and self-devaluation. Working from the premise that he has failed not because of his own inadequacy but because others are working against him, he distorts more and more of the facts to fit his delusional scheme and gradually develops a comprehensive, systematized framework that is impervious to logical attack.

As one might expect, paranoiacs can be extremely dangerous, for they may decide to take the law into their own hands and give their enemies the punishment they so obviously deserve. Many people, including husbands and wives falsely accused of infidelity, have been killed by paranoiacs intent on righting the wrongs they feel have been done them.

Manic-depressive reactions. The central characteristic of manic-depressive reactions, which account for something over 6 percent of first admissions to mental hospitals, is an exaggerated elation or depression. Against this background, there are a variety of other symptoms in keeping with the prevailing mood. A patient may show only the elated reaction (*manic type*), only the depressive reaction (*depressive type*), or an alternation between them (*circular type*) with a cycle of a few minutes to several months. With or without treatment, these disorders tend to run their course and clear up spontaneously, though they may recur. The possibility that their onset and remission are correlated with changes in blood chemistry is currently under investigation.

Individuals who show manic-depressive reactions tend to be conscientious, outgoing, sociable, and energetic. Often they show evidence of a constitutional tendency toward exaggerated mood swings, with overenthusiasm and elation when things go well and extreme dejection when things go badly. They also tend to be overly self-demanding and self-critical, assuming all the blame for failures they could not possibly have avoided.

In the manic reaction the individual seems to be trying to escape his difficulties in a whirlwind of activity. This is an exaggeration of the fairly common reaction in which a person tries to forget a broken love affair by going on a round of parties and convincing himself and everyone else that he is having a wonderful time when actually he is just one step away from tears. The manic patient is full of ideas, optimism, and elaborate projects that are never completed. He drives himself night and day and shows poor judgment in his use of time, money, and other resources. Occasionally his reaction may be so severe that he shouts incoherently, has hallucinations, and becomes thoroughly disoriented; but more often it is mild enough that most people see him simply as a person with unusual energy and enthusiasm.

In the depressive reaction the symptoms are essentially the opposite. The individual turns his rigid conscience against himself and suffers agonies of discouragement and dejection, with a slowing down of thought and activity. Feelings of unworthiness, failure, and guilt dominate his consciousness. Such reactions may be quite mild or so severe that the patient becomes immobile, has hallucinations and delusions centering about his guilt, and becomes disoriented regarding time, place, and person. He feels that his unethical thoughts are as sinful in themselves as if they were carried into action, and he may even be convinced he actually *did* commit some horrible deed that he may have had fantasies of committing. This orgy of self-blame evidently serves two defensive objectives: (1) the self-punishment helps to atone for his "sins" and (2) his admission of complete worthlessness enables him to give up the struggle temporarily and regress to dependence. But these defenses may overshoot their mark, and suicide is always a real danger in psychotic depressive reactions.

Involutional psychotic reaction. An involutional psychotic reaction may develop during the involutional or change-of-life period—roughly between forty and fifty-five for women and between fifty and sixty-five for men. It is much more common among women than among men and accounts for about 6 percent of first admissions to mental hospitals.

Involutional reactions are essentially "agitated depressions," in which the individual is overactive and depressed at the same time. They usually begin with restlessness, insomnia, unprovoked spells of weeping, and excessive worry about minor matters. As the reaction becomes more acute, the individual becomes increasingly depressed and apprehensive and develops strong feelings of worthlessness and self-condemnation. He may become preoccupied with some real or imagined sin that he feels can never be forgiven. He is in utmost despair and feels there is absolutely no hope.

His misery is usually accompanied by restlessness or agitation in which he may pace the floor, weep, wring his hands, pull his hair, bite his lips, and cry aloud at his fate. Hypochondriacal delusions are common, to the extent that he may insist his stomach is rotting away or his brain is being destroyed by some dread disease. Yet despite his depression and anxiety, the individual suffering from an involutional reaction may not be disoriented and may realize that he is ill and needs help.

During the involutional period in life various glandular and other physiological changes commonly lead to some emotional instability and feelings of depression, especially in women. Coupled with this predisposing factor are new stresses in the life situation. A person at this age comes to realize that youth is over and that life is rushing by him. He comes face to face with the fact that he is committed to whatever life pattern he has established—that a good part of his life energy is spent and that he cannot start over. Actual severe losses at this time, such as the loss of a loved one or heavy financial reverses, are especially stressful.

Most people are adaptable and well enough prepared for this life period to be able to take it in stride and make the necessary changes in their self-concept. The involutional patient is usually a rigid, overconscientious person with a tendency toward self-blame. He is dissatisfied with the way he has lived his life, and the realization of its finality brings self-recrimination and a feeling of hopelessness. His anxiety is somewhat allayed by self-punishment, but the stress situation is so self-devaluating that personality decompensation remains, and recovery is not usually spontaneous. Modern methods of treatment, however, have been unusually successful in clearing up these disorders.

DISORDERS

ASSOCIATED WITH BRAIN PATHOLOGY

There are a number of conditions in which the brain and nervous system may be damaged or their functioning impaired. In addition to sensory-motor disturbances like paralysis, incoordination, and convulsive seizures, such damage may bring disturbances of psychological functioning with impairment of intellectual functions, emotional shallowness and instability, and deterioration in conduct and standards.

Mental disorders associated with organic pathology are classified as *acute* or *chronic*. In acute disorders the pathology is temporary and usually reversible; in chronic disorders it is permanent. Disorders associated with severe vitamin deficiency, for example, are classified as acute disorders because they clear up quickly with massive doses of vitamins, whereas disorders associated with syphilis are classified as chronic, since lasting brain damage is involved. This distinction is not a hard and fast one, however; sometimes an acute disorder clears up for the most part but leaves some residual symptoms, and in other cases a chronic disorder shows apparent improvement with time. Cells in the cortex do not have the power of regeneration, and when they are destroyed, the damage is permanent; but the brain does have considerable potential for reorganization and compensation, and often intact areas can gradually take over functions formerly handled by the damaged areas. Sometimes this process of *vicarious functioning* leads to a gradual improvement in behavior and mental processes.

With extensive brain damage or upset of brain cell metabolism, physiological rather than psychological factors play the dominant role, and the nature and amount of the damage directly influence the symptom picture. With less extensive damage, however, psychological rather than physiological factors play the dominant role. Individuals with good stress tolerance can compensate for considerable brain damage or pathology without showing any serious impairment of intellectual or emotional functions, whereas marginally adjusted or unstable individuals may develop mental disorders with only slight brain damage. Interestingly enough, when the brain injury necessitates hospitalization, the rate and degree of recovery are influenced by the patient's attitude toward the life situation to which he must return. If he is eager to go back to his family and job, the outlook is much more favorable than if he dreads returning to an unpleasant life situation.

The conditions that may bring about these disorders include brain injury, brain tumor, certain infectious diseases, toxic and metabolic disturbances, endocrine disorders, and the brain deterioration that may come with old age. The actual disorders cover the entire gamut of abnormal behavior. In some cases there are predominantly neurotic symptoms; in other instances, there are psychotic symptoms or symptoms which are typical of the character disorders.

With the increasing longevity of people in this country, the mental disorders associated with old age have become a major health problem and account for over a fourth of all first admissions to mental hospitals. Two types of brain damage are common with old age: (1) gradual deterioration and atrophy of brain cells comparable to the general deteriorative changes elsewhere in the body and (2) hardening of the arteries leading to the brain, resulting in inadequate circulation, faulty nutrition of brain cells, and, in some cases, hemorrhages in the brain.

Older members of our society also face especially difficult stresses, for as a people, we value youth and beauty and have little reverence for age. Anyone who has led a busy, productive life finds it hard to be relegated to the side lines where no one needs him or asks his advice or looks to him for important decisions. The death of a life partner and a narrowing circle of old friends may leave big empty places in his life and make the world seem much less secure and friendly. Chronic poor health may erode a previously cheerful outlook. The necessity of being financially dependent on one's children is especially galling and self-devaluating.

But here, as in the case of other disorders, the outcome is not determined mechanically by either the inner stress of brain damage or the outer stresses of the life situation. The answer that the individual gives in such circumstances depends also on his maturity and personality integration—his lifetime assumptions and attitudes.

CHARACTER (PERSONALITY) DISORDERS

The disorders lumped together as character disorders have little in common except that primarily they seem to represent distorted personality development rather than decompensation under stress. They tend to involve a direct *acting out* rather than the indirect defense of the self seen in the various symptoms of the neurotic or psychotic. Four types of character disorders are described below.

Antisocial (Psychopathic) Reaction

One of the most fascinating and baffling disorders is that in which an individual who otherwise seems normal is lacking in conscience development and in any feeling of warmth for and loyalty to other people. In this category we find unprincipled businessmen, confidence men, impostors, crooked politicians, prostitutes, and assorted delinquents and criminals.

The dynamics of the antisocial or psychopathic personality are not fully understood. There seems a good possibility that this disorder is related, in certain cases at least, to a constitutional or acquired malfunction of the higher brain centers, which are concerned with adaptive behavior and normally act as inhibiters over the lower, more primitive neural centers (Lindner, 1944).

Whatever the role of organic factors, childhood environment seems to play a major role in shaping the psychopath's antisocial behavior patterns (Levy, 1951). Many of these individuals come from respected families where the parents put up a good front for the public but remain somewhat indifferent to their children and fail to provide good models for their ethical development. The children typically are denied normal affectional relationships; and at the same time that they are ignored, they may be overindulged in such matters as expressing their aggressions and their desires. By precept and example, the parents often emphasize the importance of appearances rather than values and may encourage the development of personal charm and poise as tools for manipulating others.

The product of this kind of background is likely to be an individual who has learned to gratify his immediate needs without considering the rights of others or even his own long-range needs. A startling but in many ways classic case of a psychopathic personality is described below (Galvin and MacDonald, 1959, pp. 1057, 1059-1061):

"On November 1, 1955, eleven minutes after leaving Denver, a 4-engine airliner exploded and crashed with the loss of 44 lives. Two weeks later a 23-year-old man confessed that he had placed in his mother's luggage, a time bomb consisting of a timer, hot shot battery, blasting caps and 25 sticks of dynamite. Following a plea of insanity, he was committed to hospital for psychiatric examination. . . ."

At the hospital, the young man retracted his confession, which he claimed he had made under pressure. He denied ever having wished to kill his mother and claimed that he had not blown up the aircraft, an act which he knew was wrong "both morally and legally."

The patient's history revealed that his mother had placed him in an institution for fatherless boys when he was six years old. Three years later the mother married a wealthy rancher, but she refused the boy's repeated requests to come home. School records reveal he was poorly adjusted and felt his mother did not love him. At eleven, he was expelled from the school for stealing. At sixteen, he lied about his age (with his mother's help) and enlisted in the Coast Guard, but within six months he went A.W.O.L. and subsequently was discharged. In the next two years he held over twenty-five different jobs.

". . . In March, 1951, he forged over 40 checks for a total value of approximately $4,500. . . . He was arrested in September, 1951, in Texas, after crashing through a road block at high speed and was sentenced to 60 days imprisonment for bootlegging and carrying a concealed weapon." He faced trial for his forgeries, but was released early in 1952 on five years' probation. The following year, he married a girl he had met while taking some college courses. This was the first girl he had "really cared for." Although he made friends easily, he had only one close friend other than his wife.

"When his stepfather died in October, 1954, his mother inherited over $90,000. In 1955, she purchased a drive-in for him and went to live with him. Although his mother had told him that he was to be in charge of the business, she interfered considerably in its management and there was increasing friction between them. During this year he became very irritable and short tempered. At the same time, he continued to be very dependent upon his mother. The drive-in was not a financial success and in September, 1955, it was closed for the winter months. The patient then worked as a night mechanic. This was his 45th job since leaving school."

After being arrested and sent to the hospital for psychiatric examination, following the plane explosion, he occasionally seemed preoccupied and depressed but for the most part was cheerful and outgoing. "His cheerful mood might have been considered inappropriate in the circumstances, but he was being encouraged almost daily by an attorney to expect a favorable outcome at the trial. Between interviews he carried on lively conversations with others in the ward and he entered with zest into recreational activities.

"There was no evidence of phobias, obsessions, thought disorder, hallucinations or delusions. Testing of sensorial function showed no abnormality and he appeared to be of average intelligence. . . ."

In the opinion of the examiners, the patient was a sociopathic personality but legally sane; he was therefore returned to jail to await trial. "One month after his return to jail, he made a suicidal gesture by tightening his socks around his throat. He did not suffer any ill effects but the following day he was readmitted to the hospital because of his bizarre behavior. He claimed that people were against him and were trying to poison him. A patchy amnesia, intermittent disorientation, absurd as well as correct answers to simple arithmetical problems, together with other symptoms suggested . . . simulated insanity."

A few days later, the patient confessed to having placed a time bomb in the luggage of his mother, who was flying to Alaska to visit a relative. He had unsuccessfully tried to persuade her not to go until after Thanksgiving. He described his reaction as follows:

" 'I tried to tell her how I felt about it. She just said she wouldn't stay, she wouldn't give me any reason at all, no reason why she didn't want to stay. I thought it was the last time she was going to run off and leave me. I wanted to have her to myself for once. Since I was just a little kid she'd leave me with these people, those people. I wanted to get close to her, everytime I'd get close to her she'd just brush me off like I was a piece of furniture, as if I didn't mean more to her than nothing. If she gave me money I was supposed to realize that was enough. I just wanted to do things with her, to sit down and talk to her—just like everybody else's mother would do.

" 'I just had to stop her from going—yet it seemed I had to be free from her, too. She held something over me that I couldn't get from under. When the plane left the ground a load came off my shoulders, I watched her go off for the last time. . . .'

"In subsequent interviews, he was alternately callous and remorseful regarding the tragedy. 'I just felt if it killed somebody that was tough. It seemed the odds were big enough, there was more fun that way. I just didn't think about the other people on the plane. I don't think it's hit me yet. I guess I thought I could keep it all inside of me and forget about it. I finally decided I couldn't live with it myself.' "

The patient showed little conscious guilt over what he had done; his emotions seemed to be those of fear, anxiety, and despair. He admitted that he decided to fake suicide when he realized he would be found guilty; this was after learning that his attorney had discovered where he had bought the dynamite, timer, and battery. In the opinion of the psychiatric examiners, there was no evidence of psychoses.

Dyssocial Reaction

A child who grows up in the home of a professional criminal or in a slum area where antisocial attitudes are common may develop a personality that is fairly mature and well-integrated but is built around values that the larger society regards as undesirable. Many delinquents and criminals fall in this category. While they may show courage, loyalty, imagination, and many other traits generally regarded as desirable, their loyalty is to only a segment of the society, and their courage and imagination are used to win antisocial goals. Although such individuals may,

of course, show personality decompensation in the face of severe stress, their training in "toughness" and emotional insulation often gives them a high stress tolerance.

Sexual Deviation

A sex deviation is a method of achieving sexual satisfaction which is considered undesirable by society and for which there may be criminal penalties. Very little is actually known about the incidence of such behavior because it rarely takes place in public and because our social taboos make many people reluctant to discuss it even when they have been the victims of sex crimes.

Normal adult heterosexuality is the end result of a long process of development and differentiation, and the sexual patterns reached in adulthood depend on the individual's training and experiences. Deviations may result if the individual fails to accept and learn the role appropriate for his sex, or if he is handicapped by misinformation, or if he represses his sexuality so that normal differentiation and development are impossible. Contrary to general opinion, minor sexual crimes like peeping and exhibitionism are usually committed not by oversexed individuals but by sexually inhibited ones.

Under conditions of prolonged sexual frustration, such as that experienced by prisoners serving long sentences, people with normal sexual development may eventually give in to homosexuality or other deviate practices. Upon return to a more normal situation, however, they usually drop this substitute behavior and resume their previous sexual patterns.

Most cases of serious sexual offense involve individuals suffering from general personality disorganization. In a study of three hundred convicted sexual offenders in New Jersey, Brancale, Ellis, and Doorbar (1952) found only 14 percent to be psychologically normal.

Sixty-four percent were mildly or severely neurotic, and the remainder could be classified as pre-psychotic, psychotic, brain-damaged, psychopathic, or mentally deficient.

There are many types of sexually deviate behavior. Five of the most common will be described briefly here.

Exhibitionism. Some deviates achieve sexual gratification by exposing their genitals in public or semipublic places, usually to members of the opposite sex or to children; sometimes the demonstrations are accompanied by suggestive gestures or masturbatory activity. The exhibitionist is eager for signs that his victim is impressed or shocked and is let down if his demonstration does not produce this effect. Typically, he is a quiet, submissive, "nice" individual who feels inadequate in personal and sexual relationships, has a very puritanical attitude toward the evils of sex, and is inadequately informed about it. Often he has serious doubts about his masculinity and is using this relatively safe way of proving himself. In most instances, exhibitionists respond quite well to psychiatric treatment.

Pedophilia. In pedophilia the sex object is a child. Because of the possible damage to the child through manipulation, penetration, or other sexual abuse, pedophilia is a serious offense. Pedophiliacs are a diverse group in age and cultural background; most of the older ones are married, and many have children of their own. On the surface they are self-assertive and aggressive, and they often use force to carry out their sexual impulses. They tend to be either (1) individuals who feel inadequate and inferior and focus their attention on children to avoid possible failure and self-devaluation in normal adult relationships; (2) older men with fears about their potency, who have a basically psychopathic make-up; or (3) mentally ill individuals whose ethical restraints have been lowered by their mental disorder.

Rape. In some cases rape is attempted or committed by manics or schizophrenics, but usually a rapist is a psychopathic personality who has failed to develop normal ethical controls and who has strong aggressive and hostile tendencies. He often has a past record of other kinds of antisocial actions.

A rapist usually shows no esthetic preference in his choice of victims and may simply decide to rape the first woman he can, regardless of age or appearance. He may seriously injure or even kill his victim if she struggles against him.

Promiscuity. A pattern of deviation that occurs most often among girls under eighteen is that of having a succession of transient sexual relationships. Although promiscuity often leads to prostitution, the underlying causes of promiscuous behavior are other than a desire for money or gifts.

A number of dynamic patterns may be involved here. (1) A girl—or older woman—who feels unattractive, alone, and unwanted may slide into a pattern of promiscuity because it proves her desirability. (2) Promiscuity may represent a blind rebellion against a strict, authoritarian background in which the individual wants to "show" her family and perhaps also to hurt them; with such motivation, there is commonly a swing back to strict, prudish behavior after a time. (3) The promiscuous behavior may be part of a broader picture of psychopathology.

Homosexuality. This category of deviation includes various types of sexual relationships between members of the same sex. Our society condemns such behavior, but it has existed throughout man's recorded history and has even been regarded favorably in some cultures. According to the Kinsey study (1948), 4 percent of American men are exclusively homosexual, 18 percent reveal as much homosexual as heterosexual behavior in their histories, and about half the male population has at one time had some homosexual experience. Although considerable emphasis has been placed on the supposed femininity of homosexual men and masculinity of homosexual women, such patterns are the exception rather than the rule.

It may be that constitutional factors can predispose an individual toward homosexuality, but such factors have not been demonstrated. Nor does endocrine balance seem to be the key. Some homosexuals reveal an endocrine imbalance, but so do some heterosexuals, and many homosexuals show no imbalance. The same individual may shift from one pattern of behavior to the other without apparent change in endocrine functioning, and treatment with sex hormones does not ordinarily influence the direction of sexual behavior. Homosexual tendencies seem more related to abnormal early experiences—early homosexual seduction or a home situation in which the child has for some reason learned a sex role opposite to his normal one. This can happen, for example, when there is a strong identification with the parent of the opposite sex or when a girl is brought up like a boy because the parents wanted a boy.

Addiction to Alcohol or Drugs

Although many aspects of alcoholism and drug addiction are not yet fully understood, these reactions may be regarded as two more of the ways in which an individual who feels threatened and inadequate may respond.

Alcoholism. Contrary to popular belief, alcohol is not a stimulant but a depressant that numbs the higher brain centers and thus lessens their inhibiting control. Aside from this release, which may lead him to say or do things he would normally inhibit, the alcoholic may find that drinking gives him a sense of well-being in which unpleasant realities are minimized and his sense of adequacy is increased.

Three to four million Americans drink excessively. Of these, about three fourths are classified as *symptomatic drinkers*. Although they drink too much, they manage to maintain some control over their consumption and to carry on their work. The others are the "alcohol addicts" and are called *chronic alcoholics* or *alcoholics with complications*. They have lost control over their drinking, usually after a period of excessive drinking. In both groups the excessive drinking is a symptom of some underlying maladjustment in which the individual feels he needs the crutch of alcohol to help him live with his problems.

Although there is no one personality constellation characteristic of all alcoholics, they tend in general to be immature, dependent people who have an unrealistically high level of aspiration and an inability to tolerate failure. They thus have a high level of chronic tension and anxiety which alcohol alleviates temporarily. Unfortunately, as they come to depend more and more heavily on it, they tend to regress steadily to a lower level of initiative, responsibility, and general adaptive functioning.

Three psychotic reactions are associated with excessive drinking. (1) *Pathological intoxication* is a condition in which a person with low tolerance to alcohol, perhaps because of exhaustion or emotional stress, overreacts to even a moderate amount and may become hallucinated, disoriented, and violent. In this case the alcohol only touches off the reaction and is not the primary cause. (2) *Delirium tremens* is a reaction of disorientation, tremors, hallucinations, and intense fear. It occurs in the long-time excessive drinker largely as a result of dietary deficiency and metabolic upset and can usually be cleared up by massive doses of vitamins and a better diet. (3) *Chronic alcoholic deterioration* is an overall personality deterioration that may come with habitual excessive drinking and the disorganization of the whole life pattern that this eventually involves.

Drug addiction. About forty thousand people in this country are addicted to drugs, most of them to heroin or morphine. Like alcohol, drugs bring a temporary sense of power and self-esteem, with a corresponding release from anxiety and tension.

About 5 percent of drug addicts are normal individuals accidentally addicted, perhaps through medical use for pain over a long period. The rest are for the most part teenagers and young adults who lack good ethical controls and become addicted through thrill-seeking curiosity or gang pressures to conform. Sometimes drugs seem to be a means of revolt against the authority of family or society. Once addicted, the individual needs ever increasing amounts of the drug to produce the same desired effect or merely to avoid the intense physical discomfort caused by his craving.

Drugs like heroin or morphine cause actual physical addiction that can be escaped only by an extremely painful process of withdrawal, usually in a hospital. And addicts commonly have become so *psychologically* addicted that they go right back to the use of drugs when they are released. Marijuana does not produce physiological addiction but is dangerous because it often is a stepping stone to other drugs such as heroin. It also impairs motor coordination and thinking and thus may lead to reckless, unrealistic behavior. Emotional dependence on any of the drugs is essentially an escape from reality.

PSYCHOSOMATIC DISORDERS

The disorders labeled "psychosomatic" have in common the channeling of anxiety and other emotional tensions through various bodily organs. They represent both *defenses* against emotional tensions and the *effects* of such continued tensions on bodily organs. They are often called "diseases of adaptation" because they are precipitated largely by our difficulties in adapting to psychological stresses. They may involve almost any bodily organ or system.

In all psychosomatic disorders there is evidence of prolonged emotional tension which for some reason has not been discharged through the usual channels of physical activity, talking out, or fantasy. The tension may be the product partly of an unfavorable life situation and partly of unfavorable personality characteristics such as feelings of dependence, ambivalence, or hostility. Since the cause of the tension is often repressed, the individual may be quite unaware of it; in other cases he may recognize the source of his difficulty but be unable to do anything about it.

When prolonged emotional tensions are given no direct channel of expression, they are sometimes short-circuited through a particular organ of the body and manifest themselves in such various disorders as peptic ulcers, skin disorders, migraine headaches, or bronchial asthma. These disorders are in no way "imaginary"; they are cases of physical pathology in which the original causes are primarily psychological. The symptoms may be the same as those in a disorder of primarily organic origin—often, indeed, it is difficult to distinguish between the two.

Although we do not know why one organ rather than another is selected in psychosomatic illnesses, it may be that the one affected is constitutionally weak or has been made especially vulnerable by prior illness. A person who has had a serious respiratory infection, for example, may be prone to bronchial attacks or similar respiratory disorders when he is under emotional tension. Another partial explanation for why one or another organ is affected may be that various emotional states have different effects on visceral activity—for example, the physiological changes accompanying hostility and resentment are different from those accompanying fear. Some of the most commonly observed patterns of psychosomatic disorders are summarized in the chart below.

Although most psychosomatic disorders do not greatly interfere with the individual's

---

TYPICAL PSYCHOSOMATIC PATTERNS

	Incidence	*Typical Background*
High Blood Pressure	Much more common among females.	Ambivalence toward dominant, overprotective mother and repressed hostility toward those on whom individual currently feels dependent.
Migraine	Much more common among females.	Perfectionistic tendencies combined with high intelligence, underlying insecurity, rigid conscience, and critical attitude toward others. If plans upset, individual reacts with intense but suppressed anger and anxiety.
Peptic Ulcers	Much more common among males.	Chronic anxiety, hostility, or resentment. Often high level of aspiration and aggressiveness with underlying feelings of dependency and inadequacy.
Bronchial Asthma	Somewhat more common among males.	Repressed emotional tension resulting from over-dependency and fear of loss of support.
Skin Disorders	Somewhat more common among males.	Immaturity with ambivalent feelings toward those on whom individual is dependent; repressed hostility evidently directed against self. Frequently associated with feelings of helplessness, exhibitionistic tendencies, and sexual problems.
Obesity	Sex ratio equal in childhood; later more common among men.	Lifelong pattern of overeating apparently as a compensatory mechanism providing some pleasure and relief from tension and frustration in other life areas.

ability to make adjustments in most areas of living, they are costly answers to stress. They often cause irreversible tissue damage and, as in severe cases of bleeding ulcers, occasionally result in death.

We have seen in this chapter that *all* behavior is an attempt by the organism to meet inner and outer demands as best it can. There are three main criteria for deciding whether a particular action is effective or ineffective, or somewhere on the continuum between. (1) Does the action meet the demands of the situation—or is it an unrealistic solution to the actual problem at hand? (2) Does the action meet the overall needs of the individual—or is it self-defeating to his long-term maintenance and actualization needs, or perhaps too costly in terms of the time and energy involved? (3) Finally, is the action compatible with group welfare—or does it satisfy individual needs at the expense of other people's well-being? In applying these criteria it is necessary to remember that an individual rarely finds *perfect* solutions to his problems. The effective person is one whose resources are adequate for handling most life situations in a generally successful way—and, equally important, one who is confident of his own basic adequacy and worth. He is free not only to meet his problems in a task-oriented way but also to strive toward continued growth and self-fulfillment.

Some of the handicaps to effective behavior are fixations or distortions in development, a faulty frame of reference, weak inner controls, inadequate competencies, and ineffective habits. Many people manage to muddle through in spite of such handicaps, leading "normal" if incomplete lives. But their resources for handling stress are seriously limited, and problems that other people might handle easily may exceed their adjustive ability—resulting in a decompen-

sation of personality that may lead anywhere from a mild neurosis to a complete breakdown of coordinated functioning. In some types of mental disorder, of course, an organic condition rather than excessive stress may be the principal causative factor.

The disintegration of personality organization and adjustive ability under conditions of excessive stress typically involves some or all of the following characteristics: (1) the predominance of irrational and unconscious reactions, (2) the exaggerated use of ego defense mechanisms to cope with anxiety, (3) the development of vicious circles in which defense piles on defense and perception becomes increasingly distorted, (4) a lowered integration of behavior, and (5) the appearance of specific symptoms ranging in severity from mild confusion to delusions and hallucinations.

Although it is difficult to classify mental and emotional disorders either by symptom or cause, the following classifications have been generally accepted by the psychiatric profession. *Transient personality disorders* are those brought about in fairly stable people by conditions of acute or special stress—combat conditions, civilian catastrophes, or unusually difficult life situations. Such disorders usually clear up when the stress situation passes. *Neurotic disorders* generally have their origin in faulty personality development which has left the individual feeling inadequate and threatened in the face of ordinary life stresses. Some of the common patterns of serious neurotic disorders are anxiety reaction, dissociative reaction, conversion reaction, phobic reaction, obsessive-compulsive reaction, asthenic reaction, and neurotic depressive reaction.

In the *functional psychotic disorders* personality has become so disorganized that the individual's contact with reality is seriously impaired. Delusions and hallucinations are common. The four chief patterns of functional psychoses are schizophrenic reactions, paranoid reactions, manic-depressive reactions, and involutional psychotic reactions. These and other maladjustive behavior patterns may also be found in *disorders associated with brain pathology*.

Disorders which seem to represent distorted development more than decompensation under stress are the *character disorders* such as antisocial reaction, dyssocial reaction, sexual deviation, and addiction to alcohol or drugs. Physical rather than behavioral symptoms are characteristic of the *psychosomatic*

disorders, in which anxiety and other emotional tensions are channeled through various bodily organs, causing such reactions as peptic ulcers and migraine headache.

For the most part, mental and emotional disorders develop through mechanisms over which the individual has little conscious control. Although modern methods of therapy have had remarkable success in treating most of these disorders, the best defenses against them are a realistic frame of reference and the personal resources that make effective behavior possible.

REFERENCES

The following list includes both the references cited in this chapter and a selected number of additional books and articles for outside reading.

Arieti, Silvano, ed. 1959. *American Handbook of Psychiatry*. New York: Basic Books, Inc.

Brancale, Ralph, Albert Ellis, and Ruth R. Doorbar. 1952. "Psychiatric and Psychological Investigations of Convicted Sex Offenders: A Summary Report." *The American Journal of Psychiatry, 109*, 17-21.

Burton, Arthur A., ed. 1959. *Case Studies in Counseling and Psychotherapy*. Englewood Cliffs, N. J.: Prentice-Hall, Inc.

Coleman, James C. 1956. *Abnormal Psychology and Modern Life*. 2nd ed. Chicago: Scott, Foresman and Company.

Dahl, Robert. 1959. *Breakdown*. Indianapolis: The Bobbs-Merrill Company, Inc.

Fabing, Howard D. 1955. "New Blocking Agent Against the Development of LSD-25 Psychosis." *Science, 121*, 208-210.

Freeman, Richard V., and Harry M. Grayson. 1955. "Maternal Attitudes in Schizophrenia." *The Journal of Abnormal and Social Psychology, 50*, 45-52.

Galvin, James A. V., and John M. MacDonald. 1959. "Psychiatric Study of a Mass Murderer." *The American Journal of Psychiatry, 115*, No. 12, 1057-1061.

Gorlow, Leon, and Walter Katovsky, eds. 1959. *Readings in the Psychology of Adjustment*. New York: McGraw-Hill Book Company, Inc.

Haines, William H., and Robert A. Esser. 1950. "Case History of Ruth Steinhagen." *The American Journal of Psychiatry, 106*, 737-743.

Horney, Karen. 1950. *Neurosis and Human Growth*. New York: W. W. Norton & Company, Inc.

Jaco, Egbert Gartly, ed. 1958. *Patients, Physicians and Illness*. Glencoe, Ill.: The Free Press.

Jahoda, Marie. 1958. *Current Concepts of Positive Mental Health.* New York: Basic Books, Inc.

Kaplan, Harold I., and Helen L. Kaplan. 1959. "Current Theoretical Concepts in Psychosomatic Medicine." *The American Journal of Psychiatry, 115,* No. 12, 1091-1096.

Kinsey, Alfred C., and others. 1948. *Sexual Behavior in the Human Male.* Philadelphia: W. B. Saunders Company.

Levine, Seymour. 1960. "Stimulation in Infancy." *Scientific American, 202,* No. 5, 80-86.

Levy, David M. 1951. "Psychopathic Behavior in Infants and Children: A Critical Survey of the Existing Concepts." *American Journal of Orthopsychiatry, 21,* 250-254.

Lindner, R. M. 1944. "A Formulation of Psychopathic Personality." *Psychiatry, 7,* 59-63.

Luchins, Abraham S., and Edith Hirsch Luchins. 1959. *Rigidity of Behavior.* Eugene: University of Oregon Publications.

Mark, Joseph C. 1953. "The Attitudes of the Mothers of Male Schizophrenics Toward Child Behavior." *The Journal of Abnormal and Social Psychology, 48,* 185-189.

Marmor, Judd, and E. Pumpian-Mindlin. 1950. "Toward an Integrative Conception of Mental Disorder." *Journal of Nervous and Mental Diseases, 111,* 19-29.

Menninger, William C. 1948. *Psychiatry in a Troubled World: Yesterday's War and Today's Challenge.* New York: The Macmillan Company. By permission of the author.

Miller, James G. 1957. "Mental Health Implications of a General Behavior Theory." *The American Journal of Psychiatry, 113,* 776-782.

Myers, Jerome Keeley, and B. H. Roberts. 1959. *Family and Class Dynamics in Mental Illness.* New York: John Wiley & Sons, Inc.

National Committee Against Mental Illness. 1959. *What Are the Facts About Mental Illness in the United States?* Washington, D.C.: The Committee.

Nice, Richard W. 1958. *Crime and Insanity.* New York: Philosophical Library, Inc.

Posner, Rita. 1951. "A Decompensating Obsessive-Compulsive Neurosis." *Case Reports in Clinical Psychology, 2,* No. 2. 69-74.

Public Health Service. 1958. *Patients in Mental Institutions, 1955. Part II. Public Hospitals for the Mentally Ill.* Washington, D.C.: U.S. Department of Health, Education, and Welfare, Public Health Service.

Reed, Charles Frederick, and others, eds. 1958. *Psychopathology: A Source Book.* Cambridge, Mass.: Harvard University Press.

Thorpe, Louis P., and Barney Katz. 1948. *The Psychology of Abnormal Behavior: A Dynamic Approach.* New York: The Ronald Press Company.

White, Robert W. 1956. *The Abnormal Personality.* 2nd ed. New York: The Ronald Press Company.

THE SOCIAL

SETTING

OF BEHAVIOR

The Development and Structure of Organized Groups

Functioning of Organized Groups

Collective Behavior

Group-Individual Interaction

In talking about individual behavior, we have been confronted again and again with the importance of its social context. The ways we develop, our attitudes and values, our goals and the means we select to achieve them, the problems we encounter in pursuing our goals, our characteristic patterns of adjustive behavior—all these are influenced continuously by our group memberships and the roles we play in these groups. The extent to which we are "group creatures" has been well described by Cartwright and Zander (1953, p. 3):

"If it were possible for the overworked hypothetical man from Mars to take a fresh view of the people of Earth, he would probably be impressed by the amount of time they spend doing things together in groups. He would note that most people cluster into relatively small groups, with the members residing together in the same dwelling, satisfying their basic biological needs within the group, depending upon the same source for economic support, rearing children, and mutually caring for the health of one another. He would observe that the education and socialization of children tend to occur in other, usually larger, groups in churches, schools, or other social institutions. He would see that much of the work of the world is carried out by people who perform their activities in close interdependence within relatively enduring associations. He would perhaps be saddened to find groups of men engaged in warfare, gaining courage and morale from pride in their unit and a knowledge that they can depend upon their buddies. He might be gladdened to see groups of people enjoying themselves in recreations and sports of various kinds. Finally he might be puzzled why so many people spend so much time in little groups talking, planning, and being 'in conference.' Surely he would conclude that if he wanted to understand much about what is happening on Earth he would have to examine rather carefully the ways in which groups form, function, and dissolve."

Historically, man was long studied as though he were a self-contained unit. Only in the last twenty years or so have psychologists begun to appreciate fully the importance of man's social setting in shaping and changing his reactions and to investigate systematically the various aspects of group functioning. But despite the fact that research in this area got off to a slow start, literally hundreds of studies have now been conducted on nearly every aspect of social behavior, and many more are currently in progress.

One of the most significant findings emerging from the study of groups has been the realization that there are many parallels between individual and group functioning— that most groups develop, face stresses, make adjustive responses, and disintegrate in ways that closely resemble the functioning of individuals. The behavior of a group, like that of an individual, depends on both its inner structure and its setting, including the demands of larger groups of which it is a part. To understand the behavior of husband and wife in an individual family unit, for example, you need to know the individuals involved and also whether the family is in a society that practices polyandry, polygamy, or monogamy.

Thus we find that many of the concepts developed in our discussion of individual behavior apply also to group behavior. But since we are dealing with a different level of functioning we shall also find some characteristics that are different. For example, groups usually form to meet the needs of individuals, whereas an individual organism could hardly be said to be formed to meet the needs of its constituent organs. Also, the human being, as a unit, has consciousness, whereas the group has no parallel "group mind."

In the present chapter we shall be concerned primarily with the structure and functioning of organized groups, which have been the subject of the most research and also offer the closest parallels to individual behavior. We shall also discuss the behavior of collectivities (unorganized groups such as masses and crowds) and highlight some of the ways in which groups and individuals influence each other.

THE DEVELOPMENT AND STRUCTURE
OF ORGANIZED GROUPS

The organized groups in our lives have the most potent and continuing social influence on us, whether we are members (and hence subsystems in the larger units) or outsiders. Our identifications as Californians or New Yorkers, management representatives or union men, students or faculty members, Republicans or Democrats, Presbyterians or Roman Catholics affect in a thousand little ways how we see ourselves and each other and what behavior we regard as appropriate for us.

Group Formation and Change

In general, the needs of individuals are the basis for the formation of groups. Groups may be formed to provide security for their members, to carry on economic activities, to furnish opportunities for social experiences, to educate the young, or to achieve any of a thousand other goals. As individuals, of course, we are born into a number of already formed groups and hence may find ourselves belonging to some groups that actually do not meet our needs very well. But when a new group is formed, it usually is set up to meet the needs of those who form it, and it is perpetuated and remains strong and healthy only as long as it continues to meet the needs or purposes of its current members. Even when groups demand personal sacrifices

from their members, as when a soldier is expected to risk his life for his country, their primary function is still that of benefiting the membership as a whole.

How groups are formed. Many groups form more or less spontaneously by the mutual agreement of a number of people who share common interests or are faced with a common threat. For example, property owners in a community may band together in a mutual-aid group when their property values are endangered by a proposed city freeway. Such spontaneously formed groups are often loosely structured, and they may quickly dissolve if the immediate need for them passes. In other instances, however, such groups may serve continuing and changing needs and may come to be highly organized. A group formed to consider community problems in an unincorporated village, for example, may expand and organize to the extent that a local government is formed.

Sometimes groups are formed not by mutual agreement but largely through the activities and persuasive powers of a particularly articulate person. Dorothea Dix was instrumental in establishing groups for improving the care of the mentally ill; Mary Baker Eddy was the founder of Christian Science; labor unions in this country got their start mainly through the efforts of pioneer organizers such as Samuel Gompers. Although leader-formed groups are often designed to meet the needs of their entire membership, sometimes a leader forms a group to serve his own selfish interests. In either case, however, the group will remain strong only as long as the members believe that their own purposes are being furthered.

New groups are also formed, through election or appointment, by larger groups already in existence. In such cases the new group is set up to perform various functions considered essential by the parent body. For example, a club may set up a committee to handle the details of an annual dance.

Obviously, the way a group is formed will strongly influence the role expectation and behavior of its members, their freedom of action, and the climate of the group. For example, members of appointed groups may have their jobs and their relationships laid out for them; leader-formed groups may expect the leader to take most of the initiative; members of groups formed by mutual agreement are likely to feel personal responsibility and to have more freedom of action.

Characteristic patterns of change. Many organized groups tend to grow in size and complexity up to an "adult" or optimum level of growth, becoming increasingly effective in achieving their purposes and meeting the needs of their members. The historian Toynbee, among other students of group behavior, has suggested that organized groups—much like individuals—pass through characteristic stages of development: (1) a formative, youthful period during which the group is vigorous, dedicated to its aims, and highly productive; (2) a period of conservative middle age during which initiative and dedication are reduced and the group rests on its laurels, content with the progress it has made; and (3) a period of old age and disintegration during which internal conflicts and inconsistencies within the group gradual-

ly lead to its decline and fall. Rome, for example, had its period of youth and vigor during which it conquered much of the known world and made remarkable technological and cultural advances, its period of middle age during which it tended to maintain its gains rather than to implement them or show further creativity, and its period of old age during which it suffered corruption, decline, and eventual fall to the barbarians some five hundred years after its founding.

But groups by no means always follow this pattern. Many factors, either within the group or in its environmental field, can change the direction of its development or keep it from changing at all. Many groups remain small and ineffectual for the entire period of their existence. Others have a sudden spurt in effectiveness because changes in their environment promote their growth. The trade union movement of the nineteenth century, for example, was enormously stimulated not only by the spread of industrialization but also by the contemporary wave of humanitarianism and reform.

Structural Characteristics of Organized Groups

As a group develops and achieves some stability in its organization, it becomes structured. Positions of authority and responsibility emerge, different jobs are assigned to different people (specialization of function), and rules and regulations are developed. In the broadest sense group structure includes any relatively stable characteristic of the group's organization. Six such dimensions will be discussed here: (1) power structure, (2) leadership structure, (3) communication structure, (4) role structure, (5) sociometric structure, and (6) ideological structure. The position of any given member in the group depends on the part he plays in all these relationships.

Power structure. In the animal kingdom there typically emerges a hierarchy of power based on physical prowess. On a simple level this can be seen in the order established when pigs, cats, chickens, or other animals are placed in a situation where only one can eat at a time. In one such study, for example, Masserman (1946) placed a number of cats in a cage where they could obtain food only by pressing a lever that released food pellets during limited periods when a red light was on. An eating order was soon established in which the physically superior cat pressed the lever first after the light went on and so on down to the weakest or most passive cat, who ate last.

Human groups, too, develop hierarchies of power, but they are usually on some basis other than physical superiority. Thus we find hierarchies not only in such highly organized groups as the armed services and large corporations but also in school systems, neighborhood gangs, and families, though the power structure may be less apparent and even less important in some of these groups than in others.

The individual's position in the power structure will determine what he can and cannot do, how autonomous he can be, and whether he must show deference to someone above him. We are continually seeking things from people in power positions—we may try to get a teacher to change our grade, a counselor to permit us to skip a course requirement, an employer to give us a job, a supervisor to recommend us for a promotion, or a loan company official to finance our new car. In approaching these power figures, our behavior is likely to be courteous and deferential in contrast to the way we may deal with those on a par with us or those over whom we have power. Studies show, too, that we are more likely to imitate the dress, attitudes, and other behavior of people in high power positions than of those in power posi-

tions equivalent to or below our own (Lippitt, Polansky, and Rosen, 1958). Advertisers take advantage of this tendency when they show their products being enjoyed by well-known business leaders or other power figures.

Those low in the power hierarchy are much more helpless in an autocratic structure than in a democratic one. In a democracy, for example, the ordinary citizen can vote for people to represent him, complain to his congressman, write letters to the editor, even run for office. This opportunity for participation gives him a feeling of identity with the group and a personal involvement in its goals that are often lacking when all the power resides in a few top people.

Still another aspect of the power structure that affects the individual's behavior is the kind of control devices used by those in power. The feelings and reactions induced by the coercion and suppression of contrary views will be far different from those induced when the individual is free to accept, criticize, or reject the ideas of those in authority.

Power relationships also affect and are affected by the various other aspects of the group's structure. Some of these mutual influences will become apparent as our discussion proceeds.

Leadership structure. Closely related to the power structure, but not synonymous with it, is the leadership structure of the group. Whereas the power of a person may be defined as his ability to influence or determine the fate of others, the leader is primarily concerned with mobilizing group energy and with planning and coordinating group action. Although the leader usually occupies a high power position, sometimes there is a "power behind the throne" who delegates the leadership responsibility to others but keeps the real power in his own hands.

Types of leadership. Groups differ greatly in their leadership structure. In informal or loosely organized groups, especially where there is unanimity of purpose, leadership may be virtually nonexistent or constantly shifting. In highly organized groups, on the other hand, leadership becomes an important characteristic of group structure. Such groups may be led by an individual or by a committee or other subgroup. Two leaders will often emerge—a task specialist and a social specialist, the one concerned with directing the group toward its specific goals and the other with maintaining the functional harmony of the group itself (Bales, 1958). Leadership may be autocratic or democratic or somewhere in between.

The type of leadership in a group affects both group and individual behavior, as was vividly demonstrated in a classic study by Lewin, Lippitt, and White (1939). In this investigation clubs were formed of ten-year-old boys matched as to age, intelligence, economic background, and so on, and three different types of adult leadership were practiced in the various groups. In the *authoritarian* groups the leader set the group goals, controlled all activity with step-by-step directions, and evaluated the boys' work. In the *laissez-faire* groups the leader simply stood by and answered when spoken to: the groups were entirely on their own in planning and assigning work. In the *democratic* groups members and leader discussed and determined policies and assignments together. The factor of possible personality differences was controlled by having each leader and all the boys operate in at least two different climates.

Differences in performance and other reactions were striking. In the autocratic groups performance was fairly good, but motivation was low and the boys worked only when the leader was present to direct them. The laissez-faire groups did less work and work of a poorer quality. The boys in the democratic groups showed more interest in their work and more originality and kept on working whether the leader was present or not. There was more destruction of property and more aggressiveness and hostility in the autocratic groups, but the hostility tended to be channeled toward a scapegoat member or toward the working materials rather than toward the leader. Members of autocratic groups were also more dependent and more submissive, showed less individuality, and gave less friendly praise to each other. Morale and cohesiveness were lowest in the laissez-faire groups, highest in the democratic groups.

In general it appears that while autocratic leadership may be efficient for meeting immediate and temporary crisis situations—as in the fighting of wars—it tends to defeat its own purposes if it is maintained over a long period of time, for it usually reduces the initiative and creativity of the individual members and subgroups, thus eventually reducing the adaptive potentiality of the group. On the other hand, democratic leadership appears to have greater long-range survival value for a group because it places a minimum of restraint on the initiative and creativity of its members and hence tends to promote the adaptability so necessary for meeting changing conditions and demands.

The role of leaders. The actual role of leaders in shaping human affairs is a subject of some dispute. Many social psychologists and sociologists attribute great powers to leaders and consider them key influences in shaping history, while others believe that the leaders merely symbolize what their followers want and exert influence over the group only insofar as they go in the direction that the group wants. History gives examples which seem to support both these contentions. A particular social situation must usually exist before a particular kind of leader can emerge and be accepted: a leader like Hitler, for example, could come to power only during a period of great social and economic unrest. Yet often a group can be led in any of several directions by a strong leader, and often the particular personality, abilities, ideas, and strengths or weaknesses of a leader have made a contribution of their own to the course of history. As Tannenbaum and Mas-

sarik (1957, pp. 8-9) point out, there is always a complex interrelationship between the particular leadership situation, the personality of the follower, and the personality of the leader:

"The *personality of the follower* (as it manifests itself in a given situation) becomes a key variable with which the leader must

RELATIONSHIPS BETWEEN PERSONALITY AND BEHAVIOR IN SMALL GROUPS

Behavior in Groups	*Personality Variables*						
	Intelligence	*Adjustment*	*Extroversion*	*Dominance*	*Masculinity*	*Conservatism*	*Empathy*
Leadership	+	+	+	+	+	−	+
Popularity	+	+	+	?	+	+	+
Total activity	+	+	+				
Task activity	+	+	+	+	+	+	
Social-emotional activity (positive)	+	+					
Social-emotional activity (negative)	−	−					
Conformity		−	?	−		+	

In a comprehensive analysis of research since 1900, Mann (1959) attempted to find what consistent relationships, if any, emerged between personality traits of individuals and the behavior of the individuals in groups. Despite great variety in the personality variables studied and in the means of measurement, he was able to group most of the personality measures into seven dimensions frequently isolated in analytic factor studies. The chart above summarizes his findings: a plus shows consistently positive correlations; a minus, consistently negative correlations; a question mark, contradictory findings. Where no symbol appears, the evidence was inadequate to allow computations. Most correlations were quite low; the highest was between intelligence and leadership. Correlations were influenced by the types of personality measurement (self-ratings versus objective criteria, for example) and also by situational factors like the nature of the population, the sex of group members, and the size and past history of the group. Mann emphasizes that some of his findings may be reversed by later studies in which the variables are more precisely controlled and the measurements taken more consistently.

deal. The needs, attitudes, values, and feelings of the follower determine the kinds of stimuli produced by the leader to which the follower will respond. The *personality of the leader* (also manifesting itself in a situation) influences his range of perception of follower and situation, his judgment of what is relevant among these perceptions, and thence his sensitivity to the personality of the follower and to the situation. The leader's personality also has impact on his behavioral repertoire (action flexibility) and on his skill in selecting appropriate communication behaviors."

Any comprehensive theory of leadership must take into account *the personal characteristics of the leader, the motives, attitudes, and problems of the followers, and the demands of the particular situation.*

Many subtle factors may enter into the leadership structure and its effects on group members. For example, among the Arapesh (p. 54), the leaders had to be drafted for their positions and were eager to surrender leadership responsibilities as soon as other qualified people could be found to take their places. In our own culture, on the other hand, most people are eager to be promoted to positions of responsibility.

In a dangerous situation the presence of a leader may give group members a feeling of strength and security. One of the techniques in brainwashing has been to remove the officers and regular leaders and then to remove the "emergent leaders" who arise from the ranks to take their place. Isolated and leaderless, men often find it harder to keep their perspective and their self-confidence.

People do not always choose or follow the ablest leaders. Uninformed people who are weary from frustration and discouragement may fall prey to a demagogue who exploits their misery. Sometimes, too, people will follow a popular leader out of loyalty to him or lack of confidence in themselves despite clear evidence that the best interests of the group are not being served.

Obviously we must understand the leadership structure of a group, including the attitudes of leaders and members toward each other, if we are to understand the behavior either of the group as a whole or of individuals within it.

Communication structure. Essential for coordinating the activities of individuals and subgroups that form a larger group is the process of communication. Many studies have been made of the effect of different patterns of communication in small groups. Heise and Miller (1951) found that if a group task involves the exchange and coordination of considerable information, it is more efficient to have one individual in a central coordinating position than to have an open exchange of ideas—but that this increased efficiency is obtained at the cost of group morale. Other studies confirm the finding that when channels of communication are restricted, morale is low among individuals who are not in a position to know what is going on and to help in making decisions (Gilchrist, Shaw, and Walker, 1954; Shaw, 1954).

Although free communication can be fairly effective in a small group, as the size and complexity of a group increases, problems of communication multiply and restrictive patterns of communication become typical. A private in the army who has what he considers a worth-while idea for improving the combat efficiency of his unit does not communicate his idea directly to the commanding general of the division but places it in the proper channels.

The established channels of communication in any group reveal a great deal about its power and leadership structure, for the individuals occupying high positions are usually at the top or the hub of the communication system. In fact, autocratic leaders often attempt to control the whole communication system in order to maintain their position of power. Thus they may censor the information that goes to the group members, or they may deliberately fabricate misinformation that they think will enhance their power position.

Where the existing information channels are restricted by autocratic leadership or are so poorly organized that they do not keep the members of the group adequately informed on topics of importance to them, informal channels of communication called "grapevines" tend to develop. Sometimes the information carried by these grapevines is amazingly accurate, but more commonly it is rumor and conjecture.

Ideally, a communication system should provide for a two-way exchange of information and ideas. Adequate two-way communication between leaders and followers gives the group as a whole the benefit of each member's ideas, gives the individual members a feeling of personal involvement in group goals, and gives the leaders one important basis for making or evaluating decisions. Many large businesses have become increasingly aware that adequate communication between management and employees not only improves employee morale but also increases the efficiency and productivity of the overall operation.

Communication has become so important in all aspects of group functioning that its study has evolved into a new field of science. *Information* or *communication theory* represents an attempt to analyze communication patterns and processes and to develop a set of principles that will facilitate the effective exchange of information and ideas.[1]

Role structure. Seldom is the membership of a group homogeneous, with members all alike, having the same jobs, the same rights, and the same responsibilities. In almost every group there is some specialization of function. Social roles develop which facilitate the smooth operation of the group and help it to achieve its goals. And as we saw in Chapter 2, the members occupying the different positions or roles are expected to do certain things and not others, to have certain privileges and certain limitations, to dress, speak, and perhaps even walk and sit in a certain way. As members of many subgroups, all of us have many roles which we act out according to our picture of what is expected of us—and our picture of ourselves.

Some roles must be followed more rigidly than others. In general, if the group's organization is flexible and somewhat fluid, roles may not be clear-cut, and individuals may have considerable leeway in interpreting their roles. In a rigidly organized group, however, where responsibilities and permissible behavior are clearly specified, there may be little opportunity for individual interpretations of roles. A maid at a formal banquet must not serve guests from the right, enter into the conversation, or dress like the guests any more than the guests may get up and start clearing the table.

Different groups obviously will develop different patterns of roles for their members, though comparable groups often develop similar roles. For example, studies of boys' gangs have shown that the following roles are typically developed (Redl and Wattenberg, 1951):

Leaders—As a result of physical strength, intellectual ability, courage, or some other characteristic, one individual in the group tends to emerge as the natural leader. This leader gives instructions, settles disputes, coordinates activity, sets an example for the others, and often serves as a group conscience. When a member of the gang gets

---

[1] For an introduction to communication models and their use, see Wilbur Schramm's article on page 507.

into trouble with outsiders, he may justify his behavior by blaming the leader: *"He* told me to do it."

Advocates—Often there are youngsters in juvenile gangs who are more facile with words or ideas than the leader but who lack his organizing ability or his boldness in action. These group members may be cast in the role of negotiators with rival gangs or defenders of the group against adult disapproval and are expected to be masters of the alibi and skilled at rationalization and clever negotiation. They play a role roughly analogous to that of lawyers or diplomats.

Clowns—Many juvenile groups have their court jester—a boy or a girl who is expected to be funny. Sometimes this member differs from the others in physical appearance (he may, for example, be very tall or thin or fat), and sometimes he is below par in other skills demanded by the group. By combining clowning and self-display, he can gain some status in the group or at least the tolerance and seemingly affectionate regard of other members.

"Fall guys"—Often there is a member whose alleged ineptness, mistakes, or simply bad luck gets him blamed for almost everything that goes wrong for the group. The presence of such a scapegoat tends to relieve the others of the feelings of inferiority and insecurity that would otherwise result from group failures.

Mascots—In some cases the group adopts a mascot—an individual who is younger, physically handicapped, or otherwise different from other members of the group in a way which they consider inferior. The mascot is usually well accepted by the group, providing he sticks to his role and does not attempt to participate in the group as a full-fledged member.

Because individuals bring their personal needs with them when they enter a group, they sometimes develop roles that interfere with the group's progress. Thus the child who has been dominated by his parents may rebel against the authority of even a democratic group leader and become a nonconformist and noncooperator. A child who feels unpopular and stupid may take on the role of a perpetual disrupter of group activity

To understand the behavior of a given individual, we must understand the role *he thinks* he is playing. Often the individual does not perceive his role as outsiders do and fails to realize that his behavior is inappropriate. For example, the man who is promoted to the position of supervisor may think his new role calls for very authoritative, formal relationships with the men in the group to which he has recently belonged. In thinking of his role in this way, he is likely to antagonize the group whose cooperation and effort are necessary to his success.

It is not only individual members of a group who have roles to play. Subgroups also take on specialized functions. Groups like the American Red Cross, the AFL, the Air Corps, a state conservation bureau, and a city police force all have specific roles in our society. Subgroups, like individuals, may promote the goals of society as a whole or may have roles quite inconsistent with the welfare of the larger group. Criminal gangs are a clear example of the latter type of subgroup.

Sociometric structure. The sociometric structure is the pattern of personal attractions within the group. This pattern can be determined by having each person in the group name the two or three other members whom he likes best or with whom he would most like to perform some specified task. In this way it is possible to find out where the friendship links are, which members are well liked generally, and which members are "isolates." Those who have many friendship links, showing that many other members choose them, are called "stars." They usually wield considerable power in the group because there is a tendency for others to admire and accept their values.

A diagram of sociometric structure—called a *sociogram*—will often reveal clusters, or cliques, within the larger group. The members of these cliques are joined by mutual friendship bonds but generally remain aloof from other members of the group. Often their attitudes and behavior are influenced more by the clique than by the larger group

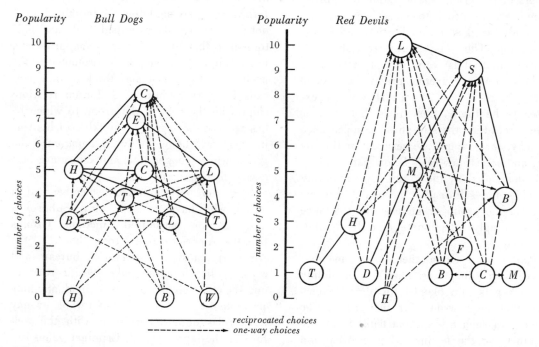

The above sociograms, showing the friendship choices in two groups of boys at a summer camp, reveal the different internal organization that resulted from two different types of leadership. The Bull Dog leader (initial C) was skillful in organizing and integrating the group's activities, shared responsibility, and showed interest and appreciation of low-status members. When his team was losing a tug-of-war, he shouted encouragement and started a rhythmic chant; his teammates took it up and eventually won the contest. His group became a closely knit, well-organized one with high morale. In the Red Devil group, on the other hand, the outstanding feature is the gap between the leaders and the majority of the members. Here the leader was chosen because of his daring and athletic skill; he showed little ability to organize or integrate the group's efforts but simply gave orders or did a job himself. He was cliquish and imperious, and when his group was failing in competitive games, he became vindictive and ridiculed his own teammates. With repeated defeats, the Red Devils blamed the other side for cheating and showed disorganization and internal feuding. Observers agreed that the two groups had boys of comparable ability and that the Bull Dogs consistently won because of their better team organization (Sherif and Sherif, 1953).

of which it is a part. For this reason teachers, supervisors, and others in a position of authority often find it necessary to break up cliques to keep them from undermining the program and purposes of the broader group.

The sociometric structure is also closely related to the power structure and role structure of the group. Individuals occupying high power positions in a business organization, for example, tend to form rather exclusive cliques, often held together by common problems, purposes, and efforts at mutual assistance in maintaining power positions. The same thing happens among teen-agers, suburbanites, psychiatrists, and racketeers—in any situation where individuals see themselves as having a similar group status and role and similar interests to defend.

An individual's position in the sociometric structure of a group will largely determine the gratification he receives from membership in that group. The individual who is valued and receives warmth and acceptance is likely to gain much more satisfaction from his group membership than is the sociometrically isolated individual. Studies have shown that in classroom groups the "isolate" is usually the first to give up when the group encounters difficulties—for example, when a class project is not going well. He is also more likely to become ill or to create disciplinary problems than are other class members (Redl and Wattenberg, 1951). It is probable that the same characteristics apply to isolates in other types of small groups.

Ideological structure. It is probably not possible to understand the behavior of organized groups without understanding their general ideological structure—their attitudes, purposes, and basic philosophy. The ideological structure of a group is roughly comparable to an individual's frame of reference—and like the assumptions and attitudes of an individual, it inclines the group to perceive and cope with its problems in a characteristic and consistent way. As might be expected, the ideological structure of a group also influences the perceptual patterns of the individual members. In a study of the Papago, Navaho, and Hopi Indians, Thompson (1951) found, for example, that children from the three tribes responded in quite different ways to Rorschach inkblots and that the responses that were characteristic in each tribe seemed to reflect the attitudes and general philosophy of the group as a whole.

As in the case of the individual, unrealistic or distorted assumptions by a group interfere with effective behavior and can result in the failure and eventual disintegration of the group. An extreme example of how an unrealistic ideological structure can lead to unadaptive group behavior is provided by the curious "cargo cults" of Melanesia (Worsley, 1959). From occasional contacts with white missionaries and traders, the primitive people who belong to these cults have been impressed with the white man's "magic." They have seen the "cargo" (pidgin English for trade goods) that the white man gets by some unknown means and have interpreted the Christian message of the returning Messiah as a promise that a "cargo" would eventually come to them, bringing a millennium. Knowing nothing about modern production and merchandising, they have concluded that the white man does not work but gets his cargo simply by writing "secret signs" on scraps of paper. In attempting to discover the white man's secret, the cultists usually work out rituals "in imitation of the mysterious European customs which are held to be the clue to the white man's extraordinary power. . . .The believers sit around tables with bottles of flowers in front of them, dressed in European clothes, waiting for the cargo ship or airplane to materialize;

other cultists feature magic pieces of paper and cabalistic writing" (p. 121). During outbreaks of religious frenzy the cultists may kill their pigs, destroy their gardens, and break their most sacred taboos. Although the hoped-for cargo never arrives, the cults live on—attributing their failure to some error in ritual rather than to an unrealistic premise.

A group's ideological structure may be formally stated or implicit in the culture of the group. Thus in the United States the Constitution provides an explicit statement of political and social values; in England custom, tradition, and common law create an unwritten constitution. In some cases, a group formally professes one ideology but implicitly accepts another; in the Soviet Union, for example, a ruling clique preaches a classless society. Often we can learn a great deal about the underlying ideological structure of a social group by examining its myths and legends, which typically are symbols of group values and ideals. The stories which American children learn about George Washington, Abraham Lincoln, Paul Bunyan, and Johnny Appleseed, for example, serve to perpetuate the philosophy and aspirations of our culture.

FUNCTIONING OF ORGANIZED GROUPS

Structure and function are so highly interdependent that it is difficult to separate them even for discussion. In the present section, however, we shall be focusing less on the continuing organization of the group and more on the processes that occur in the course of its transactions with its environment. We shall find that group behavior, like individual behavior, has both inner and outer determinants.

The Motivation of Group Behavior

Groups, like individuals, have needs to meet and goals to attain. Whether a group's purposes are political, military, religious, economic, or social, it must do two things to keep going. First, it must be ready to take active measures to maintain and strengthen itself; and second, it must solve problems related to the achievement of its purposes. Thus group motives are roughly analogous to the strivings of the individual toward self-maintenance and actualization.

Maintaining structural and functional equilibrium. An organized group strives to maintain its general organization and ide-

ology in much the same way that an individual strives, unconsciously as well as consciously, to maintain his physical well-being, his frame of reference, and his general personality organization. Groups also try to restore a state of equilibrium when normal functioning or organizational structure is disrupted. The tendency of groups toward self-maintenance has been well described by Thompson (1956, p. 75):

"A human community, which is an organization of human organisms, actively builds up and maintains in the course of development its structure-functional wholeness or integrity. . . . If this integrity or wholeness is disturbed by injury or adverse environmental influences (e.g., decimation by an epidemic, climatic change from warm to cold or from moist to dry, etc.), it tends to be re-created as far as possible by appropriate . . . activities on the part of the community . . . so that the normal state tends to be re-established or a new adaptive norm of structure and function established. This trend toward self-recovery and self-rehabilitation on the part of the community operates, if possible, in the case of interference with its normal activities from without (e.g., enemy raids . . .) and from within (e.g., overpopulation in relation to the food supply . . .)."

This tendency of groups to maintain or restore their organizational and functional equilibrium can be seen in the case of small groups as well as larger ones. If the leader of a small military unit is killed during an enemy attack, a new leader usually emerges, and the unit attempts to maintain its functional efficiency. Similarly, the loss of a member in a small family may lead to changed relationships and responsibilities as the rest of the group attempts to establish a new organizational equilibrium. Stresses that upset the equilibrium of a group also result in an increase in its tension level as resources are mobilized to deal with the danger.

Threats to the organization of the group can come from without or within the group and can take many forms. One common form of danger throughout man's history has been aggressive attack by other groups. Where the group is strong enough to defend itself against such attacks, it survives, though often at great cost in lives and material resources. Where the group is not strong enough to defend itself successfully, it is taken over by the aggressor, who may destroy it completely or permit it to exist in some modified form. In other instances, outside threats may take the form of ideological or economic warfare. Here the battle may be for men's minds or for markets that will benefit the economy of the victor.

Threats from *within* the group may also come in many forms. Crime, dissension, economic fluctuations, subversion, moral decadence—all of these may threaten or undermine societies. In our industrial economy, rapid technological progress is con-

stantly creating new products and production techniques to which existing industries and businesses must be alert if they are to survive in a competitive market.

Although we have been talking primarily in terms of large social groups, it can readily be seen that small groups and subgroups are also subject to a wide variety of maintenance problems. Even the family group must face inner and outer threats —emotional immaturity on the part of one or more members, dissension over family roles, the machinations of a would-be "home wrecker," economic changes which threaten job security.

Achieving group purposes. Besides maintaining structural and functional equilibrium, groups must accomplish the purposes for which they were formed. The goals of a group may be very simple or highly complex and difficult to achieve. The goals of a bridge club, for example, would be very easy to achieve as compared with those of a political party trying to get its candidates elected and its program put into effect. But in each case the group works to fulfill its reason for being. On a much broader scale, the goals of society as a whole seem to be the fulfillment or actualization of the human species. Again we may quote Thompson (1956, pp. 73, 76):

"The directive activities of a human community, as well as those of other species in the life-web as a whole, are not primarily a 'struggle for existence,' but rather they are primarily a creative, cooperative development directed toward fulfillment of biological ends. . . .

"[Through its economic machinery, its child-rearing practices, its system of symbols and its coherent values, etc.] the human community builds and perpetuates itself and its culture and strives to reach its normal actualization. This striving is only to a limited extent purposive, that is, at a conscious level and accompanied by foresight of a goal. It consists to a large extent of activities and processes at the unconscious level, but nonetheless developmental and directive toward biological ends."

Much as the goals of an individual may be vague or well defined, realistic or unrealistic, desirable or undesirable from the standpoint of overall adjustment, so the goals of a group may have these properties. And as with an individual, a group suffers in health and effectiveness if its goals are vague, unrealistic, or undesirable. Vague goals will not elicit the energy and enthusiasm of group members; unrealistic goals invite failure; undesirable goals create conflicts with other groups and often within the group itself.

Often outside pressures lead to a sharper delineation of group goals and motivate individual members to work harder to achieve them. As a result of the pressures of the "cold war," for example, we have been witnessing a re-examination of the values and purposes of our society and an attempt to clarify the immediate and long-range goals for which our country should be striving. In similar fashion, the individual who is faced with crisis tends to re-evaluate his needs, goals, and ultimate purposes.

In summary, then, the behavior of groups, as well as of individuals, seems to be motivated both by a need for self-maintenance and by an urge to accomplish the reasons for being. Task-oriented and maintenance-oriented behavior may, of course, be combined in various patterns, and often the two affect each other. A group's very existence may be threatened by its failure to achieve important goals, as when it fails in economic competition or in war. And failure to maintain internal strength—for example, to reconcile dissension or eliminate subversion—may impair or destroy the group's ability to achieve its goals. Overconcern with self-maintenance, on the other hand, may interfere with efficient task behavior by the group in much the same way that self-centeredness and a pathological need for self-defense may impair individual effectiveness.

We should realize, of course, that groups —like individuals—may fool themselves as to their "real" motives. They may try to keep themselves in power by dishonest or ruthless means, rationalizing that it is really for the good of the people. Action taken to save face or get revenge or salve wounded pride is often not recognized for what it is by the doer. When asked to state their goals, both individuals and groups tend to resort to high-sounding phrases: they want to believe their goals are noble and worthy, and unconsciously they try to convince both themselves and others on this score.

Mechanisms of Group Adjustment

A group's efforts to meet its maintenance and actualization tasks—to adjust—may be effective or ineffective. An effective group may try to accomplish its purposes by strengthening its organization and efficiency, by training personnel, by improving morale, and by taking steps to meet members' personal needs. Another group may simply try to hold what it has by various security mechanisms; in a political group, for example, these may be police forces and intelligence agencies (Gillin and Nicholson, 1951). An unstable group or one that feels highly threatened may resort to various nonadjustive means of defense. Instead of trying to solve its problems in constructive ways, it may use a device like scapegoating, which protects the members from feelings of self-devaluation and provides a vent for their hostilities.

The behavior potentials of groups. Both effective and ineffective groups develop typical adjustive patterns. The potentials of groups for adjustive behavior are parallel in many ways to those we have discussed on the individual level. There are, of course, obvious differences, for groups do not have organic unity or consciousness as individuals do. They must depend on the adjustive resources of individual members, acting in concert.

1. Learning and problem-solving ability. Groups, like individuals, have the ability to solve problems, to make decisions, to learn new skills or insights, to put new plans into operation in new situations. They are not automatons. In trying to meet their goals, they can select from their environment the resources they need, and they can continually evaluate and respond to the demands made upon them by other groups or by the larger society.

In achieving goals and meeting demands, groups have both advantages and disadvantages that individuals do not have. Being composed of more discrete elements, they can develop far greater specialization of function, can cover much more geographical and ideological ground at the same time, can do more things at once, and can assess a problem somewhat more accurately because several perceivers and evaluators take in information and are able to check and compare their impressions. On the other hand, the members of a group do not work together as automatically or as smoothly as the parts of a body do. Different members may be acting on different information or from different frames of reference. They have a more serious communication problem than the parts of a body appear to have. And finally, not being joined physically in space, members can simultaneously belong to many other groups, some pulling in opposite directions.

2. Use of past experiences. Groups, like individuals, can record their experiences and hence "remember" them even over several generations. In solving problems, they can study the records of other groups' experiences and use the lessons that they have learned. They can also transmit their findings to their children in an effort to perpetuate the traditions and the values that they feel enrich their lives.

3. Habitual responses. Groups, like individuals, have the ability to develop habitual, relatively automatic patterns of response to repetitive situations. Business firms send form letters in response to similar inquiries, and a family allocates about the same amounts of each monthly pay check to food, rent, utilities, and other fairly consistent expenses. Such habitual patterns simplify the business of living and free us to concentrate on the new elements and new problems in our lives. At the same time, however, routines may prevent creativity in the areas in which they operate; habitual patterns need to be re-examined from time to time to see if other behavior might be more adaptive.

4. Emergency resources. Groups do not operate at peak capacity all the time. Like individuals, they need reserve resources to cope with emergency situations. In individuals these reserves are released automatically under emotion. Groups, of course, do not have glands to secrete adrenalin or heart action or respiration to speed up. Instead they are dependent on the reserve energy of their individual members, who may be emotionally aroused by a threat to the group. These individual reactions may be readily aroused if the threat is obvious, but in other cases arousal depends on a leader's ability to make the members believe that an emergency exists.

Not all emergencies are solved by releasing extra energy, however. When time permits, a group can appeal to inactive members, assign different roles, work out better communication or leadership, call on unused skills, or develop new skills. This is similar to the way an individual may cope with an emergency by learning new skills or organizing his efforts more efficiently.

5. *Frame of reference.* Groups, like individuals, integrate the lessons of experience into a frame of reference that largely determines how they see and respond to future situations. They operate on the basis of certain assumptions about what is true, what is right or valuable, and what is possible. They develop certain ideas and attitudes about themselves and others. Thus one group prizes novelty and excitement; another, tradition and custom. Different societies have prized honesty, chicanery, extravagance, frugality, religious revelation, experimental evidence, spiritual values, material values, graciousness, bluffness, individualism, and conformity. The goals sought by any group and the means taken to achieve them depend on these common basic assumptions and attitudes in much the same way that an individual's goals and actions depend on his own frame of reference.

Pressures toward conformity. Groups tend to develop characteristic ways of doing things and, concurrently, strong feelings that these are the ways things *should* be done—that these are the "normal" ways, the "right" ways. Typical patterns of speech and other behavior and typical attitudes and values not only become characteristic of a given group but acquire a mandatory character. Political parties expect all loyal members to support the party platform. Church groups issue official statements concerning approved beliefs and disapproved behavior. The workers in a plant may exert considerable pressure on ambitious members not to speed up beyond the established norm. An adolescent girl may find it necessary to dress and behave in certain ways if she wants to belong to the crowd.

The norms of larger social groups are usually embodied in laws, customs, and group ideology. In small groups, norms may appear in formal rules and regulations, or they may be unwritten laws learned by all members through participation in the group. Whether formal or informal, the group's standards serve as criteria of conduct for the members of the group and specify the range of tolerable behavior for `members in good standing.

Reasons for conformity pressures. Group pressures toward conformity are often decried today; yet they develop inevitably as a group tries to maintain itself and achieve its goals. In fact, no group could long function as a unit without some uniformity and discipline of its members. A football team without training rules or an established practice time would probably not win many games, and a political party would suffer if its candidates openly supported greatly differing positions. Uniformity of opinion also can increase efficiency when a group must act quickly. A group with one voice can determine its direction and reach its goal faster than a group with many voices urging different actions.

Group pressures toward uniformity thus serve basic needs of the group. If the pressure to conform is too strong, however, it can stifle individual creativity and lead to rigid, unadaptive behavior on the part of the group as a whole—for a group's fundamental resources are the initiative and enthusiasm of its individual members. In the long run, group interests are probably best served when rules and regulations are limited to those areas where unanimity is essential to coordinated functioning.

Intensification of conformity pressures in crises. A group that feels quite safe and secure is best able to tolerate variations in the ideas and purposes of its individual members. Pressures toward conformity are likely to increase in times of danger to the group, as in wartime, when coordinated effort is necessary to meet the threat of a common enemy. We can see a parallel here to the way an individual under stress tends to increased conservatism and to rigidity of behavior.

In general, pressures toward conformity are greater in a homogeneous group than in a group whose members are highly dissimilar to start with. They are greater in any situation in which the members feel that individual and group goals can be best achieved by uniformity. They tend to be greater in autocratically organized groups than in democratically organized ones.

Techniques for inducing conformity. The actual pressures that groups exert to achieve conformity to their standards take many forms. Often they involve material and psychological rewards. Advancing to higher positions in the group or earning awards and honors that increase status and prestige may be possible only through conformity. But society also relies heavily on fear of punishment as a deterrent to deviant behavior. Members who create difficulties for the group or threaten it by their deviant behavior may be expelled. Members who break group laws or customs may be punished by loss of status and by fines or imprisonment. In extreme cases, such as those involving murder or treason, the individual may forfeit his life. Informal social controls are often more influential, however, than formal, legal ones.

An interesting example of strict social control is the form of ostracism practiced by a small and very strict religious group in this country. Any member of this religious community who breaks a rule of the church is systematically "shunned." Church members are forbidden to eat or drink with him, to sell to him or buy from him, and to employ him or accept employment from him.

The techniques a group uses to enforce its standards depend partly on its type of organization. Autocratic groups tend to rely on censorship, coercion, and intimidation; democratic groups tend to rely more heavily on persuasion, conversion, and education. Whatever techniques are used, group controls are intended to maintain the group and its existing power structure, to make individual behavior conform to acceptable patterns, and to perpetuate the group's culture by transmitting it to the younger or newer members.

Norms may change. Typically, the standards and values of a group are constantly changing in response to new conditions within and outside the group. New group norms usually evolve slowly, but sometimes lasting changes come about quite suddenly in response to a crisis. Only in rare cases of isolated and otherwise stable cultures do group norms persist virtually unchanged for an indefinite period. This was the case in Japan until the middle of the nineteenth century, when the government ended many generations of carefully guarded isolation by opening its doors to Commodore Perry and the eventual assimilation of Western ideas. The many changes in Japanese culture since that time—and even since World War II—have been dramatic.

Our own country is, of course, in a period of unusually rapid change in the norms both of our culture as a whole and of our various subgroups. The thrift and frugality valued by our pioneers seem old-fashioned in an economy that depends on planned obsolescence—where products are designed to be out of date in a few years and stores are filled with disposable items made to be used once and thrown away. Puritan serious-mindedness seems out of place among all the lures to "casual living." And even our much-vaunted individualism, we are told, is being lost by the "organization man."

Rapid changes in social norms threaten the integration of the group and sometimes present a real danger. If old anchorages are torn away before the foundations for new ones can be laid, members tend to become confused, uncertain of their values, and suggestible to oversimplified "answers."

Nonconformists. Despite pressures toward conformity, every large group has its share of people who do not conform. Some of these deviants—like our criminals—are emotionally immature or have learned distorted values that make them unable or unwilling to conform to the norms of society —though they may conform rigidly to the norms of their own deviant subgroup. But many nonconformists in man's history have been men and women of maturity and vision—individuals like Columbus, Galileo, Roger Bacon, Billy Mitchell, and Jane Addams. Nonconformists like these perform lasting services to their society by initiating necessary or desirable changes in group norms, even at the cost of great personal sacrifice.

Unfortunately, it is often hard for society to evaluate its nonconformists accurately. Even when there is an honest attempt to weigh historical and scientific evidence in judging new ideas, present perspective is always limited, and the decision of the present is often different from that of later generations. Sometimes, too, a group's judgment of its nonconformists is distorted because the group feels its stability threatened by the new ideas; in this case its reaction may be defense-oriented rather than task-oriented.

Factors in Group Effectiveness

In much the same way that we can evaluate the personality and behavior of an individual as effective or ineffective, we can evaluate the structure and behavior of a group. A group may be internally strong and healthy but in constant conflict with its environment; or it may meet the demands of the larger culture but fail to achieve its own goals. An effective group may be defined as one that is internally strong and able to move ahead toward its own goals while successfully coping with external demands made on it.

A number of factors contribute to group effectiveness. We shall discuss some of the more important ones in the following pages: (1) success in meeting needs of group members, (2) favorable inner and outer conditions, (3) efficiency in using available resources, (4) appropriateness of group structure, (5) clear delineation of goals, (6) high level of cohesiveness, loyalty, and morale, and (7) degree of past success. It will become apparent that none of these factors by itself tells the whole story and that the relation of any of them to group effectiveness is usually circular—high morale, for example, promotes effectiveness, which in turn promotes high morale.

Success in meeting needs of group members. As we have already noted, a group's capacity for action depends on the energy and initiative of individuals. Only if the members feel that the group is meeting their own needs are they willing to exert themselves on the group's behalf. Individual needs may be met by a group in various ways—by the advancement of specific group goals or by the security, status, camaraderie, or leadership opportunities that group membership provides. If their association with a group does not help members meet their own needs—or if it actually interferes with personal need satisfaction—they will become apathetic and may even drop out of the group. A group composed of unwilling or resentful members is not likely to be effective in its performance.

Favorable inner and outer conditions. A group is greatly handicapped if it lacks the skills or other resources it needs to achieve its goals or if its environment is highly unfavorable. As with an individual, the ability of a group to solve its problems effectively depends upon both its resources and the difficulty of its tasks, including all the external obstacles it must

A FAMILY AS A SMALL GROUP

Organization Requirements

Role — Members need similar concepts as to what husband, wife, and children should be like, and what the duties, responsibilities, and rights of each should be; they also need flexibility, ability to change roles in changing conditions. Divorced couples often show wide discrepancies in role expectations.

Communication — Clear, two-way communication is needed. If any member feels unable to express negative feelings, closeness is threatened; unvoiced feelings, commonly expressed indirectly, are more disruptive than those directly expressed.

Leadership and Power — Our society tends to expect partnership between husband and wife and alternation of leadership role in different types of situations; children are usually given more voice in family affairs as they grow older. In successful marriages, wives look to husbands for leadership more often than husbands to wives.

Ideological — Agreement on chief values, goals, priorities, strategies, overall organization of household is essential.

Integrative Tasks

Meeting Maintenance Needs — Maintenance needs include: (1) emotional support, security, and encouragement for all members; (2) mutual honesty, consideration, loyalty; (3) techniques for handling inevitable conflicts constructively; (4) wherewithal for meeting physical needs.

Meeting Actualization Needs — Actualization needs include: (1) establishment of climate for satisfaction and growth of individual members; (2) establishment of responsible, participating unit in community and larger society; (3) bringing up children equipped to meet challenges of their world; (4) implementing and passing on cultural and other values.

overcome. Serious obstacles may not prevent a tightly knit, well-trained group from achieving its goals; by the same token, internal weaknesses may not really hamper a group if it does not meet very difficult problems; but if both inner and outer conditions are unfavorable, effective action is unlikely.

When faced with new tasks or environmental obstacles, a stable group with high stress tolerance can make the necessary adjustments without a major upheaval or damage to its basic integrity and functioning. Stress tolerance in groups is the outcome of many factors, such as high individual dedication to group goals, efficient organization, good leadership, high ego-strength of individual members, and confidence in their ability to succeed—approximately the same factors that lead to effectiveness in individuals. An unstable group, on the other hand, is easily upset by difficult new problems and may fail to hold together under stress. If such a group *does* succeed in making the necessary adjustments in its structure and functioning, the change is likely to involve an extensive and energy-consuming upheaval that greatly lowers the effectiveness of group performance until new norms and procedures are established.

Efficiency in using resources. Whereas *effectiveness* can be defined as successful performance, *efficiency* is the extent to which good use is made of available resources. In a highly favorable environment, top efficiency may not be required for effective performance. A good football team may win games against mediocre competition without half trying, and Girl Scouts selling cookies in a sympathetic suburban community may meet little sales resistance, however efficient or inefficient their presentation. But the more efficiently a group operates, the better able it is to cope with stresses or unexpected problems. Further-

more, an efficient group is likely to succeed with a minimum expenditure of energy and resources. In recent years we have witnessed the development of *management engineering*, a whole new field devoted to analyzing business organizations and making recommendations about how they can make better use of their human and material resources.

Appropriateness of group structure. Not all groups need the same kind of structure to be effective; rather, each needs the type of structure appropriate to its tasks. Some tasks require complex and fairly rigid organization, whereas others can be accomplished by a relatively unstructured group. Overorganization can be as detrimental to successful group functioning as can underorganization.

All the dimensions of structure discussed earlier in this chapter enter into group effectiveness or ineffectiveness. For effectiveness, leaders must understand clearly what the group is trying to accomplish, must have the particular knowledge and skills called for, and must be able to commandeer and coordinate the various efforts of individual members and subgroups. Communication patterns must meet both individual and group needs. Long-term roles and immediate tasks for members must be clearly understood; in the long run, roles must be reasonably comfortable for those who hold them and must be within their competency. Conflict between individual members or between factions must not be great enough to disrupt group functioning. And, finally, the effective group must have a realistic frame of reference, sound values, a constructive approach, and, in most cases, a readiness to entertain new ideas.

Clear and realistic goals. An effective group has positive, clearly delineated goals to give it direction and to insure that individual efforts are coordinated toward the same ends. It is primarily task-oriented rather than maintenance-oriented.

Studies show that one way to get maximal personal involvement in the group's goals is to have the members participate in their formulation. For example, in one study (Ziller, 1957) military aircraft crews were put into situations where a decision was required, and four different techniques of decision making were compared: (1) *authoritarian*—the leader's decision was the group's decision and there was no discussion; (2) *leader-suggestion*—the leader stated his opinion first and then permitted group discussion; (3) *group-leader census*—the leader stated his opinion but only after group discussion and a census of the opinions of the group members; (4) *leader-chairman*—the leader guided a discussion without revealing his own opinion. The reactions of the crews indicated that they felt most satisfaction with the group-leader census technique and least with the authoritarian technique. It was also found that when the decision-making process was group-centered rather than leader-centered, the crews were willing to make greater sacrifices to achieve group goals—for example, to undertake more dangerous combat missions. Many other studies have shown that decisions in which members participate are more effective in changing behavior than decisions made by leaders and passed on as orders.

Cohesiveness, loyalty, and morale. Cohesiveness is an intangible force that holds the members of a group together. It is associated with feelings of common purpose, closeness, mutual understanding, appreciation, and empathy. Its most basic requirements are clear-cut, generally accepted goals and an effective group organization where members have confidence in each other to do whatever is required. But cohesiveness also develops from (and, in turn, leads to) group traditions, symbols, ceremonials, and sometimes a special jargon. Shared experiences—whether crises, recreational activities, or everyday routine—further tend to strengthen the intangible ties between the members of a group. Perhaps inevitably, large groups with a complicated organization and with few opportunities for personal contact tend to be much lower in cohesiveness than most smaller groups.

The more cohesive a group, the more personal loyalty its members feel and the less likely they are to abandon it when the going gets rough. A cohesive group tends to have high morale—a prevailing mood of confidence in its ability to cope with its problems. Faced with the same external demands, a high-morale group may maintain and even strengthen itself, whereas a low-morale group may go to pieces. The history of warfare is replete with illustrations of the importance of morale and esprit de corps in determining the effectiveness of combat units under stress. A group with high morale, like a confident individual, is likely to behave in a task-oriented way; a group with low morale, like a discouraged and self-doubting individual, is likely to concentrate on self-maintenance and defense.

The story of the famous Carlson Raiders of World War II not only illustrates the effectiveness of a highly cohesive group but indicates some of the factors that contribute to cohesiveness and morale (Sherif and Sherif, 1956, p. 166):

"In this unit, reciprocal expectations were stabilized among men in terms of the functions necessary for an explicitly formulated goal. This stabilization process involved minimizing or eliminating those traditional distinctions between officers and enlisted men which did not seem essential for coordinated action and clear outlining of the plans followed and their purpose. Officers were expected to demonstrate their worth as leaders of activity. Carlson, in particular, made himself the model in consistently meeting high expectations for his behavior.

"The result of these efforts to foster an in-group structure in which high expectations for behavior were standardized and consistently met was astounding group solidarity, even under terrible combat conditions of Guadalcanal and other battles which broke down many other units and individuals in them. It became virtually unnecessary for Carlson to exert formal disciplinary measures. Modes of behavior were standardized and internalized by members of the units. Thus, activities toward group goals were carried out with zeal and enthusiasm stemming from the men themselves and not from direct external compulsion."

Cohesiveness and morale are not static qualities; they may vary greatly with successes, setbacks, or changes in the environment. Generally speaking, the morale of a group varies in much the same way that the prevailing mood of an individual varies with changing conditions in his life situation. Like the individual, however, the group usually has a predominant or relatively consistent morale level, reflecting its feelings about its past and present accomplishments, its anticipations for the future, and the confidence of the group members in each other.

The extent to which cohesiveness and morale may change under altered conditions is shown dramatically in the report of what eventually happened to Carlson's Raiders (Sherif and Sherif, 1956, pp. 166-167):

"There came a time when the men were weary of combat and expecting a rest period, when Carlson could not fulfill the high expectations that his role demanded. Apparently this was beyond his control; his outfit was ordered back into combat and his requests for material comforts for the men were denied. Being a loyal Marine officer, he answered the men's questions and complaints evasively, refusing to put the blame on the higher echelons. As far as the men were concerned, he was 'letting them down.' His previous behavior seemed like trickery; he was just another 'brass hat.'

"As a result of this breakdown in stabilized expectations, morale was low. In contrast to the earlier period of solidarity, there was 'hell in the ranks.' Carlson and the values emphasized in the Raiders became objects of ridicule and resentment."

Past success. With groups, as with individuals, nothing succeeds like success. A past record of satisfactory achievement seems to validate the present leadership and organization of a group and increases its cohesiveness, morale, and stress tolerance—and thus makes for continued or even increased effectiveness in the future.

The effect of failure depends on the group itself and on the context in which it occurs. In some instances failure may lead to the disorganization or disbanding of the group. But if the group members have participated in formulating group goals, they may continue or even intensify their efforts in the face of adversity or defeat. We have only to recall the vicissitudes of our own Revolutionary army under Washington to see both the effects of a long series of failures in lowering the morale of the group and the power of dedication and determination to bring eventual victory.

Pathology of Organized Groups

As we have seen, groups, like individuals, tend to maintain their stability by various means and try to restore it when it has been upset. As in the case of the individual, a group's loss of equilibrium brings an increase in tension level and in maintenance-oriented activity. When efforts to restore equilibrium are successful, a group can once again channel its efforts toward achieving its purposes. But when they are unsuccessful, disequilibrium usually becomes more pronounced, and the group may go through stages of decompensation similar to those we traced for individuals: (1) alarm and mobilization, (2) resistance, and (3) exhaustion—the end of the group as a unit.

Decompensation of a group, as of an individual, may result primarily from inner weaknesses or from severe adjustive demands. For example, a group handicapped by superstitions, distorted values, member rivalries, inefficient patterns of communication, or lack of essential skills would be especially vulnerable even to minor stresses. On the other hand, invasion by a powerful neighbor or a succession of unpreventable catastrophes that left a group without food or shelter or means of escape to a more favorable setting might overtax the adjustive capacities of even a strong, stable group.

The sequence of group decompensation is vividly illustrated in the case of the Xetas, an Indian tribe recently discovered in southeastern Brazil (*Time*, 1959). The Xetas have a stone-age culture and are believed to be the most primitive humans in existence.

"They have no agriculture, know no metal, make no pottery. They sleep on the ground instead of in hammocks as most Brazilian primitives do. Their weapons are bows and arrows and stone axes. Their knives are sharp flakes of stone. They eat everything that they can find or kill in the jungle: fruit, insects, snakes, roots too fibrous for white men's stomachs" (p. 62).

The alarm and mobilization period evidently began for this tribe when it was driven back into rugged mountain country by stronger tribes and by the white man. This pattern of resistance was successful to the extent that the Xetas managed to hide from the civilized world for several hundred years, but the weaknesses within the group and its inhospitable environment doomed it to eventual exhaustion. Having been flushed out of hiding by starvation and the wooings of an anthropology professor (who hoped the surviving members of the tribe would be given government protection in a jungle preserve), the Xetas seem to be a dying people. Not more than 250 of them now remain, living in small bands and shifting camp every few days.

Short of actual group breakdown and exhaustion, there are many conditions in groups that can be considered pathological. Distrust of members for one another, repressive leaders who meet their own needs at the expense of the other members, subgroups who disregard the general welfare, overconcern of the group with maintenance and self-defense, pathological fear or hate of an enemy—all these are unhealthy conditions that cripple a group and keep it from being maximally effective in much the same way that disease or faulty adjustive habits can incapacitate an individual. Our own society has been criticized for tending to create "outer-directed" persons who find security in conformity (Riesman and others, 1950). Fromm (1955) deplores what he calls the "market orientation" of our society, in which people regard themselves as commodities with a certain market value, and he cites our fantastic rates of alcoholism, homicide, and suicide as measures of socially induced maladjustment. Our social and economic patterns have provided material well-being, but perhaps at the cost of satisfying other needs.

Pathological behavior may be typical of a group over a long period of time, as when it arises from faulty organization or attitudes, or it may be a temporary phenomenon, as when people panic in trying to get out of a burning building. For some reason, emotional reactions seem to be more easily elicited in a group setting, whether the group is an organized one or an accidental collection of individuals, as in a theater fire. Even in a classroom the fear or hostility or defiance of one member may spread quickly, and students may as a group indulge in pathological behavior that they would never exhibit in isolation.

Can sick groups be treated and cured as sick individuals can? With a group, as with an individual, success of treatment evidently depends somewhat on whether the patient is willing to admit he is sick and needs help. When group members acknowledge the group's weaknesses and are eager to correct them, they often can work out better structure and procedures or can be helped toward more effective functioning by objective, trained outsiders.

COLLECTIVE BEHAVIOR

Man's social behavior is not limited to his roles in organized groups. Another type of social behavior is *collective behavior*—behavior in which he is part of less structured and often transitory groupings. These include groupings as diverse as rioting mobs, festival and convention crowds, viewers of television programs, and citizens concerned with political issues. Such groupings are called *collectivities*. Key differences between them and organized groups are summarized in the chart on page 273.

In the study of collective behavior there has been a tendency to concentrate on its sometimes violent and irrational aspects. This may be partly because extreme behavior has a special fascination and thus has received disproportionate emphasis. But it also seems true that men acting collectively tend to behave less thoughtfully and with less attention to ethical and social restraints than do men acting individually or in organized groups. A partial explanation is that collectivities often form in unusual, unstructured, emotion-arousing situations for which the individuals involved have no customary pattern of response.

Collectivities are commonly classified as (1) crowds, (2) masses, and (3) publics.

Crowds

Crowds provide the most common examples of frenzied and irrational group behavior. They are collectivities in which the participants are in *close physical contact* and have some *common focus of attention*. The focal situation is seen as somehow out of the ordinary—perhaps severely threatening or perhaps promising some goal desired by all. If the crowd feels physically endangered or otherwise threatened, the emotions aroused are predominantly negative ones. In other crowd situations, however, such as religious festivals or pep rallies, excitement and satisfaction may be anticipated, and the emotions aroused are largely positive. In either case there is a sense of urgency about the situation—a feeling of the need to take immediate action or to participate in some emotional experience.

If the situation is unstructured and unfamiliar, as is often the case, the participants are uncertain about how they should respond and thus look to each other for direction. Under these conditions the members of a crowd become highly responsive to each other and to the undercurrent of emotion and expectation; their own mounting feelings of excitement and urgency are in turn communicated to others, and a circular reaction is under way. Even in a spectator crowd, when moving about is limited, members communicate their emotions to each other and the crowd develops a definite mood. This phenomenon of *social contagion* accounts for both the tremendous force and the irrationality of much crowd behavior. As responsiveness to the crowd increases, members become increasingly *less* sensitive to other influences that would normally help guide their behavior—the realistic demands of the situation, ethical restraints, feelings of propriety, social controls.

Not all members of a crowd are equally active or influential. At one end of the continuum are those who emerge as informal leaders, helping to initiate action and encouraging others to follow suit. At the other end are those who just go along because of group pressure. But even though these latter members do not take an active part, the mere fact of their staying in the crowd tends to strengthen its power.

Individuals have the greatest potential influence when a crowd first begins to take shape and the direction of its action is not yet clear. The leader who emerges quickly can often sway a crowd to one line of action or another—stirring up an angry lynch mob,

KEY DIFFERENCES BETWEEN ORGANIZED GROUPS AND COLLECTIVITIES

	Organized Groups	*Collectivities*
Membership	Members are selected and identified by established methods	Members are those who happen to be participating
Leadership	Leaders are selected and identified by established methods	Leaders are whomever the group is following at the moment
Norms	Are governed by established rules, traditions	Have no established procedures for making decisions, establishing or enforcing norms, or disciplining nonconformist members
Relation to Larger Society	Norms are usually (but not always) in accord with values of larger society	Norms often oppose or modify behavior norms of larger society

for example, or restoring law and order. But once a crowd acquires direction and force, the individual tends to be carried along by its momentum, and group pressure becomes so great that individual deviation is difficult or virtually impossible.

Types of crowds. Crowds vary in several important dimensions. Some crowds, like a rioting mob, are *spontaneous* groups that form in novel, unanticipated situations. Their norms emerge as the crowd takes shape, and individuals may find themselves engaged in looting or violence that was not part of their original intention. Other crowds, like those found at political conventions or sporting events, are *conventional* crowds; they meet by prearrangement and behave in the standardized ways that have come to be considered appropriate in such situations. Yet even here the crowd setting is an essential stimulus, and "conventional" behavior may be quite different from the members' customary decorum: the antics of conventioneers, for example, or the wild shouting of football fans occur only in the setting of a convention hall or a crowded stadium.

Crowds may be *manipulated* or *nonmanipulated*. A manipulated crowd may be swayed, whipped into a frenzy, or even formed in the first place to foster the special purposes of some individual or group. The goals of political rallies, revival meetings, and Communist "youth festivals" are quite different, but all are staged for a specific purpose and involve some degree of crowd manipulation. Nonmanipulated crowds are guided throughout by emergent leaders and by factors inherent in the situation.

A crowd may be primarily *active* or *expressive*, depending on its objective. An active crowd undertakes some joint action, which can range from storming a citadel of corrupt power to booing the referee or making a mass demonstration of protest against poor working conditions. An expressive crowd, like that found at a revival meeting, seeks some sort of subjective experience.

Examples of crowd behavior. The three examples described below will show both the common elements and some of the wide variations in crowd behavior. Each is spectacular in its own way.

1. Panic at the Iroquois Theater fire. Panic behavior usually takes place in the face of a sudden, overwhelming danger in which immediate escape seems to offer the only hope of safety. If escape routes are either limited or blocked altogether, ordinary social controls tend to give way to blind fear and desperate attempts at personal survival. The frantic, irrational behavior of a crowd in panic usually increases the original danger. This was true in the case of the famous Iroquois Theater fire in Chicago in 1903. The panic of the audience, and its disastrous consequences, are described below by the actor Eddie Foy, who was performing in the theater when the fire occurred and tried unsuccessfully to keep the crowd in order (Foy and Harlow, 1928, pp. 280-281, 283-286):

"I began shouting at the top of my voice, 'don't get excited. There's no danger. Take it easy!'—and to Dillea, the orchestra leader, 'Play! Start an overture—anything! But play!' Some of his musicians were fleeing, but a few, and especially a fat German violinist, stuck nobly.

"I stood perfectly still, and when addressing the audience spoke slowly, knowing that these signs of self-possession have an equally calming effect on a crowd. Those on the lower floor heard me and seemed to be reassured a little, but up above and especially in the gallery, self-possession had fled; they had gone mad. . . .

"As I left the stage the last of the ropes holding up the drops burned through, and with them the whole loft collapsed with a terrifying crash, bringing down tons of burning material—and with that, all the lights in the house went out and another great balloon of flame leaped out into the auditorium, licking even the ceiling and killing scores who had not yet succeeded in escaping from the gallery.

"The horror in the auditorium was beyond all description. There were thirty exits, but few of them were marked by lights, some even had heavy portieres over the doors, and some of the doors were locked. . . .

"They were finally burst open, but meanwhile precious moments had been lost. . . . The fire escape ladders could not accommodate the crowd, and many fell or jumped to death on the pavement below. . . .

"But it was inside the house that the greatest loss of life occurred, especially on the stairways leading down from the second balcony. Here most of the dead were trampled or smothered, though many jumped or fell over the balustrade to the floor of the foyer. In places on the stairways, particularly where a turn caused a jam, the bodies were piled seven or eight feet deep. . . . The heel prints on the dead faces mutely testified to the cruel fact that human animals stricken by terror are as mad and ruthless as stampeding cattle. . . .

"Never elsewhere did a great fire disaster occur so quickly. It is said that from the start of the fire until all the audience were either escaped or killed or lying maimed in the halls and alleys the time was just eight minutes. In that eight minutes more than five hundred lives went out. The fire department arrived quickly after the alarm and extinguished the fire in the auditorium so promptly that no more than the plush upholstery was burned off the seats. . . ."

WHY DOES PANIC OCCUR?

Is panic simply the result of "emotional contagion"? To investigate the causes of panic reactions, Mintz (1951) designed an ingenious experiment in which groups of subjects were given the task of pulling cones out of a bottle as quickly as possible—a task necessitating cooperation, as the drawing at left will show. With no reward or punishment and only the incentive to do as well as students at a nearby university, all groups got all their cones out in less than a minute—some in only ten seconds. Even when an accomplice screamed excitedly to create an emotional atmosphere, no "traffic jam" occurred. But when a competitive situation was created, the results were quite different. In this variation of the experiment, water started flowing into the bottle at the "go" signal, and subjects were told that those whose cones got wet would be fined, whereas those whose cones stayed dry would be rewarded. Traffic jams occurred in most cases, and in over half the cases most of the cones were still in the bottle after one minute. Mintz suggests that in a theater fire, cooperative behavior can be rewarding only if everyone cooperates; if only a few do not, then the others see that their only hope of escape is by competition, and the result is a stampede.

The typical sequence in panic behavior seems to be (1) perception of overwhelming danger and arousal of intense fear, (2) feelings of helplessness and desperation with no appropriate action evident, (3) feeling of urgency to do *something*, resulting in random, unadaptive behavior or in blind mimicking of others' actions. Passengers on a sinking ship, for example, may jump overboard, swamp the lifeboats, or even trap themselves by rushing below decks.

Often, as in the example given, there is a partial or complete blocking of whatever escape route might have been available earlier. In the terrible Coconut Grove night club fire in Boston in 1942, the doors opened inward, and the crowd pressed so hard against them that no one could get them open. Because there was a breakdown of normal communication, those in the rear kept crowding ahead, not realizing that they were making escape impossible. The inability to appraise the action possibilities realistically or to alter an unsuccessful course of action are extreme forms of the narrowing and rigidity of both perception and action that we have seen to be typical in any severe stress situation which the individual feels incompetent to handle.

2. The storming of the Bastille. A riot is an orgy of violent behavior by a crowd in whom a high level of tension and hostility has been built up, often over a long period of frustration and grievances. A classic example is the storming of the Bastille at the start of the French Revolution. In attacking it, the people were attacking the symbol of all the fear and oppression they had so long endured (Morris, 1893, pp. 271-273):

" 'To the Bastille! to the Bastille!' again rose the shout. Surging onward in an irresistible mass, the furious crowd poured through the streets, and soon surrounded the towering walls of the detested prison-fortress. A few bold men had already cut the chains of the first drawbridge, and let it fall. Across it rushed the multitude to attack the second bridge.

"The fortress was feebly garrisoned, having but thirty Swiss soldiers and eighty invalids for its defence.

"A chance shot was fired from the crowd; the soldiers answered with a volley; several men were wounded; other shots came from the people; the governor gave orders to fire the cannon; the struggle had begun.

"It proved a short one. Companies of the National Guard were brought up to restrain the mob,—the soldiers broke from their ranks and joined it. Two of their sub-officers, Elie and Hullin by name, put themselves at the head of the furious crowd and led the people to the assault on the fortress. . . .

"Delaunay [the official in charge of the fortress] proposed to capitulate, saying that he would yield if he and his men were allowed to march out with arms and honor. The proposition was received with shouts of sarcastic laughter.

" 'Life and safety are all we can promise you,' answered Elie. 'This I engage on the word of an officer.'

"Delaunay at this ordered the second drawbridge to be lowered and the gates to be opened. In poured the mass, precipitating themselves in fury upon that hated fortress, rushing madly through all its halls and passages, breaking its cell-doors with hammer blows, releasing captives some of whom had been held there in hopeless misery for half a lifetime, unearthing secrets which added to their revengeful rage.

"Elie and Hullin had promised the governor his life. They miscalculated their power over their savage followers. Before they had gone far they were fighting hand to hand with the multitude for the safety of their prisoner. At the Place de Grève, Hullin seized the governor in his strong arms and covered his bare head with a hat, with the hope of concealing his features from the people. In a moment more he was hurled down and trodden under foot, and on struggling to his feet saw the head of Delaunay carried on a pike. . . ."

A rioting crowd usually has a specific objective, which may have great symbolic significance, as in the case of the Bastille. The crowd members have come to share a common evaluation of the situation. Mounting tension and hostility tend to weaken customary behavioral controls; the common urge to achieve a much-desired end seems for the moment to justify violent, lawless action. The individual, feeling himself part of a group movement, often loses his sense of personal responsibility: the *group*, not he, is the acting agent and hence is responsible. Also, of course, the fact that so many other people are behaving in the same way makes the behavior seem more acceptable. In this way the most deviant, extreme behavior may be momentarily rationalized.

As the crowd mobilizes around a common objective, there is considerable pressure on individuals to conform, with a general feeling that those who do not are traitors to the cause—that all members should feel the same way, share the common definition, and support the action. Since the individual tends to assume that the vocal elements in the crowd represent the opinion of the whole and that none of the other members has any misgivings, he may be swept along with the crowd. His tendency to conform to crowd pressures may be still further increased by fear of retaliation if he expresses contrary ideas or tries to leave the group.

After accomplishing its immediate goal, a rioting crowd may relax and break up, often with feelings of guilt. Sometimes, however, its success gives the crowd a sense of power

and unanimity that leads to further violent behavior.

3. The Nazi party rallies at Nuremberg. The crowds at the colorful annual party rallies that the Nazis held at Nuremberg assembled by prearrangement with agreed-upon objectives and norms carried over from previous rallies. They gathered expecting to participate in emotional but socially sanctioned crowd behavior, and their emotional reactions were skillfully manipulated by the leaders. Thornton Sinclair, who witnessed the rally of 1936, described the Nuremberg party rallies as "one of the most remarkable of the Nazi creations," designed "to build up Third Reich traditions as quickly as possible" and to create loyalty and enthusiasm for the *Volksfuhrerstaat* (people's leader state). The following is a partial account of the rally he witnessed (1938, pp. 570-572, 576-577):

"In 1936, forty-five thousand Labor Service men, using the newly improved Zeppelin Field, passed in review before the *Führer*, marched around behind the crowded stands, and then entered the opposite end of the field in mass formation, filling a large part of it. The picture of discipline and precision, they shouldered spades as one man. Well spaced, using numerous flags, they presented a striking picture. *Arbeitsdienst* [Labor Service] leader Hierl reported to the *Führer*, who shouted, 'Heil Arbeitsleute,' and they, as with one voice, replied, 'Heil, mein Führer.' With individuals and groups speaking and the whole 45,000 at times singing, they went through lines to the following effect:

" 'The hour has come when once a year we lay aside our work and appear before the *Führer*. We stand in common work and uniform. No one is too good to work for the fatherland, and thus this service has become the duty of all. The *Führer* wants to give peace to the world and we are ready to follow him where he leads. . . . We carry the fatherland in our hearts, we praise the *Führer*, and our whole lives will be one great labor service for the German people.'

"Then they sang their song, 'God Bless the Work,' after which Hitler spoke shortly. Hitler answered that he was so filled with emotion it was difficult to reply. . . ."

In a dramatic, emotionally charged atmosphere like this one, clever leaders can manage a crowd in such a way as to strengthen their hold on it and increase its solidarity and unquestioning dedication to a cause. Carefully staged crowds have also been used to show outsiders the strength and enthusiasm of a movement and to induce fear of nonconformity. Crowds thus can become powerful instruments of social control and expansion.

Masses

Masses are collectivities in which the members are stimulated by the same event but are not, like the members of crowds, in physical contact or subject to the effects of interstimulation. The term *mass man* has the connotation of an essentially isolated, anonymous individual. But though based on the individual reactions of many people, mass behavior in the form of *consumer selectivity* can create or topple giant businesses, sweep an unknown singer to fame and fortune, or elect one president rather than another. Thus the power of the mass is very real.

With our modern methods of communication, a mass may now contain hundreds, thousands, or even millions of people. Membership, potentially at least, may come from all walks of life and all social classes. There is no leadership or other internal structuring, and since the members are separated from each other spatially, for the most part they do not know each other and may not even be aware of themselves as belonging to a

"consumer unit." Thus the key factors in determining mass behavior are the effects of the stimulus situation on the individual, especially on his motives and attitudes.

Consumer selectivity. As already suggested, the power of the mass lies in its ability to select or reject what is offered—whether it be a particular television program, toothpaste, magazine, movie, automobile, cigarette, religion, or political viewpoint. The importance of consumer selectivity can be seen readily in the almost obsessive concern with television ratings that estimate the size of a given program's audience and hence the number of potential customers being reached by its advertising. The problem of capturing a mass market for products has given special importance to product design and to highly specialized advertising appeals—appeals directed specifically at the particular mass audience for which a given product is intended.

Two types of research are commonly involved in trying to assess and understand particular mass markets: (1) *market research*, which attempts to estimate the number of potential customers for a given product, such as a new television program, automobile, or electronic gadget, and (2) *motivation research*, which is concerned with understanding consumers' motivation in buying a certain type of product. Are potential buyers of a new automobile, for example, more interested in acquiring a status symbol or economical transportation? On the basis of market and motivation research, manufacturers and advertisers can determine ahead of time both the size of the potential market and the product image that will be most likely to appeal to this group. The same type of research, of course, can go into efforts to "sell" a political candidate or an idea.

Mass persuasion. Through advertising and propaganda, mass persuasion is carried out today on an unparalleled scale. Although advertising is concerned chiefly with selling products and propaganda with selling ideas, both are aimed at capturing the favorable reactions and subsequent allegiance of the anonymous mass man. Thus both are concerned with the two kinds of research already mentioned—finding where and how big the market may be and determining what product image will be most appealing to the consumer.

Publics

Although not entirely distinct from a mass, a public can be defined as a group of people who are (1) confronted by an issue that is important to them, (2) divided in their opinion as to how to resolve it, and (3) engaged in exchanging views on it through forums, discussions, or other means. A public thus tends to be more aware of itself as a unit and to have more communication between its members than a mass; it is less transitory and less emotional than a crowd. Although the public is without internal organization, it may have spokesmen.

The issue. The issues around which publics form are not only matters on which people disagree but matters on which people are assumed to have the *right* to disagree. Thus the members of a public are not subject to the same conformity pressures they would meet if their opinion challenged a basic ideological assumption of the culture.

Some issues may arise spontaneously as social problems develop and people seek to define and solve them collectively. Some are brought into focus by newspapers, news programs, and other media concerned with the public interest. Often, however, issues are brought to the public's attention by special interest groups which try to promote their own definition of the issue in order to shape public opinion. Thus we may be told that our choice is between unlimited military spending and a weak national defense, between a closed shop and a crippled labor movement, between intellectual training and training for life adjustment. Commonly an interest group oversimplifies the issue and fails to acknowledge many of the possible alternatives; it plays upon our tendencies to believe what we want to believe and to distort or screen out contradictory ideas. In fact, even when an issue is presented as objectively as possible, we usually do not weigh all the facts impartially but tend to form an opinion that is congruent with our existing assumptions, values, and motives— and appropriate to our social position and status.

Public opinion. Officials who are charged with carrying out the public's wishes need to keep in close touch with public opinion —especially if they are dependent on public support for keeping their jobs. The public may express its opinions in a number of ways—by voting, by giving or withholding financial support, and by cooperating with or resisting the policies of those in power.

A precise way of measuring public opinion has become available in recent decades through the development and refinement of opinion polls. Such polls now have the advantage of going beyond simple "for" and "against" dimensions to give a much more detailed picture of the different opinions that people hold. Among the many problems that must be considered in making a reliable opinion poll are choosing a representative sample of the particular group being polled, eliciting truthful answers, framing questions that will reveal the various shadings of opinion, determining the relation between expressed opinion and actual behavior, and, finally, assessing the effects of the polls themselves on subsequent opinion. Although the techniques for solving these difficulties cannot be discussed here, they are crucial to the success of any attempt to understand and predict the behavior of publics.

GROUP-INDIVIDUAL INTERACTION

In this chapter our attention has been focused primarily on the structural and functional characteristics of groups as entities. Ultimately, however, our concern is with individuals—with how their group setting affects *them* and how they, in turn, affect *it*.

Group Influence on the Individual

Many of the so-called effects of the group on the individual are actually not effects of the group as an active agent so much as effects of the individual's interpretation of his own role and adequacy in a group situation. Thus the actor with stage fright is jittery not because of anything the audience is doing to him but because he feels "on the spot" and fears he may not live up to expectations.

The actual effects of any group setting on an individual depend, of course, on many factors, including the size, purposes, structure, prestige, power, and efficiency of the group, whether the individual is a member or an outsider, and what other groups may be influencing him.

Trait pattern and sense of identity. The traits we develop depend in large part on the kinds of social interaction we experience. Through our social interactions we can learn to be competitive or cooperative, suspicious or trusting, hostile or friendly, dependent or independent. Not only are the obviously social traits shaped in this way but even such seemingly personal traits as patience and courage. Each cultural group, as we saw in Chapter 2, tends to develop a basic personality type with a characteristic cluster of attitudes, assumptions, values, competencies, and general view of life.

As Sherif and Sherif (1956, p. 630) have noted, even our sense of identity is derived in large part from our association with various groups: "A central portion of the individual's sense of personal identity, his ego-attitudes defining his status and role relations with others, his prestige concerns, the level of his future goals is derived from groups of which he is a part or aspires to be a part." This close relationship between an individual's self-concept and his group identifications helps to explain many aspects of social behavior, including the success of groups in making individual members conform. The individual maintains the norms and values of a group partly because its strength contributes to his own feelings of adequacy and security.

Especially influential in shaping our sense of identity and determining which traits we shall develop are the many *small* groups with which we are associated—for it is these groups that confer or withhold the status and recognition that matter most to us, and it is through our participation in these small groups that we meet or fail to meet many of our basic psychological needs. We feel impelled to adopt certain goals, accept certain standards and values, and behave in prescribed ways not so much at the urging of the culture as a whole as because these are the goals, standards, values, and limitations of our family, friends, neighbors, business associates, or others whom we respect or admire—and upon whose good opinion our own feelings of adequacy and worth largely depend. LaPiere (1954, p. vi) maintains that the striving for acceptance and recognition in close groups of this kind explains much of human behavior. Social control, he says, "is exercised by relatively small and intimate groups, and it induces conformity to the norms or standards of the group by operating on the individual's desire for social status—more precisely, his need for a kind of status that only such groups provide." In a study of the psychology of status, Hyman (1942) similarly found that most people adopt the standards and norms of relatively small reference groups rather than of society as a whole.

The extent to which an individual builds his own identity around that of his reference groups is clearly brought out in cases where membership and reference groups are not the same. An individual in the middle class economically and according to other people's evaluation may identify himself as a member of the upper class and use the standards of this higher social group in selecting his home, automobile, recreational activities, political philosophy, and social attitudes. The factory worker who identifies himself as a rank-and-file laborer will have standards of performance and personal relationships with his fellow employees different from those of the factory worker who holds a comparable job but sees himself as merely in training for a much higher position. The foreman in a factory often finds himself in a dilemma because his reference group affiliations are unclear—he is a part neither of management nor of rank-and-file labor. Similarly, individuals in an ethnic minority who reject their own group but are unable to win acceptance in another typically experience much conflict and insecurity.

In a complex society like ours, a certain amount of conflict in the values of one's different reference groups is almost inevitable. The norms a man accepts as a church member or a family member may conflict with the norms of his business associates or his country club. In general, a person accepts the norms of groups that do most to meet his needs and avoids or drops out of groups that offer him no satisfaction or actually threaten his feelings of adequacy and worth.

Distortion of perception and judgment. The desire for group acceptance and approval can lead to remarkable distortions in individual judgment and even in perception. This was illustrated in an experiment by Asch (1952, 1955) in which several groups of seven to nine college students were asked to choose which of three lines on a card (right) matched the length of a standard line on a second card (left). One of the three

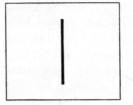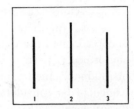

lines they could choose from was actually the same length as the standard line; the others differed from the standard by anywhere from three fourths of an inch to an inch and three fourths. In each group there was only one "innocent" subject—seated always in such a position that he would not announce his own guess until after most or all of the other group members had announced their choices. Everyone but the innocent subject had previously been instructed to make a *unanimous wrong* choice on most of the trials after the first two. Thus, after hearing the false judgment given by the planted majority, the minority subject had to choose between denying the evidence of his senses and contradicting the judgment of the group.

Under such pressure, minority subjects accepted the majority's wrong selections in 36.8 percent of the trials. (Control subjects who matched the lines under ordinary circumstances made mistakes less than 1 percent of the time.) Some individuals, however, were able to stand up to group pressure much better than others: about a fourth of the 123 minority subjects clung consistently to their independent judgments, whereas certain individuals yielded to the majority decision on almost every trial. When the test subjects were interviewed after the experiment, it was found that some had yielded out of fear of seeming "different," even though they continued to believe in the correctness of their own judgments. Others assumed that, although their own perceptions clearly *seemed* correct, the majority could not be wrong. In a few cases perception itself was apparently distorted so that the subject was not consciously aware of yielding to group pressure. (All the subjects who yielded later underestimated the number of times they had conformed.) Even subjects who consistently maintained their independent judgments tended to be considerably disturbed by their disagreement with the majority and reported later that they had been seriously tempted to go along with the group in order to avoid seeming inferior or absurd. In spite of this conflict, however, they felt they should maintain their individual judgment until actual measurement of the lines proved them wrong. Other studies of conformity have shown that the more adequate an individual feels, the more independent of group pressures he tends to be.

In-group and out-group attitudes. Individuals who closely identify with a group and feel that their own status depends largely on *its* status have a tendency to perceive their own group as objectively better than other groups. The same kind of perceptual distortion that makes an individual less aware of his own failings than of other people's operates to give group members a favorable view of their fellow members and a depreciating or suspicious view of outsiders. Many prejudices are thus a direct outgrowth of our group identifications rather than personal experience or personality factors. A suggestion or criticism coming from another in-group member may be accepted as helpful and constructive, whereas the same criticism from an outsider is apt to arouse defensiveness or resentment. In direct proportion to the extent an individual identifies with a group, he tends to defend it from attack or threat and to rationalize its mistakes so as to keep it in a favorable light.

Satisfactions and frustrations. Not all groups afford their members either the same satisfactions and frustrations or the same balance between them, and not even all members of the same group have the same pattern of pluses and minuses. Usually those of higher status have more personal opportunities, more security, and broader potential satisfactions. Those low on the scale or those who belong to subgroups regarded as undesirable or inferior usually find their sources of satisfaction sharply limited and their frustrations many. Those excluded from groups they regard as desirable may find life predominantly frustrating.

A successful, efficient group with high morale tends to provide more satisfactions to members than a deteriorating or seriously threatened one. Citizens in a town where the only industry has gone bankrupt find their satisfactions suddenly curtailed and changed because of their group membership. An unstable society offers its members contradictory values and shifting foundations on which to build their lives. Many of the conflicts and frustrations we all experience are the result of unsolved problems, contradictions, tensions, and rapid changes in our society. The fortunes of a group, the kind of group it is, and the problems it is facing all influence the satisfactions and frustrations that accrue from membership in it. Whether an individual devotes his major efforts to maintenance or to actualization often depends as much on his social setting as on personality factors.

Our sense of our own worth is strongly influenced by our pattern of group memberships and our status within the groups to

The degree to which an individual's perceptions and attitudes depend on group factors was shown dramatically in two experiments by Sherif and Sherif (1953, 1956). In each experiment, boys at a summer camp were divided into two groups which were then housed separately and pitted against each other in athletic contests. In each case the boys came to ascribe desirable traits to members of their own group and undesirable traits to members of the other group. Personal frustration resulted in intense hostility. After losing a tug-of-war, one group burned the other group's flag (left). The other group retaliated, and a series of bunkhouse raids ensued, accompanied by accusations of cheating and other expressions of hostility. Pleasurable activities like eating and shooting off fire crackers became occasions for the boys to throw food at each other and call each other names. Not until the groups had to work together to solve problems that were important to both and that neither could solve alone, like discovering the source of trouble in the water supply (right), did the boys begin to lose their hostility, mingle across group lines, and eventually ascribe favorable characteristics to each other.

which we belong. Acceptance in a high-status group usually enhances our feelings of worth. Being looked up to and consulted by others makes us feel worthy and important. By the same token, if we belong to a despised minority group, we may be unable to see ourselves as having any worth. Condemnation by other members of our group or rejection by a group to which we would like to belong also tends to lower our feelings of worth. It is hard to maintain a favorable view of ourselves if those we admire do not value us.

Social stimulation. In the interstimulation of crowd situations we see another kind of social influence on individual behavior. The individual who goes wild at the winning touchdown or who tramples over others in his effort to escape a burning building is responding to the heightened emotionality and irrationality of those who are in a similarly uncertain and highly suggestible state.

Less dramatic instances of such social contagion can often be observed even in small, organized groups. In a classroom the restlessness or defiance of one or two students may quickly spread to the rest. In a group with high morale and esprit de corps, individual members feel buoyed up by each other's presence and become more effective; a demoralized group, on the other hand, saps members' personal confidence and decreases their effectiveness.

Encouragement or hampering of growth. Some patterns of social interaction or social climate promote traits that are personally satisfying and conducive to continuing personal growth. Others tend to promote unhealthy, stultifying traits or even suicidal ones. Beginning with the experiment with autocratic, democratic, and laissez-faire leadership (p. 253), studies have consistently shown that a democratic setting fosters personal responsibility, helpfulness, and self-control, whereas an authoritarian setting tends to induce dependence and apathy and often gives rise to repressed tension and hostility. Pentony (1956), for example, found that nursery school children from democratic homes were more socially active, more constructive in their play, and more intellectually curious than children from other types of homes. In Chapter 3 we noted other kinds of early social experience that help to shape an adequate, confident, and self-actualizing individual.

Influence of the Individual on the Group

Since individuals are the "human resources" of groups, it is only as members have or develop the necessary skills that a group can achieve its goals and meet its needs. A group can hardly be more mature or task-oriented than the individuals within it, since ultimately it is individuals who actually make and implement group decisions. Thus, any group reflects to some extent the particular ideas, needs, purposes, and competencies of its members. Members with serious personality weaknesses, prejudices, and immaturities may disrupt the group and prevent it from reaching its goals just as able, dedicated members help insure success.

Leaders, as individuals, have an especially potent influence on the group, for their role is a pivotal one on which the functioning of many others depends. The personal traits of a leader will determine the values he will promote and the degree to which he will serve the group or make the group serve him. A leader can deploy the group's resources wisely or ineffectively, can inspire dedication and enthusiasm or resentment and division among the membership, and may raise or lower the sights of the group as a whole. Often in the course of history one individual with imagination and persistence has tackled a problem that seemed hopeless and has succeeded in enlisting enough cooperation and support to work out a solution. Depending on its leadership, a group may move toward reasoned action, emotionalism, apathy, or violence.

Yet one man can sell only if another will buy, and a leader is a leader only as long as he is being followed. If the rank-and-file members disapprove of what is advocated, the leader may be unable to implement his policies, however sound. This is especially true in a democratic group, where group action depends on some degree of voluntary cooperation; but even in a dictatorial group, where behavior can be manipulated irrespective of personal convictions, the progress of the group will be affected by whether individuals give the minimum essential cooperation or respond enthusiastically. Thus every group is greatly influenced by a need to make itself attractive to its members and to help them achieve their personal goals. In the long run the progress and even the survival of a group depend on the imagination and effort of the ordinary individuals within it.

In this chapter we have examined the structure and functioning of groups and have found several parallels as well as differences between individuals and groups. We have found that organized groups have several dimensions of structure which, taken together, help to determine their stability and effectiveness. Groups, like individuals, have goals, purposes, and needs and may show primarily task-oriented or primarily defense-oriented behavior. For groups, as for individuals, an emphasis on self-maintenance and self-defense at the sacrifice of more constructive activity is a pathological condition. Factors that contribute to group effectiveness include successful meeting of members' personal needs, favorable inner and outer conditions, appropriate degree and kind of group structure, clear-cut and realistic goals, cohesiveness, high morale, efficiency in the use of resources, and a past record of success.

Our social field often includes various kinds of unorganized groups known as *collectivities*. In a *crowd*, where people in close physical proximity are mutually stimulated by an unusual situation, individuals experience the effects of social contagion and are likely to participate in emotional, irrational behavior. A *mass* is a group of individuals who are stimulated by the same situation but are not in physical contact or direct communication with each other. The power of a mass lies in the collective ability of many people acting individually to select such things as consumer goods, ideas, and political officeholders. A *public* is a group of people who are unified in their concern over a particular issue but have differing opinions about it, which they express through such means as voting, financial support or nonsupport, and opinion polls.

The individual, as a subsystem in various social units, is subject to continuing and pervasive social influences that shape both his development and his behavior. But he also influences his social field and, with other individual members, provides the energy and resources that make group behavior possible. The values, competencies, and level of maturity of the individual members ultimately determine how effective any group can be in achieving its own purposes and meeting the needs of its members.

REFERENCES

The following list includes both the references cited in this chapter and a selected number of additional books and articles for outside reading.

Asch, Solomon E. 1952. *Social Psychology*. New York: Prentice-Hall, Inc.

Asch, Solomon E. 1955. "Opinions and Social Pressure." *Scientific American, 193*, No. 5, 31-35.

Bales, Robert F. 1958. "Task Roles and Social Roles in Problem-Solving Groups." *Readings in Social Psychology*. 3rd ed. Eleanor E. Maccoby, Theodore M. Newcomb, and Eugene L. Hartley, eds. New York: Henry Holt and Company.

Bass, Bernard M. 1960. *Leadership, Psychology, and Organizational Behavior*. New York: Harper & Brothers.

Bonner, Hubert. 1959. *Group Dynamics: Principles and Applications*. New York: The Ronald Press Company.

Browne, Clarence G., and Thomas Simon Cohn. 1958. *The Study of Leadership*. Danville, Ill.: The Interstate Printers and Publishers.

Cartwright, Dorwin, ed. 1959. *Studies in Social Power.* Ann Arbor: University of Michigan Press.

Cartwright, Dorwin, and Alvin Zander, eds. 1953. *Group Dynamics: Research and Theory.* Evanston, Ill.: Row, Peterson and Company.

Deutsch, Morton. 1959. "Some Factors Affecting Membership Motivation and Achievement in a Group." *Human Relations, 12,* No. 1, 81-95.

Fiedler, Fred E. 1960. *Leader Attitudes and Group Effectiveness.* Urbana: University of Illinois Press.

Foy, Eddie, and Alvin F. Harlow. 1928. *Clowning Through Life.* New York: E. P. Dutton and Co., Inc.

Fromm, Erich. 1955. *The Sane Society.* New York: Rinehart & Company, Inc.

Gilchrist, J. C., Marvin E. Shaw, and L. C. Walker. 1954. "Some Effects of Unequal Distribution of Information in a Wheel Group Structure." *The Journal of Abnormal and Social Psychology, 49,* 554-556.

Gillin, John, and George Nicholson. 1951. "The Security Functions of Cultural Systems." *Social Forces, 30,* 179-184.

Glanzer, Murray, and Robert Glaser. 1959. "Techniques for the Study of Group Structure and Behavior: I. Analysis of Structure." *Psychological Bulletin, 56,* No. 5, 317-332.

Gordon, Thomas. 1955. *Group-Centered Leadership: A Way of Releasing the Creative Power of Groups.* Boston: Houghton Mifflin Company.

Hare, Alexander Paul, and others, eds. 1955. *Small Groups: Studies in Social Interaction.* New York: Alfred A. Knopf, Inc.

Hartley, Eugene L., and Gerhart D. Wiebe. 1960. *A Casebook in Social Processes.* New York: Thomas Y. Crowell Company.

Heise, George A., and George A. Miller. 1951. "Problem Solving by Small Groups Using Various Communication Nets." *The Journal of Abnormal and Social Psychology, 46,* 327-335.

Hyman, H. H. 1942. "The Psychology of Status." *Archives of Psychology,* No. 269.

LaPiere, Richard Tracy. 1954. *A Theory of Social Control.* New York: McGraw-Hill Book Company, Inc.

Lewin, Kurt, Ronald Lippitt, and Robert K. White. 1939. "Patterns of Aggressive Behavior in Experimentally Created 'Social Climates.' " *Journal of Social Psychology, 10,* 271-299.

Lippitt, Ronald, Norman Polansky, and Sidney Rosen. 1958. "The Dynamics of Power." *The Study of Leadership.* Clarence G. Browne and Thomas Simon Cohn, eds. Danville, Ill.: The Interstate Printers and Publishers.

Lindzey, Gardner, ed. 1954. *Handbook of Social Psychology.* Cambridge, Mass.: Addison-Wesley Publishing Company, Inc.

Mann, John H., and Carola Honroth Mann. 1959. "The Importance of Group Task in Producing Group-Member Personality and Behavior Changes." *Human Relations, 12,* No. 1, 75-80.

Mann, Richard D. 1959. "A Review of the Relationship Between Personality and Performance in Small Groups." *Psychological Bulletin, 56,* 241-270.

Masserman, Jules. 1946. *Principles of Dynamic Psychiatry.* Philadelphia: W. B. Saunders Company.

Mintz, Alexander. 1951. "Non-Adaptive Group Behavior." *The Journal of Abnormal and Social Psychology, 46,* 150-159.

Morris, Charles. 1893. *Historical Tales: French.* New York: The R. H. Whitten Company.

Pentony, P. 1956. "Home Environment and Nursery School Behavior." *Australian Journal of Psychology, 8,* 61-65.

Raven, Bertram H. 1959. "The Dynamics of Groups." *Review of Educational Research, 29,* No. 4, 332-343.

Raven, Bertram H., ed. 1959. *A Bibliography of Publications Relating to the Small Group.* Los Angeles: University of California.

Redl, Fritz, and W. W. Wattenberg. 1951. *Mental Hygiene in Teaching.* New York: Harcourt, Brace and Company.

Riesman, David, and others. 1950. *The Lonely Crowd: A Study of the Changing American Character.* New Haven, Conn.: Yale University Press.

Shaw, Marvin E. 1954. "Some Effects of Unequal Distribution of Information upon Group Performance in Various Communication Nets." *The Journal of Abnormal and Social Psychology, 49,* 547-553.

Sherif, Muzafer, and Carolyn W. Sherif. 1953. *Groups in Harmony and Tension: An Integration of Studies on Intergroup Relations.* New York: Harper & Brothers.

Sherif, Muzafer, and Carolyn W. Sherif. 1956. *An Outline of Social Psychology.* Rev. ed. New York: Harper & Brothers.

Sinclair, Thornton. 1938. "The Nazi Party Rally at Nuremberg." *Public Opinion Quarterly, 2,* 570-583.

Stogdill, Ralph Melvin. 1959. *Individual Behavior and Group Achievement.* New York: Oxford University Press.

Tannenbaum, Robert and Fred Massarik. 1957. "Leadership: A Frame of Reference." *Management Science, 4,* No. 1, 1-19.

Thelen, Herbert Arnold. 1954. *Dynamics of Groups at Work.* Chicago: The University of Chicago Press.

Thibaut, John W., and Harold H. Kelley. 1959. *The Social Psychology of Groups.* New York: John Wiley & Sons, Inc.

Thompson, Laura. 1951. "Perception Patterns in Three Indian Tribes." *Psychiatry, 14,* 225-263.

Thompson, Laura. 1956. "The Societal System, Culture and the Community." *Toward a Unified Theory of Human Behavior.* Roy R. Grinker, ed. New York: Basic Books, Inc.

Time. 1959. *73,* No. 1, 62-63.

Worsley, Peter M. 1959. "Cargo Cults." *Scientific American, 200,* No. 5, 117-128.

Ziller, Robert C. 1957. "Four Techniques of Group Decision-Making Under Uncertainty." *Journal of Applied Psychology, 41,* No. 6, 384-388.

PART 3

RESOURCES FOR EFFECTIVE LIVING

An Adequate Frame of Reference

Intellectual Competence

Emotional Competence

Social Competence

Professional Resources

INTRODUCTION

In Parts 1 and 2 we have emphasized the view of man as a unique creature with the capacity to assign value and meaning to his experience, to select and evaluate stimuli in terms of his needs and purposes, to think creatively, and to choose and initiate a course of action. We have noted the importance of man's social field as well as of his own unique make-up in shaping his development and behavior. And we have seen how man strives not only to maintain his physical and psychological well-being but also to grow and to fulfill his potentialities as a human being.

It has also been suggested in these chapters that man, being self-aware and lacking most of the built-in controls that guide the behavior of the lower animals, must develop for himself the know-how and know-why of successful living. In Part 3 we shall take a closer look at just what this involves.

Of first importance is a realistic and otherwise adequate frame of reference. Chapter 9 discusses the implications for behavior of the individual's assumptions concerning fact (what is), value (what should be), and possibility (what could be). To behave effectively and make the most of himself, man must begin with an accurate picture of himself and his environment; he also needs reliable values to give meaning to his life and to guide him in choosing goals and making decisions; and he must be able to appraise realistically his possibilities for self-growth and for achievement. Implicit in an adequate frame of reference, too, is the individual's ability to accept himself and to assume responsibility for directing his own life.

Chapters 10, 11, and 12 examine emotional, social, and intellectual competencies as basic resources for effective living. Assuming that the individual has an adequate level of physical health, his success in coping with both the usual and extraordinary problems of life depends to a great extent upon his abilities to direct and control his emotional resources, to establish and maintain satisfying interpersonal relationships, and to make the best use of his intellectual capacity in learning, solving problems, and making decisions. Chapter 13, finally, presents a survey of the professional resources which are available for helping individuals with adjustment difficulties.

The World Health Organization has defined health as "a state of complete physical, mental and social well-being and not merely the absence of disease or infirmity." Personality Dynamics and Effective Behavior has tried to reflect this concept, which suggests the need for the full development and utilization of our adjustive resources—biological, psychological, and social—in achieving a personally satisfying and socially useful way of life.

AN ADEQUATE
FRAME OF
REFERENCE

Assumptions Concerning Fact

Assumptions Concerning Value

Assumptions Concerning Possibility

In tracing the pattern of human development (Chs. 2 and 3), we noted how each individual gradually builds up a unique frame of reference—a set of basic assumptions concerning fact, value, and possibility—which gives him a meaningful picture of himself and of his world. We may think of these assumptions as a basis for the individual's answers to the three key questions "Who am I?" "Where am I going?" and "Why?"

Without some frame of reference an individual would be incapable of consistent or purposeful action. In evaluating new experiences and choosing appropriate modes of response, he must draw upon what he has learned—rightly or wrongly—from past experiences. His basic assumptions may be accurate or inaccurate, conscious or unconscious, rigidly maintained or tentative and subject to disproof. But in any case they color his perception of each new situation. To the extent that his assumptions about either himself or his environment are inaccurate, his behavior is likely to be ineffective.

In this context we may distinguish between the relatively permanent and consistent aspects of an individual's frame of reference and the temporary distortions that often occur under special conditions. We have seen in earlier chapters how strong motives can commandeer and distort cognitive processes and how emotions can easily subvert rational processes in a stressful situation; and the automatic operation of the ego defense mechanisms provide a further source of error. Temporary distortions in a person's frame of reference, however, do not necessarily reflect inaccuracies in the long-range assumptions on which he bases most of his adjustive action. These relatively permanent assumptions are our chief concern here.

An adequate frame of reference carries the conviction of truth while remaining fluid enough to allow for correction and expansion. The individual should feel free to act as though his assumptions were correct but remain alert to information that may prove them false. This is essentially the attitude expressed by Gandhi (1948, p. 5) in his autobiography:

"I am far from claiming any finality or infallibility about my conclusions. One claim I do indeed make and it is this. For me they appear to be absolutely correct, and seem for the time being to be final. For if they were not, I should base no action on them."

An individual's ability to maintain an adequate frame of reference—to test his present assumptions and to remain open to experiences which contradict them—depends, of course, upon his having a basic sense of personal adequacy. Even experiences which require a person to modify his self-concept may be accepted so long as they do not undermine his basic feelings of confidence and ultimate worth. In this context Carl Rogers (1951, p. 513) has described "psychological adjustment" as existing "when the concept of self is such that all the sensory and visceral experiences of the organism are, or may be, assimilated . . . into a consistent relationship with the concept of self."[1] Similarly, Combs and Snygg (1959, p. 243) define an adequate personality as "one capable of admitting any and all experiences and of integrating this experience into his existing self structure. Such a person can acknowledge his experience, allow it entrance to his consideration, and relate it in some fashion to the existing concepts he holds of himself and the world about him."

To be able to accept all his experiences, the individual must first of all accept himself. As we examine the basic components of an adequate frame of reference, we shall have many occasions to note how the capacity for growth and improvement develops from a person's ability to see and accept himself *as he is*.

[1]This concept is basic to Rogers' system of psychotherapy. See his article, "A Theory of Personality and Behavior," on page 449.

ASSUMPTIONS CONCERNING FACT

The foundation of an adequate frame of reference is the individual's picture of how things really are—who he is and what he is worth, what the rest of the world is like (including the people in it), and how he fits into the overall picture. It is on the basis of what he assumes to be *fact* that the individual develops his assumptions of *value* (what is good or worth while) and *possibility* (what can be changed or improved). At the heart of his reality assumptions, of course, is his picture of himself.

Self-Identity

If you were to approach several strangers at random and ask them to answer in three sentences the question "Who are you?" you might get such answers as the following:

"I am Mrs. Royce Masterson. I was just voted one of the ten best-dressed women in this city. My husband is the well-known architect."

"I'm Bill Jackson. I guess you could call me a bum. I've never had much ambition."

"I'm Mark Walton. I'm an actor. I'm doing odd jobs until I can get a break in television."

"I'm Mrs. Peterson. I'm just a housewife. I have two children, and they take most of my time."

"Why do you want to know? I'm me. I'm myself."

In spite of their brevity, such answers probably reveal a good deal about the self-concept of these individuals—about their sense of identity and the value they place on themselves and on various goals. But such answers also raise important additional questions. Is Mrs. Masterson's identity, for example, really synonymous with her reputation as a well-dressed woman and her status as the wife of a prominent architect? And if so, is this an adequate identity for a mature, self-directing, and self-actualizing individual? Obviously a realistic and clear-cut self-picture depends upon something more.

Sources of self-identity. An individual's sense of identity grows from his knowledge and experience of himself as both "object" and "process." He is aware of himself not only as a physical entity with certain attributes but also as a self-aware being with the capacities for knowing, striving, and doing. He is not only John Holt, brown hair, brown eyes, 5 feet 11 inches tall, 160 pounds, 125 I.Q., 23 years old, son of Mary and George Holt, Presbyterian, graduate of Eastern University, and assistant advertising manager for Scott Department Store at a salary of $5500 a year. He is also a self-directing human being who can set goals, initiate action, exert self-control, say "yes" and "no," assume responsibility, and plan for the future. All of this—and much more—is implicit in John Holt's use of "I" and "me" and "mine."

As we noted in our discussion of human development, everyone's sense of identity is shaped in large part by his environment—the way other people react to him, what they say about him and expect of him, his status in various groups, the kinds of problems he encounters, and the success he has in meeting them. His environment normally acts as a kind of sounding board that tells him who he is and how well he is doing. A person's identity also incorporates his various ego-extensions—the individuals, groups, possessions, ideas, and values (all part of his environment) with which he closely identifies.

Some criteria for an adequate identity. Although outside influences always play a part, a mature sense of identity must stem ultimately from *inner* sources. The self-directing individual is independent of outside influences in the sense that he has thought out his own values and decided on his own goals. He experiences himself as the originator of his own acts. His self-concept is consistent within itself and also with his ideals and actual behavior. He may identify himself closely with other people and work hard to achieve group goals, but he remains aware of himself as an individual whose personal identity is something quite apart from that of any group. He is not afraid to be different if "being different" means acting in the light of his own values, knowledge, and experience. Only as an individual approaches this kind of independence does continuing growth and self-actualization become possible.

The goal of establishing a clear-cut and relatively independent sense of identity is, of course, a very difficult one to achieve. As we noted in Chapter 8, groups not only make it possible for us to satisfy our material needs but also make us feel adequate, secure, and worth while. If the individual doubts his own ability, the strength of the group to which he belongs gives him confidence. If he questions his worth, the status afforded him by the group reassures him. If he feels isolated and unloved, the friendship of the group makes him more secure. If he is confused about how to behave, his role in the group delineates a path he can follow. Being unsure of himself, the individual faces a constant temptation to establish his own identity by merging it with that of a group.

Thus the modern tendency toward conformity can be seen as a search for psychological as well as material security. But as May (1953, p. 32) has pointed out, the individual whose sense of identity derives mainly from outside sources leads a precarious existence:

"Every human being gets much of his sense of his own reality out of what others say to him and think about him. But many modern people have gone so far in their dependence on others for their feeling of reality that they are afraid that without it they would lose the sense of their own existence. They feel they would be 'dispersed,' like water flowing every which way on the sand. Many people are like blind men feeling their way along in life only by means of touching a succession of other people."

The outer-directed man is hardly free to develop his own potentialities. Nor can he even guarantee his own security by simply "not being different," for he is always dependent on outside forces. To the extent that security is possible and desirable, it stems from an individual's knowledge of himself and from his confidence that he can meet most situations successfully.

Self-Evaluation

Like our self-identity, our self-evaluation depends both on how we see ourselves and how we think others see us—and also how we would *like* to be. Indeed, by comparing these three images of self, we sometimes get an important clue to how accurately we are evaluating ourselves. The individual who considers himself capable and mature but finds that other people are consistently critical of what he does should probably sit down and take stock—as should the individual who thinks he is consistently *over*rated by others.

Obviously, we should not accept uncritically the evaluations of other people—particularly of our own families and others who are so ego-involved that they perhaps see us less clearly than a perceptive stranger would. On the other hand, it is generally true that when most people see us very differently from the way we see ourselves, our self-image is somehow inaccurate, and we are probably headed for trouble. Similarly, the individual whose self-ideal has little relationship to his present self-image is likely to encounter continual failure and frustration. A realistic assessment of one's assets and liabilities, achievements and failures, limitations and potentialities seems essential both for effective functioning on a day to day basis and for the fullest development of self.

Picture of assets and liabilities. In evaluating his assets and liabilities, the average person may consider only such obvious characteristics as his physical health, personal appearance, intelligence level, and socioeconomic background. A more adequate evaluation, however, would include his aptitudes and abilities in every area of competence—physical, intellectual, emotional, and social—as well as such constitutional factors as his energy level, resilience, and temperament pattern. It would also be related to his personal aspirations (a poor sense of pitch is a liability to a musician but probably not to a businessman) and to his particular environment (physical skills may be essential in a hunting or fishing society but are relatively unimportant in our own). A particular trait can be considered an asset or liability only in the context of (1) the individual's overall pattern of traits, (2) how much it helps or hinders the individual as he tries to achieve his basic goals, and (3) the extent to which it can be modified.

Often our most crippling limitations are the ones of which we are least aware. The college student who blames his lack of social success on his physical appearance or his financial limitations is probably overlooking the real cause of his failure—perhaps his lack of concern for other people, his irresponsibility, or his tendency to show off. Only when these social and emotional liabilities are assessed realistically do change and improvement become possible.

Unfortunately, it is usually much more difficult to admit inner limitations than outer ones, such as physical handicaps or environmental restrictions, and a good deal of our energy goes into defensive devices that keep us from seeing where we are wrong. The ability to recognize—and ultimately overcome—such limitations depends upon a determination to look at ourselves objectively, a knowledge of what to look for, and a willingness to accept what we see.

If a person is basically insecure, he may need help to accomplish these tasks. But most of us feel adequate enough to accept the fact that we have certain limitations and to face them with a constructive rather than a defensive attitude. For such people, a better understanding of the basic competencies required for effective adulthood (Chs. 10, 11, and 12) can provide a useful starting point for self-improvement.

There are some limitations, of course, that cannot be changed and with which we must learn to live. A great many people suffer from physical handicaps such as impaired vision or hearing, malformation or loss of limbs, and various chronic ailments. To mention just one category, some two million people in the United States have serious limitations in powers of movement, speech, and vision due to cerebral vascular accidents or "strokes." For some people, even personal appearance can be a kind of physical limitation. Girls in particular may find that a crooked nose, big feet, excessive height or weight, or even freckles make them feel inferior to other people. Or a boy may find that being considerably smaller than his contemporaries constitutes a serious limitation. These characteristics are not really physical handicaps, since the person living with them may be perfectly healthy and capable, but they do sometimes create special problems of adjustment in a society that places such a high premium on good looks.

Each of us must live with certain limitations in ability too. In a highly competitive culture such as ours, we are often forced to admit that we come off second best—or worse—in athletic ability, mechanical ability, artistic ability, intellectual ability, or some other area of performance. This ordinarily is not devaluating unless it begins to seem that everyone else can do *something* well and that we are good at absolutely *nothing*. It is only when an individual falls consistently below the norm in areas that seem important to him that inferior ability constitutes a serious limitation.

There are also various situational limitations with which we must learn to live. Being a janitor's daughter, belonging to an ethnic minority, or having to accept responsibility for the care of aging parents may limit an individual's opportunity for certain kinds of recognition or accomplishment.

There is no one-to-one relationship between the assets and liabilities an individual has and the success he makes of his life. It is difficult to imagine more severe limitations than those of Helen Keller, totally blind and deaf from the age of nineteen months. Yet Miss Keller's accomplishments, in terms not only of personal achievement but also of service to others, have been so great that she has become a symbol of inspiration to handicapped and non-handicapped people alike. Few of us can look at her life without feeling that we are half wasting the resources at our own command.

Feelings of adequacy and worth. As we have often noted, one of the greatest handicaps to personal effectiveness is self-devaluation. From feelings of inadequacy and unworthiness we acquire a defensive orientation that discourages growth and positive accomplishment. Such feelings usually develop from an unrealistic picture of ourselves in relation to other people. As Warters (1949, p. 157) has pointed out, whether failures and personal limitations become devaluating depends upon the way we interpret them:

"If I meet a frustrating situation that makes me feel completely inadequate, I do not feel inferior because of my inadequacy unless others make me feel that, in being inadequate, I am less good, less intelligent, less strong, or in some other way less worth while than they are. I am made to feel different in an undesirable way, and so I feel inferior."

Often, of course, an individual thinks other people consider him inferior simply because he falls so far short of his *own* aspirations. The pattern usually includes not only unrealistic aspirations for oneself but also an idealized picture of others. We continually compare our assets, achievements, status, and behavioral standards with those of other people. Such comparisons may lead to a realistic appreciation of individual differences and a more or less objective picture of our own assets and liabilities—or to an exaggerated sense of inadequacy.

The latter is most likely when we use an unrealistic basis for comparison. Thus we may match ourselves against the very best person in a given field and feel devaluated because we do not measure up, not realizing that the vast majority of people are no better and perhaps are worse than we are. Or we may exaggerate the overall gifts and personality characteristics of people who have made a remarkable achievement in only one field. We fail to realize that they are much like us, make mistakes as we do, have problems of their own, and perhaps are actually inferior to us in some areas—and that in their chosen fields they have excelled not only because of superior ability but also because of hard work and various chance factors. Finally, we may suffer devaluation when we exaggerate the importance of our own liabilities—whether these be a bad complexion, a large nose, poor athletic ability, or low socioeconomic status. Today more than ever before, envious comparisons are encouraged by advertising, movies, magazines, and television, which give an idealized picture of life and are geared to making us aware of what we are not and have not. Some envious comparisons are inevitable and nor-

SELF-EVALUATION

AND OTHER CHARACTERISTICS

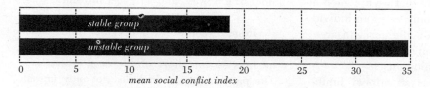

mean social conflict index

Although a person's self-concept cannot be observed directly, a number of studies have demonstrated its far-reaching influence on subjects' perceptions, defenses, and methods of attacking problems. In one such study subjects classified as "stable" or "unstable" (on the Guilford-Martin Inventory of Factors GAMIN) were asked to rate themselves on a list of traits in four different ways: as they thought they were, as they hoped they were, as they feared they were, and as they thought others regarded them. The stable group rated themselves more highly than the unstable group did, and, as the above graph shows, had a lower score on the social conflict index—that is, there was less discrepancy between their self-ratings and the way they thought others would rate them. They were also better liked, better adjusted socially, less situation-dominated, and showed less defensive behavior (Brownfain, 1952).

Another study showed that feelings of adequacy and success may depend more on self-acceptance than on actual achievement. One hundred students in an educational psychology class were assessed on self-acceptance (Bills Index of Adjustment and Values) and anxiety (Taylor Manifest Anxiety Scale) and asked to indicate their grade expectations for each of three examinations. On the basis of their achievement and their self-acceptance ratings, the students could be classified into four groups, as described below. Regardless of their actual test performance, the self-acceptant students tended to be optimistic, nonanxious, and noncompetitive; the self-rejectant ones, anxious and unrealistic in goal-setting (Mitchell, 1959).

Self-Acceptant Underachievers	Failed to reach expected achievement but least anxious of all groups.
Self-Acceptant Overachievers	Surpassed their expectations; consistently expected and got high grades, sometimes despite mediocre ability; industrious but not anxious, saw selves as mature, worthy, well-liked.
Self-Rejectant Underachievers	Started with unrealistically high expectations; after failure set progressively lower goals; least motivated of all groups, gave up easily.
Self-Rejectant Overachievers	Consistently surpassed their expectations yet most anxious, nervous, unhappy of all; strongly competitive, highly motivated, studious. Feelings of incompetence, failure, unworthiness prominent.

mal, and some may even act as worth-while incentives; but when we are left feeling worthless and inadequate, we need to re-examine our own assets and the values we consider to be really important.

Sometimes self-devaluation comes from feelings of guilt rather than from conviction of inferiority. Here again the problem usually arises when we measure ourselves against unrealistic standards. Perhaps we have an idealized conception of human nature which leaves no room for normal sexual urges, anger, resentment, jealousy, or even pride. Often guilt feelings incurred during childhood over "sinful" misdemeanors carry over into adult life. In Chapter 10 we shall discuss the difference between normal and morbid guilt. Guilt becomes pathological when we condemn ourselves for failing to live up to impossible standards and when we find forgiveness impossible.

Although effective behavior requires that we face up to our limitations and shortcomings, it also requires that we maintain a feeling of basic adequacy and worth. The findings of modern psychology and psychiatry have shown repeatedly the fallacy of believing that the only way to insure socially desirable behavior is to make people feel guilty, humble, and unworthy. We are coming to realize, rather, that self-devaluation not only stifles an individual's potential for growth and creative activity but, through the unconscious operation of defense mechanisms, may also lead to such socially undesirable characteristics as aggressiveness, hostility, and a condemning attitude toward others.

In summary, then, adequate knowledge of self involves both (1) a realistic assessment of one's own assets and liabilities and (2) a recognition that weaknesses and limitations need not be defeating and do not detract from one's ultimate worth as a human being. With a realistic acceptance of oneself, the individual, instead of continually setting his goals on the

basis of what he *should* be able to do or what he *should* want to do, can act on the basis of what he feels *able* to do and what he really *wants* to do. This reorientation in reality frees the individual for spontaneity and for growth within the range of his own capacities.

Knowledge of One's World

An individual's ability to make effective adjustments depends upon the assumptions he makes about his world as well as those he makes about himself. He can interact effectively with his environment, making the most of its resources and being the least restricted by its limitations, to the extent that he has a reasonably full and realistic environmental picture. Everyone has laughed at tales of the city slicker who makes a fool of himself on the farm or of the country bumpkin who blunders along in the big city. Each is at the mercy of an unfamiliar environment.

Usually more serious, though often less obvious, are the mistakes that most of us make every day because we are similarly handicapped by misconceptions or inadequate knowledge about our environment. We make foolish decisions, suffer unrealistic fears, and forego many possible satisfactions. Just as a young child may be frightened when he wanders from the familiar world of his own backyard, so an adult loses confidence and the ability to act effectively once he is outside those areas where he has the necessary knowledge to anticipate and cope with adjustive demands. As adults, we face the continuing task of widening the boundaries of our own "backyards" and expanding the areas in which we can act effectively—and without fear.

Environmental opportunities and limitations. For an adequate picture of his world —and of himself—the individual first of all needs to understand the opportunities his environment affords and the limitations and responsibilities it imposes upon him. This involves something more than a knowledge of what goals are available and what means are practicable. The effective individual understands the extent to which he is both dependent upon and free from the physical and socio-cultural field in which he lives. He tries to anticipate the problems he will have to face and to identify the competencies he will need. He attempts to build up a background of knowledge—political, economic, social, scien-tific—that will provide a reliable guide for his behavior. He tries to understand the structure and functioning of his society and the reasons behind its written and unwritten rules. He makes an effort to distinguish realistically between environmental limitations that can be overcome and those that he must learn to live with and between legitimate social pressures and those that infringe unreasonably on his individuality. He tries to relate his own pur-

PERCEPTION OF THREAT

Stimulus Situation	*Threat Perceived*	*Defense Undertaken*
Impending drought	Divine anger	Religious ceremonies
Impending drought	Scientific	Drawing on food resources; irrigation, manipulation of nature
Impending drought	No threat seen	No defense attempted

Adapted from Gillin and Nicholson (1951)

Depending on one's assumptions of fact, value, and possibility, the same stimulus situation may be perceived quite differently—and met accordingly with different responses. For example, as shown in the chart above, an impending drought may be regarded as evidence of divine anger, understood on a scientific basis, or not seen as a threat at all. The defense undertaken would depend on the threat as defined by the viewer rather than on the objective stimulus situation. The need for an accurate picture of "reality" is obvious.

In general, a dominance-oriented culture tends to see any threat as an attack and its own defense as a counterattack. When actual danger is great, this attitude is conducive to objective security, but it is likely to produce high anxiety and perpetual warfare. A submission-oriented group is more vulnerable to actual danger but, except when a threat materializes, tends to have greater psychological security and peace of mind.

poses to those of other people, and he recognizes his responsibilities as a member of society. He strives to understand community and national and world problems and to see their implications for him as a responsible human being.

Thus it is clear that independence and self-direction do not mean cutting oneself off from society. While making his own decisions and accepting responsibility for his own actions, the mature individual recognizes his personal limitations and those imposed by his environment, and he seeks help when he needs it. He also recognizes his relatedness to other people and his obligations as a social being. He does not have to "prove" his independence by becoming a professional nonconformist, though he is prepared to go against the tide when it seems important to do so. In describing the characteristics of the self-actualizing individuals whom he studied, Maslow (1954, p. 209) emphasizes this distinction between genuine independence and carping nonconformity:

". . . the self-actualizing person practically never allows convention to hamper him or inhibit him from doing anything that he considers very important or basic. It is at such moments that his essential lack of conventionality appears, and not as with the average Bohemian or authority-rebel, who makes great issues of trivial things and who will fight against some unimportant regulation as if it were a world issue."

A reasonable respect for social conventions in no way detracts from an individual's integrity, and it enables him to avoid senselessly hurting or fighting with other people.

The people in one's world. An adequate environmental picture also involves a realistic picture of the people who share one's world. More important than a theoretical appreciation of "individual differences" is an understanding of the needs people have, the problems they face, and the reasons for their behavior. As we shall see in a later chapter on social competence (Ch. 11), the ability to function effectively in a social setting depends to a large extent on the ability to see things—including ourselves—through the eyes of other people.

ASSUMPTIONS CONCERNING VALUE

Although our values depend heavily upon our reality assumptions, they are distinct from fact or information in their reference to what is *desirable* or what *ought to be,* rather than what *is.* Because they imply goals to work for in the future as well as standards for measuring the present and the past, values are also related closely to our assumptions concerning possibility.

Defining Value

In any discussion of values, we are immediately frustrated by difficulties of definition. Is a value an object or an experience or an idea? Are values absolute or relative? Are a person's values reflected more accurately by what he says or by what he does, or can a single individual have more than one standard of values? These are some of the questions that must be considered in any attempt to work out an adequate system of values.

As a first step toward a workable definition of value, we may note that values, however universal, seem to be meaningful only in terms of some personal reference point. Whatever an individual sees as desirable—because, for him, it is practical or precious or beautiful or good—has worth for him and is therefore a value. If his own experience does not make an object or enterprise desirable, then for him it is not a value. Psychologically, values determine our choices; we choose one objective over another on the basis of our own values. Herrick (1956, p. 138) regards values as "the relation existing between the thing sought and the satisfaction it gives, or may give, the seeker."

Values as meaning and guides. In relating "the thing sought" to "the seeker," Herrick has suggested two aspects of values: (1) they embody the *meaning* an individual attributes to things, including his evaluation of what is desirable and what is not, and (2) they serve as guides to action. Both aspects are implied in the useful definition of value formulated by Clyde Kluckhohn (1954, p. 395):

"A value is a conception, explicit or implicit, distinctive of an individual or characteristic of a group, of the desirable which influences the selection from available modes, means, and ends of action."

Every individual operates according to a system of values, whether it is verbalized and consistently worked out or not. In selecting goals, in choosing modes of behavior, in resolving conflicts, he is influenced at every turn by his conception of what is good and desirable. Although everyone's value system is in some degree unique, an individual's values are usually grounded in the core values of his culture. These core values reflect a culture's orientation to five basic human problems (F. Kluckhohn, 1956):

1. *Human-nature orientation*—Is human nature basically good, bad, or neutral? Does the individual have an intrinsic worth?

2. *Man-nature orientation*—Is man a helpless pawn, or does he have free will? Is he the "center" of his universe, or is he of no more significance than other forms of life?

3. *Time orientation*—Should man live for the present or in preparation for the future?

4. *Activity orientation*—What kind of activity is most valued? Making money? Being a good hunter? Service to mankind? Contemplation?

5. *Interpersonal-relationship orientation*—What is the dominant or desired relationship among members of the group? Is it competitive or cooperative, friendly or hostile?

Against the background of the answers generally given to these questions in his culture, the individual develops his personal system of values. And depending on his conception of what is desirable and good in human life, he selects certain goals over others and patterns his behavior according to standards of what he believes to be right and worth while. The way a man carries on his business activity, the kind of relationships he has with his wife and children and with his friends, the degree of respect he has for other individuals (and for himself), his political and religious activity—all these reflect the individual's values, though he may scarcely have thought them through.

Values, of course, are not the only determinants of behavior. Any given act reflects the individual's immediate motivational pattern and various situational factors (such as the means and goals available at the time) as well as his relatively permanent assumptions concerning value.

Conceived and operative values. A person's values have varying degrees of affective reinforcement and ego-involvement. Most people who have studied values systematically make some distinction between conceived and operative values. *Conceived* (or normative) values are conceptions of the ideal. For the most part these are the values which the culture teaches and the ones most likely to be talked about in any discussion of "morality" or "ethics." But conceived values, even though held with a good deal of intellectual conviction, sometimes have little practical

SOME VALUE CONFLICTS
IN AMERICAN SOCIETY

To clarify our individual and group goals, we need a well-defined and coherent system of values. Here is a summary of one attempt to identify some current conflicts in American values (Naegele, 1949).

Initiative
vs. Passivity

Belief in the value and effectiveness of individual initiative conflicts with the tendency to wait passively for a lucky break or for automatic advancement through seniority

Liberty
vs. Conformity

Belief in the value of the individual and the importance of freedom of conscience conflicts with admiration for efficient mass organization in which the individual must subordinate his goals to those of the group

Responsibility
vs. Determinism

Belief in the moral responsibility of the individual for his own acts conflicts with the tendency to seek out causes over which the individual has no control

Equal Opportunity
vs. Pull

Belief in equal opportunity for all conflicts with the readiness to take advantage of personal influence and special privilege in order to move ahead

Brotherly Love
vs. Competition

Belief in responsibility for one's fellow man conflicts with the determination to look out for one's own interest in any competition ("Good guys finish last")

Social Equality
vs. Success

Belief in the ideal of social equality conflicts with the determination to achieve financial success and acquire the various symbols of higher social status (expensive home, car, clothes; exclusive neighborhood, schools, clubs; etc.)

Saving
vs. Spending

Belief in the virtue of thrift, both for the individual and the nation, conflicts with the individual drive to display success symbols and a national economy based on increasing consumption

Simplicity
vs. Show

Belief in the virtue of humility and lack of ostentation conflicts with admiration for visible proof of financial success

Playing Safe
vs. Taking Risks

Belief in the virtue of responsibility and conservatism conflicts with admiration for bold gambles for high stakes influence on behavior. For example, an individual who conceives of human equality, nonviolence, service to mankind, and complete honesty as fundamental values may not be guided by them in his actions even when circumstances would make it fairly easy for him to do so. *Operative* (or factual) values, on the other hand, are the criteria an individual actually uses in making choices. As Clyde Kluckhohn puts it (1954, p. 402):

"Values are operative when an individual selects one line of thought or action rather than another, insofar as this selection is influenced by generalized codes rather than determined simply by impulse or by . . . temporary expediency."

A person's "real" values, then, must be analyzed not only in terms of what he says but in terms of what he does in situations that involve an element of choice. The intensity with which a value is felt can often be measured, too, by how much time and energy the individual is willing to expend in following it and what satisfactions he is willing to forego in its behalf. Finally, value strength can be gauged subjectively by how much satisfaction or guilt the individual experiences when he is true to a value or violates it.

Sometimes the discrepancy between an individual's conceived and operative values indicates an alarming schism between his "idealized" and "real" self. The businessman who professes to accept the golden rule but violates even the most basic business ethics, the woman who extols selfless mother love but governs her child with refined cruelty, and the politician who speaks of freedom but denies fellow citizens the right to vote are only very obvious examples of an all too common phenomenon. Sometimes a person holds dual standards without realizing it, sometimes knowingly from a conviction that the ends justify the means. Unfortunately, as Emerson

said, "The end preëxists in the means," and we tend to become what we do, not what we say.

It is rarely if ever possible, of course, to bring conceived and operative values into complete harmony. The man who places a high value on nonviolence will usually fight rather than be killed, and the man who values complete honesty may lie to protect a friend. The complexities of human nature and human society make utopia an ideal against which to measure our progress rather than a goal we can realistically hope to achieve. But this does not invalidate conceptions of the ideal nor strip them of their practical value. Salvador de Madariaga, a Spanish diplomat and political essayist, has made the point well (Smith and Lindeman, 1951, p. 123):

"Our eyes must be idealistic and our feet realistic. We must walk in the right direction but we must walk step by step. Our tasks are: to define what is desirable; to define what is possible at any time within the scheme of what is desirable; to carry out what is possible in the spirit of what is desirable."

To practice responsible self-direction, an individual must find meaning in his world and have criteria by which to choose and evaluate; if his values are vague and inconsistent, his behavior becomes aimless and confused. Values are necessary, too, for the stability and effectiveness of society, which cannot function unless its members agree on certain standards of responsible behavior and share basic purposes.

We have already commented on the havoc created in our own day by the crumbling of our traditional picture of the universe and, with it, many of our most basic values.[1] As physical and philosophical boundaries fade

[1] For an existential analysis of today's spiritual and cultural crisis, see William Barrett's article, "The Encounter with Nothingness," page 514.

before the advances of science and technology, men have become less sure of their role in the universe and more uncertain of their ability to guide their own destiny. Some people cling rigidly to the values of an earlier and more stable period, only to find themselves continually at odds with a changing world; others, no more wisely, discount *all* traditional values because *some* have proved invalid; still others pay lip service to traditional values but have little faith in them as practical guides. Symptoms of confusion and insecurity are seen in the increasing incidence of mental illness in the United States and our often deplored trend toward conformity.

Sources of Value

One assumption men have been forced to make in the present century is that we are barely on the threshold of understanding the physical, spiritual, mental, and moral forces in our universe. Few people today have the effrontery to claim they have found the final answers. Where, then, can the individual find reliable values, and how can he determine their validity? How can he arrive at a system of values that is stable and at the same time flexible enough to survive change? The complexity of the problem is well stated by Sinnott (1955, p. 147):

"One of man's chief problems is to determine what the basis of a moral code should be, to find out what he *ought* to do. Is the right that which is the word of God given to man in the Ten Commandments? Is it what is revealed to us by conscience and intuition? Is it whatever will increase the sum of human happiness? Is it that which is the most reasonable thing to do? Is it whatever makes for the fullness and perfection of life? Above all, is there any absolute right, anything embedded, so to speak, in the nature of the universe, which should guide our actions? Or are right

and wrong simply relative, dependent on time and place and culture pattern, and changing with environment and circumstance? What, in short, is the basis of our moral values? These questions are of vital importance in a day when intellectual power threatens to outrun moral control and thus destroy us."

In organizing his universe into a meaningful pattern and developing a system of values, man can turn to three chief sources of understanding: (1) *science*, which can help man better to understand himself and the universe in which he lives; (2) *experience*, which relates, both for the group and the individual, the consequences of various types of behavior in terms of need-satisfaction, happiness, and fulfillment; and (3) *belief*, which gives subjective validity to religious and ethical concepts about the meaning and proper conduct of human life. No one of these sources seems sufficient in itself, nor is any of them infallible.

Science. Science has the advantage of providing information that has been checked and rechecked by objective methods. But fact is impersonal and, except as it is interpreted, does not contribute to meaning or provide a guide for action. Even the value of searching for truth—the basic premise of science— cannot be "proved" scientifically. Probably the greatest scientist of our age, Albert Einstein, acknowledged that "the scientific method can teach us nothing else beyond how facts are related to, and conditioned by, each other" (1950, pp. 21-22):

"One can have the clearest knowledge of what *is*, and yet not be able to deduct from that what should be the *goal* of our human aspirations. Objective knowledge provides us with powerful instruments for the achievements of certain ends, but the ultimate goal itself and the longing to reach it must come from another source. And it is hardly necessary to argue for the view that our existence and our activity acquire meaning only by the setting up of such a goal and of corresponding values. The knowledge of truth as such is wonderful, but it is so little capable of acting as a guide that it cannot prove even the justification and the value of the aspiration toward that very knowledge of truth. Here we face, therefore, the limits of the purely rational conception of our existence."

How, then, does science serve us in the search for a comprehensive system of values?[1] Allport (1959, p. 137) suggests at least a partial answer when he states that "although moral values cannot be derived from natural data nor from science, they can in some sense be validated (confirmed or disconfirmed) by the activity of science." Hate, for example, can be judged "bad" on the basis of scientific evidence that it interferes with the healthy functioning of both the individual and society.

In providing us with more complete information about the human organism and human society, the biological and social sciences offer a clear illustration of how science—while remaining "ethically neutral" in its pursuit of truth—can help man in his search for more reliable values. Thus the findings of anthropology, while showing that many so-called "basic" values are relative only to a particular culture, have also shown that some values seem to have a universal validity. Drawing upon the evidence uncovered thus far, Clyde Kluckhohn (1954, pp. 418-419) argues convincingly against the acceptance of complete cultural relativity:

"Some values are as much givens in human life as the fact that bodies of certain densities fall under specified conditions. These are founded, in part, upon the fundamental biological similarities of all human beings. They

arise also out of the circumstance that human existence is invariably a social existence. No society has ever approved suffering as a good thing in itself. As a means to an end (purification or self-discipline), yes; as punishment—as a means to the ends of society, yes. But for itself—no. No culture fails to put a negative valuation upon killing, indiscriminate lying, and stealing within the in-group. . . .

"Reciprocity is another value essential in all societies. Moreover, the fact that truth and beauty (however differently defined and expressed in detail) are universal, transcendental values is one of the givens of human life—equally with birth and death."

As science discovers more about the "givens" of human life and the various factors that encourage or interfere with the fulfillment of human potentialities, we gain increasingly reliable criteria for developing sound values. There is a trend toward the acceptance of self-actualization—whatever it is called—as one ultimate criterion of value. That is, we can call those things "good" which contribute to the physical, psychological, and spiritual health of the human being. Thus the theologian Paul Tillich (1959, p. 194) states that "our knowledge of values is identical with our knowledge of man . . . in his essential nature." And the psychiatrist Kurt Goldstein (1959, pp. 187-188) maintains: "Value is a characteristic of the true being of man. . . . It is 'being' as it appears in man's self-realization. . . . Health appears . . . as the prototype of value."

A similar viewpoint is expressed by the biologist Herrick (1956, pp. 147-148) when he pinpoints the relationship between science and human values:

"Since life is intrinsically valuable to the organism that has it, whatever is good for the organism is a value. Having so defined goodness, science can tell us what is good *for us* under specified conditions and, if we must

---

[1]For a further consideration of this problem, see Hobbs' article, "Science and Ethical Behavior," on page 528.

make a choice of goods, may help us to decide which of them is most likely to prove most desirable in the end. . . ."

Since human capacities—physical and psychological—can be realized only in a social setting, values conducive to *self*-fulfillment will generally also promote the welfare of the *group* and of other individuals in it. On a very practical level this means that the individual recognizes the value of following the rules of the game if he wants to achieve his own purposes. It also means that he recognizes his relatedness to his fellow men and values them for their intrinsic worth. It is in the process of relating himself not only to his immediate loved ones but to all mankind that the individual is best able to fulfill his own potential as a human being.

Although science has thus helped man greatly in his search for reliable values, the average person takes a somewhat defensive attitude toward new scientific information when it seems to undermine his value system. Because his values are so basic to his feelings of adequacy and security in a vast, changing, and sometimes unpredictable world, he likes to think that they represent final truths. Copernicus' discovery in the sixteenth century that the earth moved around the sun, rather than the sun around the earth, met with fierce opposition because it seemed to diminish man's importance and to invalidate most of what he believed in.

Resistance to a heliocentric theory seems foolishness to us today, and yet—because of a felt need to defend our picture of the world and the values that derive from it—we tend to be similarly frightened by the discoveries of our own scientists as they probe deeper into the mysteries of the universe. What can be the value of an individual life if, as the highly respected astronomer Howard Shapley maintains, the cosmos contains at least one hundred million planetary systems suitable for organic

life? Shapley himself offers one answer (1958, p. 149):

"The new discoveries and developments contribute to the unfolding of a magnificent universe; to be a participant is in itself a glory. With our confreres on distant planets; with our fellow animals and plants of land, air and sea . . . with all these we are associated in an existence and an evolution that inspires respect and deep reverence. We cannot escape humility. And as groping philosophers and scientists we are thankful for the mysteries that still lie beyond our grasp."

In an age in which every year brings fantastic progress in the various sciences, we need to develop a positive orientation toward the changing facts of life. New information is not necessarily a threat, even when it requires changes in our present value structure. Rather, every increase in knowledge furnishes the potential for a somewhat more adequate frame of reference.

Experience. In the life of the group and of the individual, many values originate from experience. Through our libraries and museums, we can draw upon the experience of men and nations throughout the world since the beginning of human history. We can trace the rise and fall of past oriental and occidental civilizations and examine the causes which led to their downfall. We can observe the effects of dictatorships on human welfare and contrast these governments with more democratic forms of social organization in terms of their long-range contributions to human happiness and social progress. We can observe the effects of greed, selfishness, and ignorance in creating general human misery and leading to warfare. We can note the almost unbelievable cost of man's incessant conflicts in terms of lives, property, and suffering and their futility in solving his basic problems. These and many other lessons can be learned from man's history, and although we cannot always scientifically prove the teachings to be accurate, they, too, confirm certain values and invalidate others.

In guiding our political and social lives, we operate on the basis of assumptions (somewhat similar to the hypotheses of the scientist) which we continually modify and expand so that they agree more closely with the "facts" of our experience. Tack after tack has been taken through history as men have tried to determine what values they should follow—individually and collectively—to find happiness and to fulfill their destiny as human beings. Usually a society changes slowly, almost grudgingly, by a series of small modifications. At certain critical times in history, however, one human personality, or several, may lead society to accept a new set of values and to put them into action, as our own founding fathers did during the period of the American Revolution. Norman Cousins (1958, p. 16) suggests how they were able to work this "magic" of winning acceptance almost overnight for a new system of political values:

"The answer is to be found in the history of ideas. An idea does not have to find its mark in the minds of large numbers of people in order to create an incentive for change. Ideas have a life of their own. They can be nourished and brought to active growth by a small number of sensitive, vital minds which somehow respond to the needs of a total organism, however diffused the parts of that organism may be. These minds sense both the need for change and the truth of ideas that define the nature of change. When the ideas are articulated and advocated, the popular response is not merely the product of logic reaping its gains but of a dormant awareness coming to life."

Often in the history of ideas new values, once articulated, have been readily accepted because people have *known* them to be right on the basis of their objective and subjective experience. In the long run, most of the values that actually influence our behavior are validated by the satisfaction we experience in pursuing them. Hence experience becomes a key factor in determining the values we follow and the ones we discard.

Religion. Science and reason can support but never supply the values that give ultimate meaning to human life and enable men to answer their persistent questions about such problems as suffering, evil, and death. For these final truths, mankind has traditionally looked to religion, whose answers derive primarily from revelation—the disclosure of God and God's will to man. Although theologians have used logic, reason, and historical arguments to help prove the existence of God and the validity of their beliefs, the "proof" of religious truth must rest finally on faith. People who have received strength and comfort from their religion have an unshakable belief in the reality of God; but the correctness of their belief can never, by argument alone, be made convincing to anyone who has not shared a similar experience. In the well-known words of Pascal, "The heart has its reasons which reason does not know."

Religion as we customarily think of it in its institutionalized form is built upon the successive revelations of God to man as recorded in tradition and sacred literature. Typically, it involves not only a formal system of belief that can be passed on from one generation to the next but also a system of worship and a system of social relationships. In many ways, such organization helps religion to better fulfill its function. Unfortunately, however, as religion becomes highly formalized, there is a danger of its losing its vitality and becoming for many people a religion *about* God rather than a religion *of* God. The dogmas, traditions, and even buildings of the church may gradually assume more importance than the truths they were intended to house and protect.

Only when religion becomes thus dependent on its formal trappings is it vulnerable to the attack of science, whose end, like that of religion, is truth. The long-standing war between science and theology seems an unnecessary one. In discounting various traditional teachings of Judaism and Christianity, such as the Biblical account of creation, science cut away the artificial props of religion which many people had come to identify with ultimate truth; but it has left unharmed the foundations of faith and perhaps even strengthened them. The explanations of myth, while often necessary to fill the gaps in man's knowledge, have always been less satisfactory than fact as the basis for a concept of man and his universe that is worthy of their Creator.

Lewis Mumford (1951, p. 90) points up the continuing role that religion must play in a scientific age if man is to approach fulfillment:

"Instead of abandoning religion as science extends the province of objective description, we must rather increase its scope, so that our subjective contributions will be as adequate and as disciplined as our objective descriptions. The despiritualization of the world . . . has not brought us closer to reality, but has shut out that aspect of reality which only the fully developed human person with a rich subjective life can cope with."

Mumford's statement suggests the need for a religion that is a good deal more than a packaged philosophy. Besides relating the individual meaningfully to his God and fellow man, spiritual values should integrate the whole of a person's life. The conceived values which derive from his religious faith must harmonize with the operative values that guide his behavior, so that in a sense his life *is* his religion. Clark (1958) distinguishes four levels of religious faith:

1. Stimulus-response verbalism. This is a childhood level of verbalization, a conditioned response.

2. Intellectual comprehension. There is some thinking through and understanding but no real caring or carrying through into real life.

3. Behavior demonstration. The individual's actions demonstrate real belief more clearly than do his words, even though an intellectual comprehension may be lacking.

4. Comprehensive integration. Religious beliefs are well understood and integrated into behavior.

Much contemporary criticism of religion is directed at what Clark calls "stimulus-response verbalism." In their search for certainty in a time of change and confusion, many people have embraced formal religion without thinking through its values or integrating them into their lives. But the faults of formalization are not *necessary* faults of religion, which remains today the primary and perhaps the only source of ultimate values for mankind.

Criteria of a Sound Value System

In discussing values, we have emphasized that the individual needs a value system to give both meaning and direction to his life. To a great extent, each individual must construct his *own* value system, drawing upon the truths he finds in science, experience, and religion to build a framework for his life. While some of his values may have a universal validity, others will be relative only to his culture or even to him as an individual. There is no single system of values that can be prescribed as absolutely "right" for one and all. Any adequate value system, however, must meet the general criteria discussed below.

Integration and faith. An adequate value system is both internally consistent and integrated with the individual's total personality. It is something in which he can reasonably have a good deal of faith. An integrated value system also implies a *hierarchy* of values, which enables the individual to choose confidently between things of greater and lesser importance and to be relatively undisturbed by frustrations that interfere only with the attainment of short-range goals. When values are thus integrated with each other and with the individual's overall personality structure, they provide guidance for *all* behavior, simplifying everyday decisions and clarifying ultimate goals.

Values come alive in direct proportion to how much faith the individual has in them. Faith helps close the gap between conceived and operative values and enables the individual to achieve a sense of wholeness in everything he feels and says and does. His behavior reflects an intellectual and emotional surety; there is relatively little conflict between "ought" and "want." This is the kind of faith illustrated in the lives of men whose actions seem in complete harmony with their deepest wishes. Maslow (1954, pp. 220-221) describes it as one characteristic of the self-actualizing people he studied:

"I have found none of my subjects to be chronically unsure about the difference between right and wrong in his actual living. Whether or not they could verbalize the matter, they rarely showed in their day-to-day living the chaos, the confusion, the inconsistency, or the conflict that are so common in the average person's ethical dealings."

The kind of faith that encourages self-actualization is quite different from dogmatic faith, which seems to reflect fear and uncertainty more than it does positive conviction. Dogmatic faith tends to box the individual in and interfere with his spiritual and intellectual growth, whereas dynamic faith pushes him ahead to clearer insights. And as May points out (1957, p. 185), religion has no monopoly on dogma:

"Dogmatic faith is the kind of faith we cling to when we are scared. It's like building a stockade around yourself. The hope is that if you can protect yourself with these particular beliefs, then you can hide behind them and be safe. You may feel safe, to be sure, temporarily, but you achieve that security exactly at the cost of the failure to grow. Your life becomes increasingly drab, you have blocked off the human spirit by blocking yourself behind a stockade of dogma. Now in our age this is as prevalent in science as it is in religion. . . . I think most of the dogmatic faith in the 20th Century so far has been faith in progress, faith in mechanical happiness, faith in riches. These have to do not with religion as such, but rather with a crystallizing of dogma of a particular cultural period, and a hiding behind that dogma as though that would then give one security and freedom from anxiety."

In a transitional age such as ours the achievement of reasoned faith is more difficult—and, if there is to be any pattern in our lives, more important—than in times of greater stability. Some people wrongly use the fact of cultural relativity to support the specious argument that *no* value can have any real validity and that the "right" values, therefore, are whichever ones seem most immediately useful. Other people seek security in the face of uncertainty by accepting ready-made the values of their various reference groups—their culture, their socioeconomic class, their church —without thinking them through. Often a further problem is created here when the values of these different groups are inconsistent with each other, so that to live by them the individual must either divide his life into "compartments" or be in constant conflict with himself. Inconsistent faith, dogmatic faith, and lack of faith fail equally to provide the guidelines an individual needs to behave effectively in a changing world and to grow toward self-fulfillment.

Realism and flexibility. To behave effectively and find satisfaction in his environment, the individual needs values that can stand the test of reality and are relevant to the kinds of problems he must deal with. This means that his value system must provide meaning and practical guidance in a world that is far from being the utopia he might like to create. Madariaga's statement (p. 302) that "our eyes must be idealistic and our feet realistic" is very relevant here. An individual needs some conception of the ideal, but if his values have no touchstone in reality, they are apt to create frustration, conflict, and guilt. We need values that give direction and purpose as we go about the real business of living.

A realistic value system implies the need for a certain amount of flexibility. Fundamental values may remain relatively stable, but they must be refined and their compass extended as the individual's understanding broadens. The person whose values today are exactly the same as they were ten years ago has failed to grow in one important dimension. Values must keep pace with changes in the individual himself, in his life situation, and in his physical and sociocultural environment.

Even the process of physical maturation requires some recentering of values. As one grows older, for example, physical excellence and "youthfulness" must be reweighed as values against creativity, self-understanding, and other satisfactions which belong more properly to maturity. The tendency in our culture to worship the external attributes of youth makes this reorientation of values very difficult for many people.

Marriage and family problems also necessitate an extension and recentering of the value system, as do problems connected with one's life work. The college student deciding on a vocation, the middle-aged man who realizes belatedly that he hates his "good" job and would find much greater satisfaction in another line of work, the older man who is being forced to retire but wants to continue a productive life—all these individuals face problems, peculiar to their age and situation, which require realistic and clearly defined values for their solution. Spiritual values, too, are subject to continual redefinition and extension as the individual's knowledge and experience broaden. A realistic value system must remain flexible enough to grow.

Meaning and satisfaction. A final consideration in judging the adequacy of any value system is the amount of satisfaction that the individual derives from living by it—whether it gives meaning to his life and a sense that he is fulfilling the purposes of his existence. Cantril (1950, p. 166) goes so far as to suggest that "the ultimate criterion against which to judge the rightness or the goodness of any action is whether or not an individual himself senses that it will contribute in the long run to the possibility of his experiencing greater satisfaction in living." Dorothy Lee, an anthropologist who has made intensive studies of value in other cultures, also emphasizes subjective satisfaction as a universal criterion of value (1959, p. 165):

". . . we experience value when our activity is permeated with satisfaction, when we find meaning in our life, when we feel good, when we act not out of calculating choice and not for extraneous purpose but rather because this is the only way that we, as ourselves, deeply want to act."

We can thus see that an adequate value system is basic to an adequate identity and a sense of personal responsibility and self-direction. In this context Cantril (1950, p. 163) notes that when value-choices consistently bring the satisfactions an individual anticipates, he develops a faith in the reliability of his choices —a self-assurance—that enables him to find great satisfaction in everything he does:

"He does not have to rely on the extraordinary, the unusual, or the exotic. He searches for adequate resolutions of more immediate problems, not for final answers; he wants the respect of others, not their praise; he wants their understanding, not their adoration. He engages in activities to satisfy himself through his own participation in them, not to impress others."

Our search for values is not a perusal of vague, ethereal concepts which bear no rela-

tion to daily life; it is a quest for the value realities which must be experienced if life is to be lived to its fullest. The broader the individual's knowledge and experience—whether it be his personal experience or that accumulated by his culture—the greater is the possibility of his developing a system of values that will give real meaning, purpose, and satisfaction to his existence.

ASSUMPTIONS
CONCERNING POSSIBILITY

As Cantril has noted (1950, p. 33), "It is characteristic of man that he has the capacity to recognize that what is, does not have to stay as it is, and that there may be something he can do about it." Life derives meaning and direction not only from the values a man believes in but also from his assumptions about what he can hope to accomplish and what kind of person he can become. Even while solving problems of immediate and practical concern, the individual is aware of the goals, aspirations, and purposes he hopes ultimately to achieve. How his life will be shaped, then, depends on his assumptions about what is possible as well as upon his opportunities, resources, and ideals.

Usually the person who feels that he has been thwarted in doing what he wanted with his life is the one who has not taken the initiative for self-direction nor recognized the tremendous range of possibilities that were open to him. *Freedom* of opportunity is in many ways synonymous with *knowledge* of opportunity. As Allport notes (1955, p. 85), "a person widely experienced and knowing many courses of conduct has many more degrees of freedom. It is in this sense that the broadly educated man is freer than the man narrowly trained." To be self-directing, the individual

needs to know the range of choices open to him and the probable effect of his choices in terms of the present and future. And, of course, he needs to know what kind of a future he wants for himself if his present choices are to make sense.

Goals and Means

In discussing the dynamics of human behavior, we have repeatedly shown how important it is for both individuals and groups to have realistic and satisfying goals—and to develop the know-how for achieving them. We have also pointed to the continuing process of change in ourselves and our world which leads to endless readjustment in our goals and means. We are continually replacing old expectancies with new ones.

In setting our goals, we depend heavily upon our assumptions of possibility—of the opportunities which we think are available to us. Although some people invite failure and frustration by setting their goals too high and trying to reach the impossible, many more fail to recognize or take advantage of the vast range of opportunities that *do* fall within their reach. They lack a feeling for the potentialities of their life situations. As Sinnott (1955,

p. 82) points out, many of the differences between individuals are not those of ability or
opportunity but rather those of motivation
and purpose:

"All of us have known men and women of
very modest natural gifts and with intelligence
quotients no more than respectable, whose
ambition and enthusiastic purposefulness were
so strong as to carry their possessors on to
high achievement. Many too are those endowed
with great inborn abilities who, through lack
of determination and desire, never bring them
to full fruition."

The person who drifts through early adulthood without having a fairly clear idea of
where he wants to go and without assuming
real responsibility for directing his own life
often experiences a growing sense of frustration and dissatisfaction as he approaches middle age. At a time when he should be realizing
important goals and experiencing the rich satisfactions of maturity, he is bogged down in re-
grets over his lost opportunities. The pattern
of his life seems set—but the pattern has little
meaning and yields little satisfaction.

Although it is usually possible to establish
new goals for one's life, it becomes increasingly difficult as the individual is caught up in
the habits, routines, and responsibilities of his
middle or later years. In young adulthood, on
the other hand, most people have a very wide
choice of what to do with their lives—if they
are mature enough to identify, investigate,
and evaluate their opportunities. This is the
time for asking the question, "Where do I
want to go?"—for looking ahead to long-
range goals and for preparing to meet the obstacles that may stand in the way of achieving
them.

Yet instead of taking the initiative in establishing a direction for their lives, many young
people let circumstances make their decisions
for them. Even the choice of a vocation,

in which the average working person can
expect to spend forty-five years of his life,
is often made with little more thought than
one might give to the purchase of a new
automobile.

One difficult problem here, of course, is
balancing the present against the future. The
self-actualizing person is concerned not only
with the future but also with gaining as much
satisfaction as possible from the present. He
does not wait for a vague tomorrow to begin
living. However, he is aware that present decisions dictate the kind of tomorrow that will
come about, and he attempts to relate present
realities to future possibilities in such a way as
to achieve adequate satisfaction and fulfillment in living. Thus the young woman who
finishes school need not mark time until she
achieves her cherished goal of marriage but
may pursue worth-while interests that will
bring satisfactions whether she marries or remains single.

In examining the possibilities in one's life
situation, it is important to note that maintenance and actualization needs can be met by
many different sorts of goals. Just as the individual can meet his food requirements in
any number of different ways, so many different paths are open for satisfying the needs for
security, adequacy, love, and self-fulfillment.
Combs and Snygg (1959, p. 358) make the
point that the ability to distinguish between
needs and goals is an important key to self-
actualization:

"The mere fact of perceiving 'I do not *need*
to do this' or 'I need to be adequate but not
necessarily in this way' in itself provides a
freedom to explore new and more satisfying
means of achieving need satisfaction. The very
perception that 'I do not *have* to be married,
or a doctor, or richer than my neighbor' in
order to achieve adequacy, opens the doors
for the consideration of new possibilities and
new directions."

When the achievement of a particular goal is blocked by personal or environmental limitations, other goals for meeting the same need can usually be substituted—if the individual is alert to the opportunities open to him. Seldom, in this country at least, is the individual so restricted that he is unable to select and achieve satisfying goals. Self-fulfillment is *everyone's* potential, not merely that of a relatively few people who are favored by circumstance. As Jung points out (1959, p. 70), real growth and accomplishment always originate from *within* a person: an individual's "environment cannot give him as a gift that which he can win for himself only with effort and suffering. On the contrary, a favorable environment merely strengthens the dangerous tendency to expect everything to originate from outside—even that metamorphosis which external reality cannot provide, namely a deep-seated change of the inner man. . . ."

Possibilities for Self-Growth

We live in a competitive, materialistic world in which much of our energy is directed, quite naturally, toward the attainment of tangible goals. Such goals are likely to be genuinely satisfying, however, only when they contribute in some way to self-expression and self-growth. Ultimately we are concerned with self-actualization—with becoming the kind of person we would like to become.

As we have already said, there are many avenues to self-fulfillment and many alternate goals which will provide nearly equal satisfactions if the individual can see and take advantage of his opportunities. Usually the most serious obstacles to self-fulfillment are not in the individual's environment, as we so often think, but in his own personality structure—in his emotional immaturity, perhaps, or in his inability to get along with other people.

Even when we are objective enough to recognize our own personality difficulties, there is a temptation to take the attitude, "I wish I were different, but I guess there's nothing I can do about it. That's just the way I am." It is true, of course, that each of us has certain limitations imposed by heredity and environment, limitations that we must learn to live with. It is also true that personality and behavior are shaped to a large degree by forces beyond our immediate control. Thus we tend to explain the behavior of the juvenile delinquent in terms of an unhappy home, economic insecurity, or bad companions—tacitly excusing the individual from personal responsibility.

But while it is important to recognize the influence of environmental factors and past experiences, it is equally important to remember that the self—as knower, striver, and doer—is also an important determinant of behavior. With our capacities for evaluating and choosing, each of us has a considerable measure of freedom in shaping his own life. And having recognized our weaknesses, we can do much to overcome them if we assume that self-improvement is possible and approach it realistically.

Change is slow. A realistic approach to self-improvement is essential, for an attempt at self-improvement can be defeated by over-optimism and grandiose aspirations as well as by the attitude that "there's nothing I can do." Habit and the individual's need to defend his present self-structure make sweeping personality changes unlikely; the assumption that one can develop new traits and behavior patterns simply by deciding "This is the way I'd like to be from now on" only invites failure and discouragement. As Combs and Snygg point out (1959, pp. 349-350), there are limits to the individual's capacity for tolerating changes in his perceptual field, and unless he maintains a certain amount of stability in his assumptions, he will feel less adequate and secure than before he began trying to change himself:

"The basic need of the organism for the maintenance of organization forces each of us to protect ourselves against sweeping changes in self. We cannot 'lift ourselves by our bootstraps' overnight. . . . Changes in the self come about slowly and over a considerable period of time. This is not to say, however, that there is not room in the perceptual field for movement and change to occur. As a matter of fact, the self is in a constant process of change throughout its existence. There is always a degree of freedom in the selection of perceptions, a certain amount of 'slack' within which choice may occur. It is even possible that if this 'slack' is consistently taken up in the same direction over a period of time, a considerable degree of change in the self may be brought about."

Whether trying to learn new competencies or seeking to correct faulty patterns of adjustment, the individual stands a much better chance of success when he strives for improvement rather than for perfection. Each of us has an ideal of the kind of person he would like to be. But unless our ideal-self is attainable and fits *us*, it will be largely ineffective in motivating and guiding our self-growth. And even when our self-ideal is realistic, it can only be achieved slowly and by small steps.

It is by a series of such small changes that we accomplish major changes in self. Indeed, our real satisfactions are found in the day-to-day progress we make, not in the achievement of some seemingly ultimate goal that will signal that we have "arrived." In fact, ultimate goals are largely an illusion, for as we achieve certain goals, new ones always present themselves. As Gordon Allport suggests in the title of his book, *Becoming,* we never reach a point where growth is no longer possible or desirable. The term "self-actualization" is too often taken to imply a finished product rather than a continuing process and a continuing source of deep satisfactions.

The importance of self-acceptance. Despite the seeming paradox, it is true that in order to *change* himself, the individual must first accept himself *as he is*. Too often the recognition of personal inadequacies leads to an attitude of self-rejection which, far from acting as a spur to self-improvement, actually interferes with growth. Instead of attacking his problems in a task-oriented way, he typically becomes bogged down in a system of ego-defenses that obscure the real source of difficulty. The first need of the person who is threatened by feelings of guilt and inferiority is to protect himself against devaluation.

A chief function of all types of psychotherapy is to provide a supportive atmosphere in which there is little need for such defenses. Encouraged by the accepting attitude of the therapist, the individual gradually develops an appreciation of himself as a person who, like other human beings, has both strengths and weaknesses. Only when he can look at his own shortcomings objectively, without feeling that they undermine his essential worth as a person, is he able to do something about overcoming them. It is an obvious fact, but one too often overlooked, that we can only build on the structure of what we are now.

Although a person with severe feelings of guilt or inferiority may be unable to overcome them without professional assistance, the, average individual can move toward greater self-acceptance by acquiring a clearer picture of his many resources and by increasing his understanding of what it means to be a human being. Thus the first two parts of this book have aimed at providing an appreciation of both the problems and potentialities of the "normal" individual. We become most free to develop our enormous potential when we not only recognize our opportunities but also stop looking for perfection in ourselves and others.

The need for positive action. Although self-knowledge and self-acceptance are important first steps in increasing personal effectiveness, they are *only* first steps. In the long run, we become more adequate by *behaving* more adequately in actual situations. The educator's maxim that children "learn by doing" applies equally well to the problem of improving our intellectual, emotional, and social competencies as adults. Accepting the inevitability of occasional failures and frustrations, we must put ourselves into new situations where we can test ourselves and, through experiences of success, increase both our felt and actual adequacy. This "educational" process has been well described by Combs and Snygg (1959, p. 362):

"Effective change in self is a process of becoming involved in experiences or predicaments and working one's way out of them again. To do this successfully, however, requires a real appreciation of the personality in operation. The things we try must fit the selves we are. One of the greatest sources of discouragement in self help is the attempt to try to be what one is not or to do something in the way another person does it. The experiences we seek need to be selected in terms of our own personalities. To force ourselves into experiences in which we must be what we are not for any length of time is almost

ADJUSTMENT LEVEL

AND ACCURACY OF SELF-PICTURE

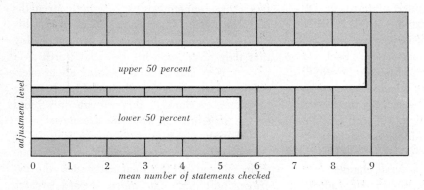

The well-adjusted person is better able to admit his faults than the poorly adjusted individual, who is more apt to feel threatened by the perception of undesirable traits in himself and thus rejects or distorts such perceptions in order to maintain a favorable self-picture. This is illustrated by a study in which sixth-grade children were asked to check anonymously which of twenty statements of undesirable behavior were true of them. All statements described behavior likely to be true of all children—for example, "I sometimes waste time when I should be working," and "I sometimes talk back to my mother." The children also took the California Test of Personality *which measured their level of adjustment. As the chart above shows, the children who were in the upper 50 percent in adjustment level admitted over half again as many undesirable behavior traits as those who were less well-adjusted (Taylor and Combs, 1952).*

certain to result in increased feelings of inadequacy."

The warning against trying to fit ourselves into another person's mold is an important one, which brings us back to the need for a clear-cut sense of identity. Our value assumptions are also important here, for to move consistently ahead toward self-fulfillment we must have at least tentative answers to such questions as "What is important to me?" and "What do I really want to make of my life?"

The Greek oracle said "Know thyself"; Emerson said "Trust thyself"; and the Danish philosopher Kierkegaard said "Choose oneself." These are the challenges for the self-actualizing person. He must know who he is and what he can hope to become; he must have confidence in his ability to direct his own life; and he must choose to be himself and to take responsibility for what he does.

In this chapter we have classified the interrelated assumptions that comprise a person's frame of references as assumptions of *fact*, of *value*, and of *possibility*. Although the distinctions are not always clear-cut, this classification is a useful one for analyzing what is meant by an adequate frame of reference and for showing how effective behavior grows out of a realistic picture of oneself and one's world.

What Carl Rogers calls an "openness to experience" is perhaps the most important foundation for an adequate frame of reference —and for effective behavior. A defensive orientation, though it may be successful for a time in protecting the individual's good picture of himself, is ultimately self-defeating. Here threatening situations are "screened out" or perceived in a distorted fashion and "processed" on the basis of false assumptions; this leads to the selection of an inappropriate pattern of action; divergent feedback fails to show the error because it too seems threatening and is therefore perceived inaccurately or screened from awareness altogether. Thus a faulty frame of reference, when protected by a defensive orientation, becomes increasingly out of tune with reality—and increasingly inadequate as a guide to adjustive action.

We have seen that the individual's assumptions must be relatively stable if he is to trust them as guides in making decisions and taking action. At the same time, however, they must remain flexible enough so that he can modify them whenever new information or changes in his life situation make his present frame of reference inadequate. To behave effectively and to realize his potentials for self-actualization, the individual must look at himself and his world realistically, continually reappraising his assumptions of fact, value, and possibility in the light of all the available information.

REFERENCES

The following list includes both the references cited in this chapter and a selected number of additional books and articles for outside reading.

Allport, Gordon W. 1950. *The Individual and his Religion: A Psychological Interpretation.* New York: The Macmillan Company.

Allport, Gordon W. 1955. *Becoming: Basic Considerations for a Psychology of Personality.* New Haven, Conn.: Yale University Press.

Allport, Gordon W. 1959. "Normative Compatibility in the Light of Social Science." *New Knowledge in Human Values.* Abraham H. Maslow, ed. New York: Harper & Brothers.

Brownfain, John J. 1952. "Stability of the Self-Concept As a Dimension of Personality." *The Journal of Abnormal and Social Psychology, 47,* 597-606.

Cantril, Hadley. 1950. *The "Why" of Man's Experience.* New York: The Macmillan Company. Reprinted by permission of the publishers.

Cantril, Hadley. 1958. *The Politics of Despair.* New York: Basic Books, Inc.

Cantril, Hadley, and Charles H. Bumstead. 1960. *Reflections on the Human Venture.* New York: New York University Press.

Clark, Walter Houston. 1958. *Psychology of Religion, An Introduction to Religious Experience and Behavior.* New York: The Macmillan Company.

Combs, Arthur W., and Donald Snygg. 1959. *Individual Behavior.* Rev. ed. New York: Harper & Brothers. Copyright 1959 by Arthur W. Combs and Donald Snygg. Published by Harper & Brothers, New York, and reprinted with their permission. See especially Chapter 16, "How People Can Help Themselves."

Cousins, Norman. 1958. "What the Founding Fathers Believed." *Saturday Review, 41,* No. 12, 15-17 ff.

Dodson, Dan W. 1958. "Reassessing Values in the Present Age." *Journal of Educational Sociology, 32,* 49-61.

Einstein, Albert. 1950. *Out of My Later Years.* New York: Philosophical Library, Inc.

Gandhi, Mahatma. 1948. *The Story of My Experiments with Truth.* Washington, D.C.: Public Affairs Press. Quoted in *The "Why" of Man's Experience* by Hadley Cantril, New York: The Macmillan Company, 1950.

Gillin, John, and George Nicholson. 1951. "The Security Functions of Cultural Systems." *Social Forces, 30,* 179-184.

Goldstein, Kurt. 1959. "Health As Value." *New Knowledge in Human Values.* Abraham H. Maslow, ed. New York: Harper & Brothers.

Herrick, C. Judson. 1956. *The Evolution of Human Nature.* Austin: University of Texas Press.

Jung, Carl G. 1958. *The Undiscovered Self.* Boston: Little, Brown and Company.

Kluckhohn, Clyde, and others. 1954. "Values and Value-Orientations in the Theory of Action." *Toward a General Theory of Action.* Talcott Parsons and Edward A. Shils, eds. Cambridge, Mass.: Harvard University Press.

Kluckhohn, Florence. 1956. "Value Orientations." *Toward a Unified Theory of Human Behavior.* Roy R. Grinker, ed. New York: Basic Books, Inc.

Köhler, Wolfgang. 1959. *The Place of Value in a World of Fact.* New York: Meridian Books, Inc.

Lee, Dorothy. 1959. "Culture and the Experience of Value." *New Knowledge in Human Values.* Abraham H. Maslow, ed. New York: Harper & Brothers.

Kuenzli, Alfred E., ed. 1959. *The Phenomenological Problem.* New York: Harper & Brothers.

May, Rollo. 1957. "The Relation Between Psychotherapy and Religion." *Personal Problems and Psychological Frontiers.* Johnson E. Fairchild, ed. New York: Sheridan House.

May, Rollo. 1953. *Man's Search for Himself.* New York: W. W. Norton & Company, Inc.

Maslow, Abraham H. 1954. *Motivation and Personality.* New York: Harper & Brothers.

Maslow, Abraham H., ed. 1959. *New Knowledge in Human Values.* New York: Harper & Brothers.

Menninger, William C. 1953. "Self-Understanding for Teachers." *NEA Journal, 42,* No. 6, 331-333.

Mitchell, James V., Jr. 1959. "Goal Setting Behavior As Function of Self-Acceptance, Over- and Under-Achievement, and Related Personality Variables." *Journal of Educational Psychology, 50,* 93-104.

Morison, Elting E., ed. 1958. *The American Style: Essays in Value and Performance.* New York: Harper & Brothers.

Moustakas, Clark E., ed. 1956. *The Self: Explorations in Personal Growth.* New York: Harper & Brothers.

Mumford, Lewis. 1951. *The Conduct of Life.* New York: Harcourt, Brace and Company.

Naegele, Kaspar. 1949. *From de Tocqueville to Myrdal: A Research Memorandum on Selected Studies of American Values.* Unpublished; Values Study Project, Harvard University.

Rogers, Carl R. 1951. *Client-Centered Therapy.* Boston: Houghton Mifflin Company. Copyright 1951 by Carl R. Rogers.

Rogers, Carl R. 1958. *Becoming a Person.* Austin: The Hogg Foundation for Mental Hygiene, The University of Texas.

Samler, Joseph. 1959. "Basic Approaches to Mental Health: An Attempt at Synthesis." *Personnel and Guidance Journal, 37,* 638-643.

Shapley, Harlow. 1958. *Of Stars and Men: The Human Response to an Expanding Universe.* Boston: Beacon Press, Inc.

Sinnott, Edmund W. 1955. *The Biology of the Spirit.* New York: The Viking Press, Inc. Copyright 1955 by Edmund W. Sinnott.

Smith, T. V., and Eduard C. Lindeman. 1951. *Democratic Way of Life.* New York: New American Library of World Literature, Inc.

Taylor, Charles, and Arthur W. Combs. 1952. "Self-Acceptance and Adjustment." *Journal of Consulting Psychology, 16,* 89-91.

Tillich, Paul. 1959. "Is a Science of Human Values Possible?" *New Knowledge in Human Values.* Abraham H. Maslow, ed. New York: Harper & Brothers.

Warters, Jane. 1949. *Achieving Maturity.* New York: McGraw-Hill Book Company, Inc.

EMOTIONAL

COMPETENCE

Components of Emotional Competence

Strategies for Improving Emotional Competence

Dealing with Problem Emotions

One of the dimensions of personal experience is the emotional or *affective* dimension. As we size up a problem and try to cope with it, we feel pleased, uneasy, elated, angry, or perhaps worried about the situation or our role in it. As we undertake a course of action, we may feel enthusiasm or distaste or perhaps dread. Whatever the situation, we tend to have feelings of some kind about what we are seeing and thinking and doing. Thus emotional processes are not isolated phenomena but components of general experience, constantly influencing and influenced by other processes going on at the same time.

Emotional reactions, of course, include not only feelings but also various chemical and neurological processes, such as those mentioned in Chapter 5. These physiological processes, however, are regulated largely by the autonomic nervous system, and there is little we can do to control them directly. Therefore we will be primarily concerned here with emotional competence on a psychological level—with some of the ways for discouraging negative emotions, encouraging positive ones, and expressing both negative and positive ones in healthful and constructive ways. The person who achieves emotional competence in these respects will be little troubled by the physiological aspects of emotion.

Emotional competence is greatly dependent on an accurate frame of reference and on overall maturity. How we perceive a situation—its meaning for us—determines what emotions will be aroused. If we see no threat, we feel no fear—however great or small the real danger. If we see our performance as superior, we feel elated regardless of the realities of the situation. And if we see ourselves as unfairly treated, we feel angry whether or not our perception is accurate. If we see ourselves as inadequate and unlovable, we feel perpetually anxious and discouraged whether we really are inferior and unlovable or only think we are.

Barring major changes in our life situation, most of us have a continuing, characteristic pattern of emotional reactions that is an important part of our life style. Saul (1947, p. 159) says:

"Every person has his own individual emotional constellation arising out of the emotional influences and experiences of his own childhood (always including congenital, physical, social and other related factors . . .). This 'nuclear constellation' is an important part of the core of every personality. . . . *No personality . . . is understood unless this nuclear constellation is clearly seen and comprehended.*"

We are as consistent and predictable in our emotional reactions as in our perceptual habits, thought patterns, prejudices, and other aspects of our approach to life. The events that arouse emotion in us, the type and degree of emotion they arouse, and our ways of expressing and controlling it all enter into this nuclear pattern which is unique for each individual.

COMPONENTS

OF EMOTIONAL COMPETENCE

In order to understand the components of emotional competence, we need to understand the ways in which we differ in our emotional reactions and the degrees of difference that seem to be within the normal range. These differences will be discussed under two head-ings: (1) the pattern of emotional experience, and (2) the pattern of expression and control. We shall then outline some of the causes that underlie the development of our characteristic emotional patterns.

Pattern of Emotional Experience

Although we often assume that other people "feel about the same way we do," there is considerable evidence that such is not the case. We seem to differ greatly in the depth and range of our feelings, in our moods, and in the proportion of our positive and negative feelings.

Depth of feeling. Some people apparently feel great intensities of emotion; they react to the ups and downs of living with intense joy, intense disappointment, and intense concern. Others, whether from constitutional limitation or defensive learning, are not easily stirred to either enthusiasm or distress but seem to be insulated from any strong feelings. Most of us are somewhere in between.

Emotional competence would seem to require sufficient depth of feeling to allow active, vigorous, healthy participation in living. Although wide differences in emotionality seem to be within the normal range, the extremes at either end are unadaptive. Overreaction to every minor situation squanders the individual's resources, whereas a very shallow reaction usually indicates a defense orientation with its rigidity and narrowing of perception.

In terms of their intensity, emotions may be described as *mild, strong,* or *disintegrative.* Interestingly enough, different intensities of emotion are apparently related to quite different physiological processes.[1]

1. *Mild emotions.* Prescott (1957, p. 396) has described the physiological effects of mild emotion as follows:

[1]This description of the different functions and effects of mild, strong, and disintegrative emotions draws heavily on conceptions developed in Prescott's **Emotion and the Educative Process** (1934) and **The Child in the Educative Process** (1957).

"Mild emotion, whether it is pleasant or unpleasant, produces modest increases in the rate at which all processes involved in the ingestion, digestion, distribution, assimilation, and metabolism of energy-releasing materials are carried on. . . . The sense organs also function more discriminatively, so that perceptions are sharpened. The over-all effect of these functional changes in body processes is to increase alertness and to focus the person's attention upon the meaning-producing factors in the situation. It also increases moderately the amount of energy being transmuted in the brain and central nervous system, the muscles generally, and the visceral organs. In other words, the effect of mild emotion, both pleasant and unpleasant, is generally tonic to all normal body processes. So the person feels 'pepped up' and invigorated."

2. *Strong emotions.* Strong emotions present a quite different picture. We have already described briefly (Ch. 5) the physiological changes that take place with the strong active emotions that one typically feels under frustration, conflict, or pressure. In this case there is an emergency mobilization for immediate, more or less violent action, and the stepping up of physiological processes is both more selective and more extensive. Processes related to digestion are suspended and the mouth becomes dry, whereas heartbeat, blood pressure, respiration, and adrenalin production are all increased. The capillaries along the alimentary canal constrict, while those in the brain and the large muscles enlarge for better circulation. Red blood cells from the spleen and sugar from the liver are released into the blood. Even the factor that induces blood clotting in injuries is increased—just in case. Carbon dioxide production may increase by as much as 60 percent. In the strong depressive emotions like grief, on the other hand, no action is usually called for, and action potentials are restricted accordingly: pulse rate, blood pres-

PATTERNS OF EMOTIONAL RESPONSE

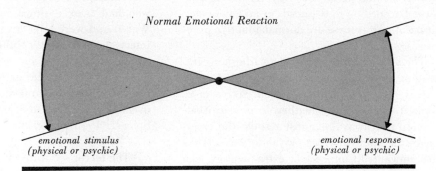

Normal Emotional Reaction

*emotional stimulus
(physical or psychic)*

*emotional response
(physical or psychic)*

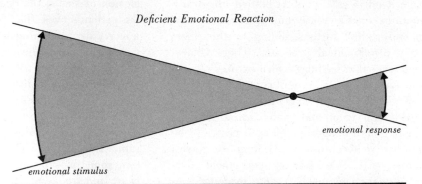

Deficient Emotional Reaction

emotional response

emotional stimulus

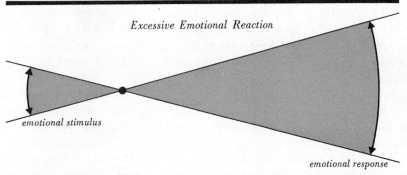

Excessive Emotional Reaction

emotional stimulus

emotional response

Adapted from Menninger, 1945.

*In a normal emotional reaction, stimulus and response are proportionate
in intensity. An imbalance in either direction—a strong stimulus evoking
a negligible response or a negligible stimulus evoking an intense response
—indicates some degree of emotional maladjustment.*

sure, and respiration are all depressed, and carbon dioxide production may be 30 percent under normal (Dumas, 1932; Prescott, 1957). In both cases—in strong active and strong depressive emotion—the energy release is patterned according to the needs of an emergency situation. Thus these are normal adaptive processes.

The circumstances of modern life, however, seldom allow for the direct use of the extra energy produced by the strong active emotions. Usually we can neither do physical battle nor run away but must resolve the emergency in more indirect or subtle ways. Thus the unwanted, unneeded, extra energy can constitute a hazard to us unless we learn to drain it off in safe ways. If bottled up, strong emotions can increase our level of tension uncomfortably, further adding to the emergency physiological processes. There is also the danger that feelings denied expression will be driven below the level of consciousness and may then find expression in unhealthy ways.

Although emotional mobilization may be adaptive on a temporary basis, it ceases to be adaptive if it continues very long. In Selye's studies (p. 172) we saw that permanent physical damage can result from a prolonged attempt to adapt to severe, long-lasting stress. In our anxious age, worry and strain too often result in a chronic emotional mobilization which prevents optimal functioning and eventually depletes our adaptive energy. The various psychosomatic ailments are disorders in which physiological functioning has been disrupted by the effects of long-continued emotional tension.

3. *Disintegrative emotions.* In addition to our mild and strong emotions, both of which may be normal and healthy, we occasionally experience *disintegrative* emotions. These may be the outgrowth of normal emergency emotions too long continued, or they may be precipitated by overwhelming stress. In such circumstances, as we noted in Chapter 7, even

a stable personality may develop a transient mental disorder, and an unstable one may decompensate to a full-blown psychosis.

The intensity of disintegrative emotions is well illustrated by observations of soldiers who had broken down in combat in World War II and were later given sodium pentothal interviews. Under the influence of this drug, which produces effects somewhat similar to those of hypnosis, the patient can "relive" his combat experience and discharge some of his overwhelming fear and anxiety (Grinker and Spiegel, 1945, p. 80):

"The terror exhibited in the moments of supreme danger, such as at the imminent explosion of shells, the death of a friend before the patient's eyes, the absence of cover under a heavy dive bombing attack is electrifying to watch. The body becomes increasingly tense and rigid; the eyes widen and the pupils dilate, while the skin becomes covered with fine perspiration. The hands move about convulsively, seeking a weapon, or a friend to share the danger. The breathing becomes incredibly rapid and shallow. The intensity of the emotion sometimes becomes more than they can bear; and frequently at the height of the reaction, there is a collapse and the patient falls back in bed and remains quiet for a few minutes, usually to resume the story at a more neutral point."

Range of feeling. We all tend to experience unpleasant emotions when our strivings are blocked or our values threatened—whether by forces outside us or by internal factors. We experience pleasant emotions when we achieve our goals or anticipate doing so or when we receive some confirmation of our values. Thus the actual events that please or displease us are as varied as our strivings and interests. In general, reaching maintenance goals yields satisfaction or relief, whereas attaining or making progress toward actualization goals yields elation or joy. When we fail to reach maintenance goals, we have feelings of frustration, loss, and general upset. When we fail to reach actualization goals, we feel, in addition, a certain amount of disappointment and perhaps self-condemnation.

Some people seem to experience only general "for" and "against" feelings. Others experience subtle nuances and fine shades of difference. Each of us, however, develops a characteristic repertoire of emotional reactions.

The chart on page 324 shows the usual progress of differentiation of emotions from the primitive excitement of early infancy into first delight and distress and later the more precise emotions of jealousy, elation, shame, guilt, worry, and all the rest. Typically, as old age approaches, there is a constriction and simplification of the emotional repertoire. Although the physical processes associated with maturation and aging evidently lay the groundwork for these changes, they are by no means automatic. Both cultural patterns and personal attitudes help shape the patterns of feeling that become typical in later maturity.

A wide range of appropriate emotional reactions adds richness to our experience. The failure to develop a full repertoire usually indicates general immaturity, faulty attitudes, or an unconscious defense against emotional involvement.

Moods. In addition to our somewhat transitory specific feelings, we tend to have general background moods that last longer and color the whole situation or activity in progress. Our mood may be one of zest and anticipation, one of discouragement and hopelessness, or perhaps one of nagging worry. Whatever its quality, our mood is an important determiner of our stress tolerance, level of energy, and degree of task or defense orientation. We have probably all had the experience of being in a bad mood and finding that molehills looked like mountains or of being in an especially good mood and sailing through a situation that normally would upset us.

Moods tend to fluctuate through a fairly predictable cycle somewhat independently of external events, but the length of the cycle and the difference between crest and trough are individual matters. People often find it interesting to keep a record of their moods every morning for a few months in order to see if they can detect a regular pattern.

The extreme mood fluctuations of the manic-depressive patient are only a more extreme example of the fluctuations in mood that seem to be typical of the human species. The individual who feels that his mood swings are beyond the range of the "normal" should seek professional counsel.

Positive or negative orientation. Both positive and negative emotions are normal, healthy reactions to certain types of situations. We all experience some of both, and the person who feels he should have only positive feelings is making unrealistic demands on himself. Yet a preponderance of negative feelings is unhealthy and maladjustive. Negative feelings indicate that the individual feels thwarted or threatened in some way, and such a perception, as we have already seen, tends to induce defense-oriented behavior. Furthermore, the fearful or resentful person is constantly on the lookout for new dangers and thus tends to see only what confirms his worries and fears. Such a person has trouble maintaining satisfying relationships with other people, and in time his chronic emotional mobilization may even have serious effects on his physical health. Thus a preponderance of negative emotions not only prevents present effectiveness but also interferes with the development of greater competence and maturity.

A predominance of positive feelings, on the other hand, is characteristic of the emotionally healthy person. Repeated studies, both clinical and experimental, have shown that love, sympathy, and other positive feelings are conducive to self-esteem, adequacy, and self-actualization. Although our feelings are, of course, somewhat dependent on what life brings us, this is only part of the story; some people manage to have a predominance of positive feelings despite great adversity, whereas others are constantly fearful, angry, and resentful in what looks to us like a favorable situation. It is our attitudes and values that chiefly determine whether an experience will be gratifying or frustrating to us. Except under the most extreme stress—as in a concentration

EMOTIONAL CHANGES WITH AGE

Infancy		*Maturity*		*Old Age*
Undifferentiated response. Random behavior.	Process of differentiation and integration.	Mature emotional sensitivity and control. Maximum differentiation of response and aesthetic feeling.	Process of consolidation and some disintegration.	Constricted response. Preservative behavior.

Excitement

Distress {
Anxiety
Fear
Shame
Anger
Disgust
Jealousy
Disappointment
Restless
  uneasiness
}

Grief
Worry
Self-pity
Guilt feelings
Querulousness
Irritability
Boredom
} Depression

Delight {
Joy
Elation
Hopeful
  anticipation
Affection
Sex love
}

Mystical
  ecstasy
Possessive
  satisfaction
Benevolence
Gustatory
  sensuousness
} Content

Apathy and Passivity

Adapted from Banham (1951)

camp, for example—the emotionally competent person can usually manage to keep the balance on the side of the positive emotions.

Pattern of Expression and Control

People vary not only in their patterns of emotional experience but also in their patterns of expression and control. Some are effusive and demonstrative, freely expressing their feelings in words, gestures, and other behavior. Others hide their feelings—sometimes just from other people, sometimes from themselves as well. Sometimes "admirable" emotions are expressed freely, while disapproved ones are concealed or denied. These may be culturally induced patterns, but usually they serve individual needs and purposes too.

Clearly not every emotionally competent person will have exactly the same pattern of expression and control. As with the experience of emotion, "normal" covers a wide range. The following three characteristics, however, are associated with competence in emotional expression and control: (1) a balance of spontaneity and control, (2) a habit of channeling emotion constructively rather than suppressing it, and (3) an avoidance of distorted and disguised expression.

Spontaneity and control. Sometimes emotional reactions are out of proportion to the situation. With inadequate inner controls, we may overreact emotionally to routine situations, flying off the handle or bursting into tears; with too rigid controls, we may be unable to "let ourselves go" at all. Neither extreme is desirable. Emotional health requires both the freedom to express our feelings without embarrassment or guilt and the ability to control emotional expression according to the requirements of the situation.

Constructive channeling versus suppression or repression. When direct expression of our feelings brings us pain or when we are taught to be ashamed and afraid of our feelings, we may unconsciously resort to emotional insulation or repression to protect ourselves from hurt or self-devaluation. Thus we may try to stay aloof from emotional involvement altogether so that, whatever happens, nothing can hurt us; or we may drive our unwanted feelings below the level of consciousness; or we may turn all blame inward so that we can keep only kindly feelings toward those around us. Although these ruses enable us to maintain our self-esteem and may provide a temporarily more comfortable way of living with our feelings, they are usually unadaptive in the long run. Once aroused, feelings press for expression in some way, and we ignore or deny them at our peril.

Accepting and acknowledging our feelings does not mean that we act out all hostile or destructive impulses, for emotional competence requires that our actions be in keeping with our long-term goals and values. But feelings that are acknowledged and accepted stay under our potential control; we can then decide whether and how to express them, and we can work out sensible and satisfying patterns of expression and control. Repressed feelings, on the other hand, are beyond the range of our direct control and thus can do untold mischief.

Surprising as it may seem, one of the primary tasks of psychotherapy customarily is to reintroduce the individual to his own real feelings.[1] Typically in the course of therapy there is first an avalanche of negative feelings and then, as these are worked through in a sympathetic and unthreatening atmosphere, a shift to a predominance of positive feelings as the individual finds himself again tapping the mainstream of his own deepest experience.

Direct versus disguised expression. Feelings that are denied direct expression may find outlets in disguised ways. Hostility, for example, may be expressed through nagging

[1]For an elaboration of this point, see Carl Rogers' article on page 449.

or cynicism; and anxiety and fear may be expressed through chronic fatigue. In some cases the strain of suppressing the emotions may be relieved by the development of a psychosomatic ailment such as asthma, hay fever, or a type of dermatitis where the skin itself "weeps." None of these reactions satisfies either the individual or those around him. His destructive feelings are increased instead of lessened, and he usually is unaware of the real motive power behind his reactions. Often he is bewildered by his own behavior. He can hardly learn more effective patterns of expression until he understands the reasons for his present reactions.

The healthy use of emotional resources cannot be achieved by rigid control. Effectiveness in emotional expression and control, like effectiveness in other forms of behavior, means that both inner needs and outer demands are taken into account. Nor is emotional competence something that can be achieved once and for all. Although we can learn to look at emotion-arousing situations differently and thus reduce our susceptibility to unpleasant emotions, emotional experience is often beyond our conscious control. Thus everyone has the continuing problem of finding personally satisfying and constructive ways to express his emotional tensions.

Determinants of Emotional Patterns

The reasons for the differences in our characteristic emotional patterns are complex and not completely understood. The following factors, however, evidently contribute to the picture.

Constitutional make-up. We have already seen that even newborn babies show wide differences in excitability. Some are easily aroused; others are phlegmatic. Undoubtedly these original reaction tendencies are partly responsible for later differences in depth and range of emotion. Yet they cannot be the whole story, for anxious, insecure children can *learn*

not to let themselves feel deeply; and the shallowness of affect typical of psychopathic personalities also seems to be learned.

Some individuals are apparently more prone to mood swings than others, and both the length of the cycle and the intensity of the moods involved seem to be largely constitutionally determined. It is not known, however, whether constitutional factors play a part in shaping a predominantly positive or negative orientation, or whether they influence our pattern of expression and control.

Early training. From our earliest training we learn to regard our emotions as something to be encouraged and expressed or as something to be denied and hidden. These early attitudes affect our subsequent emotional development. If we are taught to recognize and accept our real feelings, regarding them—even the negative or violent ones—as part of our normal human equipment, then normal emotional development can proceed. Learning appropriate patterns of expression and control is, of course, a continuing developmental task, for with the new problems of each life period, somewhat different emotional patterns become appropriate.

Unfortunately, in meeting its needs for harmony and stability, society too often encourages the inhibition of potentially disruptive emotions rather than the constructive channeling of them. Thus a child may be taught to be ashamed of his anger and to avoid expressing it at all, especially when his hostility is directed at adults or brothers and sisters. In addition, he may get little help in learning either how to work off his feelings or how to change his attitudes in ways that will discourage the arousal of intense negative emotions. The resulting build-up of emotional tension makes the child unusually susceptible to other negative feelings—and so a vicious circle is sometimes inaugurated. Under such circumstances it is unlikely that a child will develop either a normal emotional repertoire or the patterns of expression and control that are part of maturity and competence.

The alternative to inhibiting the child's emotions is helping him accept them as natural (even when they make him feel like kicking his baby sister) while at the same time teaching him the need for appropriate modes of expression. Basic to the process of emotional growth, of course, is the realization that other people's feelings can be as vulnerable as one's own. With the right kind of guidance a child will learn gradually but easily that both he and other people are much happier when his destructive emotions are vented in nondestructive ways. This means learning, among other things, that at certain times and in certain places some means of expression work out better than others and that talking out his feelings is sometimes better than acting them out. If the stresses of his life are within his ability to handle, he will thus gradually increase not only his self-control but also his ability to accept frustration and delay.

Frame of reference. To understand an individual's emotional responses, we must understand his frame of reference. Both the feelings a person has and the way he expresses and controls them depend on his basic assumptions and attitudes about what is true, what is right, and what is possible. He reacts to a situation according to its apparent meaning in terms of his own needs and purposes.

If an individual's level of aspiration is too high or too low and his self-expectations unrealistic, he will never have a chance to experience feelings of success and adequacy. If he regards the world as a dangerous, hostile place, he will interpret whatever happens as confirmation of this view and will constantly feel anxious and threatened. If he feels guilty about what are actually normal feelings, he will keep subjecting himself to unnecessary anxiety and self-condemnation—from which he will then have to protect himself by various conscious and unconscious defensive maneuvers.

Whether an individual has a predominance of positive or of negative feelings also depends heavily on whether he is primarily task-oriented or defense-oriented—which again depends upon his underlying assumptions and attitudes about himself and his world. His positive or negative emotional reactions then further reinforce his predominant orientation toward task-achievement or self-defense. Again we see the close interrelation and circular role of these processes.

The social field. The kind of social climate in which people function has a great deal to do with their emotional patterns. People who live in a highly competitive, hostile, aggressive society tend to develop aggressiveness and hostility, with an underemphasis on love and sympathy. And an autocratic social climate, as we have already noted, tends to elicit hostility, which is sometimes channeled through scapegoating behavior. On the other hand, a prevailing social climate of warmth and friendliness tends to elicit love, compassion, and other positive emotional responses. The warlike Comanches and the peaceful Hopi of our Southwest provide a dramatic contrast in dominant emotional patterns induced by the social field.

The channeling of emotions, as well as their arousal, is strongly influenced by the social field. Some societies tolerate gossip but prohibit physical attack. Some regard any expression of pain or fear as a sign of cowardice or lack of manliness—a pattern somewhat common among primitive peoples who live under adverse conditions in which fear and pain are undoubtedly common underlying feelings. Some social groups expect loud lament when a family member dies; others expect stoic acceptance. Some encourage free expression of feelings; others set up elaborate, formal rituals through which all expression must take place.

The same principles apply, of course, to the framework of family life. In a prevailing climate of bickering and tension, hostility and other negative emotions are continually aroused and expressed in rather direct, destructive ways. In a warm, happy family, on the other hand, love and other positive emotions are likely to be dominant, and members learn to keep negative feelings from disrupting the family harmony.

Inadequate, infantile parents or disturbed emotional relationships in the family may be reflected in fixations and distortions in children's development that carry over into adulthood. As Saul (1947, p. 205) has pointed out: "Adults generally maintain with amazing exactness the emotional patterns of their childhood relationships to the members of their families." Although immature patterns may be outgrown in a more favorable setting later on, there is no guarantee that this will occur. More typically, much effort is needed and sometimes professional help.

The field situation influences our emotional reactions in another way as well. As we saw in Chapter 8, social contagion in a crowd may lead to strong emotional arousal in the individuals and to behavior that they would never normally permit themselves. When those around us are responding with intense emotion, as in a crisis or panic, their reactions make it harder for us to keep our own equilibrium. In the same way, we are responsive to the general level of morale of those around us.

If others are discouraged and depressed, our own spirits may be dampened. If others are excited and enthusiastic, they may carry us along with them. It is hard to remain serene and constructive in an atmosphere of dissension and suspicion. A healthy social climate is thus of immeasurable help to us in our attempts to attain emotional competence, whereas an unhealthy social climate may subvert our best efforts.

Special conditions. Other factors, many of them transient, may also affect our emotional responses. Fatigue, illness, or a residue of upset from previous stress may make us unduly sensitive so that we overreact to minor irritations. Alcohol lowers normal cortical controls, and people under its influence tend to react overemotionally. Brain damage or the deterioration of brain tissue accompanying old age may bring a lessening of emotional control so that the individual is easily moved to tears or laughter.

Another special condition which often upsets our emotional reactions is the familiar vicious circle. Inadequate emotional patterns complicate our lives in geometric progression. The emotionally incompetent person, by virtue of his very incompetence, continuously creates much more severe problems for himself than the emotionally competent person usually ever has to face.

STRATEGIES FOR IMPROVING EMOTIONAL COMPETENCE

Most people are troubled about their feelings from time to time. Some wish they could feel more deeply and spontaneously; others wish they could learn not to fly off the handle so easily; still others have irrational fears or feelings of hostility that they cannot conceal yet do not know how to express without inviting retaliation. Although building greater emotional competence depends first and foremost on building healthy attitudes toward ourselves and our world, there are also specific steps we can take to help insure that our emotional equipment will play a constructive and enriching role in our lives instead of inducing stress.

Understanding and Accepting Emotion

The first step in improving our mastery over our emotions is to understand them. Much misery comes from sheer ignorance. Many people worry about mood swings that are actually quite normal, feel a loss of self-esteem over normal sexual urges, or suffer agonies of shame and guilt because of occasional feelings of hostility toward parents or others whom they love. Although an understanding of emotional processes will not automatically solve problems of expression and control, emotional competence starts with a healthy and realistic attitude toward emotion as part of one's equipment for living.

Knowing what is emotionally healthy and unhealthy, normal and abnormal, can enable us to evaluate our own emotional habits realistically and see what and where we should try to change. We need to realize that emotional processes serve the adaptive functions of reinforcing motivation and regulating the amount of energy we have available according to the needs of the situation. Mild emotions, both positive and negative, are healthy and invigorating in their effects and help make our experiences meaningful. No less normal are the strong emotions we experience in emergency situations. These, too, serve an adaptive function, providing extra energy when we need it or, in the case of strong depressive emotions such as grief, cutting down on the energy available when our need is not for action but for a readjustment in our frame of reference. Yet it is important for us to realize that any strong emotion brings widespread physiological changes and that for long-term health we must (1) find safe ways of relieving tension and discharging the extra energy and (2) manage our lives so that emotional mobilization does not persist and become chronic.

Functioning with Emotions Instead of Fighting Them

One important strategy in directing our emotional reactions is learning to function with them instead of attempting the impossible task of fighting them. Bottling up our feelings or trying to deny them can only get us into trouble.

Much unnecessary emotional arousal and behavior disorganization can be avoided by adequate preparation for specific life demands that are likely to arise. We have fire or disaster drills in our schools so that children will know what to expect and what to do in case of emergency. In the training of combat troops, simulated warfare is necessary to give the men essential knowledge and skills for coping with actual combat. In less dramatic situations, it is often helpful to rehearse or role-play situations like job interviews or speeches. A certain amount of preparation for marital and vocational adjustments can be accomplished by discussion and study of possible trouble spots and of ways others have solved their problems. When we understand a problem and know what it involves and what it demands of us, the situation tends to lose its emergency character; we can usually approach it with considerable confidence and a corresponding freedom from disruptive emotion.

Some stress situations, of course, will evoke strong emotion no matter how thoroughly we have tried to prepare ourselves. As we have pointed out, such emotion serves a useful adaptive function if we know how to handle it. If the soldier in combat does not experience fear, he will hardly be normal and, lacking the extra energy that fear provides, will probably not fight as well. But if he regards fear as a sign of cowardice and devotes his energy to trying to deny and hide it, he will have less energy for dealing with the actual dangers and will, in addition, be handicapped by continual inner conflict.

Finding Constructive Ways to Express Feelings

When strong feelings are aroused that cannot be expressed directly for practical reasons, it is important, as we have seen, to find safe ways of releasing the extra energy that is produced and thereby relieve the tension. There are many ways in which this can be done. Any physical activity will help—the more strenuous the better. It can even take the constructive form of cleaning out a garage or closet or washing a car. Talking things out with a trusted friend or a counselor is usually helpful. Just getting our fears, anxieties, disappointments, hostilities, and even loves out into the open where we can see them for what they are helps us to discharge much of the tension they have created. Writing, painting, and working on a hobby are other ways. Fantasies, in which we "tell off" someone who has crossed us or imagine what we would like to do to him if we could, sometimes help us work off hostile feelings. If we realize that nursing a grudge can do us serious harm physiologically, we will be less apt to allow ourselves this luxury.

Keeping a Sense of Humor

A sense of humor is an important emotional resource. The person who can remain objective enough to appreciate the incongruities of a situation is less likely to be overwhelmed by it. Laughter is perhaps as healthy and effective a way of reducing negative feelings as has yet been discovered.

Sometimes, of course, what passes for humor is really an expression of hostility, as when we attempt to feel superior by making other people appear ridiculous. Similarly, the so-called humor of many smutty jokes seems to represent an immature method of satisfying sexual tensions or showing off. In his study of a group of self-actualizing adults, Maslow (1950) found that his subjects tended to appreciate

subtle wit rather than broad humor and that their humor tended to be lacking in hostility.

An ability to use and enjoy humor is both a cause and a result of our attitudes. A defense-oriented person can seldom see anything funny about himself. On the other hand, one who can enjoy a good joke on himself is helped thereby to maintain a task-oriented approach to his problems.

Accentuating Positive Emotions

Since it is important to emotional competence and even to good health that positive feelings predominate, we should do what we can to keep the balance on the positive side. Although we obviously cannot decide "Now we shall start having only positive feelings," there is much we can do to encourage healthy emotions. We can choose the activities that seem most likely to yield rich satisfactions while they are being done. We can concentrate on actualization strivings instead of maintenance ones—on growth instead of on keeping what we have. Rather than nurse a grudge against someone, we can explore ways of building a better relationship with him. Instead of playing a martyr role and wallowing in self-pity, we can tackle projects that will center our attention outside ourselves. We can make a deliberate effort to be more acutely aware and appreciative of the assets that we usually take for granted.

Much of this boils down to the task of building positive attitudes. Unfortunately, it is much easier to endorse the merits of equanimity, courage, patience, and cheerfulness than it is to adopt these attitudes under trying circumstances. We cannot put on positive attitudes as easily as we change into new clothes. Nonetheless, it seems true that a major change in attitude is usually a prerequisite for any major improvement in emotional patterns.

The key to attitudinal change is not a simple resolve to "think positively" in the sense of denying that a problem exists. A real change in attitude depends, rather, upon an ability to see the problem in a new light. This means facing up to it realistically and evaluating it in relation to one's self-concept, needs, and purposes. The person who can see his disappointments and frustrations in perspective will not get "steamed up" emotionally over a broken date, the mistakes of a bumbling bridge partner, or his mother's insistence on straightening his tie. Even major frustrations can be taken with considerable equanimity by the individual who can be objective enough to see that they do not necessarily reflect on his adequacy or interfere with the achievement of his important goals. And defeat can quite literally be turned into victory if it points out mistakes to avoid instead of serving as the occasion for self-pity and discouragement.

If negative feelings predominate and we cannot seem to do anything about them, we may be the victims of unconscious attitudes and defenses which keep us from seeing things in their true perspective. In such cases professional counseling may be necessary to help us examine the real basis for our emotional difficulties and, with this better understanding, achieve a more positive orientation. Counseling and psychotherapy will be discussed in Chapter 13.

The Question of Tranquilizers

In recent years a great deal of public and scientific attention has been focused on the use of so-called tranquilizers and other tension-reducing drugs. Early experiments with these drugs in mental hospitals brought dramatic results: many patients who had been seemingly impervious to treatment of any kind were able at last to benefit from psychotherapy; some could even resume their normal life activities. In most cases, tranquilizers seem to have the effect of reducing anxiety and tension and improving psychological integration and stress tolerance. But they cannot correct the faulty attitudes and response patterns which are often at the root of mental disturbance.

The remarkable success of the tranquilizing drugs in treating mental illness has tended to obscure the fact—at least in the public mind—that they cure symptoms rather than eliminate causes. Thus many people have turned to tranquilizers as a means of reducing the tension and strain of everyday living. Some have found that the drugs make them feel much better and more capable of dealing efficiently with their problems; others have been able to detect no appreciable results; and still others have suffered undesirable side-effects which seem to outweigh any benefits. A great deal of research is being done to evaluate the drugs more fully and to improve them. At the present time, however, it seems that at best they are crutches which are valuable primarily in times of severe stress. Used indiscriminately, they are dangerous to the extent that they may produce harmful side-effects and/or obscure the need to come to grips with the original source of tension.

DEALING WITH PROBLEM EMOTIONS

The general strategies already outlined for improving emotional competence are, of course, applicable to all the emotions. In addition, however, it will be useful to explore the unique aspects of several of the emotions that most often present problems for us. Although we will discuss them one at a time, it should be emphasized that in our actual experience they rarely occur in isolation. Fear, anxiety, and hostility, for example, commonly go together.

Fear and Worry

Fear is an emergency reaction to situations viewed as dangerous. Since no life is free of hazard, fear is a normal and justified experience. Yet many people feel it is a sign of cowardice to feel or show any fear. It is especially difficult for men in our culture to admit their fears because of our prevalent stereotype of the male as a strong, confident provider under whose protection his family can feel secure. Thus, although his job or social situation may make him feel inadequate and frightened, a man may not dare reveal these feelings to others for fear they will be interpreted as signs of weakness. In fact, however, most of his confreres are in the same boat, struggling to appear more courageous and confident than they feel.

Although we often think of fear as being aroused only by external danger or threat of danger, many fears reflect rather the individual's special vulnerability to certain kinds of stress, usually the outgrowth of early painful experiences. Thus an individual who was rejected as a child may be so oversensitive that he continually fears being rebuffed by his adult associates—even when they accept and like him. Another person may carry into adulthood a fear of the dark or of being left alone. Sometimes, too, fears undergo displacement or substitution through the working of ego defense mechanisms, so that the individual develops irrational fears or phobias (Ch. 7). Thus adult fears may no longer be simple reactions to current external threat but highly complicated reactions. Unfortunately, as our fears become disguised, they become increasingly difficult to handle.

Closely related to fears are the nagging worries that often keep us in a turmoil. Most of our worries are about things that never happen or about things that have happened and cannot be changed. Only a small percent concern real dangers that we can do something about. Worry, like fear, *can* be constructive in keeping us sensitive to impending danger, but it is more often negative in its effects because it tends to a narrowing of the perceptual field, to a paralysis of positive action, and to a fearful, self-defeating approach to our problems.

Distinguishing between realistic and unrealistic fears. The first step in dealing with fear or worry is to try to understand its cause. Is it elicited by a real danger? Is it proportional to the actual degree of danger, or is it exaggerated? Is it reasonable or irrational? Is it born of the present situation, or does it reflect a pervasive feeling of inadequacy and inferiority? Is it related to early trauma?

Probing and self-examination will not, of course, yield a sudden harvest of insights. Just as it is hard to find what we are looking for in a storeroom where half of the packages are labeled improperly, so it is difficult to identify the hidden meanings behind the things we do and feel. But in approaching fear as something to be recognized and understood instead of something to be denied and hidden, we have taken the first step toward competence in handling it.

Knowing what to expect and what to do. Since fear stems from a feeling of helplessness, the best insurance against it is actual adequacy and competence. Obviously we cannot know ahead of time all the situations we will face, but we can foresee many fairly probable ones and prepare ourselves for those. With good all-round intellectual, emotional, and social competencies and specific preparation for a vocation, marriage, parenthood, and aging, for example, we will be able to maintain a constructive, task-oriented approach in meeting the normal problems to be expected in these areas—although unusual stress or overwhelming catastrophe may, of course, still prove too difficult for us.

If there are certain types of situations in which we commonly feel fear, we can often identify and then work to develop the skills we need to carry on despite the fear. As we become more proficient, we may find our fear lessening, though we can never expect to banish fear completely. Some actors, for example, suffer agonies of stage fright throughout their professional careers. Fortunately, they are able to learn to function effectively despite their fears by mastering the skills needed in their profession. By knowing what to expect and what to do, they are able to carry on.

Taking action. Fear tends to paralysis and paralysis to further fear. Action—almost any action—can break this circle and lessen feelings of fear even when it does not lessen the actual danger. The actor usually loses his stage fright once the action begins. The soldier in combat who has something to do is less apt to go to pieces emotionally than the one who must remain immobile. During the London blitz the fire wardens, who were above ground and exposed to the bombs, suffered fewer emotional breakdowns than the civilians who were safe in subterranean shelters. Although the wardens were in greater actual danger, they had duties to perform that kept them busy, absorbed their attention, and used the extra energy that fear made available.

Taking action of some sort—the best we can see at the moment, presuming it is not completely senseless or harmful—implies also a willingness to take calculated risks. As we have noted in earlier chapters, effective behavior in any area requires the ability to act decisively even in the face of doubt. When fear is involved and a wrong choice may bring serious consequences, action sometimes becomes very difficult. But if we wait for absolute certainty, we will wait forever.

Anxiety

Anxiety, or psychic pain, is a normal protective device which, like physical pain, serves as a warning of danger. As we saw in Chapter 5, it differs from fear in being more vague and dif-

fuse. Even irrational fears (phobias) are directed toward some specific object or situation, but anxiety—sometimes called "free-floating" fear—is typically experienced as a generalized feeling of uneasiness and foreboding. Without knowing why, the individual is apprehensive of impending disaster. Sometimes, as we have noted, the disaster he unconsciously dreads is a breaking through of his own repressed feelings and desires.

A certain amount of anxiety is probably an inevitable by-product of modern life. Most of us feel vaguely apprehensive about the possibility of accident, illness, failure, economic disaster, and war. Because such dangers are often ill-defined in our thinking and only partially understood, they tend to generate continuous mild anxiety. A complicating factor, too, would appear to be the difficulties we encounter in our quest for values and meaning in our fast-changing society. As May (1953, p. 37) has put it: "We are anxious because we do not know what roles to pursue, what principles for action to believe in. Our individual anxiety, somewhat like that of the nation, is a basic confusion and bewilderment about where we are going."

Anxiety can hamper us in two basic ways. In the first place, anxiety beyond a very minimal level leads to a defensive orientation which makes us less able to face our problems objectively and to work effectively toward their solution. Our perception narrows; we become more rigid and less inventive; and we develop a spiraling need to protect ourselves by rationalization, projection, repression, and other ego defenses. In the second place, prolonged anxiety keeps our bodies chronically mobilized for emergency action when no appropriate action is evident. The harmful effects of such continued physiological mobilization have already been described. It might be added, too, that anxiety deprives us of much of the enjoyment of living. (In Chapter 7 we noted the role that anxiety typically plays in the development of neurotic disorders.)

Obviously there is no easy rule for coping with anxiety. Because its source is unclear and often below the level of consciousness, anxiety is more difficult to attack than fear. Until the individual knows *why* he is anxious, he can do little to overcome his feelings. We can do much to *prevent* unnecessary feelings of anxiety, however, by developing an adequate frame of reference. Knowledge and acceptance of oneself, a realistic appraisal of one's opportunities and limitations, realistic and clear-cut goals, and a satisfying value orientation—these eliminate the most common sources of anxiety.

We should also be alert to such common symptoms of anxiety as chronic fatigue, worry, depression, indecision, insomnia, and unexplained stomach upsets. When we recognize these early warnings, we can sometimes analyze the possible sources of trouble and so deal with them on a conscious level. Often a trusted friend can help by serving as a sounding board, but in cases of severe and persistent anxiety the services of a professional counselor or psychotherapist may be required. Anxiety, like physical pain, can serve the useful function of warning us that something is wrong. Only when we ignore it is it likely to become severely crippling in its effects.

Hostility (Anger, Resentment, Hate)

The origin of hostility usually lies in frustration. As Saul (1947, p. 109) has noted:

". . . there is probably no impairment, frustration, conflict or friction of any kind which does not result in hostility as a reaction, and this hostility seeks to express itself in some way. Hostility is probably the psychologic correlate and perception of the body's automatic physiologic response to any irritation or threat, that is, of its physiologic mobilization for fight or flight."

Hostility, then, can be seen as a normal device intended to help the organism serve its needs through aggressive action. But since it is as often unadaptive in modern living, we are taught early in life that it is a dangerous emotion and often grow up feeling guilty about our hostility and not knowing how to cope with it. This is especially true of hostility toward those closest to us. We feel so strongly that we should love our parents and our children, for example, that it is often impossible for us to admit that we have any negative feelings toward them. Yet anyone close to us will frustrate us sometimes, so that occasional feelings of hostility toward loved ones are inevitable.

Because we have learned to deny our hostile feelings, hostility—like fear—may wear many masks. The Overstreets (1956, p. 68) describe some of its various disguises:

"As a personality trait, and not merely a response to some specific stimulus, hostility has various expressions: hypercriticalness, for example; readiness to belittle and disparage; a habit of nagging; a tendency to hold grudges; many-sided prejudice; cynicism; suspicion of people's motives; xenophobia; 'patriotism' that seems to have no content except hatred for some enemy; a way of bringing every conversation around to something that can be deplored or viewed with alarm; quickness to take offense and to see personal opponents as public enemies; a readiness to exploit, humiliate, and intimidate; a habit of defining success in terms of status and power over others; and contempt for the 'soft' enterprises of reconciliation."

Hostility may also be turned inward in a "hate campaign" against oneself, finding expression in migraine headaches, peptic ulcers, or other psychosomatic afflictions or in feelings of depression and self-recrimination. In the background of an intrapunitive person is often a fear of not being loved or being unworthy of love, together with a rigid conscience and a high level of aspiration. After punishing himself, such a person is often able to revert to a more normal outlook again. However, an individual with recurrent feelings of severe depression or despondency should seek professional assistance.

Although hostility is a normal part of our adjustive equipment, we differ greatly in the degree and frequency of our hostile feelings. As we have seen, some cultures value and encourage hostility and aggressiveness, whereas others discourage such traits. A repressive, frustrating social setting creates much more hostility in its members than one that provides many satisfactions and few frustrations—witness the aggressiveness and scapegoating common among socially frustrated groups. In addition, each individual has a personal balance sheet of successes and failures, loves and hates, gratifications and frustrations which, together with his self-attitudes, affects the degree of hostility he feels.

What can we do about hostile feelings that we recognize but see no direct way of expressing without incurring retaliation or other undesired dividends? The following are points to keep in mind.

Understanding our hostile feelings. As with other emotions, competence in dealing with hostility begins with an understanding and acceptance of our feelings instead of moral self-condemnation. This does not mean nourishing all our gripes, grudges, and hates. If we feel hostile, we need to recognize this as a fact of life; but then, since continuing hostility usually disturbs our physical and psychological well-being as well as our social relationships, we need to try to understand why we are angry or resentful and do whatever we can to keep these feelings from becoming chronic.

Hostile feelings are often a justifiable and normal reaction to a difficult situation, but sometimes they are the result of immature attitudes and unrealistic expectations. An immature person is easily upset and angered by minor delays, disappointments, discourtesy or hostility in others, or sudden changes in plans.

Although everyone becomes vulnerable to such trivial irritations when he is very tired or under severe stress, under normal circumstances a mature individual is able to see molehills as molehills and not as mountains; he is not aroused to wasteful and inappropriate anger at every obstacle. A habit of overreacting to minor frustrations often indicates underlying feelings of inferiority as well as emotional immaturity.

Expressing the feelings. When feelings are intense, expression of some sort is highly desirable to lessen the tension and dissipate the extra energy that has been made available. Several "safe" ways of doing this were suggested on page 330. Usually there are many kinds of physical activity possible that will serve the purpose without complicating the problem further. Release through words or through creative media can be equally effective.

Expecting some hostility from others. As we learn to accept and tolerate hostility in ourselves, we must also learn to accept it in others, even when it is directed against us. Perhaps the most essential aspect of dealing with overt hostility in adulthood is to be prepared for it and to give up the notion of wanting everyone to love and appreciate us. Although there is a certain justice in reacting angrily to the seemingly unjustified anger of another person, this is a form of self-indulgence that seldom pays off. Two people preoccupied with defense against each other or with retaliation for past offenses only feed and perpetuate their feelings of hostility. If we can see another person's anger, especially when it is disguised, as a problem for him rather than as a threat to us, we can often make the response that will lessen his tension and thus make a better relationship possible.

Guilt and Depression

Man universally experiences a sense of guilt when he violates or falls short of the standards he accepts for himself. This recognition of responsibility for failure is a necessary concomitant of self-direction, and guilt is potentially a normal, useful emotion that can lead to a correction of error and a reparation of damage. But when guilt persists without leading to redirection of effort or when it focuses on self-condemnation and self-devaluation instead of on future improvement, then it is morbid and pathological. Our earlier discussion (p. 86) of the differences between mature and immature conscience also has relevance here.

Normal versus morbid guilt. Normal guilt feelings can usually be dealt with through confession of guilt (to oneself, to a minister or priest, or to a well-chosen confidant), a sincere effort at reparation, and then a willingness to accept forgiveness and to look to the future instead of the past. This sequence normally leaves one better equipped to avoid the same mistake on subsequent occasions. In the case of morbid guilt, however, the individual cannot be convinced that the slate will ever really be wiped clean, and he ordinarily requires professional assistance from a psychotherapist to help him with this problem.

With morbid guilt, the individual magnifies his transgression out of all proportion, feels that he has committed an unpardonable sin, and suffers such pervasive feelings of unworthiness and depression that there is no joy left in anything he does. Usually too, the individual suffers from feelings of anxiety and apprehension stemming from his belief that somehow he will be "punished for his sins." Such morbid guilt feelings usually reflect immature, rigid, unrealistic standards that no human being could possibly follow; with an implacable but unrealistic conscience, the individual is foredoomed to perpetual failure.

Sometimes, of course, such individuals project their guilt to others—thus freeing themselves of blame and protecting their sense of worth. Another unconscious defense against guilt is reaction formation (p. 202).

Depression as a component of guilt. Severe or morbid guilt feelings are usually accompanied by feelings of depression. Some degree of depression is, of course, a normal reaction to setbacks that keep us from reaching our goals; but while severe depression—though unadaptive—occasionally seems warranted by the realities of the situation, many depressive reactions are unrealistic in relation to the objective situation and reflect immaturity, faulty attitudes, and unconscious self-punishment for failure to live up to self-demands. For example, an individual with an unrealistically high level of aspiration and a compulsion to excel may suffer deep feelings of unworthiness, guilt, and depression over inconsequential failures that in no way threaten his long-term record. Another common source of depression is conflict over hostile or sexual desires which the individual considers unethical and evil. When a person tries to hide such desires even from himself, repression, guilt, anxiety, and depression (as a form of self-punishment) may then follow.

In simple cases of self-condemnation for perceived failure, the self-punishment seems to atone for the "misdeed," and in the course of time the individual usually regains his emotional balance. But where repression is involved, the cycle of conflict, guilt, anxiety, and depression may be a continuing one, and the individual may need professional help to extricate himself. In cases of severe depression, suicide is always a real possibility. Those close to a seriously despondent person should do what they can to see that he receives help.

Grief

Grief is a universal reaction to bereavement, found even among animals. It is apparently based on a close identification with the person or thing that has been lost; in a sense, the bereaved feels that a part of himself is gone. This is especially apparent with the death of a close family member, but much the same reaction may occur in public mourning over the death of a well-loved national figure. The Britisher's personal concern for the welfare of the royal family is a striking example of such identification.

Grief is often complicated by feelings of hostility, guilt, and depression, especially when the grief-stricken individual has had ambivalent feelings toward the lost loved one. When death comes, he feels vaguely responsible and is depressed by his inability to make amends. Guilt and depression are almost inevitable, of course, when the individual has actually been involved in some way in the event that caused the death, as in an automobile accident.

Death is not the only source of bereavement and grief. An individual's wife may leave him, or his son may commit a crime and be sent to prison. The loss of an eye or a limb is a very real bereavement. Even the loss of possessions can bring grief if the possessions have supplied important emotional supports and gratifications for the individual and, in a sense, are viewed as extensions of himself.

Ordinarily, grief is worked through with time. This process of "grief work" may include talking, crying, mourning in other ways, and rearranging life details into a new pattern. The free expression of sorrow—and of guilt and hostility if these are involved—seems to facilitate readjustment and prevent the development of depression later on. As intense feelings of loss and hurt lessen, the bereaved individual gradually comes to accept his circumstances and to re-evaluate and rebuild the pattern of his life. With very intense grief or grief complicated by guilt and depression, however, this comeback becomes relatively more difficult.

Like other problem emotions, grief must be dealt with from the viewpoint of the individual involved. While he is experiencing intense grief, well-meaning admonitions to "keep a stiff upper lip" or "consider how many people are worse off" are likely to do more harm than

good. The psychological needs of the bereaved, rather, are freedom to express his feelings and, a little later, support as he tries to build a new life. There is a growing feeling that, except in unusual circumstances, it is a mistake to prescribe tranquilizers to help a grief-stricken person float calmly through the period when grief work is normally accomplished. Delaying the reaction to loss may in the long run make an adjustment more difficult. In severe cases, of course, where an individual might otherwise be overwhelmed by the intensity of his feelings, tranquilizers may help him over the crisis until he is able to work through his feelings in a normal way.

Love

Despite its central importance in human affairs, love, as a psychological phenomenon, has received very little scientific study. In fact, many psychology books do not even have the term *love* in the index, and where the term is used, it is ordinarily in connection with sex and marriage rather than in terms of its more general place in human relationships. Yet it would probably be agreed that an ability to give and receive love is one of the most important of all emotional competencies, for all the evidence points to the necessity of love for normal human development and functioning.

Why human beings have such a great need and desire for love has been the subject of considerable speculation. Fromm (1956) believes that love develops from man's awareness of his separateness and his need to overcome the anxiety this separateness brings by achieving union with someone or something. But he stresses the point that the only healthy union is one in which the integrity of the individual is not threatened. For example, man can achieve a feeling of union through dependence on another individual or through conformity to the group, but in so doing, he surrenders his own individuality; likewise, he can achieve union through dominating others, but here the others suffer. Only through love, Fromm feels, can the needed sense of union be achieved without loss of individuality and integrity on either side.

The meanings of love. Many people have tried to define love. Prescott (1957, p. 358) has described valid love in terms of the following components:

"1. *Love involves* more or less *empathy* with the loved one. A person who loves actually enters into the feelings of and shares intimately the experiences of the loved one and the effects of these experiences upon the loved one.

"2. One who loves is deeply *concerned for the welfare*, happiness, and development *of the beloved*. This concern is so deep as to become one of the major organizing values in the personality or self-structure of the loving person. . . .

"3. One who loves finds *pleasure in making his resources available* to the loved one, to be used by the other to enhance his welfare, happiness, and development. Strength, time, money, thought, indeed all resources are proffered happily to the loved one for his use. A loving person is not merely concerned about the beloved's welfare and development, he does something about it.

"4. Of course the loving person seeks a maximum of participation in the activities that contribute to the welfare, happiness, and development of the beloved. But he also *accepts fully the uniqueness and individuality of the beloved and . . . accords* [*him*] *full freedom to experience, to act, and to become what he desires to become*. A loving person has a nonpossessive respect for the selfhood of the loved one."

Usually we think of love in terms of a relationship between two individuals, but as Fromm points out (1956, p. 46) mature love involves "an *attitude*, an *orientation* of char-

acter which determines the relatedness of the person to the world as a whole. . . . If a person loves only one other person and is indifferent to the rest of his fellow men, his love is not love but symbiotic attachment, or an enlarged egotism." Beyond one's continuing close personal attachments there needs to be a valuing of all human beings and an eagerness to form new bonds with others.

There are also, of course, somewhat unique components in the love we feel for a parent, a child, a friend, and a mate. Fromm (1956) delineates five somewhat different love relationships, as described below.

1. *Brotherly love.* Perhaps the most basic kind of love is that for all of one's fellow men. Fromm (p. 47) describes it as "the sense of responsibility, care, respect, knowledge of any other human being, the wish to further his life." Unlike the love of man and woman or mother and child, brotherly love is in no way exclusive. It is the orientation to all human relationships which finds expression in the Biblical injunction to "love thy neighbor as thyself."

2. *Motherly (parental) love.* Here Fromm emphasizes the parent's unconditional affirmation of his child's life and needs. Parental love involves care and responsibility for the child's well-being and growth, together with a willing acceptance of the fact that his life is his own. The parent assumes responsibility for a life entrusted to his care and finds his happiness in seeing that life fulfilled. True motherly love is nonpossessive.

3. *Erotic love.* Fromm (pp. 52-53) describes erotic love as "the craving for a complete fusion, for union with one other person. It is by its very nature exclusive and not universal . . . ." Typically, of course, erotic love finds its culmination in the framework of marriage.

It is in erotic love that we typically see the greatest investment of self in the happiness and well-being of the other person. Paradoxically, it seems to be in the climate of such complete fusion that the individual feels the most complete freedom to be himself and to express his own deepest aspirations. This is brought out by Maslow (1954, pp. 239-240) in his study of self-actualizing people:

"One of the deepest satisfactions coming from the healthy love relationship reported by my subjects is that such a relationship permits the greatest spontaneity, the greatest naturalness, the greatest dropping of defenses and protection against threat. In such a relationship it is not necessary to be guarded, to conceal, to try to impress, to feel tense, to watch one's words or actions, to suppress or repress. My people report that they can be themselves without feeling that there are demands or expectations upon them; they can feel psychologically (as well as physically) naked and still feel loved and wanted and secure."

Thus even erotic love, if healthy, nurtures the individuality and integrity of both lovers. Not all erotic attachments achieve this, of course. Often in such relationships *infatuation* is mistaken for love. Dr. Henry A. Bowman suggests these points of distinction between the two (Adams, 1951):

"Infatuation may come suddenly but love takes time.

"Infatuation can be based on one or two traits (usually plus sex appeal) whereas love is based on many traits.

"In infatuation the person is in 'love' with love, whereas in love, the person is in love with another person.

"In infatuation the other person is thought of as a separate entity and employed for self-gratification. In real love there is a feeling of identity with the other person.

"Infatuation produces feelings of insecurity and wishful thinking whereas love produces a sense of security.

"In infatuation you may suffer loss of ambition and appetite, or be in a daze, whereas in love you work and plan to please the other person.

"The physical element is much more pronounced in infatuation than in love.

"Infatuation may change quickly but love lasts."

Although infatuation may not last, it is a powerful force while it holds sway. It provides rose-colored spectacles for its victims, and when the urgency surrounding it leads to a hasty marriage, the individual may find himself married to someone he scarcely knows, whose weak points come to him as quite a shock.

Many other irrational elements may also make it difficult for a person to tell if he is really in love. For example, even a relatively mature individual may convince himself that he wants to get married because he is in love when actually he wants to have someone take care of him, to insure his sexual satisfactions, or to protect himself from loneliness. Often, too, the individual is indoctrinated with the romantic notion that there is only one person in the world who is right for him; and in his eagerness to believe he has found that person, it is easy for him to convince himself that he is in love.

Genuine erotic love grows out of shared experiences of many kinds. The climate of a happy marriage is not necessarily one of complete harmony at all times; but it is one in which the bonds of love are deepened, by shared problems as well as happiness, and one in which both partners can continue to grow as individuals. The latter point is particularly important, for a love which feeds on dependency is apt to destroy itself. Erotic love, like brotherly and parental love, nurtures the growth of the loved one as an individual.

4. *Self-love.* There is a widespread belief that while loving others is a virtue, loving oneself is a vice. Self-love, according to this theory,

not only reveals a shameful lack of humility but also prevents love for others. Actually, since love implies care, respect, responsibility for and knowledge of its object, it should be clear that self-love is a necessity for emotional competence. As we have seen, we all have a need for self-acceptance and self-esteem, and there is ample clinical evidence that only if this need is met can we be free to love others. It is true that a selfish person cannot love others, but he has no love for himself either. Selfishness and self-love, far from being identical, are mutually contradictory. The individual who is able to love productively loves both himself and others. Self-deprecation and self-rejection interfere with healthy social relationships and play a prominent role in maladjustment and mental disorder.

5. *Love of God*. In discussing religious love, Fromm (p. 83) emphasizes again man's "need to overcome separateness and to achieve union"—in this case, union with God. Allport (1955, p. 96) describes the mature religious sentiment in a similar fashion, rejecting the theory that religion is merely a defense against fear:

"While religion certainly fortifies the individual against the inroads of anxiety, doubt, and despair, it also provides the forward intention that enables him at each stage of his [development] to relate himself meaningfully to the totality of Being."

People of all times have tried to fathom the governing principle in the universe and relate themselves to it. Sometimes this principle has been conceived as a personal deity, sometimes as abstract truth and justice, sometimes in other terms. But men of every age have been eager to give devotion to the highest reality they can conceive and to align their efforts with cosmic purposes.

The ability to love. The ability to love is not a gift apart. Like other emotional com-
petencies it depends upon such factors as our self-understanding, our general level of maturity, and our freedom from the need for self-defense.

The ability to give and receive any kind of love begins in a healthy infant-mother relationship and then expands as we build satisfying relationships with other family members, friends, and eventually a mate and children of our own. But as we have seen, it can be impaired by early rejection, by generalized attitudes of suspicion and distrust, by emotional immaturity and egocentricity, or by a continuing predominance of negative feelings. Thus an individual with a high level of hostility and a strongly negative approach to life is unlikely to develop deep love for anyone. In fact, when such individuals marry, it is often with the notion of two people standing together against a hostile world—indicating a defensive and self-centered orientation that is not conducive to a genuine love.

Usually a minimally favorable emotional climate in childhood is necessary if the individual is to be able to give and receive love in later years. Yet long-held patterns of self-doubt, fear, and cynicism can be dissipated by a growth in self-understanding and the experience, finally, of being accepted by others. In the following section we shall examine some of the ways in which emotional handicaps can gradually be overcome.

Emotional "Weak Spots"

The achievement of emotional competence is complicated for most of us by the presence of emotional "weak spots" or "scars." Painful and frightening experiences—particularly those in childhood—are apt to create psychic wounds which never completely heal. As a result, we are left with a particular vulnerability to certain kinds of stress. Learning to recognize and deal with such weak spots is a necessary emotional competency.

Sources of trauma. Emotional weak spots are most commonly caused by terrifying events, severe deprivations and frustrations, and faulty parent-child relationships. The extent to which any event or situation creates trauma depends, of course, upon the emotional and intellectual resources of the individual. In general, children are more vulnerable to trauma than adults because they lack the experience and maturity that are necessary to cope with many difficult situations and put them in proper perspective. Childhood experiences that often leave emotional scars are family deaths and separations, severe illnesses, and accidents. Often without warning, the child is exposed to a dangerous and seemingly hostile world with which he feels inadequate to cope. Such experiences are not altogether different from those of soldiers thrust without adequate preparation into terrifying combat situations.

Few of us escape at least minor traumas. It is terribly devaluating to a boy, for example, to be beaten up in the schoolyard by the local bully and then taunted for running away. Similarly, when we make a social blunder, forget an important speech, or drop an easy fly ball that brings in the winning run for the other team, we suddenly feel terribly inadequate. Even when we forget such events with the passage of time, the emotional reaction they engendered remains a part of us and is apt to be reactivated in similar situations. Emotional scars are commonly caused, too, by guilt-arousing sexual experiences in childhood, such as participating in forbidden sexual acts or being sexually assaulted by an older person. Often the child is ashamed and afraid to talk about such experiences and may later "refuse" to remember them. But many times they complicate his sexual adjustment as an adult.

Aside from specific traumatic events, the general circumstances of our upbringing may leave emotional scars which time only partial-ly heals. A person who has grown up in a poverty-stricken family may find it difficult as an adult to achieve a real feeling of security, despite the degree of financial and social success he enjoys. His need for tangible indications of security is insatiable. The deprivation of love during childhood can have even more devastating effects, as we have seen. Many of our emotional difficulties have their roots in faulty patterns of relationship with our parents—rejection or overprotection, perfectionism or overindulgence. The lasting effects of such relationships depends, of course, on many individual factors.

In recognizing the sources of emotional weak spots, the idea is not to affix blame—on our parents or elsewhere—or to admit defeat. Rather, by understanding the reasons behind the way we react, we can hope to improve our emotional competence.

Some general effects of psychic wounds. Although the human system tends to restore its equilibrium after distortion or stress, many psychological wounds—like many physical ones—leave a certain amount of residual damage. Thus we find that people usually "snap back" after being thrown badly off balance for a time by the death of a loved one, financial reverse, or social disgrace; but seldom do such experiences leave them totally unscarred.

One common residual effect of a psychic wound is *reaction sensitivity*—the tendency to be acutely sensitive to those elements in a total situation which bear some possible relationship to an earlier painful experience. Thus a person whose home has once burned down may thereafter tend to perceive any unidentified odor as the smell of smoke. An individual who grew up in the midst of marital tension and unhappiness may hesitate to marry because he is more sensitive to the potential risks of marriage than its potential satisfactions. The person who has been rejected by his parents may see indications of rejection or loss of love in even the best-intentioned behavior of his spouse. The reactivation of such feelings takes place automatically, as a result of emotional conditioning, and therefore is not easily subject to voluntary control.

Unfortunately, early traumatic experiences sometimes create major blocks to growth. Because we fear repetition of the experience, we tend to avoid situations in which painful feelings might be reactivated. This makes it all but impossible to develop the competencies and attitudes we need as effective adults. Again we find that conditions are ripe for the development of a vicious circle. The pattern has been clearly described by Maslow (1954, pp. 43-44):

"In a fairly insecure person every external influence, every stimulus impinging on the organism is somewhat more apt to be interpreted insecurely rather than securely. For example, a grin is apt to be seen as a sneer, forgetfulness is apt to be interpreted as insult, indifference is apt to be seen as dislike, and mild affection as indifference. In such persons' worlds then, there are more insecure influences than there are secure ones. We might say that the weight of evidence for him is on the side of insecurity. And so he is pulled steadily, even though slightly in the direction of more and more extreme insecurity. This factor is of course reinforced by the fact that an insecure person tends to behave insecurely, which encourages people to dislike and reject him, which makes him more insecure, which makes him behave still more insecurely—and so on in a vicious circle. Thus he tends, because of his inner dynamics, to bring about just what he fears most."

Methods of "working through" psychic wounds. Because early traumas can have such unfortunate effects on subsequent personality development and behavior, modern clinical psychology has emphasized the importance of "working through" painful experiences and removing the emotional blocks they create. Our discussion thus far has dealt with the problems of recognizing the sources of emotional weak spots and understanding how they can affect behavior. This knowledge is a necessary prerequisite for working through traumatic experiences and minimizing their long-term effects. Now we are ready to examine some specific procedures that facilitate the "healing" of emotional wounds: catharsis, insight, and re-education.

1. *Catharsis.* The term *catharsis* refers to the discharge of emotional tensions, either by talking them out or by "reliving" the painful experience which engendered them. In common parlance it means getting things off your chest. Catharsis is particularly helpful in overcoming the embarrassment or shame associated with social failure, and it is invaluable as a means of reducing the tensions associated with anxiety, fear, hostility, and guilt. By verbalizing a trauma, we also get the experience out into the open where we can look at it more objectively and thus begin integrating it into our ego-structure.

Catharsis may take any of various forms. The Eskimos have long used the device of role playing, in which they act out their failures and embarrassing experiences within a group so that everyone can laugh about them together. We have previously noted the use of catharsis in the treatment of mental disorders induced by combat situations; under the influence of a drug such as sodium pentothal the patient almost literally relives his battle experience and thus is able to discharge much of the emotional tension he has built up. Typically, we achieve catharsis by talking out our feelings.

It is often difficult to begin working through a problem by catharsis, because it brings to consciousness many of the painful feelings we have been trying to hide. Very often it is not until a great deal of tension has been built up that our feelings burst out in a flood of expression. To voluntarily undertake and carry through with catharsis, we must be convinced that this often painful process is worth while.

There is a danger in catharsis if one "spills out" to the wrong person—one who might reinforce the fear and anxiety, the guilt and resentment the individual is trying to rid himself of. In severe cases, a professional therapist may best be able to help the individual accept his feelings and integrate a traumatic experience into his ego-structure. In less severe cases, a minister or a doctor or an emotionally mature and discreet friend is able to provide the listening ear and the comments which lead the way to insight.

2. *Insight.* Catharsis often enables us to gain insight into the ways an emotional trauma has been affecting our behavior. When much of the emotion associated with a past experience has been discharged, we are able to see the experience more objectively and may discover that we have been overreacting to it. We may find that we have devalued ourselves unnecessarily, or our aspirations were unrealistic, or that our childish interpretation of an event was inaccurate. We begin to see *why* we feel the way we do—why a small amount of criticism, even if it is constructive, hurts our feelings and makes us feel inferior; why we would rather keep a piece of defective merchandise than face a sales clerk and ask him to take it back; why we are afraid to argue with people even though we are churning with anger over something they have said; why we feel so self-conscious with members of the opposite sex.

Usually these insights come to us only as we are able to tolerate them. We seem able to protect ourselves against perceiving our weaknesses until such time as we can accept these perceptions without feeling unduly threatened by them.

3. *Re-education.* It is a mistake to assume that the battle is wholly won when a person has achieved insight into his emotional behav-

ior. Understanding a faulty emotional reaction does not automatically improve it. Emotional re-education is a long and laborious process.

To overcome faulty emotional reactions, the individual needs to put himself into situations where he can experience positive feelings. He can overcome a fear of social gatherings, for example, by participating in such gatherings and having the experience of being accepted. He can learn to reveal his feelings without the fear of disapproval as he discovers that a greater openness of expression makes his interpersonal relationships more rewarding rather than more threatening.

This process of re-education becomes possible as the individual achieves enough insight into the reasons for his negative reactions to realize that they *can* be changed. To put oneself deliberately into a situation that has previously been painful, one must be convinced that the risk of being hurt again is less than the likelihood of achieving new satisfactions. The first step takes courage and determination, but each experience of success tends to make subsequent steps much easier. Fortunately, positive emotions tend to perpetuate themselves just as negative ones do, and the first increase in self-confidence provides the basis for a new and more healthy pattern of reaction. Learning how to break old emotional patterns and help establish new ones is an essential component of emotional competence.

We have seen in this chapter how an individual's constitutional make-up, his early training, the social climate in whch he lives, and particularly his frame of reference all help to determine the pattern of emotional responses that he develops. Depending on these factors, his emotions may be deep or shallow, specific or general, and preponderantly positive or preponderantly negative. Similarly, his emotional expression may be balanced or uncontrolled, constructively channeled or suppressed, healthful or damaging. For every individual, this emotional dimension of personal experience is an important, characteristic part of his life style.

But although each of us develops a consistent and continuing "nuclear emotional constellation," we need not remain the same today, tomorrow, and forever. If we find that our emotional patterns are immature and disruptive, we can take steps to improve them— not by fighting our emotions but by under-standing and accepting them, learning to express them constructively, and accentuating those that are positive rather than negative. Taking these steps in adulthood is not an easy matter, for by then there have been years of practice in the faulty patterns that have produced unhappy experiences, negative emotions, and unconscious defenses; but working through these emotional obstacles and handicaps can lay the groundwork for building true emotional competence.

REFERENCES

The following list includes both the references cited in this chapter and a selected number of additional books and articles for outside reading.

Abrahamsen, David. 1958. *The Road to Emotional Maturity*. Englewood Cliffs, N. J.: Prentice-Hall, Inc.

Adams, Clifford R. 1951. *Preparing for Marriage: A Guide to Marital and Sexual Adjustment*. New York: E. P. Dutton & Co., Inc.

Allport, Gordon W. 1955. *Becoming: Basic Considerations for a Psychology of Personality*. New Haven, Conn.: Yale University Press.

Banham, Katharine M. 1951. "Senescence and the Emotions: A Genetic Theory." *The Journal of Genetic Psychology*, 78, 175-183.

Blanton, Smiley. 1956. *Love or Perish*. New York: Simon and Schuster, Inc.

Cannon, W. B. 1931. "Again the James-Lange and Thalamic Theories of Emotion." *Psychological Review*, 38, 281-295.

Dreikurs, Rudolf. 1946. *Challenge of Marriage*. New York: Duell, Sloan & Pearce, Inc.

Dumas, G. 1932. *Nouveau Traite de Psychologic*. Paris: Felix Alcan.

English, Oliver S., and Gerald H. J. Pearson. 1955. *Emotional Problems of Living: Avoiding the Neurotic Pattern*. Rev. ed. New York: W. W. Norton & Company, Inc.

Fromm, Erich. 1956. *The Art of Loving*. New York: Harper & Brothers.

Grinker, Roy R., and John P. Spiegel. 1945. *War Neuroses*. Philadelphia: The Blakiston Company.

Inglis, Brian. 1959. *Emotional Stress and Your Health*. New York: Criterion Books, Inc.

Maslow, A. H. 1950. "Self-Actualizing People: A Study of Psychological Health." *Symposium #1 1950 Values in Personality Research*. Werner Wolff, ed. New York: Grune & Stratton, Inc.

Maslow, A. H. 1954. *Motivation and Personality*. New York: Harper & Brothers.

May, Rollo. 1953. *Man's Search for Himself*. New York: W. W. Norton & Company, Inc.

Menninger, Karl A. 1945. *The Human Mind.* 3rd rev. ed. New York: Alfred A. Knopf, Inc. Illustration adapted by permission of the publisher, Alfred A. Knopf, Inc. Copyright 1930, 1937, 1945 by Karl A. Menninger.

Midwest Conference on Character Development. 1930. *The Child's Emotions.* Chicago: The University of Chicago Press.

Overstreet, Harry and Bonaro. 1956. *The Mind Goes Forth.* New York: W. W. Norton & Company, Inc.

Prescott, Daniel A. 1934. *Emotion and the Educative Process.* Washington, D.C.: Committee on the Relation of Emotion to the Educative Process, American Council on Education.

Prescott, Daniel A. 1957. *The Child in the Educative Process.* New York: McGraw-Hill Book Company, Inc. By permission from *The Child in the Educative Process*, by D. A. Prescott. Copyright 1957 by McGraw-Hill Book Company, Inc., New York.

Rogers, William F. 1950. "Needs of the Bereaved." *Pastoral Psychology, 1,* No. 5, 17-21.

Saul, Leon J. 1947. *Emotional Maturity: The Development and Dynamics of Personality.* Philadelphia: J. B. Lippincott Company.

Sorokin, Pitirim A. 1959. "The Powers of Creative Unselfish Love." *New Knowledge in Human Values.* A. H. Maslow, ed. New York: Harper & Brothers.

Stevens, S. S., ed. 1951. *Handbook of Experimental Psychology.* New York: John Wiley & Sons, Inc.

Wenger, M. A., and others. 1956. *Physiological Psychology.* New York: Henry Holt and Company.

SOCIAL

COMPETENCE

Foundations of Good Interpersonal Relationships

Improving Our Social Competence

Man is a social creature, and his success in dealing with others will greatly influence the course of his life and the satisfactions he derives from it. Success in attracting a desired mate, in establishing a happy marriage, in raising children, in achieving occupational advancement, and in making friends depends heavily upon the individual's skill in dealing with other people. The electronics engineer who antagonizes his subordinates because he has never learned to offer criticism in a courteous and constructive way is handicapped professionally even though he may know a great deal about the intricacies of electronics. Many people become "unpopular," fail in their work, ruin their marriages, raise maladjusted children, and go through life feeling alone and friendless because they are unable to establish satisfying relationships with others. Man is dependent upon his fellow human beings for the satisfaction of his most basic psychological needs as well as for his physical survival. Our richest experiences are *shared* experiences.

The importance of learning to get along with others applies, of course, not only to individuals but to groups and even nations. The political, social, economic, and technological complexities of the modern world have put a premium on the ability of very disparate peoples to understand and work with each other. Although in this chapter we shall confine our discussion to interpersonal relations, much of what we shall say applies to intergroup relations as well.

FOUNDATIONS OF GOOD INTERPERSONAL RELATIONSHIPS

In spite of the importance of good human relations, most of the available literature on this subject has been in the form of popular books and articles which typically list what the authors consider to be simple steps to popularity and success. Actually, of course, there are no "simple" techniques which can be applied effectively without a broad appreciation of the principles and attitudes underlying real social competence. For example, the technique of praising the other person, often emphasized in popular writings, may backfire if the praise is insincere or used primarily to make the other person more amenable to our own wishes. In this sense, popular approaches are often misleading, and many people who adopt them in order to win affection and good will are shocked to discover that, instead, they are reaping a harvest of dislike and hostility.

The present chapter will discuss some of the general principles of good interpersonal relationships and then, in the context of this broader understanding, outline some specific ways for improving social competence. Although it is useful and often necessary to talk about various "social skills," it is important to remember that good human relations depend in the long run upon *attitudes* rather than techniques.

A Recognition of Mutual Rights, Needs, and Responsibilities

Psychologists have looked with disfavor upon most popular writings about social skills not only because they tend to greatly oversimplify the problem of good interpersonal relations but also because they typically have a "sales" approach. The emphasis in such works is on influencing and sometimes even exploiting others without adequate regard for their own needs and purposes.

Perhaps the first step in developing good relations with others is to remember that all relationships are *inter*relationships—that they involve mutual responsibility. As other people set the atmosphere of our daily life, so we help to set the atmosphere of theirs. Their approval or disapproval affects us; our approval or disapproval in turn affects them. Many of us are extremely sensitive to wounds which other people have inflicted upon us. We talk about our parents having been too critical, of having made us feel inadequate, or of having been overly indulgent and leading us to expect more than the world is prepared to give us; but we less frequently conceive of ourselves as having influenced our parents. It is a rare person who, even when he is grown up, can look back and see how he contributed to making his mother into a nag. It is an unusual student who thinks of himself as being a source of satisfaction or disappointment to his teacher, an exceptional employee who can see how he might be a contributing factor to his employer's short temper. But each of us does play a part in the lives of those people who come in contact with us.

Our relationship with others is a reciprocal affair, and we have much to do not only with the satisfactions or displeasures we derive from it but also with the satisfactions or displeasures it provides other people. The recognition that our attitudes and actions have a profound effect on others is thus one key to establishing satisfying relations with them—both parties must contribute if the relationship is to prove mutually satisfying. This is particularly true of intimate relationships, such as those with parents, mates, and friends. It is necessary to concentrate on what we contribute as well as what we receive.

Very often, faulty interpersonal relationships result from a marked discrepancy in the amounts of effort or emotional investment contributed by the parties involved. In a marriage, for example, the structuring may be such that one person is relatively indifferent while the other puts in 90 percent of the effort necessary to keep the marriage going. Similarly, a friendship may become arranged in such a way that one person must always take the initiative in maintaining it. Where such discrepancies exist, the individual putting in most of the effort is likely to feel somewhat hostile and devaluated, though he may not show it on the surface. It is questionable whether good interpersonal relationships can actually be established and maintained on an intimate basis without the parties involved contributing roughly equal amounts of effort and emotional investment.

The realization that our behavior may have a profound effect on others is a first step, but we must then decide how we wish to affect others—what kind of relationship we wish to establish. In general, it would seem that truly satisfying interpersonal relationships can be established only within the context of a democratic approach—an approach which recognizes the right of other persons to individuality. They must be granted "life space." This does not mean that we must accept another person's beliefs or values but rather that we acknowledge his right to his own convictions while maintaining the same right for ourselves. In short, a democratic approach involves mutual respect and feeling for the dignity and rights of the other person. *Mutual* respect, whether in work or play or marriage, tends to *mutual* satisfaction. This democratic approach brings depth, meaningfulness, and freedom to interpersonal relationships, qualities which are unlikely to be realized in an authoritarian approach or through adoption of the exploitive concepts so often emphasized in the popular literature on "dealing" with others.

Closely allied to our respect for the other individual's need to be accepted as a person in his own right is our ability to think in terms of his needs and purposes. In interpersonal relationships each individual has certain needs

MISUNDERSTANDING THE NEEDS
AND GOALS OF OTHERS

Many intergroup and interpersonal problems stem from the failure of one party to understand the frame of reference of the other. Such lack of understanding was demonstrated clearly in a study comparing the opinions of labor and management about the job factors most important to workers. From a list of seventy-one items, employees at several companies were asked to choose the five job factors that were most important to them personally. Fifty executives from the companies and forty-two union officers were asked to rank the same items in the order they thought the workers would give them. Results for the ten items most frequently mentioned by the employees are shown in the table below. (A rank of 40+ means that the item was not ranked among the first forty items.)

Job factors	Em-ployees	Exec-utives	Union Officers
Job security—employment stabilization	1	2	2
Opportunities [in the company] for advancement	2	4	18
Compensation—base pay	3	1	1
Employee financial benefits (pensions, etc.)	4	8	19
Practice of informing you of your job status (successes and failures)	5	40+	40+
Type of work	6	7	39
Vacation and holiday practices	7	3	8
Profit-sharing plans	8	13	40+
Physical working conditions (on the job)	9	5	4
Company's attitude toward employees (liberal or conservative interpretation of policies)	10	6	6

In general, both employers and union officials overemphasized the importance of economic factors in determining worker satisfaction and morale. The workers' desire to be kept informed of their job status—fifth in their rankings—was not even included in the first forty items listed by either the executives or the union leaders. Surprisingly, company executives were considerably more accurate than union officers in judging the importance of some of the factors—for example, advancement opportunities and type of work (National Industrial Conference Board, 1947).

which he attempts to meet—whether these be for affection, social approval, feelings of self-worth, increased adequacy in attaining certain goals, or simply feeling related to others. Where the relationship tends to meet one person's needs but frustrates or fails to meet the needs of the other person, it becomes difficult to maintain. Thus even the most generous and devoted friend may become tired of a relationship in which he is continually forced to lend money to his friend and is never repaid.

For a relationship to meet the needs of both parties, there needs to be a commonality of purpose. The importance of such shared purposes in establishing mutually satisfying relationships and the harmful effect of a lack of such commonality can be illustrated in many ways. In time of war, common purposes unite nations in alliances, but after the war is over, differences in purposes tend to emerge, and conflicts result. In our highly competitive society, the matter of conflicting purposes is readily apparent in business transactions which are profitable to one party but not to the other and in political activities, advertising, and sports. Labor-management disputes often arise over the seemingly incompatible needs and purposes of the two groups. Too, there are many personal and family problems which center around conflicting purposes: parents may want their sons and daughters to remain under their domination even after they reach young adulthood; a girl may want to get married while her boy friend doesn't; a married couple may find themselves "incompatible" due to the failure of each partner to meet the needs of the other. Similarly, friendships do not usually long endure unless there is a commonality of purpose, as well as mutual confidence, respect, and shared experiences.

Cantril (1950, pp. 112-113) emphasizes the importance of common purposes when he points out that loyalties develop only when we feel that certain of our needs will be satisfied by continuing a particular relationship:

"Loyalties are mutual in so far as our activity in carrying out our purposes helps other people carry out their purposes. We have no loyalty to a person, a group, a symbol, or an inanimate object that does not in some way help us to act effectively. Hence in peacetime people in many democratic countries have less feeling of loyalty to their 'country' than they do during war times, since in times of peace there are not so many clear-cut common purposes to be furthered by action.

"Friendship involves a high degree of mutual aid in carrying out the purposes of each party. Gibran wrote, 'Your friend is your needs answered.' If friendship is to prove enduring, it must provide for mutual development, mutual and independent experiences of . . . value. Friendships of our early childhood, our school days, our army life, or those we make during a vacation or a long steamer voyage so often prove transient because the purposes that brought us together at the time have dissolved with the changing situation. We no longer need each other."

All men have certain needs in common, as well as their own individual needs. It is in satisfying the needs-in-common that we become "socially competent," and it is in satisfying the particular needs of certain individuals that we form the lasting relationships that provide one of life's major satisfactions. The recognition of every man's dependence upon his fellow human beings finds expression in the age-old guide to good human relations: Do unto others as you would have them do unto you.

The honesty, consistency, and concern implied by the golden rule are necessary not only from a moral standpoint but from a practical one. Lying, deceit, failure to keep confidences, and other evidences of a lack of integrity in our dealings with others are fatal to good interpersonal relationships. The businessman who cheats his partner—like the husband who is unfaithful to his wife—creates conditions which make a good relationship impossible. Dishonesty destroys any common ground for mutually satisfactory give-and-take.

The golden rule implies more, however, than simply refraining from doing harm to others. Perhaps the Biblical phrasing, "love thy neighbor as thyself," gives better expression to the concept, suggesting the need for an attitude of positive care and concern toward our fellow men. Mere adherence to the "rules" and a pseudointerest in other people rarely hide an essential indifference toward their welfare, much less envy or resentment when their good fortune seems greater than our own. It can be very irritating, of course, when someone else gets a good grade or a promotion or a pay raise that we think we deserve as well; and too often in such cases, we give ourselves a great deal of credit for merely hiding our resentment. But it is only as we develop the capacity to find satisfaction in the good fortune of others, while continuing to strive for our own purposes, that we can develop genuinely satisfying relationships with other people. As suggested in the last chapter, brotherly love is essentially an orientation to life rather than a rule for getting along. It comes from the feeling of closeness with all men.

By recognizing that each of us has needs and purposes that must be met, we can foster relationships that will satisfy them—not only for ourselves but for the others in the relationships. And with the security and satisfaction that accrues from having his needs met, each individual will become better able to contribute to the meeting of the other person's needs.

An Understanding of Self and Others

Our view of ourselves and others has a great deal to do with the type of relations we are able to establish. Often we have a false view of our own "stimulus value." We may see ourselves as generous, while others view our alleged generosity as an attempt to be a "big shot" or as a means of getting others indebted to us; we may view ourselves as brilliant and witty conversationalists, while others think we talk too much about trivial things; we may view ourselves as highly endowed in leadership qualities, while others view us as bossy and domineering. We may tend to be hostile, overly competitive, pompous, demanding, self-centered, or over dependent on others without realizing it. Because we are often unaware of our negative stimulus value to others, we may be quite bewildered by their apparent ingratitude, by their obvious lack of appreciation of our merits and abilities, and by the continual friction we experience in our dealings with them. We do not easily recognize that the way others react to us is usually the result of the way we have acted toward them.

It is useful to examine our behavior to see if there are immature, irrational, or defensive components which damage our relationships with others. The more common traits of this sort are egocentricity, deceit, overdependency, a strong tendency to rebel against any authority, a prevailing attitude of hostility toward others, rigidity, and defensive strategies such as showing off or bragging. These and other sources of difficulty are elaborated in the chart on page 357. It can be noted here, however, that such traits may vary in generality—that is, a person may show them in marked degree only in given situations with given individuals —and hence their effect on an individual's interpersonal relationships may be more detrimental in dealing with some people than with others.

Similarly, our view of others is of crucial importance in our relations with them. If we tend to view people as generally egocentric, selfish, and prone to dishonesty, we shall establish a different type of relationship with them than if we view them as generally honest, kind, and prone to do the right thing as they see it. Most of us, of course, tend to make discriminations and to avoid lumping everyone

PERSONALITY CHARACTERISTICS
AND INTERGROUP ATTITUDES

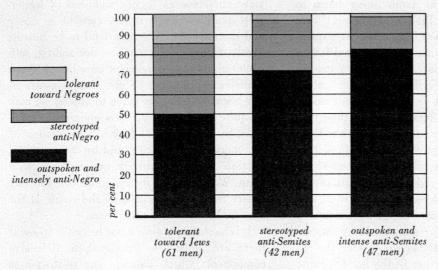

tolerant toward Negroes

stereotyped anti-Negro

outspoken and intensely anti-Negro

per cent

| tolerant toward Jews (61 men) | stereotyped anti-Semites (42 men) | outspoken and intense anti-Semites (47 men) |

Various studies suggest that prejudice is often associated with personality traits that make the individual distrustful of or antagonistic toward *any* outside group. The graph above, for example, shows the results of a study comparing the attitudes of one hundred and fifty veterans in Chicago, Illinois, toward Negroes and Jews (Bettelheim and Janowitz, 1950). In the majority of cases, tolerance toward one group was correlated with tolerance toward the other, and vice versa.

In another study (Hartley, 1946) college students were asked to judge thirty-five nations and races on the Bogardus Social Distance Scale, which includes the following possible ratings: (1) Would *exclude* from my country, (2) As *visitors only* to my country, (3) To *citizenship* in my country, (4) To employment in my *occupation* in my country, (5) To my school as *classmates*, (6) To my street as *neighbors*, (7) To my club as *chums*, (8) To close *kinship* by marriage. Among the groups to be rated were listed three fictitious ethnic groups—the Daniereans, Pireaneans, and Wallonians—which the subjects accepted as real. Interestingly enough, students who discriminated against the groups with which they were familiar showed a similarly prejudiced attitude toward the nonexistent groups. Other students, by contrast, were consistently free of discrimination toward any group; still others took a consistently intermediate position.

A generalized attitude of prejudice toward outsiders seems to be associated with a personality pattern best characterized as "authoritarian." An extensive study in Berkeley (Adorno and others, 1950) found that individuals who rated high in prejudice typically came from homes in which discipline was harsh, parents were both idealized and feared, family status was a matter of concern, and people in general were inclined to be regarded with a moralistic and suspicious attitude.

into a particular category, but some individuals are generally suspicious of others and wary of getting too close to them, as a result of early training and experiences which led them to distrust other people. On the other hand, some of us make the opposite error in our assessment of other people. That is, we overestimate their desirable qualities such as good judgment, honesty, and concern for others. More often than not we are ultimately disillusioned by the discovery that these people are less perfect than we had thought, and our relationships with them deteriorate. Even when this fails to happen, such people are likely to sense that we expect more of them than they are able to give, and thus they are apt to feel somewhat hostile toward us. It is important not to continually expect too much of others, for this hurts both them and ourselves.

Often we tend to be overly impressed by certain individuals because of their money, family, position, or other characteristics. They are "big shots" in our world, and we are eager to establish friendships with them without fully realizing that a lack of common interests and differing personality traits can make a satisfying relationship impossible.

Another common source of difficulty in gaining a realistic view of others is that many of our relationships are competitive. We are continually in competition—for jobs, social status, material possessions, and even in most of our recreational pursuits. As a result, we often tend to evaluate people in terms of their intellectual abilities, their job performances, or their recreational skills rather than in terms of their total personalities. Thus we may classify people as good bridge players but know little else about them, even though we have spent many hours around the bridge table together.

In this context, it may be noted that a characteristic shared by many people is a strong "I" or "me" orientation—they are primarily interested in themselves and in what a given situation or individual has to offer them. A primary concern for oneself and one's purposes is normal and natural, providing it is tempered by respect and concern for the other person as well. But when self-interest reaches a point of egocentricity, it is likely to prove a serious handicap in getting along with others. Again we come back to the basic principle of commonality of purpose as a fundamental of good interpersonal relationships.

In close relationships especially, it is important that we try to understand the motives, expectations, problems, values, and general personality make-up of the other person involved. What does he hope to gain from the relationship, and what satisfactions is he actually receiving? It is important, too, that we be aware of our *own* real motives. In a marriage, we may expect—without realizing it—to gain satisfaction from dominating the other person and playing "the head of the house"; or we may hope to bolster our feelings of adequacy by leaning upon our spouse and pouring out our problems. Obviously, such motives offer little possibility for building a sound marital relationship. But once we face them honestly, it is often possible to work out new ways for satisfying our own needs and at the same time meeting those of the other person.

Adequate Structuring

As the term suggests, "structuring" an interpersonal relationship means giving it shape or form—defining it in terms of limits, responsibilities, and roles. For a relationship to be successful, each person must know what is expected of him and, in turn, let others know what he expects of them. Such expectations, of course, must be mutually comfortable and satisfactory.

In many cases, structuring is inherent in a situation—for example, there is general agreement in our culture about the type of relationship that is appropriate between teacher and student, employer and employee, lieutenant and private, bishop and parish priest. But in most of our more personal relationships—such as those involving husband and wife, parent and child, or friend and friend—the structuring must be determined by the parties involved. Realizing this fact is important for building good interpersonal relationships, since all relationships *do* become structured with time, whether or not the individuals take any active measures to insure their development in a particular direction.

To take a simple example, we may examine the behavior of a young couple who are dating. Unless they take active measures to structure the situation in terms of permissible limits of affection, of behavior with others, of mutual effort in maintaining their relationship, of courtesy and honesty in dealing with each other, such limits will eventually become established simply by what actually takes place —whether or not these limits are satisfactory for the individuals involved. Once certain patterns have been established, it becomes increasingly difficult to change the structuring. For example, the girl who has permitted sexual intimacies will find it much more difficult to limit such behavior thereafter than if she had structured the affectional limits differently in the first place.

Unfortunately, structuring is sometimes predetermined by the existence of certain emotional limitations. A person may habitually establish competitive relationships, no matter how inappropriate they may be in some situations, as in marriage. Or he may always be cooperative, so that he is unable to say "no" even when it needs saying. When a person can see in retrospect that he has tried to carry over a type of relationship from a situation in which it is appropriate to another in which it is inappropriate, he can begin to avoid making the same mistake by evaluating new situations in advance, thereby maintaining some control over the structuring.

Many of us are rather naïve in the matter of structuring interpersonal relationships which are appropriate to the situation and person. Often we unwittingly encourage others to be overly familiar or to take advantage of us— and then blame *them* for an unsatisfactory relationship that has been largely of our own making. It is always important to examine in advance the type of relationship that is desirable—whether between employer and employee, executive and secretary, husband and wife, father and daughter, or friend and friend —and to take active measures to establish and maintain the relationship in the form we consider appropriate.

Effective Communication

When lines of communication are open between individuals, each is likely to understand the attitudes, point of view, and feelings of the other person. When lines of communications are closed or when communications are misunderstood, there is apt to be conflict. Even in old friendships or established marriages, misunderstandings stemming from inadequate communication can cause serious trouble. One factor in a failing marriage is usually the inability of the partners to talk about their problems with any degree of objectivity or mutual understanding. Eventually such a communication breakdown may reach the point of almost total silence, signaling the failure of the relationship. Each has given up trying to "get through" to the other.

One common communication difficulty stems from our tendency to think of communication solely on cognitive and verbal levels —in terms of ideas and words. Actually, one crucial aspect of communication—and of good interpersonal relationships—is the understanding of *feeling*. The distinction between cognitive and affective elements in communication has been well summarized by Martineau (1957, pp. 133, 139-140) :

"Superficially we think that words are the only form of communication, because we live in such a highly verbal atmosphere. Yet in actuality there is a far greater amount of non-verbal communication going on all the time through the use of other symbols than words. . . . Besides expressing logical thought, our words and our actions are also indicative of the emotions, attitudes, moods, and intention of the speaker. Whenever we speak, we are offering two different kinds of clues. One is manifested by the thought content. The other is at the level where intuition operates, where the speaker conveys his feelings, his intentions, his motives."

There are many situations when we are called upon to answer feelings rather than spoken words, and when we fail to perceive these feelings, we may do and say things which hurt or anger the other person. Similarly, we often find it difficult to communicate our *own* feelings adequately. Many of us have learned during early childhood to conceal our fear, anger, and even our love; we tend to be embarrassed by emotion or even ashamed of it and to feel we must do or say that which is socially expedient or expected of us in a given situation. Often people do not know how to express their feelings even when they want very much to put them into words; a young suitor, for example, usually has a great deal of difficulty in conveying his feelings to his loved one when he proposes marriage. When the individual's feelings are ambivalent, it is usually even more difficult to express them clearly; the young bride who is both smiling and crying and the youth who both loves and hates his parents would probably have difficulty in explaining their feelings.

Child psychologists maintain that children are quite sensitive to the feelings of other people and that they can sense irritation, love, and fear even before they can understand any spoken words. Some adults seem to retain this childhood skill of sensing the feeling behind the words of others and show a great deal of intuition and understanding in dealing with people. Too many of us, however, put our emphasis on the literal meaning of words and tend to take verbal communications at face value. If someone replies to our question, "How are you today?" with "Fine, thank you," we may accept his answer without noting the lack of positive feeling behind it which indicates that he is actually feeling anything but fine. Or when we ask someone, "Do you mind if I . . ." and he politely says "Not at all . . . ," we may miss the note of irritation in his voice which means that he *does* mind a good deal.

Another common difficulty in communication stems from differences in background and experience. It would be difficult for a Pigmy from the jungles of equatorial Africa to communicate efficiently with a businessman from the United States, since their backgrounds of knowledge and experience are so different. In much the same way, it is often difficult for labor and management to understand each other's point of view, or for a lower-class husband to understand his middle-class wife; although they seem to be talking about the same problem, they often fail to "communicate." Here it may be helpful to note that communication involves a sender, a message, and a receiver. If the sender is unclear about what he is trying to communicate, if he codes his message in a misleading or unclear way, or if the receiver lacks the background to understand the message, the communication is not likely to succeed.[1] And, of course, the more divergent the frames of reference of the parties involved, the more likely the message is to be misunderstood. Conversely, commonality of assumptions, values, and motives tends to facilitate accurate communication.

Even at best, accurate communication is more difficult than it would appear. It often

[1] See Wilbur Schramm's article, "Communication Theory," on page 507.

seems that if a statement *can* be misunderstood, it *will* be misunderstood. Yet effective communication is essential for good interpersonal relationships; and the more intimate and sustained the relationship, the more important it becomes.

IMPROVING OUR SOCIAL COMPETENCE

Having examined some of the key factors determining the nature of interpersonal relationships, we are now ready to consider some specific ways of improving our social competence. As will become apparent, these are essentially applications of the general principles we have already discussed. It should be reemphasized that social skills are of little use and can ultimately be self-defeating unless they are grounded in attitudes of respect and concern for the people with whom we are dealing.

Helping Others Feel Approved and Adequate

As we have already noted many times, when a person feels threatened, he tends to become defensive, hostile, and less capable of perceiving situations accurately or evaluating them objectively. Many difficulties in our interpersonal relationships are the result of the fact that we somehow threaten the other person—that we endanger his feelings of adequacy and worth or seem to stand in the way of his accomplishing his purposes. In this connection Rogers (1959) has emphasized the individual's need for "positive regard" from others—his desire to experience approval and acceptance from them.

Often, of course, we are unaware of the mannerisms and traits that elicit defensive reactions from other people and cause friction and misunderstanding. We may be highly competitive in our relationships with them, striving to prove our own adequacy without realizing that we may at the same time be un-

dermining theirs. We may tend to judge and criticize rather than to understand and try to help. We may express our own views in a dogmatic way that seems to defy contradiction or even discussion. We may be too proud to admit our mistakes or to apologize to others when an apology is indicated. Or we may try to handle complicated situations when they are too "hot"—that is, when the other person is obviously upset emotionally and unable to look at things objectively.

When we understand another's need for reassurance, for affection, for feeling important, for being accepted, for being "right," we can usually help him satisfy these needs without in any way jeopardizing our own. Many of the difficulties in human relations stem from a false assumption, as Combs and Snygg suggest, that the only alternatives in dealing with other people are to sacrifice *our* interests to theirs or *theirs* to ours. A third and much better alternative, they suggest (1959, p. 322),

". . . is an approach to human interaction which says in effect: 'I am a person of dignity and integrity. I believe you are too. I have no need to attack you nor will I permit you to attack me.' This is a position which is neither attack nor appeasement. It is not concerned with winning or losing. . . .

"Appeasement interferes with the achievement of adequacy. It destroys the dignity of the appeaser. Attack violates the integrity of others and brings into being the negative effects of threat. The position we speak of maintains the dignity and integrity of the behaver without either violating the rights of others

COMMON SOURCES OF DIFFICULTY
IN INTERPERSONAL RELATIONSHIPS

Egocentricity

A concern with one's own interests to the extent of being insensitive to the welfare and rights of others. The egocentric individual is incapable of establishing anything but the most superficial relationships.

Deceitfulness

A tendency, often accompanying egocentricity, to take an exploitive approach to interpersonal relationships. Sometimes deceit extends to outright lying and stealing, but more commonly it shows itself in the efforts of an "operator" to manipulate people and situations to his own advantage.

Overconformity

An emphasis on getting along with others at the expense of personal integrity, often accompanied by a tendency to be overawed by the authority of those whose good opinion seems important—and, in turn, to be authoritarian and hostile toward those considered inferior.

Rebelliousness

A tendency to rebel against all authority and to become hostile and uncooperative at the slightest suggestion of being "bossed." Sometimes rebelliousness takes the form of flouting all of society's mores and manners in an ill-conceived attempt to assert one's independence.

Overdependency

A tendency to lean excessively upon others for either material aid or emotional support and to rely upon them for making one's decisions. The overdependent person contributes little or nothing to a relationship and usually loses his self-respect as well as the respect of the other person. Occasionally, underlying feelings of dependency are concealed by an exaggerated show of independence (e.g., refusing to become "indebted" to anyone) which is equally destructive of close relationships.

Hostility

A tendency, usually associated with authority problems, to be antagonistic and suspicious toward other people. When hostility is openly expressed, it creates immediate problems in a relationship. Equally harmful in the long run, however, are such covert expressions of hostility as being gossipy or overly competitive.

Inferiority Feelings

A basic lack of self-confidence or self-esteem which may be expressed either in oversensitivity to "threat" or in exaggerated efforts to prove one's own adequacy and worth by such techniques as boasting, showing off, and being hypercritical of other people.

Emotional Insulation

An inability to make the necessary emotional investment in a relationship, for fear of being hurt.

or relinquishing one's own in the process. . . . It is a position equally applicable to relationships between individuals or nations."

Sometimes we behave in threatening ways because we ourselves are insecure; sometimes because we don't stop to consider the other person's needs or the extent to which his good picture of himself depends upon what *we* say and do. We are so preoccupied with our own needs and desires that we neglect to take into consideration those of another person. In considering marriage, for example, many people think only, "Will this person make me happy?" Rarely do they ask themselves the question, "Will I make this person happy?" Such an approach not only disregards the rights and needs of another individual but is ultimately self-defeating, for a successful marriage de-

pends upon the active cooperation of both parties and their mutual efforts to understand and fulfill each other's needs.

Putting yourself in the other person's place. When we examine our own reactions to various people, we can see more clearly how a person contributes either to the success or to the failure of a relationship by making the other person feel either more or less adequate. It is usually pleasant to be around people who obviously like and accept us. Their attitude raises our self-esteem and makes us feel secure and relaxed with them. On the other hand, people who are hypercritical of us or who accept us with obvious reservations tend to make us defensive and ill at ease. Although most of us are able to tolerate some constructive criticism, we soon reach a point where we become defensive and hostile.

PERSONALITY FACTORS INFLUENCING
OUR PERCEPTION OF OTHER PEOPLE

How accurately we perceive the traits of other people seems to depend a great deal on (1) whether we like them or dislike them and (2) the importance in our own personality of the trait being judged (Vroom, 1959)

Typical Distortions in Perception

Perception of people we like	We tend to project to them our own assumptions and attitudes, especially those that are most central to our concept of self. We perceive most accurately the ways in which they are *similar* to us, least accurately the ways they are *unlike* us.
Perception of people we dislike	We tend to see them as basically different from us and to assume that their assumptions and attitudes are contradictory to our own. We perceive most accurately the traits *unlike* our own, least accurately the traits *similar* to our own.

Going a step further, it might be pointed out that we rarely enjoy being around any person who is hypercritical, overdemanding, and negativistic in his attitude, even when we are not the target of his displeasure. Perhaps we feel that he will be equally critical of us when our back is turned, or we dislike the gloomy picture he tends to paint of the world around us. If, on the other hand, a person is reasonably positive and understanding in his attitude toward others, we expect that he will probably react to us in the same way. Understanding and approval minimize the need for defensiveness in any interpersonal relationship.

In all our interpersonal relationships, but particularly when we find ourselves in serious disagreement with another person or severely critical of his behavior, it is often useful to ask ourselves what *we* would do in his circumstances. There will always be some margin of error in our interpretation, but we can reduce this by practicing the technique and by improving our knowledge of the other person's background and life situation. Role playing can be a very useful strategy here. In the case of family conflict, for example, the various members of the family can take each other's parts and play out a situation that has commonly caused trouble. Only the situation and the roles are decided in advance; the "play" evolves as each role player tries to think and feel and act like the person whose part he has taken. Variations of this technique have been successfully used by many psychotherapists (see p. 418). Through the role-playing process conflicting feelings and points of view are brought out into the open, and all participants gain a better perspective of both themselves and others. The groundwork is thus laid for a mutually satisfactory resolution to the conflict.

Approving of the other person while disapproving of what he does. Accepting and approving of a *person* does not mean that one accepts and approves of everything he does or *says*. In dealing with both children and adults, it is often necessary to make a clear-cut distinction between one's attitude toward the person and one's attitude toward his behavior. For instance, if a child steals something, it is likely to do much more harm than good to call him a thief and obviously reject him. It is far better to make it clear to the child that he is loved as a person but that his behavior has been wrong and presents a problem that must be worked out. This makes it unnecessary for the child to withdraw or become hostile and defensive in his attitude; it enables him to feel that he is worthy of love and to look at his behavior objectively as something that needs to be changed.

In dealing with adults, too, it is often necessary to separate one's disapproval of their attitudes or behavior from any disapproval of them as persons. The adult, even more than the child, is often so ego-involved in his views and behavior that any criticism is interpreted personally and viewed as a threat to his self-esteem. By making it clear that we disapprove of the deed but not of the doer, we are better able to disagree with the individual and discuss his behavior or attitudes in an objective manner without unnecessarily arousing his defenses.

Expressing praise and appreciation. We all like to receive sincere praise and appreciation. We can remember how proud we felt as children when our parents praised our efforts and accomplishments, and most of us have a continued need for evidence of approval. In adult life our accomplishments are, unfortunately, usually taken for granted unless they are very outstanding. The breadwinner, the homemaker, and the oldster who still tries to do his bit too often have to scratch for acknowledgment of their efforts. As a result, many of us do not receive the praise and appreciation we need for bolstering our self-esteem, sense of adequacy, and need for approval. This is particularly unfortunate because it has repeatedly been shown in experimental studies that praise usually motivates us toward increased effort and tends to bring out warm, positive feelings toward others.

Actually, sincere praise and appreciation should be easy to bestow, for everyone has traits that merit praise, such as generosity, neatness, conscientiousness, a sense of humor, or an ability to cook. Often, too, we can pass on to the individual the compliments others have paid him. Most people find that the quality of their interpersonal relationships improves when they develop a habit of deliberately giving credit where credit is due, verbally and with overt recognition—not just by refusing to detract from another's good points. Such praise is almost always welcome, except in the case of a highly suspicious person who may tend to be rather cautious about accepting it; and if it is sincere and based on fact, even he will probably appreciate it.

It is important, of course, to make a clearcut distinction between honest praise and insincere flattery designed to exploit the other person. Although some people suffer from such marked inferiority feelings that they grasp at flattery as a drowning man might grasp at a straw, most of us sooner or later recognize insincere flattery for what it is and come to distrust and dislike the person giving it.

Learning how to give criticism. Although there are times when it is necessary to be critical and "tough," it is usually better to temper the hurt of criticism by pointing out the individual's strong points first, thus putting him in a more receptive frame of mind. If an employee is reprimanded for talking too much on the job, he is more likely to respond in a constructive way if it is first pointed out to him that his contributions to the company are greatly appreciated and that he is considered to be a good worker and valued member of the organization. The wife who must criticize her husband for being untidy around the house will get a much more favorable hearing if she

tells him first how much she appreciates his thoughtfulness in other respects. Such an approach avoids making the individual feel that he is being criticized for minor faults while his more important positive contributions are unappreciated.

Criticism does great harm to a relationship when it is vindictive or spiteful. Even if it is intended to be genuinely helpful, criticism never serves a constructive purpose when it harks back to old mistakes which are beyond correction and would better be forgotten. Yet as the Overstreets note (1956, p. 104),

"Wherever we turn in today's world, it seems, we find human beings who look guardedly or vengefully at one another across barriers of old mistakes: mistakes that have never been openly acknowledged and that are still, in many cases, being defended; mistakes that, even where an effort has been made to straighten things out, have never been forgiven— much less forgotten."

Usually it is much more helpful to try to understand *how* and *why* a mistake occurred than *who* made it. When a person is repeatedly confronted with an error of the past, any regret he may have felt over the incident will gradually turn into defensiveness and resentment.

Criticisms made publicly also tend to force the person being attacked into face-saving and retaliatory behavior. The husband or wife who criticizes his spouse—or his children—in front of friends seldom accomplishes any constructive purpose. Besides showing an insensitivity for the feelings of the person being criticized, public criticism is also embarrassing to the outsiders who happen to be present. Thus it may harm not one relationship but several.

Giving the other person a good reputation to live up to. Most of us attempt to live up to the reputations or roles that other people create for us. This principle is used in the armed forces when the soldier is given a medal for his bravery in action. He now has the reputation of a brave man to live up to, and he becomes a model for others.

In all areas of life, "tags" usually stick to the people who acquire them, in spite of the fact that such labels may not have been too accurate in the first place; somehow or other we tend to become what other people say we are. Unfortunately, this tendency holds true whether the reputation is a good one or a bad one. The child whose mother takes every opportunity to point out his bad behavior and to tell him that he is incorrigible will probably behave accordingly. The husband or wife who receives nothing but nagging criticism may give up trying to be a good mate and actually come to warrant the criticisms that have been made. On the other hand, the employee who knows he is regarded as a resourceful, imaginative worker will try hard to live up to this picture.

In deliberately creating a good role for another person, it is necessary, of course, that it be a generally realistic one that he can live up to. And continual reinforcement is required until the role becomes an habitual part of that individual's self-perception and behavior. For example, the husband who wants his wife to become a better cook can take the first opportunity that arises to compliment her on her cooking, as when she does a better job than usual or successfully tries a new recipe. If she responds to this encouragement and tries again, he further compliments and encourages her. Chances are, if this continues, she will actually become the fine cook he has made her see herself.

It is unfortunate that we so often try to make changes in the behavior of others by nagging criticism and self-righteous demands which make them so defensive that it is all but impossible for them to attack their problem objectively. It is in helping people become more adequate and secure, rather, that we enable them to grow and improve. A person who constantly feels threatened can hardly approach his shortcomings in a task-oriented way.

Maintaining One's Own Integrity

When social skills are emphasized, we often get the mistaken impression that the goal is simply to avoid friction and to get along with other people at all costs. While it is essential to be sensitive to the needs of others, it is equally essential to maintain one's personal integrity —to have the courage to disagree and take a clear-cut stand when one believes others are wrong. Although tact is an important ingredient in building and maintaining friendships, personal integrity is probably the most essential ingredient of all.

Taking a stand when it is indicated. To win the respect of others—and to maintain our own self-respect—we must stand up for what we believe whenever an important issue is at stake, even though our position may elicit antagonism from those who feel we are endangering their purposes. The old saying that one is known for one's enemies as well as one's friends is relevant here. There is a story that when Confucious was asked the question, "If you are a really good person, will everyone like you?" he replied, "No, the good people in the community will like you, but the bad people will dislike you." The hostility we sometimes engender when we stand up for our beliefs need not be devaluating or anxiety-arousing for us if we are prepared for it and if we have faith in our own position. The mature adult does not expect everyone to love and appreciate him, nor does he need universal approval in order to feel adequate as a person.

Everyone distrusts the person who tries to be all things to all men. There is truth in the statement that only one's good friends will tell one the truth even if it hurts. Others are usually so intent on maintaining cordial relationships that even in the face of direct questions they will be evasive or even deceitful rather than say anything that might endanger the relationship. How such situations are handled, of course, is very important in determining whether honest disagreement will help the individual or arouse his ego defenses. But it should be remembered that truthfulness with one's friends implies a confidence in *their* integrity as well as one's own—a faith in their ability to look at all the facts objectively and to face their problems realistically.

Learning when and how to say "no." For many people, one of the most difficult things in the world is to say "no." We often buy things we don't want, attend social functions that don't interest us, accept responsibilities in social groups we dislike, and otherwise get into difficulties in our personal relationships by our inability to say "no" at the right time. Not infrequently we become angry or resentful because we feel other people are imposing on us or taking advantage of our good nature, but in tracing matters back, we can usually see that we have been partly at fault; if we had said "no" earlier, the entire matter could have been avoided.

Our difficulty in saying "no" apparently stems from our underlying fear of disapproval and hostility from others. We are often so eager to make everyone like us that we become too susceptible to social pressure. Sometimes, too, we find it hard to say "no" because we put ourselves in the other fellow's position and feel sorry for him.

As we become more mature in our social relations, we gradually come to realize that most people respect a firm negative answer more than a grudging consent. Furthermore, we have a right and a need to protect ourselves against excessive demands. The time to act is at the moment it becomes apparent that we are getting into something in which we don't want to become involved. A courteous but emphatic "no" at the right time—whether in dealing with salesmen or overly aggressive dates—is essential to avoid involvement in sit-

uations that may become more difficult to deal with as they progress.

When we have to say "no" to someone, we can often temper our refusal by suggesting some acceptable alternative. In turning down an invitation, a person may make it clear that he would be happy to accept one at a later time. In refusing to take the chairmanship of a fund drive, he may volunteer to help out in some other capacity. The graduate assistant who marks the papers for a college course may tell a student that he doesn't feel justified in raising the student's test grade but offer to refer the problem to the course instructor. Sometimes, of course, there are no reasonable alternatives—for example, some of the many demands on our time and pocketbooks must simply be met with a courteous but unequivocal "no." But in dealing with friends and loved ones, it is usually possible to temper negative responses and thus eliminate or minimize the arousal of hostility.

Being Sensitive to the Requirements of the Situation

Social expectations range from the fundamentals of good manners to highly complex role requirements; many customs and requirements are peculiar to a particular ethnic or religious group, age bracket, sex, or social class. To meet the varied expectations of different people in different situations requires both a knowledge of social customs and an ability to sense what is appropriate.

Sensitivity to the requirements of a situation is basic to social competence. By knowing what is expected of him, the individual is freed of much self-consciousness and fear of doing the wrong thing. And by knowing what to expect of others, he is in a position to understand and give consideration to their feelings.

Respecting social conventions. The argument is often raised that it is more important to be oneself than to worry about good manners. While it is certainly true that strict adherence to the rules of etiquette can never substitute for personal integrity or a genuine concern for others, it is equally true that a disregard for social conventions is more often a sign of self-centeredness than an expression of real integrity and independence. Good manners are merely agreed-upon forms for showing other people that we respect them and do not wish to hurt their feelings. A boy may consider it foolish to open the car door for his perfectly healthy date; but his failure to do so, if the girl expects it, says in effect, "Your feelings are of no concern to me."

While formality and propriety can certainly be overdone, in general there are few things as unattractive as the sight of the unmannered person—whether a child or an adult—in the act of "being himself." The child who learns that "please and thank you are magic words that open many doors" is more apt to become the adult who applies the lubricant of good manners to the social machinery of his day and in so doing prevents its deterioration and breakdown. It is always helpful to know the proper form in making introductions, in dating, in table manners, and in all social practices. Such a simple matter as not knowing the meaning of R.S.V.P. on an invitation may prove to be embarrassing to the individual and inconvenient to his host.

In this context we may note the importance of developing a feeling for what is appropriate in a given situation, whether there are any social rules to cover it or not. On a simple level this can mean knowing what kinds of jokes will be well received in different situations. On a more complex level it may mean knowing how to conduct oneself when involved in an automobile accident. Although some people seem to have an innate sense of the appropriate, their ability is less likely a "gift" than the result of experience and training.

Understanding role requirements. Sensitivity to the requirements of one's social role is also important to good interpersonal relationships; people will inevitably feel uneasy and at odds with the minister who acts like a playboy, the teacher who acts like a juvenile delinquent, or the sixty-year-old woman who tries to dress and act like a flirtatious girl of seventeen. When someone does not conform within reasonable limits to the expectations for his role, other people find his behavior confusing and become uncertain about how to behave in return. A lack of structuring— or highly unconventional structuring—makes everyone feel insecure. For example, an employer who insisted on telling his employees about his marital problems, his worries about the business, and his fears of becoming an alcoholic would be creating almost insurmountable problems in interpersonal relations and in morale. He would not be playing a role to which his employees could comfortably relate—or which would enable them to feel secure in their jobs.

Social competence also requires considerable flexibility in role playing since, as we have previously noted, each of us is called upon to play a variety of roles each day in order to maintain successful relationships in our homes, our businesses, and our various social groupings. The individual who is unable to shift roles as the occasion warrants is likely to make other people uncomfortable or even hostile. This does not mean, of course, that we should be puppets who are manipulated by the strings of social expectation. Success in role playing, like social competence in general, depends upon the individual's having a basic integrity and an understanding of both the value and limitations of social convention.

Learning to Communicate More Effectively

Although the basic requirements for communication simply involve a sender, a message, and a receiver, meaningful communication does not automatically take place whenever two people talk to—or at—each other. Everyone has had the experience of talking to a person who appeared to be thinking only of what he was going to say next. Here little real communication was going on. As one exasperated college girl said about her date: "He spent the entire evening talking about himself and ended up thinking he knew all about me." To build and maintain good interpersonal relationships, we must be as skilled at listening to and interpreting what other people say and feel as we are at expressing ourselves.

As a "sender," the individual has to know what he is trying to communicate and how to code the message in such a way that the receiver can interpret it accurately. If the sender is unclear as to the message he is trying to convey or if he fails to code the message so that it is meaningful to the person he is communicating with, the message is not likely to be received accurately. The high incidence of failure here is evidenced by our frequent use of statements such as "I didn't mean that" and "You misunderstood what I was trying to say."

To further complicate matters for the sender, communication involves much more than simply the logical formulation and expression of some particular thought. The sender must also face the problem of his own personal stimulus value. If he is viewed as prone to exaggerating, as suspicious and hostile toward others, as too weak to take a stand on any issue, or as confused and inconsistent in his convictions, this will probably influence how his messages are received. The sender's status, mannerisms, personal appearance, and authority position may influence how the receiver interprets a given message; similarly, the receiver should be aware of how his own attitudes, motives, and values influence the way in which he views the sender and interprets his message.

As suggested earlier in this chapter, there are many situations in which we are called

upon to answer feelings rather than spoken words. The person who is insensitive in this respect often unknowingly does or says things which hurt or anger other people; we characterize him by saying, "Every time he opens his mouth, he puts his foot in it." Although there are no simple rules for improving one's sensitivity to the needs and feelings of others, the following techniques are often very helpful.

1. Let the other person talk, even if it is small talk and seemingly unimportant; the very lack of significant content may give us an opportunity to detect the feeling behind his words. An increased sensitivity to voice, intonation, posture, and facial expression will help us understand what people *want* to say as well as what they *do* say. In general, a great deal of the lack of social competence stems from talking too much oneself and not listening enough. We are so preoccupied with our own aspirations, tensions, and problems that we do not even notice that another person may be under considerable pressure to discuss a problem with us. We use his every sentence as a springboard for turning the conversation back to ourselves.

2. Ask questions involving the word *feeling* rather than *thinking*. For example, we might ask an employee who is opposed to a new method, "How do you feel about this method?" rather than "Why do you think this method won't work?" If he takes advantage of this opening to express his feelings, what he says may make it apparent that he is opposed to the new method not because he doesn't think it will work but simply because he wasn't consulted about it during the planning stage. Providing him with the opening to discuss his reaction not only gives him a chance to express his feelings but also suggests that his feelings matter.

3. Mirroring or reflecting the feelings of others, without standing in judgment, is often helpful. This is one essential method used in psychotherapy. For example, the therapist

DIFFICULTIES IN COMMUNICATION

Behavior	Norm A	Communication	Norm B	Communication
Being "cruel" to animals	Animals are like other forms of material property.	A man who treats animals harshly does not consider them to be very valuable.	Animals are like humans in being sensitive to pain.	A man who is cruel to animals is indifferent to others' pain and probably abuses his own children.
Allowing "junk" to accumulate in front yard	A man's front yard is his castle; it reflects his interests, not his class position.	A man in whose front yard many things accumulate is interested in many things.	A tidy front yard is a mark of respectability.	A man whose front yard is untidy is contemptuous of middle-class virtues.
Collecting rare books	Rare books are matters of good taste as well as a good investment.	A man who collects rare books is more interested in enduring satisfactions than in fleeting pleasures.	Rare books are marks of over-refinement.	A man who collects rare books is probably neglecting more practical things.

We communicate to other people through all our behavior, not just through spoken or written words. And even more than with verbal communication, our actions are apt to be misunderstood by people whose norms are different from our own. The chart above, for example, shows how behavior prompted by one set of assumptions (Norm A) might be interpreted by a person with a different frame of reference (Norm B). We can facilitate accurate communication—and hence increase the likelihood of being able to maintain good interpersonal relationships—by remembering that all our actions "say something" to other people and by trying to make sure that our behavior communicates what we intend.

Adapted from Newcomb (1950)

may listen to the individual's statements about his wife and then reflect—by repeating or paraphrasing—the feelings which the individual has expressed, in this way helping him to bring his feelings out into the open where he can examine them for what they are.

Through the use of these simple techniques, it is often possible to detect the underlying feelings of others and to deal with interpersonal relationships more effectively.

The social skills we have discussed in this chapter are applicable to all types of interpersonal relationships, ranging from marriage and close friendships to the most casual and transient acquaintanceships. In general, people are eager to have a wide circle of acquaintances and to be well liked by others, for such popularity helps raise one's self-esteem, provides many opportunities for pleasant social interaction, and enables one to meet a wide range of interesting people. But "popularity" in this sense is only a by-product of real social competence, which is better measured by one's ability to build meaningful, lasting, and mutually satisfying relationships with the people whose lives closely touch one's own. In analyzing the essential characteristics of a group of self-actualizing individuals, Maslow found (1954, p. 218) that most of these people actually had a relatively *small* circle of people they counted as their friends:

"Partly this is for the reason that being very close to someone . . . seems to require a good deal of time. Devotion is not a matter of a moment. One subject expressed it so: 'I haven't got time for many friends. Nobody has, that is, if they are to be *real* friends.'"

The desire for popularity can be a booby trap if it leads the individual to conform rigidly to popular tastes, expectations, demands, and pressures—if he feels that he must act and even think like the others in his peer group. The person who keeps up a busy social life while failing to build more meaningful relationships with his family and a few close friends cannot be called socially competent. The striving for popularity as an end in itself usually indicates a selfish orientation and a lack of sureness about one's own adequacy and worth. The person who knows himself and is at ease with himself is relatively independent of the need for this kind of approval. At the same time, he enjoys a greater capacity for both giving and receiving the satisfactions that only interpersonal relationships can afford. Ultimately the ability to get along with others rests upon the ability to get along with oneself.

REFERENCES

The following list includes both the references cited in this chapter and a selected number of additional books and articles for outside reading.

Adorno, T. W., and others. 1950. *The Authoritarian Personality.* New York: Harper & Brothers.

Allport, Gordon W. 1954. *The Nature of Prejudice.* Boston: Beacon Press, Inc.

Beach, Leslie R., and E. L. Clark. 1959. *Psychology in Business.* New York: McGraw-Hill Book Company, Inc.

Bernard, Jessie S. 1957. *Social Problems at Midcentury: Role, Status, and Stress in a Context of Abundance.* New York: The Dryden Press, Inc.

Berrien, Frederick K. 1951. *Comments and Cases on Human Relations.* New York: Harper & Brothers.

Bettelheim, Bruno, and M. Janowitz. 1950. *Dynamics of Prejudice.* New York: Harper & Brothers.

Blake, R. R., and J. S. Mouton. 1955. *Theory and Practice of Human Relations Training.* Austin: The Hogg Foundation for Mental Hygiene, The University of Texas.

Bonner, Hubert. 1953. *Social Psychology: An Interdisciplinary Approach.* New York: American Book Company.

Cantril, Hadley. 1950. *The "Why" of Man's Experience.* New York: The Macmillan Company. Reprinted by permission of the publishers.

Cantril, Hadley, and Charles H. Bumstead. 1960. *Reflections on the Human Venture.* New York: New York University Press.

Cartwright, Dorwin, and Alvin Zander, eds. 1953. *Group Dynamics: Research and Theory.* Evanston, Ill.: Row, Peterson and Company.

Combs, Arthur W., and Donald Snygg. 1959. *Individual Behavior.* Rev. ed. New York: Harper & Brothers. Copyright 1959 by Arthur W. Combs and Donald Snygg. Published by Harper & Brothers, New York, and reprinted with their permission.

Fromm, Erich. 1955. *The Sane Society.* New York: Rinehart & Company, Inc.

Goffman, Erving. 1955. "On Face-Work: An Analysis of Ritual Elements in Social Interaction." *Psychiatry, 18,* No. 3, 213-231.

Hartley, E. L. 1946. *Problems in Prejudice.* New York: King Crown Press.

Jahoda, Marie. 1959. "Conformity and Independence." *Human Relations, 12,* No. 2, 99-119.

Jennings, Helen Hall. 1950. *Leadership and Isolation—A Study of Personality in Interpersonal Relations.* New York: Longmans, Green and Company.

Martineau, Pierre. 1957. *Motivation in Advertising: Motives That Make People Buy.* New York: McGraw-Hill Book Company, Inc.

Maslow, A. H. 1954. *Motivation and Personality.* New York: Harper & Brothers.

Mursell, James L. 1953. *How to Make and Break Habits.* Philadelphia: J. B. Lippincott Company.

National Education Association, Adult Education Service Division. 1951. *Dynamics of Participative Groups.* Boulder: University of Colorado.

National Industrial Conference Board. 1947. "Factors Affecting Employee Morale." *Studies in Personnel Policy, 85.*

Newcomb, Theodore M., 1950. *Social Psychology.* New York: Dryden Press.

Overstreet, Harry and Bonaro. 1956. *The Mind Goes Forth.* New York: W. W. Norton & Company, Inc.

Riesman, David, and others. 1950. *The Lonely Crowd: A Study of the Changing American Character.* New Haven, Conn.: Yale University Press.

Rogers, Carl R. 1959. "A Theory of Therapy, Personality, and Interpersonal Relationships, As Developed in the Client-Centered Framework in Psychology." *A Study in Science.* Sigmund Koch, ed. New York: McGraw-Hill Book Company, Inc.

Ruesch, Jurgen, and Gregory Bateson. 1951. *Communication: The Social Matrix of Psychiatry.* New York: W. W. Norton & Company, Inc.

Sullivan, Harry Stack. 1953. *The Interpersonal Theory of Psychology.* New York: W. W. Norton & Company, Inc.

Vroom, V. H. 1959. "Projection, Negation, and the Self Concept." *Human Relations, 12,* 335.

INTELLECTUAL COMPETENCE

Learning

Problem Solving and Decision Making

Creative Thinking

Man's greatest adjustive resources are his intellectual gifts—his superior capacity for learning, reasoning, and imagining. It is largely by virtue of these resources that he has been able, as a species, to master so many facets of his environment and establish his supremacy over other members of the animal kingdom. And on the individual level, the person who develops and learns to use his intellectual capacities effectively has a decided advantage in adjusting to life problems and is likely to enjoy greater material and psychological benefits—ranging from high earning power and status through enhanced feelings of adequacy and worth which come from being able to handle a wide range of problems. In the present chapter we shall discuss the development of intellectual resources under three categories: (1) learning, (2) problem solving and decision making, and (3) creative thinking.

LEARNING

In Chapter 3 we outlined the general role of learning in development, noting that practically everything a person strives for, thinks, feels, and does is influenced by what he has learned in the past. We also noted some of the distinctions between *associative learning*, which is based upon a mechanical association between stimulus situations and response tendencies, and *cognitive learning*, which depends more upon the exercise of reason and imagination. In our present discussion we shall be concerned primarily with learning as a means for achieving greater personal maturity and self-direction—for developing both the know-how and the know-why for living. Obviously this involves something more than the mere acquisition of information or the learning of response patterns by rote, though both of these may sometimes play a part.

In analyzing the factors in effective learning, we must take into consideration the characteristics of the person who is learning, the nature of the task to be learned, the way the individual goes about learning it, and the outcome of learning.

The Learner

What the individual brings to a learning situation in terms of personality traits, motivation, and general background has an important influence on what he is *willing* to learn, what he *can* learn, and how *efficiently* he will learn it.

Maturity. In planning school curriculums, educators place considerable emphasis upon the importance of physiological maturity in determining readiness for learning. Regardless of his interest and the instruction he may receive, for example, a child cannot learn to read, to write, to work long division, or to ride a bicycle until the structures which are basic to these skills have reached a certain level of maturation. Physiological maturity, however, is not the entire story. Learning ability is also related to psychological maturity in terms of such traits as the ability to concentrate one's energies on a particular learning task, to tolerate frustration, and to look at new information and ideas objectively. Immaturities that commonly hamper learning—in everyday life as well as in academic situations—are overdependence, lack of self-discipline, uncertainty about goals and values, and unwillingness to take an active role in acquiring new skills and concepts. We can predict a great deal about what an individual is likely to learn from a particular situation on the basis of tests measuring his intellectual, social, and emotional maturity.

Previous learning. What an individual is capable of learning is always limited by what he already knows. He cannot learn algebra without having first mastered arithmetic, and he cannot understand the dynamics of psychopathology without having learned the basic principles of normal behavior. It is in recognition of this principle that, in teaching, so much emphasis is placed upon introducing new skills and concepts in an orderly fashion, always building upon what has been learned before. An adequate background becomes increasingly important as one goes up the scale from simple associative learning to learning that involves reasoning and problem solving.

In nonacademic life, particularly, people encounter all sorts of unnecessary learning difficulties and failures because they do not take the time or trouble to build up an adequate background in the area they are trying to master. Even in college many students get into trouble because they ignore the suggested prerequisites for the courses they want to take. Another kind of deficiency is the failure to develop the tools or techniques for efficient learning. The student who is untrained in study skills, for example, will have a great deal more difficulty in mastering formal learning tasks than one who knows how to schedule his time, outline and organize material, and so on. With training and practice most college students could easily double their average reading rate of about three hundred words per minute. Listening skills, which are involved in so much learning both inside and outside the classroom, are even more seriously neglected by most people (Nichols and Stevens, 1957).

Motivation. The basic motivation for learning is found in the human organism's normal tendency to explore and make sense of its environment. With time this general tendency is differentiated in terms of specific needs, interests, and goals, so that we are motivated to learn things that tie in directly with our purposes while remaining relatively uninterested

in learning other things. If curiosity is disapproved or punished, as it is by some parents and by some societies, the natural incentive for learning is greatly dulled.

Learning is encouraged when it is rewarded by material or psychological satisfaction. In a school situation, where the subject matter to be learned may bear little relationship to the learner's immediate interests and purposes, motivation must sometimes be induced by the manipulation of rewards and punishments. In general, however, the successful teacher is the one who manages to relate learning tasks to the experiences and purposes of his students— to get them ego-involved in the learning situation. In much the same way, the mature college student can do much to improve his learning efficiency by making his studies as meaningful as possible and relating them to both his present interests and his long-range purposes and goals.

Motivation for learning is usually increased, too, by association with people who value intellectual competence and take a positive approach to the discipline of study. The approval of intellectual achievement by those we like and admire—whether family, friends, or teachers—is a powerful incentive to learning.

Resources. Competence in learning always presupposes a level of intelligence adequate for mastering the tasks at hand. In general, the higher an individual's I.Q., the more capable he is of mastering complex learning tasks and of learning with a minimum of time and effort. Other resources that facilitate learning are the ability to see and organize relationships, good study habits, good health and a high level of energy, freedom to devote the time and attention necessary for mastering a particular task, and—where they apply—special abilities such as those in music, art, and science.

Important as they are, however, a high level of intelligence and good general resources do not automatically insure effective learning. If a person is immature, poorly motivated, or lacking in learning opportunities and background, his intellectual potential may never be realized. And on the other hand, a mature outlook, strong motivation, and a favorable environment can go far toward compensating for minimal resources. Related to all these factors is the individual's frame of reference, especially his self-concept.

Frame of reference. The information, assumptions, and attitudes that comprise an individual's frame of reference determine in large part what he sees and learns. The range of information that will be meaningful to him, the way he will interpret new material, whether he will look at facts objectively or distort them to match his preconceptions—these facets of learning, and many more, are influenced by the individual's picture of himself and of his world. Misinformation, faulty assumptions, or negative attitudes in relation to a particular task will obviously hamper effective learning. Indeed, learning something new often depends upon "unlearning" what one has learned before. This may be relatively easy or very difficult, depending upon how closely it involves one's basic concept of self.

In general, a person's self-structure determines whether a learning situation is perceived as a threat, as a matter of no importance, or as a challenge. Usually an individual is eager to tackle learning tasks which he feels competent to handle and which tie in with his needs and purposes. On the other hand, he usually tries to avoid those tasks for which he feels inadequate—even though he may be strongly ego-involved—or to approach them with an attitude that encourages failure. Combs (1952, p. 668) illustrates the circular effect of a faulty self-concept upon learning with the example of a child who conceives of himself as unable to read:

"Such a child is likely to avoid reading and thus the very experience which might change his concept of self is by-passed. Worse still, the child who believes himself unable to read, confronted with the necessity for reading, is more likely than not to do badly. The external evaluation of his teachers and fellow pupils, as well as his own observations of his performance, all provide proof to the child of how right he was in the first place!"

Similarly, there are scores of people in everyone's acquaintance who deny themselves the opportunity to learn anything about art or music or mathematics because they falsely conceive of themselves as unable to "draw a straight line," or to "sing a note," or to "add two plus two." Most of us never realize all of our learning potential, partly because we only try to learn those things that fit into our existing self-concept.

Other characteristics of the learner such as inner conflict, anxiety, and maladjustment may also, of course, influence his ability to learn.

The Task

There are four characteristics of the learning task itself which influence how the learner should approach it and the ease with which he can master it. These are the type of task, its size and complexity, its clarity, and the conditions under which it must be learned.

Type of task. Whereas the learning of *motor* skills usually requires time and practice to train the muscles to function with the necessary strength and coordination, *verbal* learning can often be mastered at a single sitting. With nonmotor learning, *meaningful* material is much easier to learn and retain than that which must be learned by *rote*. Another distinction that influences the ease of learning and the approach one takes to it is that between *formal* and *informal* learning. Formal learning, such as that in a school setting, is facilitated by the clarity of the task, the availability of guidance, and the knowledge of progress provided by student-teacher conferences and examinations. Motivation, on the other hand, is often greater in informal learning, which usually ties in more closely with everyday interests and goals.

Size, complexity, and familiarity of task. In general, the smaller the amount of material to be learned, the easier the learning task. The extent to which difficulty is increased with additional amounts of material depends very largely, however, upon the kind of material to be learned. It is much greater for meaningless material such as nonsense syllables or digits than it is for meaningful material such as a passage of prose or poetry. But with *any* kind of verbatim or rote learning, an increase in the amount of material brings an increase not only in the total learning time but also in the average amount of time required for learning each unit. A list of seven nonsense syllables, for example, is within the memory span of the average college student and can be learned in a single presentation; but a list of ten syllables might require as many as eight or nine presentations. With meaningful material that does not require verbatim memorization, increased length has a relatively small effect on rate of learning.

The complexity of material and its familiarity are other factors that influence learning difficulty. Although added complexity tends to increase the time required for study and understanding, this factor may be offset if the learner is familiar with the material in a general way and has an adequate background for understanding it. Familiarity tends to encourage learning even when motivation is relatively low—a principle which teachers apply by trying to relate new concepts to what their students already know.

Clarity. The clarity with which a learning task is defined seems to be an important variable in the learning process, although it has not been extensively studied. Probably every student has had the frustrating experience of listening to a teacher who failed to make clear the points he was trying to communicate or whose assignments were vague and ill-defined. In general, it would appear that the less clear the learning task, the more time and effort the learner will have to spend in mastering it—if he can master it at all.

One reason we often fail to learn what we should from our everyday experiences is that the essential elements are never pointed up clearly, either because they are too complex and interrelated or because we are too ego-involved to see them for what they are. One function of professional counselors and psychotherapists is to clarify the key dimensions of the problems the individual is trying to deal with.

Task environment. The conditions under which learning takes place represent another important variable of the learning task. If the individual's learning is socially disapproved, if conditions of study are unfavorable, if essential tools or resources are lacking, if time pressures are severe, or if other life demands are distracting, the difficulty of the learning task is increased over what it would be in a more favorable environment. Other aspects of the task environment, such as a democratic versus authoritarian learning climate (Ch. 8) and the quality of instruction available, are also significant in determining the ease and effectiveness of learning.

Procedure

Learning efficiency assumes first of all that the learner is adequately motivated to put forth effort and that he possesses the intellectual and other resources necessary for mastering the particular task at hand. When these qualifications are met, the outcome of learning effort then depends largely upon the learner's method of attack. In general, the goal is to learn and retain as much as possible with a minimal expenditure of time and energy. Since specific study skills are thoroughly covered in elementary texts,[1] we shall simply outline some of the basic procedures for fostering effective learning, particularly as they apply to a school situation.

Using the best facilities and resources. Although some aspects of the task environment are beyond the learner's control, others are of his own choosing. A first step toward making efficient use of learning time and effort is to choose a good place to study—a spot that is well-ventilated, well-lighted, and as free as possible from distractions. The necessary texts, reference books, and other study materials should, of course, be readily available.

[1]See, for example, the annotated bibliography on page 534.

Familiarity with available resources also facilitates the effectiveness of learning effort. Most college students could save a great deal of time and avoid much misguided effort if they had a better knowledge of library facilities and a greater skill in using them. Learning efficiency is sometimes impaired, too, by the failure to utilize opportunities for questions and discussion with teachers and other experts whose training in a particular area is superior to our own.

Establishing a study routine. Scheduling a place and time to study, and sticking with this study pattern until it becomes habitual, is of great importance to efficient learning. The routine that is established should permit the achievement of as many goals as possible dur-

MEANINGFULNESS AND LEARNING

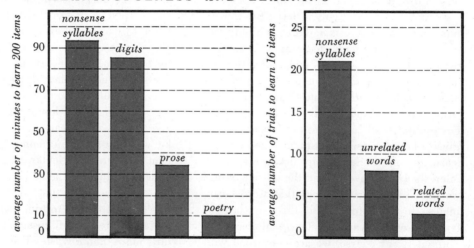

Various studies have shown that ease of acquisition is directly related to the meaningfulness of the material to be learned. The graph at left, for example, shows the amount of time required to learn equal amounts of four different kinds of material. As we might expect, the formal structuring of poetry makes it even easier to learn than meaningful prose (Lyon, 1914). A similar study using nonsense syllables, unrelated words, and related words—all three letters in length—affirms the conclusion that meaning and context facilitate acquisition. The graph at right shows the number of trials necessary to learn fifteen items of three different kinds of material (Guilford, 1934).

ing the course of a day or week, and it should provide for an appropriate balance between study and other activities. When a schedule seems impossible to maintain, it should be re-evaluated—probably with an eye to cutting down the number of recreational and extra-curricular activities. A college schedule which is realistic in terms of study demands will still permit a reasonably balanced life, but it is a mistake to think that formal learning—which is, after all, the main business of college—can be sandwiched in between outside activities that may provide more immediate pleasure. Actually, of course, the student who works out a good schedule and sticks to it is apt to find that he has *more* free time at his disposal, sim-ply because he is making much more efficient use of his day.

Building interest and motivation. As we have noted, a main reason why informal learn-ing usually comes so easily is that it ties in with our immediate interests and thus is highly mo-tivated. With academic learning it is usually possible to foster interest and motivation by taking an active approach to a subject and making a deliberate attempt to relate it to ex-isting interests and to other areas of study. Few subjects are uninteresting when one be-gins to be informed about them. The more we learn, the more relationships between separate interests are discovered and the more pleasure we take in exploring things that were mean-ingless to us before. And thus we become launched on a voyage of intellectual discovery. Ultimately, of course, we are concerned with balancing *depth* of learning with necessary *breadth* of learning needed by an integrated and cultured person.

The clarification of goals and values is an important aspect of building motivation for college work. When a student takes time to think through the relationship between what he makes of his present educational opportu-nities and what he hopes to make of his life later, he becomes much more willing to put

forth the concentrated effort that is necessary for success in college.

Maintaining an active mental set. By delineating his goals, so that he can see clearly where he wants to go and what he must do to get there, the learner also helps establish a favor-able mental set. Taking an active approach to learning means, for one thing, making an ef-fort to organize material in terms of (1) what is most important to an overall picture of the subject, (2) what is of lesser importance but still essential, and finally (3) what is unim-portant or irrelevant. Discussing what one has learned with others, integrating it with one's overall frame of reference, questioning doubt-ful points, and following up new interests with further study are other procedures which en-courage both learning and retention.

Preparing for examinations. Usually the knowledge that one will have to apply what he has learned in practical situations or be tested upon it by a formal examination acts as a stim-ulus to effective learning and recall. The time to begin preparing for an examination, of course, is when the learning task is begun. Dis-tributed study, periodic review, and overlearn-ing all encourage long-range retention and give the learner real confidence in what he knows. Last-minute cramming may get a stu-dent through a particular examination, but his understanding will be so poor and his rate of forgetting so high that what he has learned will be of little use to him thereafter. Further-more, lectures and discussion periods are often little more than a waste of time for the student who puts off all his reading until the last few days before the exam.

When a student builds up knowledge of his subject as he goes along, he can then use his final review time to prepare for the particular type of examination he will be required to take. For an essay examination, demanding re-call rather than simple recognition, it is impor-tant to review in depth and to organize one's knowledge in terms of major ideas and relationships. In reviewing for an objective examination, on the other hand, it may be better to concentrate on a good overall view of the material in order to recognize points which the exam brings up.

Adequate preparation is obviously the first defense against examination jitters, but sometimes test situations elicit anxiety on the part of even the most able students. This is to be expected, for an important examination represents a potential danger to long-range goals, to feelings of self-worth, to the relationship with one's parents, and so on. It is the student who accepts a certain amount of anxiety as *natural*, while resolving to function well in spite of it, whose performance shows little impairment under the stress of the test situation. In fact, up to a certain level, anxiety may even *improve* performance.

Promoting positive transfer. Although psychologists generally assume that all of a person's experiences affect his later behavior in one way or another, very little is actually known about how previous learning affects the ease with which we can understand and master other related tasks. The available evidence seems to indicate that some transfer is possible if there are identical elements in the two learning situations or if they can be understood in terms of the same general principles. Transfer of ideational learning is never automatic, however, but depends upon the learner's ability to perceive the points of similarity between the old and the new. There is always a danger, too, of seeing more similarity than actually exists, in which case previous learning may actually interfere with learning something new. Too, learning tasks which involve similar but not identical elements may lead to confusion, as in the case of taking both Spanish and French at the same time.

Educators are particularly concerned with promoting the transfer of academic learning to real-life situations. The psychologist, for example, can teach people the principles which enable them better to understand human behavior, but he has no control over whether they will apply this understanding in their dealings with others or in improving their own effectiveness. To increase the likelihood of appropriate transfer and of using what we have learned, we must foster the practice of looking for general principles, studying their range of application, seeing how they relate to one another, and organizing them into a coherent and consistent frame of reference. These, of course, are the same procedures that facilitate learning itself.

Feedback

In Chapter 6 we saw how man continuously modifies his adjustive responses on the basis of feedback—the return information he receives concerning the progress or outcome of his behavior. With respect to the learning process, feedback not only tells the learner whether he is proceeding satisfactorily but also serves as reward or punishment.

Knowledge of results. Many studies have shown that adequate feedback facilitates both motor and ideational learning. When the learner must work in the dark, with little or no information about how much he has accomplished or whether he is learning the right things, his learning efficiency is impaired. Under such conditions both motivation and self-confidence are likely to suffer. And, of course, he is very likely to learn errors which he will later have to unlearn. For these reasons, frequent short tests in a formal learning situation are often more useful than occasional long ones.

Sometimes the learner is so ego-involved with test results that it is difficult for him to perceive feedback accurately or to put the information to good use. If he receives a poorer grade than he expected, for example, he may become defensive and concentrate on trying to prove that the test was unfair or the scoring invalid rather than on trying to understand where he went wrong and why. Even good test papers should be studied for the information they provide about the desired direction of learning.

In everyday life situations, the variables are so complex that it often becomes very difficult to relate feedback information accurately to the learning situation. Thus a divorced person may be confident that he has learned enough from the failure of his first marriage to insure his now being able to establish a successful marital relationship—he will not again make the mistake, for example, of living near his in-laws or of letting his wife work. But he may never see the *real* causes underlying his marriage failure—perhaps a lack of common purposes or values—and thus may later discover,

EFFECT OF LEARNING METHOD
ON RETENTION AND TRANSFER

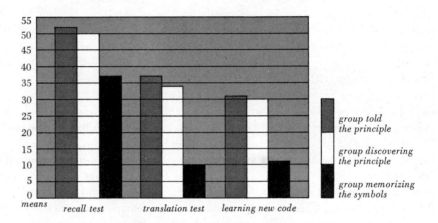

The abilities to remember what one has learned and to apply it to related situations seem to depend a great deal upon the mastery of general principles. This was illustrated in a study in which college students were asked to learn a code alphabet made up of triangles and other abstract symbols. Each subject was given a sheet of paper on which the symbols to be learned were printed under the corresponding letters of the regular alphabet. One group of subjects was also given a written explanation of the principle on which the code was based; a second group was told that the code was based on a principle, but the members had to discover it for themselves; a third group was simply instructed to memorize the code. The graph above shows the performance of the groups on three subsequent tests in which subjects had to (1) recall the code alphabet itself, (2) translate paragraphs written in the code, and (3) learn new code alphabets based on similar principles. On all three tests, the two groups who had learned the principle did significantly better than the memorization group (Forgus and Schwartz, 1957).

much to his bewilderment, that his second marriage is no more successful than his first. Many individuals continue making the same mistakes due to their inability to evaluate feedback information. Both in school and in our everyday lives, we often need expert guidance if we are to perceive feedback information accurately and apply it in correcting our failures.

Reward and punishment. Feedback reinforces learning when the return information is a source of satisfaction. Such rewards as good grades, praise, increased understanding, and progress toward specific goals all tend to reinforce what has been learned and to motivate further learning. Divergent feedback, on the other hand, has the effect of a punishment, but its results may vary. Poor grades, for example, spur some students to increased effort while making others discouraged and apathetic or else so defensive that they cannot look at their failure objectively as a learning experience. The effect of divergent feedback upon the learning process is directly related to the learner's goals, his attitudes toward learning, the standards of performance he sets for himself, and his general feelings of adequacy or inadequacy. Thus we see again the key role of the individual's frame of reference in shaping the entire course of learning. In the next section we shall have occasion to note its equally important influence on problem solving and decision making.

PROBLEM SOLVING
AND DECISION MAKING

Life presents a never-ending succession of problems to be solved and decisions to be made. In fact, as we saw in Chapter 6, the entire adjustive process is essentially one of perceiving and evaluating problems and then selecting the particular course of action that seems most likely to meet both the demands of the situation and the overall needs of the individual.

Much of our problem solving is habitual and automatic. Once we have found effective ways to handle the routine problems of everyday living, we need to devote little or no further thought to them. There are many situations, however, which require a fresh and creative approach. In our work, in our relationships with other people, in our role as citizens, we must use our full intellectual capacities to analyze the problems we encounter and work out the best solutions. Indeed, even some of the problems for which we *do* have habitual solutions merit a more thoughtful approach than we give them, for our habitual ways of seeing and doing things can become outmoded with changes in circumstances and in ourselves. All too common is the mother who still sees her married daughter as her "little girl" and treats her accordingly. On a group level, too, we can see how changes in the world situation have often forced us to make an "agonizing reappraisal" of our habitual ways of dealing with international problems.

Common Difficulties
in Defining and Evaluating the Problem

Basic to the effective solution of any new problem is defining it accurately. It is often our failure to see the dimensions of a problem —or even to recognize that a problem exists— that accounts for our failure to respond effectively. In discussing the methods of science, Albert Einstein and Leopold Infeld (1938, p. 95) wrote:

"The formulation of a problem is often more essential than its solution, which may be merely a matter of mathematical or experimental skill. To raise new questions, new possibilities, to regard old problems from a new angle, requires creative imagination and marks real advance in science."

Much the same principle seems to hold true in everyday life. With our intellectual equipment and the sources of information available to us, we should be able to find reasonably good solutions to most of our problems, but we are often thrown off the track by our inability to see a problem for what it really is. Our failure here may stem from several sources, among which are faulty assumptions and attitudes, a rigid mental set, an ego-defensive orientation, stress and emotion, and a tendency to oversimplify complex problems.

Faulty assumptions and attitudes. If false information is fed into an electronic computer, there is little probability that it will come up with valid answers. Similarly, our reasoning powers and "common sense" may fail to provide us with good solutions to problems when we start out with false premises. If we assume that marital success can be achieved without any real effort on our part, if we permit our desires to obscure the odds against us in a business venture, or if we assume that material possessions will automatically insure a happy life, we are likely to encounter serious difficulties in dealing with problems in these areas. Any major inaccuracy in a person's frame of reference is a potential source of error in problem solving.

We have previously pointed up the importance of a realistic frame of reference in solving life's problems, and we have indicated some of the major sources of distortion. However, we should again emphasize our propensity to perceive and accept information and ideas which are compatible with our existing assumption and attitudes and to reject or dis-

tort whatever is not. Hence faulty assumptions and attitudes tend to be self-perpetuating, although the setbacks of failure may, of course, cause us to revise some of them with time.

Rigid mental set. To meet the demands of any given situation, the individual must be able to examine it in various lights. Too often, efficiency in problem solving is impaired by the tendency to think there is only one way to look at a problem and only one possible solution for it. Implicit in a flexible mental set is a questioning and critical attitude, which Berrien (1951, p. 45) describes in this way:

"It is a way of thinking characterized by a kind of disrespect for the old answers, the established rules, or the accepted principles. These are not held in reverence as the inevitable and final authority, but are accepted as currently useful generalizations which may at any time be sloughed or revised if new observations fail to support the generalizations. Ideally, there is a flexibility in thinking and a breadth of observation unrestricted by preconceived notions of what one ought to experience in any given situation."

A rigid mental set is often the result of cultural biases. We fail to see the real dimensions of many problems because our perspective is limited by the cultural setting in which we live. We learn certain approved ways of perceiving and dealing with problems and are prone to think of these as the only "right" ways; if we are aware of other approaches at all, we consider them inferior or ridiculous. There is an old story of an American who ridiculed his Chinese friend for putting food upon the graves of his loved ones—a foolish custom, he pointed out, since the dead could not eat. Whereupon the Chinese friend replied that what the American said was true but that the custom was no more foolish than the American one of putting flowers on the graves of loved ones—for neither could the dead see or smell.

Often we are unaware of how much our various group affiliations influence the way we analyze and respond to problems. However, we can readily see the differences which may stem from membership in groups such as labor or management, North or South, and lower, middle, or upper class. Sometimes, of course, cultural biases are exaggerated by group pressures which force the individual to conform to group-approved views and procedures.

Established ways of dealing with problems —whether originally worked out by the individual or imposed upon him from outside— tend to be reinforced by habit, for it requires less effort to handle problems in the same old ways than it does to re-examine them. As we shall see in the following paragraphs, mental rigidity is sometimes a by-product, too, of an ego-defensive orientation or of emotion and stress.

EFFECTS OF RIGID MENTAL SET

The manner in which a rigid set can interfere with effective problem solving was illustrated in a study involving 2709 subjects from high schools, colleges, and adult education courses (Luchins, 1942).

Subjects were asked to solve the following problems involving the measurement of water:

Problem number	Given the following empty jars as measures			Obtain this amount of water
	A	B	C	
1	29	3		20
2	21	127	3	100
3	14	163	25	99
4	18	43	10	5
5	9	42	6	21
6	20	59	4	31
7	23	49	3	20
8	15	39	3	18
9	28	76	3	25
10	18	48	4	22
11	14	36	8	6

Problem 1 is a simple illustration. Problems 2-6 are "set-producing" problems which must be solved by the formula B—A—2C. Problems 7-8 and 10-11 are "crucial" problems which can be solved either by this roundabout method or more directly with only two jars. Problem 9 can be solved only by the two-jar method.

Control subjects who worked only the introductory problem and one other before tackling the "crucial" problems used the simple method in all but a few cases. In the experimental groups, however, 50 to 75 percent of subjects used the longer, set-produced method; and on Problem 9, which could be solved only by the two-jar method, 50 to 90 percent failed to find a solution. Experimental subjects who had been told to write "Don't be blind" at the top of their papers made somewhat fewer "set" responses than the others, but even here 50 percent followed the set formula on the first two crucial problems. Analysis of the results showed that rigidity had little relationship to the subjects' age, intelligence, or educational level.

Defensive orientation. In previous chapters we have noted that an individual who feels threatened and insecure tends to be more concerned with protecting his basic feelings of adequacy than with coping directly with a problem. In arguments, for example, he may be intent only on proving he is right rather than on giving objective thought to the facts of the matter or examining his viewpoint critically. The individual whose behavior is directed primarily at protecting an inaccurate self-concept shows considerable resistance to accepting new information or to facing unpleasant problems. His problem-solving ability is also impaired by a tendency to rationalize away his errors, which makes it difficult for him to learn from his mistakes.

The handling of problems in which we are ego-involved is often complicated by such a defensive orientation. For example, a parent usually finds it hard to understand or deal effectively with a delinquent child, for his identification with the child and his feelings of parental adequacy are likely to prevent him from approaching the problem with any objectivity. Similarly, marital problems are often difficult to handle because both husband and wife are too ego-involved to remain flexible and objective. When a task orientation can be maintained, on the other hand, the individual is better able to look at the problem realistically, consider a wide range of alternative solutions, and finally select the most appropriate course of action.

Emotion and stress. We are often exhorted to "put aside" our emotions in order to think clearly and reasonably. Unfortunately, this is easier to say than to do, for not all of our emotional processes can be consciously controlled. Whether we like it or not, we cannot banish fear or hate or joy or anticipation simply by resolving to do so. And in dealing with many situations, we may not even recognize the fact that we *are* emotionally involved. We may *think* we are being perfectly objective in our

approach to a family problem, for example, not realizing that our analysis of the situation is strongly colored by our complicated emotional relationships with parents or other family members.

As we saw in Chapter 5, it is under conditions of severe stress that emotions have the most dramatic effects in distorting cognitive processes—making it difficult for us to think efficiently when we need to most, in times of crisis. Fear may exaggerate the severity of the problem and generate an attitude of apprehension which makes it all but impossible to follow any course of action; anger may lead to impulsive and ill-considered action; and anxiety may markedly restrict one's ability to see problems clearly or to formulate alternative solutions. Indeed, severe stress of any kind narrows our perceptual field and causes our behavior to become rigid and stereotyped. Sometimes, too, our overall problem-solving ability is impaired by an unfavorable life situation that makes seemingly impossible demands upon us. We may even feel that just one more straw would cause us to break down. Often we are under the pressure of so many different but not necessarily crucial problems that we cannot devote sufficient time or energy to solving *any* of them—or perhaps cannot even concentrate our attention on a specific one. Preoccupation, worry, and conflict over serious problems can even impair our ability to solve relatively simple, routine problems. We tend to make mistakes that would be unimaginable under ordinary circumstances, and later marvel at how "stupid" we have been, asking ourselves, "How could I *ever* have done that?"

When one recognizes that he is under considerable emotional stress, it is often wise—if conditions permit—to put off decisions until the problem and alternative solutions can be more reasonably and calmly assessed. Particularly in solving important problems in one's life, it is essential to have adequate time, relative freedom from the pressures of other major problems, and freedom from excessive social demands that the problem be solved in a particular way. Often one can increase the likelihood of making good decisions by anticipating and preparing for problems which otherwise might induce considerable emotion and strain.

Oversimplification. In our earlier discussion of the processing of problems (Ch. 6), we noted our tendency to simplify problems to make them more easily understandable. This is both necessary and desirable, providing we simplify the problem by delineating its key dimensions—by reducing it to the lowest common denominator. Many problems are not as complicated as they first appear once we have gotten down to the essential elements.

Unfortunately, however, in the process of defining a problem, many people oversimplify it by omitting some of its key facets. Thus we have all heard individuals offering easy solutions to problems ranging from improving international relationships to dealing with women. Although their answers may appear persuasive at first glance, they are not valid answers since they do not take into consideration certain key dimensions which must be considered if the solution is to prove successful.

Some Aids in Problem Solving

As the foregoing discussion suggests, competence in problem solving depends first of all upon personal maturity and adjustment. Each of the formal aids to problem solving is limited in its usefulness if there are personality characteristics which make it difficult for the individual to look at his problems objectively or to admit the possibility of more than one solution. The individual who is relatively free of such handicaps, on the other hand, can improve his effectiveness in solving problems by applying various intellectual "strategies" such as those we shall discuss in the following

pages. Used singly or in combination, they are valuable safeguards against the all too common errors imposed upon us by "common sense."

Logic and semantics. Over two thousand years ago Aristotle developed a technique called the *syllogism* for testing whether a given conclusion or generalization follows legitimately from the premises on which it is based. Although we tend to think of logic as an artificial exercise for the intellect, actually we use syllogistic reasoning every day, though usually not the full form. When the toddler stands with his hand gingerly suspended two inches from the stove and says "Hot! Burn!" he has stated one premise and the conclusion of a syllogism:

All hot things burn.

This stove is a hot thing.

Therefore this stove burns.

Similarly, the man who says "Women drivers!" to his wife in a derogatory tone is really saying:

All women are poor drivers.

You are a woman.

Therefore you are a poor driver.

But here the conclusion, although "logically" correct, is based upon a false premise, for all women are *not* poor drivers. This illustrates the greatest limitation of syllogistic reasoning: if we begin with a false assumption, we can never depend on our conclusion. Applying the devices of formal logic can help us with our problems, however, by forcing us to state our premises fully, so that we can examine them objectively and determine whether they are valid.

Much cloudy thinking can be avoided if we can remain alert to the following sources of error, which underlie many of the false premises from which we reason.

1. Overgeneralization from limited experience. If a person fails to consider whether his own experience has been typical or whether it has been broad enough to justify *any* broad conclusion, he may make sweeping generalizations which have no support in fact. Thus a man may conclude that blondes are more frivolous than brunettes after having had dates with only two or three girls in each category.

2. Misapplying general rules. If he fails to translate the abstract and general into the concrete and specific, a person may apply general principles—valid in themselves—to specific situations where they do not apply. Thus the general rule that a person should be honest does not necessarily mean he should tell a girl at a party that her dress is inappropriate.

3. Mistaking correlation for causation. When two things go together, people often jump to the conclusion that there is a direct causal relationship between them. For example, the fact that in this country there are fewer Negroes than white people in the professions has been construed by some to suggest that Negroes are lower in intelligence—a conclusion which experimental studies have failed to support. When we mistake correlation for causation, we may be overlooking the operation of one or more additional factors which are responsible for the relationship.

4. Dichotomous (all-or-none) thinking. In an effort to simplify problems, we often classify individuals or situations according to the extremes of a continuum. Thus a person may be seen as absolutely good or bad, right or wrong, honest or dishonest. Such dichotomous thinking, of course, obscures all sorts of gradations as well as the fact that few traits are revealed by an individual in all situations. Thus a person may be highly honest in situations involving friends, relatively honest in his business transactions, but dishonest in dealing with people he considers to be his enemies.

5. Thinking in terms of stereotypes. Stereotypes represent another type of oversimplification. A certain attribute of a group or of individual members in a group is abstracted and regarded as the primary characteristic of every member. Thus the American is materialistic, the Scot is close-fisted, and the Frenchman is a great lover. Such categorizations usually give us a false picture of the group as a whole and are even more misleading when we apply them to individuals, who may not fit the stereotype at all. Stereotypes are, of course, necessary to some extent in thinking about large numbers of people whom we cannot possibly view individually. However, they can be seriously misleading if applied to individual cases.

6. Failure to recognize multiplicity of causes. Still another kind of oversimplification is attributing an event or situation to a single cause. Having seen statistics which show juvenile delinquency to be much more prevalent in slum areas than in better residential neighborhoods, we may conclude that a good slum clearance program will eliminate delinquency. Such a conclusion overlooks such factors as emotional disturbances, lack of parental guidance, and gang associations as possible causes of delinquent behavior.

There are many other reasons why we accept false premises—and then let "logic" lead us to false conclusions. One is the naïve assumption that any idea accepted by the majority is necessarily valid. Another is the tendency to let our like or dislike for a person influence our evaluation of his ideas. We need to continually clarify and evaluate the premises from which we reason if logic is to serve us as a tool for clear thinking.

Important to the effective use of logic are the techniques of *semantics*, the branch of linguistic science concerned with the relationship between words and the reality they are intended to represent. Words are symbols for objects and ideas; by using words we are able to refer to things which are not physically present. But when the meaning of words becomes distorted or imprecise, our thinking becomes cloudy, and we may be led to accept a distorted picture of reality. Semantic confusion is most readily illustrated in arguments where several people, using the same words, are actually talking about quite different things. The same type of confusion often enters into our individual thinking when the symbols we use are inaccurate. In "talking to oneself" as well as in trying to communicate with others, it is important to define terms and to make them as precise a representation of reality as possible.

In semantic analysis there are three trouble spots to watch out for particularly. First, symbols often change with time. The word *liberal*, for example, has quite a different meaning today from what it did thirty-five years ago. Second, the same word may have quite different meanings for different individuals, especially if it is one that commonly arouses an emotional response, such as the word *sex*. Finally, words for abstract or general concepts can be misleading when applied to a concrete or specific situation unless their meaning in this particular instance is precisely defined. For instance, what do we mean when we call someone a *gentleman?* Is he any male? Is he an upper-class male? Or is he a man whose inherent gentleness entitles him to be named such? Our ability to manipulate linguistic symbols can either facilitate or interfere with effective thought, depending upon how accurately our symbols mirror the reality with which we must ultimately deal.

Authority and expert opinion. Reliance upon the advice of an authority is one of the oldest problem-solving methods known to man, and certainly in a complicated culture such as ours we would find it impossible to deal with many of our problems if we did not have experts to call upon. We depend upon the specialized skills and training of the doctor, the lawyer, the political economist, the electrician, the architect, and the television repairman to supplement our own areas of knowledge. Indeed, one mark of intellectual competence is the ability to recognize the limitations of one's own experience and know *when* and *where* to turn for additional information and advice.

In seeking the help of experts, the individual need not forfeit responsibility for making his own decisions. He must first of all check his authorities carefully to determine by what right they *are* authorities. He must question and verify. Usually he must look not just to one expert but to several, to see if there is agreement among them. And he must determine for himself when he has adequate information on which to base a decision. Frequently, the value of an expert may lie in his ability to help the individual comprehend fully the dimensions of his problem and the variety of ways in which it might be dealt with.

Most people tend to be fairly critical in choosing their authorities in such well-defined fields as medicine and law. But the same individual who insists on having the advice of the best lawyer in the city for help with his legal problems may take his personal problems to friends and relatives who are poorly qualified to give advice. In many cases, too, we mistake experience for wisdom. The new mother who consults the experienced mother of six children will not inevitably get sound advice on child rearing; indeed, the advice may be very bad. Another danger is that of accepting information or advice as valid because it comes from someone we like personally, from someone whose prestige is great in another field, or from a large and influential group.

For the person who chooses his authorities carefully and tries to validate what they say, the opinion of others can be an invaluable aid in problem solving. Ultimately, however, the individual must base his decisions upon his own judgment and values if he is to be a self-directing person.

Group problem solving. There is ample experimental evidence to indicate that some kinds of problems can best be solved by people working as a group rather than individually. Anyone who has had the experience of participating in an effective committee has witnessed the sharing of ideas and experiences, noticed how the faulty logic of one member was checked by the thinking of others, recognized how creative thinking was sparked by the interchange of ideas, and finally seen a solution or plan of action developed which successfully embodied ideas from several different persons.

Every experience of working with a group is not necessarily a happy one, however. Against the saying that "Two heads are better than one," we must match another: "Too many cooks spoil the broth." Sometimes group problem solving is time-wasting and inefficient and can even frustrate the initiative of individual members. The success of many groups in solving problems which might otherwise defy solution should not obscure the fact that some types of problems can best be handled by individuals.

When group strategy is indicated, the following principles should be considered if the group is to function effectively:

1. The individuals participating should be directly concerned with the problem and prepared with enough background information to discuss it intelligently.

2. Participants should be task-oriented rather than ego-oriented—primarily concerned with solving the problem rather than promoting their own ideas or influence.

3. The entire problem should be clearly reviewed before an attempt is made to attack it.

4. The leader or leaders of the group should see that each member is given the opportunity to express his views and that the group has ample time to evaluate various suggestions before arriving at a final conclusion.

5. The group should formulate its conclusion precisely and develop a plan for putting it into operation. If a solution has not been agreed upon, the group should make specific recommendations for a further attack on the problem.

Many of man's problems are solved in a group setting—whether it be an informal family group, a legislative committee, or a team of research scientists. When proper safeguards are employed against inefficiency and the stifling of individual initiative, group strategy—by pooling the creative and problem-solving resources of many individuals—can often achieve remarkable results.

A basic strategy for problem solving. Whatever specific techniques we may rely upon in solving everyday problems, we can often improve our effectiveness by following a strategy which James Mursell has labeled the W-E-D approach. The name is derived from the three basic steps in problem solving: (1) obtaining a comprehensive picture of the problem as a *whole*; (3) identifying the essential *elements* of the problem and ordering them in terms of their relevance to the overall picture; and (3) gathering and ordering the necessary *details* for completing the picture and putting a plan of action into effect.

Although it may occasionally be preferable to vary the order of these three steps, and in the case of emergencies demanding immediate action to abandon them altogether, the W-E-D approach represents a systematic and efficient strategy for evaluating and solving most everyday problems. Mursell (1951, p. 24) illustrates their practical application with the following example:

". . . a first-rate administrator, when he is taking charge of a new enterprise, proceeds according to our basic pattern. He is not likely to start, the very first day, making radical changes here, there, and everywhere, even though his fingers may be itching to do so. Instead, he begins with a careful and comprehensive study of the situation. He scrutinizes the records, examines organizational charts, interviews key personnel. For quite a long time he listens much and says little, keeping an open mind. But gradually, certain broad conclusions, certain general ideas about policy and practice shape up in his thinking. Not until these have become fairly clear is he ready to roll up his sleeves, go into action, and modify the innumerable details that must be changed to give his views effect."

In using this approach special emphasis may be given to the identification of essential elements—for it is impossible to deal efficiently with detail until these elements have been identified. As Mursell (1951, p. 65) points out, "Once the essentials in any undertaking are located, the work is very often half done, and quite often, nine-tenths done." In essence, the problem has been defined, and the alternative solutions are likely to become readily apparent.

The solutions we develop on the basis of these three steps—whole picture, key elements, and relevant details—are ordinarily tested in application. When we put a carefully thought-out solution into effect, we sometimes find that we have made errors in our evaluation of the problem. On the whole, however, with experience and training we can become surprisingly adept at analyzing problems and anticipating the probable consequences of proposed solutions. When used by either an individual or a group, the W-E-D approach facilitates an efficient attack and acts as a safeguard against the all too common tendency to become hopelessly bogged down in relatively unimportant details.

These principles of problem solving are applicable to the most diverse problems. Mursell (1951) cites the climbing of Mount Everest and the Arctic explorations of the famous explorer Stefansson as cases in point. In line with the W-E-D approach, the first phase of the attack on Mount Everest was an overall survey of terrain and climatic factors; the second phase was the selection of a feasible attack route and the location of approach camps; and the third phase involved the han-

dling of the myriad details of food, oxygen, and other essential equipment.

Similarly the explorer Stefansson, by bringing together data concerning the Arctic and analyzing the essential elements of the problem of surviving there, was able to make long journeys in the Arctic relying mainly on the country for food and shelter—journeys which other white men considered impossible and which even the Eskimos never attempted. Stefansson credited his success to his college education; he had developed competence in problem solving in college and had applied what he had learned to a situation far removed from the academic world.

These experiences refute the criticism we sometimes hear that nontechnical education is of little use outside the "ivory tower." Equally important, they demonstrate the importance of keeping in close touch with reality—of testing our formal knowledge and translating it into terms that have practical significance. Problem solving is a competency that makes or breaks lives. When an individual's hindsight is always better than his foresight, or when he is continually surprised and disappointed by the way things turn out, it is time for him to take stock of his problem-solving skills.

Some Aids in Decision Making

The careful and systematic analysis of a problem does not automatically gear the individual for action. Often he must choose between two or more solutions which seem to be about equally good in terms of the risks they involve, the satisfactions they promise, and the amount of time and effort they demand. We noted in Chapter 6 (pp. 191-192) that in formulating the best line of action the individual evaluates possible solutions in terms of such questions as the following: Would this solution be realistic? Can I predict the outcome of this action? Would the risk be too great?

Would the action be consistent with my standards? Would too much effort or anxiety be involved? Decision making, in other words, is essentially a process of weighing possible satisfactions against risk and probable cost.

Relatively few of the problems we encounter in the course of our everyday living have clearcut, ideal solutions. In choosing one line of action, we may forfeit the satisfactions promised by another. Sometimes our choice is not even between two good alternatives but between the lesser of two evils. And because we cannot control all relevant variables or anticipate chance factors, we can never be entirely sure that a decision will work out according to plan. In spite of the difficulties inherent in making decisions, however, we must continually choose how to act—or else be acted *upon*. Self-direction implies the assumption of responsibility for oneself and the willingness to take calculated risks. Recognizing that occasional failures are inevitable, we can substantially improve our odds for success by following the general principles outlined below.

Avoiding impulsive action. Acting in haste is an excuse we hear offered to explain everything from buying inferior merchandise to quitting a job at the first sign of difficulty. Whenever snap judgments are made—but especially in areas where the individual has little knowledge and experience—the likelihood of error is great. Sometimes, of course, a poor decision is of relatively little consequence, and we might rather gamble on an easy choice than waste the time and effort required for evaluating alternate possibilities. But if the decision is an important one that will have long-range effects, it is wise to examine it carefully and often to "live with it" for a time before committing oneself to action. The high percentage of failure of impulsive wartime marriages is a matter of record.

The maxim "look before you leap" suggests the value of preparing for future decisions as well as carefully exploring alternative solutions to important problems of the moment. Preparation for marriage and work, for example, should begin long before the time for decision arrives. A thorough understanding of the problem and a thinking-through of alternative solutions also facilitate the ability to make *good* compromises—those that sacrifice smaller satisfactions for larger ones—while safeguarding against any momentary temptation to make compromises that will later prove untenable—as, for example, serious compromises in values and standards that we later find difficult to live with.

Accepting a reasonable level of satisfaction. Perhaps as dangerous as impulsive action on major decisions is the inability to act until an "ideal" solution can be found. The person who always insists upon maximum satisfactions often becomes the victim of vascillation and indecision. Indeed, the strain of suspending judgment indefinitely can be so great, if a major decision is involved, that the individual's ability to deal with even the routine problems of living suffers considerably. Even if a superior solution is ultimately found, it may not justify the tremendous cost in anxiety and strain.

In deciding about something as important as marriage, of course, a person is right in demanding a high level of satisfaction and taking the time necessary to think through his decision carefully. But even here it becomes necessary at last to take a calculated risk, recognizing that any choice is apt to have some negative aspects—marriage even to a seemingly "ideal" person entails a loss of freedom, the assumption of new responsibilities, and other factors that must, of course, be weighed against the larger satisfactions that marriage can provide.

Besides increasing the difficulty and strain of decision making, perfectionism also tends to create dissatisfaction with choices after they have been made. To use the example of marriage again, the individual who demands absolute satisfaction may be tremendously upset by minor irritations in his marriage that another person would consider inconsequential.

When it comes to problems that are routine or unimportant from a long-range point of view, perfectionism has even less to recommend it. The person who debates interminably over what to wear, how to spend the evening, what restaurant to go to, or even what car to buy is wasting more time and energy than any of these decisions justifies.

Reducing the negative aspects of choice. Most decisions involve an element of conflict. We are aware that our choices have certain negative as well as positive aspects, and as a result we both fear and look forward to the action we are about to undertake. The balancing of plus and minus factors is complicated, as we saw in Chapter 5, by the fact that dread increases more sharply than anticipation as the time for committing oneself to a decision gets closer.

The fundamental principles of ambivalent or approach-avoidance behavior can be summarized as follows (Miller, 1944):

1. The tendency to approach a goal having positive value is stronger the nearer the subject is to it. This may be called the "approach gradient."

2. The tendency to avoid a goal having negative value is stronger the nearer the subject is to it. This may be called the "avoidance gradient."

3. The strength of avoidance increases more rapidly than the strength of approach as the subject gets nearer to the goal.

4. The strength of approach or avoidance tendencies varies with the strength of the drive upon which they are based. An increased drive raises the height of the entire gradient.

It is when there is approximate equality of strength between approach and avoidance tendencies that conflict is most severe. Thus the individual who is about equally torn between the desire to marry and fear of losing his freedom is likely to experience severe conflict as his wedding date nears. The balance can be tilted in the direction of marriage either by building up the positive aspects of the choice or by reducing the negative ones. Strengthening the approach gradient, however, is usually a less satisfactory way to resolve conflict than is reducing the avoidance gradient. As Phillips puts it (1956, p. 178):

"Except in very mild cases of human conflict, a pat on the back, a 'pep' talk, and similar 'forward push' techniques would all seem not only to have short-lived effects but also to run the risk of increasing tension because of the calculable effect of such efforts to push the person farther up on the approach gradient, thus indirectly increasing his avoidance tendencies and consequently increasing the conflict and the tension he experiences."

There are various techniques that an individual can use to minimize the negative aspects of choice. Among them are the following:

1. He can clarify his picture of the actual dangers involved in his decision, thus eliminating vague anxiety over the unknown.

2. He can build up the competencies that will enable him to cope with the foreseeable trouble spots. For example, adequate vocational preparation increases the probability of success in a challenging job; the development of social competencies will reduce the need for fearing difficult yet desired new relationships.

3. He can put the decision into proper perspective. Many decisions are of such relatively small importance in terms of long-range consequences that even if the worst happens, nothing much is lost. Recognizing this reduces the fear involved in making a decision.

Being prepared to back up a decision. Although it is often foolish to maintain an obviously wrong decision, there are many times when decisions are rescinded without first being put to a fair test. Usually this follows from the failure to really commit oneself to a choice. The indecisiveness that may have preceded the decision is carried over after the decision is put into effect.

Many marriages fail because one of the partners withdraws at the first sign of difficulty. No matter how good a decision is, it must be implemented by positive action. It would be difficult to think of *any* interpersonal relationship, or any job, wherein difficulties do not occasionally arise. These may sometimes make it advisable to modify a decision in order to make it more workable but will not usually require its complete abandonment. A general who commits his forces to a certain battle area may modify his plan of attack according to how circumstances develop, but while there is a reasonable chance for success he will not cut and run.

Maintaining a reserve of resources. Rarely is it advisable to throw all caution to the winds and venture everything on any one decision. " 'Tis the part of a wise man," said Cervantes, " to keep himself today for tomorrow, and not venture all his eggs in one basket." Conservation of resources is necessary if, in the event of failure, one is to be assured of a second chance.

Second chances sometimes are no more than the opportunity to make a first decision finally work by calling on available reserves. A man who begins his business on a small, experimental basis may not become a millionaire overnight, but neither will he become bankrupt. He is more likely to spot trouble in certain areas of operation and make changes that will put his business on a more solid foundation; or if the first venture fails, he will not be left entirely without resources. Similarly, the young man or woman who does not summarily abandon his education when love beckons, but either postpones marriage or works out an arrangement for combining it with further schooling, is maintaining reserves that considerably reduce the risk of failure. Even the all-

out emotional expenditure demanded in a relationship like marriage should be backed up with reserves in the form of developing one's interests and potentialities as an individual.

Developing clear-cut values as guides. Much indecision, vascillation, and cognitive strain result from a lack of clear-cut values to guide us in making our choices. Values not only indicate the direction of choice but, as May has noted (1953, pp. 217-218), provide the sense of conviction which enables us to implement our decisions with an investment of self:

"Ethical judgment and decision must be rooted in the individual's own power to evaluate. Only as he himself affirms, on all levels of himself, a way of acting as part of the way he sees reality and chooses to relate to it—only thus will the value have effectiveness and cogency for his own living. For this obviously is the only way he can or will take responsibility for his action. And it is the only way that he will *learn* from his action how better to act next time, for when we act by rote or rule we close our eyes to the nuances, the new possibilities, the unique ways in which every situation is different from every other. Furthermore, it is only as the person chooses the action, affirms the goal in his own awareness, that his action will have conviction and power, for only then will he really believe in what he is doing."

Since the solution of most problems permits a wide degree of choice, it is obvious that the person who has a clear sense of identity, well-defined goals, and an adequate system of values will have an easier time making decisions than the person who is not sure who he is, where he is heading, or what is really important to him. The alternative to being guided by one's own values is to rely upon the advice and values of others. The person who follows the latter course often finds himself making decisions which are inconsistent not only with each other but with his concept of self.

Ultimately, of course, the validity of an individual's values will determine the satisfactions he derives from following them. Often we must choose between a decision that promises material gain and one that favors self-expression and self-growth; or between a decision that promises immediate satisfaction and one that will further our long-range purposes and perhaps yield greater satisfactions at a later date; or between a decision that will bring personal gain and one that will help others. Usually we must try to maintain some kind of balance between these extremes. Whatever the nature of our decisions, the important thing is that they be our *own* and consistent with the values in which we believe. This idea was given eloquent expression by former secretary of state Dean Acheson (1950) in a statement in which he explained his reasons for having taken a severely criticized stand on one of the "hot" issues of the day:

"The safe course is to avoid situations which are disagreeable and dangerous. Such a course might get one by the issue of the moment, but it has bitter and evil consequences. In the long days and years which stretch beyond that moment of decision one must live with one's self; and the consequences of living with a decision which one knows has sprung from timidity and cowardice go to the roots of one's life."

Minimizing the Effects of Faulty Decisions

A certain percentage of decisions must be expected to go wrong because of human limitations and chance factors which cannot be controlled. When an individual experiences failure, he usually finds it of value to examine the possible reasons *why* he has failed, so that he does not keep making the same mistake over and over again. The tendency to deny that a mistake has been made, or to rationalize mistakes by decrying unfavorable circumstances or to project blame for them onto other people is a major stumbling block to the development of increased competence in making choices. The reason why so many second marriages fail is that one or both partners are "repeaters" who have never realistically analyzed the mistakes made in a first marriage.

Often it is possible to salvage a good deal from a faulty decision. If, after three or four years of premedical training, a young man decides that his choice of a medical career was a mistake, he may still, after careful investigation and reliable vocational counseling, be able to use his education to good advantage in a profession not completely alien to medicine —perhaps as a biologist, a laboratory technician, or a veterinarian. After the failure of a marriage, professional help is often valuable in helping everyone concerned make the best of the changed situation, especially if children are involved. With a business failure, nothing may be left except a backlog of good will and a very small financial reserve with which to build again, but the good will alone is of inestimable value in any new venture. Most of us have far more inner strength in dealing with failures and disasters than we realize, and although we may be momentarily damaged, we can usually rally our hopes and resources for a new assault on our goals.

CREATIVE THINKING

Creative thinking—thinking which produces new methods, new concepts, new understandings, new inventions, new works of art —is at the very root of human progress. The history of civilization is the history of man's creative triumphs, from his use of fire to his investigations of outer space.

In a general sense, all problem solving is creative; each problem is unique in certain respects, and each solution requires the integration of ideas into new and meaningful patterns. On another level, creativity may manifest itself in the speculations of the philosopher and the hypotheses of the scientist; on still another, in the works of the painter, the sculptor, the composer, the novelist, and the poet. Then, too, on the everyday level, there is the creative thinking that changes one's own personality. It can produce insights into some phase of oneself or one's world which one has not seen before—insights which may drastically alter one's assumptions, motives, and ways of behaving. In every case and at every level, creativity brings into existence something that is new.

Because psychologists know relatively little about that level of special talent we call genius, Maslow (1959) makes a distinction between "special talent creativeness" and "self-actualizing creativeness." In the latter sense, creativity becomes a general characteristic of normal human functioning. This agrees with Rogers' thesis (1959, p. 72) that the urge to create is an inborn tendency in man:

"The mainspring of creativity appears to be the same tendency which we discover so deeply as the curative force in psychotherapy— *man's tendency to actualize himself, to become his potentialities.* By this I mean the directional trend which is evident in all organic and human life—the urge to expand, extend, develop, mature—the tendency to express and activate all the capacities of the organism, to the extent that such activation enhances the organism or the self. This tendency may become deeply buried under layer after layer of encrusted psychological defenses; it may be hidden behind elaborate façades which deny its existence; it is my belief however, based on my experience, that it exists in every individual and awaits only the proper conditions to be released and expressed."

The Process of Creativity

In recent years psychologists have become increasingly interested in trying to identify the factors involved in the creative process and the personality traits that facilitate or hamper creative thought. What is involved in the creation of something new—whether an object or an idea? And why does one person become a highly original and productive thinker when another, with similar intelligence and other resources, seems only able to follow the lead of other people?

Relation of creativity to higher mental processes. Despite the importance of creative thinking, there is little scientific evidence to explain just what cognitive processes are actually involved; but in dealing with complex problems, these five steps ordinarily seem to occur:

1. Orientation—pointing up the problem.

2. Preparation—saturation of the mind with all available data.

3. Incubation—a rest period for the thinker, in which the problem is not worked on consciously, though presumably it continues to be attacked by the thinker's mental processes, even during sleep.

4. Illumination—the point at which the solution occurs to the thinker.

5. Verification—the critical and often scientific evaluation of the solution.

As these steps indicate, the creative process involves a great deal of hard work. Even though a moment of inspiration, or illumination, can occur, it is usually the final integration of elements and details that have been painstakingly assembled. A lifetime of study may prepare the way for the "sudden" flash of insight. "No great thing," said the philosopher

Epictetus, "is created suddenly, any more than a bunch of grapes or a fig."

Aside from its problem-solving aspects, we actually know very little about creativity. The processes involved in creating poetry, art, and music often defy description, although the compulsion to create and the satisfaction achieved through creation have been described by many artists.

Relation of creativity to personality traits. Another way of viewing creativity is in relation to the personality traits of the individual—in terms of motivational, attitudinal, and other determinants without which the creative act could not have occurred. Various investigators have emphasized different traits in this connection. Basic requirements listed by Rivlin (1959) in a study involving high school students are:

1. Above average intelligence.
2. Skill in a particular area (called "talent," "technique," or "technical ability").
3. Training and/or experience in the area in which there is skill.
4. An opportunity to utilize or actualize 1, 2, and 3.
5. The personality characteristics that facilitate the functioning of 1 through 4.

Other traits that have been mentioned as essential to the creative person include flexibility in thinking, openness to new experience, courage, faith, enthusiasm, self-assertiveness, esthetic sensitivity, originality, and honesty. Curiously enough, Roe (1953)—after studying a number of leading artists and scientists in several fields—found only one trait that was shared by all: the willingness to work long and hard. Of course she assumed a basic minimum of intelligence, ability, and other traits essential to their particular area of creativity.

It has long been popular to think of creative genius as being closely related to personality maladjustment and mental illness. Indeed, history is replete with the names of highly creative persons—Van Gogh, Wagner, Poe, and so on—who suffered from serious personality problems, and psychoanalytic theory has often identified creativity as a form of neuroticism. The consensus of most current investigators, however, as Anderson (1959, p. 248) has pointed out, is that:

". . . creativity is an expression of a mentally or psychologically healthy person, that creativity is associated with wholeness, unity, honesty, integrity, personal involvement, enthusiasm, high motivation, and action.

"There is also agreement that neurosis either accompanies or causes a degraded quality of one's creativity. For neurotic persons and persons with other forms of mental disease, such assumptions as the following are offered: that these persons are creative in spite of their disease; that they are producing below the achievements they would show without the disease; that they are on the downgrade, or that they are pseudo creative, that is, they may have brilliant original ideas, which, because of neurosis they do not consummate."

Perhaps a convenient way of distinguishing here between "special talent creativeness" and "self-actualizing creativeness" is by saying that the former may make itself apparent despite personality handicaps while the latter is based upon those characteristics that make for integration, wholeness, unity, and fulfillment as a human being.

Factors Facilitating Creativity

In discussing what facilitates creativity, it is again convenient to distinguish between "special talent creativity" and "self-actualizing creativity." The former obviously requires special skill, usually based on training and experience as well as inborn capacity. The latter depends much more on the psychological health and integration of the individual. And, of course, for any type of higher level creativity a minimum level of intelligence, information, and opportunity are essential. For our immediate purposes we shall assume that the individual has the intelligence or whatever other special skills are required for the creative product he is trying to create. Beyond this point there are a number of additional factors which appear to be of crucial importance in creativity. In examining these factors, we shall be concerned with what creative thinking accomplishes for the individual who is coping with personal problems as well as with the role of creative thinking in scientific or artistic accomplishments.

Openness to new experience. A number of investigators, including Rogers and Maslow, have emphasized the importance of being open to new experience. Such openness is the exact opposite of defensiveness, where new experiences that are incompatible with or threatening to the self-structure are prevented from entering consciousness or are permitted entrance only in a distorted form.

Openness to new experience implies a tolerance for conflict and ambiguity, a lack of rigid categories in thinking, a rejection of the notion that one has all the answers. It is, in a sense, a childlike quality, for the young child is a natural explorer and experimenter who embraces every new experience with open arms and an open mind and who constantly "creates" with thoughts, with words, with pencils and paints. It is only as people grow older that they become timid and conservative both in accepting new experiences and in reacting to them. By carefully conforming to all the customs and folkways of their society and placing security before curiosity, many adults cut themselves off from new experiences and new concepts—and thereby close the door on creativity.

Human progress has always depended most on those who refuse to be satisfied with the old ways of thinking and acting, those whose ideas break away from traditional patterns, those whose minds are endlessly receptive and flexible and active. This, of course, does not mean that all thinkers who break with traditional ways of viewing things or who are "dreamers" are creative and productive. However, most high-level creativity does involve new ways of seeing and doing things. What we mean in essence here is well described by Susanne Langer (1951, p. 8):

"The limits of thought are not so much set from outside, by the fulness or poverty of experiences that meet the mind, as from within, by the power of conception, the wealth of formulative notions with which the mind meets experiences. Most new discoveries are suddenly-seen things that were always there. A new idea is a light that illuminates presences which simply had no form for us before the light fell on them. We turn the light here, there, and everywhere, and the limits of thought recede before it."

Motivation and set. As we noted, Roe has emphasized the importance of motivation among creative thinkers in terms of their willingness to work hard and long. The dedication of great artists and scientists has sometimes caused them to lead lives of hermit-like isolation, sacrificing the comforts and companionships of ordinary existence in a single-minded drive toward a chosen goal. Although in many more cases powerful motivation has simply served to keep the creative thinker from straying off course, without forcing him to discard or damage healthy interpersonal relationships, the time often comes when he must choose between the safety and security of ordinary living and the danger and uncertainty of pioneering. Frequently, the creative way is the lonely, painful way; history offers many examples of men who paid for their creativity by suffering loneliness, misunderstanding, ridicule, poverty, even death. Thus the motivation of the creative thinker often must be strong enough to overcome fear. Creativity demands courage.

Besides motivation, a general mental attitude, or set, toward creativity—whether in terms of problem solving or self-expression—would also appear to be important. Guilford (1957), for example, refers to "evaluative abilities," one factor of which is a general sensitivity to problems—the ability to recognize that things are wrong or that they can be improved. Without such awareness, he points out, creative thinking would never get started. Along with this evaluative and critical mental set goes a questioning attitude, which has been described by Osborn (1953, pp. 228-229) as follows:

"The *question* technique has long been recognized as a way to induce imagination. . . . Imagination has to be guided by stabs such as 'What *about* . . . ?' and 'What *if* . . . ?' And always it must be prodded with 'What *else?*' and again 'What *else?*' By bombarding our imaginations with such queries we can pile up a quantity of ore in the form of all kinds of ideas —good, bad, and indifferent. Out of that ore, our own judgment, or the judgment of others, can refine gold in the form of good ideas."

This mental set seems to be a key factor in creative thinking as it applies to solving the everyday problems that most of us are concerned with. Solutions to problems often seem so obvious to us after we have arrived at them that we wonder how we could have missed recognizing them earlier. The answer is simple: most of us make too few attempts to get away from—or even to evaluate—the beaten track, the status quo, the traditional ways of thinking and acting.

Social stimulation. In discussing creativity, there is a natural tendency to concentrate on individuals—great artists, great writers, great inventors—and to ignore the importance of the social setting. Yet, as historians and sociologists point out, some periods and some societies have fostered creativity, while others

have inhibited it. In Renaissance Italy the time was ripe for a great artistic flowering; in the United States at the beginning of the twentieth century the inventions and innovations of men like Ford and Edison were welcomed with open arms. But in medieval Europe freedom of scientific investigation was restricted, and in modern totalitarian states innovations in art have been suppressed. In our own society we have been prone to encourage and support creativity that promises physical improvements in our daily living more than creativity that promises esthetic satisfactions. It is of interest to note also that in science, technology, and even business and government we have come to place increasing emphasis on the creative team, often at the expense of the creative individual who may not be suited to working in a "team" setting.

The creative thinker is probably more valuable today than ever before. On the national level we must produce our share of great integrative and creative thinkers if we are to hold our own among the other nations of the world. On the personal *and* the national level, we must think creatively if we are to meet successfully the complex problems of our times and achieve that sense of self-fulfillment that represents the realization of our potentialities as human beings.

In this chapter we have examined a number of valuable strategies for improving intellectual competence. We have also seen how the usefulness of these strategies is limited by the personality characteristics and maturity level of the individual who applies them. The improvement of problem-solving competence by application of the W-E-D approach, for example, presumes that the individual has adequate resources for solving the problem, that he feels secure enough to look at the facts objectively and maintain a task orientation, that he has defined his values and knows what goals he is heading for, and that he can tolerate a reasonable level of frustration without becoming defensive or discouraged.

Although we have discussed learning, problem solving, decision making, and creative thinking as involving special skills and procedures, there are certain general strategies which facilitate competence in all these areas. Among these are the building of interest and motivation, the maintenance of an active and inquiring mental set, and the habit of checking one's generalizations and looking for new ideas and relationships. The application of these and the other procedures we have discussed can go far to insure not only academic success but competence throughout life in building the know-how and know-why for effective living.

REFERENCES

The following list includes both the references cited in this chapter and a selected number of additional books and articles for outside reading.

Acheson, Dean. 1950. "Statement on Alger Hiss." *New York Herald Tribune*, March 1. Quoted in *The "Why" of Man's Experience* by Hadley Cantril, New York: The Macmillan Company, 1950.

Anderson, Harold H. 1959. "Creativity in Perspective." *Creativity and Its Cultivation.* Harold H. Anderson, ed. New York: Harper & Brothers.

Berrien, Frederick K. 1951. *Comments and Cases on Human Relations.* New York: Harper & Brothers.

Burton, William H., Roland B. Kimball, and Richard L. Wing. 1960. *Education for Effective Thinking.* New York: Appleton-Century-Crofts, Inc.

Cantril, Hadley, and Charles H. Bumstead. 1960. *Reflections on the Human Venture.* New York: New York University Press.

Combs, Arthur W. 1952. "Intelligence from a Perceptual Point of View." *The Journal of Abnormal and Social Psychology, 47,* 662-673.

Drevdahl, John E. 1956. "Factors of Importance for Creativity." *Journal of Clinical Psychology, 12,* 21-26.

Einstein, Albert, and Leopold Infeld. 1938. *The Evolution of Physics.* New York: Simon and Schuster.

Forgus, R. H., and R. J. Schwartz. 1957. "Efficient Retention and Transfer As Affected by Learning Method." *The Journal of Psychology, 43,* 135-139.

Garfinkel, Harold. 1960. "The Rational Properties of Scientific and Common Sense Activities." *Behavioral Science, 5,* No. 1, 72-83.

Guilford, J. P. 1934. *Laboratory Studies in Psychology.* New York: Henry Holt and Company.

Guilford, J. P. 1957. *A Revised Structure of Intellect.* Report of Psychological Laboratory, No. 19. Los Angeles: University of Southern California.

Hovland, C. I. 1951. "Human Learning and Retention." *Handbook of Experimental Psychology.* S. S. Stevens, ed. New York: John Wiley & Sons, Inc.

Johnson, Donald M. 1955. *The Psychology of Thought and Judgment.* New York: Harper & Brothers.

Langer, Susanne K. 1951. *Philosophy in a New Key.* Cambridge, Mass.: Harvard University Press.

Luchins, A. S. 1942. "Mechanization in Problem Solving: The Effect of Einstellung." *Psychological Monographs, 54,* No. 6, whole No. 248.

Lyon, D. O. 1914. "The Relation of Length of Material to Time Taken for Learning and the Optimum Distribution of Time." *Journal of Educational Psychology, 5,* 1-9, 85-91, 155-163.

Maltzman, Irving, Seymore Simon, David Raskin, and Leonard Licht. 1960. "Experimental Studies in the Training of Originality." *Psychological Monographs, 74,* No. 493, 1-23.

Maslow, Abraham H. 1959. "Creativity in Self-Actualizing People." *Creativity and Its Cultivation.* Harold H. Anderson, ed. New York: Harper & Brothers.

May, Rollo. 1953. *Man's Search for Himself.* New York: W. W. Norton & Company, Inc.

Miller, Neal E. 1944. "Experimental Studies of Conflict." *Personality and the Behavior Disorders.* Vol. I, J. McV. Hunt, ed. New York: The Ronald Press Company.

Mursell, James L. 1951. *Using Your Mind Effectively.* New York: McGraw-Hill Book Company, Inc.

Nichols, Ralph G., and L. A. Stevens. 1957. *Are You Listening?* New York: McGraw-Hill Book Company, Inc.

Osborn, Alex F. 1957. *Applied Imagination: Principles and Procedures of Creative Thinking.* Rev. ed. New York: Charles Scribner's Sons.

Phillips, E. Lakin. 1956. *Psychotherapy: A Modern Theory and Practice.* Englewood Cliffs, N.J.: Prentice-Hall, Inc.

Rivlin, Leanne Green. 1959. "Creativity and the Self-Attitudes and Sociability of High School Students." *Journal of Educational Psychology, 50,* No. 4, 147-152.

Roe, Anne. 1953. *The Making of a Scientist.* New York: Dodd, Mead & Company.

Rogers, Carl R. 1959. "Toward a Theory of Creativity." *Creativity and Its Cultivation.* Harold H. Anderson, ed. New York: Harper & Brothers.

Stein, Morris I., and Shirley J. Heinze. 1960. *Creativity and the Individual: Summaries of Selected Literature in Psychology and Psychiatry.* Glencoe, Ill.: The Free Press.

Vinacke, William E. 1952. *The Psychology of Thinking.* New York: McGraw-Hill Book Company, Inc.

PROFESSIONAL

RESOURCES

Personality Assessment

Counseling

Psychotherapy

There is today a tremendous range of resources available to the individual who needs help in solving his problems. He can go to a lawyer for legal advice, consult a medical doctor for physical ailments, have an architect assist him in designing his home, obtain the services of an interior decorator in planning the furnishings, and command the services of specialists in many other areas. And as modern psychology and psychiatry have come of age, people are increasingly turning to specialists in these areas for assistance with marital, occupational, educational, and other life problems.

Basically, psychological assistance for the individual may involve three key functions: personality assessment, counseling for life plans, and psychotherapy or treatment of personality difficulties. Whatever the reason the individual seeks the aid of a psychologist or psychiatrist, the initial step is usually that of personality assessment. This provides the information about the individual which is essential for helping him with most problems—whether the problem be a relatively simple one such as choosing the best kind of vocational training or a more complicated one such as serious personality maladjustment.

In the present chapter we will briefly consider the major methods of personality assessment and the more general counseling and therapy methods used in aiding the individual. Our primary purpose here is to gain some understanding of the nature and range of psychological assistance available for helping us to cope with life problems.

PERSONALITY ASSESSMENT

The entire process of personality assessment might be described as an attempt to identify the unique characteristics of the individual—the extent to which he possesses given traits and the unique patterning of these traits in his personality make-up. For example, in testing the individual's intelligence, we are concerned with the amount of this trait he possesses in comparison with other people. Thus his I.Q. may show him to be below average, average, or superior in intelligence. But usually we are not content to stop here; his intelligence level must be related to his interests, level of aspiration, and other traits—as well as his life situation—if we are to make an accurate assessment of its significance in his behavior.

The Purpose of Personality Assessment

The major goals of personality assessment are: (1) to ascertain personal resources, (2) to reveal typical modes of adjustment, and (3) to diagnose personality difficulties.

In assessing personal resources, the psychologist is mainly concerned with the individual's general intellectual level, special abilities, interests, and related traits. Thus to help the adolescent plan his education, it would be important to know his general level of intelligence, the areas of study he would find most interesting, and the fields his abilities would best fit him for.

In dealing with typical modes of adjustment, the psychologist is most interested in discovering the patterning of motives, abilities, and adjustive action. Such traits as extroversion-introversion and dominance-submission as well as the individual's ego-defensive patterns would also be of interest.

In diagnosing personality difficulties, the psychologist focuses attention on the individual's level of maturity, the assumptions, attitudes, and values which underlie his adjustive behavior, his level of competence in various areas, the conflicts and problems which may be causing trouble, and his general level of anxiety. Here, too, of course, the patterning of his ego defenses is of immediate relevance, particularly in relation to the various categories of abnormal behavior—for example, the extent to which the individual reveals psychosomatic, neurotic, or psychotic tendencies or action patterns.

While we may focus on a specific goal of the assessment process, it is usually essential to make a thoroughgoing evaluation of the individual for any of the three purposes indicated. Thus, while the psychologist may use the psychological assessment data for different purposes, he usually needs to include some assessment of resources, typical adjustive patterns, and any personality difficulties.

Requirements for Accurate Assessment

Before we undertake a review of various assessment procedures, we will find it worth while to consider the basic requirements of any useful assessment technique.

Validity. The first requirement of an assessment method is that it be *valid*. This simply means that the assessment device must measure what it says it measures. For example, an intelligence test must yield an accurate evaluation of the individual's level of intellectual ability—in terms of his ability to learn, the complexity of concepts he can handle, and so on. Some traits are much more difficult to measure than others, and with a trait such as honesty or courage, the problem of validity in psychological testing can be most difficult. It is hard to devise tests of honesty or courage in which high scores actually correlate well with honest or courageous behavior in real life.

Reliability. The second characteristic required of an assessment technique is that it be *reliable*. This means that the score the individual attains will not fluctuate markedly if he is

tested again. For example, if he attains a superior score on a reliable intelligence test, it can be assumed that he will attain a comparable score if he is retested at a later time. This, of course, assumes that the trait in question tends to remain constant over long periods of time. Barring brain damage, such constancy is true for many traits, such as intelligence, but other traits, such as anxiety level or stress tolerance, may fluctuate markedly, and here reliability becomes more difficult to demonstrate. However, psychologists have worked out reasonably satisfactory statistical techniques for demonstrating reliability.

Objectivity. The characteristics of validity and reliability imply that the assessment device is *objective*. This means that different psychologists using the same assessment method would arrive at approximately the same rating or score for the individual. On an intelligence test, objectivity is relatively easily attained. The individual either passes or fails certain items or tasks, and the examiner need only assign him a score in relation to his performance. In an interview type of assessment, however, it is often much more difficult to achieve this criterion of objectivity—interviewers may vary considerably in their ratings, depending upon the methods used—but a certain level of objectivity must be maintained if the assessment procedure is to be valid and reliable.

Standardization. A fourth requirement of an assessment technique is that it be *standardized*. In essence this means that the score an individual achieves for a certain trait should be capable of being compared with the scores which a large representative group have attained. For example, it is only because intelligence tests have been administered to large numbers of individuals that we can know whether a particular I.Q. is low, average, or high or ascribe a centile rank to an individual, indicating what percentage of the general population would be below him in intelligence and what percentage would be above him.

Methods of Assessment

In seeking to develop an integrated picture of the individual, psychologists use a wide range of assessment methods. For our purposes we may divide these various procedures into six general categories: (1) maximal performance tests, (2) rating scales, (3) inventories, (4) projective methods, (5) interview assessment, and (6) activity assessment. Some of these procedures are designed for use with a single individual, while others are group tests which allow many subjects to be measured at the same time. Some require the active cooperation and/or participation of the subject; others do not.

Before turning to a discussion of actual methods of assessment, we may also note that there are essentially three ways of viewing the personality traits of the individual. We may consider the traits as the individual himself sees them—as when we ask him to indicate whether a number of statements are true or false in regard to himself; we may consider his traits as others see them—as when we ask a friend or interviewer to rate him; or we may consider the traits in terms of his performance in actual test situations—as when we use intelligence tests where the individual's actual performance is the basis for assessing his intelligence. We shall see that modern methods of assessment cover all three of these approaches.

Maximal performance tests (speed and power tests). In general, a maximal performance test requires an individual to accomplish certain standard tasks. In an intelligence test this might be the solving of certain problems by reasoning, the defining of certain words, or the accurate identification of certain analogies. The main intent of this type of test is to demonstrate the full extent of the existence of a certain trait.

Maximal performance tests may be divided into two common types: those requiring speed and those requiring power. A speed test usu-

ally sets a time limit on the accomplishment of a particular task. In an intelligence test, for example, the individual may be required to figure out the key to a code within a certain number of seconds or be considered to have failed the item. Here we are concerned with efficiency and level of functioning in terms of time. The power test, on the other hand, measures the level of intellectual functioning in terms of ultimate achievement—in terms of the difficulty and complexity of problems the individual can solve if he is given all the time he needs.

Maximal performance tests are extensively used and, on the whole, highly accurate. However, these tests require the subject's cooperation if they are to provide an accurate assessment of various traits.

Rating scales. The rating scale is most often used when we are dealing with traits that are difficult to measure by performance on set tasks. Aggressiveness, honesty, and sympathy are examples of traits most easily measured by having the subject himself or those who know him well rate him on these qualities. A rating scale item for aggression might be as follows:

a) Not aggressive—tends to be passive

b) Moderately aggressive

c) Very aggressive—tries to dominate social situations

Some rating scales have as many as seven alternatives or ask the subject to check the appropriate point on a continuum.

Self-rating on a given trait, while it may be informative, is, of course, a very subjective evaluation; the subject may be influenced by whether he thinks a high or low rating on a given trait is good or bad. Thus an individual who considers being either passive or very aggressive as undesirable might tend to rate himself as moderately aggressive even though he actually is very aggressive. Of course, when other people do the rating, it is obvious that their impressions of the subject may also be in error, but since they are presumably less ego-involved, fewer defensive measures would be likely to influence the ratings. It may be of interest to note that the discrepancy between a subject's view of himself and the view others have of him gives us one measure of his self-knowledge. The less insight a subject has into himself, the more one would expect his score to deviate from those of the other raters.

Rating scales may also, of course, be used by trained interviewers for rating many traits such as poise, personal appearance, ability to grasp the essential features of problems, and so on. In general, a well-designed rating scale may reach a high level of validity and reliability, whether the rating is done by the subject, by someone who knows him well, or by a trained interviewer.

Inventories. An inventory is usually made up of a series of direct questions that a subject is required to answer about himself. It is widely used to measure traits relating to mode of adjustment, temperament, interest, attitudes and the like. The questions may range from very general questions concerning the presence or absence of certain traits (somewhat like the items on a rating scale) to very specific questions about likes and dislikes, worries, habits, preferences, interests, and so on. The subject is usually required simply to answer "yes" or "no" or "true" or "false" to the given question or statement, but some inventories include an intermediate category of "uncertain" or "cannot say." Examples of possible inventory items are:

I often feel as if things
were unreal.   Yes   No
I frequently have nightmares
which disturb my sleep.   Yes   No
When I am disappointed I
like to talk about my hurt
with someone else.   Yes   No

An inventory that has been carefully designed and whose results have been carefully examined statistically may be highly accurate in its appraisal of traits. Although a typical subject may not know himself well enough to respond accurately or may intentionally distort his answers and thus impose a certain limitation on the inventory, there are means of correction even for these deficiencies. For example, one commonly used inventory has three scales whose sole purpose is to give the examiner an indication of the test-taking attitudes of the subject. Thus, if the subject has been distorting his answers, this tendency shows up in a high score on one of the validity scales. In this way, inventories may be designed to detect faulty test-taking attitudes.

Projective tests. A projective test consists of an unstructured stimulus to which a subject is required to give meaning. For example, he may be shown an inkblot and asked to tell what he sees in it, or he may be shown a picture and asked to make up a story about it. In performing such tasks, the subject is forced to organize and interpret the ambiguous stimuli, thereby revealing a good deal about his conflicts, level of aspiration, cognitive patterns, defense mechanisms, and other aspects of his personality make-up. In this way, projective techniques emphasize the ways in which the subject's ego-structure tends to determine his interpretation of experience and the patterning of his adjustive actions. Because there are no definitely right or wrong answers, projective tests are difficult to fake and help to circumvent ego defenses which might otherwise bias test performance.

The degree of structuring of the material in projective tests may vary considerably. Thus the Rorschach inkblot test is relatively unstructured; in the Thematic Apperception Test, where the subject is shown a picture and asked to make up a story about it, the degree of structuring is somewhat greater; and in the Sentence Completion Test, where the subject is asked to complete a sentence such as "The thing I dislike most about people is . . . ," the test borders on the structured method of the inventory.

Projective tests are widely used by clinical psychologists in the diagnosis of personality disorders, but they have serious limitations such as the necessity of drawing all sorts of inferences about the subject's personality make-up from his test behavior. Accurate interpretation of the subject's responses requires a high degree of training and skill on the part of the examiner, and the meaning of a given response is not always readily apparent even to highly trained psychologists. In fact, experimental investigations concerning the validity and reliability of projective techniques indicate that these tests do not justify the confidence which many psychologists place in them. But refinements in projective techniques are continually being made, and they undoubtedly represent one valuable approach to personality assessment—particularly in tapping the unconscious levels of personality and studying the patterning of traits.

Interview assessment. The interview assessment technique is probably the oldest of the methods for making judgments about personality traits. For centuries men have assumed that they can "size up" another person by talking to him for a period of time.

The interview is usually defined as a face-to-face conversation between two people, conducted so that one person can obtain information from or evaluate the other. This description of the interview situation belies, however, the wide range and complexity of the interview process itself. For example, the interview may vary from a simple set of questions designed to gather certain information, to the stress interview designed to see how a given subject will function intellectually and emotionally in a difficult situation, to the technically complex therapeutic interview, which may involve both assessment and therapy. The interviewer may simply talk informally or may follow a standardized procedure.

While interview techniques are widely used and of undoubted value, their reliability and validity are often difficult to demonstrate. Error may be injected by the subject who is trying to make a good impression and is skillful at answering questions and putting up a good front. In other instances sources of error stem from the examiner himself. For example, a discrepancy of social class between interviewer and interviewee may change considerably the kind and extent of information that the interviewer obtains. Other difficulties may stem from the interviewer's biases, values, unconscious motivations, and limited range of experience. For example, the interviewer may tend to slant the interview in the direction of obtaining certain kinds of responses from the subject without even being aware of it, or the interviewee may respond in terms of what he thinks the interviewer wants to hear rather than in terms of what he actually feels or believes. Too, the assumptions and values of the interviewer are bound to affect his evaluation of the data he does obtain, biasing some of his inferences without his awareness.

While it can be readily seen that the interview has many disadvantages as a method of assessment, it is nevertheless a highly valuable technique in the hands of a skilled interviewer; and interviewing skills can be taught and improved upon through experience. In fact, in making many complex decisions about an individual's ability to function in certain types of situations, the interview often appears to be more reliable than psychological test data.

Activity assessment. The technique of activity assessment, or behavior sampling, may be used either when the trait in question is a type of ability involving physical coordination or when it is so complex that the underlying traits associated with it are unknown or impossible to measure by other assessment procedures. In such instances the examiner tries to duplicate as closely as possible the real situation in which this ability is expected to function. From the subject's behavior he then attempts to assess his ability. In activity assessment the psychologist does not accept either the subject's word or the word of those who know him but rather depends on the subject's actual performance in a real life situation or one that simulates life as closely as possible.

Three commonly used types of activity assessment are the time sampling method, the incident sampling method, and the controlled diary method. In the *time sampling method* the subject is observed in a real life situation at selected intervals. The extent of a subject's cooperativeness might be assessed from observing his actual behavior on the job several minutes a day over a period of several days or even weeks. In the *incident sampling method* the investigator either sets up a given situation or takes advantage of certain naturally occurring incidents to assess the individual on a given trait. For example, the individual may be placed in a situation designed to reveal his leadership abilities, or such abilities may be assessed by noting critical incidents in his relationships with fellow employees. In the *controlled diary method* the subject is required to keep a careful account of his own behavior, feelings, or thoughts in given situations over a period of time.

When activity assessment methods are practical, they have certain advantages over psychological tests and interview methods in that data are obtained in either actual life situations or close-to-life situations and thus do not simply reflect the opinion of the subject or interviewer. Considerable caution is necessary, however, in generalizing from the individual's behavior in one type of situation to his possible behavior in other situations. Thus an employee may demonstrate tact, patience, and understanding on the job and behave quite differently at home; similarly, the child may be very cooperative in the classroom in the presence of the teacher, while he may be quite disruptive in outside situations. Again we are faced with the complexity of trait organization and the necessity for carefully evaluating assessment data.

There are other assessment methods that do not seem to fit readily into these six categories. Among these is the evaluation of expressive behavior—as exemplified in handwriting, painting, or literary productions, including autobiographies. Such methods often represent valuable adjuncts to the assessment methods we have described, but in considering such methods, the problems of validity, reliability, and standardization must be reckoned with.

Integration of Assessment Data

As we have mentioned, the use of a single test score for prediction is highly risky, and, in general, assessment data are meaningful only when enough are available to provide an integrated picture of the individual. When we are using assessment data in connection with problems of life adjustment—in marital counseling, occupational counseling, or psychotherapy—it is essential to consider not only the psychological assessment data but medical and sociological data as well. For example, in psychotherapy it is essential to rule out the possibility that organic conditions such as brain tumors, rather than a psychological disturbance, may be causing symptoms such as depression; and it may be highly relevant to understand the general nature of his life situation. In short, a total meaningful picture of the individual includes medical, psychological, and sociological data.

In discussing the integration of assessment data, we may review our discussion of trait variability in Chapter 3 (pp. 75-78). As we have noted, we have no absolute standard of measurement for assessing most traits, but rather assign the individual a *trait position* on the basis of how he compares with other individuals. We do not say that he has "x" quantity of a given trait but that he has more or less than such and such a percentage of individuals thus far tested. For example, we can say that the given individual is average, below average, or above average in intelligence—or we can be more precise and say that such and such a percentage of people fall below him in intelligence and such and such a percentage above. Thus he might rank at the 60th centile, indicating that 60 percent of the population fall below him in this trait and 40 percent above.

Certain other characteristics of traits, such as their *consistency* and *durability*, must also be considered in evaluating assessment data. Under conditions of emotional upset, fatigue, or deprivation, we can expect shifts in the degree to which normally consistent traits are manifested in behavior. Records show, for example, that in prisoner-of-war camps many men resorted to stealing, informing, and other practices which would have been abhorrent to them under normal conditions. Under these severe conditions the value of survival became prepotent over many other traits which would normally have been consistent characteristics of the individual's personality make-up. In considering trait consistency, then, we must expect fluctuations to arise with changes in mood, motivation, ego-involvement, stress, and other conditions under which a given test is administered. Even reliable psychological tests may yield different results from time to time due to fluctuation of specific traits in the individual's trait hierarchy.

With respect to trait durability, it is generally true that a person's basic trait structure is established some time before he reaches adulthood, but human beings can and do change in trait characteristics. Thus a confirmed sinner may reform; an individual may turn from honesty to dishonesty or vice versa; and traits

such as sympathy may become dulled by unfortunate experiences with others. However, certain traits such as intelligence tend to maintain their trait position throughout the individual's lifetime. The I.Q. is not likely to vary more than a few points from childhood to old age—barring brain damage, of course.

The *generality* of a given trait—the extent to which it is exhibited in the behavior of the individual—must also be considered in the evaluation of assessment data. Some traits, such as nervousness, self-control, and volatile temperament, seem to be quite general in nature. Other traits, such as honesty, shyness, and loyalty, may vary considerably from one situation to another. If we measure such a trait in only one or a limited number of situations, we may be wrong in assuming that the trait is usually characteristic of the individual.

As we have already emphasized, the extent to which a given trait determines the actual behavior of an individual depends upon the relationship of that trait to his total personality make-up or trait pattern. An individual may rate high in honesty, yet if he is an exceptionally ambitious individual, this ambition may override his honesty in situations that can be used to his own advantage. Thus, of two individuals who obtain the same score on honesty, one may be found to be honest in nearly every situation while another, faced with particular circumstances, may resort to any number of dishonest practices. From the measurement of a single trait, we cannot predict that the behavior of an individual with a given score will be similar to that of another individual obtaining the same score.

COUNSELING

Psychological counseling refers in general to assistance with problems such as educational, vocational, and marital planning and adjustment. Thus psychological counseling can be distinguished from psychotherapy, in which the primary objective is the overcoming of personality problems. Personality problems, however, may be of crucial importance in hindering educational, occupational, and marital adjustment, and the psychological counselor is sensitive to such problems even though he may not attempt the needed psychotherapy himself. Counseling differs from psychotherapy in one other respect: it usually requires only a limited number of contacts with the client, as contrasted with psychotherapy where there are usually numerous contacts over an extended period of time.

Counseling Goals and Procedures

In general, psychological counseling is directed toward one or more of the following objectives: (1) to assist the individual in gain-

MENTAL HEALTH IN AMERICA

In a recent nationwide survey (Gurin, Veroff, and Feld, 1960), trained interviewers questioned 2460 Americans about their mental health problems and how they handled them. The subjects were selected to be representative of the total population in such characteristics as age, sex, education, income, occupation, and place of residence. Among the findings from this study were the following:

Severe Emotional Crises

Asked if he had ever felt he was going to have a nervous breakdown, one out of five people interviewed replied "Yes."

—Of these, nearly half had consulted a professional source of help.

—Among those who had experienced an emotional crisis of this magnitude, the largest group (about 40 percent) blamed it on something external to themselves, the most frequently mentioned reason being a death, illness, or separation involving a loved one. Another large group (about 20 percent) mentioned as the reason a physical illness of their own.

Serious Problems

Asked if he had ever had a problem in which professional help would have been useful, nearly one in four interviewees replied "Yes."

—One out of seven said he had actually sought help of some kind for past problems.

—Among those who sought help, the problems most frequently mentioned were those centering around marriage (42 percent), personal adjustment difficulties (18 percent), and children (12 percent).

—Among those who sought help, 42 percent consulted clergymen, 29 percent physicians in general, 18 percent psychiatrists or psychologists, and 10 percent social agencies or marriage clinics. People who saw their problems as

ing a more realistic picture of himself—particularly in relation to his assets and liabilities, interests, values, modes of adjustment, and related personality traits; (2) to assist the individual in achieving a better understanding of the problem with which he is trying to cope—for example, by supplying information, by posing the problem from different points of view, and by delineating the key dimensions of

the problem; and (3) to assist the individual in working out an effective solution to his problem—a solution which the client can put into effective operation.

In working toward these objectives, the psychological counselor may use a variety of specialized techniques in addition to the assessment procedures which we have delineated. One of his first steps is to establish rapport

---

stemming from personal defects were the ones most likely to consult a psychiatrist.

—Among those who sought help, 58 percent stated unequivocally that they had been helped; 14 percent said they had received help, but with qualifications; about 20 percent said they had not been helped.

Day-to-Day Problems

Subjects were also asked how they handled their day-to-day worries and periods of unhappiness—problems *not* ordinarily seen as requiring professional assistance. Many people reported that they simply let the situation run its course (for worries, 34 percent; for periods of unhappiness, 23 percent). Others used prayer (worries, 16 percent; unhappiness, 33 percent), tried to do something about the problem on their own (worries, 14 percent; unhappiness, 6 percent), or turned to formal or informal sources of help (worries, 28 percent; unhappiness, 22 percent). Those seeking help utilized the following resources:

	Day-to-day worries	Periods of unhappiness
Sources of Help		
Informal		
Spouse	56	17
Parents	4	9
Children	3	4
Other family	8	16
Friends	12	31
Other acquaintances	4	3
Formal		
Clergyman	4	5
Doctor	3	3
Mental health specialist	1	1
Not ascertained	5	11

with his client. *Rapport* refers to the feelings of trust, confidence, respect, and understanding which make it possible for the client to confide completely in the counselor. In other words, the client must feel free to react honestly to the assessment procedures which may be used and to discuss his problem as he sees it without reservation. Once rapport has been established, counseling may follow either of two general directions—*directive* or *nondirective*.

Directive counseling. In directive counseling the counselor takes the attitude of the authority who is in a position to give the client direct advice. In essence he tells the client what he considers the best solution to his problem.

This procedure is often criticized by counselors who use a nondirective approach. They insist that instead of helping the client to organize his own resources and teaching him to make his own decisions, the directive method tends to reduce his sense of responsibility and of adequacy in dealing with his problems; with the directive method, these critics feel, a type of father-son relationship is established in which the counselor assumes the role of a highly authoritarian father. Such objections, however, do not necessarily invalidate a directive approach for certain types of problems. For example, a directive approach would often appear indicated when the client's chief need is for information or reassurance or when lack of time dictates an immediate decision and the client is too immature or emotionally upset to get over this particular hurdle on his own. In the latter case, however, once the emergency is past, the counselor might encourage the client to take more responsibility for his decisions or obtain psychotherapy to overcome deep-seated personality problems.

Nondirective counseling. In nondirective counseling the counselor places the primary responsibility on the client for working out a solution to his own problems. The counselor largely restricts himself to supplying information the client may need—concerning job op-

portunities and the availability of certain kinds of training, for example, or the results of tests as to the client's own interests, values, and abilities. He then further helps the client clarify his thinking about himself in relation to the problem—helping him to see the key dimensions of the total situation in which he finds himself. The nondirective counselor tries to avoid suggesting decisions and solutions so that the final responsibility for the outcome of the counseling rests on the client himself. This type of therapy utilizes the resources of the client to the fullest possible extent and insures that the counseling experience will be a growth experience for him in terms of solving his own problems and making his own decisions.

In actual practice, of course, few counselors are entirely directive or nondirective. For example, the nondirective counselor may give the client reassurance in regard to his ability to solve the problem, may supply information concerning assessment data or life problems, and so on; similarly, the directive counselor may encourage the client to utilize his own resources in thinking through the problem, in exploring various ways of coping with it, in selecting the solution which seems most appropriate, and in putting this solution into operation and taking the responsibility for the outcome. In general, it would appear that the most effective counselor, regardless of his general orientation, is the one who utilizes the client's resources to the fullest extent and makes every effort to insure that the counseling will be a growth experience for him, helping him to become more competent and self-reliant in the future.

Common Counseling Problems

In their efforts to help people make the most of their potentialities, counselors work with many types of problems. Many counselors work in schools or colleges and are particularly concerned with helping students to gain a better view of their personality assets and liabilities, to see the value of the right education in their vocational and life planning, and to deal with current problems of adjustment. Other counselors work in rehabilitation agencies and hospitals and are primarily concerned with helping persons with physical, mental, or emotional handicaps to make vocational adjustments. Still another group of counselors work in industrial settings, assisting with such problems as the development of managerial talent and the placement of employees to the best advantage and with the various personal problems of the employees. Finally, there are some counselors primarily concerned with marital planning and adjustment.

Educational and vocational planning. In educational and vocational planning, counseling is directed chiefly at helping the individual gain a better understanding of himself in relation to the educational and vocational opportunities available to him—to assist him in choosing the career best suited to his abilities and interests. Since vocational choice is one of the most important decisions the individual will ever make, such counseling can be of great value to him. All too often, however, educational and vocational choice is made on the basis of the individual's limited experience or in terms of his parents' aspirations and pressures. In such cases, of course, adequate information concerning his interests and abilities and the complex and rapidly changing occupational picture is usually lacking—particularly in terms of long-range occupational trends. Often, too, a career is chosen for its glamor or the amount of money the individual thinks he can make rather than for the opportunities it provides for the individual to develop his interests and potentialities.

The values and purposes of vocational counseling are summarized by Hahn and MacLean (1950, pp. 43-44), who point out that the student's difficulties in planning on his own often stem from:

". . . his failure to understand himself in relation to the socio-economic world in which he lives and will live. Parents, radio, movies, advertising, and magazine romances have often filled his head with fantasies about himself, the world of work, and the world of school and college. Our task is to make available to him counselors who can help with self-evaluation, strip away his illusions and replace them with the realities concerning his measured personal assets and liabilities; show him how these may be adapted to ready him for a personally satisfying and socially useful job; inform him as to the range and kind of vocations in which he might find his optimum employment and as to the rewards and hazards of these; and, when his choice is made, indicate the school and college curriculums which will best make him ready."

Perhaps we should add here the caution that experimental evidence does not demonstrate the infallibility of educational and vocational counseling. But although it is not infallible in helping the student find the field most suited to him, it can provide him with the basic information necessary for making his final choices.

Marital planning and adjustment. Marriage is another crucial decision which most young people face—crucial in that it can promote the happiness and growth of each partner or lead to frustration and disillusionment. And here again we often find the decision based upon unrealistic and irrational considerations. For example, couples may lack an understanding of the real motives that prod them into getting married—such as wanting to lean upon someone, to avoid loneliness, to get away from living with parents, or because all their friends are getting married and it seems the appropriate thing to do. Often, too, couples confuse infatuation with love or get married with the mental reservation that if it doesn't work out they can divorce and remarry. Because of the complexity of factors that determine marital happiness and because the counselor is dealing with two people in interaction rather than with a single individual, marital counselors can predict no more than the *probability* of success for a particular marriage. They perform a very valuable function, nevertheless, by providing individuals who are planning marriage with information about themselves, about the types of problems and conflicts they are likely to encounter in their particular marriage, and about the importance of such factors as common interests and values and an attitude of determination to make the marriage a success.

Post-marital counseling can also be of great help in improving the happiness of marriages and in saving marriages that are failing—providing, of course, that both partners really want to make a success of it. Marital counseling is particularly indicated when the couple have reached the point where communication is beginning to break down and they are no longer able to cope with their problems or arrive at workable compromises by themselves.

The function of the counselor here is to help the marriage partners express their feelings about their problems and understand the real sources of trouble. Often couples diagnose their marital difficulties incorrectly and can only be helped to see them objectively and unemotionally with the assistance of a trained counselor. When the problems have been clarified, the counselor can also help the couple to work out appropriate solutions for them. When, as often happens, only one of the individuals concerned really wants to make the marriage a success, it is unlikely that the counselor can do very much except clarify the situation for the person who desires help and perhaps give him emotional support during the marital break, if it comes about.

It should be emphasized once more that modern approaches to counseling do not force the values of the counselor on the client; rather, the client is helped to understand himself and his problems more clearly, so that the way is paved for *his* making choices that will prove desirable.

PSYCHOTHERAPY

As we have noted, psychotherapy deals in general with the treatment of personality difficulties. At the present time there are many who practice psychotherapy—medically trained psychiatrists and psychoanalysts, clinical psychologists, and psychiatric social workers, as well as various charlatans who merely call themselves psychologists or psychotherapists. The chart on page 409 summarizes the training of qualified personnel in this field. Needless to say, it is important when seeking help with personality and adjustment problems that the individual go only to a qualified psychotherapist, for psychotherapy is an exceptionally complex process and requires the highest degree of skill and responsibility.

Goals of Psychotherapy

No matter what techniques are used, the basic objective of all psychotherapy is to improve the individual's patterns of coping with life demands. Implicit goals in this general objective are: (1) increased understanding and acceptance of reality in relation to the self and the environment—that is, a more realistic frame of reference; (2) the development of more effective techniques and competencies for coping with problems; and (3) personality growth toward maturity and toward self-actualization.

Specific goals in therapy may vary considerably from one patient to another—depend-

PERSONNEL IN PSYCHOTHERAPY

	Professional Requirements	*Legal Requirements*	*Type of Therapy*
Psychiatrist	M.D. degree plus specialized training in mental hospitals or clinics	Must have an M.D. degree	Uses physical therapy (drugs, surgery, shock, etc.) and/or psychotherapy
Neurologist	M.D. degree plus specialized training in treating disorders of the brain and nervous system	Must have an M.D. degree	Specializes in treatment of organic psychoses by physical methods of therapy
Clinical or Counseling Psychologist	Ph.D. in psychology plus internship training in psychological assessment, counseling, and psychotherapy	No legal qualifications in most states	Administers and interprets psychological tests and/or practices psychotherapy
Psychoanalyst	M.D. degree plus extensive training in theory and practice of psychoanalysis	Status and training not yet defined by law	Practices an intensive system of psychotherapy based to a greater or lesser extent upon Freudian theory
Psychiatric Social Worker	M.A. in social work plus supervised experience in outpatient clinics or social service agencies	Status and training not yet defined by law	Works mainly with social aspects of patient's problem and sometimes counsels other members of family
Psychiatric Team	In both clinics and mental hospitals a psychiatrist, clinical psychologist, and psychiatric social worker often work together in gathering medical, psychological, and sociological information about the patient and planning a coordinated program of treatment. In mental hospitals the team may also include a specially trained psychiatric nurse.		

ing upon his resources, the time he has available for therapy, his immediate needs, the severity of his adjustment problems, and related considerations. For one patient the goals may be very limited; for another they may be quite comprehensive and involve major personality changes. In some instances the goals are primarily supportive—the aim is to help the patient cope with his immediate problems by strengthening his existing adjustive patterns. In other instances the therapy goals may be little concerned with the immediate or day-to-day problems of the patient but be focused on long-range changes in personality and the achievement of deep self-understanding.

The psychotherapist may have to work within certain severe limitations. For one thing, he cannot suddenly undo the entire past history and present life situation of the patient, nor can he expect major personality changes to be made except over a long period of time. Too, rigidities and other personality traits of the patient may severely limit the possible goals of therapy; or the patient's life situation may be so unfavorable that he operates under a continual load of anxiety and discouragement, making it almost impossible for him to profit from anything but the most superficial form of supportive therapy. Indeed, in some cases psychotherapy has little chance of success, and in others minor improvements are all that can be hoped for.

Some Key Factors in Psychotherapy

In discussing some of the key factors which determine the goals, course, and outcome of psychotherapy, we should emphasize that all psychotherapy depends upon the patient's inner tendencies toward psychological integration and health—just as the practice of physical medicine depends upon the patient's inner tendencies toward biological integration and health. Without these basic assets of the patient, neither the physician nor the psychotherapist could hope that treatment would be very successful.

The patient. Obviously one important determinant of the course and outcome of therapy is the patient himself—and his reason for seeking therapy. Usually an individual obtains psychotherapy when he is anxious and uncomfortable or dissatisfied with his behavior. Here the patient who comes to a psychotherapist is much like the patient who goes to see a dentist because he has a toothache—and in both instances the patient usually puts off the visit as long as possible or until his discomfort becomes intense enough to force him to take action. In some instances the patient is forced to seek psychotherapy by relatives, court action, or other outside agencies. Therapy may still be successful in such cases if the patient realizes he needs it—but if he comes only under pressure, there is usually little that can be done for him. In short, the patient's motivation for seeking therapy is a very important consideration in his ability to profit from it.

The psychotherapeutic process is also influenced by the patient's resources. If he is seriously handicapped by immaturities, rigidities, and defensive patterns, the therapy is likely to take longer and to be more limited in its objectives; on the other hand, if the patient has a realistic frame of reference and relatively good intellectual and other competencies, the goals of psychotherapy may be more ambitious and achieved in a relatively short-range period—particularly if the patient is strongly motivated to change and improve his mode of adjustment.

And as we have noted, the life situation of the patient is often an important factor in determining the success or failure of therapy. The prognosis is much more favorable, of course, when it is in the patient's power to improve his life situation, but unfortunately this is not always possible. Disturbed children, for example, may be the helpless victims of a home environment which continually generates tension and anxiety. In such cases the focus of treatment may be on modifying the home situation rather than the child—that is, on creating an environment conducive to successful adjustment rather than maladjustment. With problems stemming from a marital relationship, too, it is often necessary to treat both husband and wife if psychotherapy is to have a good chance of success.

The therapeutic relationship. Many psychotherapists consider the relationship established between the patient and the therapist to be the most important factor in the entire therapeutic experience—particularly when therapy continues over an extended period of time. Especially important in the therapeutic relationship between patient and therapist are the following:

1. Acceptance. The patient needs to feel that he is accepted by the therapist as a person of worth and value. This is extremely important in psychotherapy, since the patient is usually harassed by inner conflicts and fears which tend to self-devaluation. An attitude of "positive regard" by the therapist enables the patient to feel comfortable, to relax his defenses, and to communicate freely with the therapist about his problems.

2. Permissiveness. In order for the patient to relieve his emotional tensions and come to grips with his problems, he must feel free to bring up any thought or feeling that he wishes. If the therapist appears shocked at what the patient says, if he criticizes the patient, or if he appears to be taking a judgmental attitude, the patient will hesitate to discuss the basic feelings and conflicts that may actually be at the root of his difficulties. For example, a homosexual patient might find it impossible to come to grips with his sexual problem if the psychotherapist seemed shocked by his discussion. Often patients bring up superficial problems during the early stages of therapy until they feel that they can trust the therapist and that

he will accept whatever it is that they must tell him.

3. Understanding. The patient needs to feel that the therapist understands him and what he is trying to communicate. This means that the therapist must be capable of seeing things from the patient's point of view. Implicit in understanding, too, is empathy—which means that the therapist is not only able to see the situation from the patient's frame of reference but to experience the feelings and emotional components of the situation *as if* he were the patient—without, however, losing his objectivity or identifying with the patient (Rogers, 1951).

4. Sheltered reality-testing. The therapeutic relationship must provide an environment in which the patient can safely explore his innermost feelings and thoughts and "try out" various ways of handling his problems before applying them to real life problems.

Other aspects of the patient-therapist relationship will be discussed in our description of the various methods of psychotherapy.

Emotional release and learning. Once the patient has developed rapport with the therapist and has learned that he can express himself without being criticized or condemned, he often gives way to an outpouring of long bottled-up emotions—his fears, hostilities, and anxieties. And as we have noted in our discussion of emotional competence, it is this ability to release pent-up emotional tensions—to get feelings out in the open where they can be seen for what they are and dealt with accordingly— that paves the way for understanding one's problems and taking a more constructive attitude toward them.

Although emotional release, or *catharsis*, is often an important first step, the entire psychotherapeutic procedure is basically a learning experience in which the patient gains new insights into his own behavior, achieves new ways of viewing his problems, and is helped to find better techniques for coping with them.

One might ask why, if psychotherapy is essentially a process of learning, it is not possible to achieve similar results by reading a book or taking a course. Actually, personality changes often can be achieved in these ways, but the individual who is in need of therapy is usually too emotionally involved and defensive to profit very much from such "objective" approaches. He tends to perceive his problems in inaccurate and distorted ways, often denying various aspects of his experience—homosexual impulses, for example, or hatred of his mother—which he finds particularly threatening to his feelings of adequacy and worth. Only in a therapeutic relationship, where he receives the unconditional support of the therapist, is the individual able to drop his ego defenses and face his problems in a task-oriented way.

Various specific learning concepts are applicable to psychotherapy. Thus many early traumas and weak spots may be worked through by means of "reconditioning" experiences. The main point, however, is that psychotherapy is not some mysterious force that changes the person but rather provides a learning situation in which the individual is able to acquire new ways of perceiving, new and more realistic assumptions for guiding his behavior, and new skills and techniques for handling his problems.

Theory, procedures, and values of the therapist. In much the same way that the resources, frame of reference, and other assets and liabilities of the patient influence the course and outcome of therapy, so also do the personality theory, techniques, and values of the therapist himself. Some therapists rely primarily upon such techniques as asking the patient questions, reflecting and clarifying his feelings and thoughts, and interpreting the meaning of his communications to him; other therapists heavily emphasize free association and dream analysis as the essential procedures for getting behind the patient's repressions

and resistances and coming to grips with his problems; and still other therapists, while using some of these techniques, also use hypnosis or sodium pentothal in their therapy interviews. Some therapists tend to be directive and others nondirective in their general approach to therapy. Often the theoretical orientation and techniques of the therapist will dictate the type of patient he will accept for treatment. If he feels that a particular individual is unlikely to respond to his method or approach, he will probably suggest that the individual seek the help of another therapist.

The value system of the therapist can also be an important consideration in the therapeutic process. (For a summary of some of the value orientations underlying various systems of psychotherapy, see the chart on page 413.) Although it is generally agreed that the therapist should not force his values on the patient, it is inevitable that his value system will have some influence upon the therapeutic process.

Types of Psychotherapy

There are a number of "schools" of psychotherapy, each somewhat different in terms of the personality theory on which it is based and the therapeutic procedures it utilizes. In the following pages we shall briefly describe five of these schools or types of psychotherapy: (1) client-centered therapy, (2) psychoanalysis, and neo-analytic therapies, (3) psychobiology, (4) relationship psychotherapy, and (5) group psychotherapy.

Client-centered therapy. Client-centered (or nondirective) psychotherapy has been developed largely by Carl Rogers. It is grounded on the theoretical assumptions that man has the capacity to be self-directing and to realize his inherent potentialities through rational thought processes, although certain stumbling blocks or irrational processes can enter in and lead to conflict, anxiety, and thwarted growth.

VALUE ORIENTATIONS UNDERLYING
VARIOUS SYSTEMS OF PSYCHOTHERAPY

Below are summarized four of the value orientations underlying current systems of psychotherapy (Lowe, 1959). Criticisms have been advanced against each of them—and many therapists, rather than adhering strictly to a given orientation, have tried to incorporate valid concepts from various approaches. Whatever the psychotherapist's value orientation, it is usually reflected in both the goals and procedures of treatment.

Naturalism

This view takes two important forms: (1) Tendency to view behavior in terms of bodily needs and processes—an orientation strongly entrenched in classical psychoanalytic theory with its emphasis on basic instinctual drives such as sex and aggression. (2) Logical positivism—the view that all concepts used in psychology must be subject to experimental validation and that science, by increasing man's understanding and control of himself and his world and by improving his well being and comfort, is the ultimate answer to his problems.

Culturalism

Emphasizes man's social nature and the importance of his "adjusting" to other people and to society. Two viewpoints are included here: (1) Notion that maladjustment stems basically from individual's isolation from other people and that ultimate goal of psychotherapy is to lead the individual back to others by improving his interpersonal skills and relationships. This represents the general orientation of relationship therapy. (2) Notion that psychotherapy should be directed toward helping the individual to "adjust" to the values of our democratic society.

Humanism

Human nature is seen as essentially rational and good, with man tending toward self-direction and self-actualization under favorable conditions. The goal of psychotherapy is to foster these natural tendencies by drawing on the patient's own inner resources for the solution of his problems. This value orientation is typical of client-centered and so-called eclectic therapists.

Theism

Emphasizes man's dependence on God and maintains that his problems have their ultimate solution in religious faith, which gives meaning to a person's existence and provides guides for coping with problems of human relations, marriage, family, work, and so on. Religious faith and love of God also give the individual the strength he needs for coping with fears, feelings of isolation, and inner weaknesses.

Rogers views these stumbling blocks as centering around an incongruence between the individual's self-concept and reality—in the sense that various feelings, thoughts, and events which threaten his feelings of adequacy and worth are screened from awareness or perceived and symbolized in distorted ways. This process of self-defense ultimately leads to a lack of integration or wholeness of the self and to maladjustment. The client becomes anxious, and his basic actualization tendencies are blocked.

For those who accept this theoretical position, the basic function of the therapist becomes one of providing a therapeutic situation in which the client can lower his self-defenses and look objectively at the conflicts that are bothering him. To achieve this, the therapist creates an atmosphere in which the client feels unconditionally accepted, understood, and valued as a person. In such a climate the client becomes increasingly free to express feelings and thoughts which have in the past been denied awareness or distorted in awareness— and his self-concept becomes reorganized to accept these experiences. As this reorganization of the self continues, his self-concept becomes increasingly congruent with his experience, now including experiences which previously would have been denied or distorted because they were too threatening. As the blocks to growth are removed, the client achieves integration and wholeness, and his natural tendencies toward actualization again assert themselves. Now he becomes more open to his experiences and less defensive, more self-accepting, and more effective as a self-directing person.

In the actual therapeutic process the primary responsibility rests upon the client, who can proceed in his own way and at his own rate. The therapist plays a relatively passive role, since he assumes that the patient is inherently able to solve his own problems. Approaching the client with as few preconceived notions as possible of what his problems may be or how they can be resolved, the therapist is essentially nondirective throughout the entire process of therapy. He works with the material presented by the client, repeating or reflecting —and sometimes clarifying—certain of the client's feelings and thoughts but even here confining himself as much as possible to the client's own words. The emphasis is at all times on utilizing to the maximum extent the client's own potentials for expressing, understanding, and resolving his conflicts.

As a consequence of considerable observation and research, Rogers concludes that client-centered psychotherapy follows an orderly and predictable sequence of development. The steps are as follows: (1) creation of the therapeutic relationship, (2) expression by the client of feelings and thoughts which had formerly been denied or distorted, (3) insight and increased self-understanding, (4) positive steps toward resolving his conflicts, and (5) termination of treatment. The latter step is again left to the client, who arrives at a point where he feels he no longer needs the support of the therapeutic relationship. The duration of therapy depends, of course, upon the resources of the client and the nature of his problem, but it is relatively short as compared, for example, with psychoanalysis, which may take several years.

Psychoanalysis. As developed by Sigmund Freud, psychoanalytic therapy has emphasized (1) the important role of irrational and unconscious processes in maladjustive behavior, (2) the origin of personality difficulties in early childhood experiences, and (3) the conflict between social prohibitions and the individual's basic instinctual drives such as sex and hostility.[1] Psychoanalysis is an intensive therapy which may last from one to several years. It is not unusual for the patient to see

[1]For a discussion of the personality theory upon which Freud based his method of therapy, see William Menninger's article on page 437.

the psychoanalyst for a fifty-minute therapy session several times each week.

During the initial phases of therapy the patient is taught the basic rule of saying everything that enters his mind—regardless of how trivial or embarrassing it may seem to him. This is the method of *free association*, whose purpose is to surmount the patient's defenses and bring repressed feelings and thoughts into consciousness. In the process of free associating, however, the patient usually continues for some time to repress certain feelings and thoughts which he finds too threatening to talk about even in the accepting atmosphere of therapy. The therapist helps the patient overcome these blocks, known as *resistances*, through the technique of *interpretation*. Initially, this may merely mean pointing out to the patient that he is still repressing something, but later in therapy the psychoanalyst is likely to make interpretations designed to help the patient bring the repressed material into the open and understand its significance. Another technique often used to help the patient understand himself is *dream analysis*—the assumption here being that dreams often have symbolic meanings that reveal much about the patient's unconscious desires and conflicts.

As the patient and therapist interact in the process of therapy, the relationship between them becomes complex and emotionally involved. Often the patient carries over and applies to the therapist attitudes stemming from his relations with people in his past. Thus he may view the therapist as a father figure and react to him accordingly. This phenomenon, known as *transference*, is basically irrational from the point of view of the realities of the situation. For example, the patient who reacts to the therapist as he did to his own father may carry over attitudes of dependency or fear of disapproval which are inappropriate when applied to the therapist. Once the transference is firmly established, an important part of psy-

choanalytic treatment is helping the patient to understand the irrational nature of his transference and its relevance to early experiences with some important person in his life. When the transference is handled in this way, the patient matures in his ability to deal with important figures in his present life situation—to see them more objectively without carrying over a residue of irrational attitudes from the past. For example, he may be able to relate to his wife as a person in her own right without continually comparing her with his mother and expecting her to behave toward him in comparable ways.

In general, psychoanalytic therapy is presumed to follow an orderly sequence not unlike that in client-centered therapy—beginning with the free expression of emotions, gradual achievement of insight and understanding, and the working through of conflicts by emotional re-education.

In concluding our brief description of psychoanalytic therapy, we may note that there have been a number of departures from classical psychoanalytic theory and practice. Notable are those of Carl Jung and Alfred Adler.

1. Jungian analysis. Feeling that Freud overstressed the role of sexual factors in motivation, Jung broke with his teacher in 1911. His own theory has emphasized the idea that personality development and structure involve a pattern of opposite traits and tendencies such as passivity versus aggressiveness and thoughts versus feelings. In the normal person these opposing tendencies are presumably integrated in such a way as to permit normal functioning and personality growth, while in the maladjusted person one particular pole has achieved pathological ascendancy. Therapy then is directed toward the restoration of balance. Jungian therapy is also notable for its emphasis upon the achievement of a religious or spiritual outlook to provide meaning and guidance in living. Probably the most controversial of Jung's ideas is the theory that man has a *col-*

TECHNIQUES IN PSYCHOTHERAPY

Free Association
Patient is directed to express every random thought and feeling; the free flow of associations leads to the gradual uncovering of repressed material and underlying conflicts. Typically the patient assumes a relaxed position, as on a couch, and the therapist remains to the side and rear so as not to intrude on patient's awareness.

Reflection
Therapist simply repeats part or all of patient's statement, usually in patient's own words but sometimes rephrased for clarification. Reflection may be used to: (1) help patient clarify his thoughts and feelings, (2) help patient consider what he has just said more objectively, (3) reassure patient that he is being understood, and (4) guide the interview by emphasizing key thoughts and feelings.

Associative Anamnesis
Therapist keeps patient focused on the core of his problem by repeating only certain key words of patient's statements or stressing these in a questioning tone of voice.

Questions
Therapist directs discussion along certain lines by asking patient to elaborate on a statement or by asking questions such as "How did you feel?" "What did you think?" "Tell me more about that."

Interpretation
Therapist analyzes what patient has said and suggests what it may mean or shows how it relates to other statements and actions of patient. Some therapists use little or no interpretation; others use it freely to help patient understand himself.

Dream Analysis
In the most common method of dream interpretation, the technique of free association is applied to the *manifest content* of a dream—the content as it appears to the dreamer—until gradually the *latent content*—the symbolic meaning—comes to light, revealing repressed desires, inner conflicts, and fears. Assumption is that ego defenses are lowered during sleep, permitting repressed material to gain symbolic expression.

Role Playing
Patient and therapist, or several patients together, act out each other's roles in a simulated conflict situation. Patient thus gets more objective view of his own reactions, can express emotions in a "safe" setting, and gets a better conception of problems and viewpoints of others. Patient also gains practice in developing better social skills.

Hypnosis
This is useful in some cases for identifying repressed material that is at root of patient's difficulties and for working through traumatic memories.

lective unconscious, a storehouse of inherited memories stemming from the long history of the human race. These common memories presumably account for similarities in the dreams and folklore of peoples from very different cultures.

2. Adlerian therapy. Adler's theory of personality emphasizes an active, creative self-structure that plays a central role in the individual's attempts to organize his experience and fulfill himself as a human being. It holds that a person's behavior is determined chiefly by his *life style*—the basic pattern of motives, attitudes, and habits that he has developed in keeping with his concept of himself. As an inherently social being, his deepest and most pervading need is to establish a place in relation to his social group, but his view of himself and his abilities determines the path he takes. Thus an active but insecure child may try to win his place by showing off, whereas a passive child who is convinced of his ineptness may learn to use his helplessness as a means of controlling the other members of the family.

According to Adlerian theory, all human beings early in life have some awareness of inferiority—everyone else is bigger and more able than they. Coping with life demands is largely a process of compensating for these feelings, with behavior aimed at establishing feelings of adequacy. Maladjustment and neurosis develop when the individual learns to choose personally or socially destructive means of compensation or to overcompensate, striving not for adequacy but for superiority over others. An "inferiority complex"—an Adlerian concept—enables the individual to avoid participation in an area where he does not want to run the risk of failing. He may use both physical and mental handicaps—real and imagined—in this way.

For the causes of present maladjustment, the therapist looks not to irrational instincts or early conflicts but to present goals and values. The individual's perceptions, attitudes, and actions are all viewed as supporting his present purposes, although he is not always aware of these purposes. Rationalization may convince him that he is always trying to help people out of altruism, whereas in therapy it may come out that he is really trying to demonstrate his superiority or keep people dependent on him. The Adlerian therapist draws on a variety of techniques including dream analysis, psychodrama, and group therapy; he takes an active, directive role in guiding the course of the interviews and in analyzing and interpreting the information that comes to light. Therapy is directed toward helping the individual to (1) understand his present life style—the goals which actually have been most important to him and the maladaptive behavior patterns he has been using to pursue them—and (2) develop the feelings of adequacy that will enable him to choose both more satisfying goals and more efficient means.

Psychobiology. As formulated by Adolf Meyer and his followers, psychobiology might be characterized as a well-organized eclectic system of therapy which emphasizes the interrelatedness of psychological and biological processes. On a psychological level, particular emphasis is placed upon detecting attitudes, values, and habits which are immature, defensive, or otherwise ineffective—and hence which contribute to frustration, anxiety, and lowered integration. Sociological factors are also evaluated so that the therapist can obtain as complete an understanding of the patient as possible. As the total dynamic picture emerges, the patient's problem is formulated in the simplest possible terms and a thorough program of treatment is worked out.

In the therapeutic process both the patient and the therapist take an active role. Responsibility is placed upon the patient for sincerely trying to make the most effective use of each session of psychotherapy and for following through on whatever decisions are made. The therapist himself is highly directive—both in helping the patient to see the nature of his problem and in working out a satisfactory solution. In general, he draws upon any and all psychotherapeutic techniques, using those which seem best suited to the requirements of the individual case. In addition, he may plan a program covering the patient's activities during most of the day—a program designed to help modify undesirable attitudes and habits. Throughout the therapy program, emphasis is placed upon helping the individual achieve a better synthesis of the various facets of his personality.

The personality theory underlying psychobiology has never been precisely formulated but is largely eclectic like the therapy itself. Its distinguishing feature is perhaps its great emphasis upon viewing the individual as a whole person—a psychobiological organism —functioning in a given life situation.

Relationship therapy. Relationship therapy has been heavily influenced by the thinking of Harry Stack Sullivan, who stressed the importance of disturbances in the patient's interpersonal relationships—in his dealings with parents, wife, family, and friends. The basic premise of therapy is that maladjustment stems from the patient's conflicts with and isolation from other people and his consequent feelings of loneliness, rejection, and worthlessness. Thus treatment is directed toward improving the patient's social competencies and leading him back to other people—toward helping him achieve satisfying relationships with others and adjust more effectively to his social environment. It is assumed that he can find "wholeness" and be an adequate person only by relating effectively to other people—particularly those of importance in his everyday living.

An important therapeutic tool in relationship therapy is *psychodrama*, as developed by J. L. Moreno. In psychodrama the patient is

encouraged to enact on a stage a life situation or experience relating to his difficulties. The particular situation utilized may be suggested by the patient or by the therapist. Immediately before the psychodrama session the situation is briefly outlined—for example, the patient's wife has told him that she is in love with someone else and is planning to leave him. This serves to set the dramatic situation, but from here on, the patient is on his own and enacts the scene spontaneously. Before the session starts, the role of the other person or persons in the situation may be given to a supporting cast called *auxiliary egos*—persons trained to play various roles and to facilitate interaction in the dramatic situation. In the process of enacting the situation, the patient may achieve a good deal of emotional release—perhaps expressing his fears, resentments, and feelings of devaluation—while at the same time he gains insight into the reactions of others and learns how to react spontaneously and effectively to the demands which arise in the course of the dramatic situation. The events taking place in the dramatic situation may be analyzed later in interview sessions with the director or therapist.

A less formal technique which has developed out of psychodrama is *role playing*. Here the patient may enact a particular role in the interview situation with the therapist; or, in group therapy, a situation may be chosen and different roles assigned to particular patients. In both psychodrama and role playing, the main focus of therapy is upon the patient's learning to see situations from the point of view of other people, to become more aware of his own stimulus value, and to become more flexible and skillful in his interpersonal relationships.

Group psychotherapy. A relatively new therapeutic approach which has had considerable success in dealing with certain kinds of problems is group psychotherapy. The therapist selects several patients—usually six to

SOURCES OF HELP AND INFORMATION

The following organizations may be helpful in suggesting sources of qualified psychotherapeutic help.

American Psychiatric Association
1700 18th Street, N.W.
Washington 9, D.C.
 (Will give the names and addresses of qualified local psychiatrists, if any.)

American Psychoanalytic Association
36 West 44th Street
New York 36, New York
 (Will give the names and addresses of qualified local psychoanalysts and psychoanalytic institutes, if any.)

Veterans Administration
Washington 25, D. C.

Division of Abnormal and Clinical Psychology
American Psychological Association
1333 16th Street, N.W.
Washington 27, D. C.
 (Will give the names and addresses of qualified local clinical psychologists, if any.)

Family Service Association of America
215 Fourth Avenue
New York 3, N.Y.
 (Will give the names and addresses of local psychiatric clinics, if any; will also make referrals to other community facilities such as qualified psychiatrists, psychologists, and child guidance clinics.)

The following organizations distribute free or low-cost literature on many aspects of mental health. Free publication lists are available.

The National Association for Mental Health, Inc.
10 Columbus Circle
New York 19, New York

National Institute of Mental Health
Bethesda 14, Maryland

American Association of Marriage Counselors
104 East 40th Street
New York 16, New York

Association for Family Living
32 West Randolph Street
Chicago 1, Illinois

National Council on Family Relations
1219 University Avenue, S.E.
Minneapolis 14, Minnesota

Child Study Association of America
9 East 89th Street
New York 28, New York

Children's Bureau
Washington 25, D.C.

National Council on Alcoholism
2 East 103rd Street
New York 29, New York

American Association on Mental Deficiency
20 North Street
Willimantic, Connecticut

National Association for Retarded Children
99 University Place
New York 3, New York

eight—who presumably can profit from working together on their problems. Ordinarily the individuals in such a group have similar educational and cultural backgrounds and are trying to cope with essentially similar problems. The group typically meets for about an hour and a half session from one to three times per week.

In guiding the process of therapy, the therapist usually focuses on the *interaction* taking place in the group, in terms of feelings and thoughts, rather than on the individual members. Most therapists who use this technique contend that the proper handling of the group creates a therapeutic atmosphere which enables each person involved to help both himself and others in exploring problems and arriving at tenable solutions. There are, of course, differences among group therapists in terms of both theory and practice. Some tend to be Freudian in their theoretical orientation and others eclectic; some tend to be highly directive in handling the group interaction and others nondirective.

In some respects, group therapy has a number of advantages over individual therapy. For one thing, it helps to remove feelings of isolation and of being different, since each participant soon discovers that other members of the group have similar problems and often more severe ones. In hearing others discuss their problems in an accepting group atmosphere, the individual loses some of his resistance to facing his own problems and talking about them. Too, in the process of this mutual sharing of problems, he is likely to achieve new insights and to see his difficulties in a broader perspective. Finally, the group situation provides an opportunity for "social reality-testing" and the improvement of interpersonal skills.

It should be noted, however, that some people feel more secure in individual therapy or have problems that cannot easily be resolved in a group setting. It has been found that groups not infrequently tend to focus on surface problems rather than coming to grips with the deeper conflicts of the patients involved. However, when the members of the group are properly selected and when the group interaction is directed by a skillful therapist, group therapy can be very successful.

In this chapter little attempt has been made to compare or evaluate the various approaches to psychotherapy. All of the methods here discussed have had a good degree of success, and as yet we lack sufficient knowledge to say definitely what method will be most effective for a given individual with a given type of problem. It should also be noted that many therapists who identify themselves with one or another of these systematic approaches are far from orthodox in either theory or practice but use whatever principles and procedures seem to work best for *them*. Finally, no formal therapeutic approach can make up for a lack of appropriate skills and human qualities in the therapist.

It should be apparent from even this brief discussion that there are many factors a person should consider in seeking psychotherapeutic help. Probably of greater importance than the theoretical orientation of the therapist is his ability to establish genuine rapport with the particular individual in question—for a good therapeutic relationship, as we have noted, is the cornerstone of *all* successful psychotherapy. Obviously practical matters such as time, cost, and the availability of psychotherapeutic assistance in a particular locale must also be taken into consideration. Most important, however, is the realization that professional resources *are* available for helping most people deal more effectively with problems of personal adjustment. By using those best suited to their particular needs, many more individuals could save themselves the high cost of muddling through.

REFERENCES

The following list includes both the references cited in this chapter and a selected number of additional books and articles for outside reading.

Adler, Alfred. 1956. *Individual Psychology of Alfred Adler.* Heinz L. Ansbacher and Rowena R. Ansbacher, eds. New York: Basic Books, Inc.

Adler, Kurt A., and Danica Deutsch, eds. 1959. *Essays in Individual Psychology: Contemporary Application of Alfred Adler's Theories.* New York: Grove Press, Inc.

Alexander, Franz, and others. 1946. *Psychoanalytic Therapy: Principles and Application.* New York: The Ronald Press Company.

Allen, Robert M. 1958. *Personality Assessment: Psychometric, Projective, and Other Approaches.* New York: Harper & Brothers.

Brammer, Lawrence M., and Everett L. Shostrom. 1960. *Therapeutic Psychology: Fundamentals of Counseling and Psychotherapy.* Englewood Cliffs, N. J.: Prentice-Hall, Inc.

Burton, Arthur A., ed. 1959. *Case Studies in Counseling and Psychotherapy.* Englewood Cliffs, N. J.: Prentice-Hall, Inc.

Cattell, Raymond Bernard. 1957. *Personality and Motivation Structure and Measurement.* Yonkers-on-Hudson, N. Y.: World Book Company.

Chance, Erika. 1959. *Families in Treatment.* New York: Basic Books, Inc.

Cronbach, Lee J. 1960. *Essentials of Psychological Testing.* 2nd ed. New York: Harper & Brothers.

Dorcus, Roy M., ed. 1956. *Hypnosis and Its Therapeutic Applications.* New York: McGraw-Hill Book Company, Inc.

Freud, Sigmund. 1949. *Collected Papers.* Vols. I-IV. London: The Hogarth Press.

Gorlow, Leon, and Walter Katkovsky, eds. 1959. *Readings in the Psychology of Adjustment.* New York: McGraw-Hill Book Company, Inc.

Guilford, J. P. 1959. *Personality.* New York: McGraw-Hill Book Company, Inc.

Gurin, Gerald, Joseph Veroff, and Sheila Feld. 1960. *Americans View Their Mental Health: A Nationwide Interview Survey.* New York: Basic Books, Inc.

Hadley, John M. 1958. *Clinical and Counseling Psychology.* New York: Alfred A. Knopf, Inc.

Hahn, Milton E., and Malcolm S. MacLean. 1950. *General Clinical Counseling in Educational Institutions.* New York: McGraw-Hill Book Company, Inc.

Hall, Calvin S., and Gardner Lindzey. 1957. *Theories of Personality.* New York: John Wiley & Sons, Inc.

Harper, Robert A. 1959. *Psychoanalysis and Psychotherapy.* Englewood Cliffs, N. J.: Prentice-Hall, Inc.

Ingham, Harrington V., and Leonore R. Love. 1954. *The Process of Psychotherapy.* New York: McGraw-Hill Book Company, Inc.

Jahoda, Marie. 1958. *Current Concepts of Positive Mental Health.* New York: Basic Books, Inc.

Jung, Carl G. 1939. *The Integration of the Personality*. New York: Farrar & Rinehart, Inc.

Lowe, C. Marshall. 1959. "Value Orientations—An Ethical Dilemma." *The American Psychologist, 14*, No. 11, 687-693.

Lynn, David B. 1959. "A Model Man for Applied Psychology." *The American Psychologist, 14*, No. 10, 630-632.

May, Rollo. 1957. "The Relation Between Psychotherapy and Religion." *Personal Problems and Psychological Frontiers*. Johnson E. Fairchild, ed. New York: Sheridan House.

May, Rollo, Ernest Angel, and Henri F. Ellenberger, eds. 1958. *Existence: A New Dimension in Psychiatry and Psychology*. New York: Basic Books, Inc.

Meyer, Adolf. 1948. *Commonsense Psychiatry*. Alfred Lief, ed. New York: McGraw-Hill Book Company, Inc.

Moustakas, Clark E. 1960. *Psychotherapy with Children: The Living Relationship*. New York: Harper & Brothers.

Moustakas, Clark E., ed. 1956. *The Self: Explorations in Personal Growth*. New York: Harper & Brothers.

Mowrer, O. Hobart. 1953. *Psychotherapy: Theory and Research*. New York: The Ronald Press Company.

Munroe, Ruth L. 1955. *Schools of Psychoanalytic Thought*. New York: The Dryden Press, Inc.

Patterson, C. H. 1959. *Counseling and Psychotherapy: Theory and Practice*. New York: Harper & Brothers.

Pervin, Lawrence A. 1960. "Existentialism, Psychology, and Psychotherapy." *American Psychologist, 15*, No. 5, 305-309.

Phillips, E. Lakin. 1957. *Psychotherapy*. Englewood Cliffs, N. J.: Prentice-Hall, Inc.

Rapaport, David. 1959. "The Structure of Psychoanalytic Theory: A Systematizing Attempt." *Psychology: A Study of a Science*. Vol. 3. Sigmund Koch, ed. New York: McGraw-Hill Book Company, Inc.

Rogers, Carl R. 1951. *Client-Centered Therapy*. Boston: Houghton Mifflin Company.

Rogers, Carl R. 1958. "A Process Conception of Psychotherapy." *The American Psychologist, 13*, No. 4, 142-149.

Rogers, Carl R. 1959. "A Theory of Therapy, Personality, and Interpersonal Relationships, As Developed in the Client-Centered Framework." *Psychology: A Study of a Science*. Vol 3. Sigmund Koch, ed. New York: McGraw-Hill Book Company, Inc.

Standal, Stanley W., and R. J. Corsini, eds. 1959. *Critical Incidents in Psychotherapy*. Englewood Cliffs, N. J.: Prentice-Hall, Inc.

Sullivan, Harry Stack. 1953. *The Interpersonal Theory of Psychiatry*. New York: W. W. Norton & Company, Inc.

Symonds, Percival M. 1956-1958. *Dynamics of Psychotherapy: The Psychology of Personality Change*. Vols. I-III. New York: W. W. Norton & Company, Inc.

Walker, Nigil. 1957. *A Short History of Psychotherapy in Theory and Practice*. London: Routledge & Kegan Paul, Ltd.

Watson, Goodwin. 1958. "Moral Issues in Psychotherapy." *The American Psychologist, 13*, No. 10, 574-576.

PART 4

EXPLORATIONS IN PERSONALITY AND BEHAVIOR THEORY

A Selection of Readings

Prepared by Dr. Alvin Marks

Los Angeles State College

INTRODUCTION

The student of any of the physical sciences usually must enter graduate study before getting his introduction to the unknown. But it is quite a different story for the student of psychology. With his very first course he becomes aware that he has arrived at the frontiers of his discipline. Its very newness is one reason why psychology is such a fascinating science.

Not too long ago such concepts as systems theory, cybernetics, self theory, game theory, and information theory (to mention only a few) were unheard of. Although many of these theories are in a very tentative state and may eventually be discounted in whole or part, they have already contributed substantially to psychology by giving us new ways of looking at human behavior. They represent the continuing search for new theories that will explain the known facts more adequately and suggest new avenues of research.

The serious student must know the theories of his discipline if he is to see it in perspective, because every science gets direction from its theorists. The following reading selections are intended to give the reader a capsule view of some of the major frontiers in personality and behavior theory. The selection of articles is purposely broad in order to indicate the breadth of research being done. The editor has also tried to provide enough variety that each reader will find something of special interest and be motivated to do more extensive reading in that particular area.

Because of their broad coverage, the following articles are not grouped formally, although their order follows roughly that of the text. Some selections, of course, relate to several chapters. The reader should keep in mind that many of the ideas he will encounter in the following pages are both speculative and controversial. He should consider them as tentative proposals and attempt to evaluate them critically.

THE GENERAL NATURE
OF THEORY CONSTRUCTION

by Melvin H. Marx[1]

Some apparently simple scientific questions can turn out to be very complex. For example, just what is a theory? Why are theories needed? How are they constructed? This article partially answers these questions and suggests some criteria for evaluating a scientific theory. Dr. Marx is Professor of Psychology at the University of Missouri.

Introduction

Direct empirical measurement is generally agreed to be the fundamental task of natural science. An impressive array of highly reliable and useful scientific knowledge has been accumulated in this way. However, it is not always possible to answer scientific questions *simply* by means of direct observation and measurement. Many phenomena appear to be too remotely and too tenuously related to the immediately observable variables to permit so direct an approach. Furthermore, there are problems of underlying general relationships between apparently unrelated phenomena that can not easily be attacked by strictly empirical methods. For these reasons all modern natural sciences have developed a large number of theories, or abstract explanatory principles ... ultimately based upon but [not] entirely reducible to bare empirical measurements.

A number of problems involving the relationship between the empirical and the theoretical components of science have arisen in the rapid scientific emergence of psychology, with its long-time philosophical orientation and its intimate connection with matters of great practical significance. The actual use of theory in psychology does not appear to have kept pace with the formal recognition of the principles of theory construction. The following discussion aims at exposing the common ground that all theory construction shares, in the hope of stimulating more effective general consideration of the basic problems.

Basic Assumptions

The arguments that follow depend upon the acceptance of certain assumptions, the implications of which are often overlooked in contemporary theory construction and theory criticism. They tend, unfortunately, to be accepted in principle but ignored in practice. They may be briefly stated as follows:

1. The ultimate aim of all natural science is explanation and *understanding* and not simply prediction and control in a practical sense, as is often assumed. Brown[2] has pointed out that inability to predict or control earthquakes has not prevented the significant scientific development of seismology, and has argued that human behavior is probably in the same situation. In both cases "the causes are too obscure, intricate and inaccessible" for exact prediction. It is nevertheless true that we can investigate and understand these phenomena, and so modify our behavior accordingly. Theory, or general explanation, is the ultimate objective of science.

2. In the development of any scientific theory it is impossible to avoid direct dependence upon *empirical* operations. That is, any scientific theory, as distinguished from less rigorous "speculation," must refer back to previous empirical reports as well as point forward to new obser-

[1]From **Psychological Theory: Contemporary Readings**, Melvin H. Marx, ed., New York: The Macmillan Company, 1951, pp. 4-18. Copyright 1951 by The Macmillan Company, New York, and used with their permission.

[2]W. Brown, "Facing the Facts," **Proceedings of the Twenty-Fifth Anniversary Celebration of the Inauguration of Graduate Studies, 1910-1935**, Herbert Wynford Hill, ed., Los Angeles: University of Southern California Press, 1936. pp. 116-121.

vations. It must be recognized, in addition, that some kind of bias, whether or not it is explicitly recognized, underlies all empirical measurements, regardless of how automatic and mechanical they may appear. It is thus not possible to separate completely the empirical from the theoretical components of scientific inquiry. . . .

3. All scientific investigation has one essential characteristic whose implications psychologists are particularly prone to overlook. It is *socio-linguistic behavior.* That is, it demands communication to others. "Observations" therefore always imply report, or *verbal statements,* and the same is of course even more obviously true of constructs and hypotheses (although other forms of symbolic expression than words may sometimes be used). The fact that psychology has developed, historically, as a science of "experience" *and* "behavior" should not be allowed to confuse the issue. . . .

General Characteristics of Theories

Scientific theorizing is always an attempt to overcome the local limitations of direct observations, and to generalize beyond the immediate data. Several general characteristics of theories may now be described.

1. All theories aim at explanation, which means the establishment of *functional relationships between variables*. These must be stated in words or other symbols, and may thus be considered to be descriptive statements, or propositions, at varying levels of abstraction and comprehensiveness.

2. A theory is both a *tool* and an *objective*. Which of these functions is emphasized largely depends upon the degree of confidence—or social acceptability, and thus "factualness"—that it has achieved. It should be emphasized that no final or absolute theories (or laws) are to be expected in science. The best example of this is probably the sudden and revolutionary changes which occurred in physical theory towards the end of the last century. In this connection, however, it should also be recognized that classical Newtonian mechanics was not refuted, but was rather re-evaluated, as a result of the development of quantum and relativity theories.

When a theory is regarded only as an objective, the danger is that its provisional, tool-like character will be overlooked. . . .

3. Theories are always *relative* to the bias not only of the theorist, but also of the various observers upon whose empirical reports he has depended.[3] It may again be emphasized that some selectivity or bias in this general sense is inevitable in all observations. A common error is to talk and act as though theories somehow transcend the limitations of direct observation and logical inference, and so either are or are not "true," or truly representative of "reality." This point of view seems to overlook the necessarily man-made nature of the more or less abstract propositions that we call theories and laws. All problems of ultimate "reality" are entirely extra-scientific questions, or "metaphysical" ones. . . .

4. It follows that alternative theoretical approaches can be directly compared, scientifically, only if they make *different predictions* within the same observational framework. Scientifically, their value is a matter of empirical test, rather than philosophical or logical test, or even practical application. . . .

Major Elements of Theory Construction

Theory construction depends upon three major types of verbal statements, or propositions. Although their nature is often somewhat obscured by variations in usage, they may be most usefully differentiated as:

1. *Empirical* propositions. These are statements of "fact," of what has been observed.

2. *Hypothetical* propositions. These are statements of supposition, or conjecture, of what is predicted in observation.

3. *Theoretical* propositions. These are more or less general statements, of varying degrees of abstractness and comprehensiveness, concerning functional relations among variables. . . .

It is the hypothetical type of verbal proposition that forms the link between the empirical

[3]Cf. Morris R. Cohen and Ernest Nagel, **An Introduction to Logic and Scientific Method,** New York: Harcourt, Brace and Company, 1934; and H. M. Johnson, "Pre-Experimental Assumptions As Determiners of Experimental Results," **Psychological Review,** 1940, **47,** 338-346.

propositions, or facts, and the theories. The implications of a theory can be tested only by means of specific predictions, or experimental hypotheses. These are questions which must be answered empirically. The hypothesis is thus the backbone of all scientific theory construction; without it confirmation or rejection of theories would be impossible. Establishment of empirical propositions is referred to as *inductive*, in contrast with the complementary development of the logical implications of theories, or the *deductive* phase of scientific investigation. . . .

Theoretical and empirical propositions are characteristically tied together, in hypotheses of varying degrees of remoteness from direct observational test, by means of logical inferences called *symbolic constructs*. These are a special type of concept, or symbol, and serve the same general function as the theory itself; that is, they help to fill in the gaps which must always exist in the empirical data.

As Pratt[4] has clearly pointed out, all concepts contain both *more than* and *less than* the empirical data from which they are derived. The concept "dog"—"dog in general," that is—is at the same time more meaningful than the observation of any particular dog since it summarizes in a single word or other symbol the essence of an infinite number of observations, and less meaningful since it invariably loses in concreteness and individuality. Dangerous as concept-formation therefore is, it is nevertheless an absolutely essential step in the formation of scientific theory.

The example of "dog" represents a type of concept which can be directly reduced, by means of a relatively simple pointing operation, to particular observations (that is, experiencing a concrete dog). The dangers of concept-formation are even more pronounced, however, when a more complex type of concept is attempted. This is the type which is *constructed* on the basis of observations. Thus, the concepts—or, more specifically, the constructs—"motive," "habit," "gene," and "atom" cannot be built on observations in the same relatively simple and direct manner that the concepts "dog," "food pellet,"

and "chair" can be. Symbolic or logical constructs are *inferred* on the basis of observed relationships between objects and events. This characteristic results in an unfortunate tendency toward ambiguity which is especially marked in a complex field like psychology. It also suggests the importance of a careful analysis of such constructs, which are necessarily involved in theory construction, whether or not they are explicitly and formally recognized.

The three basic elements of theory construction are schematically shown in Figure 1. The characteristic of each element which is considered most essential, scientifically, is indicated along the continuum from practical affairs to science. The three continua may be considered in turn.

1. With regard to the empirical foundation of science, it may be freely granted that the everyday type of observation constitutes the groundwork for both the origin of scientific problems and the preliminary conceptual and theoretical formulations. However, notwithstanding the ability and ingenuity of some especially keen observers and reporters in literature, art, and related fields, some degree of *control* must be developed if science is to advance. This simply means a reduction in the ambiguity of the data, through naturalistic or experimental techniques, and their assignment as functions of definitely known variables. Further consideration of this important problem is beyond the scope of the present discussion.

2. *Operational validity*, or the open and clearly stated relationship of the construct to its empirical basis in operations producing the data, is the most essential characteristic of construct-formation. Animistic concepts and others with what Reichenbach[5] has called "surplus meaning" may be tolerated in the early, pre-scientific development of a field but their replacement by constructs more closely and necessarily tied to the data must occur for scientific advance.

The *intervening variable*, as first proposed by Tolman, offers an ideal opportunity for this kind of conceptual development. Most effectively

---

[4]Carroll C. Pratt, **The Logic of Modern Psychology**, New York: The Macmillan Company, 1939.

[5]Hans Reichenbach, **Experience and Prediction: An Analysis of the Foundations and Structure of Knowledge**, Chicago: The University of Chicago Press, 1938.

used, it *means* nothing more than certain stated empirical operations. For example, Hull's construct of habit strength $(_SH_R)$ quite literally *equals* (that is, is identical with) whatever empirical data result from variation in the four stated determinants: number of reinforcements, amount of reinforcing agent, time between stimulation and response, and time between response and reinforcement. Once the problem of some particular dependent variable has been settled, these four operations completely delimit what is meant by habit strength.[6] Of course, there still remains the problem of relating *this* "habit strength" to other versions of the same general concept; but that is by no means a unique problem, and the important advantage in this case is that one can at least tell directly what the theorist or experimenter means by "habit strength." Furthermore, if the particular construct—that

[6]The author is pointing out here that a construct such as Hull's habit strength $(_SH_R)$ should have a clear relationship to the operations (varying the amount of reward, the number of rewards, etc.) which produce the empirical data that he conceptualizes as habit strength **(Editor's note).**

is, the particular operations which define it— proves to be experimentally ineffectual or otherwise inadequate, appropriate modifications can be readily made. Such operationally controlled flexibility is an enormous advantage in the clarification of the construct and its relation to empirical data.

It should be recognized that this extremely close coupling of constructs to empirically manipulable variables is not essential to operational validity. However, some degree of reduction of conceptual terms to equivalent empirical sentences is needed. This point will be elaborated in a later section.

3. *Testability* is the absolutely essential characteristic of any scientifically useful hypothesis. Obviously an explanation that cannot be tested in some way cannot be given an empirical evaluation. It is necessary to note that the scientific test cannot be intuitively made, and thus rest on unknown bases, as is common in everyday life. . . .

It follows from the foregoing considerations that scientific progress is marked by a progressive shift from left to right in the diagram in

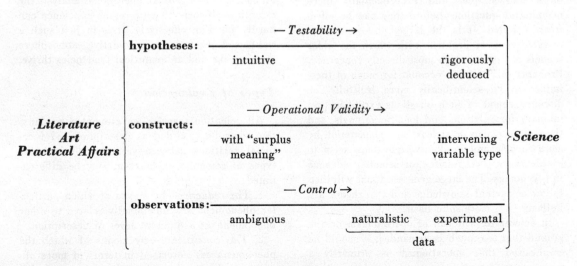

Figure 1. The Three Basic Elements of Scientific Theory Construction

Figure 1 for all three phases of theory construction. In each case there is a reduction in ambiguity of relations between the various components, and an increasingly clear and often formal differentiation of their respective functions. The fact that scientific progress results in increasingly less natural and less lifelike concepts and theories obviously increases the difficulties of popularization and translation into practical action, but is hardly avoidable. . . .

Objections to Operationism

There has been a great deal of misunderstanding and confusion with respect to the problem of operationism and its relation to intuitive functions. Some of this may be traced to certain kinds of pressures and motives which tend to restrict scientific work to the left side of the diagram in Figure 1. For example, there is the tendency to ask highly general, practically important but experimentally meaningless questions, and the attempt to translate these too directly into theory construction and research programs. These problems come, of course, out of everyday life situations but must be broken down into simpler and experimentally more meaningful questions before they can be effectively handled. It is the large, philosophically-oriented type of problem with which the older schools or systems were most directly concerned. Probably this helps to account for much of their failure to be scientifically more fruitful. The discouragement of such questions except in preliminary formulations and long-range goals, and their replacement or at least supplementation by more specific and productive questions, seem to be necessary prerequisites for scientific advance in psychology. The large generalizations will then follow as factual knowledge and . . . theory are built up on a more solid basis. . . .

In answer to criticism of operationism on the ground that too much is demanded, it should be emphasized that operationism is primarily a more or less formal attempt to *stimulate critical evaluation* of the relationship between logical constructs and their supporting empirical data. All concepts do not need to be defined literally in terms of the precise physical operations involved. But it is fair to ask that the observational basis of any concept be made as explicit as possible—that, at least, this particular problem be recognized as a problem and not simply ignored, as is very often the case. If this is not adequately done the concept is certainly open to serious question, as are any conclusions based upon its use.

The need for careful operational analysis is greatest in just those areas of psychology where it is most difficult to apply. This situation has no doubt been responsible for a certain amount of the resistance to operationism that has appeared. Inner needs, phenomenological fields, personality structures, and the like become scientifically productive concepts only in so far as their observational bases can be directly evaluated in some way or the other. . . .

In summarizing this discussion, it may be well to stress the fact that all scientifically useful concepts in psychology are derived, ultimately, from observations. Failure to identify and localize the intuitive aspects of theory construction has been a major methodological defect in many of the higher-level types of theoretical work. Without some degree of willingness to subject all concepts to a critical, operational analysis the essential self-correcting processes in science can hardly function effectively. It is in just such a tight and exclusively speculative atmosphere that cultlike and antiempirical tendencies thrive.

Types of Explanation

All scientific theories, as attempted explanation, may be regarded as descriptions of functional relations between variables. Two major types of scientific explanation may be differentiated:

1. The *reductive*—by means of which particular phenomena are functionally related to other phenomena at a different level of description.

2. The *constructive*—by means of which the phenomena are described in terms of more abstract, or higher-order, constructs and hypotheses.

The two types of explanation are shown diagrammatically as they apply to psychology in

Figure 2. Let us suppose that the behavior datum which we want to explain is a fairly simple one, say a description of an animal being presented with a certain type of food and eating. The chain of *reductive* explanation would then go approximately as follows: the eating behavior occurs because of certain stomach contractions and neurophysiological events, and these in turn occur because of certain biochemical conditions, etc. The *constructive* type of explanation would start with the same behavior, and might proceed along the following line: the eating behavior occurs because of food deprivation (construct of hunger drive) which under similar conditions previously has been paired with the giving of food (construct of reinforcement) to produce a certain behavior tendency (higher-order construct of habit), etc. . . .

A certain amount of controversial discussion has arisen over the relative merits, within psychology, of these two types of explanation. . . . Without attempting to evaluate [the arguments] it may simply be stated that whatever type of explanation seems to be most useful should be adopted, and as a matter of fact it would often

be very difficult to separate the two types in actual practice. They are complementary, rather than mutually exclusive, and ought to be regarded as such.

Levels of Explanation

A somewhat related and equally sterile controversy has developed within recent years in regard to the relative merits of the *field-theoretical* and the *stimulus-response* types of theoretical and experimental approach. It seems necessary to emphasize that these types of theoretical approaches are also to be regarded as supplementary, if not actually complementary, rather than mutually exclusive. . . . It ought to be evident to any detached bystander that many kinds of scientific attacks are possible upon different levels of complexity, or molarity, which however measured must always be regarded as upon a continuum. . . . The only scientific test of any type of theoretical approach is its ability to generate fruitful experiments or other observations and to lead to more satisfactory and more comprehensive theories. No scien-

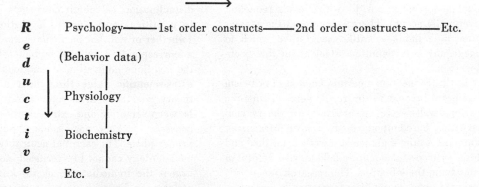

Figure 2. Two Types of Scientific Explanation

tific development in the field of psychology today justifies the enthusiastic acceptance of any single type of theoretical-experimental orientation.

A glance at the situation in physiology may be helpful in pointing up comparable problems in psychology. The physiologist may concentrate upon more and more detailed and refined analysis of highly technical problems within any one organ system, which has been the orthodox procedure as a matter of fact; or he may concern himself with more molar inter-relations of the various systems, as Cannon has done in his work on "homeostasis." There seems to have been no wholesale or concentrated effort within physiology to dispense with either approach, or even to treat them as in any way opposed to each other. They are recognized as complementary and necessary functions. There likewise seems to be no essential reason why the same calm acceptance of different purposes and approaches should not occur within psychology.

The problem of "reductionism,"[7] stimulated within recent years by the increasing popularity of the field-theoretical or holistic type of approach, has produced a great deal more heat and confusion than light and understanding. There is only one possible answer, scientifically, as to whether so-called emergent behavioral functions can be successfully "reduced" to more primary and less complex ones within the same field. The answer must be a pragmatic one, entirely dependent upon the extent to which such reduction eventually occurs. There is, again, at the present time no reliable scientific basis upon which to make any very definite statement on this problem. . . .

In this connection a certain amount of criticism has been directed within recent years against the various well-developed programs of theory construction based upon research with infrahuman animals. Again, a glance at a well-established and highly successful scientific field may be helpful in clarifying the situation. The research geneticist's primary, and many times practically exclusive, concern is with fundamental genetic functions, wherever they may occur. He has so intensively

studied the fruitfly for the same reasons that the psychologist has so intensively studied the rat—convenience, ease of experimental control, large amount of previous work, etc. It would be difficult if not impossible to point to a single fundamental genetic discovery based upon human research, or for that matter upon many other animal forms than *Drosophila*. There seems to be no reason why the behavioral scientist should not be allowed an equally unimpeded opportunity to employ infrahuman animals in the same general way and for the same general purpose—the investigation of basic animal functions, regardless of the degree to which the results may ultimately be related to human problems.

In conclusion, it may again be emphasized that a diversity of interests and approaches is not only desirable but inevitable in as complex and heterogeneous a field as modern psychology. More rather than less experimental research and empirically-oriented theory is needed at all levels of explanation—the strictly molecular as well as the broadly molar. However, it must also be emphasized that regardless of the level of complexity, or molarity, worked at the psychologist is obliged to follow the general principles of scientific theory construction, as outlined in the preceding sections. One of the most immediate needs in contemporary psychology is for a more realistic attitude towards these general methodological requirements. A major obstacle to more effective scientific progress seems to be a general disinclination to submit constructs and theories to a critical and rigorous operational analysis (whether or not that particular term is used) and a corresponding failure explicitly to recognize the invidious infiltration of emotional beliefs and extra-scientific value throughout all phases of theory construction. A more careful distinction between scientific and extra-scientific elements is necessary to keep both kinds of values in their proper place. The essential neutrality of scientific methodology cannot be sacrificed, no matter how urgent the immediate needs for knowledge and action may be, without a corresponding loss of the effectiveness of science as a uniquely successful tool for the establishment of objective explanatory propositions of a high degree of empirically-tested probability.

[7]E.g., E. H. Sloane, "Reductionism," **Psychological Review**, 1945, **52**, 214-223.

TOWARD A GENERAL THEORY
FOR THE BEHAVIORAL SCIENCES

by James G. Miller[1]

As we noted in Chapter 1, a general theory of behavior has long been the goal of many biological and social scientists. In 1949 scientists from several disciplines met at the University of Chicago to consider whether, at this stage of human knowledge, it was possible to formulate a theory that would cover all aspects of behavior. The term "behavioral sciences" was coined to refer to the major areas involved—history, anthropology, economics, political science, sociology, social psychology, psychology, psychiatry, medicine, physiology, and mathematical biology. In the following selection James G. Miller, one of the participants, gives his interpretation of the general behavior systems theory which has evolved from the work of this group thus far. Dr. Miller is Professor of Psychiatry and Chief of the Mental Health Research Institute at the University of Michigan.

. . . We have assumed from the start that any adequate theory of behavior would represent in large part a selection from among viewpoints—some even from opposing schools—which have already been stated succinctly and capably. Our quest was *not* for originality with a capital "O."

We chose certain working assumptions, not because we were certain they were more valid than alternatives chosen by other theorists, but in order to get on with the task. First, we agreed to accept as confirmation of theorems only *objective* phenomena available to public inspection by more than one observer, excluding private experience. Second, we tried when possible to state hypotheses *quantitatively*, so that they might be precisely testable and could subsequently be corrected. Third, we attempted to make statements capable of being disproved as well as proved, by *crucial experiments*. Finally, . . . insofar as possible we employed dimensions of the natural sciences related to the centimeter-gram-second system.

[1]From **The American Psychologist**, 1955, **10**, No. 9, 514-519. Adapted from a paper delivered, among other places, at the Conference on the Evolution of Behavior, sponsored by the American Psychological Association and the Society for the Study of Evolution, at Arden House, Harriman, N.Y., on Tuesday, April 5, 1955.

General Behavior Systems Theory

Of the various possible integrations of the relevant data, we have found most profit in what we call *general behavior systems theory*. Systems are bounded regions in space-time, involving energy interchange among their parts, which are associated in functional relationships, and with their environments. General systems theory is a series of related definitions, assumptions, and postulates about all levels of systems from atomic particles through atoms, molecules, crystals, viruses, cells, organs, individuals, small groups, societies, planets, solar systems, and galaxies. General behavior systems theory is a subcategory of such theory, dealing with living systems, extending roughly from viruses through societies. Perhaps the most significant fact about living things is that they are open systems, with important inputs and outputs. Laws which apply to them differ from those applying to relatively closed systems.

All behavior can be conceived of as energy exchange within an open system or from one such system to another. Any exchange of energy across a boundary results in some alteration or distortion of the energy form. Those specific functions of systems which we can stipulate and whose magnitude we can measure in a relative scale, we will call "variables" if they are within the system and "parameters" if they are in its environment. Each system except the largest of all—the universe—has its environment. The system and its environment together constitute a suprasystem. Each system except the smallest has subsystems, which are any components of an organism that can affect a variable.

Inputs and outputs may be either coded or uncoded. Coding is a linkage within subsystems whereby process A_1 is coupled with process A_2 so that either will elicit the other in the future. Coding involves conditioning, learning, or pairing of two processes in a system and the memory or retention of this union over a period of time. Any action is uncoded unless—like speech or gesture —it has some added significance as a result of such a bond. It then conveys information.

All living systems tend to maintain steady states of many variables, by negative feedback mechanisms[2] which distribute information to subsystems to keep them in orderly balance. Not only are subsystems ordinarily kept in equilibrium, but systems are also usually in balance with their environments, which have outputs into systems and inputs from them. This prevents variations in the environment from destroying systems, either by collapse or by explosion. There is a range of stability for any parameter or variable in any system. It is that range within which the rate of correction is minimal or zero and beyond which correction does occur. Inputs (or loads), either coded or uncoded, which, by lack or excess, force the variables beyond the range of stability constitute stresses and produce strains within the system. These strains may or may not be capable of being reduced, depending upon the equilibratory resources of the system.

The above general statement can be translated into terminology of several behavioral sciences. In individual psychology, for instance, the system has generally been known as the organism; the input, as the stimulus; and the output, as the response. Uncoded inputs, we have recognized, can result in strains or disequilibria within the organism which are known as primary or somagenic

drives. Coded inputs result in secondary, learned, acquired, or psychogenic drives. Reduction of strains is called drive satisfaction. When inputs or loads create strains great enough to call into play complex subsystems to restore equilibrium, we sometimes refer to such processes as "defense mechanisms." When these mechanisms fail, severe disruption of the steady state of the organism, known as mental or physical illness, or ultimately death, occurs. The total of the strains within the individual resulting from his genetic input and variations in the input from his environment is often referred to as his values. The relative urgency of reducing these individual strains determines his hierarchy of values.

Specific Aspects of the Theory

System. Our definition of "system" is very general, and at first sight might appear to apply to almost everything in the world. And, of course, the function of general theory is to be inclusive. However, it may be helpful to indicate what is not a system. The dark-colored half of the Pied Piper was not a system. The opposing lines of two football teams in scrimmage, independent of their backs, would not ordinarily be considered together as a system. If the Headless Horseman of Washington Irving had not been fictional, he could not have held his head in his arm and yet behave like an intact system. All the blondes in the United States are themselves not a system unless they are organized by some sort of communication, like the Red-headed League of A. Conan Doyle. In simple, naive, common-sense terms, then, a real system is all of a thing. Even though it is possible to construct a conceptual system which includes grandpa's mustache, Chinese hokku poetry, and the Brooklyn Bridge, this would not correspond to a real system of general systems theory, because these things are not surrounded by a single boundary, are not continuous in space-time, and do not have recognizable functional interrelationships.

Some may wonder whether "system" is identical with "Gestalt." Are there laws of the whole which do not apply to specific parts? We hold that both the parts, or subsystems, and the whole behave according to similar laws. However, the

---

[2]For an explanation of negative feedback, see the selection by Morgan and Stellar, page 499 **(Editor's note).**

fact that subsystems are equilibrated together by system-wide organizing processes (even though these mechanisms can be explained by the behavior of component parts) means that there are characteristics of the whole which do not apply to any part. This is true of systems at every level.

Boundary. Boundaries of systems are not always clear-cut and round like the rind of a watermelon. Sometimes they have intricate geometrical design, more like the surface of a branching coral, but even more complex than that. A naval task force maneuvering blind at sea can be a system, even though its boundary is complicated and in continual flux. It is a system organized by communications which require at least a small filament of contiguous space-time of ether, to transmit radio, radar, or other signals. When a typhoon hits the *Caine* and her sister destroyers, wiping out radio and radar contact, then the flotilla is no longer a system, because usual functional interrelationships are impossible. Communications make feasible complex organizations of systems, like the American Psychological Association or the United Nations. A given individual or behaving subsystem can, of course, be part of several systems at the same time, equilibrating at least partially with all of them. To deal with this fact the concept of "role" has been developed in social psychology.

Subsystems. How could one disprove our contention that every system except the smallest has subsystems? The answer is that if one found a homogeneous distribution of energy in any system, so that no boundary between its subsystems was discoverable, then that system would have no subsystems. How does one locate a boundary, i.e., a region where energy or information exchange is significantly less than inside or outside the system? One decides upon the order of magnitude of difference in rate of exchange of information or energy which one will accept as indication of a boundary. Let us call this amount d. This differs according to the level of system with which one intends to deal. Then, having decided on this, one can empirically locate the boundary as that region where there is d less interchange of energy and information than either outside or inside. In general, d is progressively less from larger systems to smaller so that ordinarily it is great for societies, less for individuals, and much less for cells.

We know a good deal about the input-output relations of the peripheral sensory and motor subsystems, but it is extremely difficult with present methods to determine these relations for processes in the human central subsystems. Electronic technicians know that if there is only one subsystem between two test electrodes which contact the input and the output respectively, 100 per cent of the variance will be in that subsystem; if, however, there are two subsystems, and there is no way to put a test electrode between those systems, all the variance may be in Subsystem A; all of it may be in Subsystem B; or the variance may be accounted for by an infinite set of possible combinations of the relationships between the two. Extremely complex mathematics is required to study the input-output alterations of multiple systems whose components cannot be isolated. For this reason precise study of central subsystems of the individual—often said to be the main variables of his "personality"—presents a difficult or impossible scientific problem by present methods.

Coding. In living organisms the important process of coding, which makes it possible for energy exchange also to be information exchange, is accomplished by at least three means, which are perhaps basically the same, but which for convenience can be classified as (*a*) instinct; (*b*) imprinting;[3] and (*c*) conditioning or learning. The first is irreversible; the second may be; and the last is reversible. Instinct is a "wiring in" of the relationship before birth, either in the endocrine or in the nervous system. Imprinting is "wired in" before birth or hatching and stamped in by "social releasers" during early hours after birth or hatching. Conditioning or learning is usually acquired after birth, and it may be lost.

As the link between energy theory and information theory, the process of coding is of prime importance. While both the biological and the

---

[3]Imprinting is the name given to rapid (and often irreversible) learning that takes place, without specific reward, at a particular stage of development in some birds and animals—usually within the first few hours or days of life. It has been demonstrated, for example, that goslings become attached to the first large moving object they see after hatching, whether this be their mother (as would normally be the case) or a human being **(Editor's note)**.

social sciences share a dual concern with energy transfer and information transfer, the predominant emphasis of the biological sciences is energy transfer, whereas that of the social sciences is information transfer. The social sciences deal chiefly with verbal or symbolic behavior. Information theory[4] abets the union of the natural and the social sciences, but is probably more likely to be useful to the latter. General behavior systems theory incorporates most aspects of modern information theory, but it is more encompassing, for it deals with the transmission of both information and energy, and with the relationships between information and energy transfer. . . .

Equifinality. The concept of *equifinality* advanced by Bertalanffy[5] explains purposive behavior in animals and men more effectively than vitalistic assumptions, and also more consistently with our general theoretical framework. Teleological notions of goal striving are not necessary if we accept this principle. It operates only in open systems [in which] materials necessary to create and maintain a certain organization may be selected from the input and surplus products or wastes be rejected in the output. For example consider a chemical system made up of two solutions, silver nitrate and hydrochloric acid, which when combined precipitate silver chloride. If an indefinitely large input of both substances is available and output is possible for this system, then the rate of precipitation will become constant at a specific equilibrium level. Moreover, this rate will not depend on the amounts of silver

[4]For an introduction to information theory, see Wilbur Schramm's article on page 507 **(Editor's note)**.
[5]Ludwig von Bertalanffy, "The Theory of Open Systems in Physics and Biology," **Science**, 1950, **111**, 23-29.

nitrate and hydrochloric acid present at the beginning of the experiment. There could be either a dram or 100 gallons of each. Rather, it depends on the solubility characteristics of the components (H^+, Cl^-, Ag^+, and NO_3^-). This reaction, then, looks as if it always strives teleologically toward the same goal—that is a specific rate of precipitation—no matter whether the system at first was poor or rich in silver nitrate or hydrochloric acid. Actually, however, it is clear that this "equifinal" result is determined by the nature of the constituents of the system.

We contend that this is true of all behaving systems. Whether an infant be three months premature and weigh two pounds or be born of a diabetic mother and so weigh fifteen pounds, he will ordinarily be of normal weight a few months later. The small one will grow more rapidly than an average baby and the big one less rapidly. This may appear like vitalistic teleology, but it can be explained simply by stating that the constituents of human subsystems determine what their equilibrium levels shall be. Many of these together, in turn, fix the size of the child.

So the "goals" which "impel" the rat to run the maze, the woman to marry, and the candidate to file for public office, can be interpreted as internal strains which elicit efforts to achieve inputs of energy and information that will reduce the strains toward an equilibrium point. And no matter whether he is nurtured at court to become Pharaoh or cast away in the bullrushes, a man will search until he finds an environment with inputs capable of diminishing the particular drives within him— strains established by his genetic inputs as modified by later inputs of energy and information, by learning or acculturation. . . .

PSYCHOANALYTIC THEORY

by *William C. Menninger*[1]

One of the most influential and controversial theories in the history of psychology has been the psychoanalytic theory of Sigmund Freud (1856-1939). Many psychologists criticize psychoanalytic theory on the grounds that it cannot be validated scientifically, and even Freud's most sympathetic followers have disagreed with some of his conclusions. But most psychologists would agree that Freud's achievement in developing the first comprehensive theory of personality was a truly remarkable one and that he has contributed significantly to our understanding of the dynamics of human behavior, particularly in his formulation of the unconscious. Graduating from the University of Vienna's medical school in 1881, Freud early became interested in the origin and treatment of mental disorders and by the turn of the century had worked out the major principles of his psychoanalytic theory. For the remainder of his long and distinguished career he continued to revise and expand his ideas, drawing heavily on his intensive clinical studies of individual patients. In the following selection the major aspects of Freudian theory are summarized by Dr. William Menninger, a prominent psychiatrist, who, with his brother Karl, developed the famous Menninger Foundation in Topeka, Kansas.

. . . Though some persons express disagreement with some of Freud's observations and conclusions, they do so in most instances without having carefully studied his original reports. Even psychiatrists who are critical have accepted and obviously utilize much more of Freud's contribution than they seem to recognize. There are, of course, others who are poorly informed about the progress in this field and are either ignorant of, or blind to, the many changes in the theoretical concepts postulated, altered, or added, not only by Freud himself but by many of the followers of the school that grew around his studies.

Regardless of our personal or scientific opinions of Freud and his work, many of us feel that through his stimulus psychiatry was given a new birth. It was converted from a purely descriptive science, largely preoccupied with psychoses, into a dynamic, rational system capable of serving as a basis for interpreting psychopathology. Such interpretations are applicable to the acts of every-

day behavior as well as to the great variety of human illnesses described as neurotic reactions.

It may be helpful for the sake of orientation to amplify the meaning of the word *psychoanalysis*. Psychoanalysis was the term employed by Freud initially to refer to a method of treatment. It is still used in this sense to identify a technique that is applicable in a very limited number of personality disturbances. In the process of using it as a treatment, however, Freud accumulated an enormous amount of material. As he attempted to evaluate and classify his data, he developed a psychological theory. As a consequence, when one speaks of psychoanalysis, he may refer to this psychological theory. The term "psychoanalysis" also refers to a research technique. Obtaining data by a process of clearing away, stratum by stratum, the abnormal psychic material is a process Freud likened to the excavation of a buried city. In both instances the find was apt to prove surprising, and emphatically so in the case of psychoanalytic investigation. All three of these features, namely, a method of treatment, a psy-

[1]From **Psychiatry: Its Evolution and Present Status** by William C. Menninger, Cornell University Press, Ithaca, 1948, pp. 50-85.

chological theory, and an investigative procedure, have continued to be characteristics of the total process of psychoanalysis.

In presenting certain features of psychoanalysis one must recognize that there are parts that can be understood completely only in the frame of the whole theory. In presenting a discussion of some specific elements, one is keenly aware of the risk of giving a totally inadequate conception of the composite whole.

I shall attempt to present in an extremely condensed fashion four of the major areas of psychoanalytic psychiatry that contribute most to the understanding of behavior: the psychosexual stages of development, the anatomy of personality in terms of the conscious and unconscious, personality physiology in terms of the Id, Ego, and Super-Ego, and, finally, some examples of the defense mechanisms used by the Ego to maintain its equilibrium.

Psychosexual Development

One of the most significant discoveries of psychoanalysis was that the events of infancy and babyhood are all-important in shaping the personality or character of the individual. Psychoanalysis turned the spotlight, perhaps, better, the telescope, on this area of development and has shown without question or doubt that it is during these early years that the basic personality structure and patterns of behavior are laid down. It is during this period that the groundwork is laid for later mental health or ill health. Since this experience occurs during a period for which the adult has amnesia, he is completely unable to explain certain attitudes or behavior in himself.

Freud's study and evaluation of the data he had gained in the treatment of his patients indicated to him that there were definite stages in infant and child personality growth and psychosexual development.

With the introduction of the term "psychosexual," additional explanation is in order. One of the most frequent criticisms of psychoanalysis is that it is too much occupied with sex. Critics are unaware, however, of the fact that to Freud the term "sex" meant far more than genital activity. It included all forms of physical gratification.

Moreover, few of these critics know that every psychiatric patient under intensive psychological treatment always brings up this subject himself. The treatment of patients led to the discovery that seeking for gratification is an instinctive drive in every person and cannot be ignored because of prudishness any more than can any other instinctive need. Even as the term is used in America, sex is one of the basic and all-pervasive motivations in life. Furthermore, everyone has some minor or major difficulties concerned with sexual life at various crucial periods of development—during adolescence, at marriage, or at other times when adjustment must be made to associates or spouse. Sexual maladjustment is accepted, even by non-psychoanalytic psychiatrists, as a major causative factor in mental illness. In any case, the misunderstanding is due both to semantic differences and to the suppression and repression of this basic human interest and activity. The result has been much resistance to the initial acceptance of psychoanalysis both as a body of knowledge and as a treatment technique. Incidentally, the American cultural taboo against discussion of this instinctual need is a significant factor in the high incidence of neuroses.

Growing up entails changing from a little animal concerned only with his own physical processes into a social being cognizant of relationships between himself and other people. This change starts in the first year of life. Very early the inherent internal forces within the child, namely, his will to live, to express himself, and to find gratification, must be integrated with his surroundings, his environment, his parents, his siblings, and the external world. It is through the initial and early experiences in the family that the child learns to relate himself to people and to develop certain techniques by which he accomplishes this.

When the infant is born into the world, we can be sure that he has no interest except selfishly to gratify his own cravings. He has certain instincts at birth, and the demand to satisfy these is his only motive in life. In his early months the infant gives nothing to anyone else; he makes no attempt to please anyone; in short, he is interested only in receiving what he wants. One may say that he follows the path of gaining all the pleasure he can and so far as possible avoiding displeasure and pain in any form. This pattern of behavior follows what is known as the "pleasure-pain principle": All effort is directed toward obtaining pleasure and avoiding pain, regardless of consequences. The term "pain" refers not only to physical suffering but also to every other sort of displeasure, unhappiness, and discomfort.

It is only after some years that the child begins to apply what is known as the "reality principle," namely, the acceptance of a limited amount of pain or unhappiness or dissatisfaction because of the promise of more gratification in the future. It is one of the changes that must occur in order for the child to become an adult psychologically.

During the first three, four, or five years of life the child has three experiences that are of paramount interest to him and through which he formulates his relations to those about him. Continuing through most of his first year is his interest in and his gratification from nursing (sucking). This is his chief contact with the external world and with those about him, and it serves as his chief source of satisfaction.

Toward the end of this year a new interest appears. Through the efforts of his parents to encourage his control of his excretions, the child's attention becomes focused on those processes. They become his chief bodily interest and in some degree replace the previously primary interest in using his mouth.

Between the second and third year the child's interest turns to curiosity about his or her sexual organs and their function, how they differ from those of others. Concurrent with and related to interest in this new area of physical gratification, is a new type of relationship to his parents and siblings.

The child passes imperceptibly from one phase to another in his development; no lines of demarkation separate one period from another. Nevertheless, it is possible to outline the various characteristics in each of these stages. The evolution of growth through these periods is referred to as psychosexual development. It is psychical development because it has to do with forms of psychological gratification. It is sexual development because it concerns various parts of the body that serve as sources of gratification. It will be apparent that the word "sexual" in this connection is obviously a much more inclusive term than laymen ordinarily consider it.

The oral stage. For a period of at least the infant's first year, sometimes longer, his chief interest in life centers around an event that occurs every three or four hours—his feeding. Not only does nursing provide satisfaction through the process of sucking and by ending the discomfort of hunger, but it is also usually a time for cuddling. Anything that happens with this frequency, with resultant gratification or lack of it, must in many ways affect subsequent attitudes concerned with the taking-in or receiving tendencies of the individual.

While the food itself serves as a source of gratification, the child also gets great satisfaction from the procedure of sucking. Carefully made studies show that children who have been bottle-fed are much more likely to be thumbsuckers than those who are breast-fed, the explanation being that the breast-fed baby usually nurses about fifteen minutes and the bottle-fed baby about five minutes. To make up the difference the bottle-fed baby often develops the habit of sucking his finger or a pacifier to obtain additional satisfaction. One of the most important elements in this feeding difference is the amount of coddling or affection that the child receives from the parent. Too often the bottle is propped up and the baby left to himself during feeding time.

There are two distinct phases in this "oral stage" of development, a sucking phase and a biting phase. It is presumed that in the earlier phase of sucking, the child regards the breast as part of himself. He makes no distinction between the breast as part of his mother and the parts of his own body. It is only after weeks or perhaps months that the child recognizes the breast as an object that can be taken away from him. As he grows and demands more food and at the same time is developing teeth, the mother is made well aware of the baby's frequent inclination to bite. Particularly is this true when the milk may not be forthcoming as rapidly as the child wishes it; in his impatience he bites the nipple. The biting is the result of frustration, the expression of a temporary resentment because the child is thwarted in gaining the oral satisfaction he wishes.

Many hang-overs of this oral phase are expressed in normal adulthood.[2] Our responses to our first experience in receiving become the prototype for our techniques of receiving, obtaining, and taking in later life. It is probable that the traits of optimism and dependence are related to this period. Certain character traits in the adult are traceable to unsatisfactory experiences in this period of life, particularly impatience, hastiness, and restlessness. The "biter" becomes the argumentative, vitriolic, and sarcastic adult.

Numerous traits are directly related to the oral process itself, as expressed by those individuals whose chief interest in life is eating in spite of gains in weight and in those who are Epicureans of the first order, to whom eating is the most enjoyable activity. Smoking is another oral gratification: the inhalation of smoke gives satisfaction related to that of sucking. Other examples are pipe, cigar, pencil, and gum chewing. An obvious expression of oral gratification is seen in the unfortunate immature individual who in later life substitutes for the earlier bottle of milk one which contains alcohol.

The anal stage. In practice, this stage of development begins whenever the parents initiate training. It is now believed that the toilet training of the child should not begin until some time in the second year. Unfavorable personality reactions are more likely to develop when it is started during the first year, for then the parent imposes a regime upon the insufficiently mature child. In that case, for a period of many months or even a year or two, the child is placed on the toilet at regular intervals several times a day. It is the intention of the parent to gain the child's co-operation by focusing his attention upon this particular procedure. It can be readily understood why any ceremony of this sort, so often repeated, and upon which the parent places so much emphasis, often emotional as well as physical, becomes of considerable importance to the child.

Certain elements in the procedure assume special significance to the child. Very early he learns that this business of urinating and defecating is a method he can use to gain love and approval, or to revenge himself and show determination. In other words, he soon finds that it is one way in which he, an infant, can have power over the adult. Every parent is familiar with the situation in which the child will not "do his duty" regardless of persuasion, pleading, or even threats. Then, as soon as he is removed from the toilet, he performs. In this way the child can express his own desires, his disapproval or hostility toward the parent and toward the idea of control. On the other hand, parents are equally familiar with the situation in which the child responds to pleas to "be a big girl" or "a big boy"; thus, learns that by doing as the parents wish, he or she can gain their love and approval.

One can also observe that the child soon becomes intensely interested not only in the process but in the product. It is literally his first creation. One can observe further that, early in his training, the child derives a very definite gratification through either the expulsion or later the retention of this product. In either case he has a sense of omnipotence, of power that is entirely his. Response to the parental emphasis on regularity and cleanliness serves to instill these characteristics in varying degrees into the personality.

In the adult, the residual expressions of the training and experience in the anal phase of infancy are even more varied than the oral expressions. This probably occurs because, with increasing age, there is increased suppression as well as repression of conscious interest in this procedure. Fundamentally this experience is the prototype of our technique of giving, and thus an important relationship between ourselves and the world. It is undoubtedly related to such character traits as perseverance, persistence, orderliness, cleanliness, and conscientiousness in one's duties. On the other hand, some of the more disagreeable personality characteristics are related to this period. It gave us our first lessons in being stubborn, in refusing to co-operate. Obstinacy has its origin in this phase of an individual's life, along with parsimony, particularly as this becomes avarice and miserliness. Toilet training gave us our first experience in how to be mean to our parents—later, to other people. Not only does the child learn that he can offend or hurt his parents by refusing to

---

[2]Because psychoanalysts regard these early experiences as extremely important in the formation of character, they have indicated by the terms "oral character" and "anal character" certain personality constellations seen in some adults. . . .

co-operate, but he can make matters much worse by soiling himself. Even the layman is familiar with such suggestive expressions as "mud slinging," "whitewashing," "painting things red," "messing things up," all of which are polite references to the sadistic tendencies that result from this training.

Genital stage. The child becomes curious about his own sexual organs in the third year. He discovers differences between himself and his sisters and his parents. The objectively observing parent knows when the child discovers his genital area and fingers it (which is referred to as "infantile masturbation"), or enjoys the stimulation of this area through bouncing, rocking, and other types of play.

Even the young child soon becomes aware that genital manipulation is taboo. All too often his innocent questions are met by rebuff on the part of his parents. As a result, most children learn early to believe that all things sexual are "naughty" or "dirty." Even more disturbing to the child is the attitude that they are "forbidden." Too often parents do not realize that interest in the genitals and sexual differences is a natural, normal phase of development.

Acquaintance with sex differences is intimately bound up with the child's attempt to orientate toward his father as a man and toward his mother as a woman. It is at this time that every little child has a conflict in relating himself to his or her parents. Extensive evidence for this has been gained from the psychoanalytic investigation of many, many individuals. The little boy initially craves the entire attention and love of his mother but recognizes some sort of competition with the father.[3] In a normal, healthy solution of his dilemma, he forms a new part of his personality, the Super-Ego (which we will discuss later), which enables him to identify himself with his father as an ally rather than as a competitor. By so doing he makes what is termed a masculine identification. To solve his problem he imitates his father in manners, dress, and behavior. Similarly the little girl goes through the same conflict in relation to sharing her father with her mother, which ends, in normal development, when she identifies herself with her mother and thus adopts a pattern for feminine identification.

In summarizing these psychosexual stages of development, it should again be pointed out that these events are important in that, first, they determine the methods by which the child relates himself to his environment and particularly to the people in it; second, they are the basis of techniques by which the child obtains gratification. In all three phases, basic character traits are initiated and patterns developed that largely determine the characteristics of that personality as an adult.

The Unconscious

The second major contribution of psychoanalytic psychiatry to the understanding of behavior is a concept of the anatomy of the personality as being divided into a conscious and an unconscious portion. None of us have clear recollections of those experiences in infancy that occurred during psychosexual development. Thus none of us have any real knowledge of the basis of many of our most outstanding personality traits—honesty or dishonesty, sociability, selfishness or unselfishness, and so forth. The average individual usually believes that he knows why he does all that he does. Sometimes, however, his explanations for his attitudes and behavior are so shallow that he himself may question their validity. Occasionally he may admit that he does not know just why he does a certain thing or why he takes a certain point of view. Human behavior is complex, and the average person has no explanation why one individual has a persistent fear of crowded places or another has frank delusions. The same would puzzle the psychiatrist without a theory of the existence of a major part of the personality—the unconscious—that motivates much of our behavior.

Originally, as the explanation of neurotic behavior, Freud postulated the existence of a large area in the individual's personality that was not under voluntary control. In his early definition of the theory he tried to explain neurotic symptoms as resulting from the interaction of forces, some of which obviously arose from a deep, un-

[3]This conflict is known as the "Oedipus situation." When the conflict is between a little girl and her mother for the love and attention of the father, it is called the "Electra situation" **(Editor's note)**.

recognized layer of the personality and others of which stemmed from a conscious level of the personality. In order to develop a functional concept, he made a topographical division of the personality into a conscious and an unconscious system. The chief source of symptoms was the conflict between the forces resident in each system. "The outcome of this conflict depended upon the economic relationship between these two sets of forces, yet the sum of the two psychic forces could practically always be considered constant." This simple theory was later amplified by Freud himself into a much more complicated one in order that he might take into account many additional factors, both within and without the personality, that he believed determined behavior.

By definition, the psychiatrist regards the unconscious as a large region of the mind that is inaccessible to conscious awareness by ordinary means of questioning or self-examination. In it are contained the inherited and racial trends. This region of the mind contains the basic energy drives. In the very small infant they are allowed free expression without restraint and without modification. As the child grows up, the primitive expressions of these drives have to be molded, cloaked, and controlled, but they remain the sources of energy. The unconscious also contains the no longer consciously remembered learning experiences of infancy and early childhood as well as all the associations established at that time.

The unconscious cannot be demonstrated like the brain, for it is not an anatomical unit. It is a concept whereby behavior can be explained. There is much evidence to support the premise of such a functional portion of the personality, perhaps the most convincing of which can be demonstrated in the process we call hypnosis. Hypnosis is a form of suggestion by which certain individuals can be placed in a trancelike state, subject to the control of the hypnotist. In this state of mind an individual may recall incidents or remember facts that he is not able to recall normally. During this trance the hypnotist can make suggestions to be carried out after the person has emerged from the hypnotic state and without the person's recalling that these acts were suggested to him.

Another very common type of evidence of the existence of the unconscious is one's dreams. Some popular opinion may regard them as nonsensical and meaningless. Nevertheless, scientifically they are recognized as a kind of thought process, which is specific for the dreamer. They always have a significant relationship to the thought process of his conscious life. The dream is a production of the unconscious part of the mind that is censored and altered before reaching the conscious part. It is usually so disguised that the average individual cannot recognize its true meaning.

Further evidence that a portion of the personality is not under voluntary control is the slip of speech. We say one thing but mean another. In an unguarded moment, when the conscious censor of the personality is "off duty," the slip of speech occurs and we express the opposite of what we intended to say. Very closely related to this type of psychological phenomena is the common experience of forgetting something that we know we know but cannot remember. The recall of a person's name, a name with which we are quite familiar, is sometimes unsuccessful, even after a special effort to remember it. It is often possible to demonstrate that in such instances, because of some unpleasant association, we do not want to recall the name, and in spite of great effort to do so the name continues to elude the conscious mind.

Recall of forgotten experiences under special conditions is another evidence of the unconscious. Only under certain circumstances can we recapture the memory of them. This is a most important phenomenon, however, because certain long-forgotten infantile and childhood experiences must be recalled in the effective treatment of some mental illnesses.

The psychoanalytic concept regards the unconscious as a powerful force in the life of every individual and not as an inert group of discarded experiences or associations. The unconscious is present at birth and exists throughout life, always remaining primitive and infantile. In other words, it is the conscious part of us that matures while the unconscious remains the same from babyhood to old age. Not only does it contain inherited instinctual drives, but it also receives many of the unacceptable interests, desires, and experiences that we must repress, that is, exclude from our conscious personality. Into the unconscious of every individual must go the erotic satisfactions of infancy, the forbidden hostile feelings toward parents and siblings, and many other unsocial wishes and even behavior that the mature adult personality cannot accept as a part of his conscious life.

The Id, Ego, Super-Ego Relationship

The division of the personality into conscious and unconscious levels does not completely explain human emotions, thought, and behavior. A further elaboration of the psychoanalytic theory describes these conscious and unconscious regions as having three functional and interrelated systems, each of which has certain characteristics and functions. Each is dependent to some degree on the others, the Id, the Ego, the Super-Ego.

The Id, which is the sum total of the personality at birth, is primitive and exists entirely in the unconscious. By primitive we mean that it is animallike, uncivilized, uncultured. It is the "it" in all of us that accounts for the demanding, selfish, inconsiderate part of all of us. If one were to verbalize its continuous theme song, it would be "it wants."

At birth, there is no Ego. As the personality develops, that conscious portion of ourselves (although part of it remains unconscious) that acts as an intermediary between the Id and the external world is called the Ego. In it reside our conscious storehouse of knowledge and the intellectual capacities to choose and to judge and to think. Its theme song, both to the Id and to the world, is "I will" or "I will not."

The Super-Ego is a third portion of the personality that grows with us. It is our internal policeman; it functions as the judge and the critic; it embraces what we call conscience. The phrase which characterizes its advice to the Ego is "you must not."

This theory of the interworking of these three parts of the personality gives us a rational basis for understanding human behavior. These do not represent physical parts of the brain but rather are functional systems, and the sum total of their expression is behavior.

The Id. The Id is that portion of the personality that constitutes most of the unconscious region. It makes up the whole of the personality at birth. The Id remains unrefined throughout life and is that part of the individual referred to popularly as "the animal in man." It has no regard for morals; it never learns or acquires what we think of as intelligence. It never "grows up"; it changes little from birth to adulthood except through the additions of certain experiences that the conscious part of the individual refuses to keep in its own house and so forces into the domain of the Id. Its only rule of existence is to seek pleasure and avoid pain, regardless of consequences.

Its function, if we may call it such, is to supply the psychic energy that the person uses in life, the will to live. Freud was sufficiently discerning to distinguish two directions or aims of motivation in the expenditure of psychological energy. He identified these as "instincts," using the term to refer to an unconscious, impelling drive toward a particular type of behavior. He believed that these two drives were related to each other and that, under ideal circumstances of adjustment, they would interact in such a way as to neutralize the overt, primitive expressions of each other. One of these instincts impels the individual toward aggressive, destructive, or hostile behavior. The other impels the individual toward erotic, constructive, or affectionate behavior.

Both of these instincts or drives are manifest in the behavior of everyone. The relationships established by one person with other people and with objects, as well as all forms of behavior, can be identified as expressions of these two motivating pressures. As suggested, the ideal adjustment implies a fusion of the aggressive and affectionate elements within the personality. When sufficiently blended with a constructive, affectionate instinct, the aggressive element loses its hostile, destructive element. When there is a failure in the fusion, one sees the direct expressions of hate and destruction.

In our culture the expressions of these drives are expected to be modified, directed, or deflected into acceptable social behavior. At best, however, the conscious ego can exert only a somewhat superficial control, so that one's ideas and action may give minor and major evidences of the predominance of either constructive or destructive impulses in a particular personality at a particular time. These drives may be vented or invested externally or turned in toward the self. In their external expressions they are constantly modified by the environmental situation. The resulting changes in the balance of the forces within the individual and between him and the outside world are the dynamic factors in personality development.

A recognition of the presence of these drives as dynamic forces is important, but even more important is an understanding of their evolution. This evolution follows a similar pattern in everyone. The drives are modified by parental training, by developmental experiences, and by many other contacts with the external world. In the infant most of the time the two antagonistic drives are so fused as to neutralize each other. Their energy is directed almost completely toward himself. As the world begins to intrude into his life with its irritations and frustrations, he expresses hostile aggression toward it. Through growth and training, if given love, the individual learns to merge the hostile with the erotic instinctual drives in order to react with toleration, and under suitable conditions to return affection. Some of the initial irritations he may absorb; others he may elude; still others he will change with his acquisition of experience and knowledge so that they cease to be irritating. As the child grows, more and more of his energy is directed away from himself and invested in the objects or the people he encounters in his environment. His reaction to them may be either hostile and aggressive or erotic and affectionate, or it may be neutral.

Individuals vary in the success with which they are able to deflect the direction of this energy from themselves to the external world. Some retain a considerable investment of the erotic drive in themselves, as manifested in many expressions of self-love. Others retain a considerable degree of investment of the aggressive drive in themselves as manifested in the neuroses, the psychoses, and many other forms of partial and even complete self-destruction.

Ideally, as one reaches psychological maturity, his mastery of the external world presumably makes it unnecessary to direct either the erotic or aggressive drives toward himself. Maturity implies aggressive constructive activity, which brings a gratifying return from appropriate investment. The directing of primitive erotic energy involves giving affection, considerate protection, and confidence to the love object, that is, the mate, who has been selected for his or her own sake and not as a mere substitute for some reluctantly abandoned earlier object, such as a parent. In maturity, the aggressive drive is so merged with the erotic drive as to provide initiative, forcefulness, strength of purpose, competitiveness, decisiveness. It no longer seeks release in any type of self-destruction or handicapping of the self. Sublimated forms of its expression are crusading, militant missionary effort, evangelism, "righteous indignation." Frustrations evoke their expression in normal persons, as do indignities and inhumanities. But ideally, the aggressive force is expressed in pure form only toward threatening or existing danger.

It is apparent then that the power of the Id is a continuous threat to the Ego. When any impulse arising within the Id is blocked in its outlet by the Ego, tension arises and is felt as anxiety.

The Ego. It is the Ego that becomes aware of anxiety because it makes up the bulk of the personality that we refer to as "consciousness." Most of it is conscious, and it represents the thinking, knowing, and feeling part of the person. The Ego begins to develop at birth, in contrast to the Id, which already is well developed at that time. As one learns from experience and gains in knowledge, the Ego expands and grows strong or is weakened, depending on those environmental factors, particularly the parents, that assist in the solution of childhood problems.

The Ego has numerous functions. It serves as the intermediary between the world, the environment outside the individual, and the inner demands, wishes, and desires that originate in the Id. Thus its first function is to make the primitive drives of the Id conform to the demands of reality. Its guiding rule, so long as it is healthy, is to accept and to modify reality. It has the function of organizing the mental processes in a coherent fashion. It has the responsibility of obtaining gratification and satisfaction from the environment. It must control and govern the crude, though superior strength, of the impulses which come from the deep unconscious. It must mold these so that they are acceptable to the world outside the personality. It must prohibit the direct expression of desires that are self-destructive or that would destroy the environment.

Even when one goes to sleep, the Ego still censors any thought processes that go on, and so one's nocturnal mental activity is forced to express itself in bizarre, distorted forms that we call dreams.

The Ego also controls all voluntary motor functions. A part of the Ego is unconscious, and through this portion of it all repression is carried on, along with other mental mechanisms (to be discussed later), without our being consciously aware of them.

The Super-Ego. The Super-Ego, the third system of the personality, is chiefly unconscious. It begins to develop in the individual during the third or fourth years as a means of partially solving the conflict in orienting himself to his parents. By developing a Super-Ego, the little child borrows strength from his parents through identification with them. He sets up an inhibiting force, a kind of police force within himself, a conscience, which keeps saying to the Ego, "You must not." Within his Super-Ego he has absorbed those standards of control presented to him by parents and teachers.

Thus the Super-Ego is both a conscious and an unconscious conscience, a critic that watches the conscious Ego deal with the strivings of the Id. When the Ego makes poor decisions, including those with which the conscience cannot agree, the Super-Ego criticizes and condemns the Ego. For instance, when one wrongs a friend, he feels remorse in proportion to his understanding of the degree or extent of his aggressions against the friend. His Ego feels guilty and seeks punishment, so that he feels he needs to make restitution. The critical Super-Ego may force him to make excessive efforts toward restitution, which may be expressed in various kinds of self-punishment, self-failure, and self-depreciation.

A knowledge of the interrelations of these three parts or systems of the personality is essential to understanding human behavior. When the equilibrium between them is disturbed, maladjustment results, and the expression of the maladjustment creates symptoms.

The Ego is the intermediary between the Id and Super-Ego and the external world. It must harmonize three powerful forces, that is, the Id, the Super-Ego, and Reality, all of which are potentially stronger than it is.

Sometimes the Ego is unable to conform to reality, that is, the external world; sometimes it is not sufficiently strong to adjust the personality to the demands of the external situation. When it is so threatened, symptoms develop; the soldier in combat frequently develops physical disturbances of his heart or his stomach. Others react by denying the reality situation by the formation of delusions or other types of falsification of the true environmental situation.

Again, if the Ego is sufficiently strong, it either holds the demands and impulses of the Id in check or modifies them into some form of expression that is socially approved. Sometimes the Ego remains loyal to reality, but the primitive wish puts on a masquerade and so disguises itself that it gains expression without the Ego's recognizing it as the forbidden desire. When this occurs, the resulting expression may be a socially approved sublimation or a neurotic symptom. When the Ego is weak, it may permit certain of these primitive impulses to gain direct expression as we see them in psychoses or antisocial behavior.

The Super-Ego dominates the Ego and is critical if the Ego fails to control the Id impulses. It is an inner judge, an unconscious arbiter of our behavior. Its blame leads to the development of feelings of guilt, which lead to self-inflicted punishment, all of which may be entirely an unconscious process.

The equilibrium of the Ego is threatened continuously from all sides. When the Ego weakens or begins to fail in its function, the individual shows the symptom of anxiety. In order to avoid anxiety the Ego develops certain devices that we call "dynamisms," or "mechanisms" that help maintain the equilibrium between these three portions of the personality. They serve as a medium of expression of the Id impulses that can be accepted by external reality. These mechanisms are a necessary part of the functional equipment of the Ego of every person, and they constitute one of the most widely accepted and most helpful portions of psychoanalytic psychiatry.

Mental Mechanisms

A slowly developing conscious Ego can control, guide, and modify the unconscious instinctual energy with only varying degrees of success. There is no one who does not experience an occasional serious maladjustment, nor are any of us completely free of eccentric or unusual traits of character and behavior. Everyone shows neurotic symptoms at one time or another. Complete control of the primitive expressions of energy is not possible all the time and under all circumstances. Psychiatric patients continuously display grossly uncontrolled or only thinly masqueraded expressions of energy that are exaggerations of the pathological behavior of everyday life.

The mental mechanisms are the devices that the personality uses, both in health and in sickness, to channel its unconscious drives. Their expressions are always apparent and conscious, but they originate in the unconscious. Therefore, their stimulus as defenses against tension induced by conflict within the personality is an automatic attempt to control the expression of primitive energy. They are not consciously activated. Once recognized, their action may be modified by a conscious decision to do so. Knowledge of these mechanisms gives us an understanding, not only of illogical behavior and ideation, but also of normal behavior.

At least seventeen different mental mechanisms have been described in psychoanalytic literature, but no classification of these is satisfactory. Some of them are a part of our growth process; thus by introjection we continuously absorb from our environment those ideals, opinions, data, and attitudes that make us what we are. Some mechanisms function primarily as defenses for the Ego against the development of anxiety and are used specifically for this purpose. Repression, mentioned earlier in this dis-

cussion, is one of these. The majority of these mechanisms are utilized both in health and in disease, but all the expressions of a few of them are always symptoms.

It is neither possible nor practical to discuss all these mechanisms in a brief space. Quite deliberately five of the more common have been selected for brief presentation as illustrative examples.[4]

One of the most common mental mechanisms is *sublimation,* the device by which we obtain gratification through the channeling of primitive energy into some type of socially approved activity. Sublimated expressions provide a healthy release of the same instinctual energy that produces symptoms in the sick individual who cannot sublimate or repress it. Although individual capacity for sublimation varies widely, much of the activity of our daily life represents this mechanism. Sublimation is always healthy, and when the individual fails to use it, he invariably displays symptoms. Thus the original aggressive drive, instead of being manifested in its raw forms of hate and destruction, is converted by sublimation into leadership, initiative, and healthy aggressiveness. All of us maintain a reservoir of hostility. In the well-adjusted individual this is drained off through many of our activities, such as a competitive athletic contest or digging in the garden or playing bridge.

Sublimation is exemplified in a major way in the choice of a vocation. Thus the nurse or the kindergarten teacher may resign her desire or hopes for children and find satisfaction in the care of many patients or children; they become the substitutes for children of her own. The primitive desire and gratification obtained in infancy through the infliction of pain or cruelty is sublimated in the butcher, and perhaps in a more refined way in the surgeon. The infantile gratification from the use of power, dominance, independence, and hoarding in the anal stage finds partial outlets in an approved fashion in the banker. Microscopic analysis of all work and play would reveal them as approved outlets for primitive energy and, as such, they represent sublimation.

[4]Other common defense mechanisms are discussed in the text on pages 198-205 **(Editor's note).**

Rationalization is a second type of mechanism that we all use frequently. Technically speaking, it is the device for explaining plausibly and thus accounting for or justifying certain feelings, ideas, or behavior. The explanation always appears to us a logical one.

All of us at times believe that our mistakes or blunders are the result of fate. We explain our feelings on the basis of the weather. When we do not do something we should, we justify our action; when we want something badly, we find good reasons for getting it. Rationalization does not refer to consciously concocted explanations but rather to apparently honest and logical thought about our attitudes and our behavior. Rationalizations may be used to justify erroneous opinions or ideas. Strong loves and hates, whether they are rational indulgences or frank prejudices, are always supported by what seem to be logical explanations. The drug addict rationalizes the reasons why he must take drugs; the deluded patient explains quite rationally to himself the reasons for his delusions. The alcoholic is sincere in his belief that he began drinking to escape his troubles or his sorrow. In general we defend our position by rationalization.

A specific type of rationalization is called idealization. By this device we avoid being critical of ourselves or of those who are very important to us emotionally. Thus the conceited, exhibitionistic individual consciously is lacking in critical judgment about himself. Lovers have an irrational fondness for each other. Blind hatred, which destroys any critical faculty, is another form of this type of rationalization.

So much of our behavior is motivated by unconscious factors that it is understandable why rationalization is such an important mechanism for our adjustment. We must rationalize in order to explain to ourselves and others why we have certain character traits, why we behave as we do, why we have certain likes and dislikes. Rationalization permits us to believe quite honestly and comfortably that we have the explanation.

Another common mechanism is *displacement*. This is a process by which the emotional value attached to one idea or person is transferred to another idea or person. The emotional attitude expressed is either out of proportion or unrelated to the object toward which it is directed.

Whenever we misplace the blame or credit for a feeling that we have, we use the mechanism of displacement. Thus the upbraiding of the roommate at the end of a hard day of classes may be a displacement of hostility toward an exacting professor. The excessive lavishing of affection on a dog may be a displacement of desire to lavish affection on some human object. An excess of anger or other emotion over any trivial incident is a displacement from emotion felt about some other situation to which it may or may not be related. When the majority of a class of students fail to make passing grades, the teacher often displaces the responsibility with a belief that the students are lazy, stupid, or eccentric. When parents fail to manage a child, they often express their sense of failure in scolding or whipping the child.

Very often displacement is used in a major way in our lives. Some individuals select as a mate a substitute mother or father and displace their feelings toward their parent in childhood onto the wife or husband. Sometimes we use displacement to keep ourselves blind or to justify our course of action. For instance, not infrequently some of us become so involved in saving the community that our families are badly neglected. The displacement of our interest and energy often protects us from recognizing the neglect and, perhaps even our resentment, toward our responsibilities to the family. Not infrequently we meet individuals whose maladjustment and dissatisfaction with their lives is taken out on everyone with whom they come in contact, whether this be the wife, the children, the employees, or merely friends.

Displacement is a kind of face-saving device that protects our Egos from seeing their mistakes and that shields us from the unpleasant recognition of our misdirected investments of emotion and interest.

One of the mechanisms that always indicates failing adjustment, even more so than displacement, is *projection*. This is the dynamism by which the individual, in order to protect himself against ideas and wishes that he cannot admit he has, projects them onto another person or object in a more or less disguised form. Even though the expressions of projection may be very mild, their use indicates a failing, or a chronically poor, adjustment.

In the latter case the individual soon acquires a reputation for his tendency to blame others for his own inadequacies. Some people always blame their partners for the mistakes in the card game; they believe they do not get the right breaks; they have the conviction that their employer, their wife, or their associates do not understand them or have been unfair to them. Unjustified suspicions are examples of projection.

By the use of this device the individual always becomes the object of attention, sometimes because of assumed persecution or sometimes by an overevaluation of ability. In either case, he believes himself to be the object of special attention and thus attributes to others an interest in and motives toward himself that are entirely false.

The extreme form of this mechanism is seen in those individuals who may, on the one hand, regard themselves as a special emissary from the Almighty, as a great leader, as the recipient of special God-given abilities, or, on the other hand, as being persecuted by the government, the FBI, the Ku Klux Klan, or some other powerful group.

Finally, another mechanism that is always a manifestation of ill health, is *conversion*. By its use the Ego channels the threatening impulse from the Id into a symbolic expression of pain, distress, or functional disorder in some part of the body. The result always is a physical symptom, either motor or sensory. In this device, as in most of the defense mechanisms, the symptom represents a compromise. The Ego denies the direct expression of the repressed wish, but the symptom is a disguised expression of this wish unrecognized by the Ego.

Minor conversions occur frequently in many of us. In most of us their appearance would not justify the diagnosis of a particular mental illness. We have stomach symptoms because of homesickness. We get a headache from some special frustration. We may develop physical symptoms either in anticipation of or as the result of a situational problem.

Conversion symptoms are most spectacularly illustrated in cases of sudden blindness, loss of voice, paralysis, anesthesia. Most of these develop under acute stress and were rather commonly seen in the combat soldier. Conversion symptoms, however, include all types of physical malfunctioning that have an emotional origin, whether this be of the stomach, heart, lungs, genital system, or other part of the body. Symptoms of this type constitute the complaints of a high percentage of patients seen by family physicians and medical specialists. Therefore, an understanding of the conversion mechanism is extremely important to all medical people.

These five mental mechanisms—sublimation, rationalization, displacement, projection, and conversion—are illustrative of the automatic devices of our mental machinery. These are methods by which the conscious Ego protects itself from the development of anxiety. They are the vehicles and modes of expression, both healthy and unhealthy, of urges or wishes that seek expression from the unconscious. They constitute the psychodynamics of the personality.

A THEORY
OF PERSONALITY AND BEHAVIOR

by Carl R. Rogers[1]

Widely known as the founder of client-centered or nondirective therapy, Carl Rogers has made additional contributions with his theory of personality and behavior and with his pioneering research on the nature of the therapeutic process itself. Both as a therapist and as a theorist, Rogers has emphasized the fundamental importance of self as the unifying and directing force in behavior; the primary function of psychotherapy, he maintains, is to provide a nonthreatening atmosphere in which the self becomes free to accept all experience and thus to realize its potential for growth. Acknowledging that his theoretical formulations reflect his clinical experience and therefore are subject to revision or disproof, Rogers has elaborated his theory of personality and behavior in terms of nineteen propositions, as stated below.

As clinical and research evidence accumulates, it is inevitable that those interested in client-centered therapy should try to formulate theories which would contain and explain the observed facts, and which would point out profitable directions for further research. This [article] attempts to report the present stage of our thinking in this matter of constructing a more generalized statement of personality dynamics and behavior. . . .

In order to present the thinking as clearly as possible, and also in order to make possible the detection of flaws or inconsistencies, the material which follows is offered as a series of propositions, with a brief explanation and exposition of each proposition. . . . Some of these propositions must be regarded as assumptions, while the majority may be regarded as hypotheses subject to proof or disproof. Taken as a whole, the series of propositions presents a theory of behavior which attempts to account for the phenomena previously known, and also for the facts regarding personality and behavior which have more recently been observed in therapy. . . .

[1]From **Client-Centered Therapy,** Houghton Mifflin Company, Boston, pp. 481-532. Copyright 1951 by Carl R. Rogers.

The Propositions

1. Every individual exists in a continually changing world of experience of which he is the center.

This private world may be called the phenomenal field, the experiential field, or described in other terms. It includes all that is experienced by the organism, whether or not these experiences are consciously perceived. Thus the pressure of the chair seat against my buttocks is something I have been experiencing for an hour, but only as I think and write about it does the symbolization of that experience become present in consciousness. . . .

It should be recognized that in this private world of experience of the individual, only a portion of that experience, and probably a very small portion, is *consciously* experienced. Many of our sensory and visceral sensations are not symbolized. It is also true, however, that a large portion of this world of experience is *available* to consciousness, and may become conscious if the need of the individual causes certain sensations to come into focus because they are associated with the satisfaction of a need. . . .

An important truth in regard to this private world of the individual is that it can only be known, in any genuine or complete sense, to the individual himself. No matter how adequately we attempt to measure the stimulus—whether it be a beam of light, a pinprick, a failure on an examination, or some more complex situation—and no matter how much we attempt to measure the perceiving organism—whether by psychometric tests or physiological calibrations—it is still true that the individual is the only one who can know how the experience was perceived. I can never know with vividness or completeness how a pinprick or a failure on an examination is experienced by you. The world of experience is for each individual, in a very significant sense, a private world. . . .

2. The organism reacts to the field as it is experienced and perceived. This perceptual field is, for the individual, "reality."

This is a simple proposition, one of which we are all aware in our own experience, yet it is·a point which is often overlooked. I do not react to some absolute reality, but to my perception of this reality. It is this perception which for me *is* reality. Snygg and Combs[2] give the example of two men driving at night on a western road. An object looms up in the middle of the road ahead. One of the men sees a large boulder, and reacts with fright. The other, a native of the country, sees a tumbleweed and reacts with nonchalance. Each reacts to the reality as perceived.

This proposition could be illustrated from the daily experience of everyone. Two individuals listen to a radio speech made by a political candidate about whom they have no previous knowledge. They are both subjected to the same auditory stimulation. Yet one perceives the candidate as a demagogue, a trickster, a false prophet, and reacts accordingly. The other perceives him as a leader of the people, a person of high aims and purposes. Each is reacting to the reality as he has perceived it. . . . This same proposition is exemplified in so-called abnormal conditions as well. The psychotic who perceives that his food is poisoned, or that some malevolent group is out to "get" him,

reacts to his reality-as-perceived in much the same fashion that you or I would·respond if we (more "realistically") perceived our food as contaminated, or our enemies as plotting against us. . . .

To the present writer it seems unnecessary to posit or try to explain any concept of "true" reality. For purposes of understanding psychological phenomena, reality is, for the individual, his perceptions. Unless we wish to involve ourselves in philosophical questions, we do not need to attempt to solve the question as to what *really* constitutes reality. . . .

While it is not necessary for our purposes to define any absolute concept of reality, it should be noted that we are continually checking our perceptions against one another, or adding them one to another, so that they become more reliable guides to "reality." For example, I see some salt in a dish. That, for me at that instant, is reality. If I taste it and it tastes salty, my perception is further confirmed. But if it tastes sweet, my whole interpretation of the situation is changed, and both in seeing and tasting I perceive the material as sugar. Thus each perception is essentially a hypothesis—a hypothesis related to the individual's need—and many of these perceptions are tested and re-tested by experience. . . . Thus the world comes to be composed of a series of tested hypotheses which provide much security. It acquires a certain predictability upon which we depend. Yet mingled with these perceptions, which have been confirmed by a variety of experiences, are perceptions which remain completely unchecked. These untested perceptions are also a part of our personal reality, and may have as much authority as those which have been checked. . . .

3. The organism reacts as an organized whole to this phenomenal field.

Although there are still some who are primarily concerned with the segmental or atomistic type of organic reaction, there is increasing acceptance of the fact that one of the most basic characteristics of organic life is its tendency toward total, organized, goal-directed responses. This is true of those responses which are primarily physiological, as well as of those which we think of as psychological. Take such a matter as the main-

[2]Donald Snygg and Arthur W. Combs, **Individual Behavior: A New Frame of Reference for Psychology,** New York: Harper & Brothers, 1949.

tenance of the water balance in the body. It has been shown that this is ordinarily maintained by the activity of the posterior lobe of the pituitary gland, which, when the body loses water, secretes more of an antidiuretic hormone, thus reducing the secretion of water by the kidney. This reaction would appear to be definitely of the atomistic type, reducible in the last analysis to purely chemical factors. But where the posterior lobe is experimentally removed, the animal drinks very large amounts of water, and thus maintains a satisfactory water balance in spite of the loss of the regulating mechanism.[3] It is thus the total, organized, goal-directed response which appears to be basic, as evidenced by the fact that, when one avenue is blocked off, the animal organizes to utilize another avenue to the same goal. The same would be true of various compensatory physiological phenomena.

In the psychological realm, any simple S-R [stimulus-response] type of explanation of behavior seems almost impossible. A young woman talks for an hour about her antagonism to her mother. She finds, following this, that a persistent asthmatic condition, which she has not even mentioned to the counselor, is greatly improved. On the other hand, a man who feels that his security in his work is being seriously threatened, develops ulcers. It is extremely cumbersome to try to account for such phenomena on the basis of an atomistic chain of events. The outstanding fact which must be taken into theoretical account is that the organism is at all times a total organized system, in which alteration of any part may produce changes in any other part. Our study of such part phenomena must start from this central fact of consistent, goal-directed organization.

4. The organism has one basic tendency and striving—to actualize, maintain, and enhance the experiencing organism.

Rather than many needs and motives, it seems entirely possible that all organic and psychological needs may be described as partial aspects of this one fundamental need. It is difficult to find satisfactory words for this proposition. The particular phrasing is from Snygg and Combs.[4] The

words used are an attempt to describe the observed directional force in organic life—a force which has been regarded as basic by many scientists, but which has not been too well described in testable or operational terms.

We are talking here about the tendency of the organism to maintain itself—to assimilate food, to behave defensively in the face of threat, to achieve the goal of self-maintenance even when the usual pathway to that goal is blocked. We are speaking of the tendency of the organism to move in the direction of maturation, as maturation is defined for each species. This involves self-actualization, though it should be understood that this too is a directional term. . . .

It is our experience in therapy which has brought us to the point of giving this proposition a central place. The therapist becomes very much aware that the forward-moving tendency of the human organism is the basis upon which he relies most deeply and fundamentally. It is evident not only in the general tendency of clients to move in the direction of growth when the factors in the situation are clear, but is most dramatically shown in very serious cases where the individual is on the brink of psychosis or suicide. Here the therapist is very keenly aware that the only force upon which he can basically rely is the organic tendency toward ongoing growth and enhancement. . . .

It would be grossly inaccurate to suppose that the organism operates smoothly in the direction of self-enhancement and growth. It would be perhaps more correct to say that the organism moves through struggle and pain toward enhancement and growth. The whole process may be symbolized and illustrated by the child's learning to walk. The first steps involve struggle, and usually pain. Often it is true that the immediate reward involved in taking a few steps is in no way commensurate with the pain of falls and bumps. The child may, because of the pain, revert to crawling for a time. Yet, in the overwhelming majority of individuals, the forward direction of growth is more powerful than the satisfactions of remaining infantile. The child will actualize himself, in spite of the painful experiences in so doing. In the same way, he will become independent, responsible, self-governing, socialized, in spite of the pain

[3]J. McV. Hunt, ed., **Personality and the Behavior Disorders**, New York: The Ronald Press Company, 1944, pp. 601-602.
[4]Snygg and Combs, op. cit.

which is often involved in these steps. Even where he does not, because of a variety of circumstances, exhibit growth of these more complex sorts, one may still rely on the fact that the tendency is present. Given the opportunity for clear-cut choice between forward-moving and regressive behavior, the tendency will operate. . . .

5. Behavior is basically the goal-directed attempt of the organism to satisfy its needs as experienced, in the field as perceived.

. . . All needs have a basic relatedness, if we accept Proposition 4, in that they all spring from and have reference to, the basic tendency to maintain and enhance the organism. These needs occur as physiological tensions which, when experienced, form the basis of behavior which appears functionally (though not consciously) designed to reduce the tension and to maintain and enhance the organism. The need itself is not necessarily consciously experienced; there are seemingly different levels of description. In hunger, for example, stomach contractions occur which ordinarily are not directly experienced. The excitation which is thus set up may be experienced vaguely and below the conscious level, nevertheless bringing about behavior which is in the direction of food, or it may be symbolized and perceived on the conscious level as hunger.

The question arises, Do all needs have their origin in physiological tensions? Are the needs for affection and achievement, for example, which seem to be significantly related to the maintenance and enhancement of the organism, biologically based? We should gain by well-planned research on this point. The work by Ribble[5] and others would seem to indicate that the need for affection is a physiological need, and that the infant who does not have adequate close physical contact with a mother-person is left in a state of unsatisfied physiological tension. If this is true of the infant, then it is easy to see how this need, like all the others, becomes elaborated and channelized through cultural conditioning into needs which are only remotely based upon the underlying physiological tension. . . .

[5]Margaret A. Ribble, "Infantile Experiences in Relation to Personality Disorders," **Personality and the Behavior Disorders,** Vol. II, J. McV. Hunt, ed., New York: The Ronald Press Company, 1944.

It is noted that behavior is postulated as a reaction to the field as perceived. . . . A man in the desert will struggle just as hard to reach the "lake" which he perceives in a mirage, as to reach a real water hole. At a more complex level, a man may strive for money because he perceives money as the source of emotional security, even though in fact it may not satisfy his need. Often, of course, the perception has a high degree of correspondence with reality, but it is important to recognize that it is the perception, not the reality, which is crucial in determining behavior.

It should also be mentioned that in this concept of motivation all the effective elements exist in the present. Behavior is not "caused" by something which occurred in the past. Present tensions and present needs are the only ones which the organism endeavors to reduce or satisfy. While it is true that past experience has certainly served to modify the meaning which will be perceived in present experiences, yet there is no behavior except to meet a present need.

6. Emotion accompanies and in general facilitates such goal-directed behavior, the kind of emotion being related to the seeking versus the consummatory aspects of the behavior, and the intensity of the emotion being related to the perceived significance of the behavior for the maintenance and enhancement of the organism.

In this goal-seeking effort which is termed behavior, what is the place of emotion, feeling, emotionalized attitudes? . . . We may think of emotions as falling primarily into two groups—the unpleasant and/or excited feelings, and the calm and/or satisfied emotions. The first group tends to accompany the seeking effort of the organism, and the second to accompany satisfaction of the need, the consummatory experience. The first group appears to have the effect of integrating and concentrating behavior upon the goal, rather than having the disintegrating effect which some psychologists have pictured. Thus, in anything but excessive degree, fear accelerates the organization of the individual in the direction of escape from danger, and competitive jealousy concentrates the efforts of the individual to surpass. . . .

The intensity of the emotional reaction appears to vary according to the perceived relationship of the behavior to the maintenance and enhancement of the organism. Thus if my leap to the curb to escape the oncoming automobile is perceived as making the difference between life and death, it will be accompanied by strong emotion. The reading of another chapter tonight in a new psychology book, a behavior which is seen as having a slight relationship to my development, will be accompanied by a very mild emotion indeed. . . .

7. The best vantage point for understanding behavior is from the internal frame of reference of the individual himself.

It was mentioned in Proposition 1 that the only person who could fully know his field of experience was the individual himself. Behavior is a reaction to the field as perceived. It would therefore appear that behavior might be best understood by gaining, in so far as possible, the internal frame of reference of the person himself, and seeing the world of experience as nearly as possible through his eyes.

What we have been doing for the most part in psychology may be likened to the early studies of primitive societies. The observer reported that these primitive peoples ate various ridiculous foods, held fantastic and meaningless ceremonies, and behaved in ways that were a mixture of virtue and depravity. The thing that he did not see was that he was observing from his own frame of reference and placing his own values upon their modes of behavior. We do the same thing in psychology when we speak of "trial-and-error behavior," "delusions," "abnormal behavior," and so on. We fail to see that we are evaluating the person from our own, or from some fairly general, frame of reference, but that the only way to understand his behavior meaningfully is to understand it as he perceives it himself, just as the only way to understand another culture is to assume the frame of reference of that culture. When that is done, the various meaningless and strange behaviors are seen to be part of a meaningful and goal-directed activity. There is then no such thing as random trial-and-error behavior, no such thing as a delusion, except as the individual may apply these terms to his past behavior. In the present, the behavior is always purposeful, and in response to reality as it is perceived. . . .

8. A portion of the total perceptual field gradually becomes differentiated as the self.

. . . We shall have much to say about various aspects of the operation of the self. For the present the point is made that gradually, as the infant develops, a portion of the total private world becomes recognized as "me," "I," "myself." There are many puzzling and unanswered questions in regard to the dawning concept of the self. We shall try to point out some of these.

Is social interaction necessary in order for a self to develop? Would the hypothetical person reared alone upon a desert island have a self? Is the self primarily a product of the process of symbolization? Is it the fact that experiences may be not only directly experienced, but symbolized and manipulated in thought, that makes the self possible? Is the self simply the symbolized portion of experience? These are some of the questions which shrewd research may be able to answer.

Another point which needs to be made in regard to the development of a conscious self is the fact that it is not necessarily coexistent with the physical organism. Angyal[6] points out that there is no possibility of a sharp line between organism and environment, and that there is likewise no sharp limit between the experience of the self and of the outside world. Whether or not an object or an experience is regarded as a part of the self depends to a considerable extent upon whether or not it is perceived as within the control of the self. Those elements which we control are regarded as a part of self, but when even such an object as a part of our body is out of control, it is experienced as being less a part of the self. The way in which, when a foot "goes to sleep" from lack of circulation, it becomes an object to us rather than a part of self, may be a sufficient illustration. . . .

It should be clear from the foregoing that though some authors use the term "self" as synonymous with "organism" it is here being used in a more restricted sense, namely, the awareness of being, of functioning.

9. As a result of interaction with the environment, and particularly as a result

[6]András Angyal, **Foundations for a Science of Personality,** New York: The Commonwealth Fund, 1941.

of evaluational interaction with others, the structure of self is formed—an organized, fluid, but consistent conceptual pattern of perceptions of characteristics and relationships of the "I" or the "me," together with values attached to these concepts.

10. The values attached to experiences, and the values which are a part of the self structure, in some instances are values experienced directly by the organism, and in some instances are values introjected or taken over from others, but perceived in distorted fashion, *as if* they had been experienced directly.

It will probably be best to discuss these two important propositions together. . . .

As the infant interacts with his environment he gradually builds up concepts about himself, about the environment, and about himself in relation to the environment. While these concepts are nonverbal, and may not be present in consciousness, this is no barrier to their functioning as guiding principles. . . . Intimately associated with all these experiences is a direct organismic valuing which appears highly important for understanding later development. The very young infant has little uncertainty in valuing. At the same time that there is the dawning awareness of "I experience," there is also the awareness that "I like," "I dislike." "I am cold, and I dislike it," "I am cuddled and I like it." "I can reach my toes and find this enjoyable"—these statements appear to be adequate descriptions of the infant's experience, though he does not have the verbal symbols which we have used. He appears to value those experiences which he perceives as enhancing himself, and to place a negative value on those experiences which seem to threaten himself or which do not maintain or enhance himself.

There soon enters into this picture the evaluation of self by others. "You're a good child," "You're a naughty boy"—these and similar evaluations of himself and of his behavior by his parents and others come to form a large and significant part of the infant's perceptual field. Social experiences, social evaluations by others, become a part of his phenomenal field along with experiences not involving others—for example, that radiators are hot, stairs are dangerous, and candy tastes good.

It is at this stage of development, it would seem, that there takes place a type of distorted symbolization of experience, and a denial of experience to awareness, which has much significance for the later development of psychological maladjustment. Let us try to put this in general and schematic terms.

One of the first and most important aspects of the self-experience of the ordinary child is that he is loved by his parents. He perceives himself as lovable, worthy of love, and his relationship to his parents as one of affection. He experiences all this with satisfaction. This is a significant and core element of the structure of self as it begins to form.

At this same time he is experiencing positive sensory values, is experiencing enhancement, in other ways. It is enjoyable to have a bowel movement at any time or place that the physiological tension is experienced. It is satisfying and enhancing to hit, or to try to do away with, baby brother. As these things are initially experienced, they are not necessarily inconsistent with the concept of self as a lovable person.

But then to our schematic child comes a serious threat to self. He experiences words and actions of his parents in regard to these satisfying behaviors, and the words and actions add up to the feeling "You are bad, the behavior is bad, and you are not loved or lovable when you behave in this way." This constitutes a deep threat to the nascent structure of self. The child's dilemma might be schematized in these terms: "If I admit to awareness the satisfactions of these behaviors and the values I apprehend in these experiences, then this is inconsistent with my self as being loved or lovable."

Certain results then follow in the development of the ordinary child. One result is a denial in awareness of the satisfactions that were experienced. The other is to distort the symbolization of the experience of the parents. The accurate symbolization would be: "I perceive my parents as experiencing this behavior as unsatisfying to them." The distorted symbolization, distorted to preserve the threatened concept of self, is: "*I* perceive this behavior as unsatisfying."

It is in this way, it would seem, that parental attitudes are not only introjected, but what is much more important, are experienced not as the attitude of another, but in distorted fashion, *as if* based on the evidence of one's own sensory and visceral equipment. . . .

Out of these dual sources—the direct experiencing by the individual, and the distorted symbolization of sensory reactions resulting in the introjection of values and concepts *as if* experienced—there grows the structure of the self. . . . The self-structure is an organized configuration of perceptions of the self which are admissible to awareness. It is composed of such elements as the perceptions of one's characteristics and abilities; the percepts and concepts of the self in relation to others and to the environment; the value qualities which are perceived as associated with experiences and objects; and the goals and ideals which are perceived as having positive or negative valence. It is, then, the organized picture, existing in awareness either as figure or ground, of the self and the self-in-relationship, together with the positive or negative values which are associated with those qualities and relationships, as they are perceived as existing in the past, present, or future. . . .

11. As experiences occur in the life of the individual, they are either (a) symbolized, perceived, and organized into some relationship to the self, (b) ignored because there is no perceived relationship to the self-structure, (c) denied symbolization or given a distorted symbolization because the experience is inconsistent with the structure of the self.

Let us look first at those experiences which are ignored because they are irrelevant to the self-structure. There are various noises going on at this moment, in the distance. Until they serve my intellectual need of this moment for an example, I am relatively oblivious to them. They exist in the ground of my phenomenal field, but they do not reinforce or contradict my concept of self, they meet no need related to the self, they are ignored. . . .

A more important group of experiences are those which are accepted into consciousness and organized into some relationship with the self-structure either because they meet a need of the self or because they are consistent with the self-structure and thus reinforce it. The client who has a concept of self that "I just don't feel that I can take my place in society like everybody else" perceives that she hasn't learned from her schoolwork, that she fails when she attempts things, that she does not react normally, and so on. She selects from her many sensory experiences those which fit in with her concept of herself. . . .

Likewise a great many experiences are symbolized because they are related to the needs of the self. I notice a book because it is on a topic I wish to learn about; I perceive neckties when I am preparing to buy one for myself. The infantryman perceives spots of freshly turned dirt in the road when these might indicate the existence of a land mine.

It is the third group of sensory and visceral experiences, those which seem to be prevented from entering awareness, which demand our closest attention, for it is in this realm that there lie many phenomena of human behavior which psychologists have endeavored to explain. In some instances the denial of the perception is something rather conscious. The client cited above, whose self-concept was so negative, reports: "When people tell me they think I'm intelligent, I just don't believe it. I just—I guess I don't want to believe it. I don't know why I don't want to believe it—I just don't want to. It should give me confidence, but it doesn't. I think they just really don't know." Here she can perceive and accept readily anyone's depreciation of her, because this fits in with her self-concept. Contradictory evaluations however are denied, by selecting and stressing other perceptions, such as that others cannot really know her. This type of more or less conscious denial of perception is certainly a frequent occurrence with everyone.

There is, however, an even more significant type of denial which is the phenomenon the Freudians have tried to explain by the concept of repression. In this instance, it would appear that there is the organic experience, but there is no symbolization of this experience, or only a distorted symbolization, because an adequate conscious representation of it would be entirely inconsistent with the concept of self. . . . The adolescent who has been brought up in an oversolicitous home, and whose concept of self is that of one who is grateful to his parents, may feel intense anger at the subtle control which is being exerted over him. Organically he experiences the physiological changes which accompany anger, but his conscious self can prevent these experiences from being symbolized and hence consciously perceived. Or he can symbolize them in some distorted fashion which is consistent with his structure of self, such as perceiving these organic sensations as "a bad headache." . . .

It should be noted that perceptions are excluded because they are contradictory, not because they are derogatory. It seems nearly as difficult to accept a perception which would alter the self-concept in an expanding or socially acceptable direction as to accept an experience which would alter it in a constricting or socially disapproved direction. The self-distrusting client cited above has as much difficulty accepting her intelligence as a person with a self-concept of superiority would have in accepting experiences indicating mediocrity. . . .

12. Most of the ways of behaving which are adopted by the organism are those which are consistent with the concept of self.

Although there are some significant exceptions to this statement (exceptions which will be discussed in the following proposition), it is noteworthy that in most instances the form of the seeking effort is dictated by the concept of self. As the organism strives to meet its needs in the world as it is experienced, the form which the striving takes must be a form consistent with the concept of self. The man who has certain values attached to honesty cannot strive for a sense of achievement through means which seem to him dishonest. The person who regards himself as having no aggressive feelings cannot satisfy a need for aggression in any direct fashion. The only channels by which needs may be satisfied are those which are consistent with the organized concept of self.

In most instances this channelization does not involve any distortion of the need which is being satisfied. Of the various ways of satisfying the need for food or for affection, the individual selects only those which are consistent with the concept which he has of himself. There are times, however, when the denial of experience, spoken of above, plays a part in this process. For example, a pilot who conceives of himself as a brave and relatively fearless individual is assigned to a mission which involves great risk. Physiologically he experiences fear and a need to escape from this danger. These reactions cannot be symbolized into consciousness, since they would be too contradictory to his concept of self. The organic need, however, persists. He can perceive that "the engine is not running quite properly," or that "I am ill and have an upset digestive system," and on these grounds excuse himself from the mission. . . . Most neurotic behavior is of this type. In the typical neurosis, the organism is satisfying a need which is not recognized in consciousness, by behavioral means which are consistent with the concept of self and hence can be consciously accepted. . . .

13. Behavior may, in some instances, be brought about by organic experiences and needs which have not been symbolized. Such behavior may be inconsistent with the structure of the self, but in such instances the behavior is not "owned" by the individual.

In moments of great danger or other emergency stress, the individual may behave with efficiency and ingenuity to meet the needs for safety or whatever other needs exist, but without ever bringing such situations, or the behavior called forth, to conscious symbolization. In such instances the individual feels "I didn't know what I was doing," "I really wasn't responsible for what I was doing." The conscious self feels no degree of government over the actions which took place. . . .

Another example of this sort of behavior occurs when many of the organically experienced needs are refused admittance to consciousness because inconsistent with the concept of self. The pressure of the organic need may become so great that the organism initiates its own seeking behavior and hence brings about the satisfaction of the need, without ever relating the seeking behavior to the concept of self. Thus, a boy whose upbringing created a self-concept of purity and freedom from "base" sexual impulses was arrested for lifting the skirts of two little girls and examining them. He insisted that he could not have performed this behavior, and when presented with witnesses, was positive that "I was not myself." The developing sexuality of an adolescent boy, and the accompanying curiosity, constituted a strong organic need for which there seemed no channel of satisfaction which was consistent with the concept of self. Eventually the organism behaved in such a way as to gain satisfaction, but this behavior was not felt to be, nor was it, a part of the self. It was behavior which was dissociated from the concept of self, and over which the boy exercised no conscious control. The organized character of the behavior grows out of the fact that the organism on a physiological basis can initiate and carry on complex behavior to meet its needs. . . .

14. Psychological maladjustment exists when the organism denies to awareness significant sensory and visceral experiences, which consequently are not symbolized and organized into the gestalt of the self-structure. When this situation exists, there is a basic or ·potential psychological tension.

. . . Conscious control becomes more difficult as the organism strives to satisfy needs which are not consciously admitted, and to react to experiences which are denied by the conscious self. Tension then exists, and if the individual becomes to any degree aware of this tension or discrepancy, he feels anxious, feels that he is not united or integrated, that he is unsure of his direction. . . .

To illustrate briefly the nature of maladjustment, take the familiar picture of a mother whom the diagnostician would term rejecting. She has as part of her concept of self a whole constellation which may be summed up by saying, "I am a good and loving mother." . . . With this concept of self she can accept and assimilate those organic sensations of affection which she feels toward her child. But the organic experience of dislike, distaste, or hatred toward her child is something which is denied to her conscious self. The experience exists, but it is not permitted accurate symbolization. The organic need is for aggressive acts which would fulfill these attitudes and satisfy the tension which exists. The organism strives for the achievement of this satisfaction, but it can do so for the most part only through those channels which are consistent with the self-concept of a good mother. Since the good mother could be aggressive toward her child only if he merited punishment, she perceives much of his behavior as being bad, deserving punishment, and therefore the aggressive acts can be carried through, without being contrary to the values organized in her picture of self. . . . This is a good illustration of most maladjustment in which the organism is striving for certain satisfactions in the field as organically experienced, whereas the concept of self is more constricted and cannot permit in awareness many of the actual experiences. . . .

15. Psychological adjustment exists when the concept of the self is such that all the sensory and visceral experiences of the organism are, or may be, assimilated on a symbolic level into a consistent relationship with the concept of self.

This proposition may be put in several different ways. We may say that freedom from inner tension, or psychological adjustment, exists when the concept of self is at least roughly congruent with all the experiences of the organism. . . . The mother who "rejects" her child can lose the inner tensions connected with her relationship to her child if she has a concept of self which permits her to accept her feelings of dislike for the child, as well as her feelings of affection and liking. . . .

The best definition of what constitutes integration appears to be this statement that all the sensory and visceral experiences are admissable to awareness through accurate symbolization, and organizable into' one system which is internally consistent and which is, or is related to, the structure of self. Once this type of integration occurs, then the tendency toward growth can become fully operative, and the individual moves in the directions normal to all organic life. . . .

One aspect of this proposition for which we have some research evidence, but which could be tested even more clearly, is that conscious acceptance of impulses and perceptions greatly increases the possibility of conscious control. . . . The sense of autonomy, of self-government, is synonymous with having all experiences available to consciousness.

The term "available to consciousness" in the last sentence is deliberately chosen. It is the fact that all experiences, impulses, sensations are *available* that is important, and not necessarily the fact that they are present in consciousness. It is the organization of the concept of self *against* the symbolization of certain experiences contradictory to itself, which is the significant negative fact. Actually, when all experiences are assimilated in relationship to the self and made a part of the structure of self, there tends to be *less* of what is called "self-consciousness" on the part of the individual. Behavior becomes more spontaneous, expression of attitudes is less guarded, because the self can accept such attitudes and such behavior as a part of itself. . . .

16. Any experience which is inconsistent with the organization or structure of self may be perceived as a threat, and the more of these perceptions there are, the more rigidly the self-structure is organized to maintain itself.

This proposition is an attempt to formulate a description of certain clinical facts. If the rejecting mother previously mentioned is told that several observers have come to the conclusion that she does reject her child, the inevitable result is that she will, for the moment, exclude any assimilation of this experience. She may attack the conditions of observation, the training or authority of the observers, the degree of understanding they possess, and so forth and so on. She will organize the defenses of her own concept of herself as a loving and good mother, and will be able to substantiate this concept with a mass of evidence. She will obviously perceive the judgment of the observers as a threat, and will organize in defense of her own governing concept. . . . If the self cannot defend itself against deep threats, the result is a catastrophic psychological breakdown and disintegration. . . .

17. Under certain conditions, involving primarily complete absence of any threat to the self-structure, experiences which are inconsistent with it may be perceived, and examined, and the structure of self revised to assimilate and include such experiences.

Here an important clinical fact, attested by many therapeutic cases, is difficult to state in ac-

curately generalized form. It is clear that self-concepts change, both in the ordinary development of the individual, and in therapy. The previous proposition formulates the facts about the defenses of the self, while this one endeavors to state the way in which change may come about.

. . . In therapy of a client-centered form . . . the client is gradually assured that he is accepted as he is, and that each new facet of himself which is revealed is also accepted. It is then that experiences which have been denied can be symbolized, often very gradually, and hence brought clearly into conscious form. Once they are conscious, the concept of self is expanded so that they may be included as a part of a consistent total. Thus the rejecting mother, in such an atmosphere, is apt first to admit the perception of her behavior—"I suppose that at times it must seem to him that I don't like him"—and then the possibility of an experience inconsistent with self—"I suppose that at times I *don't* like him"—and gradually the formulation of a broadened concept of self: "I can admit that I like him and I don't like him and we can still get along satisfactorily." . . .

If we try to analyze the elements which make possible this reorganization of the structure of self, there would appear to be two possible factors. One is the self-initiated apprehension of the new material. Exploration of experience is made possible by the counselor, and since the self is accepted at every step of its exploration and in any change it may exhibit, it seems possible gradually to explore areas at a "safe" rate, and hitherto denied experiences are slowly and tentatively accepted just as a small child slowly and tentatively becomes acquainted with a frightening object. Another factor which may be involved is that the counselor is accepting toward all experiences, all attitudes, all perceptions. This social value may be introjected by the client, and applied to his own experiences. This last certainly cannot be the major reason, since it is often known to the client that the counselor is one among a thousand in holding such a value, and that society in general would not accept the client as he is. Nevertheless this introjection of the counselor attitude may be at least a temporary or partial step toward the client's experiencing of himself **as acceptable.** . . .

A question sometimes raised is that if absence of threat to the self-concept were all that was required, it might seem that the individual could, at any time that he was alone, face these inconsistent experiences. We know that this does happen in many minor circumstances. A man may be criticized for a persistent failing. At the time he refuses to admit this experience at face value, because it is too threatening to his self-organization. He denies the fault, rationalizes the criticism. But later, alone, he rethinks the matter, accepts the criticism as just, and revises his concept of self, and consequently his behavior, as a result. For experiences which are deeply denied, however, because they are deeply inconsistent with the concept of self, this does not avail. It appears possible for the person to face such inconsistency only while in a relationship with another in which he is sure that he will be accepted. . . . .

It should also be obvious that what is being described here is a learning process, perhaps the most important learning of which the person is capable, namely the learning of self. It is to be hoped that those who have specialized in theory of learning may begin to utilize the knowledge from that field in helping to describe the way in which the individual learns a new configuration of self.

18. When the individual perceives and accepts into one consistent and integrated system all his sensory and visceral experiences, then he is necessarily more understanding of others and is more accepting of others as separate individuals.

. . . If we try to understand the theoretical basis upon which this takes place, it appears to be as follows:

The person who denies some experiences must continually defend himself against the symbolization of those experiences.

As a consequence, all experiences are viewed defensively as potential threats, rather than for what they really are.

Thus in interpersonal relationships, words or behaviors are experienced and perceived as threatening, which were not so intended.

Also, words and behaviors in others are attacked because they represent or resemble the feared experiences.

There is then no real understanding of the other as a separate person, since he is perceived mostly in terms of threat or nonthreat to the self.

But when all experiences are available to consciousness and are integrated, then defensiveness is minimized. When there is no need to defend, there is no need to attack.

When there is no need to attack, the other person is perceived for what he really is, a separate individual, operating in terms of his own meanings, based on his own perceptual field.

While this may sound abstruse, it is corroborated by much everyday evidence, as well as by clinical experience. Who are the individuals, in any neighborhood, or in any group, that inspire confidential relationships, seem able to be understanding of others? They tend to be individuals with a high degree of acceptance of all aspects of self. In clinical experience, how do better interpersonal relationships emerge? It is on this same basis. The rejecting mother who accepts her own negative attitudes toward her child finds that this acceptance, which at first she has feared, makes her more relaxed with her child. She is able to observe him for what he is, not simply through a screen of defensive reactions. Doing so, she perceives that he is an interesting person, with bad features, but also good ones, toward whom she feels at times hostile, but toward whom she also feels at times affectionate. On this comfortable and realistic and spontaneous basis a *real* relationship develops out of her real experiencing, a satisfying relationship to both. It may not be composed entirely of sweetness and light, but it is far more comfortable than any artificial relationship could possibly be. It is based primarily upon an acceptance of the fact that her child is a separate person. . . .

The implications of this aspect of our theory are such as to stretch the imagination. Here is a theoretical basis for sound interpersonal, intergroup, and international relationships. Stated in terms of social psychology, this proposition becomes the statement that the person (or persons or group) who accepts himself thoroughly, will necessarily improve his relationship with those with whom he has personal contact, because of his greater understanding and acceptance of them.

This atmosphere of understanding and acceptance is the very climate most likely to create a . . . consequent self-acceptance in the person who is exposed to it. Thus we have, in effect, a psychological "chain reaction" which appears to have tremendous potentialities for the handling of problems of social relationships.

19. As the individual perceives and accepts into his self-structure more of his organic experiences, he finds that he is replacing his present value *system*—based so largely upon introjections which have been distortedly symbolized—with a continuing organismic valuing process.

In therapy, as the person explores his phenomenal field, he comes to examine the values which he has introjected and which he has used as if they were based upon his own experience. (See Proposition 10.) He is dissatisfied with them, often expressing the attitude that he has just been doing what others thought he should do. But what does *he* think he should do? . . . If he cannot longer accept the "ought" and "should," the "right" and "wrong" of the introjected system, how can he know what values take their place?

Gradually he . . . discovers that his own senses, his own physiological equipment, can provide the data for making value judgments and for continuously revising them. No one needs to tell him that it is good to act in a freer and more spontaneous fashion, rather than in the rigid way to which he has been accustomed. He senses, he feels that it is satisfying and enhancing. Or when he acts in a defensive fashion, it is his own organism that feels the immediate and short-term satisfaction of being protected and that also senses the longer-range dissatisfaction of having to remain on guard. . . . He discovers that he does not need to *know* what are the correct values; through the data supplied by his own organism, he can experience what is satisfying and enhancing. He can put his confidence in a valuing *process*, rather than in some rigid, introjected *system* of values. . . .

. . . [Although] the establishment of values by each individual may seem to suggest a complete anarchy of values, experience indicates that quite the opposite is true. Since all individuals have basically the same needs, including the need for acceptance by others, it appears that when each individual formulates his own values, in terms of his own direct experience, it is not anarchy which results, but a high degree of commonality and a genuinely socialized system of values. One of the ultimate ends, then, of an hypothesis of confidence in the individual, and in his capacity to resolve his own conflicts, is the emergence of value systems which are unique and personal for each individual, and which are changed by the changing evidence of organic experience, yet which are at the same time deeply socialized, possessing a high degree of similarity in their essentials. . . .

Conclusion

This [article] has endeavored to present a theory of personality and behavior which is consistent with our experience and research in client-centered therapy. This theory is basically phenomenological in character, and relies heavily upon the concept of the self as an explanatory construct. It pictures the end-point of personality development as being a basic congruence between the phenomenal field of experience and the conceptual structure of the self—a situation which, if achieved, would represent freedom from internal strain and anxiety, and freedom from potential strain; which would represent the maximum in realistically oriented adaptation; which would mean the establishment of an individualized value system having considerable identity with the value system of any other equally well-adjusted member of the human race.

It would be too much to hope that the many hypotheses of this theory will prove to be correct. If they prove to be a stimulation to significant study of the deeper dynamics of human behavior, they will have served their purpose well.

A TRAIT APPROACH

TO PERSONALITY STUDY

by J. P. Guilford[1]

This selection introduces an approach to personality study that differs markedly from the clinical methods of Rogers and Freud. Maintaining that a scientifically useful theory of personality must be precise and subject to experimental verification, Guilford (with others) has used the mathematical method of factor analysis to describe personality in terms of its component traits. Dr. Guilford is Professor of Psychology at the University of Southern California.

It is natural that such a widely used word as "personality" should have a variety of definitions. After a survey of this matter, Allport[2] concludes that there are at least fifty different meanings of the term. He reports that "personality" came originally from the Latin word "persona," which was associated with the ancient Greek theater. A Greek player commonly held a mask before his face. The mask was called a "persona" because he talked through it. In time the term "persona" came to apply to the actor and eventually to individuals in general. . . .

A Trait Definition of Personality

The definition of personality [adopted by this author] starts logically from an axiom to which everyone seems agreed: each and every personality is unique. This statement includes identical twins, for it is possible to find differences even in pairs of such individuals. A person cannot be unique without differing from others. He is, of course, similar in some respects. But considering his whole pattern of characteristics, he is different from all others. It is in individual differences, then, that we find the logical key to personality, and we shall find later that it is also a most useful, operational key. *An individual's personality*, then, *is his unique pattern of traits.*

[1]From **Personality** by J. P. Guilford, pp. 2, 5-6, 21-24, 85-89. Copyright © 1959 by McGraw-Hill Book Company, Inc., New York, and used with their permission.
[2]Gordon W. Allport, **Personality: A Psychological Interpretation,** New York: Henry Holt and Company, 1937.

Traits. This definition of personality . . . emphasizes individual differences. This means that we can best know personalities by comparing them with one another. There are no absolute standards for personalities: there are only other personalities from which our frames of reference must be derived. Comparisons of personalities must therefore be made.

It is humanly impossible for us to compare one "person-as-a-whole" with another "person-as-a-whole." The act of comparison is an analytical process. In fact, the act of observation of a single person is an analytical process, as is the act of observing anything. Things, including persons, are known by their properties. An object is round, or sharp, or hard, or all of these things. A person is observed to react promptly, or vigorously, or accurately, or in all of these ways. Properties are abstractions that come by way of analysis from totalities. Our abstraction of a property from a totality does not destroy the totality; it remains the same unitary object it was before. No one can therefore truthfully claim that his abstractions, however numerous, have exhausted the object or will ever completely account for it. But this is not sufficient reason for refusing to analyze. We can extend our observations and thus approach complete coverage of the totality if we have the patience to do so.

Comparisons of individuals are thus commonly made in terms of one aspect at a time, or at least in a limited number of aspects. Persons A and B differ in aspects $c, d, e, f, j,$ and so on: persons X

and Y differ in aspects d, f, g, j, m, and t, and so on. More often, our comparisons are between a person Q and the norms (typical qualities) for the population of which Q is a member.

The aspects or properties that we have just been considering are *traits*. *A trait is any distinguishable, relatively enduring way in which one individual differs from others.* "Trait" is thus a very broad, general term. A trait of personality may be as inclusive as a general attitude of self-confidence or as narrow as a specific habit, such as a conditioned muscular contraction in response to a sound. A trait may be a characteristic indicated by behavior, as in the two examples just given, or of physical make-up. The former is a behavior trait, the latter a somatic trait. . . .

Approaches to the Study of Personality

In the study of personality, is the interest to be in persons as such or in abstractions about people in general? This question, in turn, presents another issue which, in some respects, is related to the one discussed first but also presents new aspects. Difference of opinion concerning this issue goes somewhat deeper than with the other; furthermore, it involves logical problems of scientific theory and method.

The personal view. The personal or personalistic point of view that is often held by clinicians is very well described in the following quotation from Murray:[3]

"Any conceptual formulation of man's experience . . . must necessarily do violence to human feelings. . . . This will be so because it is the substitution of heartless, denotative, referential symbols for the moving immediacy of living. By employing such a scheme, a person's vital movements, once warm and passionately felt, become transformed into a cruelly commonplace formula, which dispossesses them of unique value. . . . The artist's representation of an experience, on the other hand, is a re-invocation of the original . . . equally immediate, exciting, and intense."

[3]Henry A. Murray, **Explorations in Personality: A Clinical and Experimental Study of Fifty Men of College Age,** New York: Oxford University Press, 1938, pp. 17-18.

Such a view favors the retention of as much of the immediately given, total view of personality in scientific studies as it is possible to achieve.

The impersonal view. The basic scientist's reply to the last statement is likely to be that we must lose the individual in order that we may find him. In some respects the difference between the personal and impersonal views is like that between applied and fundamental research. The objective of applied research is to obtain the answer to a problem of immediate concern, pertaining to a particular place, time, and subgroup or population. The information obtained is of limited use, for it usually cannot be generalized. Fundamental research, on the other hand, is designed to obtain information that is more independent of particular circumstances. The results have more general significance and a larger sphere of application. . . .

Idiographic vs. nomothetic approaches. In terms of methodology, the personal or personalistic view calls for an approach that has been called *idiographic*. This means the intensive and extensive study of one person at a time. The approach is contrasted with that called *nomothetic*, which calls for the study of many individuals, each probably less extensively. The idiographic approach seeks to understand persons. The nomothetic approach seeks to arrive at general principles that apply to people generally; in this sense it represents the impersonal view.

The differences can be made clearer if we consider some basic differences in the way personality can be investigated. Whatever our views or our methods, when we undertake to study personality, we encounter three main variations. We may study different *persons* and different *traits*, and we may make observations on different *occasions*. In the typical study using the nomothetic approach, interest is likely to be centered upon one trait or a relatively small number of traits with the purpose of finding out how each trait varies in a relatively large number of persons on one occasion or on a small number of occasions. Typically, there are many persons, but few traits and few occasions are involved—perhaps only one trait and one occasion. For any trait, the main reference point will be the average trait position of the population with which the study is concerned. The average measurement is regarded as a group norm for that trait, just as it is for other traits.

In the typical study using the idiographic approach, one person or a very few persons are likely to be studied with reference to many traits. A relatively small number of occasions will probably be involved. The major interest is likely to be in the pattern of traits presented by each person. There may be some interest in *intraindividual* differences, the way in which traits differ within each person. In this connection, the person provides his own reference point, which is his own average, if a reference point is wanted. By contrast, the nomothetic approach is primarily interested in *interindividual* differences, although it can and does deal as well with the problems of intraindividual differences.

A suggested resolution. The heated debate on this issue could have been avoided if a clearer distinction had been recognized between science and technology. The impersonal view and the nomothetic approach belong to basic science; the personal view and the idiographic approach belong to technology. In every science, the individual case is properly regarded as merely an opportunity for making another observation. The single case belongs to history, not to science. Without replications, we have no science. In approaching a final goal, science aims at generalizations that apply to *classes* of phenomena, not at descriptions of particular events.

The idiographic approach is natural in dealing with the practical problems of a particular case. In this connection, however, the technologist can and does use the kind of information, the concepts, and the techniques that have been derived from the nomothetic approach of scientists. Having applied this knowledge, however, the technologist is "on his own" in completing the picture. Because information is always in short supply or its application is not always clear, the technologist may feel that the scientist, in order to be of more help, should take a personalistic approach. What the technologist may actually need, however, is more information of the kind he already has. He is mistaken, therefore, in asking the scientist to take a personal point of view. Nomothetic information contributes much to the under-

standing of individuals. Idiographic information tells almost nothing about people in general; it belongs to the individual case.

The scientist, left to himself, is likely to go where his own curiosity and personal interests lead him. It is fortunate that he has this freedom, for without it he would fail to turn up those new ideas that eventually prove to be of great importance and usefulness. Probably he could often produce more of the new methods and concepts that the technologist needs if his interests could be channeled in those directions. It is true that the scientific investigator of personality has not given as much attention as he might have to the general problem of the principles governing structures of individual personalities, thereby emphasizing the combinations and interrelationships of traits. This is partly because he needs to know the traits first, and to this problem he has given much more attention. . . .

Selecting Trait Concepts

In this [section] we shall consider the general question of what kinds of trait concepts will best serve in describing personalities from the standpoint of basic science of personality and how, in general terms, we arrive at those concepts. . . .

There are many ways of "slicing" a personality in describing it. But in whatever way this is done, we would come out with a list of descriptive categories. Since analysis of personality in some form is inevitable, how shall we decide on the way to approach it? Let us first set up some requirements for a good list of trait concepts. . . .

First, we shall consider some requirements regarding particular trait concepts, requirements that should determine whether or not the concepts ought to be generally adopted. Then we shall consider requirements regarding the total list of trait concepts, for there are certain desirable features, beyond those applying to particular traits, that apply to a total list.

Requirements regarding particular trait concepts. The first requirement is that *each term should refer to some demonstrable unity in personality.* By calling for "unities," this statement does not mean that personality should be "broken down" into its simplest "elements" or smallest "particles," by analogy to nuclear physics. It means that however complex or simple the products of analysis of personality may be, there is some degree of coherence or orderliness of the behaviors that indicates a trait. A trait name, to have unique status, should apply to an empirical concept. This test is met if we can point to some clearly observable trait indicators that are associated with it, directly or indirectly. We should find dependable behavior signs for it in performances in the laboratory, in test situations, in clinical operations, or in everyday life.

. . . Two trait concepts that are purely fictitious entities are "charm" and "impressiveness." This can be seen from a purely logical point of view. Impressions of charm or of impressiveness in a certain person can arise from quite different behaviors and different personal qualities, depending upon the person. These concepts therefore fail to meet the test of consistent signs.

Another example can be given in which empirical investigation has failed to demonstrate a unitary trait. It would seem reasonable to suppose that there is a unitary ability to analyze, in view of the fact that all of us engage in analyzing operations in one way or another in our thinking every day. A factor-analysis investigation of this hypothesis, however, failed to show that analyzing tasks of different kinds show in common a single ability to analyze.[4] Analyzing in one kind of task requires different abilities than analyzing in another. It is therefore incorrect to speak of an individual's analyzing ability, meaning that he has a characteristic position on a scale of a single trait that goes by that name. This does not mean that we do not analyze or that there is no apparent similarity between analyzing operations of different kinds. It means that a person can do well in some analyzing operations and poorly in others, and this is not a matter of unreliability of measurement or of functional fluctuation. It means that a common underlying ability to analyze is lacking. The same has been found with regard to a supposed common ability to synthesize.[5]

The second requirement for particular trait concepts is a refinement and extension of the first. It is to the effect that *each trait concept should be as exact as possible.* It should pertain to one thing and one only, and it should be capable of clear definition. This does not mean that all traits should be independent or uncorrelated. It does mean that they should be distinct in the sense of having their own consistent patterns of behavior signs. This requirement is desirable for preventing fuzzy and slippery thinking and for promoting mutual understanding among those who deal with personality or with persons.

A third requirement, not as essential, is that *a trait concept should be capable of integration into a general theory of personality.* If we believe that there is general order and system in a human personality, traits must be interrelated in logical ways. A trait concept must fit into a larger conception of personality. The development of a logical framework of theory may have to wait until many of the basic concepts are known, but sooner or later information regarding traits will lead to ideas of a more inclusive picture of some kind. Then the consistency of a trait concept with the general picture and the existence of a reasonable place for it in that picture represent another kind of test of its interpretation and its worth. . . .

Requirements regarding the list of trait concepts. *The list of trait concepts should be an economical one.* We should aim at a minimum number that will serve our purposes. The principle of parsimony that is generally recognized in science urges us to seek a much smaller number of concepts than there are phenomena to be described. There is no hard-and-fast rule regarding the ratio of concepts to phenomena, but the effort is to make that ratio small. This can be done by avoiding redundancies. Where trait concepts duplicate one another, it is possible to find more inclusive concepts under which they can be subsumed and by which they can be accounted for.

Running somewhat counter to the preceding requirement is one to the effect that *the list shall provide comprehensive coverage of the phenomena.* No significant aspect of personality should be slighted or omitted in following the urge to be economical. Like the business-minded shopper, we want to "get the most for our money" and yet

[4]Robert C. Wilson, J. P. Guilford, Paul R. Christensen, and Donald J. Lewis, "A Factor-Analytic Study of Creative-Thinking Abilities," **Psychometrika**, 1954, **19**, 297-311.
[5]Ibid.

obtain all the necessities. Each kind of technologist may find a limited number or area of concepts adequate for his purposes, but the basic scientist who adopts personality as his field of study must take a more general and impartial view of traits and give attention to them all. The trait concepts that one technologist does not find useful another one may find very important in his work.

The last requirement in our list is very difficult to satisfy. To be realistic, it can only be stated in relative terms. This requirement is to the effect that *there should be as much general agreement as possible to the list of concepts.* If the first two requirements mentioned were faithfully followed, there would be little question that we should achieve the requirement of agreement, at least among reasonable people. We have long passed the day, as Lorge has remarked, when acceptable traits can be created "by fiat." Lorge put it very clearly:[6]

"Personality traits cannot be created by the psychologist. If the concept of personality is to have meaning, it must be conceived as an aspect of the individual—an aspect susceptible to quantification. Naming a trait does not make it a trait. . . . Personality traits cannot exist by fiat alone."

Trait concepts "created by fiat" of some authority should be regarded as hypotheses, the same as any other new proposed ideas, subject to verification or rejection on the basis of empirical testing. Unfortunately, the spread of acceptance of such trait concepts has all too often been on the basis of argument and the winning of disciples.

It is easy to find examples of the fate of such concepts. Very early in the efforts to measure

personality, there arose the idea of a trait called emotional maturity. Different investigators must have had their own personal conceptions of this trait when they translated it into inventories for measuring it. Four different inventories designed to measure emotional maturity gave scores that were found to intercorrelate over the range from −.12 to +.46.[7] It is obvious that the concept, as used by these investigators, did not pass the test of empirical examination. We should expect correlations between scores measuring the same trait to be closer to .80.

A similar fate was encountered by the concept of introversion-extraversion. Several inventories developed to measure a trait by this name were obviously based upon different conceptions. Their scores were found to intercorrelate all the way from .19 to .62, none high enough to support the idea that they are alternate measures of the same trait.[8] Intercorrelations of behavior-test scores from tests proposed to measure the same trait have been even lower.[9]

These results should not necessarily be interpreted to mean that there are no such genuine traits as emotional maturity and introversion-extraversion. They mean that no unique set of trait indicators had been found to demonstrate or to represent those concepts. When such demonstrations are provided, and only then, should there be general acceptance of those and other concepts.

[6]I. Lorge, "Personality Traits by Fiat," **Journal of Educational Psychology,** 1935, **26,** 273-278.

[7]P. R. Farnsworth, "The Measure of Emotional Maturity," **Journal of Social Psychology,** 1938, **9,** 235-237.

[8]E. R. Guthrie, "Measuring Introversion and Extroversion," **Journal of Abnormal and Social Psychology,** 1927, **22,** 82-88; J. P. Guilford and J. McV. Hunt, "Some Further Experimental Tests of McDougall's Theory of Introversion-Extroversion," **Journal of Abnormal and Social Psychology,** 1931, **26,** 324-332; and J. P. Guilford and R. B. Guilford, "An Analysis of the Factors in a Typical Test of Introversion-Extroversion," **Journal of Abnormal and Social Psychology,** 1934, **28,** 377-399.

[9]E. A. Schwegler, "A Study of Introvert-Extravert Responses to Certain Test Situations," **Teachers College Contributions to Education,** 1929, No. 361.

THE PERCEPTUAL VIEW OF BEHAVIOR

by Arthur W. Combs and Donald Snygg[1]

These authors present yet another approach to the study of human behavior. The initial publication of their book Individual Behavior *in 1949 excited the psychological world with its thesis that behavior can be understood only in terms of the individual's personal frame of reference. Subsequent research by many investigators has lent support to this perceptual view of behavior. Dr. Combs teaches at the University of Florida and Dr. Snygg at the State University of New York, Teachers College, Oswego.*

People do not behave according to the facts as *others* see them. They behave according to the facts as *they* see them. What governs behavior from the point of view of the individual himself are his unique perceptions of himself and the world in which he lives, the meanings things have for him. . . .

Disregarding, for the moment, the objective facts about behavior some of us have learned, let each one of us look at his own behavior as we actually see it at the moment we are behaving. At once, we find lawfulness and determinism. From the point of view of the behaver himself behavior is caused. It is purposeful. It always has a reason. . . . Sometimes the reasons are vague and confused, in which case his behavior is equally vague and uncertain; sometimes the meanings are extremely clear and definite. But everything we do seems reasonable and necessary at the time we are doing it. . . .

From the point of view of an observer who knows the location of an exit, the behavior of a fire victim rushing back again and again to a jammed door is completely unreasonable. From the point of view of the victim in those circumstances, it is the most reasonable thing he can do because the door is the closest approximation to an exit he can find. However capricious, irrelevant, and irrational his behavior may appear to an outsider, from his point of view *at that instant,* his behavior is purposeful, relevant, and pertinent to the situation *as he understands it.* How it appears to others has no bearing upon the causes of his behavior. The important thing is how it seems to the person himself. These personal meanings which govern behavior the psychologist calls perceptions. It is [our] fundamental thesis . . . that all behavior is a function of the individual's perceptions. [Now] let us examine the fundamental premises upon which this point of view depends.

All Behavior Is Lawful

It is a necessary assumption of any science that its subject matter is regular and lawful. If this assumption could not be made, there could, of course, be no science. It is the purpose of science to discover the laws of events, but if the events with which the science deals are totally capricious and without meaning, there can obviously be no science at all. Like all science, then, we begin our study of behavior with the assumption that it is lawful and meaningful. Beginning with this assumption psychology may hope to discover the laws of behavior through careful observation and interpretation.

The Perceptual Field Determines Behavior

Behavior, we have assumed above, is lawful. To the behaver himself behavior always seems relevant, purposeful, and caused. But, if the behavior is caused, where are the causes? To the individu-

---

[1] From **Individual Behavior,** by Arthur W. Combs and Donald Snygg, pp. 16-36. Copyright © 1959 by Arthur W. Combs and Donald Snygg. Published by Harper & Brothers, New York, and reprinted with their permission.

al the causes of his behavior appear to be in the world around him and in his relation to it. As he experiences it, he eats, not because of stomach contractions, or a lowering of the sugar content of his blood, or because of habit, but because he is hungry, or because he does not wish to disappoint his wife, or just because he *feels* like eating. In any case, it seems to him that his behavior is a reasonable and necessary result of his present situation.

This situation is, of course, not the physical situation or the objective situation but the *perceived* situation, the situation as it appears to the behaver. An "hereditary" Democrat (or Republican) may believe that Republicans (or Democrats) are customarily wrong-headed, misguided, and—to some degree—enemies of society. If he believes so, he will act and vote accordingly. He will not doubt the validity of his own views and he will think that he is basing his behavior upon objective facts. It should be clear, however, to other people that his behavior is determined, not by the objective field, but by a personal, individual way of perceiving which is not identical to that of any other individual.

The "field" concept. Modern science has long since discovered that many matters cannot be understood solely in terms of the "things" with which it deals. Many of the complex events we hope to understand and predict can only be dealt with through an understanding of *interrelationships*. Even when the precise nature of these interrelationships is not known, it may still be possible to use them effectively. To deal with such interrelationships modern science has invented the very useful concept of a "field." When something occurs at one point in space apparently because something else happened at another point with no visible means by which the "cause" can be related to the "effect," the scientist often says the two events are connected in a field. This field serves as a kind of bridge between cause and effect by which the scientist can deal with a problem even though he may not be clearly aware of all intervening aspects. No one has ever seen electricity, for example, nor are we entirely certain just what it is or exactly how it works. In spite of this lack of exact knowledge, however, we are able to deal with the phenomenon by assuming the existence of an electric field. Using this field, scientists and engineers have been able to predict and control electric currents and to build devices using its properties.

A field, it should be recognized, is an inference. Whether or not it really exists in any tangible fashion, we do not know. Although no one knows exactly how this field is composed, or what it is that makes it operate, nevertheless, the concept is useful as it makes it possible to deal with events that behave predictably even though we may be ignorant of the reasons why or how. That an event can be utilized in a predictable way is sufficient to make it useful for the scientist's purposes. Thus, the field concept has proved tremendously useful to modern science; it has made it possible to by-pass some unsolved problems and to deal effectively with matters about which we do not know all we should like to know. The astronomer uses the concept to predict the orbits of the stars. The atomic physicist finds it helpful in understanding the structure of matter. The embryologist explains the determination of function by referring to the location of cells in a growth field. Psychologists, too, have found the field concept useful for the understanding and predicting of human behavior.

The perceptual field. [Here] we shall use the field concept to refer to that more or less fluid organization of meanings existing for every individual at any instant. We call it the perceptual or phenomenal field. *By the perceptual field, we mean the entire universe, including himself, as it is experienced by the individual at the instant of action.* It is each individual's personal and unique field of awareness, the field of perception responsible for his every behavior.

Several years ago a friend of mine was driving a car at dusk along a Western road. A globular mass, about two feet in diameter, suddenly appeared directly in the path of the car. A passenger screamed and grasped the wheel attempting to steer the car around the object. The driver, however, tightened his grip on the wheel and drove directly into the object. The behavior of both the driver and the passenger was determined by his own phenomenal field. The passenger, an Easterner, saw the object in the highway as a boulder and fought desperately to steer the car around it. The driver, a native Westerner, saw it as a tumbleweed and devoted his efforts to keeping his passenger from overturning the car.

In understanding this behavior it is not necessary to know what the object "really" was. Each individual in the car behaved toward it according to its nature in his own perceptual field. What a botanist or a geologist might have known about the object had no effect on the behavior of these travelers as they struggled to get the wheel. The behavior of each was determined, not by the objective facts, but by his own perceptual field. In other words, the factors effective in determining the behavior of an individual are those, and only those, which are experienced by the individual at the time of his behavior. These experiences we call perceptions and the entire field of these perceptions we call the perceptual field.

The concept of complete determination of behavior by the perceptual field is our basic postulate. It may be stated as follows: *All behavior, without exception, is completely determined by, and pertinent to, the perceptual field of the behaving organism.* The perceptual field has also been called the personal field, the private world, the behavioral field, the psychological field, the individual's life space, and the phenomenal field. The last term is derived from a school of philosophy known as phenomenology which holds that reality lies not in the event but in the phenomenon, that is to say, in the individual's experience of the event. It will be recognized that this is essentially the position we have taken—that behavior is a function, not of the external event but of the individual's perception of it. Because it is similar to the early view of the phenomenologists, perceptual psychology is sometimes called phenomenological psychology, and the perceptual field is sometimes referred to as the phenomenal field. In this [article] we will not use the term "phenomenological" but we shall occasionally use the term "phenomenal field" synonymously with the term "perceptual field," only because this synonym will serve to avoid repetition.

The Perceptual Field As "Reality"

The perceptual field is the universe of naive experience in which each individual lives, the every-

day situation of the self and its surroundings which each person takes to be reality. To each of us the perceptual field of another person contains much error and illusion; it seems an interpretation of reality rather than reality itself; but to each individual, his phenomenal field *is* reality; it is the only reality he can know. This perceptual field is far richer and more meaningful than that of the objective, physical world. We do not live in a world of objects without meaning. On the contrary, we invest the things about us with all sorts of meanings; these meanings are for each of us the reality to which we respond.

The restriction of "reality" to the attenuated field of physics means a complete abandonment of everything that we ordinarily recognize as real. A friend of mine owns a desk at which he writes and on which his friends sit and spill cigarette ashes. An inquiry about the real nature of the desk had the following results:

"It is really cellulose."
"What is that?"
"A molecular combination of carbon, hydrogen, and oxygen."
"What are they?"
"They are made up of protons and electrons."
"What are they?"
"They are really charges of electricity."
"What are they?"
"They are not matter, just waves."
"What are they?"
"Not waves in anything, just waves."
"What are they?"
"All right, waves of nothing!"

In other words, what the desk *really* is depends upon the professional perceptual field of the person who answers the question. From the point of view of chemistry, my friend owns some rather refractory and unusable cellulose; from the standpoint of sub-atomic physics he owns no matter at all. Neither science says that he has a desk because neither science deals with desks.

No matter what we are told, our own perceptual field will always seem real, substantial, and solid to us. It is the only field and the only reality we can directly experience. It includes all the universe of which we are aware—including not only the physical entities which exist for us but such other entities as justice, injustice and public opinion. It also includes experiences of love and hate, of fear, anger, and human compassion which do not exist outside the experience of people. So strong is our feeling of reality with respect to our perceptual field that we seldom question it. We accept that how it seems to us must truly be so. When others do not see things as we do, we are quite likely to jump to the conclusion that they must be either stupid or perverse; for what is right and proper seems to us so clear with respect to our own observation that no other conclusion seems warranted.

Our perceptions always have the feeling of reality at the instant of behaving. This may not be true in prospect, or in retrospect. Looking back at what we thought was so last week, we may feel now that our observations at that time were in error. But these are observations after the fact. At the time we acted, it seemed to us that the things we did, the thoughts we had, and the feelings we felt were reasonable, correct, and real. Even the murderer, at the moment he commits his crime, may feel that he is solving his problems in the only way he can under the circumstances. Later, reviewing his action, he may regret his decision and doubt the "reality" of his past thinking. On the other hand, looking forward today to the situation we will be in next week, we may plan very carefully what will be right and proper to do. When the time comes, however, we may behave quite differently because it may "seem" different at that moment. We behave in terms of the immediate meanings existing in our perceptual fields on both occasions.

Characteristics of the Phenomenal Field

A field, as it is understood in modern science, always has at least four properties: stability, fluidity, intensity, and direction. The reader may recall his experiments in his physics or science classes with iron filings and a magnet. When iron filings are scattered upon a piece of paper over a magnet they can be observed to line up in patterns of force about the magnet. That is, the iron filings placed in the electromagnetic field around the magnet respond to the force of the field and fall into patterns that reveal something of the character of the field. From the behavior of these filings it can be observed that the electromagnetic field is stable, that is, it tends to retain its character until some event causes it to change. At the same time, the field is also fluid. It can be changed, for instance, by the introduction of other magnets to the field. The intensity and direction characteristic of the field are revealed by the patterns taken by the iron filings. These same four properties are also characteristic of the phenomenal field although they are expressed in somewhat different fashion.

The perceptual field is fluid. The phenomenal field is continually changing, and thus it is sometimes difficult to study. Like the Irishman's pig which ran around so fast that he could not count it, the phenomenal field is sometimes difficult to observe because, even as we attempt to look at it, it changes. It is this fluidity of the field, however, which makes change in behavior possible. Without a degree of fluidity, the individual would be unable to adjust to the changing circumstances in which he must live his life and find need-satisfaction. The capacity for change in the perceptual field also makes learning, reasoning, remembering, forgetting, and creativity possible.

The perceptual field has stability. Although the perceptual field is highly fluid it is by no means unorganized; the organization of the field necessarily gives it a degree of stability. To live successfully each of us needs an organized, stable, predictable field. Without some stability of the field we could not live at all. . . .

The perceptual field has direction. In the same physical situation, or in objectively identical situations, the perceptual fields of different individuals will differ. Furthermore, during successive presentations of the same physical situation the perceptual field of even the same person changes. However, although the content and form of organization vary from individual to individual and from time to time, the perceptual field always has direction, i.e., it is always organized and meaningful. Our perceptions are never masses of meaningless and unrelated stimuli.

This organized characteristic of the perceptual field was first studied by the Gestalt psychologists who objected to the orthodox, stimulus-response psychology of their day and pointed out that, surely, human understanding is much more than an addition of unrelated stimuli. When we look at a picture we see much more than spots of paint; our response to a musical composition is much more than hearing a series of notes. The Gestalt psychologists pointed out that perception is always organized into what they termed a "Gestalt," or configuration. What is perceived, they said, is always a "total" and never an isolated event.

The perceptual field of any individual is both much more and much less than the field which is potentially available in the immediate physical environment. It is much more in that it includes many things not physically present. The most detailed perceptual field, however, includes only a very few of the vast (practically infinite) number of objects, details, and meanings which are present, or which might be present, in the fields of other individuals in the same physical situation. For instance, if any of us began to make a close study of the room in which we are at this moment, it is probable that we could spend months, years, or even a lifetime making a series of discoveries about it, even though we may think we are already very familiar with the room. . . .

At any given time, the field of a given individual is organized with reference to his need and the activity by which he is trying to satisfy his need at the time. The field of a professor playing golf, for instance, is very different from the field of the same professor engaged in teaching a class or in conversation with his wife. In each case, the field is organized around the activity of the moment and the perceptions occur which have bearing upon the professor's immediate problem. If thoughts of the lecture intrude into his golf game or if thoughts of his wife intrude into his lecture, it is only because: (1) the intruding activity has not been brought to a conclusion and, from his point of view, is still in progress; or (2) the intruding activity is more important to the satisfaction of the individual's need than the activity in which he is formally engaged. What is perceived is always a function of the individual's need operating in an organized field.

The figure-ground character of organization. The Gestalt psychologists observed that the meaning of any event was always a result of the relationship of any item to the totality observed. This relationship of the part to the whole they called the figure-ground relationship. The figure-ground relationship is familiar to all psychologists but the accompanying illustration . . . will show some of its salient points. If the whole

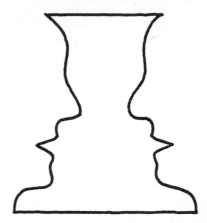

illustration is seen as a candlestick there is relatively little detail. As soon, however, as the observer looks for details in the base of the candlestick, the details in the top fade into ground. To illustrate the above point, the observer will note that the figure always is something. As long as any part of it is figure, it is meaningful. It is either a vase, a candlestick, two faces, or, at least, an undifferentiated object. When the illustration is seen as two faces there is a striking change in the character of the area between the faces as it fades down into ground. When the illustration is seen as a vase or a candlestick the same area emerges into figure, and a previously nonexistent solidity emerges that is striking. Objectively there has been no change, but the perceptual change can have a marked effect on the behavior of the observer. This process of emergence of figure from ground is known as *differentiation,* and makes possible change in our perception of events.

An example of the figure-ground relationship and its effect upon behavior may be seen in the difference between the field and the behavior of a motorist who is testing his brakes, and between the field and the behavior of another motorist who is stopping his car to avoid an imminent accident. In the first case the figure is rather diffuse and includes some awareness of his tires; consequently, he brings his car to a stop in a way that will not damage the tires. It is almost impossible for a responsible driver to bring his car to the required, abrupt stop under those conditions since, as soon as he feels the wheels slide, he eases up on the brake pedal. In a real emergency, however, the object to be avoided and the need for stopping stand out so sharply that his concern for tires drops into the ground, and the brakes are applied with violence and decision.

The effect of such a narrowing of the figure upon behavior was amusingly illustrated in the case of a young man so intent upon chasing a jack rabbit down the road with his car that he suddenly discovered he had followed the rabbit through a barbed-wire fence and into a pasture. Similar, although perhaps less dangerous, samples of intent response to figure are common in almost everyone's experiences. Perhaps one of the best examples is to be seen in our experience at a movie. Entering the theater we perceive the screen and its content as ground, the aisle and seats as figure. Having found a seat we perceive the screen somewhat more precisely as we make ourselves comfortable. At this stage, we are still aware of our surroundings, of the edge of the screen, even of the screen as a screen. Shortly, however (if the picture is a good one), the images on the screen move into exclusive figure so that we lose practically all awareness of the ground surrounding us, to the extent that we feel so "alone" with the images on the screen that we may cry unabashedly in a manner which we certainly would not had all the strangers around us been clearly in figure.

The use of these illustrations should not mislead the reader into thinking that figure exists only in the visual aspects of the field. It may occur in any sense field or in any combinations of sense fields. In taste perception, for example, the figure-ground relationship can be observed when we attempt to bring into clearer awareness some particular component of a tasty dish whose recipe we are seeking to guess. In connection with the sense of hearing, the relationship may be observed when, lying in bed, we suddenly become aware of a dripping faucet or a rattling window

which only a moment ago caused no annoyance to us at all when it existed as part of the ground of our perceptual field.

Anything in the field can become figure, including bodily fatigue, pain, and abstract ideas. As the Gestaltists have pointed out, however, two events may not appear in figure simultaneously. We may perceive [the illustration on page 470] as a candlestick or as faces but not as both at once. How an individual behaves at any moment, however, is always a function of the total perceptual field in existence at that time. The meaning of any event perceived is always a product of the relationship of that figure to the total ground of which it is a part.

The intensity with which events are experienced in the phenomenal field will be a function of differentiation and levels of awareness. Although the perceptual field includes all the universe of which we are aware, we are not aware of all parts with the same degree of clarity at any moment. For instance, we walk through the living room without paying specific attention to the exact location of the lamps and the chairs, but our behavior indicates that we are aware of them. We do not bump into them. We know they are there even though we may be intent upon other matters. Awareness of these objects is at a low level of clarity adequate for the purposes of the moment. If our needs change, however, the same chairs we were only vaguely aware of a moment ago may emerge into very clear figure; for example, if our wives suggest redecorating. Until this moment the reader, if he is sitting down, has probably been aware at only a very low level of his point of contact with whatever it is he is sitting on. Were he not aware that he is firmly in contact with something he would not behave as he does; he would be busily trying to keep himself from falling. The reader may also discover that now that we have drawn his attention to his point of contact, the perception may be in very clear figure. Other low-level-awareness phenomena like breathing, the feel of the tongue in the mouth, or of the toes inside our shoes can also be brought into clearer figure when necessary. This process by which aspects of the perceptual field are brought into clear figure is called differentiation. At any moment perceptions in the field may exist at any and all levels of differentiâtion from the vaguest to the sharpest.

We have said that behavior is always determined by the nature of the perceptual field at the instant of behaving. It follows that at whatever level of awareness perceptions exist in the field, they will have their effects upon the individual's behavior. When we perceive clearly and sharply, behavior is correspondingly direct and efficient. When we perceive only vaguely, then behavior, too, is likely to be fuzzy and inaccurate. Perceptions at low levels of awareness, it is true, will affect behavior with less precision than perceptions more clearly in figure, but as long as they exist at all in the perceptual field, they must have their expression in behavior. The mass activity elicited by a fly buzzing around the face of an uneasy sleeper is an example. In the sleeper's field the fly functions as a vague, relatively undifferentiated annoyance and his response is made accordingly. When the level of awareness is sharpened and the fly, as source of annoyance, has been clearly perceived, behavior similarly becomes more precise and direct.

It should not be supposed that all meanings existing in the phenomenal field at low levels of awareness can always be called readily into clear figure, or reported to other people. Not at all! Many aspects of experience are destined to remain in ground all our lives. Consequently it may never be possible to bring them into sufficiently clear figure to relate them to others. However, reportable or not, since behavior is always the product of the total field, even vague awarenesses play their part in our behavior. Early in this century Freud noted this effect upon behavior and based a great deal of his theory of psychoanalysis upon what he called the "unconscious." Much of people's behavior, he observed, was motivated by events discernible by him but denied by his patients. He concluded, therefore, that behavior was often controlled by unconscious impulses. This is a point of view similar to the one we hav been expressing.

Freud's description of behavior produced from low-level awareness as "unconscious," however, has turned out to be most unfortunate. The terms "conscious" and "unconscious" leave the impression of a clear-cut dichotomy instead of a continuous gradation of awareness from sharp and precise perceptions to vague and indistinct perceptions. The term "unconscious" has also been used by some people as though there were perceptions of which the individual is unaware. They have described the "unconscious" as a kind of "place" (even sometimes, as a kind of dark closet) where one could hide away things one does not want to look at. These are unfortunate aberrations of the perfectly useful idea that behavior may be significantly affected even by perceptions at low levels of awareness. . . .

Differentiation, the process of field change. Each of us is constantly searching his field for details and meanings which will better enable him to satisfy need. This process involves a continual change in the perceptual field by the constant rise of new characters into figure and the consequent lapse of other characters into ground, in the manner described above. This process, from the point of view of the behaver, is one of increased awareness of details and is, therefore, called differentiation. It is through differentiation that change in the perceptual field and, hence, change in behavior occurs.

An example of differentiation, or change in the field, may be seen in the process of becoming aware of an object. When persons are shown a figure or group of figures for varying lengths of time and asked to reproduce what they see, the first awareness is ordinarily of a vague, relatively undifferentiated whole, which then differentiates in more or less orderly fashion into more detailed parts. Since the properties of a newly emerging object are determined by its relationship to the rest of the field, at this stage it can easily be, and frequently is, distorted and misinterpreted. Illusions, hallucinations, and many cases of mistaken identity, as well as the common errors of proof reading, result. Who has not made errors like the traveler expecting a bridge, who mistakes a billboard for the anticipated span? Who has not been surprised to discover that a sign he thought said one thing on closer examination actually said something quite different?

The factors which appear to determine the nature and extent to which an event is differentiated are the need of the behaver and the opportunities for differentiation that are available.

Since the figure is the only aspect of the field of which we are clearly aware, change in the field means change in the figure. The figure may become more precise, more detailed, and more intense, or it may become larger, more vague, and more diffused. On the other hand, the figure may become so large, so vague, and so diffused that it practically merges into ground. This probably does not happen except in deep sleep or unconsciousness, as under ordinary circumstances of daily life the individual is engaged in a continual search for the means of satisfying his needs; this requires a continual emergence of new characters into figure.

In the same way the figure is constantly shifting in size it is also changing in character as new characteristics and entities arise and differentiate from the ground. Since precision of behavior can only result from precision of figure, it is this emergence into figure which is the basic cause of more effective behavior. Change in behavior occurs with differentiation in the perceptual field. Thus, learning, problem solving, remembering, forgetting, and the like are all aspects of the process of differentiation occurring in the individual's phenomenal field.

Synthesis, generalization, and perception of abstract events. It is the differentiations an individual is able to make in his perceptual field that determine the nature of his perceptions—both the direct perceptions of concrete events apprehended through our sense organs and the perceptions of complex events understood only through the medium of abstract thought. This broad use of the word "perception" is somewhat of a departure from traditional practice in laboratory psychology and a word of explanation seems in order. Historically, psychologists have used the word perception to refer only to, "a single, unified meaning obtained from sensory processes while a stimulus is present." To describe acts of knowing, understanding, or forming ideas, they have used the words "cognition" or "conception." In this book, however, the word "perception" is used to refer to *any* differentiations the individual is capable of making in his perceptual field whether an objectively observable stimulus is present or not. There seems little need for more than one process to explain these

events. Differentiations in the phenomenal field resulting in perceptions of seeing, hearing, smelling, or feeling are precisely the same as those made in conceiving, knowing, or understanding. Although the subject matter varies, the process is the same. The differentiation of an idea or a concept is not basically different from the differentiation of a scent, a sound, or the printed words on a page.

Differentiation, as we have been describing it, seems to correspond to a process of analysis. But, it may be asked, do we not synthesize as well? Do we not also see examples of generalization? Are not synthesis and generalization the opposites of differentiation? To answer these questions, it is necessary to remind ourselves that the perceptual approach to understanding behavior is concerned solely with the problem of how events are experienced by the behaver. What seems like integration, synthesis, or generalization observed from an objective point of view, becomes—observed from the behaver's own frame of reference, simply another form of differentiation. When an individual, for example, perceives that "all these things have this aspect in common," what is occurring is not an "adding up" of separate and discrete perceptions. Rather, the observer has differentiated from his field of perceptions the unifying principle that "all these things have this aspect in common." Thus, what appears on the surface to be integration or synthesis, is—from the behaver's own point of reference—a differentiation of the relationship of events to each other.

Common Perceptions
Make Communication Possible

Since the perceptual field cannot be observed directly by any other individual it may appear to the reader that in this frame of reference the causes of behavior are so secret that actual prediction of behavior must be beyond any outsider's power. Indeed, if the perceptual fields of different individuals were completely private, there would be no way of knowing another person's field and the prediction and control of behavior would, of course, be impossible. When I whistle to a dog, call to a friend, or lecture to a class, however, the dog, my friend, and the students, in a large percentage of cases, behave as if the sounds I make in my perceptual field are also present in theirs. In other words, changes in my own field are often accompanied by behavior on the part of others which indicates that a change has also taken place in their phenomenal fields.

It is probable that this relationship arises in the following way: each of us is born into a situation in which certain common characters and objects exist. For example, both the Eskimo and the South African tribesman are born into a world where things will fall if they are dropped, where there is ground under their feet, where there are people around them, where there are forms of precipitation, where there are colors and sounds to be experienced. Even among people as remote from one another as these, there is considerable agreement about the things they experience. There is even more among people in the same culture, who have many more common aspects as potential characters of their perceptual fields and of their individual "realities." Thus communication is possible through that part of the phenomenal field that is common to two persons. For instance, among most members of western society there are common gestures which make some communication possible although the spoken languages are different. However, they can do so only when the physical gesture has the same phenomenal significance. An American, to whom the nod means assent, will be unable to communicate by this means with a Greek, to whom it means negation, until he discovers the meaning of the gesture in the other's field. It is not the physical nature but the perceived character of the action that is important in determining behavior.

Communication is essentially the process of acquiring greater understanding of another's perceptual field and it can take place only when some common characters already exist. In speech, for instance, communication is possible only to the extent that the objective physical sounds or characters have the same meanings in the two fields. An American cattle fancier found his ability to communicate with a Scottish dealer much enhanced as soon as he discovered that "coo" meant not cow, as he had inferred, but calf. The same words often have very different meanings in the perceptual fields of different individuals. Even strangers of the same general culture often have difficulty communicating, but old friends who have shared many experiences can understand one another's fields so well that they can communicate and anticipate one another's behavior without using words at all. . . .

The Understanding and Prediction of Behavior

The presence of common meanings in the perceptual fields of different persons makes communication possible. It also makes possible the understanding and prediction of the behavior of other people. The relation between one's own perceptual field and one's own behavior is relatively simple and well known to each of us because of our lifelong experiences in which we have been able to observe the relationship between our own perceptions and behavior. Because of this experience, the process of reconstructing another individual's perceptual field by observing his behavior is a relatively simple and easy task, which can often be done with little training. Since behavior is always determined by the individual's perceptual field, we need only to learn to read behavior backwards in order to understand the perceptions of another person. That is, we can infer from another's behavior the nature of the perceptions which probably produced it.

As a usual thing, when we see a man scratch, we can infer that he itched. When we see him yawn, we often share his field so vividly that we are impelled to duplicate his behavior. By this kind of inference from what we are able to observe, we can understand the perceptions lying behind a great deal of human behavior. We can accomplish this by asking ourselves "Now why did he do that?" or "Under what circumstances would I have done that?" . . .

The social scientist, attempting to understand and predict human behavior approaches the problem of prediction in exactly the same manner, that is, by inference from observed behavior. What the rest of us do, often haphazardly and implicitly, however, the professional worker seeks to accomplish more explicitly, more precisely, and with greater discipline and care. . . .

DEFICIENCY MOTIVATION
AND GROWTH MOTIVATION

by Abraham Maslow[1]

In Chapter 4 the reader was introduced to some of the problems involved in developing an adequate theory of motivation, one of the central concerns in psychology today. In the following article a psychologist who has done much work in this field makes a case for distinguishing between behavior motivated by deficiency needs and that motivated by growth needs. Dr. Maslow's paper was presented as part of the University of Nebraska Symposium on Motivation, 1955; it is followed by the comments of two other symposium members who represent somewhat different points of view. Dr. Maslow is Professor of Psychology at Brandeis University.

Hans Zinsser has described the difference between philosophical and scientific theorizing by comparing the latter to a trellis which one builds out just ahead of the growing vine in the direction of its growth and for the sake of its future support. It is this latter task that I have set myself in this paper which is a portion of a larger systematic theory of general psychology. It is based mostly upon clinical and personological researches and experience, rather than upon formal experimentation but will soon be ready, I think, for the experimental test. I must warn you that the demands of system and of theory probably play a considerable role in what follows. To some extent, its existence and its particular shape are called for not only by data but also by theoretical, systematic considerations of which I cannot speak here, and which will be apparent only when the whole structure of theory is seen as a unity.

Another point that I must warn you about is this. . . . I am not *only* the disinterested and impersonal seeker for pure cold truth for its own sake. I am also very definitely interested and concerned with man's fate, with his ends and goals and with his future. I would like to help improve him and to better his prospects. I hope to help teach him how to be brotherly, cooperative, peaceful, courageous and just. . . .

It is this humanistic emphasis which is the source and the justification of what I consider to be the important questions which justify inexact and unreliable researches. They *must* be done; we don't *dare* turn away from them because we can't handle them well. We must do the best we can.

Psychology as a science in the United States has considered itself to stand in a line stemming primarily from Wundt and the German experimental psychology. . . . I remind you, with Fromm, that we have forgotten in this country another line of development and another time-honored task for psychology. Aristotle, Spinoza, James, Goldstein, G. Allport, and Fromm are a few of the names in this tradition that considers the humanistic task of psychology to be that of constructing a scientific system of values to help men live the good life, i.e., a humanly usable theory of human motivation. . . .

In recent years more and more psychologists have found themselves compelled to postulate some tendency to growth or self-perfection to supplement the concepts of equilibrium, homeostasis, tension-reduction, defense and other conserving motivations. This was so for various reasons.

1. Psychotherapy. The pressure toward health makes therapy possible. It is an absolute *sine qua non*. If there were no such trend, therapy would be inexplicable to the extent that it goes beyond

[1]From **Nebraska Symposium on Motivation, 1955**, Marshall R. Jones, ed., University of Nebraska Press, Lincoln, 1955, pp. 1-39.

the building of defenses against pain and anxiety. (Rogers,[2] Angyal,[3] et cetera).

2. Brain injured soldiers. Goldstein's work[4] is well known to all. He found it necessary to invent the concept of self-actualization to explain the reorganization of the person's capacities after injury.

3. Psychoanalysis. Some analysts, notably Fromm[5] and Horney,[6] have found it impossible to understand even neuroses unless one postulates an impulse toward growth, toward perfection of development, toward the fulfillment of the person's possibilities.

4. Creativeness. Much light is being thrown on the general subject of creativeness by the study of healthy growing and grown people, especially when contrasted with sick people. Especially does the theory of art and art education call for a concept of growth and spontaneity.[7]

5. Child psychology. Observation of children shows more and more clearly that healthy children *enjoy* growing and moving forward, gaining new skills, capacities and powers. This is in flat contradiction to that version of Freudian theory which conceives of every child as hanging on desperately to each adjustment that it achieves and to each state of rest or equilibrium. According to this theory, the reluctant and conservative child has continually to be kicked upstairs, out of its comfortable, preferred state of rest *into* a new frightening situation.

While this Freudian conception is continually confirmed by clinicians as largely true for insecure and frightened children, and while it is a little bit true for all human beings, in the main it is *untrue* for healthy, happy, secure children. In these children we see clearly an eagerness to grow up, to mature, to drop the old adjustment as outworn, like an old pair of shoes. . . .

For the writers in these various groups, . . . growth, individuation, autonomy, self-actualization, self-development, productiveness, self-realization, are all crudely synonymous, designating a vaguely perceived area rather than a sharply defined concept. . . . We just don't know enough about growth yet to be able to define it well.

Its meaning can be *indicated* rather than defined, partly by positive pointing, partly by negative contrast, i.e., what it is *not*. For example, it is not equilibrium, homeostasis, tension-reduction, need-reduction, et cetera.

Its necessity has presented itself to its proponents partly because of dissatisfaction (certain newly noticed phenomena simply were not covered by extant theories); partly by positive needs for theories and concepts which would better serve the new humanistic value systems emerging from the breakdown of the older value systems.

This paper however derives mostly from a direct study of psychologically healthy individuals. . . . The end product of growth teaches us much about the processes of growth. In a recent book,[8] I have described what was learned from this study and in addition theorized very freely about various possible consequences for general psychology of this kind of direct study of good rather than bad human beings, of healthy rather than sick people, of the positive as well as the negative. I must warn you that the data cannot be considered reliable until someone else repeats the study. The possibilities of projection are very real in such a study and of course are unlikely to be detected by the investigator himself. [Now] I should like to crystallize a little more some of the differences that I have observed to exist between the motivational lives of healthy people and of others, i.e., people motivated by growth needs contrasted with those motivated by the basic needs.

[Maslow defines a need as basic or "instinctoid" if its satisfaction is essential to the health of the organism. He includes in this category not only physiological needs such as those for food, water, and rest but also certain higher-level, psychological needs which seem necessary to healthy

[2]Carl R. Rogers and R. F. Dymond, eds., **Psychotherapy and Personality Change**, Chicago: The University of Chicago Press, 1954.
[3]András Angyal, **Foundations for a Science of Personality**, New York: The Commonwealth Fund, 1941.
[4]Kurt Goldstein, **Human Nature in the Light of Psychotherapy**, Cambridge, Mass.: Harvard University Press, 1940.
[5]Erich Fromm, **Man for Himself: An Inquiry into the Psychology of Ethics**, New York: Rinehart & Company, Inc., 1947.
[6]Karen Horney, **Neurosis and Human Growth**, New York: W. W. Norton & Company, Inc., 1950.
[7]F. Wilson, unpublished papers on art, education, and psychology, 1954.

[8]Abraham H. Maslow, **Motivation and Personality**, New York: Harper & Brothers, 1954.

functioning—for example, the need for love. The basic needs "are essentially deficits in the organism, empty holes, so to speak, which must be filled up for health's sake." But, Maslow maintains, if these basic needs are met, they lose much of their importance for motivation; the healthy individual is motivated by a tendency to *grow* rather than merely to maintain equilibrium.]

So far as motivational status is concerned, healthy people have sufficiently gratified their basic needs for safety, belongingness, love, respect and self-esteem so that they are motivated primarily by trends to self-actualization (defined as ongoing actualization of potential capacities and talents, as fulfillment of mission or call or fate or vocation, as a fuller knowledge of, and acceptance of, the person's own intrinsic nature, as an unceasing trend toward unity, integration or synergy within the person).

Much to be preferred to this generalized definition would be a descriptive and operational one which I have already published.[9] These people are there defined by describing their clinically observed characteristics. These are:

1. Superior perception of reality.
2. Increased acceptance of self, of others and of nature.
3. Increased spontaneity.
4. Increase in problem-centering.
5. Increased detachment and desire for privacy.
6. Increased autonomy, and resistance to enculturation.
7. Greater freshness of appreciation, and richness of emotional reaction.
8. Higher frequency of mystic experiences.
9. Increased identification with the human species.
10. Changed (the clinician would say, improved) interpersonal relations.
11. More democratic character structure.
12. Greatly increased creativeness.
13. Certain changes in the value system. . . .

One major difficulty with this conception as so far presented is its somewhat static character. Self-actualization, since I have found it only in

older people, tends to be seen as an ultimate or final state of affairs, a far goal, rather than a dynamic process, active throughout life, Being rather than Becoming.

If we define growth as the various processes which bring the person toward ultimate self-actualization, then this conforms better with the observed fact that it is going on *all* the time in the life history. . . . Growth is seen then not only as progressive gratification of basic needs to the point where they disappear, but also in the form of specific growth motivations over and above these basic needs, e.g., talents, capacities, creative tendencies, constitutional potentialities. We are thereby helped also to realize that basic needs and self-actualization do not contradict each other any more than do childhood and maturity. One passes into the other and is a necessary prerequisite for it.

The differentiation between these growth-needs and basic needs which we shall explore in this paper is a consequence of the clinical perception of qualitative differences between the motivational lives of self-actualizers and of other people. . . .

1. Attitude toward impulse: impulse-rejection and impulse-acceptance. Practically all historical and contemporary theories of motivation unite in regarding needs, drives and motivating states in general as annoying, irritating, unpleasant, undesirable, as something to get rid of. Motivated behavior, goal seeking, consummatory responses are all techniques for reducing these discomforts. This attitude is very explicitly assumed in such widely used descriptions of motivation as need reduction, tension reduction, drive reduction, and anxiety reduction.

. . . The physiological needs, the needs for safety, for love, for respect, for information are in fact often nuisances for many people, psychic troublemakers, and problem-creators, especially for those who have had unsuccessful experiences at gratifying them and for those who cannot now count on gratification.

Even with these deficiencies, however, the case is very badly overdrawn: one can accept and enjoy one's needs and welcome them to consciousness if (a) past experience with them has been rewarding, and (b) if present and future gratification can be counted on. For example, if one has

[9]Ibid.

in general enjoyed food and if good food is now available, the emergence of appetite into consciousness is welcomed instead of dreaded. ("The trouble with eating is that it kills my appetite.") Something like this is true for thirst, for sleepiness, for sex, for dependency needs and for love needs. However, a far more powerful refutation of the "need-is-a-nuisance" theory is found in the recently emerging awareness of, and concern with, growth (self-actualization) motivation.

The multitude of idiosyncratic motives which come under the head of "self-actualization" can hardly be listed since each person has different talents, capacities, potentialities. But some characteristics are general to all of them. And one is that these impulses are desired and welcomed, are enjoyable and pleasant, that the person wants more of them rather than less, and that if they constitute tensions, they are *pleasurable* tensions. The creator welcomes his creative impulses, the talented person enjoys using and expanding his talents.

It is simply inaccurate to speak in such instances of tension-reduction, implying thereby the getting rid of an annoying state. For these states are not annoying.

2. Differential effects of gratification. Almost always associated with negative attitudes toward the need is the conception that the primary aim of the organism is to get rid of the annoying need and thereby to achieve a cessation of tension, an equilibrium, a homeostasis, a quiescence, a state of rest, a lack of pain.

The drive or need presses toward its own elimination. Its only striving is toward cessation, toward getting rid of itself, toward a state of not wanting. Pushed to its logical extreme, we wind up with Freud's Death-instinct. . . .

This theory must be put down as an inadequate description even of deficiency motivation. What is lacking here is awareness of the dynamic principle which ties together and interrelates all these separate motivational episodes. The different basic needs are related to each other in a hierarchical order such that gratification of one need and its consequent removal from the center of the stage brings about not a state of rest or Stoic apathy, but rather the emergence into consciousness of another "higher" need; wanting and desiring continues but at a "higher" level. Thus the coming-to-rest theory isn't adequate even for deficiency motivation.

However, when we examine people who are predominantly growth-motivated, the coming-to-rest conception of motivation becomes completely useless. In such people gratification breeds increased rather than decreased motivation, heightened rather than lessened excitement. The appetites become intensified and heightened. They grow upon themselves and instead of wanting less and less, such a person wants more and more of, for instance, education. The person rather than coming to rest becomes more active. The appetite for growth is whetted rather than allayed by gratification. Growth is, *in itself,* a rewarding and exciting process. . . .

. . . Growth motivation may be long-term in character. Most of a lifetime may be involved in becoming a good psychologist or a good artist. All equilibrium or homeostasis or rest theories deal only with short-term episodes, each of which have nothing to do with each other. Allport particularly has stressed this point. Plan-fulness and looking into the future, he points out, are of the central stuff or healthy human nature. He agrees[10] that "Deficit motives do, in fact, call for the reduction of tension and restoration of equilibrium. Growth motives, on the other hand, maintain tension in the interest of distant and often unattainable goals. As such they distinguish human from animal becoming, and adult from infant becoming."

3. Clinical effects of gratification. Deficit-need gratifications and growth-need gratifications have differential subjective and objective effects upon the personality. If I may phrase what I am groping for here in a very generalized way, it is this: Satisfying deficiencies avoids illness; growth satisfactions produce positive health. I must grant that this will be difficult to pin down for research purposes at this time. And yet there is a real clinical difference between fending off threat or attack and positive triumph and achievement, between protecting, defending and preserving oneself and reaching out for fulfillment, for excitement and for enlargement. . . .

[10] Gordon W. Allport, **Becoming,** New Haven, Conn.: Yale University Press, 1955.

4. Different kinds of pleasure. Erich Fromm[11] has made an interesting and important effort to distinguish higher from lower pleasures, as have so many others before him. . . .

He distinguishes scarcity-pleasure from abundance-pleasure, the "lower" pleasure of satiation of a need from the "higher" pleasure of production, creation and growth of insight. The glut, the relaxation, and the loss of tension that follows deficiency-satiation can at best be called "relief" by contrast with the *Funktionslust*, the ecstasy, the serenity that one experiences when functioning easily, perfectly and at the peak of one's powers—in overdrive, so to speak.

"Relief," depending so strongly on something that disappears, is itself more likely to disappear. It must be less stable, less enduring, less constant than the pleasure accompanying growth, which can go on forever.

5. Attainable and unattainable goal states. Deficiency-need gratification tends to be episodic and climactic. The most frequent schema here begins with an instigating, motivating state which sets off motivated behavior designed to achieve a goal-state, which, mounting gradually and steadily in desire and excitement, finally reaches a peak in a moment of success and consummation. From this peak curve of desire, excitement and pleasure fall rapidly to a plateau of quiet tension-release, and lack of motivation.

This schema, though not universally applicable, in any case contrasts very sharply with the situation in growth-motivation, for here characteristically there is no climax or consummation, no orgasmic moment, no end-state, even no goal if this be defined climactically. Growth is instead a continued, more or less steady upward or forward development. The more one gets, the more one wants so that this kind of wanting is endless and can never be attained or satisfied.

It is for this reason that the usual separation between instigation, goal-seeking behavior, the goal object and the accompanying affect breaks down completely. The behaving is itself the goal, and to differentiate the goal of growth from the instigation to growth is impossible. They too are the same.

[11]Fromm, op. cit., p. 186.

6. Species-wide goals and idiosyncratic goals. The deficit-needs are shared by all members of the human species and to some extent by other species as well. Self-actualization is idiosyncratic since every person is different. The deficits, i.e., the species requirements, must ordinarily be fairly well satisfied before real individuality can develop fully.

Just as all trees need sun, water, and foods from the environment, so do all people need safety, love and status from *their* environment. However, in both cases this is just where real development of individuality can begin, for once satiated with these elementary, species-wide necessities, each tree and each person proceeds to develop in his own style, uniquely, using these necessities for his own private purposes. In a very tangible sense, development then becomes more determined from within rather than from without.

7. Dependence and independence of the environment. The needs for safety, belongingness, love relations and for respect can be satisfied only by other people, i.e., only from outside the person. This means considerable dependence on the environment. A person in this dependent position cannot really be said to be governing himself, or in control of his own fate. He *must* be beholden to the sources of supply of needed gratifications. Their wishes, their whims, their rules and laws govern him and must be appeased lest he jeopardize his sources of supply. He *must* be to an extent "other-directed" and *must* be sensitive to other people's approval, affection and good will. . . .

In contrast, the self-actualizing individual, by definition gratified in his basic needs, is far less dependent, far less beholden, far more autonomous and self-directed. Far from needing other people, growth-motivated people may actually be hampered by them. I have already reported their special liking for privacy, for detachment and for meditativeness.

Such people become far more self-sufficient and self-contained. The determinants which govern them are now primarily inner ones, rather than social or environmental. They are the laws of their own inner nature, their potentialities and capacities, their talents, their latent resources, their creative impulses, their needs to know themselves and to become more and more integrated and unified, more and more aware of what they really are, of what they really want, of what their call or vocation or fate is to be.

Since they depend less on other people, they are less ambivalent about them, less anxious and also less hostile, less needful of their praise and their affection. They are less anxious for honors, prestige and rewards. . . .

8. Interested and disinterested interpersonal relations. In essence, the deficit-motivated man is far more dependent upon other people than is the man who is predominantly growth-motivated. He is more "interested," more needful, more attached, more desirous.

This dependency colors and limits interpersonal relations. To see people primarily as need-gratifiers or as sources of supply is an abstractive act. They are seen not as wholes, as complicated, unique individuals, but rather from the point of view of usefulness. What in them is not related to the perceiver's needs is either overlooked altogether, or else bores, irritates, or threatens. This parallels our relations with cows, horses and sheep, as well as with waiters, taxi-cab drivers, porters, policemen or others whom we *use*.

Fully disinterested, desireless, objective and holistic perception of another human being becomes possible only when nothing is needed from him, only when *he* is not needed. Idiographic, aesthetic perception of the whole person is far more possible for self-actualizing people, and furthermore approval, admiration, and love are based less upon gratitude for usefulness and more upon the objective, intrinsic qualities of the perceived person. He is admired for objectively admirable qualities rather than because he flatters or praises. He is loved because he is love-worthy rather than because he gives out love. . . .

Disinterested, unrewarded, useless, desireless perception of the other as unique, as independent, as end-in-himself, in other words as a person rather than as a tool is the more difficult, the more hungry the perceiver is for deficit satisfaction. A "high-ceiling" interpersonal psychology, i.e., an understanding of the highest possible development of human relationships, cannot base itself on deficit theory of motivation.

9. Ego-centering and ego-transcendence. We are confronted with a difficult paradox when we attempt to describe the complex attitude toward the self or ego of the growth-oriented, self-actualized person. It is just this person, in whom ego-strength is at its height, who most easily forgets or transcends the ego, who can be most problem-centered, most self-forgetful, most spontaneous in his activities. . . .

This ability to center upon the world rather than to be self-conscious, egocentric and gratification-oriented becomes the more difficult the more need-deficits the person has. The more growth-motivated the person is the more problem-centered can he be, and the more he can leave self-consciousness behind him as he deals with the objective world.

10. Interpersonal psychotherapy and intrapersonal psychogogy. A major characteristic of people who seek psychotherapy is a former and/or present deficiency of basic-need gratification. To a larger extent than the Freudians are yet willing to admit, neurosis is a deficiency-disease. Because this is so, a basic necessity for cure is supplying what has been lacking or making it possible for the patient to do this himself. Since these supplies come from other people, ordinary therapy *must* be interpersonal.

But this fact has been very badly over-generalized. It is true that people whose deficiency needs have been gratified and who are primarily growth-motivated are by no means exempt from conflict, unhappiness, anxiety, and confusion. In such moments they too are apt to seek help and may very well turn to interpersonal therapy. And yet it is unwise to forget that *more* frequently the problems and the conflicts of the growth-motivated person are customarily solved by himself by turning inward in a meditative way, i.e., self-searching rather than seeking for help from someone. Even in principle, many of the tasks of self-actualization are largely intrapersonal, such as the making of plans, the discovery of self, the selection of potentialities to develop, the construction of a life-outlook.

In the theory of personality improvement, a place must be reserved for self-improvement and self-searching contemplation and meditation. In the later stages of growth the person is essentially alone and can rely only upon himself. This improvement of an already well person Oswald Schwarz has called psychogogy. If psychotherapy makes sick people not-sick and removes symptoms, then psychogogy takes up where therapy leaves off and tries to make not-sick people healthy. . . .

11. Instrumental learning and personality change. So-called learning theory in this country has based itself almost entirely on deficit-motivation with goal objects usually external to the organism, i.e., learning the best way to satisfy a need. For this reason, among others, our psychology of learning is a very limited body of knowledge, useful only in small areas of life and of real interest only to other "learning theorists."

This is of very little help in solving the problems of growth and self-actualization. Here the techniques of repeatedly acquiring from the outside world satisfactions of motivational deficiencies are much less needed. . . . Change becomes much less an acquisition of habits or associations one by one, and much more a total change of the total person, i.e., a new person rather than the same person with some habits added like new external possessions. . . .

The most important learning experiences reported to me by my subjects were very frequently single life experiences such as tragedies, deaths, traumata, conversions, sudden insights, which forced change in the life-outlook of the person and consequently in everything that he did. (Of course the so-called "working through" of the tragedy or of the insight took place over a longer period of time but this too was not a matter of associative learning.)

To the extent that growth consists in peeling away inhibition and constraints and then permitting the person to "be himself," to emit behavior —"radioactively," as it were—rather than to repeat it, to allow his inner nature to express itself, to this extent the behavior of self-actualizers is unlearned, created and released rather than acquired, expressive rather than coping.

12. Deficiency-motivated and growth-motivated perception. What may turn out to be the most important difference of all is the greater closeness of deficit-satisfied people to the realm of Being.[12] Psychologists have never yet been able to claim this vague jurisdiction of the philosophers, this area dimly seen but nevertheless having undoubted basis in reality. But it may now become feasible through the study of self-fulfilling individuals to have our eyes opened to all sorts of basic insights, old to the philosophers but new to us.

For instance, I think that our understanding of perception and therefore of the perceived world will be very much changed and enlarged if we study carefully the distinction between need-interested and need-disinterested or desireless perception. . . .

We may not be aware when *we* perceive in a need-determined way. But we certainly are aware of it when *we* ourselves are perceived in this way, e.g., simply as a money-giver, a food-supplier, a safety-giver, someone to depend on, or as a waiter or other anonymous servant or means-object. When this happens we don't like it at all. We want to be taken for ourselves, as complete and whole individuals. We dislike being perceived as useful objects or as tools. We dislike being "used."

Because self-actualizing people ordinarily do not have to abstract need-gratifying qualities nor see the person as a tool, it is much more possible for them to take a non-valuing, non-judging, non-interfering, non-condemning attitude towards others. . . . This permits much clearer and more insightful perception and understanding of what is there. This is the kind of untangled, uninvolved, detached perception that surgeons and therapists are supposed to try for and which self-actualizing people attain *without* trying for. . . .

[In conclusion, Maslow illustrates some basic principles of his theory by showing the differences between "needed love" (deficiency-motivated, selfish love) and "unneeded love" (the type of love experienced by growth-motivated individuals). His general remarks on these differences are reprinted below.]

The love need as ordinarily studied . . . is a deficit need. It is a hole which has to be filled, an emptiness into which love is poured. If this healing

---

[12]Paul Tillich, **The Courage To Be,** New Haven, Conn.: Yale University Press, 1952.

necessity is not available, severe pathology results;[13], [14] if it *is* available at the right time, in the right quantities and with proper style, then pathology is averted. Intermediate states of pathology and health follow upon intermediate states of thwarting or satiation. If the pathology is not too severe and if it is caught early enough, replacement therapy can cure. That is to say, the sickness, "love-hunger," can be cured in certain cases by making up the pathological deficiency. Love hunger is a deficiency disease exactly as is salt hunger or the avitaminoses.

The healthy person, not having this deficiency, does not need to give or to receive love except in steady, small maintenance doses and he may even do without these for periods of time. But if motivation is entirely a matter of satisfying deficits and thus getting rid of needs, then a crucial paradox results. Satisfaction of the need should cause it to disappear, which is to say that people who have stood in satisfying love relationships are precisely the people who should be *less* likely to give and to receive love! But clinical study of very healthy people, who have been love-need-satiated, shows that they are far *more*—not less—loving people than others.

This finding in itself exposes very clearly the inadequacy of ordinary (deficiency-need-centered) motivation theory and indicates how inescapable is the necessity for "metamotivation theory" (or growth-motivation, or self-actualization theory). . . .

Comments: David C. McClelland[15]

Maslow's paper differs from others in this series, as he himself notes, in that he addresses himself directly to the problem of trying to improve man's lot as well as trying to find out what makes him tick. He wants to help teach man "how to be brotherly, cooperative, peaceful, courageous, and just," and he searches contemporary motivational psychology to see what clues he can find which will help him in this task. What he seems to be

searching for is a scientific basis for ethics or, at the very least, for a *rapprochement* between psychology and ethics. Any comments, then, would seem to have to be directed at the task which he set himself rather than at the various things which he did not attempt to do, such as provide a thoroughly validated psychology of motivation.

Let me commend him first for his honesty in attacking this problem head on. Many clinical psychologists and even experimental psychologists hide their implicit value assumptions behind a cloak of scientific respectability, but Maslow at least begins the quest for the empirical basis for value assumptions. . . .

How does Maslow go about accomplishing his task? Basically his method is to describe the motivational states of psychologically sick and psychologically healthy people. Thus, he feels the evidence is clear that maladjusted people have basic biological needs for love, security, and status which have not been satisfied in an exactly parallel fashion to people who show physical symptoms because of vitamin deficiency. We need love as much as we need vitamin B_1. These psychological needs are present in all people; that is, they are instinctoid and though they may be modified by circumstances, they must be satisfied at least at a minimum level. On the other hand, healthy people seem not only to have these basic needs satisfied, but to have developed a new type of need for spontaneous expressive behavior or for self-actualization. It is possible to raise questions about his basic argument both at the level of the evidence which he marshals to support it and at the level of its possible ethical consequences.

In the first place, the evidence is simply not altogether clear that there are basic psychological needs which do not have to be acquired before their frustration will produce psychological illness.[16] . . . My own view, elaborated elsewhere,[17] is that given the human condition (both social and biological), certain needs are *very likely* to form very early in life. Subsequent frustration of these needs will indeed cause illness *once they*

[13]J. Bowlby, **Maternal Care and Mental Health**, Geneva: World Health Organization, 1952.

[14]David M. Levy, **Maternal Overprotection**, New York: Columbia University Press, 1943.

[15]Dr. McClelland, Professor of Psychology at Harvard University, is a noted personality theorist.

[16]Cf. Arnold Bernstein, "Some Relations Between Techniques of Feeding and Training During Infancy and Certain Behavior in Childhood," **Genetic Psychology Monographs**, 1955, **51**, 3-44.

[17]David C. McClelland, J. W. Atkinson, R. A. Clark, and E. L. Lowell, **The Achievement Motive**, New York: Appleton-Century-Crofts, Inc., 1953.

have been formed, but this still leaves open the possibility of developing the wide cultural differences in motivation observed and reported by anthropologists. Possibly what Maslow means by "instinctoid" is "very likely to be learned," but there is considerable difference in the implications of these two terms so far as a scientific basis for ethics is concerned. The former assumes a biological need for brotherliness; the latter suggests that such a need is very likely, given a certain kind of early nurturance.

Other problems arise when one considers a little more carefully the methodological assumptions he makes in studying and drawing implications from groups of psychologically sick and healthy people. To draw the conclusions he does, for example, about the motivational needs of neurotics, does he not have to assume that their condition could not be biological in nature, despite recent evidence on the effects of drug therapy? That is, what if it should turn out that the illness he attributes to a "love deficit" is due to a metabolic deficit? The assumption of environmental causation is, of course, one that most of us have felt that we can safely make, but nevertheless it should be tagged as an assumption. . . .

Even worse problems come up in connection with his choice of healthy people. Here one cannot avoid the suspicion that subjects will be chosen whose values will be congruent with those of the person who chooses them or, at the very least, of the culture of which he is a member. Who has the right to pick extraordinarily self-actualized people—Maslow, St. Paul, or Mao Tse Tung? Whatever the answer to such a question, I feel sure that they would nominate different sorts of people and that, if psychologists analyzed the nominees, we would have some conflicting conclusions as to what the motives are which lead to maximum psychological health.

The third difficulty will be considered by many to be the central one. It is, of course, Maslow's inability at this stage of the game to give any clear operational definitions of his terms. How are we to know when a person is showing needed or unneeded love? I do not mean the question in a general way, since he has given us some criteria, but I mean it quite specifically in terms of how we go about measuring the existence of these two

needs in a particular individual or group of individuals. What are the measuring devices? How is the need altered by circumstances, a question which can only be answered after we have some way of measuring it? . . . A quick look at the history of personality study shows all too readily that when theorists are faced with the ambiguous situation of describing a person's motives, without operationally defined facts, they tend to project their value systems into the ambiguous stimuli. This is true even of Freud to whom Maslow pays homage, as do all the rest of us. That is, despite Freud's empiricism, it is becoming clearer and clearer that many of his so-called scientific judgments about life, death, and the necessity for tension reduction were neither more nor less than reflections of the time, place, and culture in which he grew up. . . . This is not to say, of course, that Maslow does not have the right, even the duty, to think beyond his data to its possible implications as Aristotle and Freud did. It is to say that he becomes more and more subject to his implicit or explicit cultural and personal value assumptions the further he moves from established scientific facts.

Even assuming that these difficulties on the side of evidence can be overcome—and I for one do not think of them all as insurmountable—I am not sure that they will really tell men how to live a better life. Suppose Maslow is correct. Suppose he establishes by his method that mental disease is a result of deficiencies in the satisfaction of certain motives and mental health is a result of the development of certain other motives for self-actualization. Granted certain assumptions such as that health is better than disease, that life is more important than death, and that the individual is more important than society, then the ethical implications might be quite clear. Since these are assumptions that most of us make, the practical utility of his discoveries might be considerable, but I am not certain that they constitute a basic contribution to ethics. Certainly some complex questions can still be asked at the level of the assumptions. Is health always better than disease? Should we cure the neurotic, hard-driving, creative artist so that he becomes more spontaneous and less disciplined? Must we lose great social contributions because it is "unhealthy" to deny and reject impulses rather than accept them? For that matter, is science itself worthwhile on this basis? As a discipline it certainly seems to involve a lot of impulse rejection and control. Or is the individual's health always more important than the social well-being—a question which comes up consistently in paroling patients and delinquents? These questions are raised, not because anyone could have expected Maslow to have treated them in his paper, but because psychologists are all too ready to assume that their findings can be easily applied to ethical problems when in fact they have made very little study of ethics. Hubris is indeed the sin of scientists, psychologists included!

But with all this, Maslow could fairly answer that he never claimed that the evidence for his position was definitive, that he never intended to go deeply into questions of ethics, and that his paper was merely a reconnaissance expedition to spy out the land in a new territory. Here I must agree with him. If I have raised difficulties, it is because the task is a difficult one and not because it isn't worthwhile. On the contrary, it can hardly fail to have one very much needed effect and that is to challenge the motivational assumptions that classical theorists have made to the effect that certain biological needs are primary and that all motivational life is basically designed to produce instrumental striving in the direction of the elimination of drive. The fact is, of course, that these assumptions, made in the name of parsimony and natural law, have reflected cultural biases and the *Zeitgeist* [spirit of the time] as much as Maslow's do in a different way, and it is time someone questioned them vigorously and brought the discussion into the open. . . .

Comments: James Olds[18]

The first thing I want to do is go on record in favor of Maslow's Humanism. I believe there is something objectively good about the self-actualizing personality which Maslow describes; and I do not think this is merely a matter of personal appreciation. To put this assertion a trifle more

[18]Dr. Olds is on the faculty of the School of Medicine at U.C.L.A. He has opened up new vistas in the fields of physiology and psychology with his research on "pleasure centers" in the brain.

boldly, I believe that it is possible for the psychologist to come to scientific conclusions which constitute at the same time ethical norms. . . .

This scientific ethics will not change the fact that different cultures have different behavior norms, nor will it change the internal design of cultures. It will, however, allow evaluation of values which are causing trouble.

A value is a behavior pattern. To evaluate a value as good or bad is the job of ethics. Psychological research will permit us to evaluate values (as means to all the other values taken as ends) precisely at the point where ethics is needed, namely the point where some value is giving trouble because it conflicts with another, or no longer fits the general ends of the society. All the values will never be evaluated at once. To suggest such a massive change would be as foolish as exchanging heart, liver, and brains for a new, untested, rationally conceived set of organs. Psychology will, however, eventually give scientific evaluation of particular values whenever such evaluation is needed.

It is my belief that Maslow's humanistic and self-actualizing values will come out above their competitors when scientific evaluation becomes possible.

A second point I would like to make regarding Maslow's aim concerns the question of what is and what is not productive psychological research. My feeling is that much so-called "scientific" psychology either proves the obvious, or quixotically aims to disprove the obvious; the rest is apt to produce facts which are of a different order of magnitude from the gaps in our knowledge. There is a great tendency among people who perform such research to damn as unscientific the Maslow type of research which adjusts itself well to the gaps in our knowledge, not trying to discover nuances before the major questions are answered.

Enough good things have been said to permit a few criticisms. Maslow seems at times to be so impressed with the vagueness and inaccuracy of his own definition of self-actualization that one wonders if it would still have as much humanistic and moral value for him if psychology should succeed in breaking it down mechanistically. The question is whether we are allowed to analyse the concept into specific mechanisms in order to find out what variables influence the process of self-actualization. Is it really so impossible to analyse psychic growth into a series of specifiable applications of particular laws? My impression is that as a first step, one should cease to give the Aristotelian specification of growth in terms of the end product. The tree itself is a poor explanation of how it got to be that way. And the self-actualizing mature adult tells us little about how this individual was produced. Learning theorists would certainly expect that the acquisition of certain learned motives as against others would importantly influence the eventual amount of self-actualization. As opposed to the Aristotelian specification of growth we should at least study and analyse the progressive stages in growth and development to see how each is produced out of its antecedents and in turn produces consequences. And we should study carefully the influences of necessary "nutrients" and "catalysts" that foster and inhibit this or that aspect of the growth process.

SOME IMPLICATIONS
OF THE STRESS CONCEPT

by Hans Selye[1]

Dr. Hans Selye's theory of the general-adaptation-syndrome, outlined in Chapter 5, has been widely acclaimed as a major contribution to the fields of both medicine and psychology, being particularly helpful in explaining the psychosomatic disorders. In the following selection Dr. Selye discusses some practical implications of his theory. Note that Selye uses the term stress *in the sense of actual "wear and tear" on the body, distinguishing it from the stress-provoking stimulus, or* stressor; *this usage differs somewhat from that of the present book. Dr. Selye is Director of the Institute of Experimental Medicine and Surgery at the Université de Montreal.*

Psychosomatic Implications

Dissect your troubles. . . . [Stress] is an essential element of all our actions, in health and in disease. [Our analysis of the mechanism of stress has shown] that most of our troubles have a tripartite origin. The tweezers of stress have three prongs. Whether we suffer from a boil on the skin, a disease of the kidney, or a troubled mind, careful study of the condition will usually reveal it to consist of three major elements:

1. The *stressor,* the external agent which started the trouble, for instance, by acting directly upon the skin, the kidney, or the mind.

2. The *defensive measures,* such as the hormones and nervous stimuli which encourage the body to defend itself against the stressor as well as it can. In the case of bodily injuries, this may be accomplished by putting up a barricade of inflamed tissue in the path of the invading stressor (the microbe, allergen, and so forth). Mental stressors (orders, challenges, offenses) are met with corresponding complex emotional defensive responses, which can be summed up as the attitude of "not being done in."

3. The *mechanisms for surrender,* such as hormonal and nervous stimuli, which encourage the

body not to defend itself. For instance, not to put up barricades of inflamed tissue in the path of invaders, and to ignore emotional stressors.

It is surprising how often a better understanding of this tripartite mechanism of disease-production (and I use the word *disease* here in its widest sense, as anything that disturbs mind or body) can help us to regain our balance, even without having to ask the advice of a physician. We can often eliminate the stressor ourselves, once we have recognized its nature, or we can adjust the proportion between active defensive attitudes and measures of surrender, in the best interest of maintaining our balance.

Somatopsychic vs. psychosomatic. An enormous amount of work has been done by physicians in connection with problems of psychosomatic medicine. In essence, this specialty deals with the bodily (somatic) changes that a mental (psychic) attitude can produce. An ulcer of the stomach or a rise in blood pressure caused by emotional upsets are examples in point.

Almost no systematic research has been done, however, on the opposite of this: the effect of *bodily changes and actions upon mentality.* Of course, I do not mean physical damage to the brain, which could evidently influence the mind, but rather, such facts as that looking fit helps one to *be* fit. A pale, unshaven tramp, who wears dirty rags and is badly in need of a bath, actually does not resist either physical or mental stresses as well as he would after a shave, a bit of sunburn, a good bath, and some crisp new clothes have helped to rehabilitate his external appearance.

None of this is new. Intuitively, and merely on the basis of experience throughout centuries, these facts have long been recognized. That is why, to strengthen morale, armies insist on the spotless appearance of their men. That is also why opposite procedures are used (in some countries) for breaking down the physical and mental resistance of prisoners.

I was first introduced to these truths at the age of six, by my grandmother, when she found me desperately crying, I no longer recall about what. She looked at me with that particularly benevolent and protective look that I still remember and said, "Anytime you feel that low, just try to smile with your face, and you'll see . . . soon your whole being will be smiling." I tried it. It works.

There is nothing new here. But then, confession had been practised long before Freud; relativity was known before Einstein, and evolution before Darwin. Man did not need Pavlov's investigations on conditioned reflexes to find out that a dog can be trained to come when you whistle, or a horse to stop when you say "whoa!" Yet history shows that only the scientific analysis of these subjects by these particular men gave the concepts of psychoanalysis, the relativity of all our notions, the evolution of man's body from lower forms, and the conditioned reflexes, that philosophic impact which they now exercise upon contemporary thinking.

The existence of physical and mental strain, the manifold interactions between somatic and psychic reactions, as well as the importance of defensive-adaptive responses had all been more or less clearly recognized since time immemorial. But stress did not become meaningful to me until I found that it could be dissected by modern research methods and that individual, tangible components of the stress-response could be identified in chemical and physical terms. This is what helped me to use the concept of stress, not only for the solution of purely medical problems, but also as a guide to the natural solution of many problems presented by everyday life.

Let us take a few examples of such practical applications.

On being keyed up. Everybody is familiar with the feeling of being keyed up from nervous tension; this process is quite comparable to raising the key of a violin by tightening the strings. We say that our muscles limber up during exercise and that we are thrilled by great emotional experiences; all this prepares us for better peak-accomplishments. On the other hand, there is the tingling sensation, the jitteriness, when we are too much keyed up. This impairs our work and even prevents us from getting a rest.

Just what happens to us when we are alerted? Being keyed up is a very real sensation which must have a physicochemical basis. It has not yet been fully analyzed, but we know that at times of tension our adrenals produce an excess, both of adrenalines and of corticoids. We also know that taking either adrenalines or corticoids can reproduce a very similar sensation of being keyed up and excitable. For example, a person who is given large doses of cortisone in order to treat some allergic or rheumatoid condition often finds it difficult to sleep. He may even become abnormally euphoric, that is, carried away by an unreasonable sense of well-being and buoyancy, which is not unlike that caused by being slightly drunk. Later a sense of deep depression may follow.

We first saw this condition in experimental animals which had been given large doses of corticoids. Here, an initial state of great excitation—corresponding to the euphoria of patients—was followed by depression which might even proceed to complete anesthesia.

It had long been known that not only mental excitement (for instance, that communicated by a rioting mob or by an individual act of violence) but even physical stressors (such as a burn or an infectious fever) could cause an initial excitement which was followed by a secondary phase of depression. It is interesting to learn that identifiable chemical compounds, the hormones produced during the acute alarm-reaction phase of the G.A.S., possess this property of first keying up for action and then causing a depression. Both these effects may be of great practical value to the body: it is necessary to be keyed up for peak-accomplishments, but it is equally important to be keyed down by the secondary phase of depression, which prevents us from carrying on too long at top speed.

What can we do about this? Hormones are probably not the only regulators of our emotional level. Besides, we do not yet know enough about their workings to justify any attempt at regulating our emotional key by taking hormones.

Still, it is instructive to know that stress stimulates our glands to make hormones which can induce a kind of drunkenness. . . . The fact is that *a man can be intoxicated with his own stress hormones.* I venture to say that this sort of drunkenness has caused much more harm to society than the other kind.

We are on our guard against external intoxicants, but hormones are parts of our bodies; it takes more wisdom to recognize and overcome the foe who fights from within. In all our actions throughout the day we must consciously look for signs of being keyed up too much—and we must learn to stop in time. . . . Intoxication by stress is sometimes unavoidable and usually insidious. . . . [It] is impossible to avoid stress as long as you live and your conscious thoughts cannot gauge its alarm-signals accurately. Curiously, the pituitary is a much better judge of stress than the intellect.

How to tune down. It is not easy to tune down when you have reached your stress-quota. Many more people are the helpless slaves of their own stressful activities than of alcohol. Besides, simple rest is no cure-all. Activity and rest must be judiciously balanced, and *every person has his own characteristic requirements for rest and activity.* To lie motionless in bed all day is no relaxation for an active man. With advancing years, most people require increasingly more rest, but the process of aging does not progress at the same speed in everybody. Many a valuable man, who could still have given numerous years of useful work to society, has been made physically ill and prematurely senile by the enforcement of retirement at an age when his requirements and abilities for activity were still high. This psychosomatic illness is so common that it has been given a name: *retirement disease.*

All work and no play is certainly harmful for anyone at any age; but then, what is work and what is play? Fishing is relaxing play for the business executive, but it is hard work for the professional fisherman. The former can go fishing to relax, but the latter will have to do something else, or simply take a rest, in order to relax.

What has research on stress taught us about the way *to reach a healthy balance between rest and work?* Are there objective physiologic facts which could guide our conduct in this respect? I emphatically believe that there are, but, in order to grasp their lesson, we must turn back to what we have learned about the most general tissue-reactions to stress: cellular fatigue and inflammation. This may seem odd; you may feel that there is no conceivable relationship between the behavior of our cells (for instance, in inflammation) and our conduct in everyday life. I do not agree. All the reactions of our body are governed by general biologic laws and the simplest way to understand these is to examine how they affect the simplest tissue-reactions.

Stress as an equalizer of activities. It seems to be one of the most fundamental laws regulating the activities of complex living beings that no one part of the body must be disproportionately overworked for a long time. Stress seems to be the great equalizer of activities within the body; *it helps to prevent one-sided overexertion.*

To carry a heavy suitcase for a long time without fatigue, you have to shift it from one hand to the other occasionally. Here, local stress, manifested as muscular fatigue, is the equalizer; it acts by way of the nervous system which experiences the feeling of fatigue and thereby suggests the change-over.

In other instances, general stress may arrange the proper equalization of local activities through the intermediary of the adaptive hormones. Suppose a person has a severe infection in his left knee joint. An arthritis develops with all the characteristic manifestations of inflammation. A strong inflammatory barricade is constructed around the joint to delimit the trouble; then, various cells and enzymes will enter the joint-cavity in order to destroy the causative germs. Now, suppose both knees are infected. There develops an inflammation on both sides, but its degree will be less severe. Why? Because local stress of the inflamed territory sends out alarm-signals, through the pituitary, to stimulate the production by the adrenals of anti-inflammatory corticoids.

This arrangement is also a useful defense mechanism, because there is a limit to how much inflammation the body can tolerate. If only a small region is injured, a strong inflammatory reaction will be the best response, since inflammation has a local protective value; but if several parts of the body are simultaneously injured, the patient may not be able to stand maximal inflammatory reactions everywhere. Thus it is often in the best interests of the body as a whole to sacrifice some of its parts by cutting down local defensive activities.

This situation is quite comparable to that of a country which, when attacked on one front only, can send all its armies to the endangered region, but not when several frontiers are simultaneously invaded.

Now, since stress is a common attribute of all biologic activities, these considerations apply not only to inflammation, but to all types of biologic work. For instance, the intensity of inflammation in a knee joint may be diminished, not only by inflammation in other regions, but also by excessive muscular work, nervous activity, or anything else that requires effort. This is so because any part under stress sends out alarm-signals to coordinate resistance. For the same reason, any intense reaction in one part can influence (and, to some extent, equalize) all kinds of biologic activities in other parts of the same body.

The stress-quotient. These facts, which have been established by laboratory experiments on rats, also hold remarkably true when applied to the daily problems of man, including even his purely mental activities. In analyzing our stress-status, we must always think, not only of the total amount of stress in the body, but also of its proportionate distribution between various parts. To put this into the simplest terms, we might say that the stress-quotient to be watched is:

$$\frac{\text{local stress in any one part}}{\text{total stress in the body}}$$

If there is proportionately too much stress in any one part, you need diversion. If there is too much stress in the body as a whole, you must rest.

The importance of deviation. Deviation is the act of turning something (for instance, a biologic mechanism) aside from its course. It is not necessarily a pleasant and relaxing diversion. We have seen, for instance, how severe shock (electroshock, drug shock) can—through its general stress-effect upon all parts—deviate the body's somatic or psychic defense reactions from a habitual stereotyped course.

When the concentration of effort in any one part of our body or mind is not very intense and chronic, as we all know from experience, milder types of deviation are often quite effective (sports, dancing, music, reading, travel, whisky, chewing-gum). These do not have to act primarily through the stress-mechanism and the pituitary-adrenal axis, but they always cause a decentralization of our efforts, which often helps to restore a lopsided stress-quotient toward normal.

Deviation is particularly important in combating purely mental stress. Everyone knows how much harm can be caused by worry. The textbooks of psychosomatic medicine are full of case reports describing the production of gastric ulcers, hypertension, arthritis, and many other diseases by chronic worry about moral and economic problems. *Nothing is accomplished by telling such people not to worry.* They cannot help it. Here again, the best remedy is deviation, or general stress. By highlighting some other problem, through deviation, or by activating the whole body, by general stress, the source of worry automatically becomes less important in proportion.

This fact can be consciously used in practice. Of course, for a person who is to undergo a very dangerous surgical operation, or who finds himself on the verge of economic disaster, it is impossible to stop worrying just by deciding not to—especially if he is the worrying kind. *You must find something to put in the place of the worrying thoughts to chase them away.* This is deviation. If such a person undertakes some strenuous task which needs all his attention, he may still not forget his worries, but they will certainly fade. Nothing erases unpleasant thoughts more effectively than conscious concentration on pleasant ones. Many people do this subconsciously, but unless you know about the mechanism of diversion, it is difficult to do it well. . . .

Philosophic Implications

The wear and tear of life. . . . I have often had occasion to point out that aging, at least, true physiologic aging, is not determined by the time elapsed since birth, but by the total amount of wear and tear to which the body has been exposed. There is, indeed, a great *difference between physiologic and chronologic age.* One man may be much more senile in body and mind, and much closer to the grave, at forty than another person at sixty. True age depends largely on the rate of wear and tear, on the speed of self-consumption; for life is essentially a process which gradually spends the given amount of adaptation energy that we inherited from our parents. Vitality is like a special kind of bank account which you can use up by withdrawals but cannot increase by deposits. Your only control over this most precious fortune is the rate at which you make your. withdrawals. The solution is evidently not to stop withdrawing, for this would be death. Nor is it to withdraw just enough for survival, for this would permit only a vegetative life, worse than death. The intelligent thing to do is to withdraw generously, but never expend wastefully. . . .

. . . Life is a continuous series of adaptations to our surroundings and, as far as we know, our reserve of adaptation energy is an inherited finite amount, which cannot be regenerated. On the other hand, I am sure we could still enormously lengthen the average human life-span by living in better harmony with natural laws.

To die of old age. What makes me so certain that the natural human life-span is far in excess of the actual one is this:

Among all my autopsies (and I have performed quite a few), I have never seen a man who died of old age. In fact, *I do not think anyone has ever died of old age yet.* To permit this would be the ideal accomplishment of medical research (if we disregard the unlikely event of someone discovering how to regenerate adaptation energy). To die of old age would mean that all the organs of the body would be worn out proportionately, merely by having been used too long. This is never the case. We invariably die because one vital part has worn out too early in proportion to the rest of the body. Life, the biologic chain that holds our parts together, is only as strong as its weakest vital link. When this breaks—no matter which vital link it be—our parts can no longer be held together as a single living being.

You will note I did not say "our parts die," because this is not necessarily so. In tissue cultures, isolated cells of a man can go on living for a long time after he, as a whole, has died. It is only the complex organization of all our cells into a single individual that necessarily dies when one vital part breaks down. An old man may die because one worn-out, hardened artery breaks in his brain, or because his kidneys can no longer wash out the metabolic wastes from his blood, or because his heart muscle is damaged by excessive work. But *there is always one part which wears out first and wrecks the whole human machinery,* merely because the other parts cannot function without it.

This is the price we pay for the evolution of the human body from a simple cell into a highly complex organization. *Unicellular animals never need to die.* They just divide, and the parts live on.

The lesson seems to be that, as far as man can regulate his life by voluntary actions, he should seek to equalize stress throughout his being, by what we have called *deviation,* the frequent shifting-over of work from one part to the other. The human body—like the tires on a car, or the rug on a floor—wears longest when it wears evenly. We can do ourselves a great deal of good in this respect by just yielding to our natural cravings for variety in everyday life. We must not forget that the more we vary our actions the less any one part suffers from attrition. . . .

If we are to learn something by observing stress in nature, if we are to derive some lesson that could guide our conduct in our daily life, we must again ask ourselves, "What can we do about all this?" The development of fatigue or inflammation in an overworked organ, the production of ACTH and corticoids during stress, are obviously beyond voluntary control. So is our genetic make-up. There is something compulsive, something strictly obligatory, even in our "voluntary activities." It is all very well to say that our vitality (our adaptation energy) should be used wisely, at a certain rate, and for certain tasks, but all this is theory. In practice, when it comes to guiding human conduct, it seems that we must all bow to the great law which says that what is in us must express itself, in fact it must express itself at a speed and in directions predetermined by our own inherited structure. This is largely true, but not quite—and on the little untruth in this dictum rests my whole philosophy of life.

The need for self-expression. After a pilot has left the ground in a plane—unless he wants to kill himself—he cannot stop his motor before he gets back to earth again. He must complete his mission back to earth. Yet there is very much he can do, through voluntary choice of conduct, to get as far as possible with a given airplane and fuel supply under given climatic conditions. For instance, he can fly at a speed and on a course best suited to his machine under the prevailing weather conditions. The two great limiting factors over which, once in flight, he has no control are: the fuel supply and the wear and tear that the weakest vital part of his plane can tolerate.

When a human being is born—unless he wants to kill himself—he cannot stop, either, before he has completed his mission on earth. Yet he too can do much, through voluntary choice of conduct, to get as far as possible with a given bodily structure and supply of adaptation energy, under given social conditions. For instance, he can live and express his personality at a tempo and in a manner best suited to his inherited talents, under the prevailing social conditions. The two great limiting factors—which are set once a man is born—are: his supply of adaptation energy and the wear and tear that the weakest vital part of his body can tolerate.

So, actually, we can accomplish a great deal by living wisely in accordance with natural laws. We can determine our optimum speed of living, by trying various speeds and finding out which one is most agreeable. We can determine our course by the same empirical method, keeping in mind, however, that occasional deviations have a virtue of their own: they equalize the wear and tear throughout the body, and thereby give overworked parts time to cool down.

In my analogy you will find two weak points which are particularly instructive because they highlight the difference between an inanimate and a living machine.

First, the real fuel of life is not the combustible (food) we take, but adaptability, because the living machine can make considerable repairs and adjustments en route, as long as it has adaptation energy. With this it can assimilate caloric energy from its surroundings. Consequently, resting an overworked part in the body helps not only by "cooling it down" but also by permitting it to make major repairs and even improvements in its structure.

Second (I say "second" as a physician, but would have said "first" as a human being), the object of man is not to keep going as long as possible. This is rather charmingly expressed by the motto on the masthead of the *Journal of Gerontology*, a medical journal devoted to the study of old age: "To add life to years, not just years to life."

Man certainly does not get the feeling of happiness, of having completed his mission on earth, just by staying alive very long. On the contrary, a long life without the feeling of fulfillment is very tedious. And yet, when (and if) they analyze their lives, most people get the feeling of merely muddling through, of drifting aimlessly, from one day to another. Just staying alive, no matter how comfortably and securely, is no adequate outlet for man's vital adaptation energy. Comfort and security make it easier for us to enjoy the great things in life, but they are not, in themselves, great and enjoyable aims. . . .

The ultimate aim. As I see it, man's ultimate aim is *to express himself as fully as possible, according to his own lights.* Whether he seeks this by establishing harmony and communion with his Maker or with nature, he can do so only by finding that balance between long- and short-range aims, between sowing and harvesting, which best fits his own individuality.

The goal is certainly not to avoid stress. Stress is part of life. It is a natural by-product of all our activities; there is no more justification for avoiding stress than for shunning food, exercise, or love. But, in order to express yourself fully, you must first find your optimum stress-level, and then, use your adaptation energy at a rate and in a direction adjusted to the innate structure of your mind and body.

The study of stress has shown that complete rest is not good, either for the body as a whole, or even for any organ within the body. Stress, applied in moderation, is necessary for life. Besides, enforced inactivity may be very harmful and cause more stress than normal activity.

I have always been against the advice of physicians who would send a high-strung, extremely active business executive to a long, enforced exile in some health resort, with the view of relieving him from stress by absolute inactivity. Naturally ambitious and active men often become much more tense when they feel frustrated by not being allowed to pursue their usual activities; if they cannot express themselves through actions, they spend the time worrying about what might be going on in their business during their absence.

At the risk of sounding facetious, let me present a little motto which I developed while analyzing stress in my experimental animals, in my colleagues, my friends, and myself. It may sound trivial and purely abstract, but it is based on solid biologic laws and—at least in my case—it works. Whatever happens during the day to threaten my equanimity or throw some doubt upon the value of my actions, I just think of this little jingle:

Fight always for the highest attainable aim
But never put up resistance in vain.

Everyone should *fight* for whatever seems really worthwhile to him. On the other hand, he should aim only for *things attainable* to him, for otherwise he will merely become frustrated. Finally, *resistance* should be put up whenever there is reasonable expectation of its succeeding, but never if we know it would be *in vain*.

It is not easy to live by this motto; it takes much practice and almost constant self-analysis. Any time during the day, in discussions, at work and at play, when I begin to feel keyed up, I consciously stop to analyze the situation. I ask myself: "Is this really the best thing I could do now, and is it worth the trouble of putting up resistance against counterarguments, boredom, or fatigue?" If the answer is no, I just stop; or whenever this cannot be done gracefully I simply "float" and let things go on as they will, with a minimum of active participation (e.g., during most committee meetings, solemn academic ceremonies, and unavoidable interviews with crackpots).

Probably few people would be inclined to contest the soundness of this motto. The trick is to follow it! But that is where my assistance must stop. That is where you come in. This may sound like an anticlimactic ending, but it really should not. We all must live our own lives. No self-respecting person wants to go from cradle to grave sheepishly following the directives of another man.

THE THEORY OF GAMES

by Oskar Morgenstern[1]

One of the really exciting developments in modern social science has been the attempt to understand problem solving and decision making in everyday life by drawing an analogy to the strategy of games. Originally developed as a method of analyzing economic problems, game theory has shed new light on many areas of human behavior, as the following article makes evident. Dr. Morgenstern, Professor of Political Economy at Princeton University, has been one of the chief pioneers of game theory.

The analogy between games of strategy and economic and social behavior is so obvious that it finds wide expression in the thinking and even the language of business and politics. Phrases such as "a political deal" and "playing the stock market" are familiar reflections of this. The connection between games and these other activities is more than superficial. When they are examined by the methods of modern mathematics, it becomes evident that many of the forms of economic and social behavior are . . . identical with—not merely analogous to—games of strategy. . . .

The theory of probability arose from a study of lowly games of chance and from the desire of professional gamblers to find ways of taking advantage of the odds. Far more difficult problems are presented by games of strategy such as poker, bridge and chess. In these games, where the outcome no longer depends on chance alone but also on the acts of other players and on their expectations of one's own present and future acts, a player must choose among relatively complex strategies. Mathematically, these problems remained not only unsolved, but even untouched.

Gottfried Wilhelm Leibnitz, the German philosopher and mathematician, seems to have recognized that a study of games of strategy would form the basis of a theory of society. On the other hand, many efforts along quite different lines were made by philosophers and economists to provide a theory for "rational behavior" for individuals, business corporations, or even for entire communities.

[1]From **Scientific American**, 1949, **180**, No. 5, 22-25.

Such a theory must be quantitative, which means that it must ultimately assume a mathematical character. A theory of games fulfilling these requirements would take into account that participants in a game vary in information and intelligence, that they have various expectations about the other players' behavior, and that different paths of reaching their goal may be open to them. The theory must also allow for the fact that the position of a player (or, equivalently, of an economic individual or a firm) is often adversely affected if his opponent finds out his intentions. The player has to take steps to protect himself against this contingency, and the theory must indicate how he should proceed most efficiently—and what his countermeasures would mean to the other players. . . .

The theory of games defines the solution of each game of strategy as the distribution or distributions of payments to be made by every player as a function of all other individuals' behavior. The solution thus has to tell each player, striving for his maximum advantage, how to behave in all conceivable circumstances, allowing for all and any behavior of all the other players. Obviously this concept of a solution is very comprehensive, and finding such a solution for each type of game, as well as computing it numerically for each particular instance, poses enormous mathematical difficulties. The theory makes important use of mathematical logic, as well as combinatorics (the study of possible ways of combining and ordering objects) and set theory (the techniques for dealing with any collection of objects which have one or more exactly specified properties in common). This domain of modern mathematics is one of exceptional rigor. But it is believed that great mathematical discoveries are required to make a break-through into the field of social phenomena.

A single individual, playing alone, faces the simplest maximum problem;[2] his best strategy is the one that brings him the predetermined maximum gain. Consider a two-person game: Each player wishes to win a maximum, but he can do this only at the expense of the other. This situation results in a zero-sum game, since the sum of one player's gains and the other's losses (a negative number) is zero. One player has to design a strategy that will assure him of the maximum advantage. But the same is true of the other, who naturally wishes to minimize the first player's gain, thereby maximizing his own. This clear-cut opposition of interest introduces an entirely new concept, the so-called "minimax" problem.

Some games have an optimal "pure" strategy. In other words, there is a sequence of moves such that the player using it will have the safest strategy possible, whatever his opponent does. His position will not deteriorate even if his strategy is found out. In such "strictly determined" games, every move—and hence every position resulting from a series of moves—is out in the open. Both players have complete information. The mathematical expression of this condition is that the function describing the outcome of a game has a "saddle point." This mathematical term is based on an analogy with the shape of a saddle, which can be regarded as the intersection of two curves at a single point. One curve in a saddle is the one in which the rider sits; the other is the one that fits over the horse's back and slopes down over its sides. The seat of the saddle represents the "maximum" curve, and its low point is the "maximin." The curve that straddles the horse's back is the "minimum" curve, and its high point is the "minimax." The point at which the two curves meet at the center of the saddle is the "saddle point." In the theory of games, the somewhat more special saddle point is the intersection of two particular strategies.

The mathematical values of the strategies involved in a hypothetical game of this kind are represented in the diagram [on this page]. This shows a simple game between two players, A and B, each of whom has available three possible strategies. There are nine possible combinations of moves by A and B. The numbers in the boxes represent A's gains or losses for all combined strategies and, since this is a zero-sum game, their negatives represent B's losses or gains. A's minimax strategy is A-2, because if he follows that sequence of moves, he is sure to win at least two units no matter what B does. Similarly, B's minimax strategy is B-1, because then he cannot possibly lose more than two units whatever A's plan of action. If a spy informed A that B was planning to use B-1, A could make no profit from that information. The point where the A-2 row intersects the B-1 column is the saddle point for this game.

A \ B	B-1	B-2	B-3
A-1	2	1	4
A-2	2	3	2
A-3	2	-1	1

It may seem that B has no business playing such a game, since he must lose two units even with his best strategy, and any other strategy exposes him to even heavier loss. At best he can win only a single unit, and then only if A makes a mistake. Yet all strictly determined games are of this nature. A simple example is ticktacktoe. In perfectly played ticktacktoe every game would result in a tie. A more complex example is chess, which has a saddle point and a pure strategy. Chess is exciting because the number of possible moves and positions is so great that the finding of that strategy is beyond the powers of even the best calculating machines.

Other two-person, zero-sum games, however, have no single best possible strategy. This group includes games ranging from matching pennies to bridge and poker—and most military situations. These games, in which it would be disastrous if a player's strategy were discovered by his opponent, are not strictly determined. The play-

[2] A simple maximum problem is defined as one of "finding the behavior formula that will yield the maximum value or return" **(Editor's note).**

er's principal concern is to protect his strategy from discovery. Do safe and good strategies exist for "not strictly determined" games, so that their choice would make the games again strictly determined? Can a player in such a game find strategies other than "pure" strategies which would make his behavior completely "rational"? Mathematically speaking, does a saddle point always exist?

It does, and the proof was originally established in 1927 by the mathematician John von Neumann, the originator of the theory of games. . . . He used various basic tools of modern mathematics, including the so-called fixed-point theorem of the Dutch mathematician L. E. J. Brouwer. Von Neumann proved, by a complex but rigorous application of this theorem to the theory of games, that there is a single "stable" or rational course of action that represents the best strategy or saddle point even in not strictly determined games.

This principle can also be demonstrated in practical terms. Observation shows that in games where the discovery of a player's plan of action would have dangerous consequences, he can protect himself by avoiding the consistent use of a pure strategy and choosing it with a certain probability only. This substitution of a statistical strategy makes discovery by the opponent impossible. Since the player's chief aim must be to prevent any leakage of information from himself to the other player, the best way to accomplish this is not to have the information oneself. Thus instead of choosing a precise course of action, the various possible alternatives are considered with different probabilities.

It is in the nature of probability that individual events cannot be predicted, so that the strategy actually used will remain a secret up to the decisive moment, even to the player himself, and necessarily to his opponent as well. This type of indecision is a well-known empirical fact. Wherever there is an advantage in not having one's intentions found out—obviously a very common occurrence—people will be evasive, try to create uncertainty in the minds of others, produce doubts, and at the same time try to pierce the veil of secrecy thrown over their opponents' operations.

The example *par excellence* is poker. In a much simpler form, this type of behavior is illustrated in the game of matching pennies. Here the best strategy is to show heads or tails at random, taking care only to play each half the time. Since the same strategy is available to the opponent, both players will break even if they play long enough and both know this principle. The calculation of the best strategy grows in difficulty as the number of possible moves increases: *e.g.*, in the Italian game called morra, in which each player shows one, two or three fingers and simultaneously calls out his guess as to the sum of fingers shown by himself and his opponent, a player has nine possible strategies. His safest course is to guess a total of four fingers every time, and to vary his own moves so that out of every 12 games he shows one finger five times, two fingers four times and three fingers three times. If he plays according to this mixture of strategies, he will at least break even, no matter what his opponent does.

Let us apply these principles to a simple economic problem. Suppose that two manufacturers are competing for a given consumer market, and that each is considering three different sales strategies. The matrix on this page specifies the possible values of the respective strategies to manufacturer A: This situation does not have a

A \ B	B-1	B-2	B-3
A-1	4	1	1
A-2	0	3	1
A-3	0	0	2

single best strategy. If A chooses strategy A-1, B can limit his profit to one unit by using strategy B-2 or B-3; if A chooses strategy A-2 or A-3, B can deprive him of any profit by choosing strategy B-1. Thus each manufacturer stands to lose if he concentrates on a single sales technique and his rival discovers his plan. Analysis shows that A will lose unless he uses a combination of A-1, A-2 and A-3, each a third of the time. On the other hand, if manufacturer B fails to employ his best mixed strategy—B-1 a ninth of the time, B-2 two ninths of the time, and B-3 two thirds of the time —his competitor will gain. These mixed strategies are the safest strategies. They should be used whenever each manufacturer does not know what the other will do.

An example which illustrates in statistical terms many of the conflicts of choices involved in everyday life is the famous story of Sherlock Holmes' pursuit by his archenemy, Professor Moriarty, in Conan Doyle's story, "The Final Problem." Holmes has planned to take a train from London to Dover and thence make his escape to the Continent. Just as the Dover train is pulling out of Victoria Station, Moriarty rushes on the platform and the two men see each other. Moriarty is left at the station. He charters a special train to continue the chase. The detective is faced with the problem of outguessing his pursuer. Should he get off at Canterbury—the only intermediate stop—or go all the way to Dover? And what should Moriarty do? In effect, this situation can be treated as a rather unusual version of matching pennies—a "match" occurring if the two men decide to go to the same place and meet there. It is assumed that such a meeting would mean the death of Sherlock Holmes; therefore it has an arbitrarily assigned value of 100 to Moriarty. If Holmes goes to Dover and makes his way to the Continent, it is obviously a defeat for the professor, but—also obviously—not as great a defeat as death would be for the detective. Hence, a value of minus 50 to Moriarty is given to this eventuality. Finally, if Holmes leaves the train at Canterbury and Moriarty goes on to Dover, the chase is not over and the temporary outcome can be considered a draw. According to the theory of games, the odds are 60 to 40 in favor of the professor.

In the story, of course, this game is played only once: Sherlock Holmes, deducing that Moriarty will go to Dover, gets off at Canterbury and watches triumphantly as the professor's pursuing train speeds past the intermediate station. If the game were continued, however, Holmes' look of triumph would hardly be justified. On the assumption that Moriarty persisted in the chase, calculations indicate that the great detective was actually as good as 40 per cent dead when his train left Victoria Station!

The theory of games has already been applied to a number of practical problems. Situations similar to that of Holmes are being analyzed in that branch of operational research which deals with military tactics, the possible courses of action being various dispositions of troops or combinations of measures and countermeasures. The handling of the more complex situations that exist in economics is expected to require the aid of calculating machines. For example, two competing automobile manufacturers may each have a large number of strategies involving the choice of various body designs, the addition of new accessories, the best times to announce new models and price changes, and so on. It has been estimated that the calculations for a game in which one manufacturer had 100 possible strategies and his competitor had 200 (a not uncommon situation) would take about a year on an electronic computer.

If we now make the transition to games involving three or more persons, a fundamentally new phenomenon emerges—namely, the tendency among some players to combine against others, or equivalently in markets to form trade unions, cartels and trusts. Such coalitions will be successful only if they offer the individual members more than they could get acting separately. Games where that is the case are called essential. Coalitions will then oppose each other in the manner of individual players in a two-person game. . . .

The approach to the coalition problem in the theory of games can be shown by a three-person situation in which it is assumed that a player can achieve a gain in any given play only if he joins with one other player. The gains and losses that would result for the individual players in the case of each possible coalition are shown in [the diagram on p. 497]. Thus if A and B form a coalition, each gains a half unit and C loses one unit. What keeps the players in the game is that they all stand a chance of profit; each player's problem is to succeed in forming a coalition with one of the other two on any given deal. This simplified situation illustrates in essence much of the conflict that occurs in modern economic life.

Now the important characteristic of this type of game is that there is no single "best" solution for any individual player. A, for example, can gain as much by forming a coalition with C as with B. Therefore all three of the possible distributions of payments, taken together, must be viewed as the solution of this three-person game.

individual players / coalitions	A	B	C
A, B	½	½	−1
A, C	½	−1	½
·B, C	−1	½	½

There are, of course, many other distribution schemes that might be considered by the players. For example, one of the partners in a coalition could make a deal with the third player whereby both improved their positions (the third player reducing his losses) at the expense of the other partner. What is to prevent the participants in the game from considering all these other possibilities?

The question can be answered by introducing the concept of "domination." In mathematical terminology the various possible schemes for distribution of payments are called "imputations." One imputation is said to dominate another if it is clearly more advantageous to all the players in a given coalition. It is found, as shown in the three-person game described above, that the imputations belonging to a solution do not dominate each other: in this case all three imputations have an equal chance of being chosen; none is most advantageous to the players in each coalition. While it is extremely difficult to prove mathematically that such a solution would exist for every game with arbitrarily many players, the principle can be expected to hold true.

Now it is also found that while the imputations belonging to the solution do not dominate each other, individually they are not free from domination by imputations outside the solution. In other words, there are always outside schemes from which some of the players could profit. But any and every imputation outside the solution is dominated by one belonging to the solution, so that it will be rejected as too risky. It will be considered unsafe not to conform to the accepted standard of behavior, and only one of the imputations which are part of the solution will materialize.

These examples give an idea of the great complexity of social and economic organization. In this realm "stability" is far more involved than it is in the physical sciences, where a solution is usually given by a number or a set of numbers. In essential games, in economics and in warfare, there is instead a set of alternatives, none of which is clearly better than another or all others. One imputation in a set is not more stable than any other, because every one may be threatened by one outside the solution. But each has a certain stability because it is protected by other potential imputations in the solution against upsets from outside. Collectively they eliminate the danger of revolutions. The balance is most delicate, however, and it becomes more sensitive as the number of players increases. These higher-order games may have many solutions instead of a single one, and while there is no conflict within an individual solution, the various solutions or standards of behavior may well conflict with one another.

This multiplicity of solutions may be interpreted as a mathematical formulation of the undisputed fact that on the same physical background of economic and social culture utterly different types of society can be established. Within each society, in turn, there is possible considerable variation in the distribution of income, privileges and other advantages—which corresponds to the multiplicity of imputations or distribution schemes in a single solution in a game.

The theory also yields insight into even more delicate social phenomena. Although it assumes that every player has full information, discrimination may exist: two players may make a third player "tabu," assigning him a fixed payment and excluding him from all negotiations and coalitions. Yet this arrangement need not lead to complete exploitation of the third player. In practical economic life, for example, cartels do not annihilate all outside firms, although it would not be a technically difficult operation. Rather, in deference to socially accepted standards of behavior they allow certain outsiders a share in the industry, so as not to attract undue attention—and to be able to point out to the government and the public that "competition" exists in the particular industry.

It is surprising and extremely significant that, although the theory of games was developed without any specific consideration of such situations, the fact that they exist was derived from general theorems by purely mathematical methods. Furthermore, the theory shows—again purely mathematically—that certain privileges, even if anchored in the rules of a game (or of a society), cannot always be maintained by the privileged if they come into conflict with the accepted standard of behavior. . . .

These and many other implications can be derived from the study of simple three-person games. Games of more than three players provide further interesting insights—but at the price of great and, in many cases, still insuperable mathematical difficulties. The almost unimaginable complexity involved may be illustrated by poker, the game which, above all others, furnishes a model for economic and social situations. The subtle-

ties of poker and the countless number of available strategies—*e.g.*, the technique of purposely being caught bluffing now and then so that future bluffs may be successful—prevent the thorough analysis that would be necessary to throw light on corresponding problems in practical everyday affairs. The matrix of possible strategies for poker is so large that it has not even been calculated, much less drawn. Consider a radically simplified version of the game which assumes a deck of only three cards, a one-card, no-draw hand, only two players, three bids between them (the first player gets two, the second one), and no overbetting. Even this watered-down version of poker involves a matrix of 1,728 boxes, and computing a single best possible strategy for each player to an accuracy of about 10 per cent might require almost two billion multiplications and additions. . . .

The initial problem in the theory of games was to give precision to the notion of "rational behavior." Qualitative or philosophical arguments have led nowhere; the new quantitative approach may point in the right direction. Applications are still limited, but the approach is in the scientific tradition of proceeding step by step, instead of attempting to include all phenomena in a great general solution. . . .

ELECTRICAL ANALOGIES
FOR THE BRAIN

by Clifford T. Morgan and Eliot Stellar[1]

The following article outlines some of the analogies which cyberneticists have made between the brain and electrical concepts (see Chapter 6). As the authors warn, it remains to be proved whether the brain actually has anything in common with a computing machine—electrical analogies as such "prove nothing at all about the brain." Dr. Morgan teaches at Johns Hopkins University; Dr. Stellar is on the staff of the University of Pennsylvania Medical School, Institute of Neurological Sciences.

Science has its fads just as people do, for it is people who make science. The fads are in ideas and in lines of research, however, and they seldom are completely wrong. Since the Second World War, a fad has been gaining ground that began well before the war. The idea is to liken the brain to a set of electrical circuits, or more particularly to a computing machine, and then to see how many of the problems of human behavior could be solved and understood if the analogy could hold true.

Background. Attempts along this line began with a group in Chicago who called themselves mathematical biophysicists. At first they simply tried to devise theories for how the brain worked in behavior by using the sort of mathematical procedures that have long been in use in theoretical physics. At the same time, however, the communications engineers were devising equipments for "packaging" information in highly complex circuits, the mathematicians and electrical engineers were building more and more complex computing machines, and psychologists during the war faced problems of human beings operating such devices as gun directors and servomechanisms. All these various trends in thinking and theorizing came to a head when Wiener dubbed the new field cybernetics and published a book under that title.

It is hard to tell how far the fad will go or even whether it is a fad. At present the field of cyber-

netics is mainly a set of analogies between electrical devices and the brain. Analogies never prove anything, but they sometimes are very stimulating and lead to something else that can be proved. Some of the ideas of cybernetics are easy and convenient ways to think about physiological functions, even if they are not correct. We believe it is worth while, therefore, to put down a few of the central notions of the field.

The brain as a digital computer. Mathematicians and electrical engineers design computing machines in many ways. One way, the way that it is used in some of the vastly complex modern computers, is to use thousands of relays. Each relay can be either open or closed and thus carries along "all-or-none" information. Relays can be arranged in banks so that the action of one relay sets off a second relay and that in turn trips another relay, and so on. Such computing machines, designed with all-or-none relays, are called *digital computers.*

It is easy, of course, to make an immediate analogy with the brain. Each neuron, we know, obeys an all-or-none law. It is either on or off. Thus it is just like a relay in a computer. We have billions of neurons in our brain—more than have been put into any physical computers—and they are arranged in various sorts of banks and circuits so that one neuron going on can set off another neuron, and so on. Having likened the neurons to relays and the brain to a computing machine, we can go on with the analogy and see what kinds of circuits may be in each and how they may function.

The reverberating circuit. . . . All over the nervous system we run into [reverberating] circuits, which once started can continue themselves indefinitely until some activity comes along to stop them. The cyberneticists make much of the reverberating circuit. . . . We remember things, they say, because a reverberating loop [i.e., circuit] gets going and does not stop. They compute, too, that we have enough billion loops in our brain to take care of all the memories we could possibly file away in a lifetime. Perhaps in the end our memory is not just a matter of reverberation but rather one of change in chemical molecules of the neurons around the circuit. Even if that is the case, the loop is essential to memory because its constant activity brings about the chemical change.

Besides memory, the cyberneticists say these loops endow us with 'purpose,' 'will,' motor coordination, and even sometimes with neurosis. At least we can find analogues in electrical instruments and computing machines for such aspects of behavior. In every case the important feature of the loop is *feedback*—which means that the events in a loop can feed back to the point where they started and affect themselves. Such feedback can be either negative or positive.

Negative feedback. In negative feedback, a loop has some natural or prearranged state of activity. Whenever the events in the loop depart from that state, they check themselves through feedback. When you set the volume control of your automobile radio, for example, the loudness of the radio stays the same (within limits) even though you get nearer or farther away from the radio station. It does that because there is a negative feed-back circuit in the radio. There is a loop from the output of the radio back to its input. When the output gets too loud it cuts down the "gain," *i.e.*, the amount to which the radio signal is amplified. When the output is too weak it "opens up" the amplifier to give you a louder program. This is negative feedback, because the output makes the input do the opposite of what it is doing, and thereby the system gets to, and stays in, a stable state.

Reflexes. This kind of feedback is at work at many levels of function in the body. Take the pupillary reflex, for example. Light falling on the eye reflexly makes the pupil contract. A small pupil, however, cuts down the light getting into the eye so that the opposite sort of reflex occurs, *viz.*, dilation. This, of course, lets more light into the eye and causes the pupil to contract. If this loop of negative feedback took place in steps as we describe them, our pupils would be widening and contracting all the time. Actually the loop is at work all the time, and thus the reflex gets to a steady state and stays there within a short time after the stimulus for the eye is presented or taken away.

Hunting. Negative feedback not only accounts for steady states of this sort but also for cases of 'hunting' and 'purposeful movement.' Gun directors used in the last war and automatic missiles that hunt out and home on a target without any human direction are just two examples of such negative feedback. Each of these instruments reacts to a stimulus. When the stimulus is off the center of their 'eyes,' the loop inside them makes them turn toward the stimulus. The more they point toward the stimulus, the less the feedback forcing them to point to it. When they are pointed directly toward it they have found their target and are in a steady state. Then negative feedback is at its lowest point. The principle is the same as in the automatic volume control of the radio.

Coordination. Various sorts of motor coordination and motivated behavior can be described in the same way. We see an object out of the corner of our eye, and feed-back circuits in our brain start our eyes turning toward the object. As our eyes move, the object gets closer and closer to the center of our retina, and this cuts down the feedback turning our eyes. Because of the loop made by our eyes, the nervous system, and the stimulus, we turn to the object and stop with our eyes on it. This is only one example. Almost any case of motor coordination could be cast in the same terms.

Purpose. We can think even of motivation, purpose, and will as the outcome of loops in which there is negative feedback. When we are motivated, our 'automatic volume control' has gone off center. The drive conditions within our body start us doing something which ends up in eating, drinking, or the like. Such eating or drinking directly or indirectly changes the drive state in our body, cutting down (by negative feedback) our actions to 'satisfy' the drive. Thus, for example, we have a loop made up of drive, behavior, and food that is closed and has negative feedback in it. This kind of analogy can be made not only for motivation but also for its relatives, such as purposeful behavior, goal seeking, and 'volition.' It takes only a little imagination to extend such notions to almost any example one wants to dream up.

Positive feedback. A second kind of feedback also gives us some clever analogies. In positive feedback we have a 'vicious circle.' The output, instead of making the input do the opposite of what it is doing, makes it do the same thing. Thus if the output increases, it affects the input to make the output increase still more. Or if the output decreases, it makes the input decrease all the more. . . .

Negative feedback keeps us in a steady state—it keeps bringing us back to normal. Positive feedback, once started, however, takes us further and further away from a steady state and at a greater and greater rate. . . . When machines go into positive feedback, as they sometimes do, they go "berserk." The only way to stop them is to pull the power switch off, if you can, or wreck the machine.

Much the same thing can be said about people. Neurotic behavior can be likened to positive feedback. Something happens in the loops to change them from a normal negative feedback to a positive feedback. The loops then keep on going, getting more and more active, sweeping other loops into their orbit. If not stopped in some way or other they may take over so much of the organism that we have a first-class psychoneurosis on our hands. Obsessions, compulsive behavior, and floating anxieties, which mark the neurotic person, are all analogous to positive feed-back circuits that have been started and have not been stopped. Cyberneticists suggest that therapy by convulsive shocks or by cutting some of the pathways of the brain sometimes helps neurotics because it breaks up the positive feed-back circuits, it "clears the machine" and lets it start over again on negative feed-back principles of operation.

The brain as a television set. The cyberneticists have many ideas—enough, in fact, to fill a book—but we have time for only one more. This is an analogy of the brain to a television system. In television, pictures are transmitted from one place to another because they are electrically broken up into a code. What happens, in effect, is that a very small beam scans the picture at a very rapid rate, just as we might read the page of a book. It runs across a line, then sweeps back to scan another line, then the next line, and so on. This scanning goes on hundreds of times a second. The beam codes what it "sees" as it goes along into a series of signals that are put on the radio carrier waves and broadcast over the air. The television receiver at home is a device for decoding the television signals; by scanning the picture tube, it puts on the tube the picture that originated in the television station. . . .

Cyberneticists suggest that the nervous system works like a television system. The alpha wave, which seems to be the normal rhythm of the brain, could serve as a scanning and carrier wave. This wave could pick up "the picture" coming into the brain from the various sensory pathways, code it much as television signals are coded, then carry the signals to different parts of the cortex for decoding. The rate of scan, about 10 per second, is rather slow for a television system, but it certainly is fast enough for what the brain does. Any of the cortical areas might then act as television receivers by decoding the signals carried on the alpha waves. Such a scheme, cyberneticists point out, might solve many of the perplexing problems of equipotentiality and recovery of function in different cortical areas.

CYBERNETICS AND PSYCHOPATHOLOGY

by Norbert Wiener[1]

With his colleagues at the Massachusetts Institute of Technology, where he is Professor of Mathematics, Norbert Wiener has been largely responsible for developing the new science of cybernetics. In the following article Dr. Wiener speculates on the possible implications of computer analogies for the understanding and treatment of mental disorders.

It is necessary that I commence . . . with a disavowal. On the one hand, I am not a psychopathologist nor a psychiatrist, and lack any experience in a field where the guidance of experience is the only trustworthy one. On the other hand, our knowledge of the normal performance of the brain and the nervous system, and *a fortiori,* our knowledge of their abnormal performance, is far from having reached that state of perfection where an *a priori* theory can command any confidence. I therefore wish to disclaim in advance any assertion that any particular entity in psychopathology . . . is due to a specific type of defect in the organization of the brain as a computing machine. Those who may draw such specific conclusions . . . do so at their own risk.

Nevertheless, the realization that the brain and the computing machine have much in common may suggest new and valid approaches to psychopathology, and even to psychiatrics. These begin with perhaps the simplest question of all: how the brain avoids gross blunders, gross miscarriages of activity, due to the malfunction of individual components. Similar questions referring to the computing machine are of great practical importance, for here a chain of operations each covering a fraction of a millisecond may last a matter of hours or days. It is quite possible for a chain of computational operations to involve 10^9 separate steps. Under these circumstances, the chance that at least one operation will go amiss is very far from negligible, even though, it is true, the reliability of modern electronic apparatus has far exceeded the most sanguine expectations.

In ordinary computational practice by hand or by desk machines, it is the custom to check every step of the computation, and when an error is found, to localize it by a backward process starting from the first point where the error is noted. To do this with a high-speed machine, the check must proceed with the speed of the original machine, or the whole effective order of speed of the machine will conform to that of the slower process of checking. Furthermore, if the machine is made to keep all intermediate records of its performance, its complication and bulk will be increased to an intolerable point, by a factor which is likely to be enormously greater than two or three.

A much better method of checking, and in fact the one generally used in practice, is to refer every operation simultaneously to two or three separate mechanisms. In the case of the use of two such mechanisms, their answers are automatically collated against each other; and if there is a discrepancy, all data are transferred to permanent storage, the machine stops, and a signal is sent to the operator that something is wrong. The operator then compares the results, and is guided by them in his search for the malfunctioning part, perhaps a tube which has burnt out and needs replacement. If three separate mechanisms are used for each stage, and single misfunctions are as rare as they are in fact, there will practically always be an agreement between two of the three mechanisms, and this agreement will give the required result. In this case the collation mechanism accepts the majority report, and the machine need not stop; but there is a signal indicating where and how the minority report differs from the majority report. If this occurs at the first moment of

[1]From **Cybernetics** by Norbert Wiener, Technology Press, Cambridge, Mass., and John Wiley & Sons, Inc., New York, 1948, pp. 168-176.

discrepancy, the indication of the position of the error may be very precise. In a well-designed machine, no particular element is assigned to a particular stage in the sequence of operations, but at each stage there is a searching process, quite similar to that used in automatic telephone exchanges, which finds the first available element of a given sort, and switches it into the sequence of operations. In this case, the removal and replacement of defective elements need not be the source of any appreciable delay.

It is conceivable and not implausible that at least two of the elements of this process are also represented in the nervous system. We can hardly expect that any important message is entrusted for transmission to a single neuron, nor that any important operation is entrusted to a single neuronal mechanism. Like the computing machine, the brain probably works on a variant of the famous principle expounded by Lewis Carroll in *The Hunting of the Snark:* "What I tell you three times is true." It is also improbable that the various channels available for the transfer of information generally go from one end of their course to the other without anastomosing.[2] It is much more probable that when a message comes in to a certain level of the nervous system, it may leave that point and proceed to the next by one or more alternative members of what is known as an "internuncial pool." There may be parts of the nervous system, indeed, where this interchangeability is much limited or abolished, and these are likely to be such highly specialized parts of the cortex as those which serve as the inward extensions of the organs of special sense. Still, the principle holds, and probably holds most clearly for the relatively unspecialized cortical areas which serve the purpose of association and of what we call the higher mental functions.

So far we have been considering errors in performance which are normal, and only pathological in an extended sense. Let us now turn to those which are much more clearly pathological. Psychopathology has been rather a disappointment to the instinctive materialism of the doctors, who have taken the point of view that every disorder

must be accompanied by material lesions of some specific tissue involved. It is true that specific brain lesions, such as injuries, tumors, clots, and the like, may be accompanied by psychic symptoms, and that certain mental diseases, such as paresis, are the sequellae of general bodily disease, and show a pathological condition of the brain tissue; but there is no way of identifying the brain of a schizophrenic . . . , nor of a manic-depressive patient, nor of a paranoiac. These disorders we call *functional;* and this distinction seems to contravene the dogma of modern materialism, that every disorder in function has some physiological or anatomical basis in the tissues concerned.

This distinction between functional and organic disorders receives a great deal of light from the consideration of the computing machine. As we have already seen, it is not the empty physical structure of the computing machine that corresponds to the brain—to the adult brain, at least—but the combination of this structure with the instructions given it at the beginning of a chain of operations and with all the additional information stored and gained from outside in the course of this chain. This information is stored in some physical form—in the form of memory—but part of it is in the form of circulating memories, with a physical basis which vanishes when the machine is shut down, or the brain dies, and part in the form of long-time memories, which are stored in a way at which we can only guess, but probably also in a form with a physical basis which vanishes at death. There is no way yet known for us to recognize in the cadaver what the threshold of a given synapse has been in life; and even if we knew this, there is no way we can trace out the chain of neurons and synapses communicating with this, and the significance of this chain as to the ideational content which it records.

There is therefore nothing surprising in considering the functional mental disorders as fundamentally diseases of memory, of the circulating information kept by the brain in the active state, and of the long-time permeability of synapses. Even the grosser disorders such as paresis may produce a large part of their effects, not so much by the destruction of tissue which they involve, and the alteration of synaptic thresholds, as by

---

[2]Anastomosing is the joining of two channels. An internuncial pool is a group of neurons that connect sensory and motor neurons within the central nervous system **(Editor's note)**.

the secondary disturbances of traffic, the overload of what remains of the nervous system, and the re-routing of messages, which must follow such primary injuries.

In a system containing a large number of neurons, circular processes can hardly be stable for long periods of time. Either, as in the case of memories belonging to the specious present, they run their course, dissipate themselves, and die out, or they comprehend more and more neurons in their system, until they occupy an inordinate part of the neuron pool. This is what we should expect to be the case in the malignant worry which accompanies anxiety neuroses. In such a case, it is possible that the patient simply does not have the room, the sufficient number of neurons, to carry out his normal processes of thought. Under such conditions, there may be less going on in the brain to load up the neurons not yet affected, so that they are all the more readily involved in the expanding process. Furthermore, the permanent memory becomes more and more deeply involved, and the pathological process which occurred at first at the level of the circulating memories may repeat itself in a more intractable form at the level of the permanent memories. Thus what started as a relatively trivial and accidental reversal of stability, may build itself up into a process totally destructive to the ordinary mental life.

Pathological processes of a somewhat similar nature are not unknown in the case of mechanical or electrical computing machines. A tooth of a wheel may slip under just such conditions that no tooth with which it engages can pull it back into its normal relations, or a high-speed electrical computing machine may go into a circular process which there seems to be no way to stop. These contingencies may depend on a highly improbable instantaneous configuration of the system, and when remedied, may never—or very rarely—repeat themselves. However, when they occur, they temporarily put the machine out of action.

How do we deal with these accidents in the use of the machine? The first thing which we try is to clear the machine of all information, in the hope that when it starts again with different data, the difficulty may not recur. Failing this, if the difficulty is in some point permanently or temporarily inaccessible to the clearing mechanism, we shake the machine, or if it is electrical, subject it to an abnormally large electrical impulse, in the hope that we may reach the inaccessible part, and throw it into a position where the false cycle of its activities will be interrupted. If even this fails, we may disconnect an erring part of the apparatus, for it is possible that what yet remains may be adequate for our purpose.

Now, there is no normal process except death which completely clears the brain from all past impressions; and after death, it is impossible to set it going again. Of all normal processes, sleep comes the nearest to a non-pathological clearing. How often we find that the best way to handle a complicated worry, or an intellectual muddle, is to sleep over it! However, sleep does not clear away the deeper memories, nor indeed is a sufficiently malignant state of worry compatible with an adequate sleep. We are thus often forced to resort to more violent types of intervention in the memory cycle. The more violent of these involve a surgical intervention into the brain, leaving behind it permanent damage, mutilation, and the abridgement of the powers of the victim; as the mammalian central nervous system seems to possess no powers whatever of regeneration. The principal type of surgical intervention which has been practiced is known as prefrontal lobotomy, and consists in the removal or isolation of a portion of the prefrontal lobe of the cortex. It has recently been having a certain vogue, probably not unconnected with the fact that it makes the custodial care of many patients easier. Let me remark in passing that killing them makes their custodial care still easier. However, prefrontal lobotomy does seem to have a genuine effect on malignant worry, not by bringing the patient nearer to a solution of his problems, but by damaging or destroying the capacity for maintained worry, known in the terminology of another profession as the *conscience*. More generally it appears to limit all aspects of the circulating memory, the ability to keep in mind a situation not actually presented.

The various forms of shock treatment—electric, insulin, metrazol—are less drastic methods of doing a very similar thing. They do not destroy brain tissue or at least are not intended to destroy it, but they do have a decidedly damaging effect on the memory. In so far as this concerns the circulating memory, and in so far as this memory is chiefly damaged for the recent period of mental disorder, and is probably scarcely worth preserving anyhow, shock treatment has something definite to recommend it as against lobotomy; but it is not always free from deleterious effects on the permanent memory and the personality. As it stands at present, it is another violent, imperfectly understood, imperfectly controlled method to interrupt a mental vicious circle. This does not prevent its being in many cases the best thing we can do at present.

Lobotomy and shock treatment are methods which by their very nature are more suited to handle vicious circulating memories and malignant worries than the deeper-seated permanent memories, though it is not impossible that they may have some effect here too. As we have said, in long-established cases of mental disorder, the permanent memory is as badly deranged as the circulating memory. We do not seem to possess any purely pharmaceutical or surgical weapon for intervening differentially in the permanent memory. This is where psychoanalysis and other similar psychotherapeutic measures come in. Whether psychoanalysis is taken in the orthodox Freudian sense or in the modified senses of Jung and of Adler, or whether our psychotherapy is not strictly psychoanalytic at all, our treatment is clearly based on the concept that the stored information of the mind lies on many levels of accessibility, and is much richer and more varied than that which is accessible by direct unaided introspection; that it is vitally conditioned by affective experiences which we cannot always uncover by such introspection, either because they never were made explicit in our adult language, or because they have been buried by a definite mechanism, affective though generally involuntary; and that the content of these stored experiences as well as their affective tone condition much of our later activity in ways which may well be pathological. The technique of the psychoanalyst consists in a series of means to discover and interpret these hidden memories, to make the patient accept them for what they are, and by their acceptance, modify, if not their content, at least the affective tone they carry, and thus make them less

harmful. All this . . . perhaps explains, too, why there are circumstances where a joint use of shock treatment and psychotherapy is indicated, combining a physical or pharmacological therapy for the phenomena of reverberation in the nervous system, and a psychological therapy for the long-time memories which, without interference, might re-establish from within the vicious circle broken up by the shock treatment.

We have already mentioned the traffic problem of the nervous system. It has been commented on by many writers, such as d'Arcy Thompson,[3] that each form of organization has an upper limit of size, beyond which it will not function. Thus the insect organization is limited by the length of tubing over which the spiracle method of bringing air by diffusion directly to the breathing tissues will function; a land animal cannot be so big that the legs or other portions in contact with the ground will be crushed by its weight; a tree is limited by the mechanism for transferring water and minerals from the roots to the leaves, and the products of photosynthesis from the leaves to the roots; and so on. The same sort of thing is observed in engineering constructions. Skyscrapers are limited in size by the fact that, when they exceed a certain height, the elevator space needed for the upper stories consumes an excessive part of the cross-section of the lower floors. Beyond a certain span, the best possible suspension bridge which can be built out of materials with given elastic properties will collapse under its own weight; and beyond a certain greater span, *any* structure built of a given material or materials will collapse under its own weight. Similarly, the size of a single telephone central, built according to a constant, non-expanding plan, is limited, and this limitation has been very thoroughly studied by telephone engineers.

In a telephone system, the important limiting factor is the fraction of the time during which a subscriber will find it impossible to put a call through. A 99 per cent chance of success will certainly be satisfactory for even the most exacting; 90 per cent of successful calls is probably good enough to permit business to be carried on with

[3]D'Arcy Thompson, **Growth and Form,** 2nd ed., Toronto: Oxford University Press, 1945.

reasonable facility. A success of 75 per cent is already annoying, but will permit business to be carried on after a fashion; while if half the calls end in failures, subscribers will begin to ask to have their telephones taken out. Now, these represent all-over figures. If the calls go through n distinct stages of switching, and probability of failure is independent and equal for each stage, in order to get a probability of total success equal to p, the probability of success at each stage must be $p^{1/n}$. Thus to obtain 75 per cent chance of the completion of the call after five stages, we must have about 95 per cent chance of success per stage. To obtain 90 per cent of performance, we must have 98 per cent chance of performance at each stage. To obtain 50 per cent of performance, we must have 87 per cent of success at each stage. It will be seen that the more stages which are involved, the more rapidly the service becomes extremely bad when a critical level of failure for the individual call is exceeded, and extremely good when this critical level of failure is not quite reached. Thus a switching service involving many stages and designed for a certain level of failure shows no obvious signs of failure until the traffic comes up to the edge of the critical point, when it goes completely to pieces, and we have a catastrophic traffic jam.

Man, with the best developed nervous system of all the animals, with behavior that probably depends on the longest chains of effectively operated neuronic chains, is then likely to perform a complicated type of behavior efficiently very close to the edge of an overload, when he will give way in a serious and catastrophic way. This overload may take place in several ways: either by an excess in the amount of traffic to be carried, by a physical removal of channels for the carrying of traffic, or by the excessive occupation of such channels by undesirable systems of traffic, like circulating memories which have increased to the extent of becoming pathological worries. In all these cases, a point will come—quite suddenly—when the normal traffic will not have space enough allotted to it, and we shall have a form of mental breakdown, very possibly amounting to insanity.

This will first affect the faculties or operations involving the longest chains of neurons. There is appreciable evidence that these are precisely the processes which are recognized to be the highest in our ordinary scale of valuation. . . .

We thus see that the superiority of the human brain to others in the length of the neuron chains it employs is a reason why mental disorders are certainly most conspicuous and probably most common in man. . . .

COMMUNICATION THEORY

by Wilbur Schramm[1]

Wilbur Schramm's analysis of the communication process introduces the reader to information theory and suggests a scientific approach to some of the practical problems of mass communication. The reader who has studied the articles on systems theory (p. 433) and cybernetics (pp. 499 and 502) will note that the principles of information transfer also have important applications in these pioneer fields of study. Dr. Schramm is Professor of Communication and Journalism at Stanford University.

The Process

It will be easier to see how mass communication works if we first look at the communication process in general.

Communication comes from the Latin *communis,* common. When we communicate we are trying to establish a "commonness" with someone. That is, we are trying to share information, an idea, or an attitude. At this moment I am trying to communicate to you the idea that the essence of communication is getting the receiver and the sender "tuned" together for a particular message. At this same moment, someone somewhere is excitedly phoning the fire department that the house is on fire. Somewhere else a young man in a parked automobile is trying to convey the understanding that he is moon-eyed because he loves the young lady. Somewhere else a newspaper is trying to persuade its readers to believe as it does about the Republican Party. All these are forms of communication, and the process in each case is essentially the same.

Communication always requires at least three elements—the source, the message, and the destination. A *source* may be an individual (speaking, writing, drawing, gesturing) or a communication organization (like a newspaper, publishing house, television station or motion picture studio). The *message* may be in the form of ink on paper, sound waves in the air, impulses in an electric current, a wave of the hand, a flag in the air, or

any other signal capable of being interpreted meaningfully. The *destination* may be an *individual* listening, watching, or reading; or a member of a *group,* such as a discussion group, a lecture audience, a football crowd, or a mob; or an individual member of the particular group we call the *mass audience,* such as the reader of a newspaper or a viewer of television.

Now what happens when the source tries to build up this "commonness" with his intended receiver? First, the source encodes his message. That is, he takes the information or feeling he wants to share and puts it into a form that can be transmitted. The "pictures in our heads" can't be transmitted until they are coded. When they are coded into spoken words, they can be transmitted easily and effectively, but they can't travel very far unless radio carries them. If they are coded into written words, they go more slowly than spoken words, but they go farther and last longer. Indeed, some messages long outlive their senders—the *Iliad,* for instance; the Gettysburg address; Chartres cathedral. Once coded and sent, a message is quite free of its sender, and what it does is beyond the power of the sender to change. Every writer feels a sense of helplessness when he finally commits his story or poem to print; you doubtless feel the same way when you mail an important letter. Will it reach the right person? Will he understand it as you intend him to? Will he respond as you want him to? For in order to complete the act of communication the message must be decoded. And there is good reason, as we shall see, for the sender to wonder whether his receiver will really be in tune with

[1]From **The Process and Effects of Mass Communication** by Wilbur Schramm, University of Illinois Press, Urbana, Ill., 1955, pp. 3-13.

Figure 1.

him, whether the message will be interpreted without distortion, whether the "picture in the head" of the receiver will bear any resemblance to that in the head of the sender.

We are talking about something very like a radio or telephone circuit. In fact, it is very possible to draw a picture of the human communication system that way [as shown in Figure 1, above]. Substitute "microphone" for encoder, and "earphone" for decoder and you are talking about electronic communication. Consider that the "source" and "encoder" are one person, "decoder" and "destination" are another, and the signal is language, and you are talking about human communication.

Now it is perfectly possible by looking at those diagrams to predict how such a system will work. For one thing, such a system can be no stronger than its weakest link. In engineering terms, there may be filtering or distortion at any stage. In human terms, if the source does not have adequate or clear information; if the message is not encoded fully, accurately, effectively in transmittible signs; if these are not transmitted fast enough and accurately enough, despite interference and competition, to the desired receiver; if the message is not decoded in a pattern that corresponds to the encoding; and finally, if the destination is unable to handle the decoded message so as to produce the desired response—then, obviously, the system is working at less than top efficiency. When we realize that *all* these steps must be accomplished with relatively high efficiency if any communication is to be successful, the everyday act of explaining something to a stranger, or writing a letter, seems a minor miracle.

A system like this will have a maximum capacity for handling information and this will depend on the separate capacities of each unit on the chain—for example, the capacity of the channel (how fast can one talk?) or the capacity of the

encoder (can your student understand something explained quickly?). If the coding is good (for example, no unnecessary words) the capacity of the channel can be approached, but it can never be exceeded. You can readily see that one of the great skills of communication will lie in knowing how near capacity to operate a channel.

This is partly determined for us by the nature of the language. English, like every other language, has its sequence of words and sounds governed by certain probabilities. If it were organized so that no set of probabilities governed the likelihood that certain words would follow certain other words (for example, that a noun would follow an adjective, or that "States" or "Nations" would follow "United") then we would have nonsense. As a matter of fact, we can calculate the relative amount of freedom open to us in writing any language. For English, the freedom is about 50 per cent. . . .

So much for language *redundancy*, as communication theorists call it, meaning the percentage of the message that is not open to free choice. But there is also the communicator's redundancy, and this is an important aspect of constructing a message. For if we think our audience may have a hard time understanding the message, we can deliberately introduce more redundancy; we can repeat (just as the radio operator on a ship may send "SOS" over and over again to make sure it is heard and decoded), or we can give examples and analogies. In other words, we always have to choose between transmitting more information in a given time, or transmitting less and repeating more in the hope of being better understood. As you know, it is often a delicate choice, because too slow a rate will bore an audience, whereas too fast a rate may confuse them.

Perhaps the most important thing about such a system is one we have been talking about all too glibly—the fact that receiver and sender must be in tune. This is clear enough in the case of a radio transmitter and receiver, but somewhat more complicated when it means that a human receiver must be able to understand a human sender.

Let us redraw our diagram [as in Figure 2]. Think of those circles as the accumulated experience of the two individuals trying to communicate. The source can encode, and the destination can decode, only in terms of the experience each has had. If we have never learned any Russian, we can neither code nor decode in that language. If an African tribesman has never seen or heard of an airplane, he can only decode the sight of a plane in terms of whatever experience he has had. The plane may seem to him to be a bird, and the aviator a god borne on wings. If the circles have a large area in common, then communication is easy. If the circles do not meet—if there has been no common experience—then communication is impossible. If the circles have only a small area in common—that is, if the experiences of source and destination have been strikingly unlike—then it is going to be very difficult to get an intended meaning across from one to the other. This is the difficulty we face when a non-science-trained person tries to read Einstein, or when we try to communicate with another culture much different from ours. . . .

Messages are made up of signs. A sign is a signal that stands for something in experience. The word "dog" is a sign that stands for our generalized experience with dogs. The word would be meaningless to a person who came from a dog-less island and had never read of or heard of a dog. But most of us have learned that word by association, just as we learn most signs. Someone called our attention to an animal, and said "dog." When we learned the word, it produced in us much the same response as the object it stood for. That is, when we heard "dog" we could recall the appearance of dogs, their sound, their feel, perhaps their smell. But there is an important difference between the sign and the object: the sign always represents the object at a reduced level of cues. By this we mean simply that the sign will not call forth all the responses that the object itself will call forth. The sign "dog," for example, will probably not call forth in us the same wariness or attention a strange dog might attract if it wandered into our presence. This is the price we pay for portability in language. We have a sign system that we can use in place of the less portable originals (for example, Margaret Mitchell could recreate the burning of Atlanta in a novel, and a photograph could transport world-wide the appearance of a bursting atomic bomb), but our sign system is merely a kind of shorthand. The coder has to be able to write the shorthand, the decoder to read it. And no two persons have learned exactly the same system. For example, a person who has known only Arctic huskies will not have learned exactly the same meaning for the shorthand sign "dog" as will a person who comes from a city where he has known only pekes and poms.

We have come now to a point where we need to tinker a little more with our diagram of the communication process. It is obvious that each person in the communication process is both an encoder and a decoder. He receives and transmits. He must be able to write readable shorthand, and to read other people's shorthand. Therefore, it is possible to describe either sender or receiver in a human communication system [as in Figure 3].

What happens when a signal comes to you? Remember that it comes in the form of a sign. If

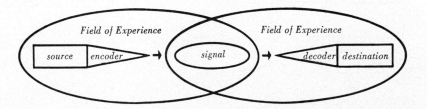

Figure 2.

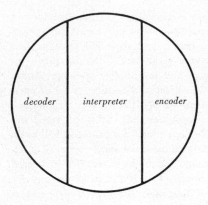

Figure 3.

you have learned the sign, you have learned certain responses with it. We can call these mediatory responses, because they mediate what happens to the message in your nervous system. These responses are the *meaning* the sign has for you. They are learned from experience, as we said, but they are affected by the state of your organism at the moment. For example, if you are hungry, a picture of a steak may not arouse exactly the same response in you as when you are overfed.

But subject to these effects, the mediatory responses will then determine what you do about the sign. For you have learned other sets of reactions connected to the mediatory responses. A sign that means a certain thing to you will start certain other processes in your nerves and muscles. A

sign that means "fire," for example, will certainly trigger off some activity in you. A sign that means you are in danger may start the process in your nerves and muscles that makes you say "help!" In other words, the meaning that results from your decoding of a sign will start you *encoding*. Exactly *what* you encode will depend on the choice of the responses available in the situation and connected with the meaning.

Whether this encoding actually results in some overt communication or action depends partly on the barriers in the way. You may think it better to keep silent. And if an action does occur, the nature of the action will also depend on the avenues for action available to you and the barriers in your way. The code of your group may not sanction the action you want to take. The meaning of a sign may make you want to hit the person who has said it, but he may be too big, or you may be in the wrong social situation. You may merely ignore him, or "look murder at him," or say something nasty about him to someone else.

But whatever the exact result, this is the process in which you are constantly engaged. You are constantly decoding signs from your environment, interpreting these signs, and encoding something as a result. In fact, it is misleading to think of the communication process as starting somewhere and ending somewhere. It is really endless. We are little switchboard centers handling and rerouting the endless current of communication. We can accurately think of communication as passing through us—changed, to be sure, by our interpretations, our habits, our abilities and capa-

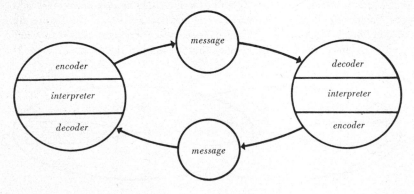

Figure 4.

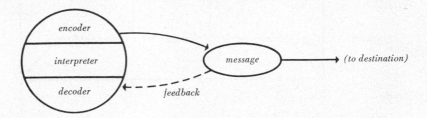

Figure 5.

bilities, but the input still being reflected in the output.

We need now to add another element to the description of the communication process. Consider what happens in a conversation between two people. One is constantly communicating back to the other, [as has been diagrammed in Figure 4]. The return process is called *feedback*, and plays a very important part in communication because it tells us how our messages are being interpreted. Does the hearer say, "Yes, yes, that's right," as we try to persuade him? Does he nod his head in agreement? Does a puzzled frown appear on his forehead? Does he look away as though he were losing interest? All these are feedback. So is a letter to the editor of a newspaper, protesting an editorial. So is an answer to a letter. So is the applause of a lecture audience. An experienced communicator is attentive to feedback, and constantly modifies his messages in light of what he observes in or hears from his audience.

At least one other example of feedback, also, is familiar to all of us. We get feedback from our own messages. That is, we hear our own voices and can correct mispronunciations. We see the words we have written on paper, and can correct misspellings or change the style. [Figure 5 illustrates what is happening when we do that].

It is clear that in any kind of communication we rarely send out messages in a single channel, and this is the final element we must add to our account of the communication process. When you speak to me, the sound waves from your voice are the primary message. But there are others: the expression of your face, your gestures, the relation of a given message to past messages. Even the primary message conveys information on several levels. It gives me words to decode. It emphasizes certain words above others. It presents the words in a pattern of intonation and timing which contribute to the total meaning. The quality of your voice (deep, high, shrill, rasping, rich, thin, loud, soft) itself carries information about you and what you are saying.

This multiple channel situation exists even in printed mass communication, where the channels are perhaps most restricted. Meaning is conveyed, not only by the words in a news item, but also by the size of the headline, the position on the page and the page in the paper, the association with pictures, the use of boldface and other typographical devices. All these tell us something about the item. Thus we can visualize the typical channel of communication, not as a simple telegraph circuit, in which current does or does not flow, but rather as a sort of coaxial cable in which many signals flow in parallel from source toward the destination.

These parallel relationships are complex, but you can see their general pattern. A communicator can emphasize a point by adding as many parallel messages as he feels are deserved. If he is communicating by speaking, he can stress a word, pause just before it, say it with a rising inflection, gesture while he says it, look earnestly at his audience. Or he can keep all the signals parallel—except one. He can speak solemnly, but wink, as Lowell Thomas sometimes does. He can stress a word in a way that makes it mean something else—for example, "That's a *fine* job you did!" And by so doing he conveys secondary meanings of sarcasm or humor or doubt. . . .

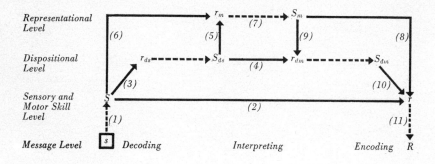

Figure 6.

Communication
in Terms of Learning Theory

So far we have avoided talking about this complicated process in what may seem to you to be the obvious way to talk about it—in the terminology and symbols of learning theory. We have done so for the sake of simplicity. Now in order to fill in the picture it seems desirable to sketch the diagram of how communication looks to a psychologist of learning. . . .

Let's start with the diagram [Figure 6], then explain it.

The diagram isn't as complicated as it looks. Remember that time in the diagram moves from left to right, and then follow the numbers and you won't get far off the road.

Begin with (1). This is the input. At the message level we have a collection of objectively measurable signs ⊡. These come to your sense organs, where they constitute a stimulus for action. This stimulus we call s. When the process gets as far as s, you are paying attention. The message has been accepted. It may not have been accepted as intended; s may not equal ⊡ ; the sensory mechanism may have seen or heard it incompletely. But everything else that happens as a result of the message in that particular destination will now necessarily be the result of the stimulus accepted by your sense organs.

Now look at (2). The message may not have to go to any other level in order to bring about a response. If a man waves his fist near your nose, you may dodge. If he squeezes your hand, you may

say "ouch!" These are learned, almost automatic, responses on the sensory and motor skill level.

But the stimulus may also bring about other kinds of activity within your nervous system. Look at number (3). The stimulus s may be translated into a grammatical response on your dispositional level—by which we mean the level of learned integrations (attitudes, values, sets, etc.) which make it so easy for you to dispose of the variety of stimuli that come to you in the course of a day. These are what we call the intervening variables.[2] Suppose the stimulus stirs up activity in this area of intervening variables. Two things may happen. Look at number (4). The response may be so well learned that it doesn't even have to go to the level of thinking. You hear a line of a poem, and almost automatically say the second line. In that case the activity is through numbers (4) and (10).

More often, however, the activity goes through number (5). Here the original stimulus has been decoded into grammar, fed through the intervening variables, and sent up to the representational level of the central nervous system, where meanings are assigned and ideas considered. Occasionally a stimulus comes to that level without going through the intervening variables—as is number (6). These stimuli create activity in the central nervous system (r_m) which is the terminus of the decoding part of the process. This is equivalent to

[2]By **intervening variables** Schramm means those variables that are inferred to be affecting responses; this differs somewhat from Marx's use of the term in his discussion of theory construction, page 428 **(Editor's note).**

the meaning or significance of the signs $\boxed{s}$. What happens in number (7), then, is what we have been referring to as interpretation. The response r_m which we call meaning becomes in turn a stimulus which sets the encoding process in action, so that (7) is both the terminus of decoding and the start of encoding. We learn to associate meanings with desired responses. And so the encoding process moves through (8) or (9). That is, we give certain orders which either pass directly to the neuro-muscular system (through 8) or are passed through the intervening variables (through 9 and 10). In any case, all this activity of the nervous system finally results in a response on the motor skill level (r), which results in output (number 11). If the output is an overt response (R), then we have another message, which may offer itself as a collection of signs $\boxed{s}$ and be accepted by still another person as a stimulus (s).

This is what we believe happens when someone says to you, "cigarette?" and you answer "yes, please," or "no, thanks." If you are interested in doing so, you can translate all that is said about the communication process in this paper into the psychological symbols we have just been using. But to make the account simpler, we are going to shift gears at this point and talk about communication effects and mass communication in the terms we used in section 1.

How Communication Has an Effect

The chief reason we study this process is to learn something about how it achieves effects. We want to know what a given kind of communication does to people. Given a certain message content, we should like to be able to predict what effect that content will have on its receivers.

Every time we insert an advertisement in a newspaper, put up a sign, explain something to a class, scold a child, write a letter, or put our political candidate on radio or television, we are making a prediction about the effect communication will have. I am predicting now that what I

am writing will help you understand the common everyday miracle of communication. Perhaps I am wrong. Certainly many political parties have been proved wrong in their predictions about the effects of their candidates' radio speeches. Some ads sell goods; others don't. Some class teaching "goes over"; some does not. For it is apparent to you, from what you have read so far, that there is no such thing as a simple and easily predictable relationship between message content and effect.

Nevertheless, it is possible to describe simply what might be called the conditions of success in communication—by which we mean the conditions that must be fulfilled if the message is to arouse its intended response. Let us set them down here briefly . . . :

1. *The message must be so designed and delivered as to gain the attention of the intended destination.*

2. *The message must employ signs which refer to experience common to source and destination, so as to "get the meaning across."*

3. *The message must arouse personality needs in the destination and suggest some ways to meet those needs.*

4. *The message must suggest a way to meet those needs which is appropriate to the group situation in which the destination finds himself at the time when he is moved to make the desired response.*

You can see, by looking at these requirements, why the expert communicator usually begins by finding out as much as he can about his intended destination, and why "know your audience" is the first rule of practical mass communication. For it is important to know the right timing for a message, the kind of language one must use to be understood, the attitudes and value one must appeal to in order to be effective, and the group standards in which the desired action will have to take place. This is relatively easy in face-to-face communication, more difficult in mass communication. In either case, it is necessary.

THE ENCOUNTER WITH NOTHINGNESS

by William Barrett[1]

One response to the loss of traditional values and beliefs in the modern period has been the development of existentialism, a school of thought which emphasizes man's need to stand on his own and to find a new identity based not on philosophic or scientific abstractions but rather on the reality of his existence—on his own experience of being. In recent years a growing number of clinical psychologists and psychiatrists have become attracted to existentialism for the insights it offers into human nature and human behavior. As Rollo May has pointed out in a recent book on this subject, the existential movement, like psychotherapy, is concerned with individuals in crisis: "When a culture is caught in the profound convulsion of a transitional period, the individuals in the society understandably suffer spiritual and emotional upheaval; and finding that the accepted mores and ways of thought no longer yield security, they tend either to sink into dogmatism and conformism, giving up awareness, or are forced to strive for a heightened self-consciousness by which to become aware of their existence with new conviction and on new bases."[2]

In this selection William Barrett traces man's present feelings of insecurity—and the development of existentialism—to the crumbling of traditional religious, sociopolitical, and scientific beliefs. Whether or not one agrees with this analysis, the issues raised merit serious thought. Dr. Barrett is a professor of philosophy at New York University.

No age has ever been so self-conscious as ours. At any rate, the quantity of journalism the modern age has turned out in the process of its own self-analysis already overflows our archives and, were it not that most of it is doomed to perish, would be a dull burden to hand down to our descendants. The task still goes on, as indeed it must, for the last word has not been spoken, and modern man seems even further from understanding himself than when he first began to question his own identity. . . .

The Decline of Religion

The central fact of modern history in the West —by which we mean the long period from the end of the Middle Ages to the present—is unquestionably the decline of religion. No doubt, the Churches are still very powerful organizations; there are millions of churchgoers all over the world; and even the purely intellectual possibilities of religious belief look better to churchmen now than in the bleak days of self-confident nineteenth-century materialism. A few years ago there was even considerable talk about a "religious revival," and some popular and patriotic periodicals such as *Life* magazine gave a great deal of space to it; but the talk has by now pretty much died down, the movement, if any, subsided, and the American public buys more automobiles and television sets than ever before. When *Life*

[1]From **Irrational Man: A Study in Existential Philosophy** by William Barrett. Copyright © 1958 by William Barrett. Reprinted by permission of Doubleday & Company, Inc., New York, and William Heinemann, Ltd., London.

[2]Rollo May, "The Origins and Significance of the Existential Movement in Psychology," **Existence: A New Dimension in Psychiatry and Psychology,** Rollo May, Ernest Angel, and Henri F. Ellenberger, eds., New York: Basic Books, Inc., 1958, p. 17.

magazine promotes a revival of religion, one is only too painfully aware from the nature of this publication that religion is considered as being in the national interest; one could scarcely have a clearer indication of the broader historical fact that in the modern world the nation-state, a thoroughly secular institution, outranks any church.

The decline of religion in modern times means simply that religion is no longer the uncontested center and ruler of man's life, and that the Church is no longer the final and unquestioned home and asylum of his being. The deepest significance of this change does not even appear principally at the purely intellectual level, in loss of belief, though this loss due to the critical inroads of science has been a major historical cause of the decline. The waning of religion is a much more concrete and complex fact than a mere change in conscious outlook; it penetrates the deepest strata of man's total psychic life. . . . Religion to medieval man was not so much a theological system as a solid psychological matrix surrounding the individual's life from birth to death, sanctifying and enclosing all its ordinary and extraordinary occasions in sacrament and ritual. The loss of the Church was the loss of a whole system of symbols, images, dogmas, and rites which had the psychological validity of immediate experience, and within which hitherto the whole psychic life of Western man had been safely contained. In losing religion, man lost the concrete connection with a transcendent realm of being; he was set free to deal with this world in all its brute objectivity. But he was bound to feel homeless in such a world, which no longer answered the needs of his spirit. . . . Henceforth, in seeking his own human completeness man would have to do for himself what he once had done for him, unconsciously, by the Church, through the medium of its sacramental life. Naturally enough, man's feeling of homelessness did not make itself felt for some time; the Renaissance man was still enthralled by a new and powerful vision of mastery over the whole earth.

No believer, no matter how sincere, could possibly write the *Divine Comedy* today, even if he possessed a talent equal to Dante's. Visions and symbols do not have the immediate and overwhelming reality for us that they had for the me-

dieval poet. In the *Divine Comedy* the whole of nature is merely a canvas upon which the religious symbol and image are painted. Western man has spent more than five hundred years— half a millennium—in stripping nature of these projections and turning it into a realm of neutral objects which his science may control. Thus it could hardly be expected that the religious image would have the same force for us as it did for Dante. This is simply a psychic fact within human history; psychic facts have just as much historical validity as the facts that we now, unlike the man of Dante's time, travel in airplanes and work in factories regulated by computing machines. A great work of art can never be repeated —the history of art shows us time and again that literal imitation leads to pastiche—because it springs from the human soul, which evolves like everything else in nature. This point must be insisted upon, contrary to the view of some of our more enthusiastic medievalists who picture the psychic containment of medieval man as a situation of human completeness to which we must return. History has never allowed man to return to the past in any total sense. And our psychological problems cannot be solved by a regression to a past state in which they had not yet been brought into being. On the other hand, enlightened and progressive thinkers are equally blind when they fail to recognize that every major step forward by mankind entails some loss, the sacrifice of an older security and the creation and heightening of new tensions. (We should bear this in mind against some of the criticisms of Existentialism as a philosophy that has unbearably heightened human tensions: it did not create those tensions, which were already at work in the soul of modern man, but simply sought to give them philosophic expression, rather than evading them by pretending they were not there.) . . .

The Rational Ordering of Society

. . . The great German sociologist, Max Weber, has provided one of the chief keys to the whole of modern history by describing its central process as the ever-increasing rational organization of human life. It is in this light too that the historical rise of capitalism must be understood: the capitalist emerges from feudal society as the enterprising and calculating mind who must organize production rationally to show a favorable balance of profits over costs. Where feudalism is concrete and organic, with man dominated by the image of the land, capitalism is abstract and calculating in spirit, and severs man from the earth. In capitalism everything follows from this necessity of rationally organizing economic enterprise in the interests of efficiency: the collectivization of labor in factories and the consequent subdivision of human function; the accumulation of masses of the population in cities, with the inevitable increase in the technical control of life that this makes necessary; and the attempt rationally to control public demand by elaborate and fantastic advertising, mass pressure, and even planned sociological research. The process of rationalizing economic enterprise thus knows no limits and comes to cover the whole of society's life. That capitalism has given way in our time, over large areas of the earth, to a form of total collectivization that has been taken over by the State does not alter the fundamental human issues involved. The collectivization becomes all the more drastic when a *mystique* of the State, backed by brutal regimentation by the police, is added to it. Collectivized man, whether communist or capitalist, is still only an abstract fragment of man.

We are so used to the fact that we forget it or fail to perceive that the man of the present day lives on a level of abstraction altogether beyond the man of the past. When the contemporary man in the street with only an ordinary education quickly solves an elementary problem in arithmetic, he is doing something which for a medieval mathematician—an expert—would have required hours. No doubt, the medieval man would have produced along with his calculation a rigorous proof of the whole process; it does not matter that the modern man does not *know* what he is doing, so long as he can manipulate abstractions easily and efficiently. The ordinary man today answers complicated questionnaires, fills out tax forms, performs elaborate calculations, which the medieval man was never called upon to do—and all this merely in the normal routine of being a responsible citizen within a mass society. Every

step forward in mechanical technique is a step in the direction of abstraction. This capacity for living easily and familiarly at an extraordinary level of abstraction is the source of modern man's power. With it he has transformed the planet, annihilated space, and trebled the world's population. But it is also a power which has, like everything human, its negative side, in the desolating sense of rootlessness, vacuity, and the lack of concrete feeling that assails modern man in his moments of real anxiety.

The sheer economic power of modern society is attended by the same human ambiguities. The rational ordering of production makes possible a material level of prosperity beyond anything known by the past. Not only can the material wants of the masses be satisfied to a degree greater than ever before, but technology is fertile enough to generate new wants that it can also satisfy. Automobiles, radio, and now television become actual needs for great numbers of people. All of this makes for an extraordinary *externalization* of life in our time. The tempo of living is heightened, but a greed for novelties sets in. The machinery of communication makes possible the almost instantaneous conveying of news from one point on the globe to another. People read three or four editions of a daily paper, hear the news on the radio, or see tomorrow morning's news on the television screen at night. Journalism has become a great god of the period, and gods have a way of ruthlessly and demonically taking over their servitors. In thus becoming a state of mind . . . journalism enables people to deal with life more and more at second hand. Information usually consists of half-truths, and "knowledgeability" becomes a substitute for real knowledge. Moreover, popular journalism has by now extended its operations into what were previously considered the strongholds of culture—religion, art, philosophy. Every man walks around with a pocket digest of culture in his head. The more competent and streamlined journalism becomes, the greater its threat to the public mind—particularly in a country like the United States. It becomes more and more difficult to distinguish the secondhand from the real thing, until most people end by forgetting there is such a distinction. The very success of technique engenders a whole style of life for the period, which subsists purely on externals. What lies behind those externals—the human person, in its uniqueness and its totality—dwindles to a shadow and a ghost.

. . . August 1914 shattered the foundations of [bourgeois civilization in Europe]. It revealed that the apparent stability, security, and material progress of society had rested, like everything human, upon the void. European man came face to face with himself as a stranger. When he ceased to be contained and sheltered within a stable social and political environment, he saw that his rational and enlightened philosophy could no longer console him with the assurance that it satisfactorily answered the question What is man?

Existential philosophy (like much of modern art) is thus a product of bourgeois society in a state of dissolution. Marxists have labored this point but without really understanding it; nevertheless, it remains true. The dissolution is a fact, but neither Existentialism nor modern art produced it. Nor is "dissolution" synonymous with "decadence." A society coming apart at top and bottom, or passing over into another form, contains just as many possibilities for revelation as a society running along smoothly in its own rut. The individual is thrust out of the sheltered nest that society has provided. He can no longer hide his nakedness by the old disguises. He learns how much of what he has taken for granted was by its own nature neither eternal nor necessary but thoroughly temporal and contingent. He learns that the solitude of the self is an irreducible dimension of human life no matter how completely that self had seemed to be contained in its social milieu. In the end, he sees each man as solitary and unsheltered before his own death. Admittedly, these are painful truths, but the most basic things are always learned with pain, since our inertia and complacent love of comfort prevent us from learning them until they are forced upon us. It appears that man is willing to learn about himself only after some disaster; after war, economic crisis, and political upheaval have taught him how flimsy is that human world in which he thought himself so securely grounded. What he learns has always been there, lying concealed beneath the surface of even the best-functioning

societies; it is no less true for having come out of a period of chaos and disaster. But so long as man does not have to face up to such a truth, he will not do so.

Thus with the modern period, man—to recapitulate—has entered upon a secular phase of his history. He entered it with exuberance over the prospect of increased power he would have over the world around him. But in this world, in which his dreams of power were often more than fulfilled, he found himself for the first time *homeless*. Science stripped nature of its human forms and presented man with a universe that was neutral, alien, in its vastness and force, to his human purposes. Religion, before this phase set in, had been a structure that encompassed man's life, providing him with a system of images and symbols by which he could express his own aspirations toward psychic wholeness. With the loss of this containing framework man became not only a dispossessed but a fragmentary being.

In society, as in the spiritual world, secular goals have come to predominate; the rational organization of the economy has increased human power over nature, and politically also society has become more rational, utilitarian, democratic, with a resulting material wealth and progress. The men of the Enlightenment foresaw no end to this triumphant expansion of reason into all the areas of social life. But here too reason has foundered upon its opposite, upon the surd and unpredictable realities—wars, economic crises and dislocations, political upheavals among the masses. Moreover, man's feeling of homelessness, of alienation has been intensified in the midst of a bureaucratized, impersonal mass society. He has come to feel himself an outsider even within his own human society. He is trebly alienated: a stranger to God, to nature, and to the gigantic social apparatus that supplies his material wants.

But the worst and final form of alienation, toward which indeed the others tend, is man's alienation from his own self. In a society that requires of man only that he perform competently his own particular social function, man becomes identified with this function, and the rest of his being is allowed to subsist as best it can—usually to be dropped below the surface of consciousness and forgotten.

Science and Finitude

The foregoing, all matters of historical fact, have also become the themes of existential philosophy. This philosophy embodies the self-questioning of the time, seeking to reorient itself to its own historical destiny. Indeed, the whole problematic of Existentialism unfolds from this historical situation. Alienation and estrangement; a sense of the basic fragility and contingency of human life; the impotence of reason confronted with the depths of existence; the threat of Nothingness, and the solitary and unsheltered condition of the individual before this threat. One can scarcely subordinate these problems logically one to another; each participates in all the others, and they all circulate around a common center. A single atmosphere pervades them all like a chilly wind: the radical feeling of human finitude. The limitless horizons into which man looked at the time of the Renaissance have at last contracted. Oddly enough, man's discovery that he himself is finite through and through —is so, one might say, from the inside out— comes at a time when there seem no longer to be any limits to his technological conquest of nature. But the truth about man is never to be found in one quality that opposes another, but in both qualities at once; and so his weakness is only one side of the coin, his power the other. A recognition of limits, of boundaries, may be the only thing that prevents power from dizzy collapse.

But, it might be argued, what makes Western civilization unique is its possession of science, and in science we find uniform and continuous progress without limits. Research goes on, its results are rich and positive, and these are brought together in ever wider and more inclusive systems. There would seem, in this process, to be no contracting of horizons either in fact or in possibility. In a certain sense this is true, and yet science in the twentieth century has come up with answers which make the ambitions of rationalism seem overweening, and which themselves suggest that man must redefine his traditional concept of reason. It would be unlikely if this were otherwise, for scientists too are men and therefore participate in the collective psyche as well as help fashion it. Religion, social forms, science, and art are modes in which man exists; and the more we come to recognize the temporal being of man the more we must recognize a unity within and behind all these modes in which that temporal existence finds its expression.

Science too—and within its own authentic sphere—has come up against the fact of human finitude. That this has happened within science itself, and not in the philosophizing about science, makes the discovery more authentic and momentous. The anthropological sciences, and particularly modern depth psychology, have shown us that human reason is the long historical fabrication of a creature, man, whose psychic roots still extend downward into the primeval soil. These discoveries of the irrational, however, lie outside reason itself; they are stubborn obstacles to the use of reason in our lives, but obstacles which the confirmed rationalist might still hope to circumvent by a cleverer use of that very tool, reason. The more decisive limitations are those that have shown up *within* the workings of reason, in the more rigorous sciences of physics and mathematics. The most advanced of Western sciences, physics, and mathematics, have in our time become paradoxical: that is, they have arrived at the state where they breed paradoxes for reason itself. More than a hundred and fifty years ago the philosopher Kant attempted to show that there were intellectual limits to reason; but the Western mind, positivistic to the core, could be expected to take such a conclusion seriously only when it showed up in the findings of science. Science has in this century, with the discoveries of Heisenberg in physics, and Godel in mathematics, at last caught up with Kant.

Heisenberg's Principle of Indeterminacy shows that there are essential limits to our ability to know and predict physical states of affairs, and opens up to us a glimpse of a nature that may at bottom be irrational and chaotic—at any rate, our knowledge of it is limited so that we cannot know this not to be the case. This finding marks an end to the old dream of physicists who, motivated by a thoroughly rational prejudice, thought that reality must be predictable through and through. The figure of the Laplacian Demon was a very striking symbol of this: Imagine, says Laplace, a Being who knows the position and momentum of every particle in the universe, together with the laws of motion governing such particles; such a Being would be able to predict all subsequent states of the universe. Physicists can no longer operate on such cryptotheological faiths, but must take their predictability only where and to the extent that it exhibits itself in experience. . . .

Godel's findings seem to have even more far-reaching consequences, when one considers that in the Western tradition, from the Pythagoreans and Plato onward, mathematics as the very model of intelligibility has been the central citadel of rationalism. Now it turns out that even in his most precise science—in the province where his reason had seemed omnipotent—man cannot escape his essential finitude: every system of mathematics that he constructs is doomed to incompleteness. Godel has shown that mathematics contains insoluble problems, and hence can never be formalized in any complete system. This means, in other words, that mathematics can never be turned over to a giant computing machine; it will always be unfinished and therefore mathematicians—the human beings who construct mathematics—will always be in business. The human element here rises above the machine: mathematics is unfinished as is any human life.

But since mathematics can never be completed, it might be argued that Godel's finding shows us that there are no limits to mathematical knowledge. True, in one sense; but in another sense it sets a more drastic limitation upon mathematical knowledge, since mathematicians now know they can never, formally speaking, reach rock bottom; in fact, there is no rock bottom, since mathematics has no self-subsistent reality independent of the human activity that mathematicians carry on. And if human reason can never reach rock bottom (complete systematization) in mathematics, it is not likely to reach it anywhere else. There is no System possible for human existence, Kierkegaard said a century ago, differing with Hegel, who wished to enclose reality within a completely rational structure; the System is impossible for mathematics, Godel tells us today. In practice, the fact that there is no rock bottom means that the mathematician can never prove the consistency of mathematics except by using means that are shakier than the system he is trying to prove consistent. Mathematics thus cannot escape finally the uncertainty that attaches to any human enterprise.

The situation is all the more vexing since mathematicians in the last half century have come up with some very troublesome paradoxes. Mathematics is like a ship in mid-ocean that has sprung certain leaks (paradoxes); the leaks have been temporarily plugged, but our reason can never guarantee that the ship will not spring others. This human insecurity in what had been the most secure of the disciplines of rationality marks a new turn in Western thinking. When the mathematician Hermann Weyl exclaims, "We have tried to storm Heaven, and we have only succeeded in piling up the tower of Babel," he is giving passionate expression to the collapse of human *hubris*; and we can be sure that mathematics has at last been returned to its rightful status as an activity or mode of being of finite man.

The concurrence of these various discoveries in time is extraordinary. Heidegger published his *Being and Time*, a somber and rigorous meditation on human finitude, in 1927.[3] In the same year Heisenberg gave to the world his Principle of Indeterminacy. In 1929 the mathematician Skolem published a theorem which some mathematicians now think almost as remarkable as Godel's: that even the elementary number system cannot be categorically formalized. In 1931 appeared Godel's epoch-making discovery. When events run parallel this way, when they occur so close together in time, but independently of each other and in diverse fields, we are tempted to conclude that they are not mere "meaningless" coincidences but very meaningful symptoms. The whole mind of the time seems to be inclining in one direction.

What emerges from these separate strands of history is an image of man himself that bears a new, stark, more nearly naked, and more questionable aspect. The contraction of man's horizons amounts to a denudation, a stripping down, of this being who has now to confront himself at the center of all his horizons. . . .

[3]This work by the German philosopher is generally considered the starting point of modern existential thought **(Editor's note).**

FREEDOM

by Gordon W. Allport[1]

To open the way for the development of an adequate psychology of personality, Gordon Allport has addressed himself to many issues which most modern psychologists have considered beyond the scope of the scientific laboratory. One such issue is that of free choice versus determinism. Dr. Allport is Professor of Psychology at Harvard University.

. . . Up to now the tug of war between free will and determinism has been marked by naïveté. Just as we have learned with some success to transcend the monolithic oppositions between mind and body, nature and nurture, we should strive for better perspective in our view of freedom and determinism. The following considerations may help.

1. In the first place, it is essential that we distinguish the viewpoint of the scientist from that of the acting person. The superior wisdom of the scientist may unfortunately blind him to the process of growth that is actually taking place. The scientist's frame of reference is like the frame of an omniscient being: to him all things have time, place, and determined orbits. But this frame is definitely not the frame of the acting person. The situation is much like that of the watcher from the hilltop who sees a single oarsman on the river below. From his vantage point the watcher notes that around the bend of the river, unknown as yet to the oarsman, there are dangerous rapids. What is present to the watcher's eye still lies in the future for the oarsman. The superior being predicts that soon the boatman will be portaging his skiff —a fact now wholly unknown to the boatman who is unfamiliar with the river's course. He will confront the obstacle when it comes, decide on his course of action, and surmount the difficulty. In short, the actor is unable to view his deeds in a large space-time matrix as does an all-wise God, or the less wise demigods of science. From his point of view he is working within a frame of choice, not of destiny. As psychologists we ought

to know, and do know, that the way a man defines his situation constitutes for him its reality. Choice for him is a paramount fact; how matters appear to the watcher on the hill is irrelevant. . . .

2. Even when we take the view of the scientist we note that certain conditions make for *relatively* more or less freedom for the individual. One of the conditions we are most sure of is self-insight. A therapist of even the most deterministic persuasion assumes that a patient who achieves a high degree of self-objectification, who sees his personal equation clearly written out, is at last in a position to weigh his inclinations, comprehend his limitations, and follow with some success a self-chosen course of action. If this were not so every system of therapy would operate on false pretense. Psychotherapy gives hope that a corrected self-image, a more rational assessment of one's behavior, will reduce compulsions, induce order, and free channels of development to accord with chosen aims. Hence even a scientific psychology concedes that self-knowledge may lead to a relative freedom.

3. Similarly, relative freedom, we know, depends upon the individual's possession of multiple possibilities for behavior. To state the point paradoxically, a person who harbors many determining tendencies in his neuropsychic system is freer than a person who harbors few. Thus a person having only one skill, knowing only one solution, has only one degree of freedom. On the other hand, a person widely experienced and knowing many courses of conduct has many more degrees of freedom. It is in this sense that the broadly educated man is freer than the man narrowly trained. Today we are witnessing the frightening things that political leaders with one-channeled

[1]From **Becoming: Basic Considerations for a Psychology of Personality** by Gordon W. Allport, Yale University Press, New Haven, Conn., 1955, pp. 82-88.

minds can do. What alarms us is their simplicist view of social and political reality. They know only one solution; and this solution is totalitarian and spurious. Their lack of tolerance and fear of dissent reflect their own lack of freedom. . . .

4. Finally, psychology knows that there is relatively greater freedom in certain modes of choosing than in others. Man's effort is not particularly effective when he tries to meet an impulse head on, by cracking his knuckles and gritting his teeth. Centering attention upon an impulse often brings with it a strong desire to perform the impulsive act. . . . And at this level freedom often seems to be a cruel illusion.

But when I stop cracking my knuckles and become momentarily reflective, asking myself whether "on the whole" this is the course of action I want to take, the picture is changed. The very act of asking "on the whole" brings with it a lessened strain and opens new pathways of decision. This moment of reflection serves to set into activity the larger systems of propriate[2] striving, and their activation may blot out or absorb incompatible segmental systems and impulses, leaving the individual free to be himself.[3]

The psychologist knows that most of the specific acts we perform ordinarily proceed in accordance with superordinate systems of motivation. If the superordinate system involves, let us say, a loyalty, then the individual, by calling the system to mind, automatically gives it precedence. Under its dominance decisions follow. The weakness of the habit theory lies in assuming that all acts, by the principles of repetition and reward, are theoretically of equal importance in

[2]Allport uses the term **proprium** rather than **self** or **ego** to refer to the aspects and functions of personality that account for its peculiar unity and distinctiveness and that seem subjectively "important" **(Editor's note)**.

[3]The point at issue here is of considerable theoretical importance. According to psychoanalytic conceptions the defeated impulse is thought to be repressed, and to continue to plague the individual from the limbo of the unconscious. I am suggesting that under certain circumstances—especially when the comprehensive propriate motive holds sway—the incompatible impulses are not normally repressed; they simply evaporate. Freud himself made a similar observation, though he did not follow through its theoretical implications. In a too seldom quoted passage he writes that he has become "mindful of the distinction between the mere *repression* and the true *disappearance* of an old desire or impulse." [Allport's italics.] Sigmund Freud, **The Problem of Anxiety**, New York: W. W. Norton & Company, Inc., 1927, pp. 82 f.

building the structure of personality. Habits appear and disappear not only in conformity with the principles of frequency and reward but also as subsidiary events in relation to a central or propriate structure. William James hastened to repair his doctrine of habits by affirming that the one ultimate act of freedom at man's disposal is his ability "to keep the selected idea uppermost," by which he meant that when we call upon our self-image we automatically reappraise, inhibit, steer, or activate subordinate courses of conduct. Higher-level systems determine the "go" of the lower, and it is for this reason that man is able to keep as closely as he does to his own major systems of value.

It sometimes happens that the very center of organization of a personality shifts suddenly and apparently without warning. Some impetus, coming perhaps from a bereavement, an illness, or a religious conversion, even from a teacher or book, may lead to a reorientation. In such cases of traumatic recentering it is undoubtedly true that the person had latent within him all of the capacities and sentiments that suddenly rise from a subordinate to a superordinate position in his being. What he had once learned mechanically or incidentally may suddenly acquire heat and liveliness and motor power. What once seemed to him cold, "out there," "not mine" may change places and become hot and vital, "in here," "mine."

I mention this phenomenon of saltatory becoming, not because it is frequent or typical but because it illustrates the complexity and lability of the organizational process. Becoming is not a mere matter of forging links to a chain. . . .

These considerations fall short of solving the problem of freedom. They urge us, however, to forego naïve solutions. That there are upper limits to the possibilities of growth in each life no one can deny. But it seems likely that these limits are movable by virtue of the capacities for reflection, for self-objectification, and to a degree by breadth of education, and by the effort an individual may put forth. From the ethical and theological points of view the stretching toward this limit, whatever it is, is as much of a triumph for a life of slight potential as for a life whose potentials are great.

VALUES, PSYCHOLOGY, AND HUMAN EXISTENCE

by Erich Fromm[1]

Trained as a psychoanalyst, German-born Erich Fromm has never limited himself to treating individual patients but has been greatly concerned with analyzing and correcting the ills of society as a whole. Although many of his ideas have met with opposition, particularly from more orthodox psychiatrists, he has done much to stimulate thought among professionals and laymen alike. In the following article we find a cross section of Dr. Fromm's views, which have been touched upon many times throughout this text.

In this paper, I want to present some substantiation and evidence for a thesis that is shared by a number of us.

The thesis is that *values are rooted in the very conditions of human existence; hence that our knowledge of these conditions, that is, of the "human situation," leads us to establishing values which have objective validity*; this validity exists, only with regard to the existence of man; outside of him there are no values.

Man and the Conditions of Human Existence

What is the nature of man, what are the special conditions of human existence, and what are the needs which are rooted in these conditions?

Man is torn away from the primary union with nature, which characterizes animal existence. Having at the same time reason and imagination, he is aware of his aloneness and separateness, of his powerlessness and ignorance, of the accidentalness of his birth and of his death. He could not face this state of being for a second if he could not find new ties with his fellow man which replace the old ones, regulated by instincts. . . . The necessity to unite with other living beings, to be related to them, is an imperative need on the fulfillment of which man's sanity depends. This need is behind all phenomena which constitute the whole gamut of intimate human relations, of all passions which are called love in the broadest sense of the word.

There are several ways in which this union can be sought and achieved. Man can attempt to become one with the world by *submission* to a person, to a group, to an institution, to a God. In this way he transcends the separateness of his individual existence by becoming part of somebody or something bigger than himself and experiences his identity in connection with the power to which he has submitted. Another possibility of overcoming separateness lies in the opposite direction: man can try to unite himself with the world by having *power* over it, by making others a part of himself, and thus transcending his individual existence by domination.

The common element in both submission and domination is the symbiotic nature of relatedness. Both persons involved have lost their integrity and freedom; they live on each other and from each other, satisfying their craving for closeness, yet suffering from the lack of inner strength and self-reliance which would require freedom and independence, and furthermore constantly threatened by the conscious or unconscious hostility which is bound to arise from the symbiotic relationship. . . .

There is only one passion which satisfies man's need to unite himself with the world and to acquire at the same time a sense of integrity and individuality, and this is *love. Love is union* with

[1]From **New Knowledge in Human Values,** Abraham H. Maslow, ed., Harper & Brothers, New York, 1959, pp. 151-164.

somebody, or something, outside oneself, *under the condition of retaining the separateness and integrity of one's own self*. It is an experience of sharing, of communion, which permits the full unfolding of one's own inner activity. The experience of love does away with the necessity of illusions. There is no need to inflate the image of the other person, or of myself, since the reality of active sharing and loving permits me to transcend my individualized existence and at the same time to experience myself as the bearer or the active powers which constitute the act of loving. What matters is the particular *quality* of loving, not the object. Love is in the experience of human solidarity with our fellow creatures, it is in the erotic love of man and woman, in the love of the mother for her child, and also in the love for oneself as a human being; it is in the mystical experience of union. In the act of loving, I am one with All, and yet I am myself, a unique, separate, limited, mortal human being. Indeed, out of the very polarity between separateness and union, love is born and reborn.

Another aspect of the human situation, closely connected with the need for relatedness, is man's situation as a *creature* and his need to *transcend* this very state of the passive creature. Man is thrown into this world without his consent or will. In this respect he is not different from the animal, from the plants, or from inorganic matter. But being endowed with reason and imagination, he cannot be content with the passive role of the creature, with the role of dice cast out of a cup. He is driven by the urge to transcend the role of the creature, the accidentalness and passivity of his existence, by becoming a "creator."

Man can create life. This is the miraculous quality which he indeed shares with all living beings, but with the difference that he alone is aware of being created and of being a creator. Man can create life, or rather, woman can create life, by giving birth to a child and by caring for the child until it is sufficiently grown to take care of his own needs. Man—man and woman—can create by planting seeds, by producing material objects, by creating art, by creating ideas, by loving one another. In the act of creation man transcends himself as a creature, raises himself beyond the passivity and accidentalness of his existence into the realm of purposefulness and freedom. In man's need for transcendence lies one of the roots for love, as well as for art, religion, and material production.

To create presupposes activity and care. It presupposes love for that which one creates. How then does man solve the problem of transcending himself if he is not capable of creating, if he cannot love? *There is another answer to this need for transcendence; if I cannot create life, I can destroy it. To destroy life makes me also transcend it.* Indeed, that man can destroy life is just as miraculous a feat as that he can create it, for life is *the* miracle, the inexplicable. In the act of destruction, man sets himself above life; he transcends himself as a creature. Thus, the ultimate choice for man, inasmuch as he is driven to transcend himself, is to create or to destroy, to love or to hate. The enormous power of the will for destruction which we see in the history of man, and which we have witnessed so frightfully in our own time, is rooted in the nature of man, just as the drive to create is rooted in it. To say that man is capable of developing his primary potentiality for love and reason does not imply the naive belief in man's goodness. Destructiveness is a secondary potentiality, rooted in the very existence of man, and having the same intensity and power as any passion can have. But—and this is the essential point of my argument—it is the *alternative* to creativeness. Creation and destruction, love and hate, are not two instincts which exist independently. They are both answers to the same need for transcendence, and the will to destroy must rise when the will to create cannot be satisfied. However, the satisfaction of the need to create leads to happiness, destructiveness to suffering—most of all, for the destroyer himself.

A third need, again following the conditions of human existence, is that for *rootedness*. Man's birth as man means the beginning of his emergence from his natural home, the beginning of the severance of his natural ties. Yet this very severance is frightening; if man loses his natural roots, where is he and who is he? He would stand alone, without a home, without roots; he could not bear the isolation and helplessness of this position. He would become insane. He can dispense with the natural roots only insofar as he finds new *human* roots and only after he has found them can he feel at home again in this world. Is it surprising, then, to find a deep craving in man not to sever the natural ties, to fight against being torn away from nature, from mother, blood and soil?

The most elementary of the natural ties is the tie of the child to the mother. The child begins life in the mother's womb and exists there for a much longer time than is the case with most animals; even after birth, the child remains physically helpless and completely dependent on the mother; this period of helplessness and dependence again is much more protracted than with any animal. In the first years of life no full separation between child and mother has occured. The satisfaction of all his physiological needs, of his vital need for warmth and affection depend on her; she has not only given birth to him, but she continues to give life to him. Her care is not dependent on anything the child does for her, on any obligation which the child has to fulfill; it is unconditional. She cares because the new creature is her child. The child, in these decisive first years of his life, has the experience of his mother as the fountain of life, as an all-enveloping, protective, nourishing power. Mother is food; she is love; she is warmth; she is earth. To be loved by her means to be alive, to be rooted, to be at home.

Just as birth means to leave the enveloping protection of the womb, growing up means to leave the protective orbit of the mother. Yet, even in the mature adult, the longing for this situation as it once existed never ceases completely, in spite of the fact that there is, indeed, a great difference between the adult and the child. The adult has the means to stand on his own feet, to take care of himself, to be responsible for himself and even for others, whereas the child is not yet capable of doing all this. But, considering the increased perplexities of life, the fragmentary nature of our knowledge, the accidentalness of adult existence, the unavoidable errors we make, the situation of the adult is by no means as different from that of the child as it is generally assumed. Every adult is in need of help, of warmth, of protection, in many ways differing and yet in many ways similar to the needs of the child. Is it surprising to find in the average adult a deep longing for the

security and rootedness which the relationship to his mother once gave him? Is it not to be expected that he cannot give up this intense longing unless he finds other ways of being rooted? . . .

Living is a process of continuous birth. The tragedy in the life of most of us is that we die before we are fully born. Being born, however, does not only mean to be free *from* the womb, the lap, the hand, etc., but also to be free *to* be active and creative. Just as the infant must breathe once the umbilical cord is cut, so man must be active and creative at every moment of birth. To the extent that man is fully born, he finds a new kind of rootedness; that lies in his creative relatedness to the world, and in the ensuing experience of solidarity with all men and with all nature. From being *passively* rooted in nature and in the womb, man becomes one again—but this time actively and creatively with all life.

Fourth, man needs to have a *sense of identity*. Man can be defined as the animal that can say "I," that can be aware of himself as a separate entity. The animal, being within nature and not transcending it, has no awareness of himself, has no need for a sense of identity. Man, being torn away from nature, being endowed with reason and imagination, needs to form a concept of himself, needs to say and to feel: "I am I." Because he is not *lived*, but *lives*, because he has lost the original unity with nature, has to make decisions, is aware of himself and of his neighbor as different persons, he must be able to sense himself as the subject of his actions. As with the need for relatedness, rootedness, and transcendence, this need for a sense of identity is so vital and imperative that man could not remain sane if he did not find some way of satisfying it. Man's sense of identity develops in the process of emerging from the "primary bonds" which tie him to mother and nature. The infant, still feeling one with mother, cannot yet say "I," nor has he any need for it. Only after he has conceived of the outer world as being separate and different from himself does he come to the awareness of himself as a distinct being, and one of the last words he learns to use is "I," in reference to himself.

In the development of *the human race* the degree to which man is aware of himself as a separate self depends on the extent to which he has emerged from the clan and the extent to which the process of individuation has developed. The member of a primitive clan might express his sense of identity in the formula "I am we"; he cannot yet conceive of himself as an "individual," existing apart from his group. In the medieval world, the individual was identified with his social role in the feudal hierarchy. The peasant was not a man who happened to be a peasant, the feudal lord not a man who happened to be a feudal lord. *He was* a peasant or a lord, and this sense of his unalterable station was an essential part of his sense of identity. When the feudal system broke down, this sense of identity was shaken and the acute question "Who am I?" arose—or, more precisely, "How do I know that I am I?" . . .

The development of Western culture went in the direction of creating the basis for the full experience of individuality. By making the individual free politically and economically, by teaching him to think for himself and freeing him from an authoritarian pressure, one hoped to enable him to feel "I" in the sense that he was the center and active subject of his powers and experienced himself as such. But only a minority achieved the new experience of "I." For the majority, individualism was not much more than a façade behind which was hidden the failure to acquire an individual sense of identity.

Many substitutes for a truly individual sense of identity were sought for and found. Nation, religion, class, and occupation serve to furnish a sense of identity. "I am an American," "I am a Protestant," "I am a businessman," are the formulae that help a man experience a sense of identity after the original clan identity has disappeared and before a truly individual sense of identity has been acquired. These different identifications are, in contemporary society, usually employed together. They are in a broad sense status identifications, and they are more efficient if blended with older feudal remnants, as in European countries. In the United States, in which so little is left of feudal relics and in which there is so much social mobility, these status identifications are naturally less efficient, and the sense of identity is shifted . . . to the experience of conformity.

Inasmuch as I am not different, inasmuch as I am like the others and recognized by them as "a regular fellow," I can sense myself as "I." I am— "as you desire me"—as Pirandello put it in the title of one of his plays. Instead of the pre-individualistic clan identity, a new herd identity develops in which the sense of identity rests on the sense of an unquestionable belonging to the crowd. That this uniformity and conformity are often not recognized as such, and are covered by the illusion of individuality, does not alter the facts.

The problem of the sense of identity is not, as it is usually understood, merely a philosophical problem, or a problem concerning only our mind and thought. The need to feel a sense of identity stems from the very condition of human existence, and it is the source of the most intense strivings. Since I cannot remain sane without the sense of "I," I am driven to do almost anything to acquire this sense. Behind the intense passion for status and conformity is this very need, and it is sometimes even stronger than the need for physical survival. What could be more obvious than the fact that people are willing to risk their lives, to give up their love, to surrender their freedom, to sacrifice their own thoughts for the sake of being one of the herd, of conforming, and thus of acquiring a sense of identity, even though it is an illusory one.

Reason and Orientation in the World

The fact that man has reason and imagination leads to the necessity not only for having a sense of his own identity but also for *orienting himself in the world intellectually*. This need can be compared with the process of physical orientation that develops in the first years of life and that is completed when the child can walk by himself, touch and handle things, knowing what they are. But when the ability to walk and to speak has been acquired, only the first step in the direction of orientation has been taken. Man finds himself surrounded by many puzzling phenomena and, having reason, he has to make sense of them, has to put them in some context which he can understand and which permits him to deal with them in his thoughts. The further his reason develops, the more adequate becomes his system of orientation, that is, the more it approximates reality. But even if man's frame of orientation is utterly illusory, it satisfies his need for some picture which is meaningful to him. Whether he believes in the power of a totem animal, in a rain god, or in the superiority and destiny of his race, his need for some frame of orientation is satisfied. Quite obviously, the picture of the world that he has depends on the development of his reason and of his knowledge. Although biologically the brain capacity of the human race has remained the same for thousands of generations, it takes a long evolutionary process to arrive at *objectivity*, that is, to acquire the faculty to see the world, nature, other persons, and oneself as they are and not distorted by desires and fears. The more man develops this objectivity, the more he is in touch with reality, the more he matures, the better can he create a human world in which he is at home. Reason is man's faculty for *grasping* the world by thought, in contradiction to intelligence, which is man's ability to *manipulate* the world with the help of thought. Reason is man's instrument for arriving at the truth, intelligence is man's instrument for manipulating the world more successfully; the former is essentially human, the latter belongs also to the animal part of man.

Reason is a faculty which must be practiced in order to develop, and it is indivisible. By this I mean that the faculty for objectivity refers to the knowledge of nature as well as to the knowledge of man, of society, and of oneself. If one lives in illusions about one sector of life, one's capacity for reason is restricted or damaged, and thus the use of reason is inhibited with regard to all other sectors. Reason in this respect is like love. Just as love is an orientation which refers to all objects and is incompatible with the restriction to one object, so is reason a human faculty which must embrace the whole of the world with which man is confronted. . . .

Feeling and Orientation to the World

If man were only a disembodied intellect, his aim would be achieved by a comprehensive thought system. But since he is an entity endowed with a body as well as a mind, he has to react to the dichotomy of his existence not only in think-ing but in the total process of living, in his feelings and actions. Hence any satisfying system of orientation contains not only intellectual elements but elements of feeling and sensing which are expressed in the relationship to an object of devotion.

The answers given to man's need for a system of orientation and an object of devotion differ widely both in content and in form. There are primitive systems such as animism and totemism in which natural objects or ancestors represent answers to man's quest for meaning. There are nontheistic systems, such as Buddhism, which are usually called religions although in their original form there is no concept of God. There are purely philosophical systems, such as Stoicism, and there are the monotheistic religious systems that give an answer to man's quest for meaning in reference to the concept of God.

But whatever their contents, they all respond to man's need to have not only some thought system but also an object of devotion that gives meaning to his existence and to his position in the world. Only the analysis of the various forms of religion can show which answers are better and which are worse solutions to man's quest for meaning and devotion, "better" or "worse" always considered from the standpoint of man's nature and his development.

Choices and Fulfillment

In discussing the various needs of man as they result from the conditions of his existence, I have tried to indicate that they have to be satisfied in some way or other lest man should become insane. But there are several ways in which each of these needs can be satisfied; the difference between these ways is the difference in their appropriateness for the development of man. The need to be related can be satisfied by submission, or by domination; but only in love is another human need fulfilled—that of independence and integrity of the self. The need for transcendence can be satisfied either by creativeness or by destructiveness; but only creativeness permits of joy—whereas destructiveness causes suffering for oneself and others. The need for rootedness can be satisfied regressively by fixation in nature and mother, or progressively by full birth in which new solidarity and oneness is achieved. Here again only in the latter case are individuality and integrity preserved. A frame of orientation may be irrational or rational; yet only the rational one can serve as a basis for the growth and development of the total personality. Eventually, the sense of identity can be based on primary ties with nature and clan, on adjustment to a group, or, on the other hand, on the full, creative development of the person. Again, only in the latter case can man achieve a sense of joy and strength.

The difference between the various answers is the difference between mental health and mental sickness, between suffering and joy, between stagnation and growth, between life and death, between good and evil. All answers that can be qualified as good have in common that they are consistent with the very nature of life, which is continuous birth and growth. All answers that can be qualified as bad have in common that they conflict with the nature of life, that they are conducive to stagnation and eventually to death. . . .

Well-being I would describe as the *ability to be creative, to be aware, and to respond;* to be independent and fully active, and by this very fact to be one with the world. To be concerned with *being,* not with *having;* to experience joy in the very act of living—and to consider living creatively as the only meaning of life. Well-being is not an assumption in the *mind* of a person. It is expressed in his whole body, in the way he walks, talks, in the tonus of his muscles.

Certainly, anyone who wants to achieve this aim must struggle against many basic trends of modern culture. I want to mention very briefly only two. One, the idea of a *split between intellect and affect,* an idea which has been prevalent from Descartes to Freud. In this whole development (to which there are, of course, exceptions) the assumption is made that only the intellect is rational and that affect, by its very nature, is irrational. . . . We cannot understand man fully nor achieve the aim of well-being unless we overcome the idea of this split, restore to man his original unity, and recognize that the split between affect and thought, body and mind, is nothing but a product of our own thought and does not correspond to the reality of man.

The other obstacle to the achievement of well-being, deeply rooted in the spirit of modern society, is the fact of man's dethronement from his supreme place. The nineteenth century said: God is dead; the twentieth century could say: man is dead. Means have been transformed into ends, the production and consumption of things has become the aim of life, to which living is subordinated. We produce things that act like men and men that act like things. Man has transformed himself into a thing and worships the products of his own hands; he is alienated from himself and has regressed to idolatry, even though he uses God's name. Emerson already saw that "things are in the saddle and ride mankind." Today many of us see it. The achievement of well-being is possible only under one condition: *if we put man back into the saddle.*

SCIENCE AND ETHICAL BEHAVIOR

by Nicholas Hobbs[1]

Although a scientist may remain ethically neutral in his search for truth, as a human being he cannot escape the ethical implications of his findings. He must consider what scientific progress means in terms of human welfare. Ethical considerations assume particular importance in the science of psychology, where increased knowledge raises the possibility that human behavior can someday be effectively controlled. In the following article the author seeks to clarify some of the issues involved. Dr. Hobbs is Chairman of the Division of Human Development and Guidance at George Peabody College for Teachers.

Some writers claim that science is ethically neutral,[2] but ethics clearly cannot be neutral about science. Ethical thought cannot escape the insistent implications of scientific findings. Indeed traditional modes of thought about ethics have been shaken to their foundations, and there have emerged the polar reactions of (*a*) rejecting science in ethics altogether and of (*b*) turning to science to find an entirely new basis for ethical theory.

Impact of Science

Three conceptions related to science have made trouble for traditional, revealed, or rationally self-evident ethical theories. One of these is the concept of probability. Probability theory is a central tool of all contemporary science. Its use generates an habitual mode of thought leading to skepticism of any conceptual system based on absolutes, as many ethical systems are. For the scientist, imperatives give way to probabilities, and ethical relativism is the consequence. A second source of disturbance in ethical thought comes from the findings of cultural anthropologists. Behavior strictly tabooed in one culture may be encouraged in another with no apparent ill effects. Ethical systems appear then to be, at least partly, the expression of a particular culture and to have

no necessary pervasive validity. . . . Finally with increasing knowledge, science has, paradoxically, become increasingly tentative about what is known. One criterion of a good theory is that it be precise enough to be disproven. Traditional ethical theories are not thought of as time limited, whereas scientific theories are regarded by scientists as expendable. A scientific theory is simply the best formulation of which scientists are capable at a given point in time, and constant revision of theories is the expected order of things. . . .

One reaction to the disturbance caused by science is to exclude it entirely from ethical thinking. This position has been taken by both scientists and ethical theorists. . . . It is said that science has to do with means but not with ends, that science can perhaps increase our understanding of human behavior but cannot help us judge whether a particular act is good or bad.

Another reaction to the disturbance caused by science is to recognize its potency in problem solving and to turn to it as a source of authority for ethical systems. . . .

Ethical Implications of Psychology

Simpson[3] has made the pertinent observation that many people today turn to science for ethical revelations, science being the twentieth century Mt. Sinai from whose heights might be brought

---

[1]From **The American Psychologist**, May 1959, **14**, No. 5, 217-225.
[2]George A. Lundberg, "Can Science Validate Ethics?" **Bulletin of the American Association of University Professors**, 1950, **36**, 262-275.

[3]George Gaylord Simpson, **The Meaning of Evolution: A Study of the History of Life and of Its Significance for Man**, New Haven, Conn.: Yale University Press, 1950.

down a new moral decalogue. Such a set of commandments, carrying all the persuasion of scientific authority, would bring new certitude and confidence to an anxious world and would relieve the individual of some sense of responsibility for the consequences of his behavior. But such a dispensation cannot come from science; science can never provide us with ethical imperatives. This is not to say that science has nothing to offer to us in our efforts to improve our ethics, or, more pertinently, to improve our behavior. Let us then turn to a consideration of some of the ethical implications of science, and particularly of psychological science.

Freedom of choice. To talk about psychology and ethics intelligibly one must first come to grips with an age-old and possibly insoluble problem: that of freedom of choice of the individual. It is a problem that psychologists would often prefer to ignore but cannot let alone. In 1880, William James[4] wrote: "A common opinion prevails that the juice has ages ago been pressed out of the free-will controversy, and that no new champion can do more than warm up stale arguments which everyone has heard." James goes on to say, "This is a radical mistake," and one is inclined to agree with him today for the issue is quickened every time psychologists get close to contemporary man and his problems.

Experimental psychologists generally seem less bothered by the problem than personality theorists and clinicians, though hewing the deterministic line is not always easy. In his book on the logic of problem solving in psychology, Benton Underwood[5] says simply and persuasively: "Determinism is a necessary assumption for the scientific enterprise." B. F. Skinner[6] is equally explicit: "If we are to use the methods of science in the field of human affairs, we must assume that behavior is lawful and determined." . . .

George Kelly and Gordon Allport, as personality theorists interested in moving psychology closer to man, cannot easily accept the axiom of determinism that seems so simple to the experimentalist. Common sense makes trouble.

Kelly's position[7] is a puzzler. He maintains ingeniously that freedom and determinism are two sides of the same coin. The behavior of a person is strictly determined by the constructs he uses to define the choice-demanding situation. However, the person does not have to accept these constraints; he may simply redefine his constructs. When he moves from lower order to higher order constructs, man gains freedom. Once a person adopts a construct, his behavior in the domain of the construct is determined by the construct; however, he remains free to redefine his constructs. Kelly does not specify what determines the choice of a superordinate construct system. If Kelly means simply that the adoption of a superordinate construct system increases the person's response repertory, his degrees of freedom, all would be well within Underwood's postulate of determinism as a necessary assumption of psychological science. But Kelly is talking about human freedom in the classical sense: Saint Ambrose was a fourth century advocate of constructive alternativism. He observed: "A wise man, though he be a slave, is at liberty." Boethius, Epictetus, Marcus Aurelius, and others have endorsed a similar "let's rise above it" attitude. Does Kelly's constructive alternativism offer more than this today? The answer is unclear. In any event, it would appear that Kelly works three concepts of freedom interchangeably: (*a*) the classical freedom-determinism type, from which he would like to extricate man, at least partially; (*b*) the degrees of freedom type, which refers simply to richness of response repertory; and (*c*) the semantic construct type, or the north-south argument, which maintains that the construct determinism requires the existence of freedom. Kelly solves the dilemmas of type *a* freedom by type *b* and *c* arguments.

Allport,[8] on the other hand, chafes under the restraints of science without really abandoning them. He first observes:

[4]William James, **Essays in Pragmatism**, New York: Hafner Publishing Co., Inc., 1948.
[5]Benton J. Underwood, **Psychological Research**, New York: Appleton-Century-Crofts, Inc., 1957.
[6]B. F. Skinner, **Science and Human Behavior**, New York: The Macmillan Company, 1953.

[7]George A. Kelly, **The Psychology of Personal Constructs**, New York: W. W. Norton & Company, Inc., 1955.
[8]Gordon W. Allport, **Becoming: Basic Considerations for a Psychology of Personality**, New Haven, Conn.: Yale University Press, 1955.

"It is customary for the psychologist, as for other scientists, to proceed within the framework of strict determinism, and to build barriers between himself and common sense lest common sense infect psychology with its belief in freedom."

But the kinds of alternatives that Allport describes do not join the issue. He first argues that, from the point of view of the actor, choice is "a paramount fact." Underwood and Skinner would not be discomfited by this. He then makes three additional points bearing not upon "freedom of choice" but rather on "degree of freedom." Allport is not at all sure that he has settled the matter: "These considerations fall short of solving the problem of freedom. They urge us, however, to forego naive solutions."

Anatol Rapoport[9] argues persuasively that, without freedom of choice, ethics is meaningless. If man is not free to choose between right and wrong, between the better and the worse part, what good is it even to talk about ethics at all? This requirement of free choice as a postulate puts the psychologist in a difficult spot, unless one is willing to accept his definition of choice. The act of choice is the primary datum for nearly all of psychological science, but the psychologist has his own definition of choice which can cause difficulty unless one understands what the psychologist is trying to do.

The psychologist is concerned with understanding and explaining behavior, mostly human behavior. One of the ways in which a psychologist tests the validity of his explanation is to make predictions derived from some explanatory system. If a particular prediction is confirmed, as through an experiment, his confidence in the system is increased. If the prediction is not confirmed, and if he is confident of the adequacy of his experiment, he must go back and rework his explanations. Psychologists, like other scientists, work to advance understanding by testing specific "if—then" equations and working the results into more general formulations. The ground rules of science say that these equations cannot contain variables which are nonrandom in their operation but which

[9]Anatol Rapoport, **Operational Philosophy: Integrating Knowledge and Action,** New York: Harper & Brothers, 1953.

at the same time are considered to be unavailable for any possible quantitative assessment. This does not mean that science maintains that all phenomena can be measured, since technical limitations . . . obviously limit what can be achieved in the way of mensuration. On the other hand, no scientific equation can contain an "X" variable which turns out to be the influence of any demon, pixie, gremlin, fate, entelechy, god, or spontaneous individual will. Now there is nothing in science that can disprove the existence and effective operation of demons, pixies, gremlins, fates, entelechies, gods, or undetermined individual choices. It is just that science is not set up to deal with these kinds of problems. There is no way for the scientist ever to write an equation incorporating such variables. The famous equation $E=mc^2$ does not suggest that engineers should build into an atom bomb a little man to decide whether or not the bomb is to explode. The psychologist cannot write such an elegant equation as this one of the physicist, but he too must write his equations without benefit of little men. Insofar as psychological science is concerned the notion of free choice is a homunculus. Psychology cannot prove that the behavior of the individual is determined, but for purposes of inquiry he must assume so and be content to live with whatever limitation this assumption may (or may not) make on his activities as a scientist.

But, one may protest, has not physics, the most advanced of sciences, had to admit ultimate indeterminancy? . . . Surely psychology does not pretend to be more rigorous than physics! No, not at all. Indeterminancy in physics means something quite different from the freedom of choice involved in human behavior. Heisenberg's principle [of indeterminancy] says that in certain restricted areas of physics an event cannot be measured because the process of measurement alters the nature of the event. This is a phenomenon very familiar to the psychologist, in whose work this kind of indeterminancy operates with a vengeance. The psychologist cannot give a person an intelligence test without altering his intelligence. But the effect is trivial, and no great harm is done by ignoring it.

And one may argue further that modern atomic physics has become a statistical science, dealing in probabilities and not in absolute predictions. The pathway of a particular molecule cannot be predicted and is random. Actually this development in physics has been comforting to psychologists, who are accustomed to dealing in probabilities. But it should be noted that there is nothing in physics that implies that a molecule chooses by an act of will to go in any particular direction. There is nothing in the probabilities and indeterminancies of atomic physics to establish the freedom of man or the existence of paraphysical influence in human affairs, as some writers fervidly assert (see, for example, A. H. Compton[10]). . . .

What we need to keep in mind is that science is one system which has been invented by man for the purpose of finding order in events which often appear to be more or less randomly organized with reference to his existence. Man has invented other construct systems to achieve the same grand purpose or to permit orderly transactions in some more limited sphere. Each of these construct systems may have its own unique validity. While it would be esthetically satisfying (and possibly, though not necessarily, more efficient) to have one overarching construct system, there is little to be gained from forcing consonance where little or none exists. The criterion for the validity of a construct system is not its consonance with another system but its utility in giving order and meaning to human experience. Within a scientific construct system, the assumption of determinism (plus randomness, perhaps) is required.

There are other construct systems where different assumptions rule. For example, the individual scientist, getting up in the morning, chooses to shave or not to shave; he construes the world with the assumption of almost complete freedom of choice. The legal system for construing the world assumes a middle position on determinism and individual freedom; the criminal behavior of the young person or of the psychotic is considered to be determined by circumstance, while the sane adult is construed as being responsible for his behavior. A religious system for construing the world obviously has to assume the effective functioning of some supra-individual influence. And a poetic system might make even other assump-

tions. It is when we attempt to shift from one construct system to another, without explicit recognition of what we are doing, that we get into trouble.

The process of choice. Earlier it was suggested that psychology might offer a description of choice with more limited meaning than the popular definition with its implication of freedom of will. Here is the way many psychologists would see the situation. An individual is confronted with a situation requiring one of a given number of possible responses. The individual brings to the situation as he perceives it a collection of hypotheses (behavior potentials, habits, personal constructs, as you like) about what he should do based on past experience, including experiences in similar situations. Within the limitations of the situation (a man in jail cannot choose to take a stroll in the park), of time available, of the individual's repertory of more or less appropriate responses, and from his habits of problem solving, the individual scans the situation and tries out various responses symbolically until there emerges into prominence (or until time runs out) a response that fits into his expectancies of establishing a more satisfactory state of affairs. He makes the response, or better, the response is made which is most prominent at the time when the response is required. The psychologist's incredibly complex task is to build a regression equation that will permit him to predict the relative prominence of various potential responses at any particular time. If this description of choice is acceptable, the psychologist can get about his business. The problem will still give him plenty of trouble, but it will not defeat him ahead of time by erecting insurmountable theoretical barriers.

There are inescapable facts, however, that make it difficult to accept the description of determined choice just offered: the introspective realness of the experience of choice itself and the insistence of feelings of responsibility for the consequences of one's own behavior. People, including psychologists, act on the assumption of freedom of choice, and no amount of talk about the ground rules of science is going to change much this primary assumption. That people are going to behave as though they have freedom of choice is an important datum that must be includ

[10]Arthur H. Compton, "Science and Man's Freedom," **Atlantic Monthly**, 1957, **200**, No. 4, 71-74.

ed in a scientific system which says they do not in fact have such freedom. There may be some comfort in face of this contradiction in noting that science not infrequently can get ahead with its business only when it does adopt a formulation at variance with daily experience.

The process of choice or of choosing is not complete with the occurrence of a particular determined event. The event itself becomes a part of the past experience of the individual, and it is also likely to alter future circumstances either for the individual himself or for others. Behavior is a product of interaction of the individual and his environment. Psychology is concerned with the nature of this interaction. Interactions that involve the welfare of individuals and of man may be described as ethical behavior, and psychology is not only interested in such interactions but has contributed significantly to their development. Thus the individual and his world are engaged in a process of continuous reconstruction of each other. Man remakes the world, and the world remakes man in an ongoing process.

The extent to which psychological science can contribute to this process of interaction valid observations about the nature of man, to this extent psychology can make a contribution to ethical behavior and then, secondarily, to ethical theory itself by supplying the philosopher with more data to work into his ethical systems.

But more pertinent, and intriguing, are the direct contributions that psychological science can make to the ethical behavior of the individual. Psychology makes its most distinctive contribution to ethical behavior by altering both the kind and the number of hypotheses that the individual brings to any given choice situation involving the welfare of others.

Psychology can (or better, will) alter the ultimately determined process of choice in a number of ways. Suppose for instance that psychology could demonstrate, what many have asserted, that the probability of a satisfactory choice occurring will be partly a function of the amount of time devoted to the symbolic manipulation of alternative courses of action. Common sense says that this is true, and the late Thomas Watson of IBM promoted the idea with his ubiquitous signs. But we really do not have much precise knowledge about what goes on when we think. If psychology can add to our understanding of the mechanisms of thought, it will make a contribution to ethical behavior.

Psychology may also increase the probability of the occurrence of ethically good responses by freeing a person to act on ethically good hypotheses that he already has but cannot use. This is what the psychologist attempts to do in psychotherapy. People may often not be able to use the knowledge they have about what is ethically good because of debilitating anxiety evoked by the anticipated consequences of efforts at constructive behavior. A common expression of this dilemma may be seen in the plight of the person who cannot risk loving for fear of getting hurt. There is the intriguing possibility that man may already know all that he needs to know to achieve fullest self-realization for himself and others. A simple factoring out of common elements in the major revealed or intuitive and rationally developed ethical systems of the world might yield say 90% of the ethical ideas that are important to have. If this commonality be found, then all the energies that go into efforts at refinements of ethical theories on the basis of new knowledge might well go into investigations of why man cannot act on available hypotheses as to what is good. Such incapacities, of course, are a primary concern of research in clinical psychology.

Regardless of the adequacy (or inadequacy) of available hypotheses about human behavior, good or bad, psychology must and will go on testing old hypotheses and generating new ones to be tested. Such is the nature of psychological science. If psychology can make widely available to people the results of a number of verified "if—then" statements about the behavior of people in relationship one with the other, the required consequence will be an improvement in ethical choices, if the description of the process of choice, given earlier, is accurate. For good to ensue from an increase in knowledge requires the assumption that we live in an orderly universe of which individual expressions of choice are an integral part. To the extent that choices are in harmony with whatever universal order there is, to that extent they should be ethically good. The incompleteness of our knowledge of the universe and of man possibly accounts in part for the large number of disparate criteria that have been suggested as bases for ethical systems. Psychology has no such confident solutions to offer. It can only accept some responsibility for continuous enquiry into man's changing behavior in an evolving world.

So far it has been suggested that psychological knowledge should result in more ethical behavior: (*a*) by clarifying the process of decision making; (*b*) by divesting repressed responses already in the individual's repertory of their anxiety-producing potential, thus making them useful in problem solving; and (*c*) by adding to the response repertory of the individual a number of alternative ways of behaving. All of this appears to be to the good.

Control of behavior. But if the psychologist at this point in the process of scanning the problem situation shifts construct systems and speculates on his personal responsibility as a scientist and a citizen, there emerges a much less sanguine view of the consequences of a constantly growing body of verified knowledge about human behavior.

As psychological knowledge grows, the possibility of more effective control over human behavior increases, with profound consequences for ethics. The very process of enquiry that promises to improve decision making also adds to the gravity of the decisions made.

Increasingly man will be able to employ the results of psychological science to manipulate his fellow man, often without his victim knowing that he is being controlled.

Developing psychological knowledge presents the same conjunction of good and evil that we have all felt so keenly in the development of atomic energy. Atomic energy can ease man of drudgery and disease, and it can also annihilate him. Psychological knowledge can bring man increased certitude, dignity, and joy, and it can also enslave him. These antinomies are among the most exciting and demanding developments of our time. They have within them the seeds of ultimate tragedy or triumph. The stakes seem to be getting even higher, and the rules of the game, embodied in ethics, ever more important.

ADDITIONAL RESOURCES

The following pages contain an annotated listing of books, pamphlets, and articles dealing with various aspects of four major life problems: education, work, marriage, and aging.

GETTING THE MOST FROM COLLEGE

Books, Libraries and You—A Handbook on the Use of Reference Resources of the Library by Jessie Boyd and others, New York: Charles Scribner's Sons, 1949. A good guide to all aspects of library usage.

A Century of Higher Education for American Women by Mabel Newcomer, New York: Harper & Brothers, 1959. A history and analysis of higher education for women, with a consideration of its special aims and requirements.

The Climate of Learning: A Constructive Attack on Complacency in American Colleges by Ordway Tead, New York: Harper & Brothers, 1958. A detailed analysis of the factors that make for an academic atmosphere conducive to genuine intellectual growth.

College and Life: Problems of Self-Discovery and Self-Direction by Margaret E. Bennett, 4th ed., New York: McGraw-Hill Book Company, Inc., 1952. Gives careful consideration to academic and other problems which face the college student and suggests some possible solutions.

College Freshmen Speak Out by Agatha Townsend, New York: Harper & Brothers, 1956. Reports a national survey in which freshmen students gave opinions concerning their social activities, professors, administrators, etc.

College Orientation by George Weigand and Walter S. Blake, Jr., Englewood Cliffs, N. J.: Prentice-Hall, Inc., 1955. A study skills manual, with special chapters devoted to mathematics and foreign languages.

The College Years: Intellectual and Personal Growth edited by Lois Murphy and Esther Raushenbush, New York: Harper & Brothers, 1960. Reports an intensive study on the aims and achievements of a group of women students during four years of college and two years beyond.

Crucial Issues in Education edited by Henry Ehlers, New York: Henry Holt & Company, 1955. A collection of writings covering various sides of such basic issues as intellectual freedom, censorship, and religious education.

Educating Our Daughters: A Challenge to the Colleges by Lynn White, Jr., New York: Harper & Brothers, 1950. A leading educator examines the college's role in educating women for their distinctive roles and responsibilities.

Education for Effective Thinking by Roland B. Kimball and Richard L. Wing, New York: Appleton-Century-Crofts, Inc., 1960. Includes a good discussion of critical thought processes.

Education for Responsible Living by Wallace B. Donham, Cambridge, Mass.: Harvard University Press, 1944. Worth-while ideas for students planning their careers.

Educational Wastelands by Arthur E. Bestor, Urbana: University of Illinois Press, 1953. A controversial attack on present-day educational practices, with a plea for a return to the "essentials."

Effective Living: An Interdisciplinary Approach by Lois Smith Murray, New York: Harper & Brothers, 1960. An orientation text and workbook designed to help the college freshman toward a better understanding of himself and of his college community. Includes readings and research from anthropology, psychology, physiology, sociology.

Effective Study by Francis P. Robinson, New York: Harper & Brothers, 1946. A very useful text-workbook on study techniques, with special emphasis on reading and vocabulary development.

Higher Education in Transition: An American History, 1636-1956 by John S. Brubacher and Willis Rudy, New York: Harper & Brothers, 1958. Traces the history of the American college and university system in terms of men, institutions, and ideas.

How to Read a Book by Mortimer J. Adler, New York: Simon and Schuster, 1940. Discusses how to learn the most—and get the most enjoyment—from good books.

How to Study by Clifford T. Morgan and James Deese, New York: McGraw-Hill Book Company, Inc., 1957. A manual of general study techniques, with chapters devoted to the specific problems of writing themes and reports, studying foreign languages, and studying mathematics.

The Idea of a College by Elton Trueblood, New York: Harper & Brothers, 1959. A thoughtful consideration of the aims and methods of the liberal arts college.

Introduction to College by Calvin J. Daane and others, Boston: Allyn and Bacon, Inc., 1958. A student-directed orientation book with sections on study skills, personal and social adjustment, vocation planning, and building a philosophy of life.

Issues in University Education edited by Charles Frankel, New York: Harper & Brothers, 1959. Essays by ten American scholars on the current status of higher education and the critical issues facing our colleges and universities.

Mental Health in College and University by Dana L. Farnsworth, Cambridge, Mass.: Harvard University Press, 1957. Valuable discussion of mental health in college.

The New Era in Education—A Comparative Study by I. L. Kandel, Boston: Houghton Mifflin Company, 1955. A comparison of education in England, France, Russia, and the United States.

On Becoming an Educated Person: An Orientation to College by Virginia W. Voeks, Philadelphia: W. B. Saunders Company, 1957. Describes the advantages of being an educated person and relates study techniques to the aims of a college education. Includes a section on personality characteristics which might handicap successful study.

A Practical Guide to Efficient Study by C. L. Gunthorp, New York: Exposition Press, 1957. Specific and practical suggestions for improving study attitudes, allotment of time, use of textbooks and lectures, writing of papers and examination, and relations with instructors.

Preface to Critical Reading by Richard D. Altick, 3rd ed., New York: Henry Holt and Company, 1956. A good discussion of the habits of critical reading and critical thinking which are necessary for getting the most out of college.

The Purposes of Higher Education by Huston Smith, New York: Harper & Brothers, 1955. Reports what teachers with widely different philosophical and educational views believe are the proper goals of higher education.

Reading Rapidly and Well by C. Gilbert Wrenn and Luella Cole, 2nd ed., Stanford: Stanford University Press, 1954. Offers many valuable suggestions for becoming a faster, more effective reader.

Reading Skills by William D. Baker, New York: Prentice-Hall, Inc., 1953. Suggests some practical aids for improving reading skills.

So This Is College by Paul H. Landis, New York: McGraw-Hill Book Company, Inc., 1954. An orientation book for college freshmen.

Student's Guide to Efficient Study by Luella Cole and Jesse M. Ferguson, 4th ed., New York: Rinehart & Company, Inc., 1960. A pamphlet designed to help the student develop more effective study habits.

Study Is Hard Work by William H. Armstrong, New York: Harper & Brothers, 1956. Offers specific suggestions for studying, with emphasis on vocabulary development, written work, and reading.

A Study of Participation in College Activities by E. G. Williamson and others, Minneapolis: University of Minnesota Press, 1954. Presents significant findings about how students use their time.

Studying Effectively by C. Gilbert Wrenn and Robert P. Larsen, 2nd ed., Stanford: Stanford University Press, 1955. Discusses ways to develop more efficient study habits.

Success in College by James C. Coleman, Frieda Bornston Libaw, and William D. Martinson, Chicago: Scott, Foresman and Company, 1960. A text-workbook covering the areas of orientation to college, successful study habits, personal adjustment, and vocational planning.

Successful Adjustment in College by J. R. Chandler and others, 2nd ed., Englewood Cliffs, N. J.: Prentice-Hall, Inc., 1958. A text-workbook covering most aspects of college life.

Teacher in America by Jacques Barzun, Boston: Little, Brown & Co., 1945. A witty and provocative discussion of the American educational scene and the teaching process.

Time-Budgets of Human Behavior by Pitirim A. Sorokin and Clarence Q. Berger, Cambridge, Mass.: Harvard University Press, 1939. Reveals interesting facts about time usage.

Toward Better Reading Skills edited by Russell Cosper and E. Glenn Griffin, 2nd ed., New York: Appleton-Century-Crofts, 1959. Worth-while aids for improving reading skill.

Using Books and Libraries by Ella V. Aldrich, 3rd ed., New York: Prentice-Hall, Inc., 1951. A concise pamphlet, with exercises, on how to use a library.

Working Your Way Through College by Kenneth C. Rathbun, Cambridge, Mass.: Cavalier Publishing Co., 1951. Helpful and practical pamphlet for students working their way through college.

VOCATIONAL PLANNING

Appraising Vocational Fitness by Donald E. Super, New York: Harper & Brothers, 1949. A survey and evaluation of available tests for identifying vocational aptitudes and skills.

Career Planning by Leonard J. Smith, New York: Harper & Brothers, 1959. Detailed material for helping the individual evaluate his aptitudes, interests, and personality traits in relation to a career choice. Includes a good bibliography of career information, a list of available psychological tests, and detachable self-evaluation tests.

Careers Ahead for College Women, Boston: Simmons College, 1959. A guidance handbook.

"A Check List of Facts about Jobs for Use in Vocational Guidance" by Robert Hoppock, *American Psychologist,* 1948, *3,* No. 9, 417-418. A detailed listing of the factors an individual should consider in deciding on a job.

The College Girl Looks Ahead to Her Career Opportunities by Marguerite W. Zapolean, New York: Harper & Brothers, 1956. Discusses fifteen career fields and the ways to prepare for and enter them. Includes sources of further information about each field.

Counseling and Psychology: Vocational Psychology and Its Relation to Educational and Personal Counseling by Milton L. Blum and Benjamin Balinsky, New York: Prentice-Hall, Inc., 1951. Points to the value of counseling and self-study as aids in making a vocational choice.

Educational and Vocational Planning by William D. Martinson, Chicago: Scott, Foresman and Co., 1959. Practical guidance for the college student, emphasizing the need for planning ahead and for assessing oneself as well as available job opportunities.

Guide to Career Information: A Bibliography of Recent Occupational Literature compiled by Career Information Service, New York Life Insurance Company, New York: Harper & Brothers, 1957. An annotated listing of more than eight hundred books and pamphlets containing job information about fifty-two occupational fields.

A Guide to Free Occupational and Vocational Guidance Literature, New York: Federation Employment and Guidance Service, 1955.

Handbook of Job Facts by Guidance Staff Editors, 2nd ed., Chicago: Science Research Associates, 1959. A concise presentation, by means of charts, of pertinent information about most lines of work, including earning and advancement possibilities, possible health hazards, and required abilities, temperament, and aptitudes.

Occupational Abstracts, Peapack, N. J.: Personnel Services, Inc. Six-page summaries of available literature on different occupations.

Occupational Books edited by S. Splaver, Washington, D. C.: Biblio Books, 1952. An annotated bibliography.

Occupational Information by Max F. Baer and Edward C. Roeber, 2nd ed., Chicago: Science Research Associates, 1958. A detailed handbook which includes the major sources of occupational information and a breakdown of **vocational fields.**

Occupational Information by Robert Hoppock, New York: McGraw-Hill Book Company, Inc., 1957. Covers the various sources of occupational information and the use of such information in counseling and teaching.

Occupational Information: Its Development and Application by Carroll L. Shartle, 2nd ed., New York: Prentice-Hall, Inc., 1952. Discusses the development and use of occupational information in vocational guidance and counseling.

Occupational Literature: An Annotated Bibliography by Gertrude Forrester, rev. ed., New York: H. W. Wilson Co., 1958. Describes general occupational literature as well as sources of information on specific occupations from "able seaman" through "zoologist."

Occupational Outlook Handbook, Bulletin No. 1215, U. S. Department of Labor, Bureau of Labor Statistics. Washington, D. C.: Superintendent of Documents, 1957. Briefly describes employment trends, qualifications, earnings, advancement possibilities, etc., for over five hundred occupations and twenty-five major industries.

Occupations and Careers by Walter J. Greenleaf, New York: McGraw-Hill Book Company, Inc., 1955. A comprehensive discussion of careers and the factors that contribute to success in them.

Occupations and Values by Morris Rosenberg and others, Glencoe, Ill.: The Free Press, 1958. Discusses the influence of values, attitudes, and personality factors on the vocational choices of college students and considers work as it affects a person's life, thinking, and role in society.

The Psychology of Careers by Donald E. Super, New York: Harper & Brothers, 1957. A thorough analysis of the factors that determine vocational success and satisfaction.

The Psychology of Occupations by Anne Roe, New York: John Wiley & Sons, Inc., 1956. Discusses the relationship between personality, intelligence, and sociological factors from the viewpoint of a clinician. Offers a new classification of occupations.

The Right Career for You by Eugene J. Benge, New York: Funk & Wagnalls Co. in association with *Modern Industry Magazine*, 1950. Emphasizes the importance of matching one's job to one's abilities and interests.

Successfully Finding Yourself and Your Job by Frederick A. Magoun, New York: Harper & Brothers, 1959. Outlines ways of determining one's vocational aptitudes and interests and sets forth procedures involved in getting a job, with special emphasis on the interview.

Summer Employment Directory, Cincinnati: National Directory Service. A free list, published annually, of employers who invite applications for summer jobs.

The Twenty-Minute Lifetime; A Guide to Career Planning by Gavin A. Pitt and R. W. Smith, Englewood Cliffs, N. J.: Prentice-Hall, Inc., 1959. A pertinent warning against easy career decisions by college graduates and a good discussion of career opportunities in particular fields such as business, science, sales, and teaching.

You and Your Job by Walter A. Lowen, New York: Greystone Press, 1958. Practical advice on job assessment, how to get and keep a job, problems of executives, how to improve a career.

Your Vocational Adventure by Jesse C. Burt, New York: Abingdon Press, 1959. A vocational "pep talk" which emphasizes the importance of pruning one-self for job choice. Includes job descriptions and sources of occupational information.

The following periodical indexes list books, pamphlets, and magazine articles describing different occupations:

Career Index, Chronicle Guidance Publications, Inc., Moravia, New York.

Guidance Index, Science Research Associates, 259 East Erie Street, Chicago, Illinois.

Occupational Index, Personnel Services, Inc., Peapack, New Jersey.

The following professional journals carry articles pertaining to vocational planning and adjustment:

American Vocational Journal, American Vocational Association, Inc., 1010 Vermont Avenue, N.W., Washington 5, D. C.

Journal of Applied Psychology, American Psychological Association, 1333 16th Street, N.W., Washington 6, D. C.

Journal of Consulting Psychology, American Psychological Association, 1333 16th Street, N.W., Washington 6, D. C.

Journal of Counseling Psychology, Student Services Building, Ohio State University, Columbus 10, Ohio.

Occupational Psychology, National Institute of Industrial Psychology, 14 Welbeck Street, London, England.

Personnel and Guidance Journal, American Personnel and Guidance Association, 1534 O Street, N.W., Washington 5, D. C.

Vocational Guidance Quarterly, American Personnel and Guidance Association, 1534 O Street, N.W., Washington 5, D. C.

MARRIAGE AND THE FAMILY

American Marriage and Divorce by Paul H. Jacobson in collaboration with Pauline F. Jacobson, New York: Rinehart & Company, Inc., 1959. Presents statistics on the occurrence, duration, and dissolution of marriage in the United States, including chances of marriage and remarriage, length of widowhood, frequency of racial intermarriage, etc.

Anticipating Your Marriage by Robert O. Blood, Glencoe, Ill.: The Free Press, 1955. Deals with college dating, sibling relationships, parents' influence on choice of mate, premarital problems, and considerations after marriage.

The Art of Loving by Erich Fromm, New York: Harper & Brothers, 1956. A psychiatrist and humanist discusses the meaning of love in its various aspects.

Becoming a Mother by Theodore R. Seidman and Marvin H. Albert, New York: David McKay Co., Inc., 1956. Sound, clearly written information and advice for any woman who expects to have children.

Before You Marry by Sylvanus M. Duvall, New York: Association Press, 1959. Readable discussion of factors to consider before marriage.

The Challenge of Marriage by Rudolf Dreikurs, New York: Duell, Sloan & Pearce, Inc., 1946. An excellent all-around treatment of marriage by a psychiatrist, emphasizing the psychological values which are involved.

Courtship and Marriage by Francis E. Merrill, rev. ed., New York: Henry Holt and Company, 1959. Readable discussion of courtship and marriage as social relationships.

Dating, Mating, and Marriage by Jessie S. Bernard and others, Cleveland: Howard Allen, Inc., 1958. A documentary case approach.

Education for Marriage by James A. Peterson, college edition, New York: Charles Scribner's Sons, 1956. An excellent book for marriage preparation which discusses the complexities of mate selection and adjustment to marriage.

Engagement and Marriage by Ernest W. Burgess and Paul Wallin, Philadelphia: J. B. Lippincott Company, 1953. A study of 1000 engaged couples and a follow-up report on 666 of these couples after marriage.

Families Are Forever by B. M. Moore and others, Austin: The Hogg Foundation for Mental Health, University of Texas, 1959. Pamphlet offering valuable study suggestions for young married couples.

Family Finance by Howard F. Bigelow, 2nd ed., Philadelphia: J. B. Lippincott Company, 1953. Points out family economic problems and ways of dealing with them.

The Family, from Institution to Companionship by Ernest W. Burgess and Harvey J. Locke, 2nd ed., New York: American Book Company, 1953. A popular book on the history of the family and its present-day function as a unit for companionship.

The Family: Its Function and Destiny edited by R. N. Anshen, rev. ed., New York: Harper & Brothers, 1959. Articles on various facets of family life.

Family, Marriage and Parenthood edited by Howard Becker and Reuben L. Hill, 2nd ed., Boston: D. C. Heath & Company, 1955. Experts in the field discuss marriage and the family as points of social interaction.

Family, Socialization and Interaction Process by Talcott Parsons and Robert F. Bales, Glencoe, Ill.: The Free Press, 1955. Describes the effects of family relationships on the individual.

Fathers Are Parents, Too; A Constructive Guide to Successful Fatherhood by O. Spurgeon English and Constance J. Foster, New York: G. P. Putnam's Sons, 1951. A good treatise on the neglected parent.

The Happy Family by John Levy and Ruth Munroe, New York: Alfred A. Knopf, Inc., 1938. An optimistic look at family life.

The Human Venture in Sex, Love, and Marriage by Peter A. Bertocci, New York: Association Press, 1949. A sensible study which stresses the potentialities of marriage and is essentially concerned with values in sex, love, and marriage.

Ideal Marriage, Its Physiology and Technique by Theodor H. Van de Velde, New York: Random House, 1943. Fine book on the physiological approach to marriage.

Instructions for Mixed Marriages by John S. Banahan, Milwaukee: The Bruce Publishing Co., 1957. A realistic, practical book for those contemplating a mixed marriage.

Love and Conflict: The New Pattern in Family Life by Gibson Winter, New York: Doubleday & Company, Inc., 1958. A realistic appraisal of modern family life.

Love or Perish by Smiley Blanton, rev. ed., New York: Simon and Schuster, 1957. A psychiatrist discusses the importance of love both to the individual and to the world.

Making the Most of Marriage by Paul H. Landis, New York: Appleton-Century-Crofts, Inc., 1955. A readable, optimistic book on the possibilities afforded by marriage.

Male and Female by Margaret Mead, New York: William Morrow & Company, Inc., 1949. An anthropologist draws on her knowledge of people and observations of other cultures to examine personal relationships between men and women.

Man and Wife edited by Emily H. Mudd and Aron M. Krich, New York: W. W. Norton & Company, Inc., 1957. Probably the best book on marital counseling.

"Marital Satisfaction and Religious Behavior" by Lee G. Burchinal, *American Sociological Review*, 1957, 22, 306-310. Supports hypotheses that couples who attend church regularly have higher marital satisfaction scores than those who attend irregularly or not at all.

Marriage by Earl L. Koos, rev. ed., New York: Henry Holt and Company, 1957. A much-used book on the problems facing couples during courtship and marriage.

Marriage Analysis; Foundations for Successful Family Life by Harold T. Christensen, 2nd ed., New York: The Ronald Press Company, 1958. A well-written text on marriage.

Marriage and Family Life: A Jewish View edited by Abraham B. Shoulson, New York: Twayne Publishers, 1959. Essays presenting a Jewish view of marriage and family life.

Marriage and Family Relations by Lawrence S. Bee, New York: Harper & Brothers, 1959. Approaches marriage from the standpoint of the individuals involved, the courtship period, the marriage relationship, and family interaction. Includes psychosociological case studies of three families.

Marriage and the Family by Ray E. Baber, 2nd ed., New York: McGraw-Hill Book Company, Inc., 1953. Careful and intelligent historical examination of marriage and family customs in America.

Marriage and the Family in American Culture by Andrew G. Truxal and F. E. Merrill, New York: Prentice-Hall, Inc., 1953. Pertinent discussions of marriage relationships such as "mixed marriages," personality differences, and economic factors.

Marriage Counseling: A Casebook, American Association of Marriage Counselors, New York: Association Press, 1958. An interesting book presenting forty-one representative marriage-counseling cases. Introduction gives an insightful picture of marriage in the United States today and the particular problems and tensions it raises.

Marriage for Moderns by Henry A. Bowman, 4th ed., New York: McGraw-Hill Book Company, Inc., 1960. Intelligent discussion which stimulates reader to think through the important considerations in marriage. Stresses that a successful marriage is something to be achieved.

Marriage Guidance by Edwin F. Healy, Chicago: Loyola University Press, 1958. Studies the problems of married couples and of those who are contemplating marriage.

A Marriage Manual: A Practical Guidebook to Sex and Marriage by Hannah M. and Abraham Stone, rev. ed., New York: Simon and Schuster, 1952. One of the finest books on marriage, written by a husband and wife who are both physicians.

Marriage, Morals and Sex in America: A History of Ideas by Sidney H. Ditzion, New York: Bookman Associates, Inc., 1953. Comprehensive review of American thought on moral codes.

Mate Selection: A Study of Complementary Needs by Robert F. Winch, New York: Harper & Brothers, 1958. Reports significant data gathered from research on complementariness in mate selection.

Modern Courtship and Marriage by E. E. LeMasters, New York: The Macmillan Company, 1957. Frank treatment of pre-marriage and marriage relationships.

Neurotic Interaction in Marriage edited by V. W. Eisenstein, New York: Basic Books, Inc., 1956. Good collection of information on the sources of problems in marriage.

One Marriage, Two Faiths by James H. S. Bossard and Eleanor S. Boll, New York: The Ronald Press Company, 1957. Examines the critical problems that couples of different religious faith should face before they marry.

Planning for Marriage by Oliver M. Butterfield, New York: D. Van Nostrand Co., Inc., 1956. A widely used text covering topics from courtship through marriage.

Predicting Adjustment in Marriage: A Comparison of a Divorced and a Happily Married Group by Harvey J. Locke, New York: Henry Holt and Company, 1951. Presents data used to predict success in marriage.

Preparing for Marriage by Clifford R. Adams, New York: E. P. Dutton & Co., Inc., 1951. A valuable guide to premarital considerations.

The Psychologist Looks at Sex and Marriage by Allan Fromme, New York: Prentice-Hall, Inc., 1951. An intelligent discussion which emphasizes the differences between romantic and enduring love and points up the importance of personal maturity in making a success of marriage.

The Psychology of Sexual Emotion; The Basis of Selective Attraction by Vernon W. Grant, New York: Longmans, Green and Company, 1957. Examines the psychological as well as physiological basis of sexual attraction.

Sex and Morality by Abram Kardiner, Indianapolis: The Bobbs-Merrill Company, Inc., 1954. Ethical problems as viewed by a sociologist.

Sex Attitudes in the Home by Ralph G. Eckert, New York: Association Press, 1956. Shows that attitudes toward sex are as important as factual information.

Successful Marriage edited by Morris Fishbein and Ernest W. Burgess, rev. ed., New York: Doubleday & Company, Inc., 1955. Comprehensive and sensible book on marriage and how to make it work.

This Holy Estate by John E. Riley, Kansas City, Mo.: Nazarene Publishing House, 1957. Stresses the sanctity of marriage vows.

Two Together; A Handbook for Your Marriage by Robert C. Dodds, New York: Thomas Y. Crowell Company, 1959. A simple and helpful book on premarital preparation by a Congregationalist minister.

Venture of Faith; A Guide to Marriage and the Home by Mary Alice Walker and H. B. Walker, New York: Harper & Brothers, 1959. Readable advice on family living drawn from the experiences of a Presbyterian minister and his wife in counseling young people and married couples.

What Christianity Says About Sex, Love and Marriage by Roland H. Bainton, New York: Association Press, 1957. Sets forth ethical principles that everyone should respect.

When You Marry by Evelyn M. Duvall and Reuben Hill, rev. ed., New York: Association Press, 1953. A practical approach to marriage and family life.

Your Marriage by Norman E. Himes and Donald L. Taylor, rev., New York: Rinehart & Company, Inc., 1955. Good general book for anyone planning marriage.

The following professional journals carry articles pertaining to marriage and family life:

Journal of Applied Psychology, American Psychological Association, 1333 16th Street, N.W., Washington 6, D.C.

Journal of Consulting Psychology, American Psychological Association, 1333 16th Street, N.W., Washington 6, D.C.

Journal of Counseling Psychology, Student Services Building, Ohio State University, Columbus 10, Ohio.

Journal of Social Psychology, Journal Press, 2 Commercial Street, Provincetown, Massachusetts.

Marriage and Family Living, National Council on Family Relations, 1219 University Avenue S.E., Minneapolis 14, Minnesota.

Social Problems, Brooklyn College, Brooklyn 10, New York.

Sociological Review, University College of North Staffordshire, Keele, Staffordshire, England.

Sociology and Social Research, University of Southern California Press, 3518 University Avenue, Los Angeles 7, California.

PROBLEMS OF OLDER PEOPLE

The Aged in American Society by Joseph T. Drake, New York: The Ronald Press Company, 1958. Covers demographic characteristics of the population, employment of the aged, pension and retirement plans, physiological and psychological traits of the aged, and housing, recreation, and education for the aged.

Aging and Human Skill by A. T. Welford, New York: Oxford University Press, Inc., 1958. A scientifically based report for those concerned with employment of older people, retirement, and adult education.

Aging Successfully by George Lawton, New York: Columbia University Press, 1946. A frank and readable handbook on growing older intelligently— of interest to young people who will one day be old—as well as to the already older person.

"**Attitudes of Middle-Aged Persons Toward Growing Older**" by Bernice L. Neugarten and David C. Garron, *Geriatrics*, 1959, *14*, No. 1, 21-24. A study of the ideas about their present and future of 40-70 year olds in Kansas.

The Biological, Sociological, and Psychological Aspects of Aging by Kurt Wolff, Springfield, Ill.: Charles C Thomas, 1959. Information from numerous studies about the effects of the biological, sociological, and psychological aspects of aging and what can be done about them.

"**Designs for Retirement**" by Daniel J. Hafrey, *Geriatrics*, 1959, *14*, No. 9, 595-599. Advocates extension of social security, flexible retirement age, care of health, and constructive use of leisure time.

Education on the Aging: A Selected Annotated Bibliography by Betty A. Ward, Washington, D.C.: U.S. Department of Health, Education, and Welfare, 1958.

"Emotional Conflicts of the Middle-Aged Man" by Robert W. Adams, Jr., *Geriatrics*, 1957, *12*, No. 9, 535-541. Describes the adjustment problems of the middle-aged man, giving some case histories.

"General Physiology of Aging" by Gerald J. Groen, *Geriatrics*, 1959, *14*, No. 5, 318-331. Discusses mainly the physical changes of aging—biochemistry, decreased sexual function, adjustment to changes in environment, onset of severe diseases.

Getting Ready for Tomorrow by Charles M. Crowe, New York: Abingdon Press, 1959. Chatty advice urging psychological preparation for old age long before it arrives.

How to Enjoy Life After Sixty; A Guide to Understanding and Enjoying the Later Years by Pierre Boucheron, New York: Archer House, 1959. Common-sense advice for older people on health, hobbies, jobs, friends, and adult education.

"Implication of Aging as Predicted by Population Changes" by G. Galsey Hunt, *Geriatrics*, 1959, *14*, No. 1, 1-7. Predicts the size of the over-65 population for the next twenty years and stresses the importance of providing good medical care for older people.

Longer Life by George H. Soule, New York: The Viking Press, Inc., 1958. A sound discussion of the problems facing older people and realistic suggestions about economic and social aspects of aging.

The New Frontiers of Aging edited by Wilma Donahue and Clark Tibbetts, Ann Arbor: The University of Michigan Press, 1957. Report of a research symposium which attempts to integrate the latest knowledge on aging and raises some thought-provoking questions.

New Goals for Old Age edited by George Lawton, New York: Columbia University Press, 1943. Articles by trained workers on the psychological and physiological aspects of growing old.

The Opportunities of Age by Claude C. Jones, Boston: Christopher Publishing House, 1959. Interviews with retired people who have remained active and some who are contemplating retirement.

"Personality Factors in Adjustment to Aging" by Robert F. Peck, *Geriatrics*, 1960, *15*, No. 2, 124-130. Suggests that overall adjustment of older people is highly related to such personality traits as mental flexibility, ego differentiation, etc.

"Psychological Stresses of Old Age" by Walter G. Klopfer, *Geriatrics*, 1958, *13*, No. 8, 529-531. Studies the "narcissistic trauma" associated with the older person's decreased capacities and changed relationships with others.

"Retirement Preparation Education—An Ounce of Prevention" by Charles E. Odell, *Geriatrics*, 1959, *14*, No. 9, 591-594. Sets forth plans for retirement preparation education programs.

"The Transition from Work to Retirement" by Margaret Pearson, *Occupational Psychology*, 1957, *31*, No. 3, 139-149. A question-raising study of men's adjustment to their retirement.

"Why Study Aging?" by James E. Birren, *American Psychologist*, 1958, *13*, No. 6, 292-296. Emphasizes the importance to the individual and society of learning what will produce happy, useful older people.

The following professional journals carry articles pertaining to problems associated with aging.

American Journal of Occupational Therapy, 250 West 57th Street, New York 19, New York.

Geriatrics, Lancet Publications, 84 South Tenth Street, Minneapolis 2, Minnesota.

Journal of Gerontology, The Gerontological Society, Inc., 660 South Kingshighway Boulevard, St. Louis 10, Missouri.

Journal of the American Geriatrics Society, Williams & Wilkins Co., 428 East Preston Street, Baltimore 2, Maryland.

Occupational Psychology, National Institute of Industrial Psychology, 14 Welbeck Street, London, W.I., England.

ACKNOWLEDGMENTS

Sources of photographs and many of the other illustrations in Personality Dynamics and Effective Behavior *are listed below. Sources of charts and diagrams based on research and of quoted material are acknowledged in the references at the end of each chapter.*

37 Adapted by permission of Dr. Edmund W. Sinnott and the *American Journal of Botany* (top) ; adapted by permission of the U.S. Fish and Wildlife Service (bottom).

49 Reprinted by permission of *Scientific American.*

57 Reprinted from *Childhood in Contemporary Cultures*, edited by Margaret Mead and Martha Wolfenstein, by permission of The University of Chicago Press, copyright 1955 by The University of Chicago (right) ; courtesy of the Museum of Modern Art, New York (left).

76 Adapted by permission of the American Psychological Association.

131 Reprinted by permission of the photographer, Vitold de Golish (left) ; reprinted by permission of United Press International (right).

137 Adapted by permission of the University of Minnesota, copyright 1950 by the University of Minnesota (left) ; photos by Wallace Kirkland, courtesy of *Life* magazine, copyright 1945 Time, Inc. (right).

141 Adapted by permission of the American Psychological Association.

143 Reprinted by permission of *Science.*

159 Adapted by permission of the American Psychological Association.

168 Adapted by permission of the Journal Press.

173 Photos courtesy of Hans Selye.

218 Photos by Paul Weller, reprinted by permission of *Scientific American.*

221 Adapted by permission of The Williams & Wilkins Co.

258 Adapted by permission of Harper & Brothers.

281 Reprinted by permission of *Scientific American.*

283 Reprinted by permission of Harper & Brothers.

321 Adapted by permission of the publisher, Alfred A. Knopf, Inc. Copyright 1930, 1937, 1945 by Karl A. Menninger.

365 Adapted by permission of Holt, Rinehart and Winston, Inc.

470 By permission of Harper & Brothers.

508-512 By permission of University of Illinois Press.

The drawings on the following pages are the work of Franz Altschuler: 37, 76, 77, 137, 141, 159, 168, 183, 221, 224, 258, 275, 314, 321, 352, 373, 376, 470, 508, 509, 510, 511, 512.

NAME INDEX

GENERAL INDEX